THE TRUTH is FUNNY

shift happens...

(Stuff you wish your mom had known to tell you!)

Published using

Lulu.com
3131 RDU Center, Suite 210
Morrisville, NC 27560DZRS

ISBN 978-0-9940625-0-5

First Edition 2015

Printed and bound in the United States of America.

Library of Congress Cataloging-in-Publication Data

Available from the publisher

Editor and Proofreader: Rose Macdonald
Cover design and book layout: Miriam Cunha
Back cover photo courtesy of: Giovanni Vidotto

This book is not intended as a substitute for medical advice of physicians. The information provided in this book is designed to provide helpful information on the subjects discussed. This book is not meant to be used, nor should it be used, to diagnose or treat any medical condition. For diagnosis or treatment of any medical problem, consult your own physician. The publisher and author are not responsible for any specific health or allergy needs that may require medical supervision and are not liable for any damages or negative consequences from any treatment, action, application or preparation, to any person reading or following the information in this book. References are provided for informational purposes only and do not constitute endorsement of any websites or other sources. Readers should be aware that the websites listed in this book may change. Although the author and publisher have made every effort to ensure that the information in this book was correct at press time, the author and publisher do not assume and hereby disclaim any liability to any party for any loss, damage, or disruption caused by errors or omissions, whether such errors or omissions result from negligence, accident, or any other cause.

THE

TRUTH

IS

FUNNY!

shift happens...

*(stuff you wish your mom
had known to tell you)*
Colette

A word of caution …

If you prefer the status quo and you are not interested in improving every aspect of your life …

This book will trigger the shift out of you!

ALWAYS READ THE SMALL PRINT!

DEDICATION

This magical work is dedicated to my daughters, Mackenzie and Madison, who have inspired me to dig deep and search for answers to becoming a strong woman and the best mom I can be …

Thank you for your patience! It would have come in handy to know some of this stuff sooner …

This book is also dedicated to you … congratulations! Life just got better!

The number one weakness for every child is a mother's worry. Every single thought you have about your children has the potential to strengthen or weaken them!

IF YOU CANNOT SEE A STRONG FUTURE FOR YOUR CHILD, WHO WILL?

Women are taught and encouraged to worry about their children as a badge of honor, instead of honoring their intuition to create a better future for every child.

It is my pleasure to share information that has the potential to change your life and the lives of all our children for the better!

CONTENTS

FOREPLAY

Are you afraid of the dark?

You know … those sleepless nights when you toss, turn, and wrestle with worries all night long?

You are not alone. The majority of humans throughout history have failed to rise to their infinite potential because they allow their "worries" to get in the way of their dreams. Most of those worries don't even belong to them!

From childhood on, many of us accumulate self-limiting beliefs as we are indoctrinated in how we are "supposed to be" through mainstream educational and religious systems, parenting, cultures and other influences. These limiting beliefs can also come from our own personal experiences as well as from concerns associated with our ancestors' experiences, projections into the future from our descendants, and even our potential descendants.

You cannot have light without dark or dark without light!

The most brilliant, successful people shine so brightly because they face their dark thoughts head on and shift them into light.

THIS BOOK IS MEANT TO BE READ OUTSIDE OF THE BOX OF CONVENTIONAL THINKING.

It is a magical book of shift … unlike any other book you have ever experienced … Each and every word and the spaces in-between each word are threads woven into a delicate tapestry of divine order designed to shift underlying energetic weaknesses into strengths to align you, your children and your ancestors with infinite potential and fulfillment of authentic desires …

Give yourself TOTAL PERMISSION to break every rule you have ever imposed upon yourself regarding how a book is "supposed" to be read. Disregard the order in which the pages are supposed to be read, the need to read an entire sentence, paragraph, page, chapter or even the whole book.

While you read this book you will notice suggestions for an energetic upgrade *EU …*

If you are in the process of reading a specific word, sentence or paragraph, and you feel compelled to stop what you are reading to see what *EU ... is* about, follow your intuition! You are tuning into the frequency of the words, and *it is* an indication that you have an underlying weakness to what you are reading. This *is* a window of opportunity to clear an energetic weakness that may be limiting you, your friends and your family.

We are the universe perceiving itself. When something stands out *it is* one way the universe communicates back to us. If you notice that you are weak to a particular word or sentence, tense your buttocks and your spine, feel your heart and let *it* go; there is no need to dwell on *it*. *It* only takes a second to let go of whatever you have been holding onto, perhaps for a very long time. If you still feel bothered, allow your intuition to lead you to a more specific shift by following the "*EUS ...*" peppered throughout the book until you shift and feel strong to what you are reading.

For example:

Many people have a weakness to losing. As you read the word **losing**, if your eye *is* drawn to *EU ... LOSING WEIGHT* and you are compelled to go there, break the rules and do *just* that! The thought of breaking the rules and **losing** your place in the book often brings up weaknesses from the collective consciousness of breaking rules and **losing** your place (home, business, job, career, relationship, etc.) which *is* also a leading energetic weakness preventing people from improving their financial situation and/or **losing** weight. Take a second to strengthen yourself to that weakness by running energy up and down your spine with the intention of clearing *it*. The opportunity to clear the weakness will never present *itself* in exactly the same way again because change *is* occurring every second of every minute of every day. Every thought *is* either working for you or against you in any given moment. There is no need to fear; you can't **lose** your place because every place you are in always has the potential to be the right place for you (or you wouldn't be there).

Perhaps when you pick up the book, it flips open to a page, and a sentence or a word catches your eye...

When I am providing an energetic upgrade for clients in private sessions, I ask them to inform me of what they want to release before the session begins in order to facilitate the most clearing possible in the time allotted. I found that as I read their emails I was automatically clearing the energetic weaknesses because I connected with the vibration of the words they used. Often when the actual session began, or after they signed up for one of my seminars or teleconferences they no longer had concerns around the issues they had initially listed, and were instead ready to clear another layer or move forward in another aspect of their lives. Consequently, I began experimenting with my business cards and magazine ads to see if I could imprint energy into them to automatically clear a person's leading weakness in the moment the cards and ads were read or seen. Over the years I have received numerous emails and phone calls from people who say that they were very upset about a problem they were facing and then they thought of me, picked up my business card and felt better. Or they would show up at one of my seminars and tell me that they picked up a magazine and *it just* happened to flip open to one of my ads and they felt guided to attend. I have taken what I learned from those experiences to a whole new level in the penning of this book.

Many people commonly use expressions such as, "If I see *it* I will believe *it*," or "seeing *is* believing," however, a human's naked eye only perceives approximately four percent of the electromagnetic frequencies. Electromagnetic frequencies are a range of frequencies emitted by the electric and magnetic fields. Very few of these frequencies can be detected by the naked eye. This means that at any given moment you are unable to see ninety-six percent of your potential! And of the four percent that you can see, *it is* likely that your perception *is* inaccurate. Many people operate under the assumption that what they see *is* what they get. And so *it is …*

You deserve the best! *It is* natural to expand and accelerate along with the universe. You are not insignificant. You are steering your reality twenty-four hours a day, seven days a week (according to the Gregorian calendar).

The truth is funny! Often stranger than fiction ... The truth *is*, there *is* no box!

Many people who shift out of limiting beliefs break into peals of laughter as they recognize how they have participated in what *just* might be a giant cosmic joke.

Universal peace *is* only possible as individuals choose to accept peace of mind. The dance of peace *is* not always a peaceful dance. The forces of rapids and currents can easily upset our craft and we often find ourselves treading water in the vast sea of the unknown. Our intuition *is* our saving grace. We can paddle to the shores of calmer waters and ride the wave of our infinite potential through insight received through our perception and intuition from the universe.

Do you *THINK* it *is* impossible to access your infinite potential *just* through the action of reading a book?

For the vast majority who **THINK** *it is* impossible, *it is* too ridiculous of a question to ask. For a smaller segment, of the population, who **FEEL** *it is* possible; *it is* also ridiculous to ask this question because the answer *is* so obvious!

How *is it* possible to automatically shift energy through the written word?

This short explanation of how we are affected by the written word *is* meant to somewhat satisfy the left-brain crowd whose minds are holding on tight to limiting beliefs and conventional thinking …

The following sentences both contain **fourteen words** describing the same event … ***dis-ease leading to death***.

Reading these sentences will be a unique experience, specific to each individual as well as a general, collective experience shared by many.

Notice the sensations, the heaviness of your body when you read the first sentence …

1) He battled for his life for four excruciating years before he succumbed to cancer.

Notice the difference in the sensations that flow through your body when you read the second sentence …

2) She danced through her pain for four years before the angels carried her home.

Just as every person *is* an individual, so *is* every word. However, as you may have noticed, the company you keep can have a huge influence on how you are perceived and how you perceive others. *It is* the same for words.

The first sentence *is* loaded with five words (***battled***, ***succumbed***, ***excruciating***, ***years***, ***cancer***) that trigger energetic weaknesses for the vast majority of humanity. Even if you have not personally experienced war, torture or disease, you may have ancestors, friends and family who have, and if you have experienced television, you have most definitely experienced *it* through the action of watching "the news."

For instance, we are bombarded by the media with stories of people who have **battled cancer** only to **succumb** after fighting in **excruciating** pain for **years**. We are also bombarded with images of people who are battling with each other in wars over imaginary lines drawn on a map.

1) He **battled** for his life for four **excruciating years** before he **succumbed** to **cancer**.

There is only one word in the first sentence (**life**) that **is** energetically strong and five words (**battled**, **excruciating**, **years**, **succumbed**, **cancer**) that are weak for the vast majority of humanity.

1) He battled for his **life** for four excruciating years before he succumbed to cancer.

The second sentence has four words (**danced**, **angels**, **carried**, **home**) that are energetically strong for the vast majority of humanity on a general level. These words are strong because **dance** evokes movement and many people believe **angels** do offer support to **carry us home**.

2) She **danced** through her pain for four years before the **angels carried** her **home**.

There are only two words in the second sentence, which have a weakening effect on the vast majority of humanity (**pain**, **years**).

2) She danced through her **pain** for four **years** before the angels carried her home.

The energetic weaknesses and strengths have a positive or negative influence on your physical well-being every time your body **feels** each word.

The psychological effects of the words **for**, **four**, and **before** are amplified through repetition of the sound. You will notice this more when you verbally express words that you are reading.

1) He battled **for** his life **for four** excruciating years **before** he succumbed to cancer.

2) She danced through her pain **for four** years **before** the angels carried her home.

The word **four is** also the **seventh** word in each sentence. You may not consciously be aware that there are fourteen words in each sentence and that the word **four is** the **seventh** word in each sentence; however, your sub-conscious and un-conscious minds are aware and attuned. Cycles of seven years, referred to as the "rhythm of the seven" relates to the seven days of the week and stages of human development that can trigger underlying spiritual weaknesses in **seven-year cycles**. At age seven, children lose their baby teeth, at fourteen, adolescents face the trials and tribulations of puberty, at twenty-one they are considered to officially be an adult, and so on. Many people make important life decisions around marriage, divorce, having children, career changes, moving, etc. in cycles of seven, at the age of twenty-one, twenty-eight, thirty-five, forty-two, forty-nine, etc.

Both sentences are loaded with words that resonate with disease, aging and dying. These are common fears that creep into the sub-conscious and un-conscious mind as part of the collective consciousness, and as such they trigger weaknesses on the psychic level from experiences of warring, losing the fight, dying, not living well, disease, pain, suffering, struggling, torturing, surrendering, etc.

I have pointed out **just** a few of the underlying energetic weaknesses that may occur as you read information. You are also absorbing information through touch, taste, sound and smell with your physical body as well as accumulating memories from the past, present and future on a psychic and spiritual level that you may not be aware of on a conscious level.

Is it possible to ride the wave of your infinite potential **just** through the simple action of reading a book and tuning into the vector? The answer **is ...** yes!

It Just Is!

Or if you prefer, you can also read this book as if **it is just** like any other book.

I have suspended all beliefs and expectations in the penning of this book. Whatever your experience as you engage in this book ... IT IS your perfect experience!

ENJOY THE RIDE!

Colette Marie Stefan

CHAPTER ONE

Words Of Advice That Would Have Come In Handy, Had You Known Them Sooner …

Looking back over my life, the choices that I made when major events and traumas, as well as seemingly insignificant events that took place, have put me on the fast track to accessing my potential to make my life and the lives of those around me better.

Pursuing knowledge of remote healing was not a conscious decision but more of a process caused by a series of life events that pushed me to search for answers.

By connecting with thousands of people over the years, I realized that there are definitive moments in all people's lives that direct them to make soul decisions through what may seem like insignificant every-day choices; yet these very choices will have a profound effect on the direction in which their lives will go.

I had and still have an inner drive to be the best version of me. My intention was that I would meet people who had an equal or greater ability than I do and thereby attract circumstances to accelerate my intuitive insight. I consciously did this after my dad made his transition, sub-consciously did it in my teens, and un-consciously did it at the age of almost three. I put out a call to dance and the universe answered!

Over the years, I have had many people say to me, "*I could never be as intuitive as you.*" This is absolutely true because I am intuitive in my own way and so are you! Some ancestral bloodlines are more favourable to intuitive ability, just as some bloodlines are more athletic. Your attitude, as you navigate troubled waters, plays a major factor in the outcome of the ongoing story of your life.

There is a love/hate relationship with intuitive ability. Being intuitive is one thing but being publicly intuitive is a whole different ball of wax. Many people throughout the years have been publicly butchered, crushed, burned, humiliated, tortured, ridiculed, murdered, labeled "crazy," institutionalized and have put the lives of their families in "grave danger" when they "came out" with their psychic skills.

There is no secret to being intuitive. We all are. There is not an original thought in the entire universe because the moment one person has a thought every being has access to that thought. I chose to take action on those thoughts and make them work for me.

Some people would like to have you think that there is a secret that you need to know, or that they have a special "gift." You are a gift! We all are! Follow your heart, put your intuition into practice, and the universe will take care of the rest. I am sharing my story from my heart – no holds barred! And everything I understand about shifting energy to date with you. You absolutely can connect with your intuition to make your life better. The universe has your back!

I would like to point out that my story is not "storybook" perfect and always a work in progress …

This is simply a snapshot of a moment we share as we co-create our reality to pioneer into uncharted spaces. The moment after this book is published and unleashed to the public, I have no doubt that acceleration of human consciousness will escalate and quickly make this information obsolete. That is my intention.

In that spirit, I will share with you some of the definitive moments in my life and a few words of advice.

We have a saying in Canada, "Get 'er done!" Here's how …

PAY ATTENTION TO PEOPLE AND EVENTS

Ancestral, astrological and planetary influences are all factors that shape our lives. The timing of the moment of a child's conception into the third dimensional plane and circumstances in the parents lives, affects their emotional and psychological state, significantly impacting and influencing their children's lives.

Your birthdate is neither an accident nor a coincidence. For example, my arrival, date via caesarean section was selected by my mother to be on the same birthdate as my Ukrainian, maternal grandmother, Anna. I have long suspected that she is of Romanian gypsy heritage.

The next major event in my life took place between the ages of two and three, when I was traveling in the back seat of a car. My mom slammed on the brakes to avoid hitting a German shepherd dog that was crossing the road. These were pre-seatbelt days and consequently I went flying head first into the dashboard.

My recollection is standing in the back seat, wearing a blue snowsuit with blood pouring down, the shock on my sister's face and wishing that I "got to wear" a pink snowsuit, too. I remember my mom's reaction as she reached into the back of the car to assess the damage and I felt her finger sink into my skull.

We were very close to the hospital and as we drove up, there was a very black man leaning against the building in the style of the "Marlboro Man." I remember my fascination at how absolutely beautiful he was (being raised in Saskatchewan, I had not ever seen a black person up to that point). I wanted my mom to "give me to him." She refused and took me into the hospital.

It was years later when I realized the accident that re-arranged the frontal lobe of my brain was also a meeting with Archangel Raphael in a near-death experience. It shifted the direction of my life in a very profound way when I realized in an energetic session, that the resentment I often felt as a child for being forced to stay on earth was my choice, not my mother's.

Years after that event, I faced the prospect of death once again, as I gave birth to my first daughter, Mackenzie on Mother's Day, Sunday, May 13. My body went into convulsions the moment my water broke. I had spent the last four months of the pregnancy on bed rest, in and out of the hospital with extremely high blood pressure.

During the long hours of delivery, I was aware of the external concern for our survival yet there was never a doubt in my mind, that my daughter and I were one hundred percent in rhythm with the steps to the dance of life. Far from death, we gave birth to a new transition into our soul's journey as mother and daughter.

When it came time for my next pregnancy and the birth of my daughter, Maddie, I used the experience of giving birth to Mackenzie to its best advantage. Maddie was born easily and effortlessly in a few hours. When I saw her beautiful face, I felt totally complete as a mother and knew that I had no need to give birth again.

THERE ARE NO ACCIDENTS

Shift happens … there are no accidents or coincidences. The people and events you encounter are not random. Once you consider that, you meet only a tiny fraction of the billions of people in the world, than you realize that every encounter is a possibility and an opportunity to shift your life into a new direction. Often there is a hidden challenge within that possibility. The universe has a great sense of humor! The more you meet the universe with laughter, the more the universe acknowledges you.

LIFE IS NOT FAIR …

My introduction to remote healing was not a gentle nudge. It was done in the style of eagles and dragons, where the fledglings are pushed out of their nest, high up on a cliff, to rise above or fall to their deaths, in a "sink or swim" mentality. It was only fitting that my dad, Maurice Joseph LePage was the catalyst! He was an entrepreneur by nature and somewhat impatient. He used to say "Shift! Or get off the pot!" (something like that) …

At the age of sixty-eight my dad collapsed at home, and within thirty-six hours was paralyzed from head to toe, unable to even breathe on his own. Upon admission to the hospital, he was kept overnight for observation, and in the morning fell again when he tried to make it across the room after a nurse told him it was his "own fault" for becoming so over-weight, and that he should make it to the bed himself.

In the afternoon, my uncle found him blue and unresponsive in his room. He was resuscitated and taken to intensive care where the diagnosis eventually came back as Guillain-Barré Syndrome, that incidentally can be a side-effect of the flu shot.

He made decisions about his business by blinking his right eye, yes or no until his business went bankrupt. My dad used to joke that the Guillain-Barré diet was the only diet that had ever worked for him. He lost over a hundred pounds as he worked to regain his ability to breathe, walk, talk and eat again.

During the time he was in and out of the hospital he had a tracheostomy that was eventually removed, replaced when he was still unable to breathe on his own and then accidentally removed while he was having a shunt put into his heart after contracting a MRSA infection at the hospital. That was a miracle in itself because against all odds he was able to breathe without the tracheostomy tube. During his stays at the hospital he fell several more times, was told by a head nurse that he was no better than an animal when he didn't make it to the toilet on time and was accidentally over-dosed a few times.

After he contracted MRSA at the hospital, everyone had to gown, glove and mask themselves every time they entered and left his room. Besides making it hot and itchy for visitors, it made it inconvenient for hospital staff to look after him.

I fought to have my dad sent to the Wascana Rehabilitation Center where he made very quick progress, was soon using the toilet again and proudly doing laps around the gym. Eventually he was able to be home again, off and on; however, he was not in great shape when he went into the hospital and his body had really taken a toll.

During the last week of his life, he found himself back in hospital and would beg me to please "just shoot him." He pointed out that if he were a horse people would have put him out of his misery. People would ask my dad if he had seen the doctor yet, and he would jokingly reply, "Yes, I have seen Dr. Phil on TV," but because his actual doctor did not make it to see him that week, the no-resuscitation order that was supposed to be in effect was not signed.

I received a hysterical call from my mom at four in the morning. She had received a call from the hospital informing her that dad had passed, I picked my mom up, and upon arrival at the hospital, she jumped out before I could park the car. It was the day before their forty-fourth wedding anniversary.

They allowed my mom to see him with the resuscitation equipment still forced down his mouth, his eyes wide open in a far from peaceful stare. When my eyes met hers and I witnessed our horror, deep in her eyes and in my heart, I knew that there absolutely had to be a better way to look after people than this. The system clearly was not equipped to handle an oversupply of patients and an undersupply of caregivers. There were good people working at the hospital, and there were also people who clearly were not following their purpose as caregivers.

It was only five weeks later that my niece, who was returning from the West Edmonton Mall from a last hurrah with three of her friends, before starting university, was in a head-on collision by a drunk driver. The girl who was driving was killed, along with the very inebriated driver of the other car. My niece was revived at the scene, stabilized and rushed to Saskatoon, Saskatchewan where she underwent several hours of surgery.

If there is such a thing as hell, that night was it. After receiving the phone call from my brother-in-law at around midnight, my sister, brother-in-law and I made the very long drive to Saskatoon from Regina without knowing what we would face once we arrived. My niece arrived by ambulance shortly after we did and we began the long wait, as she had surgery. We helplessly watched the mom who had lost her daughter be taken to the morgue to identify her child. The pain etched on her face is imprinted in my mind.

After several hours we rejoiced as doctors informed us that my niece had survived the surgery until they also informed us that she was severely brain damaged and was not expected to make a full recovery. My sister, her mom, absolutely refused to accept this fate for her daughter and immediately took steps to change it. She contacted a long distance healer who at that time was a teenager living in British Columbia. He worked on my niece from a photograph as she lay in Intensive Care in

Saskatoon, Saskatchewan. Every time he worked with her she made an improvement.

She did not recognize us when she came out of the coma but after a couple of sessions with him, she knew who we were. Every session after that she had a major improvement until she remembered what she had purchased at the mall. We knew then, that she would make a full recovery. My niece attended university months after the accident, is modeling, married, the mother of two daughters and most importantly, her true beautiful essence still shines from within.

After witnessing my niece's miraculous recovery I had absolutely no doubt that remote healing is possible, but I wanted to know how it was possible and if I could do it. Since then I have learned that everyone can!

I want to point out that a best-case scenario for ultimate patient care is a combination of science and heart. Hospitals often bring up mixed emotions because life and death are a daily occurrence within their walls. I have a deep respect for doctors, nurses, psychiatrists, psychologists and other professionals who want to integrate and provide the best care possible for their patients. These pioneers willingly put their reputation to risk and often compromise their livelihood doing it.

WHEN THE SHIFT HITS THE FAN …

My mom's identical twin made her transition six months after my dad, and my father-in-law passed a year later, after extended illnesses. Then my beloved afghan hound, Mercedes, became very ill. Letting go of her was the last straw for me. I was exhausted and felt so discouraged until I was given the gift of a little Tibetan Terrier named "Ella the Enchanting."

Tibetan Terriers were originally bred to be companions to the holy men who raised them for nomadic herdsmen in the mountains of Tibet. Known as the "Holy Dogs of Tibet" they were never sold but only given as gifts or in gratitude for favors. They are considered bringers of luck and were referred to as the "little people." Ella is the most beautiful gift! She was at my side for over a decade and it was through her that I was introduced to Tai Njio who was my first instructor in the Yuen Method TM. As I participated in the first seminar, I felt a huge weight lift from my shoulders and upon leaving, I knew that "I was born to do this!"

One month before leaving for certification in the Yuen Method TM, I studied the electromagnetic and metaphysical gifts of minerals and crystals with Karen Nugle of Hands of Spirit in Boulder, Colorado, in October of 2008.This was a very special time for me. My mentor, Tai Njio was also in Boulder, Colorado. We were very fortunate to have the time and space to connect with each other on a whole new level. It was one of the most magical times of my life.

Every plant, crystal and animal that you connect with is sharing powerful information with you, if you care to pay attention. I often imprint crystal energies and plant medicines in my energetic shifts to make them as powerful and as gentle as possible. Furthermore, the pets that find you are not an accident. You can learn a lot about yourself from them. (Dogs are very loyal and will take on your stuff easily, whereas cats only do it when they feel like it).

INFORMATION EQUALS ENERGY!

A lot of shift has sailed under the bridge, since I made the choice to follow my heart and embark on this journey … Every person and every challenge you encounter is an opportunity to hone your reality steering skills using a combination of tools to build the life you want. Everything you see around you began as a thought that was brought into reality, using specific tools. Every person you meet and every event that happens is a bit of information, a tool that can be applied to benefit you in daily life.

Different tools are required to accomplish specific tasks in specific situations. For instance, an accountant and a carpenter are going to use a different set of tools in their specific line of work on an everyday basis, yet those skills are interchangeable. A carpenter can be very efficient at keeping his or her own books, just as an accountant could have a hobby that produces fine pieces of furniture. They each apply their own unique abilities and skills while using the tools.

Either way, unused tools that are left lying around are unable to accomplish the task on their own. Unapplied information is just that, a tool that is not being used …

BE A TOOL, NOT A FOOL!

Why should you believe a word I say? The answer is … you shouldn't! Use your intuitive skills to come to your own conclusions.

When I first began my journey into the world of energetic healing, I thought I was at a disadvantage because I had no training in anatomy, quantum physics or metaphysics. I found out that was just my thinking. In reality, I was fortunate not to have a formal education in any of these fields because I did not have to struggle with letting go of unreliable information.

You are unique so as a matter of course your journey will be very different from my own. However, I have learned a thing or two, having worked with the best mentors, colleagues, clients, students, demo and radio participants over the last decade. It has been a blessing for me and a gift I am so pleased to share with you.

Looking back, the first "healer" I connected with is an amazing woman by the name of Betty Johnston who has been working with people for decades in a small house, on her farm by Milestone, Saskatchewan. My former husband and I had just purchased a house with a huge yard that I had been hard at work landscaping. We promised our daughters that we would drive into the city and take them on rides at the "exhibition." While I was in the shower that morning, I realized that I could not feel my left leg when I cut it while shaving.

There was a hospital next door to the grounds where the exhibition was being held. I didn't want to disappoint my daughters so I had my husband drop me off at Emergency and we agreed to meet at the merry-go-round in an hour. The doctors were concerned that I had MS. They wanted to hospitalize me to do more tests. I left, telling them, "I don't do MS," and limped off to meet my husband and daughters at the merry-go-round as I had promised.

The doctor from the hospital was a very caring individual and called me at home several times afterwards in an attempt to convince me to come in for more testing. Instead, I went out to see Betty at her farm. She stormed into the room and told me, "You don't have MS, it is dangerous to listen to that crap."

She lifted me off my feet, realigned me, and the feeling in my leg instantly came back. I often took my daughters to be re-aligned by her when they were figure skating and had bad falls. She was amazing!

At the time, I thought the problem was all the heavy lifting from wheel barrowing aggregates around the yard, but now I understand that the problem was an herbicide that I had been using to kill weeds. After I used it I always felt "off" but didn't pay attention because it is very commonly used in Saskatchewan and is "supposed" to be safe. I did not put two and two together until years after when I had my first private session with Kam Yuen where, in a half hour session, the residual pain and numbness were completely removed.

By the time I left Saskatchewan (again), I felt like I was the only person in the province who refused to use herbicides on my lawn. At this time, Betty is over ninety years old and still going strong, with people still showing up from all over the world to be treated by her.

It was also around this time that I began to dabble with using my intuition. I connected with a gifted psychic named Phoenix who taught me how to read the tarot. Every time I think of her, I feel like pitching a tent and doing energy work gypsy style. She was so intuitive and so much fun! This experience also led me in search of a way to intuitively communicate with animals.

When I was a little girl I SO wished that I was like Dr. John Dolittle, the central character of a children's book written by Hugh Lofting. He was able to speak with animals in their own languages. Shortly after attending my first seminar with Tai Njio, after Ella came into my life, I attended an animal communication seminar with Lynn Mackenzie who is a natural born intuitive and empathic, and who was mentored by animal communication specialist, Penelope Smith. She has combined her life-long love for animals with her passion and gifts for healing and counseling to create international recognition as an animal intuitive. Lynn Mackenzie and her spirit guide, "Lucero" a powerful Andalusian stallion, taught me that animals communicate in pictures that they flash to us. Whether we are aware or not, we are in constant communication with them and we are also flashing pictures to them. This knowledge has empowered me to communicate with animals and babies at an entirely different level.

THERE IS NO MAGIC PILL

Shortly after returning from that seminar, I received a call from my cousin informing me that a close family friend's daughter had drowned in their family pool. This call was a catalyst for change, that I was compelled to answer. I had just said goodbye to my dad, several other family members, plus Mercedes, and felt that I could not handle one more drama when I received that call; however, I knew on the deepest level of my being that it was essential that I rush to the hospital and be there for my friend.

I had just witnessed the miracle of my niece's recovery and fueled by that, I was determined that their daughter would also have a miraculous recovery. I had no doubt and was determined to have the same positive outcome for her and her family.

Every single person who has ever dived into the depths of energetic shifting will eventually have to rise to an occasion such as this. This is the most challenging lesson of all …

You are not in control of the outcome! Healing comes from within each and every person. Expectations of outcomes cause limitations because the outcome is occurring on many levels of existence, time and space and is not to be judged by the third dimensional world. What will be will be.

It was a privilege to be the intermediary between this beautiful baby, her parents and the young man who had shifted my niece over a six-month period until everyone was ready for her to make her transition. I learned so much from the experience and feel a deep gratitude for her, her parents and Dr. Adam McLeod ND, also known as Dreamhealer. He is now a brilliant, cutting-edge bio-scientist who promotes understanding of the healing process by bringing a scientific framework to healing with intentions at seminars worldwide.

SHIFT OR GET OFF THE POT!

After attending my first Yuen Method TM seminar, I took every opportunity I could to study and intern with Dr. Kam Yuen. For eight years, I did my best to attend every live event, teleconference, and booked private sessions with the fervor of a groupie following her favorite performer. Every experience was worth the effort and empowered me by strengthening my insight.

Dr. Kam Yuen is a thirty-fifth generation Shaolin Grandmaster. His innate ability to detect and use an opponent's energetic weaknesses brought him legendary fame in the western world of martial arts. His career in martial arts shifted drastically when he discovered that his ability could be used to strengthen energetic weaknesses and eliminate pain.

I completed the requirements to become a Certified Practitioner in November of 2008 and was designated by Dr. Kam Yuen to share his teachings as a Certified Yuen Method TM Instructor in January of 2010 and also completed his Mastery program in 2012.

One of the best compliments I have ever received was on Kam Yuen's radio show when he said that I was his best student ever and that if everyone were like me he would retire. It was a great pleasure for me to share his information with so many people at seminars and demos around the globe.

I have seen so many miracles occur around this brilliant man! The first time I had a session with him in person, in under a half hour he totally eliminated the sciatic pain that I had been suffering with off and on for years. It took me six months to realize that the pain was gone because he also eliminated the concern around it.

When I was in elementary school, I would rush home to catch the latest episode of my favorite television series, "Kung Fu." Glued to the screen, I wished that I could be like Cain and study with the Shaolin Masters. It was not until I had attended several Yuen Method TM seminars that I realized that Kam Yuen was the technical advisor for the Kung Fu series and that my adolescent dream had come true.

On two separate occasions, Kam Yuen told me that I am the happiest person he has ever met. The first time he said it, the words just kind of whizzed by, over my head; however, the second time he said it, it occurred to me that he has met a lot of people. I told him that it would be very difficult not to be happy around him. It is easy to be happy when you are able to make your dreams come true ...

SOMETHING DOESN'T ADD UP

I had an aversion to math ever since I was a young girl, and had barely survived high school algebra but I wanted to have an understanding of how the mechanics of energetic shifts worked through quantum physics before I attended certification of the Yuen Method TM. There are times when I will get an intuitive hit to surf the net and the exact information I need "pops" up. I came across Nassim Haramein's DVD set "Crossing The Event Horizon." Once it arrived, I became hooked on watching his presentation non-stop over and over until my family begged me, "to please turn that guy off!" Despite my reservations about math, I attended the delegate program in July of 2011 and went on to become an Emissary of the Resonance Project Foundation in November of 2011 in Tulum Mexico. Since learning this information, my energetic shifts have developed a powerful torque and spin.

Girls and Math ...

Ann Hess, an Emissary of the United Field was interviewing her fellow emissaries for their insights while attending the program in Tulum. She surprised me by asking me what my views were regarding girls and math. That question took me by surprise but I answered her question from my heart. The following is a transcript of that interview.

"For me, growing up and attending school, I found it very difficult to understand any math even as a young girl. Because everything they were telling me did not resonate with me and did not follow nature's laws. Even as a small child I would spend many hours out in nature ... it was my favorite thing to do.

"After taking the emissary program, just taking a walk down the beach and walking through the ocean is a totally different experience for me because I watch for the physics of what is occurring and I can see the big picture, the fractal nature of the

universe.

"As a woman, having given birth to two daughters, it is an amazing experience to understand that when I was young and felt that I just wasn't smart enough to understand math, it was actually that the fundamental principles of what they were teaching me were totally incorrect.

"On some level I did understand that ... now that I have the true knowledge and the true understanding of physics in a way that I can apply to my daily life it has made a huge, huge difference in the way I view everything in my life.

"I believe that for a lot of women the fractal nature of the universe is a part of them, a knowledge that we have because we are the ones who regenerate! We are the ones who give birth and for us to have that acknowledged and to view it from the Divine Feminine instead of from a masculine point of view has made me realize how totally brilliant I really am!"

The Emissary Program was FUN! – a life-changing event, with every day bringing more adventure. So many wonderful synchronicities took place. My favorite was when it was announced on the last day of the program, that Jon Anderson would be giving a free concert on the beach a half hour down the road. I was so pumped because his collaboration with John Vangelis, Friends of Mr. Cairo CD is what inspired me to paint a series of inter-galactic dragons six years earlier. It was so awesome to attend the concert with Nassim and several other emissaries. I was thrilled to meet Jon Anderson and his lovely wife after the concert, and to talk with him about my dragons. It was also a great surprise to discover that math does not have to be painful! Who would have thought that a quantum physicist could share such profound information and make me laugh! Thank you Nassim, for your great sense of humor and your infinite patience!

After a couple of years, I felt strong to working with clients. I would look up on-line what the medical community had to say about specific diseases and the body parts that were involved. I would then spread anatomy cards out around me and strengthen for my eye to go immediately to the number one weakness that I perceived. It drove my oldest daughter to distraction when she would hear me work with clients and tell them that their "what-cha-ma-call-it" next to the "doo-hickey" were not connected properly to each other and that was the root of their problem. She was attending university, studying medical sciences, and she told me, *"Mom, you can't expect people to take you seriously when you don't even know the proper names of anatomy!"* I replied, *"Well look! This person just emailed me and their tumor shrank to nothing in half an hour while I worked with them over the phone and I just received a phone call that a man whose kidneys I worked on, does not need dialysis now."*

However, I could see my daughter's point and began to study anatomy, sneaking her books at times, to absorb the information by placing the text under my pillow or under my bed, when the books were too thick.

MARKETING IS BOTH SHALLOW AND IMPORTANT!

I was bullied mercilessly when I attended elementary school. Unresolved issues from the trauma of rejection caused me to freeze in my tracks at the thought of speaking or performing in public. (To this day, I am still working on weaknesses of "being seen," especially in video!) I had no idea, whatsoever of how I was going to overcome my fear, but I was determined to succeed. So, shortly after my first Yuen Method TM seminar with Tai Njio, I began taking belly dance and burlesque dance classes to overcome my fear of being on stage. I was so shy that when I had called to register in the previous two years, I hung up when the instructor answered the phone. At my first solo performance, in a bar on a stage one year later, people complimented me on my shimmy afterwards, but it was honestly pure fear causing me to literally shake at the knees. Dancing was a fun way to "shake off" the fear of performing and speaking in public. Once I had gained enough confidence I realized that I needed to learn how to market myself, and the information I was sharing.

On my birthday, while attending certification of the Yuen Method TM in California, I sold my business without advertising it, and nine days later, I separated from my husband. I was short of cash and to the horror of my family, who wanted me to play it safe and get a "real job," I found a way to attend the Magnetize Your Audience seminar led by Callan Rush and Justin Livingston who teach heart-based businesses to market their message in a powerful way. I had so much resistance to the concept of choosing a specific audience because I wanted to yell from the rooftops, how great we all really are, and I didn't want to leave a single person out. Marketing is my least favorite aspect of this business. Callan and Justin make it easier to come to resolution with the fact that no matter how awesome your information is, if you don't learn how to market yourself, you are cheating people from hearing your message.

LOOKING GOOD IS A BUSINESS DECISION

I witnessed Hermann Mueller, founder of the Australasian Institute of Body Mind Analysis and Psychosomatic Therapy, in action at their seminar and immediately made it a priority to study with him. After completing the pre-requisites in 2010, as a Psychosomatic Body/Mind Practitioner with Carole Friesen of Core Potentials, I continued my study as a Master Practitioner and Teacher of Psychosomatic Therapy in 2011/2012 with Hermann Muller. It is such a pleasure to watch Hermann at work. His ability to read the subtle nuances of the human body is phenomenal to behold. I am truly blessed to have learned from such a gifted master; he taught me how to use my body language to present myself in the strongest way possible both on and off stage.

THE TRUTH IS FUNNY, STRANGER THAN FICTION!

One of the side effects of using your intuition is the creative genius that comes along with it. Many of the people whom I have worked with experience a spike in their creativity that moves them to express themselves through art, writing poetry, books and music, dancing, etc. It is therefore no surprise that in 2007, shortly after I returned home from completing the requirements for internship in the Yuen Method TM, Ahnje "Crystal Queen" announced her presence as the first Inter-Galactic dragon that I would be painting. Dragons represent potent and benevolent power as the ultimate rulers of all the elements; they embody primordial energy as a catalyst for change and transformation, for wisdom, infinity, longevity and movement through space.

In January of 2010, I was introduced to Ra-Sheeba, a healing modality, similar to Reiki that works directly on the chakras, the biological systems and DNA and shortly after was initiated by co-founder, Merilyn Bretherick. Ra-Sheeba celebrates the joyful expression of the divine feminine integrated with the masculine in connection with source. The ancient Egyptian symbols of Ra-Sheeba are amplified by dance and draw from crystal, indigo and Inter-Galactic Dragon energies. I was surprised, and somewhat relieved, to learn that people from all around the world were also tuning into the energy of the dragons. I have discovered that it can be a challenge to ignore a dragon when it is ready to spin its tale. To date I have completed sixteen paintings in a series called "Tails From The Vector." Each dragon is adorned with Swarovski crystals and has a tale to tell from the variations of space-time.

NOURISH THE BODY

There are so many people that I have had the pleasure to work with over the years from around the globe, some of whom prefer to quietly do their work and wish to remain behind the scenes at this time. It was through one of these connections that I met Ma Jaya Sati Bhagavati. I stayed at her ashram in Florida for the first time in July of 2009. Our meeting was very unlikely considering that I had never attended a yoga class; formally meditated in the traditional sense and that I had no desire, belief or inclination to look up to a guru. I was invited to stay at the ashram to meet with fellow colleagues. Her vibration was apparent to me within miles of driving through the gates. If you are familiar with the Goddess Kali, that is Ma! Cut through the bullshit and cut to the chase!

Ma Jaya Sati Bhagavati was able to drop an entire room into deep meditation with a snap of her fingers. In meditation with her, everyone from the most experienced traveler to a "first timer" would experience time and space in a whole new, raw and indefinable context. She traveled with you in meditation to places that you cannot even imagine. The ashram prayed for my mom when she was making her transition, so I do my best to get to Florida around that time of year to pay my respects. The following year after my mom made her transition, I went up during darshan, a social gathering to receive a blessing from Ma, to thank her for clearing karma for my mom.

I felt an electrical jolt as she gave me a hug and pressed her third eye on mine. Later, I woke up in the middle of the night to a strong pulsing sensation between my eyebrows. The next morning I was alarmed when I looked in the mirror. My third eye was literally bulging out of my forehead like a goose egg. It looked like someone had hit me with a hammer between the eyes. When I met with the people from our group for breakfast, I told them not to call an ambulance because I did not get medical insurance when I left Canada and it was not a physical problem. Their laid-back reaction was funny, for all intents and purposes we should have been concerned, but I was strong to it, and so we all took it in stride and got back to work. I was downloading information at an accelerated rate through my third eye, information that I could not process fast enough. By early afternoon, the swelling had gone down and the next day by all appearances, everything was back to normal. I highly recommend Ma's book about karma "The Eleven Karmic Spaces." It is an easy read with quality information. Her belief is that if you take care of people's physical hunger first, you can take care of their spiritual hunger by empowering people to move beyond the lines of poverty.

The affiliate ashram, The River Fund in New York, launched the concept of a fixed choice mobile food pantry that allows clients to select the items they want and use. Over the years, it has become the largest food pantry in Queens, easily serving some eight hundred households every Saturday of the week, and an average of 28,000 unique individual beneficiaries each month. The headquarters is a beehive of activity of community members dedicated to caring for other community members. It is beautiful to witness.

They also provide benefits such as access assistance by pre-screening, pre-qualification and enrollment in all of the benefits and services for which their clients qualify. This allows needy families to focus on employment rather than on wasting time chasing after the help for which they may qualify.

GRATITUDE

I have been so blessed to share experiences with so many fabulous clients, students, demo, and radio participants from around the world. Thank you for putting your trust in me, I have learned from each and every one of you.

A heartfelt thank you to my colleagues who have inspired me and my radio audience to soar to new heights: talented musician and energy mover Phil Free, co-founder of Energetic Upgrade seminars, Marc Kettenbach, founder of Energetic Well Being Process, LeRoy Malouf, founder of Intuitive Living, Karen Campbell Betten, epigeneticist, Charan Surdhar and founder of Ice Lotus, Rich Peterson.

I want take this opportunity to express gratitude for Sheila Gale who gave me my "big break" by featuring me on the "Sheila Show." This led to a gig with Darius Barazandeh, Kristen Howe and Debra Poneman, plus numerous other tele-summits and radio show appearances.

I wish to extend a huge than you to Lance Hood from Live Big Media for expertly shifting my perception so that I was able to step into my full potential when I needed it most!

I am filled with gratitude to my assistant Miriam Cunha for all her diligent work in keeping things running behind the scenes, and for designing the book cover, Rose Macdonald for your care in editing and proof-reading this book, Dr. Pat Baccili for pushing me into excellence, to my friends and family and all the people I have had the pleasure of working with throughout the years that empower me to empower you.

To my father, Maurice Joseph LePage thank you for leading the way and teaching me how to reach for the sky as an entrepreneur. It really would have been great to know some of this sooner, to ease your journey ... and to my beautiful mother Joan Charlotte LePage, for your huge heart and capacity for love. Thank you for showing me how to host an event and highlight the special qualities of everyone who attends. (I must have missed out on the "whip a meal out of nothing" gene.)

Last but not least, a heartfelt thank you to You! For taking time and energy to read this book!

CHAPTER TWO

Shifting Dark Into Light …

As a mom, you want what is best for your children; yet, the vast majority of humans throughout history have failed to rise to their infinite potential, and at this time it is still unlikely that any one individual would be able to access his or her infinite potential one hundred percent of the time due to the resonance of limiting beliefs and expectations from the collective consciousness. However, you can "raise the bar" for your children by tapping into your infinite potential to instantly access the most viable solution that will be applicable to any given situation or problem you encounter. This enables you to bring about a new level of achievement, unattainable in the context of previous measures of excellence, and to improve every aspect of your life and the lives of your descendants.

Humans are multi-faceted beings, functioning on multiple levels of influences, consciousness, existences, dimensions, time, realms and space. These various interconnections can lead to dis-ease of the body, soul and spirit. Often when people are faced with a particular disease or problem, their personal issues may appear to be similar to what others are experiencing yet the causes and processes for dis-ease are as unique to every individual and situation as are their fingerprints. At times it may seem as if the universe is conspiring against you and your children to make your lives miserable. It is more likely that the universe is mirroring back negative programming held in your sub-conscious and un-conscious mind because the universe perceives you as an infinite being and gives you more of what you feel you deserve, without limitations or judgment.

For instance, if you *feel* challenged in your career to bring in 100 K more per annum, the universe will respond by providing you with obstacles that make it more challenging to reach your goal. On the other hand, if you are energetically in alignment with easily accessing 100K or more the universe will pave your path to easily reach your goal and provide you with opportunities to receive more if you are energetically strong to asking for it. This is true in every aspect of life. People often say that if you have your health nothing else matters; however, if you place great importance on your health above all else, you may be setting yourself up to face challenges that will disrupt your health so that you can focus on it and give it even more attention. The rapid development of quantum physics has caught up with the field of medicine and is changing world-views on the infinite possibilities of healing. Medical research in behavioral medicine and the field of epigenetics shows that resistance to change commences the bio-chemical and psychosomatic process of fatal disease. In fact the very word "healing" is now outdated, and can often limit your ability to recover at quantum speed due to a mistaken belief, held by many people, that healing has to take time.

The human body contains one hundred trillion cells and three hundred million cells are replaced every minute. On the cellular membrane of these cells there are neuro-transmitters, neuro-junctions, neuro-receptors and fibers. Each acts as an antennae picking up information from the collective consciousness on the macrocosmic, microcosmic and intrinsic levels and shares that information with every other cell in your body before sending information from your body back out again to the collective consciousness. This information includes twenty-thousand or so known dis-eases that affect the human body as well as perceptions from your ancestors and descendants regarding success and failure in career, business, life-style, relationships, etc. All the microorganisms living in association with the human body consist of a variety of microorganisms, including eukaryotes, archaea, bacteria and viruses. Bacteria alone number ten more times than human cells for a total of about one thousand more genes than are present in the human genome. Advances in DNA sequencing technologies have created a new field of research, called metagenomics that allows comprehensive examination of microbial communities without the need for cultivation. These "friends with benefits" live symbiotically together with you. You provide them with a nice warm home and they reciprocate by providing essential services your biological body needs. If you unraveled the DNA from all of your cells, like a thread from a sweater, it would wrap around the world five million times. Yet, it has perfect order. The organization of all the systems of your body function perfectly. Confusion for even an instant has a profound effect on the systems in a very short period of time.

If you consider your body to be the best binary computer ever built, binary in this case, meaning two choices, weak or strong, all the information gathered by every cell is being recorded and stored in the hard drive. The hard drive of your computer would be the components of the spine and the brain. The spine and the brain are the central nervous system (CNS), and the software would be the peripheral nervous system (PNS) with every past, present and future experience documented and held in the memory of its components. You could consider your heart to be the power supply of the computer, pumping electricity to keep the computer running, while the keyboard is used to express and communicate through vibration or frequencies in the form of letters, numbers and symbols.

A computer does not fulfill its purpose unless the hard drive (CNS) and the software (PNS) are in alignment and are plugged into a supply of energy (heart). Most people have experienced the frustration of relying on a slow computer. Just as you can upgrade the hard drive of your computer when it is "running slow" from corrupt files, it is also possible, through an Energetic Upgrade, to deprogram energetic weaknesses that are stagnating your systems and causing dis-ease in your body, soul and spirit. You can upgrade your hard drive by plugging into your heart and focusing your thought on the spine for less than a split second to delete or deprogram files (thoughts, actions, words, etc.) that are not in alignment with your authentic desires, and you can re-align yourself with your heart's path.

Optimum performance is achieved by having insight to balancing your body, soul and spirit through clear perception and strong intuition. Intuition and logic are a fifty/fifty proposition. If logic is used to ask a question and to receive the answer it will only lead to more questions. Logical questions require intuitive answers.

You can maximize your intuition and perception to ask a question and then observe when your energy or another person's energy goes weak. This allows you to pinpoint the cause of the complaint and eliminate it with an energetic shift, similar to a light switch being flipped on. People often insist that a problem or concern in their life is coming from a source that is not based in truth, even though they believe they are being honest with themselves. This makes the problem more difficult to resolve and most often makes the problem worse. For instance, people often treat health problems as physical issues, but they are commonly the result of the "stress" of dealing with daily concerns and struggles with financial problems that manifest from a perception of lack. As people try to relax themselves out of the sensations of fear from lack, it creates a lack of tension in the physical body, which in turn stagnates systems and causes aging, and ultimately affects personal and business relationships. As the personality strives to meet the false obligations imposed by societal, cultural, educational and religious obligations, the soul becomes starved of purpose and the lack of authentic desire can cause an imbalance of the physical, mental, emotional and etheric bodies, which then creates more weaknesses that challenge health, fitness, relationships, careers, finances and aging.

You can experience quick and often instantaneous resolution of pain and other physical symptoms and instant clearing of inner barriers to achieving success and reaching your goals when the underlying cause of complaint is identified; once the "switches" are flipped, the influences that obstruct the flow of energy are removed layer by layer. Every shift has an effect and many problems are relieved or resolved instantly because energetic shifts are made on multiple levels of consciousness, and are aligned on all levels, existences and all dimensions. The shifting is made possible through your connection in the unified field by the "Higher Self Network" (H.S.N.).

There is a lot of talk these days about how we are all one. On many levels that feels true but what are the mechanics of it? How is it that we are all one? How is it possible that we are all separate individuals and at the same time all connected? The Higher Self Network (H.S.N.) is the unified field or network that facilitates the connection of everyone to everything. You can think of this as your ability to chat with others, similar to chatting on M.S.N. except that everyone is in constant communication on H.S.N. whether they are aware of it or not. The unified field is the space we occupy and the space that occupies us. No matter how big or small, all matter that we observe is made of atoms.

The ceaseless interactions within the human body constantly create new experiences editing the molecular structure in motion. The word, "anatomy" can be dissected into four words An-Atom-In-Me, and the sensations that people react to that many consider to be emotion, are actually energy-in-motion, an indivisible source of vast potential energy.

Information equals energy. For example, if you think of a circle as a dot, you can see discreetness or structure in it. If you add a triad in the center and polarize it (two triads, one facing down and one facing up) you have created new isolated boundaries. Every point, every boundary is a new perspective of new information which is part of the larger whole. More and more energy is created with each point and each point grows inside to create more points, on and on to infinity, yet it would never, ever exceed that first boundary. Infinite energy can be present in an infinite boundary in a so-called finite system. If we go deeper than the molecular, the atom itself is made up of 99.9999% space. There is always space! Even the atoms themselves have space between them and don't touch. Nothing touches, nothing has ever touched. Space organizes everything! The very fact that people come out of people, shows you that you are a reflection of the fractal, self-sustaining nature of Earth. You are the feedback loop! You are being informed by space or the vacuum every second of every minute of every day.

At this time humanity is evolving faster than ever before in the history of mankind as we know it, because of easy access to more information than ever before. You can no longer pretend that you are unaware of the global consequences of your actions. If there are children starving in the world, there is a part in you and every one of us that is also starving. If you turn a blind eye to the abuse animals on this earth are suffering, you abuse yourself. Your body consists roughly of seventy-percent water; therefore, if you pollute your water, you also pollute yourself.

When you get caught up in the chaos swirling around you, you lose touch with yourself and forget to benefit from your internal sensory communication systems. You are steering your reality twenty-four hours a day, seven days a week whether you are aware of it or not. When you turn your senses inward to center yourself to your singularity, you connect with the whole and allow homeostasis of the body, soul and spirit. You can upgrade your high tech equipment on a regular basis to make sure it is up to speed by checking in with yourself to be sure the steps of action you are taking are in alignment with your authentic desires.

One way of doing this is to face your problem head-on by asking yourself what the worst-case scenario in your situation could be and then play it out in your mind until you face every possible consequence. Next, take the best-case scenario and play out those possibilities. The more you pay attention to how weak energy feels to you, the more quickly you will identify when you are not in alignment. Once you identify that there is a weakness in in any given moment, you can delete the memories and attachments that are limiting you from your optimum potential until you become neutral to both extremes. Once you are neutral, you will be able to handle both extremes and be neutral to everything in-between.

Most people assume that they would be bothered more by their worst-case scenario; ironically, the vast majority of people are triggered and have a tendency to self-sabotage when they step out of their comfort zones and into their greatness. If you are unable to get neutral to your situation, it is possible for another person to connect with the information, delete the energetic blocks, and restore infinite potential through communication on the Higher Self Network for you.

I have enjoyed the pleasure of sharing this information with people from all around the world and from all "walks of life." As people are reminded that they have this ability, and then put their skills into practice in their daily lives, they become more and more proficient at identifying weak energies and facilitating change for the better, for themselves, for their loved ones and for the entire universe.

You are not an insignificant little dot that means nothing to the universe. You are the center of your universe, as is everyone else! We are all equal, we are all one.

CATALOGUE

(stuff you wish your mom had known to tell you)

The topics and categories listed in this catalogue are a compilation of the experiences and insights I have gathered from connecting with thousands of clients, students, demo participants, magicians, authors, speakers, shamans, alchemists, gurus, plant medicines and other beings, in-person, remotely and courtesy of the vector.

As mothers, we have all experienced times when our intuition tells us that there is something wrong and we need to connect with our children. Intuition is ALWAYS your best guide, however this catalogue is an invaluable resource for all moms and every other energetic practitioner as a reference to shift general weaknesses related to specific topics.

There is no right or wrong way to use your intuition. You are a unique individual and have your own style.

However …

Multiple interconnections of the human condition create many similarities between people who are suffering from a specific condition or bother. Often, a general shift in energy will have a profound effect that drastically reduces pain and discomfort, and provides instant relief for many people. There are also times when we need to dig deeper to clear the root cause by stripping away layer after layer to get to the diamond hidden within.

How to get the best results from the catalogue …

The information provided in this catalogue can be accessed on many levels. For some of you this may be your first encounter with shifting energy on a conscious level, whereas others of you may be seasoned experts … whatever the case, allow your intuition to take you where you need to go to make the most of your experience.

Subjects in the catalogue are listed alphabetically with categories and sub-categories to facilitate ease in locating the answer you are searching for. Words that pertain to the physical body and physical matter are in **bold** and words that pertain to non-physical aspects and actions are in ***italic bold***. This is to show the difference between ***non-physical*** and **physical anatomy** as well as **physical matter**.

ANATOMY

In order to shift pain or illness it is empowering to have a basic understanding of anatomy and how the systems of the **body** interconnect. As you read about anatomy in this book, there are parts of the body or systems that are in **bold** to emphasize their relationships with other body parts that are also in **bold**. The reasons why it is important for these **body parts** to have a strong relationship are both physical and non-physical. It is very rare for symptoms to actually be from the body part that is feeling the pain. These symptoms are most often referred from another body part. As you are reading any given sentence regarding **anatomy**, if one or more of the words or more than one word stands out, there is likely a weakness. This is an opportunity for an energetic upgrade. Take a second to run energy up and down your **spine** to strengthen that **body part** or **parts** with the **CNS**, to each other and to your **heart**. Then re-check that none of the words in **bold** in any given paragraph feel weak to each other. Let's use the following paragraph as an example:

> "The **cerebrum** is the largest part of the human brain. It is divided into **left** and **right hemispheres** and is connected by the **corpus callosum**, a band of nerve tissue (white matter) allowing the two halves to exchange information. Each hemisphere of the **cerebrum** is covered by a layer of gray tissue called the **cerebral cortex** and is divided into **four lobes**, the **occipital lobe**, **temporal lobe**, **parietal lobe** and **frontal lobe**."

1. If, as you read the first sentence, any of the words **cerebrum**, **left hemisphere**, **right hemisphere** and **corpus callosum** stand out, stop and take a second to strengthen that word. For instance, if the word **cerebrum** stands out and FEELS weak stop and strengthen it. Understand that you are not just shifting the word, which is a symbol for your actual **cerebrum**; you are shifting your physical **cerebrum** and once the word FEELS neutral, it is an indication that whatever the weakness was that was causing a *problem* in your **cerebrum,** has now been neutralized.

2. Next, you want to check if the **cerebrum** has a strong connection between the **left hemisphere**, **right hemisphere** and **corpus callosum**. If any of those words stand out or you notice a dip in your energy as you read them, there is likely an energetic weakness that you have an opportunity to strengthen.

3. Physical weaknesses between any two given **body parts** can originate from both **body parts** or can be caused by their *relationship* with **each other**, so it is important to check the *direction* from which the weakness originates. Check whether the **cerebrum** is weak to the **left hemisphere**, or the **left hemisphere** is weak to the **cerebrum**, if the **cerebrum** is weak to the **right hemisphere** or the **right hemisphere** is weak to the **cerebrum**, and if the **cerebrum** is weak to the **corpus callosum** or the **corpus callosum** is weak to the **cerebrum**.

4. Reread the sentence:

"The **cerebrum** is the largest part of the human brain. It is divided into **left** and **right hemispheres** and is connected by the **corpus callosum**, a band of **nerve tissue** (white matter) allowing the two halves to exchange information."

The sentence is strong when all the words in that sentence FEEL even and none of them stand out. You then move on to the next sentence:

5. Re-read the sentence:

"Each hemisphere of the **cerebrum** is covered by a layer of gray tissue called the **cerebral cortex** and is divided into four **lobes**, the **occipital lobe, temporal lobe, parietal lobe** and **frontal lobe**."

If none of the words in this sentence stand out or FEELS weak there is no need for an energetic upgrade.

6. Re-read the entire paragraph to make sure that the there are no weaknesses between the **cerebrum** and any other words in the paragraph:

"The **cerebrum** is the largest part of the human brain. It is divided into **left** and **right hemispheres** and is connected by the **corpus callosum**, a band of nerve tissue (white matter) allowing the two halves to exchange information. Each hemisphere of the **cerebrum** is covered by a layer of gray tissue called the **cerebral cortex**, and is divided into four lobes: the **occipital lobe, temporal lobe, parietal lobe** and **frontal lobe**."

7. Once all the words in the paragraph feel even, move on to the next paragraph and continue reading until another word or sentence grabs your attention.

It is not my intention that you study anatomy in this book. The study of anatomy can seem tedious because the medical community uses a foreign language in a confusing way. Also, when people are diagnosed with a disease, their first inclination is to go to the internet and medical journals to access information. Much of this information is written in first-person and has the potential to anchor symptoms onto the person reading it. I have simplified the language to describe anatomy and the anatomical connections throughout the book, without those anchors, for those of you who are interested in gaining a more in-depth understanding of how the body works to facilitate more specific energetic shifts.

If you prefer not to read about anatomy in the book, you can just scan the information for words that grab your attention and strengthen them or ignore those paragraphs altogether. I would like to point out that the action of reading words downloads them into your computer and makes the information contained within the words available when they are needed.

I know, *It* sounds too good to be true … but *it just is!*

PHYSICAL

Some words that do not regard anatomy are also **bolded** in the book. These words are **bolded** to show the difference between *non-physical* and **physical matter**.

NON-PHYSICAL

The words representing *non-physical* weaknesses in this book are highlighted in *bold italic*. These are *emotional re-actions, mental* and *psychological responses*, *psychic* and *spiritual influences* that commonly have a profound *effect* on the vast majority of the population and are often mistaken as **physical** problems. Examples are shown in the following paragraph:

> "*Dark energies* and *dark matter* are *traumas, tortures* and *illnesses* that are *deceptive* and *elusive* because they are hidden in *cords, bonds*, *vows*, *contracts*, *ties*, *access points, holes* and *threads* that are *birthing*, *cloning* and *seeding* from *frequencies*, *interferences* and *fears* from the *collective experiences* of other *dimensions, parallel universes*, *existences*, *time* and *space* that may or may not be *named, numbered* or *known*. They can cause *re-actions* that *repeat, repel, recycle* and *spread*."

If any of these words FEEL weak, there are underlying weaknesses that may be presenting as pains and discomfort in the **physical body**. As the energetic weaknesses are shifted, the pain and discomfort will lessen and in some instances completely disappear.

Read the entire paragraph to make sure that the there are no weaknesses between any of the **bold italic** words and any other words in the paragraph, particularly the ones that are **bold**.

Once all the words in the paragraph feel even, move on to the next paragraph and continue reading until another word or sentence grabs your attention.

ENERGETIC UPGRADES (*EU ...)

If you are in the process of reading a specific word, sentence or paragraph, and you feel compelled to stop what you are reading to see what *EU ... is about, follow your intuition! It is an indication that you have an underlying weakness to what you are reading. This is a window of opportunity to clear an energetic weakness that may be limiting you, your children, your ancestors, or other members of your family and friends. It is not necessary to return to what you were reading however, you can mark your place and return if you want to. Follow your intuition!

NUGGETS OF WIZDOM FROM THE VECTOR

What is the vector?

Vectors are used in science to describe anything that has both direction and magnitude. They are usually drawn, in equations as pointed arrows, the length of which represents the vector's magnitude. For instance, wind has a vectorial quantity because it blows in a certain direction at a certain speed. If you think about a quarterback throwing a pass down the field, the ball has both direction and magnitude depending on how hard it was thrown. In an equation representing this action, the direction of the vector arrow marks the ball's direction and the length represents the speed of the ball.

The only possible geometry that is in equilibrium in all vectorial directions (other than the sphere) is the cuboctahedron because the length of the radiating vectors and the edge vectors are equal.

In this book, I am referring to the vector as the moment in time and space that has the direction and the magnitude to qualify an answer that determines the best position to take in relation to one point of space with another.

It is not that the other answers are right or wrong … it is simply "the answer" that is most applicable to the question you are asking in that moment. If you take action in that moment, embracing that answer, you will achieve the best result.

SIDE EFFECTS

We release both physical and non-physical toxins and poisons through stool, vomit, sweat, ejaculate, menstrual blood and urine in the quickest way possible through physical elimination systems, including the **lymphatic system**, the **colon** (bowel movements)**,** the expulsion of the contents of the **stomach** (vomiting), the **bladder** (urination) and the **genitals** (orgasm and menstruation for women).

Do not be alarmed if you notice an increase in the volume or frequency of your elimination systems (and you are welcome!… if you are experiencing more orgasmic bliss) as you read this book. It is an indication that you are releasing energies that are not benefiting you.

"It is my great pleasure to offer an in-depth expansive way of sharing inclusive information to facilitate your journey to infinite potential at quantum speed …"

From One Mom To Another …

Colette

ADDICTION

Contrary to popular *belief*, many people with substance abuse issues are highly evolved individuals who have an innate understanding that there is more to life than meets the eye. They turn to **substances** or *actions* to fill in the gaps between the exciting times in their lives, such as when they get a promotion, win a competition, meet a significant other, etc., and the boredom of a mediocre existence.

The **brain** communicates and sends signals through a network of interconnecting **neural pathways** that have the ability to change throughout our lifetime. This ability is referred to as **neuroplasticity**. The **brain** has favorite routes that become etched through habit, just like when people go to and from work and tend to take the quickest, most familiar route. If a person suffers a brain injury, the **brain** creates new routes to compensate, in the same way that a person takes a detour when a road is blocked or under construction.

Addiction chemically alters the brain's communication system, rerouting regions of the brain that control *memory*, *decision-making*, *emotional reactions*, *reward* and *stress* regulation.

Impulsive and *compulsive* **behaviors** are controlled by the **prefrontal cortex**, located in the **frontal lobe** of the brain.

IMPULSIVE BEHAVIOR

Impulsive behavior is typically characterized by *actions* that are driven by the immediate pleasure from a **substance** or *action* and/or without consideration of consequences.

COMPULSIVE BEHAVIOR

Compulsive behavior occurs when a people are driven by a need to relieve "anxiety" and discomfort by taking a **drug** or *action* to *restore comfort*. In the beginning stages of addiction people are driven by *impulsive*, **pleasure-driven behavior** that eventually progresses to *compulsive* behavior. Once the addiction becomes *compulsive*, relief from taking a **substance** or *action* becomes more important than the negative consequences of the **drug** or *action*. The **prefrontal cortex** is hijacked by the addiction, and takes, the rest of the **brain** hostage.

There is a lot of talk these days about living for the "present." Addiction is a consequence of putting too much emphasis on the *present moment*, disregarding consequences from the *past* and denying the *future*. If you use the *present* moment to shift the *past* you automatically strengthen your *future*. You can empower yourself by becoming aware of *impulsive behaviors* and strengthening your *authentic self* to pleasures that are in alignment with your *goals*.

Progression of **addiction** relies on *memory* and learning because the **brain** is wired to a reward system that is activated by **food**, **water** and **sex** to ensure our **survival** as a species. Our reward and pleasure systems mainly come from the **mesolimbic pathway** in an area of the **brain** that is focused on survival; this is referred to as the **ventral tegmental area (VTA) that** connects with the **nucleus accumbens**, which is located in the **basal forebrain**. **Dopamine**, a **neurotransmitter** that is responsible for transmitting signals between the **nerve cells** (**neurons**) and the **brain**, is released when the reward system is *activated*, and sending pleasurable *sensations* throughout the **body**. This encourages repetition of **behaviors** such as the search for food, water and sexual encounters for pro-creation, and to ensure survival. In the case of **addiction**, it also encourages people to crave the **drug** or *action* of *choice*, despite the *negative consequences* for themselves and those around them. Many times there are blocks between the *base chakra* and the *sacral chakra.*

As the **body** gets used to a **drug** or *activity* the levels of **dopamine** decrease with each use, and tolerance for the **drug** or *activity* increases. At this point, addicts need a higher dosage to satisfy their cravings and to relieve the unpleasant *sensations* of **withdrawal**.

Every **drug** or *activity* has an *effect* on the **nucleus accumbens**, located in the **mid-brain** at the top of the **brain stem**, but different **addictions** have different *effects*. Stimulant drugs such as **cocaine** and **methamphetamines** release the most **dopamine**, whereas **alcohol** and **heroin** also stimulate **endorphins** in the **brain** causing **physical** as well as *emotional* addiction. As an addiction escalates, *emotions* and *memory* become involved in the **amygdala** of the **brain**. Eventually **thinking** of the **substance** or **activity**, or being triggered by **environmental cues** that are *associated* with the *memory*, stimulates a craving, which leads to preoccupation with the **activity** or **substance**. Over time, the preoccupation with the craving is replaced by *avoidance* of **withdrawal symptoms**.

RECOVERY

During the initial period of recovery, a person is in **withdrawal** which causes *discomfort* that many refer to as "stress." In response to this "stress," the **hypothalamus** releases **neuro-modulators**, **hormones** similar to **neurotransmitters**. These **neuro-modulators**, along with **dopamine** and

serotonin, decrease in the later stages of addiction, which often causes relapses in a person coping with the "stress" of the **withdrawal symptoms**. To aid the course of recovery, strengthen the levels of **dopamine** and **serotonin** to be in *balance* with the **hypothalamus**. The **physical** *sensations* of stress are only part of the trigger for relapse in addictive people. "Stress" is actually an *emotional* and *psychological* reaction to *unreliable information* and *half-truths* that often stem from **corporate interests**, **government**, the **medical community**, the **media**, and other organizations **tactically** designed for **profit**. *EU ... TACTICS, Pg. 494*

Many people who begin **addictive behaviors** do so to compensate for family members who are already addicted. This is very common when **alcoholism** and/or **incest** runs in a family and also for many children who start **smoking** because they are lured in by **advertising** as well as the *sub-conscious thoughts* they have absorbed at a young age from significant family members he or she wants to emulate. In the past public opinion considered it "cool" to smoke – actors and actresses commonly smoked in public or on the big screen. Today, in North America and some other countries, **smoking** is considered anti-social because of the negative health risks to both the smoker and others. **Tobacco** itself is not inherently **poisonous** or **toxic**. **Smoke** from the plant has been used by many ancient societies in rituals and ceremonies as plant medicine to chase away negative *psychic energies* or to facilitate healing at a distance. It was not inhaled and always used with respect. The **tobacco** that is smoked today, however, is not the same as **tobacco** from just a few generations ago. It is laden with **pesticides**, **chemicals**, **toxins** and **poisons** as well as negative *psychic energy* that arise from the **rape**, **pillage** and **plunder** that occurred from confiscation of land for **profit**, and the *misuse* and *misrepresentation* of the **plant**. On a **physical** level the first cigarette a person smokes is generally not a pleasant *experience*, but the *activity* quickly becomes **addictive** with each progressive cigarette.

Most people attempt to quit smoking because of **information** about the *health* risks, and the *negative reactions* from **society**. The **tobacco industry**, **cancer industry** and **quit-smoking industry** all go hand in hand, and all make a **profit** regardless of whether a person **smokes** or tries to **quit**. Many people smoke *compulsively;* instead of enjoying the *experience*, they obsess about the **negative consequences** to their **bodies** which causes more "stress" and more **negative consequences.** To give up a **substance** or *action*, the addict must be strong to the benefits of **quitting** outweighing the consequences of **continuing** with the addiction. For people watching from the sidelines, it may seem that the addict is in *denial* and justifying his or her **behavior**, but the problem is that the addict is not assessing the negative **consequences** and **benefits** accurately.

To let go of addictions a person needs to get strong to all of the following: *never* having a concern about using the **substance** or **activity** again, *always* having a *problem* with the **substance** or *activity* for the rest of their lives, *sometimes* using the *substance* or *activity* and using the **substance** or *activity forever* with *enjoyment*. For example, in the case of **smoking**, you can identify the number of **cigarettes** that are **smoked** on an average day and the ones that are actually enjoyed, and strengthen the person to fully enjoy the *experience* of smoking those **cigarettes**, while giving up the **cigarettes** that are being smoked due to *compulsive* **behavior**. Integrate the *sub-conscious, unconscious* and *conscious mind* to identify when the **substance** or *action* is a **physical need** driven by *compulsive* behaviors or an *impulsive* behavior driven by *pleasure*. Once the *mind* is integrated and the person *consciously* recognizes that the *negative effects* of **addiction** are causing far more **problems** than **benefits**, it is easier to make the *choice* to give up the **substance** or *action*.

Society looks up to people who persevere through hardship to reach their **goals,** and *judges* "quitters" as people who give up too soon. Many people have weaknesses to **quitting** and "being a quitter," even when **quitting** would be most beneficial.

Strengthen the **neurotransmitters, neuro-modulators,** the **nucleus accumbens**, **VTA**, **hypothalamus** and the **amygdala** to the **brain,** the *mind* and the **CNS** to have optimal communication. Even out **dopamine**, **serotonin** and **endorphins** to their infinite potential to strengthen re-routing of the **prefrontal cortex**.

THE "GOOD NEWS" IS:

Many **herbs, plant medicines** and **psychedelics** have been used by ancient societies to successfully treat and relieve **physical** and *non-physical* issues throughout the ages. When they are used with reverence and respect, they have a profound, beneficial *effect* on the people using them. **Substances** in and of themselves are not good or bad, although any substance can be abused.

THE "BAD NEWS" IS:

Most **psychedelic drugs** and **herbs** have been deemed illegal and have been replaced by **psychotropic drugs**, **alcohol** and **modern tobacco** to relieve the "stress" inflicted on people by **society**, mainly to satisfy **corporate interests** and to keep people working for the system.

NUGGET OF WIZDOM FROM THE VECTOR

ANYTIME YOU PLACE A SUBSTANCE OR ACTION ABOVE YOURSELF, THE BURDEN OF CARRYING IT WILL ROCK YOUR FOUNDATION. FOR INSTANCE, IF YOU PUT CARROTS INTO YOUR BODY AND YOU ARE WEAK TO THEM THEY WILL HAVE A NEGATIVE EFFECT ON YOU EVEN THOUGH MOST PEOPLE CONSIDER THEM TO BE HEALTHY, IT IS IMPORTANT FOR EVERY CELL IN YOUR BODY TO RESONATE STRONGLY WITH ANY SUBSTANCE OR ACTION THAT YOU TAKE.

AFFIRMATIONS

Pouring **energy** into **wishing** and positive **thinking** is a waste of time. The assumption that the desires of the **conscious mind** will manifest what a person desires through repeated **affirmations** leads to the frustration of unsatisfied **desires** and unexpressed potential. If the **sub-conscious** and **un-conscious mind** are not energetically aligned with **conscious desire** it amounts to **wishing**. **Wishing** for something you don't have attracts more situations of **wishing** for something you don't have. Conscious **desires** must be aligned with **choices** made on the **sub-conscious** and **un-conscious** level to manifest into reality.

Convincing yourself through repetition is not the answer. Peeling away hidden layers of energetic blocks on the **sub-conscious** and **un-conscious** level is the quickest way to understanding and achieving **authentic desires** and allowing them to come into being in the third dimensional world.

As you read the following affirmations, notice which words go weak in the paragraph, plug into your **heart** and run energy up and down your **spine** in a second or less to delete the underlying weaknesses and strengthen yourself to your true potential. When the blocks are released, you will become strong to **attracting**, **experiencing** and living your **authentic desires**.

INTEGRITY

I do not compromise my **integrity**. I am rigorously honest first and foremost with myself and therefore with everyone else. When I give my word, I do my best to keep it because I understand that my word is my *honor*, and without *honor*, they are just empty words.

IDEALS

I have lofty standards. I am dynamic in my self-empowerment, free of any **beliefs** or **expectations** that limit my potential to reach my goals. I expect to reach my goals with no **expectations** of how they will *manifest*. I follow my **insight** to stay on track. I am on track and closer to *manifesting* my lofty standards and ideals because they come from my **heart**.

LIFE FORCE ENERGY

Every **atom** in every **cell** in my **body** is a celebration of divine **source energy**. Infinite potential **flows** through me and I draw upon that energy at will. I am connected to the entire universe and I understand that **giving** and **receiving** are reciprocal. The more benefits I **give**, the more benefits I **receive**. I joyfully give from my **heart**.

PERSEVERANCE

I understand that I create my reality. I **deserve** the freedom to express my **authentic desires** through infinite possibilities. I am **able** to have what I want, and I am **ready** to be **who** I want to be. I am **willing** to take consistent steps of **action** and persevere in my commitment to achieving my **goals**.

MULTI-TASKING

It is easy for me to multi-task. When I multi-task I am able to effortlessly discern which of the many given tasks to give priority to in any given moment. It is easy for me to concentrate on a specific task undisturbed by distraction. My **body**, **soul** and **spirit** have strong boundaries, allowing all **external** and **internal forces** to flow through me without any negative effect on my potential to perform any task at hand.

PERFORMANCE

I **effortlessly** maximize my performance with minimum time and effort through the **efficient** use of every second of every minute of every day. I understand that any given moment is percolating with potential. I **utilize** that potential before it disappears forever.

ACCOUNTABILITY

I understand what needs to happen to achieve my goals. I take consistent steps of *action*, *utilizing* my skills and teaming up with others to share our skills. I am accountable for all of my *actions* and allow others to be accountable for their *actions* and outcomes.

CONSISTENCY

I have a clear concise image of my heart's desires, and effortlessly take consistent steps of *action* in my everyday goals in alignment with my path. It is natural for me to breathe life into my goals and persevere, seeing them through to the end with minimum effort. I easily release any limiting perceptions from *past, present* and *future* success or failure.

FULFILLMENT

I enjoy an *abundance* of everything – all *qualities* and **conditions** that are required for my *fulfillment*. Success comes easily for me and contributes to my joy and zest for life. Those who are close to me benefit from my joyful presence and are inspired to enjoy the beauty of life.

DISCERNMENT

I am able to make decisions with *ease* in all matters because I always have access to the correct **information** before I choose my next step of *action*. I understand what to do next because I am connected to my *insight*. I am able to increase my productivity by responding to **challenges.** The greater the *challenge,* the more rapidly I am *able* to access the most applicable answer to ensure a creative solution.

ORGANIZATION

I am well organized in every *aspect* of life. My body is a symphony of harmonious cooperation, contributing to my *health*, *fitness* and *youthfulness*. Any thought that is not in alignment with my heart's path is instantly released without *emotion*. Manifestation of my every *desire* is reflected in the perfect organization of my **physical environment**.

STRATEGIES

I always have strategies for success in place. I plan ahead with my goals in mind. I respond to subtle variances in the vector and adjust my strategy accordingly, **easily changing** my plans to optimize my success and the success of others who are affected by my plans.

ACHIEVEMENT

I am capable of accomplishing everything that I set out to achieve. The satisfaction of accomplishing my goals is the most significant achievement of all. I am **efficient** with my **time** and **energy** so that I am fully compensated for everything I do, even when appearances suggest otherwise.

MEMORY

I have an excellent **memory** with the **mental** capacity to retain or recall facts, events, impressions and previous **experiences**. My immediate, short term and long term **memory** are all intact. I have the capacity to store and preserve data for retrieval at any given time. My **memory** improves every day.

INITIATIVE

I take on projects on my own **initiative** without needing external input or encouragement. I carry out each task from start to finish to accomplish my **goals** with maximum **efficiency**, conserving my **energy** for my next energetic **start**.

INSIGHT

I have the insight to build my life with the **future** in mind. When I am faced with many answers to any given question, I can easily feel the answer that is in alignment with my **heart's purpose** and take consistent steps of **action** based on that **insight**.

BRAVERY

I bravely face all situations with true courage, daring and intrepid boldness. I act in accordance with my convictions regardless of the **criticism** of others who have not chosen my path. I handle any conflict with **ease**. I understand that **opportunities** are often disguised as **problems**, and I rise to the **challenge**.

INSPIRATION

I have an exceptional ability to transcend traditional ideas and consistently find **creative solutions** to solve any **problem** with meaningful new ideas. I am inspired to find better ways to perform any given task, embracing any apparent setback as an *opportunity* to inspire my creative fertility. As a result, I always find a better way and enjoy a position of growing leadership. My life is vastly enriched through *inspiration* and *creativity*.

WISDOM

I have the wisdom to express my personal *dignity* through **maturity**. I eagerly seek constant growth within myself to improve every area of my life and to improve the lives of those around me. I *utilize* knowledge and experience with common sense and have the wisdom to *create* with, rather than to **compete** with others.

LEARNING

I am disciplined in my development through study and learning and systematically *absorb* information to improve the abilities of my *mind*. I aspire to and have an appreciation for high intellectual and esthetic ideals thus increasing my learning and earning power. I read quickly and automatically comprehend the subject matter.

COMMUNICATION

I have excellent communication skills through the written word as well as through speech. When I speak, I am self-prepared and completely at *ease* before any group. I am articulate. Every word, the *tone* of each word, my *gestures* and my *body language* are congruent and in keeping with the information, I present. I speak from my **heart** with perfect understanding of my **subject** and an *authentic desire* to share pertinent information with others.

EXCELLENCE

I aspire to soar to great heights and aim for excellence. I improve my ability to perform complex tasks with *ease* by executing the most simple tasks with *excellence*.

INNER-PEACE

Every **cell** in my **body** is in harmony with my **heart**. My **body** is perfectly synchronized to the *effortless contraction* and *expansion* of my **heart-beat** as a reflection of the universe. The perfection of this connection strengthens my life-force energy, allowing me to easily filter any **external forces** that could negatively affect my inner peace.

POISE

I have the ability to remain poised in my *mind*, bearing and appearance under every circumstance. I gracefully *accept* any *challenge* because I understand that *challenges* are *possibilities* and *opportunities* in disguise.

GENIALITY

I have a pleasant and friendly manner, conducive to life and growth. This makes me approachable to others because they sense that I sincerely enjoy *aspects* of every new person that I meet. I give myself *total permission* to be me with no *pretense*. This stimulates **confidence** in others to do the same so that each time I meet with a person it enriches our experience.

CONFIDENCE

I have **confidence** in myself, in my ability to face any situation or any person. I am *able* to make appropriate *choices* and decisions and respond effectively to *change*. Since this thought precedes my *actions*, I am consistently pleased with my **behavior**. I value the information I receive from others who have equal or better understanding than I do. I have the ability to achieve my *authentic desires*.

LEADERSHIP

I *choose* to be a **leader**. I have the integrity and courage to take *response-ability* for my *actions* and inspire others to serve our common **goals** through a shared **vision**. I acknowledge the achievements of those who support our **goals** and give them generous credit for our accomplishments.

THE "GOOD NEWS" IS:

You can align your *sub-conscious, un-conscious* and *conscious minds* to support your goals by following your **heart** on your path to success.

THE "BAD NEWS" IS:

Many of the **desires** people **think** they have are not *authentic desires* and are therefore out of alignment with what is in the best interests of their *whole* *being*. **Goals** that are based on the **false obligations** of **society** limit potential, undermine confidence and lead to *frustration*.

NUGGET OF WIZDOM FROM THE VECTOR

LIVE SUCCESSFULLY TO BE SUCCESSFUL! YOU OWN YOUR MIND, YOUR MIND DOES NOT OWN YOU. WHEN YOU LEAD WITH YOUR HEART, THE SUB-CONSCIOUS, UN-CONSCIOUS AND CONSCIOUS MIND WILL FOLLOW, SUPPORTING YOU AND YOUR AFFIRMATIONS.

AGE REVERSAL

Although most people *accept aging* as an unavoidable consequence of living, many people struggle with common *fears* shared by the *collective consciousness* about *health* problems *associated* with *aging* and **death**. Loss of *youthful* appearance and a *fear* of being out of place in a **society** that honors youth and fights *aging* at all costs causes many weaknesses in the *sub-conscious*, *un-conscious* and *conscious* mind. The primary *emotional* weakness is *embarrassment* for people whose success is measured by their chronological age rather than by joyful living. The paradox is that the so-called "stress" created by unreliable information around *aging* is the number one reason for most people's lack of *youthfulness*. There are limitless surgeries that people routinely undergo in their fight for *youthfulness*. Unfortunately, many of these procedures do not achieve the desired, natural effect, and in fact are painfully obvious to even the most untrained eye. People are saturated by the media with 'photoshopped' images that are created by a team of makeup artists, hair stylists, photographers, lighting, etc. These images create unrealistic *expectations* that even those who are deemed to be the "most beautiful" cannot achieve on a daily basis. Minute by minute people are indoctrinated into the *limiting belief* that these are standards of beauty women should aspire to, even though they clearly conflict with the **reality** people *experience* through their interactions with others in the flesh.

To achieve **true age reversal,** you must be strong to *youthful memories* as opposed to *aging memories*. People who have *experienced* early **death** more often than *aging* in their *past lives,* have a tendency to look younger than their chronological age because their soul has *accumulated* fewer *aging experiences*. To reverse *aging* you have to identify its many causes, and clear any strong *memories* of *overcompensating* and internalizing the *fears* of *aging* from the *past*, *present* and *future*. Many of these *collective fears* revolve around **finances**, **jobs**, lack of *health*, running out of **time** to achieve **goals**, loss of *relationships*, etc. and these fears are maintained down the family line by your *ancestors* and *descendants*. *EU ... ANCESTORS AND DESCENDANTS, Pg. 63*

Resistance to change impedes people's ability to **regenerate** and *rejuvenate* because they tend to draw what they *fear* the most into their reality, thereby creating even more *fear*. On a **physical** level, the **systems** and **organs** for **elimination**, the **colon** and the **lymphatic system,** are most important to ward off *aging,* as is the **circulatory system** which carries **nutrients, oxygen** and **water** to the required locations throughout the **body**. The *fitness* in the structures of the **body** are also important, particularly the *flexibility* and *co-ordination* of the **joints** and the *spaces in-between* the **joints**. Rigid **thinking** leads to rigid **joints**. *Flexibility* of the *mind* and *spirit* play a significant role in *flexibility* of the **joints**. Strengthen the interconnections of *collagen* and *elastin* throughout the **body** and the *empty spaces* in the **body**.

Most important of all are your **cells**. They are complex units that maintain their viability and **function**, which is to carry out *metabolic activities*, by being fed a continuous supply of **oxygen, glucose** and **amino acids** that are dependent on the **environment** of the **cell** itself. **Cell** *degeneration* is an ongoing phenomenon in multicellular organisms, and it must be *balanced* by an equal amount of *cell regeneration*. As the waste from **dead cells** and **half dead cells** *accumulates* in the **tissues** and **organs** of the **body**, it is vital that this *balanced regeneration* takes place because too many **dying cells** and **cellular waste** *stagnate* **systems** and cause **aging**.

DEGENERATION

Most people think of *degeneration* as something to avoid; however, *degeneration* **(apoptosis)** of the **cells** is essential to human development because the **body** creates millions of **cells** that it does not need (**menstruation** is an example of this). To prevent **dysfunction** in the **cells** from spreading, **cells** die in response to signals from the **body** when they recognize **viruses** and **gene mutations**. **Cells** also receive signals from the **body** to continue living. They are sensitive to both **physical** and *non-physical* triggers that cause malfunctions in communication within the **cell**, leading to confusion as to which **cells** are **dysfunctional** and which **cells** should live or die.

REGENERATION

Just as the universe is *holofractographic* (*holographic* with perfect **nonlinear fractal structure**), so are our **bodies**. The **physical structure** of the systems that take in **nutrients** and eliminate **waste** are also in place on the *microscopic* level in the **cells**. For optimal *regeneration*, the **lymphatic system**, **nervous system**, **circulatory system**, etc., have to work in cooperation with each other and within themselves in the **intrinsic** (**physical body**) as well as at a **cellular** level. Many people concern themselves with what they put into their **bodies** without giving consideration to what is being **eliminated**. When *regeneration* and *degeneration* are even throughout the **cells** of the **body**, optimum *rejuvenation* takes place.

Black wholes can be created throughout the **body** to assist the **elimination** of *toxins*, *poisons*, **minerals**, **cellular** and **parasitic waste**, etc., and *white wholes* can be created to spin in **oxygen**, **glucose**, *hydration* and **nutrients** where they are needed in the **body** and the **cells**. **EU ... BLACK WHOLE/WHITE WHOLE, Pg. 93*

HUMAN GROWTH HORMONE (HGH)

HGH is produced by the **pituitary gland** to spur growth in children and adolescents, and to regulate **body composition, body fluids, muscle** and **bone growth**, **sugar** and **fat metabolism**. Its secretion naturally decreases around the age of **twenty** and again at **twenty-five** causing an increase in **adipose tissue** and a decrease in **lean body mass** in a process called **somatopause**.

HGH is secreted during the first few hours of deep sleep and *affects* every **cell** in the **body**, using **amino acids**, the building blocks of **proteins,** to support the synthesis of **molecules**. Several **peptides**, called **somatomedins,** and produced mainly in the **liver** are dependent on and also mediate **HGH**. **Somatostatin** is a **hormone** produced by many **tissues** in the **body**, mainly in the **nervous** and **digestive systems,** the **pancreas** as well as in the **hypothalamus**. It inhibits secretion of other **hormones**, including **HGH** and **TSH** (**thyroid stimulating hormone**) and stimulates rapid reproduction of normal **cells** and **tumors**. The **somatostatin** produced in the **pancreas** inhibits the production of **insulin** and **glucagon** and the secretion of **gastrointestinal hormones** in the **gastrointestinal tract**, such as **gastrin**.

Synthetic HGH is the active ingredient in a number of injectable drugs and products that promise to *reverse age-related degeneration* and to improve athletic performance. There are also sprays and pills that promise to stimulate **HGH** production. Their results differ and are dependent on the quality of the product and each individual. We can also energetically strengthen all functions of the components involved in the process of **somatopause**.

THE "GOOD NEWS" IS:

Positive thoughts that you are energetically in *alignment* with have the potential to make rapid changes that can manifest quickly in your **physical body** because your **cells** are constantly picking up **information** from your **environment** and adapting to that **information**.

THE "BAD NEWS" IS:

Negative thoughts also have the potential to make rapid changes that can manifest quickly in your **physical body** because your **cells** are constantly picking up **information** from your **environment** and adapting to that **information**.

NUGGET OF WIZDOM FROM THE VECTOR

CONSIDER YOUTHFULNESS AS A GAME THAT YOU PLAY TO WIN. ON ANY GIVEN DAY, YOU WILL ENCOUNTER MANY INFLUENCES THAT HAVE THE POTENTIAL TO AGE YOU. YOUR INTERPRETATION OF THESE EVENTS, PEOPLE, SITUATIONS, ETC., WILL EITHER SUPPORT YOUTHFULNESS OR ACCELERATE AGING.

ALLERGIES

We are indoctrinated at an early age that **allergies** are common because **allergens** are everywhere and we are unable to escape their *effects*. Methods used for detection and elimination of **allergies** are haphazard at best and often fail to alleviate the symptoms. Many **allergies** are secondary *physical* and *emotional re-actions* to various **physical substances** combined with *suppressed grief* and *sorrow*. The varied symptoms are often caused by *sensitivity* to *collective mental* blocks regarding *pain* and *dis-comfort*. When a person is diagnosed as being allergic to a particular substance, the *fear* of that specific **substance** and the need to avoid exposure to it often *triggers accumulations* of *negative emotions* that arise from seemingly unavoidable demoralizing **situations**. Obsessing over, removing or avoiding the **allergen** causes a stronger *re-action*.

People *accumulate* physical *sensations* from *suppressing* pain or *dis-comfort*, and this causes confusion in the **central nervous system** that can lead to many common symptoms of **allergies**. Asthma and other breathing issues such as **wheezing**, **sniffling**, **sneezing**, **choking**, **coughing**, etc., are quite often the result of a weakness to letting things go on the *exhale*, and sometimes an inability to take things in, creating a weakness on the *inhale*. **Inflamed emotions** of *anger* and the *irritation* of dealing with people and situations can create *inflammation*, **swelling**, **hives** and other *irritations* of the **skin**. Severe *re-actions* to **insect** and **spider bites**, **stings**, etc., are often triggered by *collective influences* of *infestations* and *infections*, **plagues**, etc., spread by **lice, fleas, cooties, scabies**, etc. *Feeling stuck* and an *itch* "to make things happen" can also cause *skin eruptions* and a need to scratch. *Itchy* **eyes** are often referred from the **reproductive system**.

Adverse *re-actions* to **pharmaceuticals** are often related to *psychic, karmic* and *spiritual* influences connected to the **medical profession, big pharmacy**, and the **practice** of **medicine**. The so-called "side effects" from taking prescribed **antibiotics, penicillin, aspirin, anti-inflammatories, antihistamines**, and **psychotropic drugs** are often down-played instead of being identified as *cause* and *effect*.

Allergic *re-actions* to **food** and **animals** are often associated with *harvesting* and *preparation*, including *traumatic memories* from experiences of **torture**, **hunting** and "being hunted" "running for your life" and a *collective grief* of *suffering* from and causing **abuse** and **cruelty** on a massive scale.

Trapped *psychic* and *spiritual* energies in your living environment can *trigger* experiences of sharing **overcrowded living spaces, imprisonment** and population control. The trapped *emotions* that people *suppress* can lead to *stagnation* of all systems and a lack of structure in the **cavities** of the **body**, in particular the **sinus cavity**. *Congestion* of the **sinuses** is a form of internal weeping.

Pollens, mold, dust and **chemicals** are commonly blamed for painful *mental* and *physical re-actions* when the *irritation* is actually coming from an inefficient **lymphatic system**. Blockages in the **lymphatic system** often accompany painful **body sites**. Sneezing is a rejection of something coming in and often occurs when people are feeling rejected or rejecting others by "blowing them off." A strong **lymphatic system** is essential to effectively handle *accumulated* and modern day toxins and poisons. **Physical** and *mental associations* of surrendering to the symptoms often stimulate aggressive *emotions* calculated to eliminate the enemy. Many people have *traumatic memories* of being forced to surrender, which are reinforced when they feel under attack by "the enemy," in this case a substance. *Emotional* and *psychological* grief from the *past* often accompanies watering **eyes**. **Nasal** drip and a runny **nose** are often referred from the **respiratory system** via weaknesses in the **colon** and/or from the **bladder** if a person is "pissed off."

Anaphylactic shock is caused by an overly intense *re-action* that is an *accumulation* of many *experiences*. It can be calmed down by shifting the *over re-action* first. Strengthen the people who are witnessing the event to remain calm, then break down the *accumulations* of *re-actions*, starting with the weakest one and quickly working through the rest.

RESULTS:

"I listened to Colette on the Sheila show and knew that I wanted her to work with me. I have never listened live to the show but on this day, I knew I needed to. I have lived in Shanghai for the past year and a half, and for a year of that, I have had extreme allergies and asthma (the medical diagnosis). Having spent more time ill than well here and with the ill episodes getting longer it was difficult for me to get strong and healthy between so that when I connected with Colette on the Sheila show I was quite weak, weary and suffering from not being able to breathe well. Also because I was so weak, I was not able to walk for more than a few steps at a time. Colette worked with me on the show and set the ball rolling. I knew the base of what was going on was emotional with the environment simply aggravating everything but I didn't have the correct tools to deal with it. The first thing Colette did was tell me that it was 100% emotional and that the causes are NEVER what we think they are. By the end of the show session, I was feeling much better with Colette strengthening my breathing and also my lower torso and then strengthening them to each other. She also opened up my throat. The show was on a Wednesday.

"Many things started changing in my body and everything that was being set in motion set me in a tailspin so I contacted Colette and scheduled a session with her for Monday. During that session, she started purging the troublesome aspects of my life that were causing the asthma and walking problems. It was bizarre the things she was pulling out of my past! She also started correcting all of the other aspects and issues up at this time.

"I scheduled another session for that Friday. That day was my first day back at work and I actually worked a 12-hour day having no problems with my breathing or my walking! So it was essentially 9 days work Colette did with me to get me from the place I was on the Sheila show to being back functioning totally! That is absolutely amazing – I have never experienced anything to be able to clear all of this in this short period of time. I'm looking forward to the shifts from the session on Friday – Colette said that my life would not look the same to me one week from then! So yeah …

"I'm making my wish list of all of the things I want to work on and will definitely work with Colette. She is warm and loving, totally nonjudgmental and so intuitive so that she can get to the heart of the issues. I am forever grateful to you Colette for your work."

Deborah Weimer, Shanghai, China

THE "GOOD NEWS" IS:

If you have been **suffering** from allergies since you were a young child growing up, it is most likely not your favorite **substance** causing the problem. It is more likely that your parents' **re-actions** to **inaccurate information** has rubbed off on you. Remove the trigger by separating the substance from **inaccurate information** and *emotional re-actions*.

THE "BAD NEWS" IS:

The triggers for **allergies** generally consist of multiple influences. Testing a **substance** alone will often feel strong for a person unless it is combined with *emotional re-actions*, *psychic* and *spiritual* influences. People who are hypersensitive with strong *emotional re-actions* have many combinations of *accumulations* to delete.

NUGGET OF WIZDOM FROM THE VECTOR

PEOPLE WHO SUFFER FROM ALLERGIES ARE REACTING TO THE COMBINATION OF MISINFORMATION ATTACHED TO A PHYSICAL SUBSTANCE AND THE COLLECTIVE INFLUENCE OF SUFFERING. ONCE THE TRIGGERS AND ACCUMULATIONS ARE DELETED, THE SYMPTOMS WILL DESIST. IF YOU ARE WORKING WITH CHILDREN, TEST IF THE WEAKNESS IS COMING FROM THE ADULTS FIRST.

ANCESTORS AND DESCENDANTS

Often when we are clearing energy, many weaknesses that are causing problems in the here and now come from unresolved issues from our **ancestors.** As we resolve issues for our **ancestors,** it shifts everyone up and down the family line, allowing the inherent strengths in the family to shine through.

You can connect with your **ancestors** across the veil and through *space-time* to facilitate change for the better for your family here on earth by clearing inherent weaknesses and strengthening specific qualities that are passed down the family line. Many families have generations of healers with occult powers that have been **suppressed** due to **fear** of being persecuted, usually because of **religion**; this suppression has limited spiritual growth for the entire line. There are only a few families that come from a lineage of shamans, shaolin masters, etc. who have been encouraged to express and hone these skills.

Common weaknesses that weigh families down are **karmic debts** that have not been cleared, ancestors who remain as **entities** after making their transition and are stuck on the earth plane, **demonic forces** that remain **attached** to families, **curses** and **spells**, **health issues**, **weight issues**, **premature aging**, inability to be happy and form **relationships**, the need to **suffer** and **struggle**, etc.

It is helpful to ask **what** happened, **when** did it happen, **where** in the maternal and paternal line did it happen, **who** and **how** many were involved, etc. As you come across these weaknesses, it is not uncommon for family members to come through across the veil to cheer you on. You can check if there is a **family member** or **guardian** who is overseeing the family in the hierarchy from across the veil and ask him or her for intervention to clear issues more efficiently.

DESCENDANTS

It is not only **ancestors** that have a huge effect on a person's potential here on earth. **Fears** for their descendants can also have a profound effect, especially on a person's **future**. There can also be **residual** weaknesses from **pregnancies** that end in **miscarriage** or are terminated in **abortions**. These are often **souls** whose intention was to dip their toes into amniotic waters, but not to complete their journey as viable human beings. They come through wanting resolution for themselves and their parents with whom they often have **soul contracts** for progression in **spiritual growth**. You can reconnect the soul to the would-be mother and father and eliminate any **emotional**, **psychological** or **spiritual weaknesses** to strengthen the benefits of their connection.

The veil between **dimensions**, **existences** and **space-time** is very thin. We can access information by connecting with our **ancestors** up and down the family line, including the ones from the **macrocosmic** as well as the **intrinsic** (**physical body**). If we connect with the holofractographic nature of the universe it stands to reason that we have **ancestors** who encompass all **time** and **space**. Our **ancestors** may be other than we think.

STARDUST

As early as nine years old, Nassim Haramein already realized that there should be some coherence to the *space* dividing everything because it connects all things. He began developing the basis for a unified hyper-dimensional theory of **matter** and *energy* that he eventually called the "holofractographic universe." Combining this knowledge with a keen observation of the behavior of nature, he discovered a specific geometric array that he found to be fundamental to creation, and from which the foundation for his unified field theory emerged. This unification theory is known as the Haramein-Rauscher Metric. It is a new solution to Einstein's Field Equations that incorporates torque and the Coriolis Effect. The Coriolis Effect can be described by the observation of water going down the drain, which shows that for every *action* there is an equal and opposite *re-action*. As the water spirals down the drain, air is spiraling up from the opposite direction.

Nassim's published paper, "The Schwarzschild Proton," lays down the foundation of what could be fundamental change in our current understanding of physics and consciousness. With the collaboration of Dr. Rauscher, Nassim Haramein wrote a scaling law for organized matter of *frequency* versus **radius**. The fundamental *frequency* of the objects is described by its *frequency* on the scale in **hertz** (cycles per second). They placed the data points from the *universal frequency* of **quasars**, the galactic center oscillation rate and radius, solar dynamics and stellar dynamics all the way down across the boundary of quantum theory level to the **Planck's length**.

Remarkably, the points lined up all the way from the **quasars** to the **Planck's (distance) length,** with the biological resolution being almost in the middle, a little bit closer to the **stars**. This is a huge scale! In the standard model of the **scaling law**, everything should have been random.

The odds of these points lining up in a non-organized universe are extremely low. Yet they do! If we lived in a random universe, the data points would be all over the place. In effect, this means you are simultaneously a **container** of the infinite potential of the entire universe and a **data transfer boundary** from the extremely large to the extremely small as you gather information and transfer it to your internal self.

You can use this **fractal scale** as a way to measure your connection within **H.S.N.** (**Higher Self Network**) to navigate the universe you live in. It gives a deeper understanding of the interconnectivity of all the **atoms** of the **body** within you and with others.

THE "GOOD NEWS" IS:

Scientists have recently discovered that **stars** contain **water**. If humans are the "event horizon" and we are mostly made up of **water**, it stands to reason that we are also **stardust**. As we let go of old paradigm limitations, our frame of reference expands to allow our true potential to shine through.

THE "BAD NEWS" IS:

For various reasons people don't bring **descendants** into the world and may believe erroneously that they are off the hook as far as problems with **descendants** go. However, every time you are intimate with a partner, there is the potential to bring **descendants** into being. Missed opportunities from unborn **descendants** who did not come through are often more problematic than the ones that do because people are unaware that they exist.

NUGGET OF WIZDOM FROM THE VECTOR

WHEN WE THINK ABOUT ANCESTORS, WE IMMEDIATELY THINK ABOUT OUR FAMILY LINEAGE IN THE THIRD DIMENSIONAL WORLD; HOWEVER, WE ALSO HAVE A SPIRITUAL LINEAGE THAT COMES FROM OUR SOUL. IF YOU ARE COMMUNICATING WITH OTHER LIGHT BEINGS, BE SURE THAT YOU ARE TAKING ADVICE FROM SOMEONE WHO IS SMARTER THAN YOU.

ARTHRITIS

The diagnosis of **arthritis** is used to encompass over one hundred related conditions that range from mild forms of **tendinitis** and **bursitis** to crippling systematic forms such as **fibromyalgia, lupus, gout, osteoarthritis** and **rheumatoid arthritis**. The common denominator of the symptoms of **arthritis** are chronic **joint pain, stiffness, redness** and **swelling** due to *inflammation* of the **joints**. Although most people think of **arthritis** as a **disease** of the elderly, it can *affect* people of all ages, including babies and children; interestingly, it does affect **women** more often than men.

Conventional medicine treats **arthritis** as a disease of old **age** and *degeneration* from **overuse,** a **disease** that needs to be managed and is without a cure. However, if we look at the symptoms of **arthritis** as **waste products** from ingested **foods**, in particular the **dyes, preservatives** and **artificial sweeteners** that *accumulate* in the **joints**, you can reverse the *effects* by breaking down **waste** and **dead materials** that attract **parasites** before they cause more destruction to the **joint**.

In general there are many underlying weaknesses that are common in people who experience the symptoms of **arthritic** conditions. On the **physical** level, one can strengthen the **lymphatic system** to *detoxify* and increase *alkalinity*, *negative ions* and the *electromagnetic* field as well as strengthening **water, nitrogen, carbon, oxygen, glucose** and **HGH** to penetrate into the **bone, cartilage** and **tendons** at the **cellular** level. One can increase the *fitness* of the **joints** and correct for **stiffness** and *rigidity* by restoring *space* between the **joints** and **resistance** from the **nervous system, circulatory system** and the **connective tissues**. In the case of children, one should check for deformities of the **joints** in **utero**. Often when there is *twisting* in the **body, disease** is blamed for it rather than recognizing that the *twisting* may be causing the *dis-ease*.

An inability to rise from a **sitting** position to a **standing** position without using **hands** to balance the **knees** is often an indication of *referred* **pain** from the **hands** to **feet, toes** to **fingers, elbows** to **knees, wrists** to **ankles** and **hips** to **jaw**. The energetic weakness can be referred from either **body part**. Strengthen the person to be able to "stand on his or her own two feet" without assistance. Then strengthen the ability to walk with confidence before taking each step.

The pain and discomfort of **arthritis** is a daily reminder of a "lack of control" over life and *fear* of the unknown. People who feel *trapped* by the unfairness of life tend to *over re-act* to the **physical** *sensations,* which causes them to over-internalize, over guard, protect and *relax* the **joints** affected. The lack of *tension* in the **joints** and *fear* of the "wear and tear" creates a vicious cycle of *degeneration*. The most common *emotion associated* with **arthritic pain** is *anger* and *suppressed anger*, along with *frustration*; this creates an *acidic environment* that attracts *infection* and *infestation*. The *diagnosis* and *mis-diagnosis*, particularly in the case of **lupus** and **fibromyalgia** contributes to the *anxiety* and *futility* of ever *experiencing* relief from life's tribulations.

Rigidity and lack of *flexibility* of the **body** is often a reflection of *rigidity* of the *mind* and *spirit*. A person's need to control, and/or his or her lack of **control** of both **self** and **others**, is the common denominator. Many people are triggered when people around them **lose control** or are "about to lose control" because it reminds them of *experiences* when they were **children** and they had no **control** over their **environment**. Hardened **arteries** and *inflammation* of the **pericardium** along with shortness of breath comes from an inability to connect with the "sweetness of life" and to take life in fully through the **breath**. Flare-ups often occur along with disturbances in *family dynamics* and an underlying *anger* at the direction that life is taking.

Our current life *experiences*, **physical environment** and *social programming* are not the only influences *affecting dis-ease* patterns. We inherit the *dis-ease* patterns of our **ancestors** as well, along with *spiritual environment*, history and *spiritual* family influences. *False obligations* and an *imbalance* of certain *aspects* in people's lives, in particular a lack of *spontaneity* are handed down and *accumulated*. Placing focus on these things causes a need to *suffer* and *struggle* with the ups and downs of life. *EU ... ASPECTS OF LIFE, Pg. 73*

On a *spiritual* level there are issues of *rejection* of painful *experiences* reflected in parts of the **physical body** which allow *psychic* energies to interfere with the **body's** ability to maintain homeostasis, (in particular *entities*, *spirit attachments* and *mismatched body parts*. *EU ... PSYCHIC CLEANSE, Pg. 419*

OSTEOARTHRITIS

Osteoarthritis is the most commonly diagnosed form of **arthritis**. It affects the **cartilage**, the tough elastic that covers and protects the ends of **bones** as a shock absorber. As the cushioning erodes, the **bones** rub against each other causing **pain, stiffness** and **swelling** in the affected **joints**. In severe cases, the **joints** become **calcified** and boney. Most people report feeling a **stiffness** and **pain** when they **wake** up in the **morning** that tends to lessen as they move their **bodies** and get on with their day. However, *fear* of *dis-comfort* from using the **joints** also deteriorates the **muscles** around the **joints** causing further disability.

Many people *relax* themselves into **sleep**, becoming so *relaxed* in the **body** that it sinks into their **mattress**. This causes the **organs** and **systems** in the **body** to become too *relaxed*, which *affects* their ability to function at optimal potential. It is important to strengthen *tension* to be optimum in order to support all the **systems** and to begin each day with *purposeful movement*. It is equally important to delete toxic *thoughts* and *self-criticism* from the *sub-conscious* and *un-conscious* mind that have been poisoning the **body** throughout the night.

RHEUMATOID ARTHRITIS

Rheumatoid arthritis is a chronic *inflammatory dis-order* that typically *affects* the small **joints** in the **hands** and **feet** by attacking the **synovium**, the lining of the **joints,** causing painful *swelling* and *stretching* of the **ligaments** and **tendons**, **bone** erosion and **joint** deformity. It can also affect the **skin, eyes, lungs** and **blood vessels. Nodules** commonly form under the **skin**, especially in the **arms**. It can occur at any *age* but typically affects women who are **forty** and older. Morning *stiffness* lasts for hours, accompanied by fatigue, fever and weight loss. Flare-ups occur and disappear, sometimes completely but as the *dis-ease* progresses it can spread to the **knees, ankles, elbows, hips** and **shoulders**.

Many of the **medications** used to treat **rheumatoid arthritis** cause **osteoporosis** by weakening the **bones** and making them more susceptible to **fracture**. It is necessary to strengthen optimum potential for the benefits of the **medication** and delete the "side-effects" through *black wholes*. *EU ... BLACK WHOLE/WHITE WHOLE, Pg. 93*

CARPAL TUNNEL SYNDROME

Carpal tunnel syndrome is commonly the name given to *inflammation*, which cause the **nerves** of the **wrists** to be compressed. This weakness is often referred from the **shoulders** especially in people who are "shouldering the burden of life" for themselves and others.

TENDINITIS

Tendinitis is the *inflammation* and *irritation* of the thick fibrous **cords** that attach **muscle** to **bone;** this causes **pain** and *tenderness* around the **joint**. It is most common in the **upper body,** in the **shoulders, elbows, wrists** and also in the **knees** and **heels**. The occurrence is more frequent in people who participate in occupations and sports that involve *repetitive motions*, awkward *positions*, frequent overhead *lifting*, forceful *exertion* and using equipment that *vibrates*. "Tennis and golfer's elbow," "swimmer's and pitcher's shoulder," and "jumper's knee," are slang that are used to describe the condition.

A lack of *flexibility* in the **joints** makes them easier to injure and is often blamed on *over-use* and *age*. *Accumulations* of *resentment* towards **self** and **others** for "having to work hard" and "struggling to survive" accumulate with the *repetitive* movements required to perform a **job**. These are common weaknesses for work-related **pain**, and *feeling excluded*, and *unable* to participate in the joys of life when it comes to **sports**.

BURSITIS

Bursitis is a painful condition due to *inflammation* of the **bursae,** small fluid filled pads that act as cushions for the **tendons** and **muscles** around the **joints**. It most commonly *affects* the **shoulders, elbows** and

hips and also the **knees, heels** and base of the **big toes**. The site is often **red** and **swollen**, and is sometimes accompanied by a **rash, bruising** and a **fever**. People often describe the pain as *stiff*, *achy* and as *sharp* or *shooting* when they are exerting **joints** that perform frequent *repetitive motions,* especially in occupations that are physically demanding such as **scrubbing, lifting, leaning**, or that involve **sitting** on **hard surfaces** with a lack of *tension* in the buttocks.

The location of the **pain** as well as the words people use to describe it can give clues to the *emotional* and *psychological* weaknesses underlying the **physical pain**. *EU ... SENSATIONS, Pg. 456*

GOUT

Gout is characterized by sudden, severe attacks of **pain, redness** and *tenderness* in **joints**, most often the **joint** at the base of the **big toe**, but also in the **feet, ankles, knees, wrists** and **hands**. The symptoms of **gout** are **acute pain** that comes on suddenly, without warning, usually at night, subsiding within twelve to twenty-four hours, but lingering for days or weeks.

High levels of **uric acid** in the **blood** form **urate crystals** that *accumulate* in the **joint**. **Uric acid** is **produced** in the process of breaking down **purines**, found naturally in the **body** and also in certain foods such as **organ meats, anchovies, herring, asparagus** and **mushrooms**. If you eat these **foods** test for weaknesses to **purines**. **Uric acid** dissolves in your **blood** and passes through your **kidneys** into your **urine**. If there is too much **uric acid** or your **kidneys** secrete too little it creates sharp needle-like **urate crystals**.

Gout is more common in **men** than women until they reach **menopause**. (Excessive **alcohol, high blood pressure, diabetes, high cholesterol** and narrowing of the **arteries** are *believed* to contribute to developing **gout**). It is more likely that the person is trying to *relax* himself or herself out of *anger*, and is *relaxing* the **circulatory system** in the process. Weaknesses in the **big toe** indicate "over-thinking problems" and an unwillingness to step forward in life to make *changes* that would solve **problems**. **Women** who are *experiencing* gout during "men-o-pause" are often "fed up" with **men** and want to take a pause from them. *EU ... MENSTRUATION, Pg. 327*

Thiazide diuretics, commonly used to treat **hypertension**, low dose **aspirin** and **anti-rejection drugs** for organ transplants can also increase **uric acid** production.

FIBROMYALGIA

Fibromyalgia is a *dis-order* of the **musculoskeletal structures** and over-amplification of painful *sensations* accompanied by fatigue, insomnia, sleep apnea, memory dysfunctions and depression. Many people often *experience tension* headaches, **temporomandibular joint** *dis-orders*, **restless legs syndrome**, *cramping* in the **lower abdomen** and **irritable bowel syndrome**. Symptoms often *accumulate* over time without one single trigger, although in some cases a single trigger such as **physical** *trauma*, **surgery**, *infection* or significant *psychosomatic stress* seems to trigger it. People often describe wide-spread **pain** as a *dull ache* on both sides of the **body** and in the **upper** and **lower torso**. Fatigue, inadequate sleep and "brain fog" are also common complaints.

Fibromyalgia is notorious for being **misdiagnosed** and even if the **diagnosis** is accurate, it still does not offer much relief. The *frustration* of dealing with an often-misunderstood condition accelerates the symptoms, and the fact that **fibromyalgia** runs in families is often blamed on certain genetic mutations; instead, the *emotional*, *mental* and *psychological* events that preceded it should be explored. Many people who have been diagnosed with **fibromyalgia** have difficulty "saying no" to other people and "yes" to putting themselves first. Much of the **pain** comes from *feeling* unable to do what they *want* to do.

LUPUS

Lupus is a chronic *inflammatory dis-ease* that attacks healthy **tissues**, **organs** and **body systems** including the **joints**, **skin**, **kidneys**, **blood cells**, **brain**, **heart** and **lungs**. The symptoms of **lupus** can be sudden or they can develop slowly, they can be mild or severe, temporary or permanent. Most people have a mild form where the symptoms flare up, improve and sometimes disappear altogether.

The most distinctive symptom is a **facial rash** resembling the wings of a butterfly across both **cheeks**; that occurs in many, but not all cases of **lupus**. Other common symptoms are fatigue, fever, joint pain, stiffness, swelling, skin lesions that appear or worsen with exposure to the sun, **fingers** and **toes** that turn white or blue with exposure to the cold and during times of *stress*, **chest** pain, dry **eyes**, headaches, confusion and memory loss. More serious consequences of being diagnosed with **lupus** are **kidney** damage leading to **kidney** failure, cognitive function of the **brain**, dizziness, behavioral changes, seizures, strokes, hallucinations, issues with the **blood** such as anemia, bleeding, blood clotting, *inflammation* of the **heart** and **pericardium**, and *inflammation* of the **chest cavity lining**.

Energetically, weaknesses for **lupus** are *ancestral, environmental, psychic* and *spiritual*. Potential **environmental** triggers are exposure to **sunlight**, certain types of **anti-seizure medications, blood pressure pharmaceuticals** and **antibiotics**. If symptoms are triggered by these **medications**, they generally reverse when people become strong to taking the medication. **Women** of child bearing *age*, between the **ages** of **fifteen** to **forty** of **African American, Hispanic** and **Asian** descent are most often *affected*.

The number one underlying cause of **lupus** is *stagnation*. *Infection* sets in, commonly in the **urinary tract** and **bladder** from suppressed *anger* resulting in yeast, salmonella, herpes and shingles, as well as *infections* of the **respiratory system**. *EU ... pH REGENERATION, Pg. 382*

Avascular necrosis, the gradual breakdown of the **bones**, eventually leads to collapse, particularly in the **hip joints,** and because **lupus** affects women of **child-bearing age**, it increases the risk of **high blood pressure** during **pregnancy** and **preterm birth**.

The symptoms of **fibromyalgia** and **lupus** are varied and many are inter-related. Break the *dis-ease* into specific symptoms starting with the weakest one first. Don't be fooled by the **diagnosis** or assume that the cause of one symptom is the same as that of another.

THE "GOOD NEWS" IS:

The one thing that the many forms of **arthritis** have in common is that no one in the mainstream **medical community** can pinpoint the reasons why it occurs other than the fact that it tends to "run in families." The study of **epigenetics** is now proving that we are not ruled by our **DNA** and **genes**. If we can pinpoint the underlying *energetic* and **environmental** weaknesses we can release ourselves from family dynamics.

THE "BAD NEWS" IS:

Most people who are diagnosed with **arthritis** are not aware of the underlying weaknesses and *suffer* and *struggle* with the symptoms, the **diagnosis** and the **pain**.

NUGGET OF WIZDOM FROM THE VECTOR

THE DISCOMFORT ASSOCIATED WITH ARTHRITIC CONDITIONS CAN BE GREATLY ALLEVIATED AS THE ROOT CAUSES OF THE

PAIN ARE PEELED AWAY, GIVING RELIEF TO MILLIONS OF PEOPLE AROUND THE WORLD.

ASPECTS OF LIFE

There are twelve main *aspects* that people are here on Earth to *experience*. When people give themselves *total permission* to enjoy every one of these *aspects,* they create *balance* in their lives.

People often strive for **success** without defining what **success** means to them. Success is often equated with **financial** earning potential, **social** position, **education**, etc.; however, there are many *aspects* to life that are separate from the "false obligations" imposed by **cultures** and **society**. If people hyper-focus on **doing** what is expected of them by the *collective influence* rather than on following their **heart**, it leads to an emphasis on **finances**, **aging**, *relationships*, **careers**, **jobs**, *health*, *fitness* and lack of *purpose*. Often people who excel in one or two of these *aspects* of life have major issues in the other *aspects*. For example, focusing on accumulating **wealth** at the expense of *relationships* with loved ones or concerns of lack of **money** takes a toll on *health*.

You can consider the *aspects* of life as people who are traveling on a raft in rough waters. If the majority of the people sitting at the front of the raft are operating at full potential but at the back, there are three or four who are not performing at all, eventually the raft becomes unstable and everyone traveling on it is at the mercy of the rapids.

The twelve main *aspects* of life are:

DO

Allow yourself to be spontaneous and impulsive; to make *heart felt choices* as well as **logical** choices.

RECEIVE

You are constantly **taking information** in from all of your senses and many times people ignore or discount that **information**. **Information** equals *energy*. *Receive* through your *senses*.

LEARN

Strengthen your *intellect* through reading, observing, communicating and processing **logical information**.

FEEL

Go inward to access the *whole* for the answer most applicable to your situation.

LEAD

Be *original*. When you have something to say, say it. Take the **lead** and strut your stuff.

CONTRIBUTE

You have unique gifts to contribute. Don't let false modesty deter you from taking *steps of action* that benefit the greater *whole*.

SOCIALIZE

No man is an island. We are all connected. Form *relationships* with **people** and **places**.

UNITE

Be vulnerable. Let go of the "shoulds" that prevent you from connecting and *communicating* with others from your **heart**.

EXPAND

It is natural to *expand* and *accelerate* along with the universe. Get out in nature and observe what the earth has to share with you.

TAKE RESPONSE-ABILITY

You are steering your **reality** twenty-four hours a day, seven days a week whether you are aware of it or not. Many people shy away from **responsibility**. *Response-ability* is just that, your *ability* to *respond* to *challenges* to empower your best outcome.

EXPERIMENT

Observe the global picture. Travel to new places and connect with other **cultures** and life-styles.

ACCEPT

Do not underestimate the power of willful ignorance. Until you **accept** where you currently are you are unable to make progressive change. If something is bothering you about someone else it is likely that they are mirroring an **aspect** of yourself that you do not want to see. **Forgive yourself** first and then **forgive** others.

THE "GOOD NEWS" IS:

You can create **balance** in your life by **centering** yourself and noticing which **aspects** you are over-or-under-estimating to allow for **recalibration**. Even out the **weight** and take part in life from your **heart**.

THE "BAD NEWS" IS:

The vast majority of people on the planet avoid introspection and concern themselves with **performing** and **competing** with each other to live their lives based on **false obligations** imposed by **society** at the expense of themselves and all beings on the planet.

NUGGET OF WIZDOM FROM THE VECTOR

WHEN THE ASPECTS ARE IN BALANCE, IT CREATES AN EVENNESS IN EVERY AREA OF LIFE. YOUR PURPOSE AS A CONSCIOUS BEING IS TO EXPERIENCE THE THIRD DIMENSIONAL PLANE TO ENABLE YOU TO BE THE BEST VERSION OF YOUR AUTHENTIC SELF.

ASSOCIATIONS

Many **emotions** such as **guilt** and **shame** are commonly stored in your **DNA** and are continually transmitted on some level, influencing every **thought** and decision you **choose** to make. The combined **frequencies** of **emotions** create a master signal or **vibration** that is expressed by every individual that is as unique as your fingerprints. For instance if your **DNA** holds an **association** of **guilt** to a successful **career**, the combined **frequencies** will attract **toxic people** and **situations** to you, not only your **career,** but also in every other **aspect** of your life until you find resolution. Even **subtle associations** that are occasional and/or brief with people who are **emotionally toxic** or **exceptionally brilliant** can profoundly **affect** your performance and **productivity**. These **associations** can be seen in the automatic processes of everyday activities such as riding a bicycle. In the beginning it requires training and **memory responses** to ensure that you are able to **coordinate** the **physical** and **mental** skills required to keep your **balance** and gain momentum. Once you acquire the necessary skills to ride a bike, these **responses** become **automatic reflexes** held in your **memory** that kick in when you hop back on a bike, regardless of the duration of time your skills have not been put to use.

Misery loves company, but it is not necessary for people who are detrimental to your **success** to have bad **intentions** for you. They may be "good" people who are not "good" for you.

THE "GOOD NEWS" IS:

When the energetic weaknesses are cleared, attracting **toxic people** can become a thing of the past for you, for your ancestors and for your descendants; this will facilitate promising, uplifting connections that resonate with **abundance** and **joy** in their wake.

THE "BAD NEWS" IS:

Negative life experiences resulting from **past**, **present** and **future choices**, from whom you **choose/chose** to **associate** with and who **chooses/chose** to **associate** with you or those whom you **choose/chose** to prioritize or not, and who **give/gave** priority to you or not, can have a profound **effect** on your success. **Choices** that people are not in alignment with can limit their **success** or undermine it and will eventually sabotage their goals.

NUGGET OF WIZDOM FROM THE VECTOR

ANYONE WHO HAS TAKEN THEIR DOG TO THE DOG PARK AND PICKED UP FLEAS KNOWS HOW QUICKLY THEY MAKE THEIR PRESENCE KNOWN AND HOW CHALLENGING IT CAN BE TO LIVE WITH THEM; HOWEVER, MOST PEOPLE MISS OUT ON MORE SUBTLE INFLUENCES THAT COULD HAVE A POSITIVE EFFECT ON THEIR LIVES.

ASTROLOGICAL INFLUENCES

Astrology is not the "cause" of anything, nor is it a "permission slip" to do anything. It is simply a universal language used throughout the universe to communicate between civilizations to describe **electromagnetic** and other **energies** that are present, in this case from the point of view of planet Earth. This description allows one to see the underlying ebbs and flows of **electromagnetic** (and other) **energies** before and as they occur. Any erratic energy should not be taken personally although each person will feel it or be sensitive to it in his or her own way according to their **etheric** body.

The moon's gravitational pull moves millions of gallons of **water** around the **planet**. The human **body** is made up of about seventy percent water. This is why people are **affected** by the pull of the **moon** and other **planets**. The cycles of the **sun** also have a profound effect on the inhabitants of the earth, the most obvious being **sunrise** and **sunset**. **Solar flares** commonly occur and produce **electromagnetic radiation** across the full spectrum of **wavelengths**. Most of these occur around Intense **magnetic fields** emerging from the **sun's** surface into the **corona** as **sunspots**.

Ancient **astrologers** divided the sky into **twelve** equal parts and named each part after a constellation of stars in an area of the sky to make up the **twelve signs** of the **zodiac**. As the **earth** orbits the **sun**, from earth it appears to move along a line, called the **ecliptic**, that is relative to the fixed **stars**. A band that extends about eight degrees on either side of this line is called the **zodiac**.

A **horoscope** is like a diagram of the positions of the **planets** and the signs of the **zodiac** in **space-time**, and of the angles made by the **planets** to each other. People who are born in a certain **constellation** at the time of their **birth** tend to share common **characteristics**; however, this is only one **aspect** of their chart as the positions of other **planets** and **houses** in their chart also have an influence. Many babies disregard their estimated arrival to be born at a specific time or date, timing their birth with **planetary alignments** and **astrological influences**.

THE "GOOD NEWS" IS:

Astrology is not about foretelling an inevitable fate. The free will within us all allows us the opportunity to become masters of our own destiny. An understanding of **astrological influences** determined by the **planetary positions** at the **time** and **location** of your birth can be utilized to help make sense of your connection with your inner self, with other people and with the universe at large.

THE "BAD NEWS" IS:

"What's your sign?" is a universal, ineffective pick-up line.

Astrologers, like all scientists, must use **knowledge** in conjunction with **intuition** to reveal probabilities and place them into **perspective** to facilitate clear choices. Dabblers in **astrology** often create more confusion than clarity. This is because they tend to focus on one important **aspect** of your **astrological chart**, generally your sun sign, which is determined by the location of the sun at your birth, and they do not regard other *planetary aspects*.

NUGGET OF WIZDOM FROM THE VECTOR

FIND AN INTUITIVE MASTER OF ASTROLOGY WITH A SOUND UNDERSTANDING OF PLANETARY INFLUENCES. USE THAT INFORMATION TO TURN PROBABILITIES INTO POSSIBILITIES BY SHIFTING ASPECTS WITHIN YOUR CHART AND CONFLICTING FORCES FROM PLANETARY INFLUENCES.

AUTHENTIC SELF

The *Authentic Self* consists of the *Holy Trinity*: **body**, *soul* and *spirit*, the blueprint for light based on the **geometry** of the **triangle**.

This is a **fundamental structure** of creation throughout the universe, the power of "all that is one," dividing into polarity before it manifests as **physical matter** through *expansion* and *acceleration*.

BODY

In order for the *soul* to incarnate onto the earth plane, it does so in a **physical body** as an expression of your *personality*. You also have *multiple personalities* living within multiple **bodies** at various points throughout history. Each time you reincarnate you create a new earthly *personality* and a new earthly **body**. Your **physical body** is the **container** of your five *senses* and four accessory *senses* with which you connect to all things of the **physical**, **material realm**.

Your *personality* has **gender, form, race, social standing, ethnicity,** etc., and is born into a specific family made of **blood, flesh** and **bone**. Through the *personality* you *experience* many of life's *challenges* and *respond* to them subject to the **limitations** of third dimensional *space-time*. In the world of the *personality*, "evil" and "good" do exist. **Evil** is not merely a lack of "goodness," but a **force** unto itself, created and *manifested* by the various people who inhabit the earth. On the other hand, your *soul* is the image of your *spirit* and is in turn created in **God's** image. Guidance is always available through *spirit* because your *spirit* is guided by **God**, or if you prefer, the perfect **structure** of the universe and your *soul* is guided by *spirit*. Ultimately your *personality* can *choose un-consciously*, *sub-consciously* and *consciously* to *accept* or *not accept* guidance provided by the *H.S.N.* (*Higher Self Network*).

SPIRIT

Your *spirit* is the highest *aspect* of yourself, the innermost part with which you connect with *God*, or if you prefer, *source energy* to substantiate everything in the *spiritual realm*.

The word "spirit" refers to the immaterial facet of humanity, the element that gives you the *ability* to have an intimate connection with *source*. Your *spirit* is devoid of all human elements and *personality* because it is a direct "fragment" of *God*.

Spirit is "all that is." It is the highest expression of individuality and you are a "chip off the old block!" Once you understand this, you can learn to see the universe from a different perspective and will be able to release *fear* and *anger* and embrace *love*. You are inundated by *external forces* that appear to attack your equilibrium and sense of peace; however, it is your *re-action* and the *internal forces* that determine the level of *fear* you *experience*. On a *spiritual* level your overall progress as a *whole being* can be measured by your lowest *vibration*.

SOUL

Human beings are *souls* who have *spirits*. *Soul* refers to the *whole person*, both the **material** and the *immaterial aspects* of humanity. Your *soul* is the expression of the perfection of *spirit* that has **human character** and links with the **human experience**.

The energy of the *soul* is sometimes referred to as the "higher self," the part of us that is guided through our *intuition* and connection to *spirit*. It contains our *mind*, *will* and *emotional reactions*, performing rational and intellectual functions to connect with everything in the *psychological realm*.

Your *soul* evolves through *choice* and *karma* in successive incarnations. It is transformed by the renewal of your *mind* as you let go of *spiritual traumas*. Perfect *balance* within the **body**, *soul* and *spirit* is essential for *spiritual evolution* to achieve optimum potential.

The **body**, *soul* and *spirit* are affected by *re-actions* to your so-called *emotions*. The *internal forces* (*what I.F.'s*) are generally on the *psychological* level (when *thoughts* from the *sub-conscious mind* and the *re-actions* to them have occurred so often that they become **neurological pathways**) and the *external forces* (*the what the E.F.'s*) usually are weak on the *psychic* level.

THE "GOOD NEWS" IS:

On any given day you have thousands of **opportunities** to express your **authentic self**. It is easy to make **authentic choices** once you recognize that the **challenges** you face are **opportunities** disguised as **problems**. When the **mind** and **spirit** are in **balance** with the **physical body**, that balances **physical presence**.

THE "BAD NEWS" IS:

People are **challenged** thousands of times on any given day to be **authentic** with **themselves** and others. Many people give their power away to **institutions**, **governments** and other **authority figures** because they want to hide from the **darker aspects** of themselves and don't want to take **response-ability** for the **reality** they are co-creating.

NUGGET OF WIZDOM FROM THE VECTOR

YOU ARE NOT A BODY WITH A SOUL. YOU ARE A SOUL. YOU HAVE A BODY TO USE AS A VEHICLE TO EXPRESS YOUR SOUL. THE BODY CANNOT CREATE. IT CAN ONLY EXPERIENCE AND BE EXPERIENCED. THAT IS ITS FUNCTION. THE SOUL AND SPIRIT SUPPORT THOSE FUNCTIONS WHEN ALL THREE ARE IN BALANCE.

AWARENESS

For the average person, ninety-five percent of the **actions** they take and words they **choose** are **re-actions** to **sensations** stimulated by the **sub-conscious** and **un-conscious** mind.

SUB-CONSCIOUS MIND

The **thoughts** that people are not aware of and the **automatic sensations** and **responses** that are stimulated by **experiences** in their **environment**, cause **chemical reactions** in their **brains**; these **chemical reactions** are transported throughout their **bodies** via their **blood**, the **circulatory** and **nervous systems**.

Often when people **re-act** to **situations**, they are taking **action** on **sub-conscious thoughts** that don't really belong to them. **External forces**, **limiting beliefs** and **expectations** from **ancestors**, **cultural influences**, **educational experiences**, **collective fears**, **religious experiences**, other **traumas** and **negative life experiences** in a **child's environment** generally shape their **sub-conscious minds** up to age **six** and **seven**. It is during these formative years that the **sub-conscious mind** is established, yet the vast majority of **parents** in today's **society** are encouraged to hand their children's **sub-conscious minds** over to strangers when they take them to daycares, babysitters etc., so that they can go to work to "provide" for them.

UN-CONSCIOUS MIND

The **thoughts** that people are not aware of, the **automatic responses** and **re-actions** that are stimulated by the **past, present** and **future,** and that their **spirit** has **experienced** are held in the **memory** of the **CNS** and the **cells**, where they create **chemical reactions** in the **brain** that are transported through their **bodies** via their **blood**, the **circulatory** and **nervous systems**. The **un-conscious limiting beliefs** and **expectations** from **ancestors**, **descendants**, **cultural influences**, **religious experiences**, **traumas**, **tragedies** and other **negative life experiences** will often have weaknesses on the **spiritual** and **psychic** levels.

CONSCIOUS MIND

The average person uses his or her **conscious mind** only five percent of the time, spending the vast majority of his or her existence on **automatic pilot**, **re-acting** and **re-solving life experiences** instead of investing himself or herself in taking **action** towards resolution. Most people have had the **experience** of lying awake at night or waking up in the middle of the night, unable to sleep because their **conscious mind** is chewing on a **problem** over and over again, like a stubborn dog with an old bone. They are unable to resolve it because the **problem** is really coming from their **sub-conscious** or **un-conscious mind**. *EU … SLEEP, Pg. 474*

The more you **think** about a **problem**, the worse it gets. **Logical questions** require **intuitive answers**. If you ask a **logical question** and expect a **logical answer**, you will only get another **question**. **Logic** and **intuition** are a fifty/fifty proposition. In the split second when the **sub-conscious, un-conscious** and **conscious minds** are congruent, you are able to access your infinite potential to **choose** the **answer** most applicable to your situation. This is often referred to as the "zero point," when you collapse the wave and transform **challenges** into **possibilities**.

The connection between **body, soul** and **spirit** occurs simultaneously within a person at every moment. When the self-awareness of any of these are not congruent as a result of the distractions of **life experiences**, people feel the corresponding **imbalance** as **physical disease** in the **body**, as **emotional** and **mental dis-ease** in the **mind**, and as a loss of **life purpose** and direction in the **soul**. Just like your favorite action figures, if you take *action* on the *creative solutions* you can have access to, then in that moment you can soar to infinity and beyond. Whether the other **answers** are **right** or **wrong**, **positive** or **negative** is not a concern; the most relevant solution to any **problem** will instantly become apparent when your **sub**-*conscious* and *un*-*conscious thoughts* are congruent with the **goals** you are aware of in your *conscious mind*.

At any given time, many radio stations via satellite are passing through the *space* people inhabit, but people do not hear them unless they take a quartz crystal and tune in to a specific *resonance* to pick up the signals. The *mind* operates in a very similar way, like a bio-oscillating crystal that can tune into any *resonance* in the entire universe.

"Looking for consciousness in the human brain is like looking inside the radio for an announcer." Nassim Haramein

THE "GOOD NEWS" IS:

You can use your **brain** and the other components of your **CNS** to automatically send *re-active thoughts* that impede your ability to solve **problems**, from the *mind* to *black wholes*, *existences*, *planes* and *parallel dimensions* in **space-time**. This will facilitate resolution for all *external forces* involved.

THE "BAD NEWS" IS:

Most people are unaware of what is truly bothering them. They could find resolution through awareness of *thoughts* held in their *sub-conscious* and *un-conscious minds* and send them to a *black whole*, but their **brains** fall out instead, especially when it comes to their **children**. It is challenging for **parents** to be *neutral* to their **children** because they love them so much.

NUGGET OF WIZDOM FROM THE VECTOR

MOST PEOPLE HAVE BEEN TAUGHT TO THINK PROBLEMS THROUGH, WITH A "THINK BEFORE YOU ACT" MENTALITY. THIS CAUSES MANY PEOPLE TO BECOME "SHEEP-LE," RATHER THAN PEOPLE. DON'T WASTE YOUR TIME OVER-THINKING! TAKE ACTION ON CREATIVE SOLUTIONS ACCESSED THROUGH CONGRUENCY OF THE SUB-CONSCIOUS, THE UN-CONSCIOUS AND THE CONSCIOUS MIND.

AWE-TISTIC CHILDREN

The vast majority of humanity strives to fit into the limited paradigm of what is *perceived* to be "normal" by society's standards. Most people *perceive* their **physical environment** through five *senses*: *sight*, *sound*, *touch*, *taste* and *smell*. They are comforted by the "normalcy" of life with other like-minded individuals because they are strong to these *senses* as well as *equilibrioception, proprioception, thermoception* and *nociception* while those labeled with **autism spectrum disorders** are not. **EU … SENSATIONS, Pg. 456*

Autism is commonly a problem of introversion (going inward) because of *over-sensitivity* to *external forces*. Often there are weaknesses in the **physical environment** in which the child lives, caused by **ancestral** and **familial** influences. It is important that both **parents** and their **children** are strong to the **physical environment** of their **home**, especially in the **main living space** and **bedrooms**.

Other negative influences from *external forces* can be **chemicals**, **toxins**, **vaccinations**, **additives**, **pesticides**, etc. that damage and stagnate the **CNS**, in utero and in early development. Unfortunately, medications that are meant to control symptoms also *affect* the **CNS** causing more *stagnation*. Strengthen both the **parents** and the **child** to any and all **combinations** of **medications** to receive one hundred percent **benefit** and delete the *negative effects*.

Autistic children are often sensitive to *electro-magnetic frequencies*, *psychic influences, multiple personalities* and changes in *atmosphere*. Their symptoms intensify when they are overstimulated by *sounds*, *sights*, *smells* that they are not familiar with, or if those stimuli are very different from those at **home**; this causes weaknesses to *leaving* the **house**, *going* to **school**, to other **students**, **teachers**, **administration** and **environment** in the **school**, *leaving* **school** and *returning* home. Strengthen these *actions* in relationship to each other one at a time and then in groups. It is vital that everyone *associated* with the child in **school**, the **medical community** and the **psychiatric community** is strong to the best interests of the **child**, the **parents** and *creative solutions*.

Often when **autistic** children are acting out with aggression and other inappropriate **behaviors** they are avoiding more *input* by creating *output*. They prefer to listen to their own *internal thoughts* because they feel safe in their own head and manipulate the people around them to be busy dealing with the aftermath of their *re-actions* to stimuli. **Autistic** children don't acknowledge normal verbal and *emotional* cues, causing *miscommunication* with their peers and **playmates**. The *emotional re-actions* of their **peers** faced with the lack of **communication** and autistic **behavior** often intensifies the *need* for the autistic child to go further inward. Strengthen all **communication** between the **lobes** of the **brain, cranial nerves, components** of the **CNS** and **PNS**. Weaknesses with *verbal communication* can also be actual **physical** weaknesses in the components of the **jaw, mouth** and **oral cavity** in general and/or they are referred from the **pelvic cavity**. Strengthen *purposeful communication* through **body language**, *tone* and most importantly through *intuition*. *EU ... PURPOSEFUL COMMUNICATION, Pg. 429*

Children who are labeled **autistic** often have many *spiritual* weaknesses leading from negative *religious experiences* and *associations* to *religious experiences* of being separated from *God*. Strengthen their connection to *source energy* from the *macrocosmic* level all the way to the *microcosmic* level of their **cells** and to the **cellular intelligence** of the **nuclei** of every **cell**.

High levels of **clostridia's** have been found in the **stools** of children who are labeled **autistic**. These are spore-forming **anaerobic bacteria** of the genus **clostridium** that are **nitrogen-fixing species** found in soil that cause **botulism** and **tetanus**. The **gut** to **brain axis** is the biochemical center for signals received between the **gastrointestinal tract** and the **nervous system**. **Microbiota (gut flora)** is a **microorganism** that lives in the **digestive tract**, benefiting the host by maximizing the absorption of **butyrates** in the **colon**, **propionates** in the **liver**, and **acetates** in the **muscle tissue** by utilizing energy from the fermentation of undigested **carbohydrates**.

Post-natal colonization of the **gastrointestinal tract** has a lasting impact on **neural processing** of *sensory input* from the **hypothalamus**, the **pituitary** and the **adrenal glands**. Strengthen the **physical** connections between the systems and **components** of **gut flora** to be at optimum potential and delete any *miasmas* of being born with *accumulations* of **toxic** substances.

ASPERGER SYNDROME (A.S.)

Asperger syndrome is an **autism spectrum disorder (ASD)** where affected children and adults are considered to be functioning at a high level although they have difficulty with **social** *interaction*, have a tendency to display *repetitive behaviors* and often focus on one major area of interest at one time. People with **Asperger syndrome** often have normal to superior IQ's but have difficulty "fitting in." Unfortunately they are often ridiculed by their **peers** and are assumed to be naïve by adults who *perceive* them to be abnormal; this *affects* their *ability* to thrive. **Autistic** tendencies can amplify *positive* as well as *negative behaviors*.

It is common for people with **A.S**. to have strong *past-life memories* that draw them to maps, globes, specific countries and enables them to amass many facts through *rote memory*. Clear any *accumulated* and *associated* weaknesses to *traumas*, **tortures** and *karma* from *past lives*. Their **vocabulary** is often extensive, yet they have difficulty *communicating* with "normal" people because they take each word literally and don't detect and apply sarcasm and other implied meanings to language. Strengthen the *relationship* between their **vocabulary**, *communication* and **speaking**.

Mainstream education is not geared for exploring individual interests, but is structured to mold viable employees for the work force. Awe-tistic tendencies of **autism** can be encouraged to blossom in individuals if they are allowed to pursue their passion for a specific subject in an **alternative educational system** until they are satisfied that they have mastered a subject and are ready to move on to a new area of interest.
*EU … LEARNING DIS-ABILITIES, Pg. 308

RESULTS:

"Hello Colette,

"Thank you for what you've done for Jacob my son, myself and truly the whole family. There aren't words to express the depth of gratitude. When my first-born child Jacob started to show signs of some major struggles I was in denial and desperate to fix things … We soon came to find out that he was to be diagnosed with Autism, ADHD, Anxiety, a language based learning disability and opposition defiant disorder. I was devastated and wanted nothing more than for my son to not be living in a state of complete torture every day.

"This is what it was like for him. He was extremely violent. I would always be covered in bruises from a sweet little boy who just couldn't control himself no matter how badly he wanted to. He had virtually no self-regulation system combined with a nervous system that is so sensitive, that just being touched gently had the impact of a ton of bricks landing on him. The guilt I could see and feel he had after these intense outbursts was heartbreaking for me as a mother to watch.

"He wouldn't look anyone in the eye, would growl and show his teeth if you tried to speak to him or even just say hello. He could not read and of course had no friends. His world was small painful and isolating for us all. I knew in my heart that there must be more that could be done.

"Oh, for sure, we did everything we could through the conventional system. The psychologist, behaviour consultant, pediatrician, psychiatrist, naturopath, aba tutoring, and every possible parenting program I've heard of in the lower mainland. This all did have a positive impact, however I was still so broken and spent most of my time in fear of my sons future. Not to mention the guilt I carried that somehow this was all my fault.

"Jacob was on five medications and was still barely making it through a day. My dear friends and support system knew of my search for natural solutions for Jacob and it was four and a half years ago (2011) when one of my angelic friends took me to a demo of Colette Stefan's. I happened to be chosen as one of the individuals to be demonstrated on that night. I had no idea to just what extent the impact of this moment would have on the rest of my life!

"I couldn't believe how Colette seemed to just know exactly what was going on and how I was feeling. Things I only shared with my best friend. I could feel myself changing right then and there. I had never believed shifting at this level was possible. I instantly began to feel some hope and relief from the pain I had been carrying. I decided to book a private session with Colette in regards to my son. To my surprise, she said Jacob, my son would not need to be there.

"I was shocked and totally relieved because I was sure he would throw something at her if she said the wrong thing. She spent an hour working with me and my son via distance. Colette started to clear issues around my son needing so much medication, his social interaction, how people perceived him. She cleared issues around his support system, better understanding him and mostly my guilt and worry.

"I lived most days in anxiety and so was very relieved to feel relaxed the following day. My son had a psychiatrist appointment the day after our first session and to my amazement the doctor suggested lowering Jacob's medication instead of adding another which is what typically happened at all of our appointments.

"This started the miraculous journey of freedom from medication. Truly this was the start of many freedoms my son would soon get to experience. Jacob started to respond to people without growling and could look people in the eyes and would even say hello. To my absolute joy, my son started to read and absorb learned information! I was so worried I would never see that day. There were clear and dramatic changes from our very first session.

"Everyone supporting Jacob, the teachers and principal at his school were so happy and astounded in Jacob's transformation. People who *had not seen Jacob in a year or two and met him again did not believe it was the same child. The people who believed nothing good would come of my son were all proved wrong!!!!*

"One of the most amazing parts was that they were shocked to find out that his continued growth and progress over the first six months Colette was working with us all corresponded with medication decreases instead of increases. My son was breaking free! The anxiety attacks that crippled him stopped and had even turned to smiles. He has continued to make such strong and steady progress.

"You would not know today, meeting Jacob, that he was diagnosed with all these labels. He is bright and has developed some amazing friendships and has many interests that he loves, such as Lego. So a child that was locked in pain and suffering has become free and expressive!

"It's the hugest gift that anyone could have ever given us. The energy clearing that Colette did has been so profound that I have been her student for the last four years and have loved learning how to shift energy proficiently and effectively from the person who basically saved my son's life from complete suffering. Thank you so much Colette. I love you with all my heart. Jacob, Geoff my husband, our little girl Alyssa and I will always be filled with gratitude."

Love always,

Nicole

THE "GOOD NEWS" IS:

The gap between "**autistic**" and "**normal**" people is closing. Many people in **society** today are somewhat **autistic** in behavior, preferring interaction with **computers** to people, relying on "virtual friends" rather than actual live people. You can see this at any public outing where people will gather for social interaction, yet ignore the people they are with in order to text and post on social outlets. They are not really *present* with the people who have taken time to **physically** be with them, nor with the **virtual friends** they are texting; yet they are considered normal.

THE "BAD NEWS" IS:

The more a family *struggles* with the *challenges* of raising an autistic child, the more the autistic child *struggles*.

NUGGET OF WIZDOM FROM THE VECTOR

FOR CENTURIES HUMANITY HAS PRAYED TO GOD(S) TO PLEASE SEND ANGELS TO OUR PLANET TO SAVE US FROM LIFE'S MOST DIFFICULT CHALLENGES. THROUGHOUT THE AGES GOD(S) HAVE ANSWERED OUR PRAYERS THROUGH OUR CHILDREN WHO ARE FULL OF PROMISE FOR A BETTER FUTURE. WE, IN TURN WE FIND FAULT IN HOW THEY ARE PACKAGED AND DRUG THEM IN AN ATTEMPT TO MAKE THEM CONFORM TO "NORMAL" STANDARDS.

BABIES

It is best to check in with babies week by week throughout the pregnancy, and to strengthen any weaknesses, as the baby is developing, rather than wait for the baby's arrival before shifting. *EU ... PREGNANCY, Pg. 398*

Once the baby arrives, immediately scan the **body** for any weaknesses or **traumas** from the **birthing experience**, especially if the baby was born by **caesarian section**, **forceps** or **vacuum delivery**. Test to be sure that all **systems** are functioning at optimal potential, for any **karma** that may have been missed, and any other weaknesses, **known** and **unknown**. Strengthen the baby to its **gender** and its **sexuality**.

Check for any **miasmas** that may affect the baby, in particular for "old souls" trapped in a baby's **body**, and any **negative memories** from **past lives** that may **affect** its **physical** and **non-physical** well-being. Quite often the temper tantrums of two and three year olds are not about them not getting their way, but are due to the **frustration** of having to rely on others when they have **memories** of being a fully functioning **adult**.

Check for any weaknesses the baby has in **relationship** to every member of the family, starting with the **mother**, then the **father**, the **siblings**, **grandparents**, **aunts**, **uncles**, **cousins**, **step-parents** and **siblings**, **nannies**, **babysitters**, **doctors**, **hospital staff**, etc. Don't forget to strengthen **relationships** with any **pets** in the family. Difficult births can be avoided if the baby and mother are in **synchronization** with each other.

Most people perceive **babies** as smaller versions of their **parents** because of their **physical limitations** and **dependence** on adults for survival; however, on a **soul level** they have just made a transition from the core of **God** to the **third-dimensional plane**. Be sure to strengthen both the **baby** and the **mother's** connection to **source**, and delete **accumulations** of **negative emotions**, **worries** and **concerns** that came up during the pregnancy and birth from the *past*, *present* and *future*. If the **mother** is not able to get *neutral* to her concerns, strengthen the **baby** to be independent from them.

Premature babies are often the result of **problems** within the **physical functions** of the **mother's body** that have not been addressed. If there are no **physical** issues, it is not uncommon for **babies** to have weaknesses and strengths to the **time, date** and **year** of their birth due to *astrological influences* and *planetary alignments*. This is often why **babies** make their entrance before or after their expected arrival date. *Planetary influences* can have profound *positive* and *negative effects* on their *ability* to fulfill their *soul purpose* in the present lifetime. Check to be sure that there is an evenness of **body**, *soul* and *spirit*, within their *authentic-self triad*. *EU ... ASTROLOGICAL INFLUENCES, Pg. 76*

On a **physical level** the **baby's structure** is more important than **bio-chemistry** or **nutrition**. **Baby bones** are not completely formed, making it easier to shift any **problematic structural** weaknesses. Test if either of their **feet** is stronger than the other from **left** to **right** and **right** back to **left**. Then starting at the **ankles**, work up to the **tibia** and **fibula** to make sure there is no *straining* or *conflic*t with each other. Strengthen the **bones** to be *elongated* with the **fibers** lining up *vertically* without any bulging to the sides. The **knees** need to be strong within themselves and in relation to each other, and strong in their connection to the **femurs**. **Kneecaps** must line up properly without being jammed or *separated* and the r*elationship* of the **sacrum** to the **hips** needs to be in *alignment*, not too far **forward** or **backward, twisted** or **turned**. Check for any *inconsistencies* within the **spine, vertebrae** by **vertebrae**, starting at the **tail bone** and working your way up, making sure that the **curves** in the **spine** are *consistent* with each other to provide *flexibility* and *spring* in movement. Also make sure that the **head** is attached to the **neck** with proper *alignment* of the **atlas** and **axis**.

Babies often have *fetal debris* and *accumulations* of **toxins, poisons, chemicals, medications**, etc., in the **cerebral spinal fluid** and other components of the **spine** that *stagnate* other **systems** in the **body**. Many **babies** who display symptoms of **colic** have a weakness in the **digestive system** that is referred from the **respiratory system**, and vice versa.

Check that the **sensing organs**, such as the **eyes, ears, nose** and **mouth** are strong to the **PNS** and **CNS**. Also strengthen the **colon, bladder** and other **elimination systems** to work within themselves and with each other. Delete any weaknesses in the **blood** and the **circulatory system**, as well as in all **organs** and **glands**; they must be strong to functioning with the **CNS**.

Newborns, infants and toddlers have very sensitive **central nervous systems** that are easily *affected* by the slightest deviation. It is important to protect children from the *adverse* **effects** of immunizations, pesticides, herbicides, chemicals, dyes and other **physical** and ***non-physical poisons*** and ***toxins*** because very small amounts that are not significant for adults can have a profoundly ***negative effect*** on immature systems. Educate yourself about vaccination and if you do choose to vaccinate your children, make sure both you and the child are energetically strong to it to avoid complications.

FEVERS

Babies often have fluctuations in their **body temperature** because their **systems** are immature and can be easily influenced by **physical** and **non-physical** ***external forces***. Clear any *emotional*, *mental*, *psychological*, *psychic* and/or *spiritual* issues that are weak for the **baby** and the **baby's parents**, **siblings**, **grandparents** and other **care-givers**. A **fever** is said to be the **body's** *response* to dealing with **viruses** and **bacteria**; however, a **fever** does not have to be induced by ***infection***. **Fever** is not beneficial for killing **pathogens** as suggested by alternative medicine because you would have to bring your **blood** to the boiling point to achieve this. If you shift your *perspective* to the possibility that **fever** is a similar condition to "hot flashes" experienced as a symptom of "men-o-pause," the problem is a malfunction of the **body's thermostat**, stuck at a high instead of normal range temperature. It is possible to adjust **body temperature** by shifting the ***energetic weaknesses*** of the **body's thermostat** and strengthening the **lymphatic system** and **endocrine system**. *Visual* people can see themselves turning down an old-fashioned **dial** to adjust the **temperature** accordingly in degrees, *tactile* people can feel for "just right" **temperature**, and *auditory* people can hear the **heating system** click on or off, or use all of the above.

AIRPLANES

It is very common these days for **babies** to travel on airlines. Many people prefer to avoid flights with **babies** because they do not want to endure a long flight next to a screaming **infant** or **toddler** who is acting up. **Babies** are very ***sensitive*** to the **noise**s and ***fluctuations*** of the **pressurized environment** of **aircraft**, including the ***emotional pressure*** the **parents** and fellow **passengers** are ***feeling***. The fussiness of **babies** and **toddlers** is often intensified by ***expectations*** of **problems** and can be avoided simply by becoming ***neutral*** to the baby crying or not crying. Make sure to clear any ***karma*** the **baby** may have with its **parents, fellow passengers, flight attendants** and the **pilots**.

If you are sitting near a **baby** on a **plane**, on **takeoff** and **landing feel** its **spine** along with yours and squeeze your **buttocks** to relieve the **pressure** in your **head**, for the **baby** and the **parents**.

THE "GOOD NEWS" IS:

Strong *intuitive communication* can **eliminate** many **problems** before they materialize. Instead of **parents** and **baby** *experiencing* the *frustration* of playing a guessing game as to why a **baby** is fussy, crying, unable to sleep, sick, etc., a mother can just test it and provide the *solution* for the **baby**. With better *communication*, the bond between **mother** and **child** is stronger and based in trust.

THE "BAD NEWS" IS:

While most moms have experienced *intuitive communication* with their **babies** and **children** at one time or another, few recognize their *ability* for *consistent intuitive communication*, and consequently they miss out on many *opportunities* to provide the most nurturing **environment** possible for their **children**.

NUGGET OF WIZDOM FROM THE VECTOR

MANY PROBLEMS THAT BABIES AND CHILDREN FACE ORIGINATE FROM THE ADULTS WHO CARE FOR THEM, IN PARTICULAR THE PARENTS AND GRANDPARENTS, ESPECIALLY IF THEY ARE BELOW THE AGE OF TEN, HOWEVER CHILDREN'S PROGNOSIS IS MORE FAVORABLE BECAUSE THEY HAVE LESS RESISTANCE TO THEIR RECOVERY AND FEWER BLOCKAGES TO THEIR HEALING PROCESS.

BIRTH AND DEATH

Birth and Death are both *transitions* of pushing through the **dark** to be received by the **light**. The process of what many call **death** is actually another *cycle* of **birth**. The journey of **birth** and **death** are similar; we enter the void to be brought into the light.

Imagine that you have a camera in the womb from conception onward with no prior understanding of what is to occur. You become *emotionally* invested, and develop a *sentimental relationship* with the **fetus**, as day by day you witness the miracle taking place before you. Suddenly one day, a light appears at the end of a tunnel and you helplessly watch the **baby** *struggle* as it disappears down that tunnel. This event could be *perceived* as *traumatic* and disturbing, similar to how many people are taught to think of **death**. It is important that people are strong to all of their *choices* regarding **life** and **death**. If there is a weakness in any of the *choices* it has a negative impact on **living** and **dying**. Energetically we can *choose* to *live well*, *not live well*, *die well* or *not die well*.

Many people who are **diagnosed** with a fatal **disease** or who are disabled by *accidents*, have a weakness to *living well* or *not living well*. There really are no *accidents*. Events often occur between individuals who want to clear *accumulated karma* with each other, or who have *associated karma* with the other people who are involved. *EU ... KARMA, Pg. 302

Serious **accidents** often bring people face to face with **death**. Whether an **accident** is "serious" or not, always ask what happened right before the *accident* because unresolved underlying weaknesses of a minor **accident** that remain unresolved often lead to more serious **accidents**: **What** was being discussed right before or during an accident, **where** did it happen and **where** were they going, **who** was involved, **when** did it happen (there are often underlying weaknesses for specific **dates**, **holidays**, **times**, **destinations**, etc.) **how** did it happen and **what** was going on in the person's life in general. Many times the weaknesses seem totally unrelated to the actual *accident*, yet when these weaknesses are cleared the person will enjoy instant or gradual *relief* from the symptoms.

Throughout the years, working with clients, I have discovered that **abortion** is something that many women are reluctant to discuss. When it does come up, it is usually initiated by the *unborn descendants* who wanted to come through, and/or from the *mixed* and *combined emotions* of the **biological parents**, their **ancestors** and their **descendants**. **Abortion** and **miscarriage** is often the result of a *contract* or *agreement* between a *soul* who wants to "dip his or her toes" in the **amniotic fluid** to *experience* the dense **physical body**, and a **woman** who is not energetically in **alignment** to becoming a **mother**. Once the *karmas* from the **parents**, **offspring**, **siblings** and **ancestors** down both lines are cleared, there is usually instant relief on both sides of the veil.

Dying is about letting go of everyone and everything. If a person has a weakness to *dying well* or *not dying well*, he or she tends to *sub-consciously* and/or *un-consciously* find a **disease**, **medical procedure**, **doctor** or *accident* to kill them. There are often underlying *karmas* with specific individuals and weaknesses to "being a killer" and/or "being killed" in *past lives* as well as *spiritual experiences* of *traumas* that people do not want to have to "live with."

It is important to resonate with people who are alive and *living well*. People with suicidal tendencies are bothered by not having a life worth living. They are often sensitive to *external forces* that weaken their *internal boundaries*, in particular, *religious experiences* and misguided information about **heaven** and **hell**.

THE "GOOD NEWS" IS:

When you make the transition from this third dimensional plane in what is referred to as **death** you are caught by **source** (*God*) on the other side. *God* understands exactly what to do.

THE "BAD NEWS" IS:

Babies are not delivered with a manual and it is quite possible that your **parents** won't have a clue what to do with you!

NUGGET OF WIZDOM FROM THE VECTOR

CONTRARY TO POPULAR BELIEF, CHILDREN COME IN TO IMPROVE THEIR PARENTS' LIVES. IF YOU HAVE BEEN CAUGHT BY A COUPLE OF IDIOTS, USE YOUR GOD-GIVEN TALENTS AND START SHIFTING THEM NOW! DON'T WAIT! IF YOU FAIL IN YOUR MISSION WHILE THEY ARE STILL ON THIS PLANE IT IS LIKELY THAT THEY WILL HAUNT YOU FROM THE GRAVE!

BLACK WHOLE/ WHITE WHOLE

The standard definition of a **black hole** is:

A **point mass** that *attracts* and *absorbs* **matter**. It's **gravitational field** is so strong that nothing, not even **light** can escape it.

The standard definition of a **white hole** is:

An **astrophysical body** that is the time reversal of a **black hole**. A **white hole** acts as a point mass that *rejects* or *ejects* **matter**.

THE POWER OF SPIN

Holofractographic theory takes into consideration, the **torsional** and **Coriolis Effect** generated by **space-time torque** as defined in the **Haramein-Rauscher Solution**. The **Coriolis Effect** is seen throughout the entire universe. This can be viewed when **water** goes down the **drain**. It does not go straight down; rather, it spirals down as **air** spirals up in the opposite direction. The **surface event horizon** is no longer smooth; it generates wave interactions of a **holographic** and **fractal** nature, resulting in the emission of **information** from the surroundings of the **black whole** (the **white hole** portion) that we **experience** as the **radiation** of **electromagnetic fields**.

Every **atom** in every **cell** of your **body** is essentially a **black whole**, as is the earth, the sun and the entire universe. They are **systems** within **systems** perfectly designed to spin what is not beneficial into a **black whole** and transmute that into possibilities through the **white whole**.

The **electrons** of an **atom** have an outward spin, propelling energy outward, around the top and bottom and back to the center; **protons** do the opposite and spin inwards. **Neutrons** spin in all directions, birthing the new when the **proton** and **electron** join forces.

You can create **black wholes** anywhere in the **body** to remove, eliminate and separate **traumas**, **poisons**, **toxins**, **chemicals**, **cellular waste**, **parasites** and **parasitic waste**, **radiation**, etc., that have **accumulated** in the **physical body**.

On the **non-physical** level, **associated fears**, **limiting beliefs** and **expectations** from the **mental**, **emotional** and **psychological** level as well as **karmic**, **psychic** and **spiritual** weaknesses can all be directed to **black whole**s. It is beneficial to create **black wholes** in the **neck**, **sacrum**, **spinal cord**, the back of the **eyes** and the **lymphatic system** (especially if it is compromised) to facilitate removal of **toxins** from the **systems**. As the **black whole** is releasing **toxins**, **poisons**, **cellular waste**, etc., you can simultaneously use the **white whole** to **replace, restore** and **integrate oxygen**, **nutrition**, **trace carbon**, **nitrogen** and the perfect **structure** of the universe into every **cell** of the **physical body** and spin calm from the pulse of the **heart beat** and the rhythm of the earth through the **white whole**.

THE "GOOD NEWS" IS:

There are no **isolated systems** in nature. **Information** is always shared by the **collective influence**. It never belongs to a particular group or individual alone, no matter how original it may seem, because copyright is not recognized by nature.

THE "BAD NEWS" IS:

The current calculations in **physics** are "re-normalized" to make theories fit and focus on the four percent that can be seen, ignoring the ninety-six percent that has been labeled *dark energy* or *dark matter*. This has resulted in complicated mathematics that provides fewer and fewer valuable applications for the advancement of humanity.

NUGGET OF WIZDOM FROM THE VECTOR

APPROPRIATE ACCOUNTING FOR THE FORCE OF SPIN UNLOCKS THE SIMPLICITY OF PHYSICS. THERE IS A FUNDAMENTAL FORCE OF ANGULAR MOMENTUM IN THE SPACE-TIME MANIFOLD, ITSELF THAT HOLDS THINGS TOGETHER. THIS SAME MOTION ALLOWS FOR FREEDOM OF MOTION THROUGHOUT THE UNIVERSE.

BRAIN

Many people confuse the **brain** with the *mind*. They are two separate things. The *mind* is the *intellectual* part of your *soul*. The **brain** is the **physical intelligence** of your **body**. When the systems of the **brain** are working at optimum potential it allows for improvement of the **body**, *soul* and *spirit*.

People study to improve their *intellect*; however, if the *brain* is sloppy in its performance, there will be challenges with *memory* and *cognizance* of the **information** that no amount of *intellect* can solve. If the computer is not plugged into a reliable energy source, it eventually runs out of power.

Neurological dis-orders can almost always be traced to confusion of the **brain**, **spinal cord**, **spinal fluid** and other components of the **CNS** that are running too slowly. **Brain cells** become clogged from **cellular waste**, **dead cells**, **degenerative enzymes**, **poisons**, **toxins**, etc., as well as from *emotional*, *mental*, *psychological*, *psychic* and *spiritual* excrement. This makes interpreting **information** very challenging because the **brain** is continually being fed **information** at an unprecedented rate in history as we know it, via the **media**, **internet**, **cell phones**, **texting**, etc.

It is beneficial to have a basic understanding of the **physical brain** to support energetic shifts and **physical potential**. The **brain** can be divided into two categories, the **conscious brain** and the **non-conscious brain**, which is not to be confused with unresolved *spiritual experiences* held in the *un-conscious mind*.

THE CONSCIOUS BRAIN

The **conscious brain** is made up of the **cerebrum** and the **corpus callosum**.

THE CEREBRUM

The **cerebrum** is the largest part of the **human brain**, divided into **left** and **right hemispheres** and connected by the **corpus callosum**, a band of **nerve tissue** (**white matter**) allowing the two halves to exchange information. Each **hemisphere** of the **cerebrum** is covered by a layer of **gray tissue** called the **cerebral cortex** and is divided into four lobes, the **occipital lobe**, **temporal lobe**, **parietal lobe** and **frontal lobe**.

OCCIPITAL LOBE

The **occipital lobe** is located at the back of the **head**. It is responsible for receiving and processing **visual** information.

You can improve *photographic memory* by deleting the *emotional overwhelm* caused by "having to remember." Gradually strengthen your ability to remember several **words**, work up to **sentences, paragraphs, more paragraphs, pages** and then entire **books**.

TEMPORAL LOBE

The **temporal lobe** receives *auditory* signals to hear and interpret *music*, *speech*, *language* and *olfactory* signals (the *sense* of **smell**). A specialized area in the back of the **left superior temporal lobe** is the location where *thoughts* are turned into **words**.

It is hrad to bliveee waht the hamun bairn is clbapae of. Ppoele are albe to raed tihs eevn if the lertets are slcarmbed as lnog as the fisrt and lsat lteter are in the rghit odrer. The rset of the lrettes can be ttollay out of odrer and popele can sltil raed it woiuhtt a porbelm. Tihs is bcuasee the biarn deos not raed ervey lteter on its own but the wrod as a wlohe. So mcuh for slpelnig bneig imorpatnat!

HIPPOCAMPUS

The **hippocampus** is the center for *short-term memory* and plays a role in *emotion*, *sexuality* and *spatial orientation*. It is an area of the **temporal lobe** and is considered to be a part of the **limbic brain**.

PARIETAL LOBE

The **parietal lobe** *perceives* and processes **physical** *sensations* of *touch*, *taste*, *pressure*, *pain*, *temperature*, *vibration*, *body image* and *awareness*, and has the capacity to store *memories* of these *experiences*.

At the junction of the **parietal** and **temporal lobes** is **Wernicke's area** that strengthens understanding of *language processes*.

FRONTAL LOBE

The **frontal lobe** is an area that controls the sequencing of **muscles** needed for **speech** and **swallowing** patterns. It is the main area for **planning**, **thinking** and **reasoning**, where all **voluntary** movement is initiated and plans are made to take **physical** or *conceptual actions* on decisions that are made. It allows people to feel *empathy*, *sympathy*, *understanding*, *irony*, *humor*, *sarcasm* and *deception*. You can strengthen the **motor activity** to integration of **muscle activity** in both directions to improve **speech**, *thought process* and understanding of the **order** of **words**.

The whole **brain** is designed to shift to different states of *relaxation*. It is important that the **left** and **right brain** and the **lobes** are integrated. The four states of the **brain** are measured in **hertz cycles** per **second**. They are **beta, alpha, theta and delta.**

BETA (arousal) is actively engaged at fifteen to forty cycles per second.

ALPHA (non-arousal) is the meditative state at nine to fourteen cycles per second.

THETA (greater amplitude) is a slower frequency that occurs when participating in activities such as driving or running at five to eight cycles per second.

DELTA (deep dreamless sleep) is at one point five to four cycles per second.

THE NON-CONSCIOUS BRAIN

CEREBELLUM

The **cerebellum** is located below the **cerebral cortex**. It *coordinates* and *controls* **voluntary** movement, *balances* the trunk of the body and influences **muscle tension** and *balance* of the **limbs**.

Common symptoms of dysfunction of the **cerebellum** include **tremors**, **nystagmus** (involuntary movement of the **eyes**) and lack of *coordination*. Paralysis does not occur from loss of **cerebellum** function. Common issues on the **physical** level **are trauma, calcification, vascular** and **lymphatic** insufficiency.

BRAIN STEM

The **brain stem** connects the **brain** to the **spinal cord**, keeping people alive even when they are asleep or unconscious by maintaining **heartbeat**, **breathing** and other **autonomic** functions whereas the **neck** and **facial nerves** communicate without going through the **spinal cord**, along with the **vagus nerve** that communicates with the **heart, lungs, stomach** and **uterus**. This is why a person who has a severed spine can still have a regulated heartbeat and even an orgasm.

The **brain stem** consists of the **medulla oblongata**, the **mid-brain**, the **pons**, the **diencephalon**, the **thalamus** and the **hypothalamus**.

MEDULLA OBLONGATA

The **medulla oblongata** is a crossing of **motor tracts** located closest to the **spinal cord** that regulate the **heartbeat, breathing**, control of the **blood vessel walls**, and the *reflexes* for **vomiting, coughing, sneezing, swallowing** and **hiccups**.

Common symptoms of dysfunction are **same-side paralysis, pupils** that are dilated and fixed, loss of *consciousness*, abnormal **breathing patterns, hiccups** and the inability to control movement, loss of **coug*h*** and ***gag reflex***. Strengthen **cranial nerves IX, X, XI, XII** to the **medulla oblongata**. *EU ... PNS (PERIPHERAL NERVOUS SYSTEM), Pg. 391*

MID-BRAIN

The **mid-brain** consists of the **nerve pathways** of the **cerebral hemispheres** and the *auditory* and *visual reflex* centers. It relays **motor signals** from the **cerebral cortex** to the **pons** and sensory transmissions in the opposite direction from the **spinal cord** to the **thalamus**.

Common symptoms of dysfunction are **pupils** that **are mid-position** to **dilated** and **sluggish** to **fixed**, loss of *consciousness, palsy* and **drooping** on one side of the **body**, abnormal **extensor muscles**, and **hyperventilating**.

PONS

The **pons** controls the **respiratory center, mouth** and **facial *sensation*** and ***expression*, chewing, eye-movement, inner-ear coordination**, and **hearing**.

Common symptoms of dysfunction are **pinpoint pupils**, loss of *consciousness*, **abnormal extensor muscles** and **respirations**, marked by sustained **inhalations**.

Strengthen **cranial nerves V, VI, VII, VIII**, to the **pons** and the **mid-brain** to **CIII** and **CIV**. *EU ... PNS (PERIPHERAL NERVOUS SYSTEM), Pg. 391*

DIENCEPHALON

The **diencephalon,** located between the **cerebrum** and the **mid-brain,** consists of several important **structures**. For the intents and purpose of *intuition* (as opposed to what most people refer to as *psychic ability*) I will focus on the **thalamus** and **hypothalamus**.

THALAMUS

The **thalamus** is a large bi-lateral (**right thalamus/left thalamus**), egg-shaped mass of **gray matter** that serves as the main synaptic relay center. It receives and relays *sensory* information from the **cerebral cortex**, including **pain** and **pleasure** centers.

HYPOTHALAMUS

The **hypothalamus** is a collection of **ganglia** (**neurons**) that are located below the **thalamus**. The **ganglia** are intimately connected to the **pituitary gland,** sensing changes in **body temperature, water balance** and **blood pressure**. The **hypothalamus** regulates homeostasis of the **sympathetic** and **parasympathetic nervous systems**; it also controls the **pituitary gland** and the **endocrine system**.

Strengthen the efficiency of the components of the **hypothalamus** for clear perception of the *sensory* input from *thoughts* and *emotions*.

THE TRIUNE BRAIN

During the 1950s, a doctor and researcher named Paul MacLean came up with a controversial new theory that humans have not one **brain**, but three. He proposed that through evolutionary time the human **brain** began to evolve and become more complicated.

The three **brains** he identified are the **reptilian brain**, the **limbic brain**, and the **neocortex**.

REPTILIAN BRAIN

The **reptilian brain** is located at the base of the **spine** at the **coccyx**, and runs up the **spine** to the **brain stem**. It is the oldest evolutionary part of the **brain**. The main responsibility of the **reptilian brain** is to ensure survival by controlling all routine **body functions** and *instinctive behavior*. Its functions are automatic but strongly influenced by the **limbic** brain and the **neocortex**.

LIMBIC BRAIN (MID-BRAIN)

The **limbic brain** is the outer skin of the **reptilian brain** that focuses mainly on survival. It operates on a *sub-conscious* level, modifying the *instinctual drives* that are first generated in the **reptilian brain** such as the urge to mate, defend, attack, nurture, eat and drink. It is an emotional processing center, dealing with *belief* and *value systems*, as well as *long-term memory*.

NEOCORTEX

The **neocortex**, the most recently evolved, third layer of the **brain,** covers the **reptilian** and **limbic brains**. It belongs to **humans** and **cetaceans** (**whales, dolphins** and **porpoises**), the only mammals with relatively similar **cortical** sizes and structures in the mammalian species. The characteristic wrinkling of the **neocortex** provides surface area for the function of more **neurons**.

THE AMYGDALA

The **amygdala** is an almond-shaped structure in the center of the **brain** that is the key to vital survival mechanisms. It has direct links to the **reptilian brain**, the **limbic brain** and the **neocortex**. It also has the ability to assess whether or not any given situation is harmless or potentially dangerous. By scanning *memory banks* for previous similar *experiences*, it instantly makes that determination. This early warning system originally developed from the most primitive of our **senses, smell**, and is linked to deep sexual urges at the *base chakra*, urges that are essential to human survival. It can be problematic if it becomes oversensitive to the storehouse of *sensations* that are connected to *emotional memories*, because it may then *re-act* not only to threats, but also to *perceived* threats.

There are three *loops* that pertain to the **amygdala**. The first two *loops* were the first to develop. One loop goes to the **hypothalamus,** causing the release of **corticotropin-releasing hormone** (**CRH**), stimulating **adrenaline** and **epinephrine**, which is commonly referred to as *fight* or *flight.*

The second *loop* goes to the **locus coeruleus** in the **reptilian brain** stem to manufacture **norepinephrine** which **imprints** *emotional memories* and *feelings* into the *long term memory banks* of the **fascia** of the **body**. **Allergies** are often triggered through *association* to the library of files stored in these *memories*.

The third and least developed *loop* is the **cortex** which provides the ability to comprehend appropriate *action* and discrimination of events, giving people choice to either *re-act* to what they are feeling, or to use the feeling to take strong *actions*. When people are triggered by *sensations* and by *re-acting* to *emotions*, the **cortex** is high-jacked by the **hypothalamus** and the **locus coeruleus**, which causes irrational behavior that is disconnected from *creative solutions*.

Tri-sensory perception (the **eyes**, **ears** and **mouth**) and secondary **senses** send a *sensory signal* to the **body** in the form of *sight*, *smell*, *touch*, *sound*, *balance*, *temperature* or combinations thereof. These *sensory signals* are intercepted by the **thalamus** that acts as a filter to decide if the stimuli received from the *environment* should be allowed any further into the **brain**. An overstimulated **thalamus** can cause oversensitivity to the *environment*.

From the **thalamus**, the signal goes to the **amygdala** which quickly processes the signal by searching through the *memory banks* to decide whether to declare an emergency or not. If the signal causes a high alert, it triggers the **hypothalamus** and the **limbic** and **reptilian brain** to go into survival mode.

If the survival *re-action* has been set in motion before the **cortex** has a chance to assess the situation, the *emotions* are now in charge and *mental sabotage* occurs. If the signal is *associated* with a situation in peoples' lives that was a strong *imprint*, the *memory* becomes more deeply ingrained into the *memory patterns* of the **body** and *mind*, causing the **nervous circuits** to be hyperactive to stimuli associated with certain *memories*.

THE "GOOD NEWS" IS:

An understanding that your **left brain** *receives*, and the **right brain** *retrieves* along with basic knowledge of the components of the **brain** itself, is beneficial for the integration of all the **physical processes** to function more effectively. For optimum function, strengthen the three **brains** all the way to the core (the **reptilian brain**) and the **lobes** of the **brain** to have optimal communication.

THE "BAD NEWS" IS:

There are many variations of situations from the *past*, *present* and *future*, that trigger thoughts from the *mind*, which in turn create *emotional* problems as well as '*emotionalizations*' of *feelings* that influence the way people *think*.

NUGGET OF WIZDOM FROM THE VECTOR

CONSCIOUSNESS LIVES IN THE SOUL, NOT THE BRAIN. YOUR BRAIN IS PART OF YOUR PHYSICAL INTELLIGENCE. IMPROVE YOUR ABILITY TO USE YOUR MIND TO DELETE STAGNATIONS IN THE BRAIN TO FACILITATE THE EFFICIENCY OF YOUR PHYSICAL INTELLIGENCE.

BREAST HEALTH AND AUGMENTATION

The breasts are the **tissue** overlying the **chest** and **pectoral muscles**. Women's **breasts** are made up of **glandular tissue** that produces milk, as well as **fatty** and **connective tissue** that determines the size of the breast.

The milk producing part of the **breast** is organized into fifteen to twenty sections called **lobes**. Within each of the **lobes** are twenty to forty smaller structures called **lobules** where milk is produced. The milk travels through branches of tiny tubes called **ducts**. The **ducts** connect and gather into around ten larger **ducts** in a similar way that grapes are attached to stems. The **ducts** eventually exit the **skin** through the **nipple** situated within a circular area of darker **skin** called the **areola**.

Connective tissue and **ligaments** provide support to the **breast** and give it shape. The **breast** also contains **blood vessels**, **lymph vessels** and **lymph nodes**. The **blood supply** for the **breast** comes primarily from the **internal mammary artery** which runs underneath the main **breast tissue**, providing **nutrients** and **oxygen** to the **breast**. Since **cancer cells** and **parasites** are not able to thrive in an **oxygen** and **alkaline** environment, it is important to strengthen the **nutrients, oxygen** and **alkalinity** to go where they are needed in the **breast**.

The **lymphatic vessels** of the breast flow in the opposite direction of the **blood supply** and drain into the **lymph nodes**. Most carry on to the **auxiliary nodes** under the **arm**, with a few draining deep into the **breast**. This is important because when **breast cancer** metastasizes, it usually involves the **sentinel lymph node**, the first in the chain. It is common for surgeons to remove this **node** to confirm metastases in a patient with

breast cancer. The purpose of the **lymph nodes** is to facilitate the breakdown of **toxins**, **poisons** and **abnormalities**. Break down the **abnormal cells** at the quantum level and spin them out to *black wholes*. If the **lymph nodes** have been cut out they are no longer able to fulfill their purpose. If they have already been removed, **re-integrate** them energetically to be able to perform their function at maximum potential. *EU ... PSYCHIC SURGERY AND TRANSPLANT, Pg. 425*

The road to hell is paved with good intentions. Clear the "pink ribbon effect" that often occurs when women are **diagnosed** with cancer. Well-meaning friends and family try to support them by purchasing pink slippers, robes, water bottles, going on runs, etc. with the intention of fighting dis-ease in the **breasts**. However, putting on their "cancer slippers" and bathrobe first thing in the morning weakens their **daily routine**. Furthermore, walking into establishments that sell these products increases the *fear* on a *sub-conscious* level for every woman and man, reminding them that disaster is right around the corner, only a lump away. This creates a *fear* of *touching* and having **breasts** *touched*, and imprints the *fear* onto the very **tissues** that they are trying to protect. Many people do not realize that much of the money for the pink ribbon campaign is used to encourage women to participate in the **industry** of **mammography**.

If a woman is considering **mastectomy**, **lumpectomy** or **breast implants**, any weaknesses for the "need to be cut" must be cleared first. People who have surgeries often have an underlying weakness of *karma* from **cutting** others or being **cut** by others. Make sure all *karma* with the **medical community** is resolved. In the case of **mastectomy**, especially of the **left breast**, test for *past-life* weaknesses of being a female warrior because in some cultures women would cut off their **left breast** to get it out of the way for the bow and arrow). *EU ... THE PRACTICE OF MEDICINE, Pg. 498*

BREAST AUGMENTATION

Every *thought* and *emotion* about any given part of the **body** is recorded in the hard drive of the **CNS** and back to that **body part**. The female **breasts** are hardest hit by negative and positive **information** because the vast majority of women are glorified, objectified or judged in our society by the size and shape of their **breasts**. **Breasts** sell! The **media**, **big business**, **scientific research**, the **medical community**, **fashion, industries**, etc., have become experts at exploiting women's breasts to such an extent that the vast majority of women are *relaxing* themselves to avoid these *external forces*, and in the process, *dis-associating* from their own **breasts**.

Many **girls** have negative "trainer bra" **experiences** ranging from being teased and ridiculed for being "flat," too small and on the opposite spectrum, for being over-developed at a tender age. Many fathers and mothers find it challenging to handle the metamorphosis of "daddy's little girl" to a grown woman, causing more confusion and conflicting **emotional**, **mental** and **psychological** issues to arise. To counter this, shift energies around over-guarding and over-protecting the **heart space**.

Many of the reasons **women** are not happy with their **breasts** come from an inability to "measure up." Lingerie is big business and intentionally creates an atmosphere of competition between women. Do you have the money to purchase our product? If not scrounge it together and our product will get you the man, or better yet, because of your beautiful **breasts**, he will be happy to purchase one for you! The **lingerie industry** is famous for wrapping their lingerie in tissues and expensive bags to make them seem like precious jewelry. In one chain, they actually have people running around with walkie-talkies to keep track of their bras to ensure none are stolen. These marketing strategies are geared to make women **believe** that the **product** that they are buying is more important than the **breasts** they are trying to convince people to adorn.

Unfortunately, many women and men fall for this advertising and end up disappointed, thereby creating a need to purchase another product that will make them feel better. Placing emphasis on any one **body part** at the expense of all the others automatically gives that **body part** too much importance, creating a minefield of **emotional**, **mental** and **psychological** weaknesses. Any talented burlesque dancer knows that the purpose of lingerie is to artfully remove it. If done correctly, a toss of the **hair**, the removal of a **glove**, the glimpse of a **thigh** are much more effective and sensual than focusing on the **breasts** alone.

For centuries women have subjected themselves or have been subjected to the dictates of the **fashion industry**, wearing corsets for that impossibly tiny waist, binding their breasts to make them appear smaller, or push up bras to create cleavage, etc. Bras can actually weaken the **ligaments** and **tissues** because they are doing the work for the **ligaments**. There is a saying, "use it or lose it;" this is true of the **ligaments** and **tissues** that support perky **breasts**, and **relaxation** of the **breasts** is also the leading cause of **disease** in the **breasts**.

Another common weakness that **women** have regarding bras is not feeling adequate to fill the cup, or the **fear** of spilling out of it. Clear all weaknesses around **not being enough** or **too much** of a woman. Some of these weaknesses can be traced back to infancy when babies are automatically measured and weighed at birth and at every check-up. Negative **educational** *experiences* of being graded can also inhibit a woman's desire to move up from an A cup, to a B, C or D after spending countless years *struggling* through the school system to get all A's.

Breasts are **organs,** and every **organ** can be *contracted* or *expanded* in size by working **cell** by **cell** from the inside out and gradually shrinking or enlarging the **atoms** through a basic principle of quantum physics: for every *action* there is an equal and opposite *re-action*. To have an effect on the **breasts'** size and shape, they need to be **re-integrated** with the rest of the **body**. Common weaknesses arise during **puberty** when **hormones** produced by the **ovaries** and **pituitary gland** stimulate the **breasts** to grow by stretching the **ducts** to branch out until they develop into a mature system of **lobules** and **ducts**.

When a woman's **menstruation** ends and the **ovaries** stop producing **hormones**, the numbers of **lobules** have a tendency to decrease **and** shrink in size along with the density of the **breast tissue**. High **breast density** means that there is more **connective tissue** than **fat**; **low density** means that there is more **fat** than **connective tissue**. The **ligaments** and **breast tissue** change with age, weight gain and loss, causing the **ligaments** to weaken and stretch leading the **breasts** to droop and lose their fullness.

The **ligaments** and **connective tissue** can be strengthened to support the **breasts** by shortening and contracting the **upper pec muscles** and adding **testosterone** to the underlying **muscles**. Make an *energetic necklace* that rests on the **clavicle** and has several chains stretching down to the **nipples** of each **breast**; then energetically tense the necklace to lift the **breasts**. Strengthen the **rib cage** to support the **breasts**.

Use *tension* to break down **tissue** from any unwanted **fat** from other parts of the **body** at the quantum level and redistribute any unwanted **fat** into areas of the **breasts** that you wish to *expand*. The idea is not to make it dense and heavy, but more like helium air balloons that fill and lift the **breasts**. If there is no excess **tissue** to redistribute, pull that energy in from the *macrocosmic energies*. To decrease **breast** size, do the opposite, *contract* the existing **tissue** and spin it out through *black wholes*.

Though the **breast** is mature after puberty, **breast tissue** is not activated until pregnancy when the **lobules** grow and begin to produce milk. The *sensation* of the milk "coming down" can be useful for **breast augmentation**. If you have not had the experience of breast-feeding a baby or being breastfed, tap into other *times* and *space* when you have.

It is normal for a woman to have **breasts** that are different in sizes and shapes. In some women this is more apparent than in others. Choose which **breast shape** and **size** is most desirable and strengthen the other breast to be even with it.

BREASTFEEDING

Modern **society** has turned the natural act of breastfeeding infants into a shameful exhibition to be hidden behind closed doors, leaving many women perching precariously on toilet seats in germ-laden stalls so as not to offend the sensibilities of other patrons in public establishments. Besides the obvious **nutritional** benefits for the baby to be nourished by a natural, *God-given product*, breastfeeding **bonds** the **mother** to the **baby** and vice-versa and decreases the potential for breast cancer to develop. The milk is always at the right temperature, and alleviates **financial** concerns because it is free. There are many hidden influences that make breastfeeding challenging for babies and their moms. If a woman is having difficulty with bringing in the milk, test for *karmas* with **big business** that are benefiting **financially** from the sale of formulas, *past-life experiences* of being a wet-nurse and *spiritual* weaknesses of starving.

THE "GOOD NEWS" IS:

The beauty of **breasts** is undeniable. They are a source of sensuality for both admirers and the women who own them; as well, they are an essential, free source of food for nursing babies.

THE "BAD NEWS" IS:

There is a lot of unnecessary slicing and dicing happening to **breasts** these days for various reasons, and there is a lot of contradictory information regarding **mammograms** and their ability to save lives. With all that attention and all that money, you would think the **medical community** would find a better way, other than a machine that has two metal plates that squeeze **radiation** into **breasts** with a very high, false positive rate. You don't see men lining up to expose their favorite organs to such a machine.

NUGGET OF WIZDOM FROM THE VECTOR

FOCUS YOUR ATTENTION ON BREAST HEALTH INSTEAD OF BREAST DIS-EASE. LOVE YOUR BREASTS, IF YOU DO NOT LOVE THE WAY THEY LOOK OR FEEL FIND A MAN TO DO IT FOR YOU ... MANY MEN WILL BE HAPPY TO COMPLY.

CANCER

There are few words in the modern vocabulary that strike more *fear* in the **heart** than the dreaded word "cancer." It definitely tops the list of "serious illnesses." When people get a "clean bill of health" at their annual **physical examination**, they can breathe a sigh of relief that they have escaped its deadly influence for one more year. The very seriousness of the **diagnosis** is one of the main reasons it is so deadly, yet serious **disease** can stem from seemingly trivial causes.*EU ... DIS-EASE, Pg. 193*

Cancer is the darling of the media. If there is ever a lull in the news, the empty space can always be filled with a cancer story. Many people with cancer ask themselves why cancer chose them. It is more likely that *thoughts* triggered from the **information**, a person's *emotional* and *psychological* and **physical environment** and/or other factors combined to make them susceptible to its *negative influence*.

Conventional *thinking* views cancer as an enemy attacking the body, an enemy that must be fought and eradicated at all costs, justifying collateral damage to the rest of the **body** and the quality of life of the survivor. Medical authorities claim that **genetic traits** determine the body's tolerance for abuse, but a *health crisis* that runs through the family is not necessarily **genetic**. If we look at the issue from a new *perspective*, we can see that it is possible that the **genes** are compromised because cancer causes changes in the **genes** instead of the **genes** causing cancer. The concept of early diagnosis is fundamentally flawed because many of the methods used to detect cancer fail to differentiate between **benign** and **malignant cells**. Common *triggers* of developing cancer are the uncertainty of *being tested* and hearing the results of **expert opinions**, **authority figures**, **research**, etc. A report commissioned by the U.S. National Cancer Institute and published in the Journal of the American Medical Association identifies both **over-diagnosis** and **mis-diagnosis** of cancer as two major causes of the growing cancer epidemic. Millions of people who in reality do not have cancer are needlessly subjected to **surgery, radiation** and **chemotherapy**.

Many women with conditions such as **ductal carcinoma in situ (DCIS)**, which is a benign condition, are **diagnosed** and treated for **breast cancer**. Similarly, many men undergo treatment for cancer when they are **diagnosed** with **high grade prostatic intraepithelial neoplasia (HGPIN)** that is a precursor for cancer. These people often undergo aggressive **radiation** and **chemotherapy** treatment for conditions they never had, and later they develop cancer from the side effects of the **poisons** and **radiation** in their bodies. Even in cases where a **tumor** is found early enough to contain it through **surgery, chemotherapy** and

radiation, the sub-population of **cancer stem cells** within the **tumors** tend to become enriched and more aggressive because of the treatment.

It is important to pinpoint where the **cancer cells** are originating. Most people assume that cancer originates in the **physical body**; however, it can originate from other *dimensions* and *existences* in *space-time* as well as from the *accumulative spiritual* and *psychic experiences* of cancer *traumas* from **ancestors**, **descendants**, and the *collective influence*. You can delete these *accumulative effects* and separate them from the **physical internal structures** by defining how many *psychic layers* there are before the **cancer cells** appear in the **body** and clear them before they manifest.

Malignant tumors may have an actual **physical source** that diagnostic tests will verify. They can be *miasmas* from *limiting patterns* of *beliefs* held through the **genetic line** that manifest through **internal body processes**, or they may be caused by **poisons**, **toxins** or **traumas** in the **physical environment** that impact the **body**.

The leading *physiological* cause of cancer is an **unevenness** of **structure** in the **cells**, **organs** and **systems** of the **body**. This can be from **left** to **right**, **right** to **left**, **front** to **back**, **back** to **front**, **up**, **down**, **inside** and **outside**. On the *non-physical* level, **unevenness** in the *aspects* of life cause *imbalance* between the *masculine* and *feminine* qualities held by an individual; that imbalance can manifest as **malignant** and **benign tumors**. This is a perfect time to *re-boot* and *re-calibrate* the **cells** to the perfection of the template of **pri-mordial cells**.

If cancer is viewed as a survival mechanism that has gone awry, you can think of it as a bunch of **cells** that have decided to gain importance by collecting with each other just as politicians do in parliament. You might be fooled into thinking that they are very important and really mean business. However, once the bantering is over and they swagger out of the building to go back to their constituencies you barely notice them. Breaking down a **tumor** and dissipating the **cancer cells** bit by bit throughout the **body** to *external* and *internal black wholes* breaks down their importance in much the same way.

In traditional medicine the goal of cancer, therapy is to concentrate the **cancer cells** so that the **tumor** can be **cut**, **burned** or **poisoned** out. Physiologically, the **lymphatic system** is built to **remove poisons**, **toxins** and waste out of the body including **cancer cells**. Use *black wholes* within the **lymphatic system's** components to make it more efficient at processing any **errant cells** that may show up in **medical**

tests; do this to avoid surgery, while the **lymphatic system** is in the process of doing its job.

Photons are quantum level particles that have *zero mass* and no *electrical charge*. They are made up of eight waves that travel at the *speed of light* to a variety of *frequencies*. This is the practical mechanism by which every **cell** knows the status of the other. Healthy **bodies** resonate to integrated *frequencies* and **high amplitude**, the maximum value registered by a *frequency* or **hertz**. **Hertz** is a measure of one complete oscillation that has occurred in a second; the faster the **hertz**, the higher the *frequency* and the *vibration*. **Amplitude** is the maximum value registered by a *frequency*.

Proton therapy is an effective radiation therapy for many types of **tumors**. It destroys **cancer cells** by preventing them from dividing and growing, just like in **standard x-ray (photon) radiation**. The difference between **standard proton therapy** and **standard x-ray radiation** is that **protons** deposit much of their **radiation** directly in the **tumor** and then stop. This allows patients to *receive* effective doses while reducing damage to **healthy tissues** surrounding the **tumor**.

Coherence of the **protons** and **photons** can create an energetic **laser point** that accelerates the **hertz** to disintegrate **tumors, cellular waste, parasitic waste** and **excessive connective tissues**, etc., by collapsing the wave and sending the particles off to be transformed by *black wholes*.

CHEMOTHERAPY AND RADIATION

Given that people are told to fight against cancer; it is not that much of a surprise that the foundation of **chemotherapy** as a weapon against cancer is a product of World Wars I and II when it was recognized that mustard gas caused the destruction of fast growing **cells**.

To combat the ill effects of **chemotherapy**, strengthen all **medications**, in all combinations to work with the person and each other to one hundred percent **infinite potential** and *delete* the *negative effects* down to **zero minus infinity**. Direct the treatment to the **cancer cells** and away from **healthy cells**. Boost the number of **white blood cells** to *recognize* and *absorb* cancer cells and inhibit their *reproduction*. Strengthen the *fitness* of the **mitochondria** in the **healthy cells**. Remove the **salt** and **water** out of the **cancer cells** and weaken the walls of the **cellular membrane**, by making them more *relaxed*. Optimize **alkalinity, oxygenation, negative ions** and **glutathione** (a powerful naturally occurring **antioxidant** in all human **cells**) in the **healthy cells**. Finally, Increase *tension* throughout the entire body.

CASE STUDY:

Over the years I have worked with many patients who have faced the diagnosis of cancer. It is challenging to find anything funny about cancer, however the lighter the attitude, generally the better the outcome ...

I was speaking at The Spring Festival of Awareness, in Naramata B.C., Canada, an annual event that celebrates alternative thinking and healing modalities. A woman in the audience came to the front and asked if I would work on her elderly father who had lung cancer, using her as a surrogate. He was in hospital in palliative care and was not expected to recover.

The following year, she was attending the festival once again as was I, and I asked her what had happened with her father. She replied that he had made an unexpected turn for the better and after several months, they removed him from palliative care, even though all his tests showed that he still had cancer. The difference was it no longer bothered him. I had energetically shifted him to let go of any concerns about cancer and dying from his mind and send them out to black wholes, then spun in reasons to live well through white holes.

She told me that typical conversations with him went something like this ..."*Dad, you have to cooperate with the doctors, they need to do tests.*", "*Why do they need to do tests?*", "*Because you have cancer.*", "*I do? Are you sure? I feel so good!*", or ... "*Dad, would you like to go for an ice-cream?*", "*I don't like ice-cream! Well, maybe I do, OK!*", or "*Dad, would you like to go to an art exhibition?*" "*Nah, I don't like art! Wait a minute, maybe I do!*"

She told me that it wasn't just the cancer he forgot, it was also many other things he didn't like. When she asked him if it bothered him that he could not remember some things, he said he felt that if it was important to remember he would, because he always remembered the people he loves. As it turned out, he did really enjoy art and was very animated in his conversations when discussing it. The following year, we met once again and her father was now at home and still doing better than expected.

THE "GOOD NEWS" IS:

At most hospitals the most common treatments for cancer are administered with sophisticated equipment by highly educated professionals.

THE "BAD NEWS" IS:

Unfortunately the treatment is very primitive: **cut**, **burn**, **poison**. A high percentage of doctors surveyed admit that they would not put themselves or their loved ones through **chemotherapy** or **radiation**; however they routinely recommend it to the vast majority of their **patients**.

NUGGET OF WIZDOM FROM THE VECTOR

LACK OF INTEGRITY IN THE ORGANIZATION OF CANCER CELLS ON THE MICROSCOPIC LEVEL IS EVEN MORE RAMPANT ON A MACROCOSMIC LEVEL IN CANCER ORGANIZATIONS. INSISTING THAT A TREATMENT THAT HAS LESS THAN A THREE PERCENT SUCCESS RATE AS THE BEST SOLUTION TO A LIFE THREATENING PROBLEM BEGS THE QUESTION … BEST FOR WHOM? CANCER IS BIG BUSINESS! DO NOT UNDERESTIMATE THE UNDERLYING FINANCIAL WEAKNESSES. CLEAR ALL KARMA WITH ALL INVOLVED.

CELL-EBRATION

Cells are considered the smallest units that make up the building blocks of life as the basic structure, function and biological unit for all known living **organisms**. **Organisms** are classified as **unicellular**, meaning that they consist of only **one cell** such as in the case of **bacteria**, or **multicellular** that make up the **plants** and **animals**. The number of **cells** varies from species to species, but the human **body** is comprised of about one hundred trillion **cells**.

Eukaryote cells that have a **nucleus**, and **prokaryotes** are cells that do not contain a **nucleus**. **Eukaryotes** can be both single-celled or part of multicellular organisms. **Prokaryotes** include bacteria and archaea. It is helpful to have a basic understanding of cell structure and their processes to facilitate energetic shifts that encourage *healthy*, vibrant cells to flourish with optimum *fitness*. It is easiest to gain an understanding of cells by *thinking* of all of your cells as infinitely smaller reflections of your body. Your **body** is a container for all of your **cells**, and just as your body maintains **elimination systems, digestive systems, nervous systems, circulatory systems**, etc., so does each cell. The ability of your cells to digest the main nutrients **of oxygen, water, nitrogen, hydrogen, carbon**, and to *eliminate* waste efficiently is a reflection of how your **body** is functioning over-all.

CYTOSKELETON

The **cytoskeleton** organizes and maintains the shape of the **cell** in a similar way that a **skeleton** keeps the components of the **body** in place. It also plays a crucial role in **cell division**. It has small rodlike structures made up of many **proteins** that support and anchor **organelles**, called **microfilaments, intermediate filaments** and **microtubules**.

Two main components of the **organelles** are the **microfilaments** and the **microtubules**. The **microfilaments** are responsible for **cell movement** through *contraction* and *expansion*, similar to **muscles,** while the larger **microtubules** are responsible for **cell division** mainly through **centrioles** that are *activated* in **cell division**.

Actin is the **protein molecule** that assembles with other **proteins** to make up **microfilaments** and **tubulin**. **Intermediate filaments** are generally made up of **heteropolymers** that combine with other subunits, depending on what type of **tissue** the **cell** is building.

CYTOPLASM

The **cytoplasm** of the cell is a gel-like substance that is enclosed within the **cellular membrane**, containing the **cell's internal sub-structures**. It is made up of eighty percent **water** and is usually colorless. Most **cellular activities** of **metabolic pathways** occur within the **cytoplasm**, including **cell division**. The **inner granular mass** is called the **endoplasm** and the outer, glassier layer is called the **ectoplasm**.

EXTRACELLULAR MATRIX

Living **tissues** are not made up of tightly packed **cells**. Just as with **atoms**, the **tissue's volume** is made up of **space**, called the **extracellular matrix**. The **matrix** is dynamic, providing structural support for the **cells** that are embedded in **tissue**, guiding the division, growth and development. It is made up of **proteoglycans** (a **protein core** with chains of **molecules** similar in make-up to starch), **water, minerals** and **fibrous proteins**. **Fibroblasts** are **cells** that are responsible for producing and organizing the nature of the **matrix**. Different parts of the body are composed of different types of **fibrous proteins**, including **collagen, elastin, fibronectin** and **laminin**.

As with all **spaces** within the **body**, it is essential that the **extracellular matrix** has the correct density and strength of structure in all directions and has a strong *relationship* with the **cells** contained within. For instance, **collagen** is the main **protein** found in animal **connective tissue**; it is the glue that holds the **body** together. It is found in **bones, skin, muscles** and **tendons**, and along with **elastin**, it allows **tissues** in the **body** to resume their shape after stretching or contracting.

Fibronectin is a **fibrous protein** that binds to other **proteins** and the **cell membranes** as anchors and connectors. **Laminin** is a key component of the **basal lamina**, a thin sheet-like structure that surrounds the **cells** in **animal tissue** providing **anchor points** and support for **cells**.

Different parts of the **body** require different **densities** of the **extracellular matrix** to provide the correct function for the **body part** involved. For instance, the **extracellular matrix** of **bones** is much denser, thick and highly mineralized to provide a **matrix** that is hard, as compared to the **matrix** of the **eyeballs** which is more flexible and transparent.

INTRACELLULAR FLUID

The **intracellular fluid** is made up of **water, dissolved solutes** and **proteins**, accounting for almost half of total **body weight. Water** moves in and out of the **cell** by **osmotic pressure**, pulling fluid from one part to another. Ideally the **osmotic pressure** is optimum between **extracellular fluid** and **intracellular fluid**. When there is a decrease of **water** within the **cell, electrolytes**, made up of **potassium, magnesium** and **phosphates**, move **water** back into the **cell** and vice-versa. If the *relationship* between the two is not *balanced* the **cells** will shrink or swell causing inefficiencies in **cellular function**. Strengthen the **inner** and **outer functions** to facilitate optimum **hydration** through evenness between the **extracellular fluid** and the **intracellular fluid**.

CELLULAR MEMBRANE

Cell membranes (plasma membranes) form a boundary between the **inside** of the **cell**, called the **cytoplasm,** and the **outside** of the **cell**, thus regulating transport in and out of the **cell**. The **cellular membrane** can be compared to the **skin** on your **body**; just as your **skin** is the container for your **skeleton, organs, blood** and other fluids, the **cellular membrane** contains the **cytoplasm** within its **cellular walls**.

Membranes sort and organize the contents of **cells** into compartments called **organelles** for efficiency and for the organization of **cells** that become specialized. The **cellular membrane** is referred to as a **phospholipid layer**, which means that it is made up of an **inner** and **outer layer**, with the **membrane** acting as both a **lubricant** for the **cell** as well as a **semi-permeable barrier** that incases the contents; it also protects the **cell** from unwanted substances.

There are also **protein molecules** embedded in the **membrane** that act as **channels** and **pumps** that move different **molecules** in and out of the **cell**, as well as **receptor proteins** that detect external signals from other **molecules** such as **hormones** and other stimuli from the outside **environment**.

The cell **receptors** send a message to the **DNA** in the **nucleus** of the **cell** to respond to the **environment,** thereby altering **cell function**. The messages that are transferred to and from the **receptors** include *emotional*, *mental*, *psychic* and *spiritual* data as well as **physical** information. All have *direct* and *indirect effects* on the *health* of the **cell** and the entire **body**.

DNA AND RNA

There are two different kinds of **genetic material**, **DNA** to encode **information** for long term storage in the **cells** and **RNA** to transport **information** and **enzymatic** function.

All **cells** except **red blood cells** contain **DNA (deoxyribonucleic acid)** and **RNA (ribonucleic acid)**. Both **DNA** and **RNA** are made up of **nucleic acids**, **proteins** and **carbohydrates** that constitute **macromolecules. Macromolecules** are **molecules** that contain a large number of **atoms**.

DNA encodes **genetic instructions** for all known living **organisms** as well as for many **viruses**. Most **DNA molecules** are made up of two **biopolymer strands** that coil around each other to form a **double helix**.

RNA plays a role in the **biological coding, decoding** and **expression** of **genes**. **RNA** is more often a single strand rather than a double strand that directs the synthesis of specific **proteins**, in particular in **viruses**.

The **genetic material** of **prokaryotic cells** (**bacteria**) is organized in a simple, circular **DNA molecule**, whereas the **eukaryotic genetic material** of the human **cells** are divided into **linear molecules** called **chromosomes**.

The **genetic information** is stored in the **nucleus** and **mitochondria** of the **cell**. There are forty-six **chromosomes** made up of twenty-two sets of **maternal** and **paternal autosomes** that pair up during division of the **cells**, as well as a pair of **sex chromosomes** that determine whether an individual is male or female. Female individuals have two **X chromosomes** (**XX**) and males have one **X chromosome** as well as one **Y chromosome** (**XY**). Eggs that are fertilized by **X** bearing **sperm** become **females** and those fertilized by **Y** bearing **sperm** become **males** at the point of **meiosis,** when a cell divides to produce **gametes**.

Foreign **genetic material** can be artificially introduced into the **cell** through a process called **transfection**. This can be inserted through **DNA** into the cell's **genome** or (mostly in the case of **viruses**) be transient.

ORGANELLES

Organelles are parts of the **cells** that adapt to specialized functions which are particular to each **organ** in the body. The **organelles** in **prokaryotic cells** are very simple and generally are not bound to **membranes**. **Eukaryotic cells** are generally more complicated with a **nucleus** and **golgi apparatus** that typically have solitary functions, as well as **mitochondria, chloroplasts, peroxisomes** and **lysosomes** that can have hundreds and thousands of functions.

RIBOSOMES

Ribosomes build **proteins** that are attached to the **rough endoplasmic reticulum**. They are not bound by **membranes** and can also be found floating freely in the **cytoplasm**.

The surface of the **rough endoplasmic reticulum** is made up of **ribosomes** that modify and transport **proteins,** while the **smooth endoplasmic reticulum** has no **ribosomes** on its surface. It is responsible for making new **membranes** and neutralizing **toxins**.

GOLGI BODY APPARATUS

The **golgi body apparatus** prepares material for **export** out of the **cell** by modifying, sorting, packaging and distributing **proteins** called **vesicles. Vesicles** are **membrane packages** that can be broken down into two main **enzymes, peroxisomes** and **lysosomes**.

Peroxisomes, in general are **enzymes** or **proteins** that are made up of **hydrogen peroxide** and are broken down into **water** and **oxygen** to neutralize dangerous **molecules** through a process called **catalase**.

Lysosomes are **vesicles** that are filled with **digestive enzymes** that break down food particles such as **lipids, carbohydrates** and **proteins** into **monomers** which are used to nourish the **cells**. They also recycle damaged or unused **organelles** and attack **parasitic waste** as well as other undesirable materials.

Specialized movement of **single celled organisms** comes from **flagella** and **cilia. Flagella** spins like a propeller on a boat, while **cilia** is more like a rudder. Some **cells** are anchored to a **tissue** in which case the **cilia** will move the **environment** rather than the **cell** to facilitate its function.

If you think of the **golgi body apparatus** as a shipping company, then the **vesicles** would be the garbage that is loaded up in packages and sorted by the **workers** (**the enzymes, proteins and organelles**), and loaded on the barges to be sent off to their destination, which In this case is through the **lymphatic system,** the **circulatory system** and the *black wholes* where they are to be broken down, recycled and processed.

NUCLEUS

The **nucleus** controls **cell** *activities*. Within the **nucleus** is the **DNA,** separated by a **double membrane** called the **nuclear envelope** that is essential to isolate and protect the **DNA** from **foreign substances,** thus allowing them to enter and leave via **nuclear pores**. The center of the **nucleus** is called the **nucleolus** that contains **ribosomes**.

It used to be thought that the **nucleus** was the **brain** of the **cell;** however, it is now considered by forward-thinking scientists as the **DNA blueprint** because if the **nucleus** is removed from **stem cells**, they are able to continue living and **organisms** without a **brain** will die. The science of **epigenetics** is now proving that **DNA** does not determine the future of the life in any **organism**; rather, the future of an **organism** is determined by the **environment**. The **DNA** in the **nucleus** sends out a message through the **nuclear pores** into the **cytoplasm** (the gel-like substance that makes up the **body** of the **cell**) where it will find a **ribosome** (**protein builder**), inserting it into the surface (**rough endoplasmic reticulum**) into the new **vesicle** (**membrane package**) to the **golgi**, that then sorts and builds other **membrane packages** (**vesicles**) that are utilized by the **cell** or transported out of it.

MITOCHONDRIA

The **mitochondria** are responsible for **cell respiration** and **metabolism. Mitochondria** are like **cells** within the **cells** that have a **double membrane** which is folded up to facilitate **aspiration**. They occur in various numbers, shapes and sizes in the **cytoplasm** of all **eukaryotic cells**. They can be considered as the driving force that generates energy for the **cell**, by releasing energy from **glucose** to be converted into **ATP**. Healthy **mitochondria** are essential to prevent aging. *EU ... MITOCHONDRIA REGENERATION, Pg. 342*

CELL DIVISION

Cell division happens when a **mother cell** divides into two **daughter cells**, leading to growth of **tissue** in **multicellular organisms** and **vegetative** *reproduction* in **unicellular organisms**. **Prokaryotic cells** divide by binary fission into **two cells** that then have the ability to grow to the size of the **original cell**. **Eukaryotic cells** more commonly undergo **nuclear division**, called **mitosis**, when the **cell** divides into two and replicates once, dividing again through **meiosis**, which results in **daughter cells** each of which has the same number and kind of **chromosomes** as the **nucleus** from the **mother cell**. This is typical of ordinary **tissue** growth. **Cytokinesis** occurs concurrently in the process of **cell division** dividing the **cytoplasm** of a **parental cell** into **two daughter cells**. It is important that the **cytoplasm**, the **nuclei structure**, the **cellular membrane**, the **extracellular fluid** and the **intracellular fluid** that make up the body of the **cell**, all have perfect structure within themselves and that they are working with every other **cell** in perfect harmony.

If you have ever enjoyed playing with water balloons, you are aware that the amount of fluid within the balloon determines the ability of the balloon to have that perfect snap required for it to bounce off other surfaces. If the **cellular membrane** has the proper amount of **fluid** and **support**, it is able to bounce with the other **cells**, allowing perfect transport of **nutrients** and **waste products** in and out of the **cell**. When every **cell** is in harmony within itself, the *communication* between all the **cells** becomes harmonious and becomes a cell-ebratory dance. The *fitness* and vitality of the **cells** allows for optimal *production*, *transportation*, *distribution* and *utilization* to thrive within the **cells** and support all systems in the dance of life.

DEATH OF CELLS

There are two ways that a **cell** can die, **necrosis** and **apoptosis**. **Necrosis** occurs when a **cell** is damaged by *external forces* such as **poisons**, **toxins**, **chemicals**, **injury**, **infection**, **inflammation** and **infestation**. If it is cut off from *life force energy* of **blood** and **oxygen**, it causes further problems within the **body**. **Apoptosis** is **programmed cell death**, meaning that the **cell** basically commits suicide in a controlled, predictable fashion, which stimulates **proteins** called **caspases** to break down the **cellular waste**. **Enzymes** known as **DNases** then destroy the **DNA** in the **nucleus** of the **cell** by shrinking it. The **cell** sends out signals to other large, specialized **cells** called **macrophages** that recognize, engulf and destroy **target cells**.

Macrophages are formed by a major group of **monocytes (white blood cells)**. They leave the **blood stream** to enter the **cells** and modify themselves, forming different structures that **fight disease**, **damaged tissue**

and *infection* with a long-term immune response that recognizes the **pathogen** and provides immunity. It is important to energetically strengthen the *relationship* between the **pathogens** and the **macrophages** to target **diseased cells** that are causing **neurological problems** such as Alzheimer's, Parkinson's, AIDS, cancer, arthritis, etc.

Every **cell** in your **body** needs to be strong within itself and strong in its *relationship* with every other **cell**. **Cells** need to work together as a team for optimum function.

THE "GOOD NEWS" IS:

A very basic understanding of the function of **cells** can be *utilized* to support every **cell** in your **body** to operate at a stronger level of *fitness*. It may seem intimidating to wade through all the **information** about **cells**, their **structure** and **functions**, however if you break the *processes* down one step at a time into smaller pieces and check for weaknesses one at a time, the weaknesses can be eliminated with ease.

THE "BAD NEWS" IS:

Cells are complicated! There are over one hundred trillion **cells** in your **body** and each **cell** *affects* every other **cell**. Many people become intimidated by the **information** instead of breaking the **information** down into smaller, manageable pieces to facilitate positive *change*.

NUGGET OF WIZDOM FROM THE VECTOR

YOUR CELLS ARE A POWERFUL FEEDBACK MECHANISM THAT GATHER INFORMATION FROM YOUR ENVIRONMENT, INCLUDING EMOTIONAL, MENTAL, PSYCHIC AND SPIRITUAL DATA AS WELL AS PHYSICAL DATA. THE DATA COLLECTED BY YOUR CELLS FROM THE MACROCOSMIC IS TRANSFERRED TO EVERY CELL ON THE MICROCOSMIC LEVEL. EVERY THOUGHT HAS A POWERFUL EFFECT ON YOUR INTRINSIC BODY AND IS BOUNCED BACK OUT TO THE UNIVERSE, AFFECTING THE COLLECTIVE WHOLE.

CHAKRAS

Every individual has vortices of energy in their *etheric body* (the *subtle body* closest to the **physical body**) that spin energy in from their *astral body* (the bridge between the **physical plane** and the *spiritual plane*) and beyond. *EU ... SUBTLE ENERGIES, Pg. 488*

The seven major **body chakras** are **aligned** along the vertical mid-line from the base of the **spine** to the top of the **head.** Like a radar dish in a research center, the **chakras** serve as **memory banks**, storing vast quantities of information from previous and current lifetimes, as well as **possibilities** in the **future.** You can think of them as rotating **tetrahedrons** that **receive** and **radiate** their own level of **consciousness** or **sensations** of awareness of energy, acting as transformers to specific points where there are **nerve plexus** or **ganglia.** The **nerve centers** that translate the **vibrations** received in the area are **nerve responses** that are experienced on a **physical** level. These **responses** are the **re-actions** people **experience** as feelings that have a direct influence on their daily lives, whether they acknowledge that influence or not.

Chakras also have **yin** and **yang aspects.** The **seven chakras** begin at the **base** at **Ren One**, the most **yin** point of the human torso, located at the **perineum**, through the midline, to the **crown** at the **Du Chanel**, where **yang** qualities culminate at the top of the **head.** They spin **yin aspects** from the **front** of the **body** and **yang** from the **back.** Both also have opposite **yin** and **yang** qualities that are symbolized by the dots within each half of the **yin/yang symbol.** *EU ... EXIT PORTALS, Pg. 220*

When both the **yin** and **yang aspects** are in alignment, they create a tremendous force field in the center of the **body**; however, **trauma** can damage the **bodily chakras**, creating weaknesses on the **physical**, **mental** and **emotional** levels. If the damage is at the point where life force energy enters the **chakra**, the delicate energies cannot get through the **etheric body** and are forced onto the **mental plane** or back to where they came from on the **astral plane.** If the energies get stuck in the **etheric body**, the life force energy **accumulates** creating **endocrine** issues in the **physical body** and **imbalances** on the **psychological** level.

The **seven chakras** are also **associated** with seven rays of **primary energy fields** that influence particular energy characteristics and colors. **Experience** through your **chakras** is much like a flower's awareness of its own beauty, opening petals as each **resonance** or **frequency** is reached, connecting the **ego** to **higher self** and **highest existence** in the search for truth.

THE "GOOD NEWS" IS:

Traditionally, mastery of **breathing techniques (pranayama)** coupled with **meditation** have been used to **balance** the rotation of energy within the **chakras** to maximize **intuition. Meditation** is a state of **being** that can also be reached quickly, in a second or less to clear issues as they arise, using the **CNS** in sync with your **heart**.

THE "BAD NEWS" IS:

As humanity gets closer to the tipping point of awareness on the planet, people tend to encounter and are required to address more and more *challenging experiences* that continue to raise the *vibration* of the *collective consciousness*. These *experiences* can *feel* uncomfortable and many people sabotage themselves by giving up on their dreams just as they are about to achieve them.

NUGGET OF WIZDOM FROM THE VECTOR

CHAKRAS ARE ANTENNAE THAT DRAW ENERGETIC CURRENTS FROM THE MACROCOSMIC INWARD, GIVING ACCESS TO RECORDS OF ALL THAT HAS TAKEN PLACE, AND WILL TAKE PLACE IN THE PAST, PRESENT AND FUTURE.

CHAKRA ONE – MULADHARA (BASE)

Muladhara is located at the **base** of the **trunk**. You can think of it as a brilliant **red** flower rooted in the earth that opens its **four petals** as it is nourished by **physical potential** in the third dimensional plane.

The **geometric symbol** associated with *Muladhara* is one of the **platonic solids**, the **cube** or **hexahedron**. The **cube** is made up of **squares** whose four corners represent the stability people *feel* from the solidity of the ground under their **feet**, from the base of their existence, and from their **physical needs** of **shelter**, **food**, **water** and **oxygen**. The **square** also represents honesty, integrity and the need to belong to, and fit in with a tribe.

The *root chakra* is *associated* with the *adrenal glands* and the *sensations* caused by *re-actions* felt when people *experience* the *emotion* of *excitement* that most people refer to as "fight or flight." **Red** is the flag of *excitement* and *volatility*, the power of awakened **Kundalini** (latent *female energy* that is coiled like a snake at the **base** of the **spine**) stimulating *passion* and *self-expression* just as the cape of a matador incites a bull. The delicate balance between individuality and the tribal energy of *group consciousness* can make it seem acceptable to shirk responsibility and justify *actions* and *re-actions* when people are influenced by their peers and want to fit in. When you are grounded in the *root chakra*, it is more likely that you will use *common sense*, not to be mistaken with **intelligence** and **intellectual ability**, as the two do not always go hand in hand. Many forward thinkers are considered the "black sheep" of their family because they choose to follow *authentic desires* that are different from the dominative energy of **group desire**.

Weaknesses in a group dynamic can cause an inability to earn sufficient **financial** resources which will allow people to live a full life without the *fear* of being reduced to slavery to make ends meet. This weakness often leads to either a distorted *perception* of image and an *attachment* to material possessions or on the opposite end of the spectrum, it can lead to a monastic lifestyle where a person is unable to fully participate in life due to lack of **financial** resources.

Chronic **constipation**, **diarrhea** and **hemorrhoids** are common in people who have difficulty letting go of unclean, *negative experiences* that they have *suffered* from in the *past*. They either beat themselves up over it or hang on with a death grip to the best days of their lives as if they have no *future* to look forward to.

If our energetic **tail** is well connected to the **physical intelligence** of Earth, it acts as a rudder when we steer strong *choices* in our **physical reality**. *EU … TAIL, Pg. 496

Men and women tap into the **earth** for **resources** and **breathe** *life force energy* into *manifestations* via the **air** they take in through their **lungs**. Women also have the advantage of connecting through **vaginal breathing** as another channel to *receive* the earth's bounty.

When you are *synchronized* to the speed the **earth** is traveling at, she will reciprocate by offering solidity through the ground you walk on. When you feel things are spinning out of control and you don't have "a leg to stand on," you can *center* yourself to her axis for *stability* and *balance* for the *acceleration* of her ever-expanding nature.

The body's *expectation* to be *sabotaged* by the *mind* arises from *negative life experiences* incurred from living the old paradigm of "survival of the fittest," and it can be *deleted* through a supportive **physical environment** at **home**, at **school** and in **business**. Many *limitations* are passed down by **ancestors**, who held the *limiting beliefs* that one needed to work hard and *struggle* for survival.

NUGGET OF WIZDOM FROM THE VECTOR

FREEDOM FROM SURVIVAL MODE IS POSSIBLE BY LETTING GO OF THE OLD PARADIGM OF SURVIVAL OF THE FITTEST, BASED ON A

MISTAKEN PERCEPTION OF LACK THAT ENCOURAGES A COMPETITIVE ATMOSPHERE WHERE ONLY CERTAIN INDIVIDUALS CAN WIN.

CHAKRA TWO – SVADHISTHANA (SACRAL)

Swadhisthana is located just below the **umbilicus** in the front, the source of the *Lower Dan Tian*, and the tip of the **lumbar** in the **back**, and is referred to as the *sacral chakra*. Its flower is **orange** and has **six** petals. The **geometric symbol** *associated* with *Swadhisthana* is the fifth **platonic solid**, the **icosahedron** representing the *utilization* of the pranic element of **water** and *universal flow*.

The *sacral chakra* is *associated* with the **kidneys** and the *sensations* causing the *re-actions* that we feel when we *experience disappointment*. It may be *disappointment* in self, in others, the thought of *disappointing* others, and/or others *disappointing* you. It tends to rise when we try to force situations instead of letting go of *expectations* and going with the *flow*.

Orange is the color of *death of the old* – not just of **physical** symptoms in the **body**, but also of old *limiting beliefs* and habits that are no longer beneficial. As *karma* is resolved it stimulates sexual energy for *creative solutions*.

Swadhisthana is related to the ability to *receive abundance* of **power, fame, fortune** and **money**. At this time **money** is the most commonly used form of *appreciation* for excellence in performance of athletic, musical and artistic endeavors. Difficulty in *receiving* money over extended periods of time often manifests on the **physical plane** as **lower back pain**. Regardless of whether it is because of a *perception* of lack, or of *overabundance*, people often confuse a **physical** *action* such as **bending** to pick up heavy objects, a **slip, fall** or **accident** as the cause of the **pain**, but *bending over backwards* for others is often the true underlying factor.

A low **libido** and **lack** of sexual interest can often be traced to a weakness in the connection of the **kidneys** to the **gonads (testes and ovaries)** and lack of *stimulation* of the **prostate gland** in men and the **g-spot** in women; this leads to an imbalance of *masculine* and *feminine* energies. The release of blocks from the *sacral chakra* both increases the potential of sexual energy and strengthens the **pelvic floor** and optimum **bladder** function.

The difference between the *root chakra* and the *sacral chakra* can seem subtle. The *root chakra* is based on **pro-creation** for **survival** of the human race, whereas the *sacral chakra* shapes *thought forms* on the *mental* level that promote *abundance* via the **kidneys**. When *Muladhara* and *Swadhisthana* are in sync with each other they combine to create a reservoir of power that can be *utilized* for athletic pursuits that require great strength.

The intimate *relationship* between the **respiratory system** and the **reproductive system** can be disrupted by blocks anywhere in the **body** from *Lung Qi*, *Kidney Qi*, the *Lower Dan Tian* and the *sacral chakra*. *Fear* and *insecurity* on the *emotional* level can manifest on the **physical** level as a dry, lingering **cough** when there is a weakness between the **lungs** and the **kidneys**. Many issues of *memory* loss and loss of *clarity* as well as black circles under the **eyes** can also be linked to a weakness from the **kidneys** to the *sacral chakra*.

When *sacral chakra* function is operating at full potential the innocence of your *inner child* is honored, and creative juices are allowed to flow unfettered by outside influences from **ancestors**, the *collective consciousness*, **societal structures** and **cultural influences**. A strong connection between the **reproductive system** and the **respiratory system** allows creative impulses to be born, and nurtured through the *breath of life*.

Creative solutions are strengthened through the separation of *feeling* from **emotions** and **thinking** to allow the integration of authentic concepts to *flow*.

NUGGET OF WIZDOM FROM THE VECTOR

RE-ESTABLISH THE INNOCENCE OF YOUR INNER CHILD. INNOCENCE IS OFTEN CONFUSED WITH NAIVETY. INNOCENCE IS WHEN YOU ARE AWARE OF THE DANGERS AND CHOOSE TO OPEN YOUR HEART, REGARDLESS. NAIVETY IS CHOOSING TO OPEN YOUR HEART TO DANGERS THAT YOU ARE UNAWARE OF.

CHAKRA THREE – MANIPURA (SOLAR PLEXUS)

There are two schools of *thought* as to the location of the *third chakra*. In Hindu tradition it is named *Manipura* and is located at the **diaphragm**, whereas other sources name it *hara* and consider its location to be at the **spleen**. I feel stronger to the location of the *solar plexus* at the **diaphragm** and that is the basis of this discussion.

The **solar plexus** is one of the gateways to the *emotional body* via the *astral body*; it is associated with fire, the color **yellow**, and the **tetrahedron**, the **four-sided pyramid** which represents the powers of *manifestation* and *creation*.

Yellow is the color of *active intelligence* and *adaptability*, a dynamic awareness and *true perception* of others without ego to comfort and heal wounds of the *inner child*. When people bravely face challenges that arise from the *solar plexus,* you can see the change in the color of their eyes, the window to their *soul*; that is most easily seen when blue eyes change to green.

Disturbances in the *solar plexus* often lead to a shut-down or *over-sensitivity* in feeling, which leads to **over-thinking** and an inability to access *intuition*. **Society** encourages men to shut down their *feeling center* at an early age making it difficult for them to feel and express feelings (big boys don't cry). Throughout history, women have also been forced to shut down their *feelings* and avoid using their *psychic gifts*; this was accomplished through persecution in the form of witch hunts, burnings at the stake, and other forms of **torture**. In modern times women have been labeled crazy, hysterical or menopausal. *Over-sensitivity* to the *sensations associated* with *feelings* often leads to an *unbalanced* nature, and *emotional* outbursts of *anger, fear, weeping*, etc., and to a lack of ability to move forward when faced with life's *challenges*.

Manipura is *associated* with three **physical body systems**: the **liver**, the **gallbladder** and the **spleen**. Chronic *anger* and *depression* are often linked to a **liver** that is not functioning at full potential and contribute to *aching* of the **tendons, menstrual issues, insomnia, dizziness**, and are often indicated by **jaundice**. A disconnect between the *solar plexus* and the *base chakra* has a negative effect on the **large intestine** and the **liver**, causing an inefficiency in *eliminating* the **toxins** that build up in the **eyes**, which in turn weakens *vision.*

An inefficient **gall bladder** often **manifests** as difficulty in making *choices* and carrying through with them. This results in *procrastination*, and the consequent delay in taking consistent steps of *action* prevents *manifesting* a person's intentions in the **physical world**. A lack of *flow* between the **gall bladder** and the **liver** causes a lack of *flexibility* in the **body** and of the *mind,* leading to *stubbornness of character*, and a **stiffness** and **rigidity** in the **physical body** that can manifest as **arthritis**.

Weaknesses within the **splee**n and the **pancreas** also *affect* **digestion** causing **indigestion, bloating** and other **stomach** issues on the

physical level; these weaknesses also **affect** a person's ability to "stomach" and **assimilate** life.

The **solar plexus** is the meeting point between energies from the **lower chakras** below the **diaphragm** and the energies from the **upper chakras** above it. Evenness of the **inhalation** and **exhalation** of the **lungs** increases the **ability** to take life in fully regardless of whether a person's breathing is shallow or deep. Many people have a tendency to hold their breath when faced with **challenges** as they wait for "the other shoe to drop." **Deleting limiting beliefs** and **expectations** of things going "from bad to worse" and other stories that come from the **sub-conscious** and **un-conscious mind** via **ancestors**, **collective consciousness, cultural influences, traumas**, **tortures** and other **negative life experiences**, can facilitate the flow of energy to be optimized throughout the **lymphatic system**, the **circulatory system** and the **nervous system**.

NUGGET OF WIZDOM FROM THE VECTOR

LET GO OF CONTROL ISSUES AND CLOSE DOORS ON OLD WOUNDS. A STRONG CONNECTION BETWEEN SWAHISTHANA WHERE EMOTIONS ARE BORN, AND MANIPURA WHERE THEY ARE CONTROLLED, MAKE IT EASY TO DIGEST AND ASSIMILATE LIFE.

CHAKRA FOUR – ANAHATA (HEART)

Anahata, the **fourth chakra**, is located at the **sternum** or the **cardiac plexus**. Its **green** flower has **twelve** petals that open to the enlightened mind, or what is commonly referred to as the "heart mind," the part of you that is striving towards awakening and compassion for the benefit of all beings. The geometric symbol associated with **Anahata** is the **merkaba**, a six pointed star made up of two superimposed **tetrahedrons**, one with the **apex** pointing up representing **fire**, and one with the **apex** pointing down to represent **water**.

The **heart chakra** governs **blood** and **circulation,** as well as the **thymus** where **T-cells** mature to fend off **disease. Perspiration** is called the "fluid of the heart" because when "we sweat it" the **effects** are not only **physical. Green** is **associated** with the cleansing powers of the growth of vegetation that Earth supplies to provide **oxygen** for all of her inhabitants. **Anahata** is the mediator of the higher **astral** and **spiritual energies** of the **upper chakras** with the **three lower chakras,** acting as a clearing center for **unconditional love, wisdom** and **truth**.

Imbalances in the *heart center* often manifest as an inability to *give* and *receive* as an expression of pure *love* and *joy*. Many people who accept a gift are unable to do so without questioning the motives of the *giver,* and many people who *give* from the **heart** have weaknesses to *receiving* from others.

Excessive chatter is the by-product of a lack of connection between the *throat* and the *heart chakras*; consequently, a person verbally tries to fill in *empty spaces* with words and the *mind*. *Balance* between these two *centers* is a *residual effect* of letting go of *bitterness*. The best way to achieve this is through *neutrality*. *Neutrality* allows your *mind* to operate independently of your *emotions* so that your *perception* is accurate, coming from a place of *non-judgment* and *non-criticism*, as an empty vessel that is *fearless*, *timeless* and *boundless*. If every situation you *experience* is just that, an **experience,** none more significant than any other, you are able to take the *good* and *bad*, *positive* and *negative* out of it and FEEL whether you are energetically in *alignment* or not.

People have a tendency to *relax* themselves out of **problems**. This **relaxation** *stagnates* all systems on the **physical** and *non-physical* level. It is essential that the connection of your **software** (**PNS**) is strong to your **hard drive** (**CNS**). **Physical potential** sits at the **base** of the **spine**. When that **potential** and your **heart** are in sync, the *contraction* and *expansion* of every **heartbeat** effortlessly supports all of the systems on the **physical**, *mental*, *emotional* and *psychological* levels. When your **heart** is supported by your **body**, it is able to work with efficiency and less effort.

Align yourself with consistent steps of *action* to follow your *heart's path* and reap the benefits of *giving* from the *heart* and *receiving* from the **heart**.

NUGGET OF WIZDOM FROM THE VECTOR

ALIGN YOURSELF WITH YOUR PHYSICAL HEART AS WELL AS YOUR HEART CHAKRA TO LIVE A JOYFUL, POWERFUL VERSION OF YOUR AUTHENTIC SELF.

CHAKRA FIVE – VISHUDDHA (THROAT)

Vishuddha is located at the **throat** just above the **collarbone**. Its flower is **light blue** with **sixteen petals** that resonate with both higher and lower *vibrations* or **aspects**. The *lower vibration* taps into the energy of the *collective influence's* need to be recognized in our third dimensional world through **care**er and **status**. If a person's **sexual drive** drops off, it is common for that energy to be redirected to the *mental plane* in an effort to prove to others that a person has "what it takes" to be successful. A *higher vibration* channels a more refined *frequency* that is connected to the *higher self* or *divine will*; it *receives information* through what many people consider *psychic gifts* and *intuitive abilities*.

The **geometric shape** *associated* with *Vishuddha* is the **octahedron** made up of **two pyramids** connected at their base to make a **diamond**. The **downward facing pyramid** represents the female or *earth aspect*, while the **upward facing pyramid** represents the *heavens* and *male aspect*, creating a chamber that is representative of the womb of the *inner-child*.

The **light blue** color of the *throat chakra* is *associated* with *integrity* and speaking in *alignment* with *truth*. Many children have been raised with an old Christian proverb that "children should be seen and not heard," and that "big boys don't cry;" they are taught to swallow their words instead of speaking them. Wounded energy held in the **throat** can manifest as **stuttering** and other problems of expression due to a lack of confidence in speaking their *truth* and having to face *retaliation*, *fear* and *ridicule*.

Accumulated unresolved grief affects the connection between the **lungs** and the **voice**, which is reflected by the *pitch* and *tone*. This affects the ability to *hear* and be *heard*. Many people get into the habit of speaking with a harsh tone without even being aware of it, especially **couples** who have lived together for a long time, **parents** to their **children**, and **children** to their **parents**. The *emotions* of *resentment* and *anger* from holding back unspoken words build up over time and often *manifest* on the **physical level** as **tumors** that "need" to be cut out. Many **thyroid** problems arise from *negative life experiences* of the **guillotine**, **hanging** and other forms of **beheading** from *past lives* in retaliation for speaking the *truth*.

Many issues held in the **tissues** of the **throat** arise from **traumas**, **tortures** and **wounds** inflicted on those who dare to speak out while others remain silent. Throughout the ages **assassination**, **torture**, **alienation** and **retribution** are often the extreme price people pay for voicing their opinion. Many more have *experienced ridicule* and *shame* to the point that a vast majority of adults surveyed would prefer death rather than giving a public speech. On a **physical** level the **mouth** and **anus** are intimately connected with each other. When people find it challenging to use their voice or have a tendency to have "verbal diarrhea" it is often referred by a weakness in the **elimination system** in the form of **constipation** or **diarrhea**.

You can delete the *karma* and the *negative life experiences* of **trauma**, **illness**, *limitations*, *fears* and *phobias* that are held in the **inner** and **outer** **meninges** of the **spine**, and you can strengthen **right** and **left brain** integration for stronger *perception* regarding *intuition* and *sensitivities* through freedom of speech. When you are aware of the *frequencies* held in your *throat chakra*, you can let go of *judgment* and *criticism* and allow words to *flow* through speech or song.

NUGGET OF WIZDOM FROM THE VECTOR

ONLY A SMALL PART OF COMMUNICATION IS EXPRESSED THROUGH THE ACTUAL WORDS YOU USE. TONE, PITCH AND RHYTHM OF THE WORDS AND THE SPACES IN-BETWEEN THE WORDS HAVE A PROFOUND EFFECT ON YOUR ABILITY TO COMMUNICATE.

CHAKRA SIX – AJNA (THIRD EYE)

The *Ajna* center sits one finger's breadth above and between the **eyebrows**. The *third eye* is also often referred to as the Eye of Siva, Wisdom Eye, Divine Eye and All-Seeing Eye. Its flower is an **indigo blue** and has **two petals** that symbolize the mind's ability to process information from the **third dimensional world**, as well as unseen *dimensions*, *existences* and *space*.

The **geometric symbol** *associated* with the *third eye* is the **dodecahedron**. Its twelve pentagonal faces are a symbol of the inner knowing we *receive* from the *ethers*, reminding us that we are both **human** and *divine*, *infinite* and **finite**.

Ajna is considered as a *sacral portal* of the divine *soul,* encouraging growth through knowledge and imagination in the pursuit of *authentic desire*. The color **indigo** symbolizes *clairsentience,* our ability to *feel clarity* through *sensations* which activate understanding of our *purpose* in the divine plan.

The two **lobes** of the **pituitary gland** are *associated* with the two **petals** of the *third eye* and act in conjunction with the **pineal gland, hypothalamus** and the *crown chakra*. The **ears, eyes** and **nose** are the *physical organs* that are directly related to **comprehension** and *perception* and are most often *affected* by *imbalances* of this *chakra*.

Sinus problems and **allergies** are symptoms of an *imbalance* of the *third eye* along with weaknesses in the **spleen** and **lungs**. *Hearing* and *vision* **problems** generally come from a weakness in the **kidneys** and a block in the **flow** of the *Qi* from the **liver**, manifested from repressed *anger*, *frustration*, *envy* and *resentment*.

When your *feelings*, *thoughts* and *emotions* are able to separate and integrate within a split second you are able to use your *thought* to *feel* whether your energy is *weak* in that given moment.

Feeling allows you to solve **problems** with *creative solutions* that come from your *inner self*. When you have a **problem**, you are looking for the best answer that is most applicable to your situation. The best answer is not *positive* or *negative, good* or *bad*; it is the **answer** that will give you the best possible result that is applicable to the situation at hand. This allows you to let go of *judgment* and *criticism* of yourself or others, and step into the new with an open heart free of *fear*.

NUGGET OF WIZDOM FROM THE VECTOR

OPEN UP TO INTUITIVE ABILITIES TO RECEIVE INNER WIZDOM. YOUR INTUITION DOES NOT COME FROM YOUR SPIRIT. IT COMES FROM YOUR SOUL, WITHOUT THINKING, AND FREE OF EMOTIONS.

CHAKRA SEVEN – SAHASWARA (CROWN)

Sahaswara is located above the **head** at the *crown*, slightly back from the center, where the intersection of the *yang channels* in the **body** and the *Sea of Marrow* meet. The *crown chakra* is known as "the lotus of a thousand petals," and also as "the gate of **Brahmani**."

The **geometric symbol** *associated* with *Sahaswara* is the master symbol of geometry, the **circle** or **sphere**, representing the undifferentiated potential of the cosmic womb through which every shape and pattern are born. The **sphere** is both bounded by its **form,** and at the same time, endlessly circular to remind us that there is no **beginning** and there is no **end**. **Spheres** within **spheres** are multi universes held within each other.

Our **spherical sun** is our source of **light**. The **light** we see is the portion of the *electromagnetic spectrum* that is visible to the human **eye**. Narrow bands of *wavelengths* produce **monochromatic light** referred to as the spectral colors of **red**, **orange**, **yellow**, **green**, **blue** and **violet**. These bands are made up of *radio*, *microwave*, *infrared*, *visible light*, *ultraviolet light*, *X-rays* and *gamma rays*. The color **violet** has the highest *frequency* of these bands, with the shortest waves and with the *frequency* that is *associated* with the *crown chakra*. An activated *crown chakra* connects us to what is beyond the element of **light** while at the same time being grounded to the unmanifested void of **darkness**. We cannot have light without dark or dark without light.

Use the *present* moment to facilitate a state of **freedom** and **independence** by releasing *trauma*, *tragedy* and *torturous* situations from the *past* to anticipate weaknesses that could flow into the *future*, thereby shifting the energies before they become a **problem.** Claim the right to be **equal** to and *resonate* with the best **man**, **woman** and **child** on the planet to end enslavement issues from discriminatory practices that rob people of their **dignity**. Strengthen your ability to fulfill your capabilities due to your **sexuality**, **gender**, **sexual orientation**, **race**, **ancestry**, **place of origin**, **color**, **ethnic origin**, **citizenship** or **creed**. Delete **sabotage** from the *mind* and increase your infinite potential.

NUGGET OF WIZDOM FROM THE VECTOR

YOUR SPIRIT IS THE GATEWAY TO THE POWER OF DIVINE WIZDOM, TAKING YOU BEYOND YOUR PHYSICAL BODY TO THE SOLAR, GALACTIC, COSMIC, UNIVERSAL AND MULTI-UNIVERSAL SPECTRUMS TO ACCESS HIGHER VIBRATIONAL REALMS.

CHAKRA EIGHT – THE UNIVERSAL HEART FIELD

Many people are aware of the *seven chakras*; however, they are unaware of the *eighth chakra*, a few inches from the *heart chakra*. It completes the expression of our *personality* as *conscious* beings. Some people may refer to this as the completion of the *ego*.

The eighth octave completes the Solfege scale …

DO-RE-MI-FA-SOL-LA-TI … DO!

When we sing it, it feels awkward if we do not complete the scale because of the missing key. The *eighth chakra*, or the *Universal Heart*, unlocks our higher *trans-personal awareness* to express our individual *heart*, *mind* and *will* by accessing the higher octaves of our *soul's* awareness.

The *eighth chakra* allows for expanded vision. If you are lost on a city street and cannot find your way, entering a building and taking an elevator to the highest floor to look out over the city will *expand* your vision to include the bigger picture. When you are able to see more of the surrounding landscape, it is much easier to gain *perspective* and find your way.

The **Ouroboros**, an ancient symbol that is seen in many **cultures** as a dragon or serpent biting its own tail, in the shape of a figure eight, represents *time*, *life*, *continuity*, *completion*, *repetition*, *self-sufficiency* and *re-birth*. Ancient texts also speak of a serpent of light resting in the heavens at the mouth of the **galactic center**. Recently astronomers have found two enormous gamma ray-emitting structures bubbling out of the center of our **galaxy** that are also in the shape of a figure eight.

NUGGET OF WIZDOM FROM THE VECTOR

THE UNIVERSAL HEART FIELD, LOCATED AT THE CENTER OF THE HEART IS A TORUS OF THE COSMIC HEARTBEAT, A GATEWAY TO EXPANDED VISION AND ASCENSION.

CHRISTMAS

One of the great misrepresentations of our time is the "holiday season." Over the last decade, I have received so many calls and emails during the holiday season asking for assistance, mostly from women who are *overwhelmed* by the additional responsibilities of **Christmas**. Creating a magical wonderland of perfection while pursuing career goals, raising brilliant children, looking great and making things look great, is hard work! That is not to say that men are not *affected*; however in our **society** women are still *expected* to automatically enjoy decorating, baking, shopping, etc., while it is acceptable for men to wait until Christmas Eve to do their shopping and brag about the leftover spoils they managed to bring to the celebration under the tree.

Many people are growing weary of a commercialized holiday season, spending money they don't have on stuff that no one really **needs** or *wants*. The only other holiday that comes close to causing as much "stress" is "Singles' Awareness Day," better known as Valentine's Day! The difference between the two, is that most people are aware of the "stress" of Christmas but many who don't actively participate in Valentine's Day are unaware of the undercurrents of energy that they are bombarded by.

Chasing after the perfect gift in crowded line-ups in crowded malls, decorating, baking, wrapping, traveling to see family and cooking the perfect family dinner(s) only to … unwrap and unravel at the ex-in-laws' not-so-perfect dinner, stand in line at the crowded mall to take back the "perfect" gift that was not so perfect after all … along with the batteries and toys that didn't work just as the credit card bills start rolling in and the flu hits. None of this seems to have much to do with the spirit of

Christmas, and yet in North American society it is not acceptable to forgo Christmas celebrations unless you are exempt through religion. *EU ...* COMMON COLD AND FLU, Pg. 153

Many people adhere to traditions around Christmas based on many different rituals from around the world. Most people are unaware of why they celebrate in the way that they do. It is helpful to break down the traditions of Christmas to break down the **overwhelm**.

THE SANTA "CLAUSE" ... WILL THE REAL SANTA PLEASE STAND UP!

The story of Santa Claus begins with Nicholas, who was born during the third century in the village of Patara that is on the southern coast of Turkey by today's map. He was raised as a devout Christian until his wealthy parents died in an epidemic while he was still young. It is said that he had a vision of Jesus who told him to "sell what you own and give to the poor," and so he did. He dedicated his life to the service of God and used his entire inheritance to assist the under privileged.

As a young man Nicholas was designated as the Bishop Of Myra and he became known throughout the land for his generosity to those in need, his love of children, and his concern for sailors and ships.

Nicholas was exiled and imprisoned under the Roman Emperor Diocletian (284-305 A.D.). After his release (343 AD) he served on the Council of Nicaea, whose goal was to preserve the unity of the church that was being threatened by conflicting claims about the nature of Jesus Christ. Nicholas left this plane on December 6, AD 343, and was buried in his cathedral church "Mana of Saint Nicholas" where a relic of pure water formed from the bones held in the tomb. In 1087 the bones were spirited away by ship merchants and laid to rest in Bari, Italy. The tomb in the crypt of the Basilica di San Nicola continues to produce the pure water year after year.

Prior to 1931, Santa Claus was depicted as a tall gaunt man or elf-like, wearing a bishop's robe and animal skins. In 1862 Santa was depicted in Harper's Magazine by Thomas Nast, a Civil War cartoonist, as an elf-like figure that supported the union. For three decades Nast drew Santa, gradually turning his tan robe into a red one. Then came the Coca-Cola® Company. It featured Santa in its ads since the 1920's, beginning with a serious looking Santa who morphed into the jolly red and white version we have had since the 1930's. That's when Coca-Cola® changed its target market from an adult pharmaceutical energy drink to a drink for the whole family, and launched a marketing campaign that featured art work from well-known artists for their ad campaign. The most successful illustration was of a modern day Santa illustrated by a Swedish artist named Hadon Sundblom. *EU … HARD CORE SOFT DRINKS, Pg. 270*

WHY WE DECORATE TREES

Christmas trees first showed up on the scene in what is now Latvia, in the early part of the sixteenth century. Merchants at Christmas fairs would outdo themselves to display their wares and attract visitors to their booths by stringing them on trees.

WHY WE HANG STOCKINGS

One of the stories depicting the kind deeds of St. Nicholas tells the tale of a poor man with three daughters. He was unable to provide dowries for his daughters therefore dooming them to being sold into a lifetime of slavery. Mysteriously, on three different occasions a bag of gold appeared in their home, providing the needed dowries. The bags of gold were tossed into a window and landed in shoes left by the fire to dry. This story began a tradition of children hanging out stockings or laying out shoes in the hopes of receiving a gift from St. Nicholas. Sometimes the gold is in the form of balls instead of bags, and often golden balls are represented by three oranges, one of the symbols of the "Gift Giving St. Nicholas."

WHY WE HANG LIGHTS

After Thomas Edison brought the incandescent light bulb into being in 1879, his close friend and president of the company presented to the public a six-foot electrically lit, rotating Christmas tree in the early 1880s. It was too expensive for the average person to purchase lights for their trees until the early 1930s, when it became standard practice to replace the more dangerous candles with electrical strands of lights.

"HE KNOWS WHEN YOU ARE SLEEPING, HE KNOWS WHEN YOU'RE AWAKE …"

Children are told from a young age that Santa is watching them and *judging* every move to determine whether they are *naughty* or *nice*, *good* or *bad*, and whether they warrant *receiving* what they *want* on Christmas day. What about the children who do not *receive* what they ask for? Does that automatically mean that even though they did their best not to be *naughty*, they did not measure up to their Santa Clause's "nice" *expectations*?

There are so many reasons that children may not **receive** what they have been asking for that have nothing to do with their behavior or even economics. For instance every year all I wanted for Christmas was a puppy. My mom was terrified of dogs and no matter how I pleaded with her and how many strays I brought to live with us, she refused to have a dog living with her until I finally wore my parents down when I was nine. Christmas morning was always a huge **disappointment** for me when I discovered that there was no puppy under the tree despite all my letters to Santa and all my prayers to God. I would rant at the injustice. I tried to be **good**! I did my **best**! What didn't I do **right**? My parents explained that Santa didn't DO dogs, only toys, etc. That would placate me for a while until I returned to school and found that several of my classmates did get a puppy from Santa. That was confirmation for me that there was something fundamentally wrong with me, and that I could not measure up to Santa's high standards.

This letter to the editor was printed in the New York Sun on December 31, 1897.

"Dear Editor:

I am 8 years old.
Some of my little friends say there is no Santa Clause.
Papa says, " If you see it in the <u>Sun</u> it is so."
Please tell me the truth, is there a Santa Clause?
Virginia O'Hanlan
115 West 95Th St."

Frances Pharcellus Church wrote the reply that was applauded around the world for his sensitivity.

"Yes, VIRGINIA, there is a Santa Claus. He exists as certainly as love and generosity and devotion exist, and you know that they abound and give to your life its highest beauty and joy. Alas! how dreary would be the world if there were no Santa Claus. It would be as dreary as if there were no VIRGINIAS. There would be no childlike faith then, no poetry, no romance to make tolerable this existence. We should have no enjoyment, except in sense and sight. The eternal light with which childhood fills the world would be extinguished. Not believe in Santa Claus! You might as well not believe in fairies! You might get your papa to hire men to watch in all the chimneys on Christmas Eve to catch Santa Claus, but even if they did not see Santa Claus coming down, what would that prove? Nobody sees Santa Claus, but that is no sign that there is no Santa Claus. The most real things in the world are those that

neither children nor men can see. Did you ever see fairies dancing on the lawn? Of course not, but that's no proof that they are not there. Nobody can conceive or imagine all the wonders there are unseen and unseeable in the world.

"You may tear apart the baby's rattle and see what makes the noise inside, but there is a veil covering the unseen world which not the strongest man, nor even the united strength of all the strongest men that ever lived, could tear apart. Only faith, fancy, poetry, love, romance, can push aside that curtain and view and picture the supernatural beauty and glory beyond. Is it all real? Ah, VIRGINIA, in all this world there is nothing else real and abiding.

"No Santa Claus! Thank God! He lives, and he lives forever. A thousand years from now, Virginia, nay, ten times ten thousand years from now, he will continue to make glad the heart of childhood."

Francis Pharcellus Church

Some **experts** will assure you that a child's discovery, usually around the age of six or seven, that Santa does not exist and that their **parents**, the **media**, their **teachers**, **friends** and **family** have colluded to deceive them, has no *negative effect*. The fact is that they have been hoodwinked by the very important authority figures that they depend on for their security and viability in this world and it does have an **effect** because for every **action** there is a *re-action*. It may even cause them to want to become politicians!

ARE YOU A REBEL WITHOUT A CLAUS?

What kind of person doesn't love to celebrate Christmas? Scrooge and The Grinch Who Stole Christmas, come to mind. If you point out to others that this complicated series of lies could be having a *negative effect* on **children** and their **parents**, many people will reply Bah! Humbug! Nonsense. Rubbish! However, the definition of the word "humbug" is "a hoax or a fraud intended to deceive."

The adults whom children *trust* to provide reliable information about how the world works, introduce them to Santa as a real figure. His existence is confirmed **in books**, **television**, **movies** and **scientific evidence** of the **half-eaten cookies**, **empty milk glasses** and **presents** under the tree on Christmas morning. Parents are compelled to *lie* about their part in Christmas, advocating that Santa is a supernatural figure as if celebrating love honestly for their children is not enough.

WHAT DO SANTA AND JESUS HAVE TO DO WITH ONE ANOTHER?

Some similarities between Santa and Jesus are that they both are eternal and can rise through the air. They both give gifts, they are both all-seeing and know when you have been **bad** or **good**, rewarding "good" behavior. They have both been **exploited** and **commercialized**.

THE "GOOD NEWS" IS:

Choosing to forgo the circus around the holidays is a huge trigger for friends, family and even total strangers. If they are criticizing you for it, whether they are **conscious** of it or not, they may be **jealous** of your **freedom**. Let go of the **guilt** and put the same fervor that you used to reserve for perfecting Valentine's Day, Halloween, Thanksgiving, Christmas, Hanukah, New Years, etc. into achieving your goals. Your **finances** will reflect it, providing you with even more **freedom** for them to criticize.

Things are not going from **bad** to **worse**. Christmas has always been commercialized and newspapers have always skirted around the truth.

All is calm. All is bright. Peace and Goodwill …

THE "BAD NEWS" IS:

Upholding traditions for the holidays is a huge distraction for average people who willingly embrace or begrudgingly participate in a diversion that essentially removes them from their goals for much of the fall season. Many are held hostage by their overspending for many months after. At the same time **big business** is getting ahead, cashing in and reaping the benefits.

NUGGET OF WIZDOM FROM THE VECTOR

TIDINGS OF COMFORT AND JOY …

THE MEDIA AND BIG BUSINESS ARE COMPLETELY UNEMOTIONAL AND FOCUSED ON THE FINANCIAL OPPORTUNITIES AVAILABLE DURING THE HOLIDAY SEASON, TARGETING THEIR ADVERTISING AT CHILDREN, TEENAGERS AND PARENTS.

THOSE WHO PUT A LOT OF EFFORT INTO THE HOLIDAYS HAVE A TENDENCY TO DO SO OUT OF SENTIMENTALITY, OFTEN SUPPRESSING THE MANY MIXED AND COMBINED EMOTIONS THAT ARE WHIPPED INTO PLAY.

STRONG EXTERNAL AND INTERNAL BOUNDARIES ARE NECESSARY FOR THE TORRENT OF DYNAMICS OF THE COLLECTIVE INFLUENCE TO PASS THROUGH WITHOUT A NEGATIVE EFFECT.

DELETE REACTIONS FROM THE ACCUMULATIONS OF CHRISTMAS PAST, PRESENT AND FUTURE AND PREPARE FOR THE NEXT MOST STRESSFUL HOLIDAY ... VALENTINE'S DAY.

CIRCULATORY SYSTEM

The **circulatory system** works closely with the **respiratory system** to supply **oxygen** and **nutrients** throughout the **body** and with the **lymphatic system** to carry **waste** and **carbon dioxide** out of the body. It also has an intimate connection with the **endocrine system,** transporting and delivering **chemical** instructions from **hormones** through the **blood stream**.

It is composed of the **heart**, the **blood vessels**, **arteries**, **veins** and **capillaries**. Technically there are two circulatory systems, the **pulmonary circulation** and the **systemic circulation** that is the system most people associate with the "**circulatory system**."

PULMONARY CIRCULATORY SYSTEM

Pulmonary circulation is a short *loop* from the **heart** to the **lungs** and back. The **blood** that is low in **oxygen** and high in **carbon dioxide** is pumped out of the **right ventricle** into the **pulmonary artery** that branches off into two directions. The **right branch** goes to the **right lung**, the **left branch** to the **left lung**.

In the **lungs** the **branches** divide into **capillaries**. The **blood** flows more slowly because the **vessels** are tiny. This allows the **gases** to have time to be exchanged between the **capillary walls** and the tiny **air sacs** in the **lungs** called the **alveoli**.

While **oxygenation** occurs the **oxygen** is taken up by the **bloodstream** and locks on to a **molecule** called **hemoglobin** that is in the **red blood cells**. The newly **oxygenated blood** leaves the **lungs** via the **pulmonary veins** and heads back to the **heart**, entering the **heart** through the **left atrium,** filling the **left ventricle** and is then pumped through the **systemic circulatory system**.

SYSTEMIC CIRCULATORY SYSTEM

Systemic circulation sends **blood** from the **heart** to every part of the **body** and back again. The **blood** travels out of the **left ventricle** to the **aorta**, through the **arteries**, **veins** and **capillaries** to every **organ** and **tissue** in the **body** and back to the **right atrium**. It then delivers **oxygen** and **nutrients** to the **cells** and picks up waste to deliver to the **lymphatic system**, going back through the **capillaries** into small veins called **venules**, then through the larger **veins** until it reaches the **vena cavae**. **Blood** from the **head** and **arms** returns to the **heart** through the **superior vena cava** while **blood** from the lower extremities returns via the **inferior vena cava**, delivering **oxygen-depleted blood** into the **right atrium**. The **blood** exits to fill the **right ventricle** and is now ready to be pumped into the **pulmonary circulation** to collect more **oxygen**.

THE HEART

Conventional medicine will tell you that the **heart** is the key component of the **circulatory system** as a pump that beats on average about one hundred thousand times a day to propel **blood** throughout the **body**. However, it is good to keep in *mind* that the **heart** knows how much to pump according to the messages it receives from the rest of the **body**. When the **body** is at rest, it pumps just enough **oxygen** needed, and when we are exerting ourselves it increases the delivery of **oxygen**.

The **heart** is located between the **lungs**, just to the left of the middle of the **chest cavity**. The heart has four chambers, the **left** and **right ventricles** and the **left** and **right atria**. The bottom of the **heart** consists of **left** and **right ventricles** that are responsible for pumping **blood** out of the **heart**. In-between the **left** and **right ventricle** is a wall called the **inter-ventricular septum**.

The **upper** part of the **heart** is made up of the **left** and **right atria** that receive the **blood** entering the **heart**. They are divided by the **inter-atrial septum**. There are four **cardiac valves**: the **tricuspid valve, the mitral valve**, **pulmonic valve** and the **aortic valve**. The **ventricles (lower heart)** and the **atria (upper heart)** are separated by **atrioventricular valves**. The **tricuspid valve** separates the **right atrium** from the **right ventricle**, and the **mitral valve** separates the **left atrium** and **left ventricle**. The **pulmonic valve** separates the **right ventricle** from the **pulmonary artery** leading to the **lungs,** and the **aortic valve** separates the **left ventricle** from the **aorta**. The **aorta** is the **body's** largest **blood vessel**.

Neurophysicists have recently discovered evidence that more than half the **heart** is composed of the same **neurons** as the **cerebral system** with its own intelligence that emits a five thousand times stronger *electromagnetic* field than the **brain**. *Heart intelligence* for *joy*, *love*, *gratitude* and *beauty* is expressed through the **heart**. Conversation between the **heart**, the **cranial brain** and the **tail brain** is a three-way dialogue in a **toroidal** feedback loop influencing *perception*, *emotional processing* and **cognitive** functions through the empowerment of being in sync with the **heart**. When your bio-computer is plugged into your *heart's intelligence*, the energetic shifts delivered through the **neurons** of your **heart** are encoded with those of your **spine** and **CNS** to your *authentic desires*. To build the life you want instead of adapting to the life you are living, you have to plug into the intelligence of your **heart**.

The **heart** is the first major **organ** to develop after conception in a **fetus**. Newly emerging scientific evidence proves that the **heart** *affects* **cells**, **water** and **DNA** in-vitro and greatly influences a person's ability to access their *intuition* and human *consciousness*. The delicate dance between the two has a profound effect on the outcome.

ARTERIES

Arteries are the thickest **blood vessels** with **muscular walls** that *contract* and *expand* to keep the **blood** moving away from the **heart** and through the **body**. The **systemic circulation** pumps **oxygen-rich blood** from the **heart** into the **aorta**. The **aorta** is a huge **artery** that curves up and back from the **left ventricle** heading down in front of the **spine** and into the **abdomen**. There are two **coronary arteries** that branch off at the beginning of the **aorta** and divide into a network of smaller **arteries** that provide **oxygen** and **nourishment** to the **muscles** of the **heart**.

The **pulmonary artery** is the **body's** other main **artery**. It is part of the **pulmonary circulation** carrying **de-oxygenated blood** away from the **heart** to the **lungs**. The **pulmonary artery** divides into **right** and **left branches** on the way to the **lungs** where the **blood** then picks up **oxygen**.

Arterial walls have three layers, the **endothelium**, **media** and **adventitia**. The **endothelium** is on the inside and provides a smooth lining for **blood** to flow through the **artery**. The **media** is made up of **muscle** and elastic **tissue**. The **adventitia** is a tough covering that protects the outside of the **artery**. As the **arteries** get further from the **heart** they branch out into **arterioles** that are smaller and less elastic.

VEINS

Veins carry **blood** back to the **heart**. They have the same layers as the **arteries**, but with less **muscle** power because they are thinner and less flexible. The two largest **veins** are called the **superior** and **inferior vena cavae,** to indicate their location above and below the **heart**.

CAPILLARIES

There is a powerful network of tiny **capillaries** that connect the **veins** and **arteries**, and transport **nutrients** and **oxygen** to the **cells**, and remove **waste products** such as **carbon dioxide**.

THE HEART BEAT

Every **heartbeat** is a **cardiac cycle**, consisting of two phases, **systole** (contraction) and **diastole** (expansion) described as the sound of "**dub**" and "**lub**."

SYSTOLE

The **ventricles** *contract*, sending **blood** into the **pulmonary** and **systemic circulatory systems**. To prevent **blood** flowing backwards into the **atria,** the **atrioventricular valves** close, creating the first sound "**lub**." When the **ventricles** finish *contracting*, the **aortic** and **pulmonary valves** close to prevent **blood** from flowing back into the **ventricles** producing the second sound "**dub**."

DYASTOLE

After *contraction*, the **ventricles** *relax* and *expand* as they fill with **blood** from the **atria**. The regular **beat** of the **heart** is a unique electrical conduction system. The **sinoatrial (SA node)** is a small area of **tissue** in the **wall** of the **right atrium** that sends a signal to *contract* the **heart muscle**. The so-called **pacemaker,** the drummer of the **heart**, keeps time, setting the rate for the rest of the **heart** to follow the *rhythm,* just like a drummer in a band. The *electrical impulses* cause the **atria** to *contract* first and then travel down to the **atrioventricular (AV node)** where the signals travel through the **right** and **left ventricles**, causing them to also *contract* and force **blood** into the **major arteries**.

BLOOD

The concept of the **heart** as a hydraulic **pump** became firmly established around mid-century and has prevailed in modern medicine ever since. However, in 1932 a scientist named Bremer at Harvard filmed self-propelled **blood flow** in a very early **embryo** in which the **heart** was not yet developed. A decade before that, another scientist from Switzerland, Rudolph Steiner had pointed out to doctors in medical lectures that **blood** is propelled by its own biological momentum and induced momentum from the **heart.** He also said that interruption in the **circulation** of the **blood** created the **flow**, not pressure.

Experimentation of ***numbing***, with ether and heated vapors, proved that the ***circulation*** of eight thousand liters of **blood** does not come from the **heart** alone. Mechanically this would require continuous lifting of approximately one hundred pounds to the height of a mile by a three hundred gram **organ**. Contemporary **biological** and **medical thinking** is that the natural propulsive force of the **blood** is naturally **inert** and forced by **pressure** to ***circulate*** through **vessels** without any clearly defined form, conforming to the shape and size of the **vessels** it travels through.

The opposite can also be argued that **blood** has its own form, the vortex of which determines the shape of the ***space*** within the **vessels** it travels through, and it is not propelled by **pressure** but by its own **momenta** and boosted by the **heart** through spiraling impulses. There are many examples of movement without **momentum** in nature such as the ***flow*** of **water** in **streams** and the **wind** in **tornados**.

The **spleen,** the **liver** and the **heart** are the **organs** that have the most direct ***relationship*** with **blood**. The **spleen** filters the **blood**, the **liver** stores it, and the **heart** moves it. Generally, a weakness in the **blood** ***affects*** one or more of these **organs**.

If there has been a **blood transfusion**, integrate the **density** of the **blood** to optimum potential with other **body fluids**. ***Delete*** any ***karma*** between the **donor(s)** and the **recipient**, and clear ***traumas*** or ***religious*** ***experiences*** of **bloodletting**, **poisoning**, etc.

BLOOD PRESSURE

What if **blood** does move independently, and **pressure** is not the cause of **blood flow** but the result of it? When **fluid mass** is subject to **force** in the form of **pressure**, it will first resist movement due to **inertia** and **viscosity**. **Fluids** with **low viscosity** ***flow*** easily because the **molecular** makeup results in very little **friction** when it is in motion, whereas high **viscosity** fluids **resis*t*** movement due to a lot of **internal friction**.

In a pressure driven system, the **pressure** rises faster than the **fluid** moves, and peaks before the **fluid velocity** peaks. When **pressure** and peak flow in the **aorta** (in the **left ventricle**), precede the peak **pressure**, it contradicts the law of inertia in **pressure *propulsion***. The **left ventricle wall** varies in thickness and is easily pierced, which is not what you would ***expect*** of a **pressure generator**. It is better ***able*** to maximize inertia with no static **pressure** in the **ventricle**.

PROBLEMS WITH THE HEART AND CIRCULATORY SYSTEM

Problems with the **heart** and **circulatory system** are divided into two categories, **congenital** and **acquired**. **Congenital heart defects** are present at birth and are sometimes indicated by **heart murmurs**; however, **heart murmurs** are common and often have no *negative effects* other than the concern because of the **diagnosis**.

ARRHYTHMIA

Rhythm dis-orders of the **heartbeat** can be caused by **congenital defect** in an underdeveloped **heart**, or they can be acquired later. Abnormally fast or slow, racing, irregular rhythms are typically treated with **pharmaceuticals**, **surgery** or **pacemakers**, and some have no noticeable *effect* on the person at all. When there is a problem with the *rhythm* of the **heart**, it is often weak on the *emotional*, *psychological*, *psychic* or *spiritual* levels, and has a weakness to **physical environment** and the *speed* the **earth** is traveling at.

CARDIOMYOPATHY

Cardiomyopathy is a *chronic dis-ease* of the **heart muscle**, generally beginning in the **myocardium** located in the **lower chambers** of the **heart**. It then progresses to the **ventricles** and **muscle cells** surrounding the **tissue** of the **heart**, leading to **heart failure** and **death**. It is the leading cause of **heart transplants** in children.

The **structure** of the **heart** and its **chambers** all need to be even from **top** to **bottom**, **side** to **side**, **front** to **back**, **inside** and **outside** in all directions within each **chamber**. Each **chamber** needs to have a strong *relationship* with the others as a *united whole*. Strengthen **elasticity** and **evenness** in all **directions**.

PERICARDIAL EFFUSION

The **heart** is surrounded by a **double-layered sac** called the **pericardium**. The *space* between the **two layers** normally has a small amount of **fluid**. **Pericardial effusion** occurs when too much **fluid** builds up, putting **pressure** on the **heart** causing limited **function**, **heart failure** and **death**.

Inflammation resulting from an **injured** or **diseased pericardium** can cause **fluid** to build up. If there have been any **surgical procedures**, test for *accumulations* of **blood**. Strengthen the **layers**, *in-between* the

layers, the **density** and **clarity** of the **fluid** and the *relationship* between the **heart**, the **pericardium**, and the **CNS**.

CORONARY ARTERY DISEASE

The most common **circulatory disorder** in adults is **atherosclerosis** where **plaque** made up of deposits of **fat**, **calcium**, and **dead cells** form on the **inner walls** of the **blood vessels** that supply the **heart**, and interfere with the smooth *flow* of **blood**. **Blood flow** to the **heart muscle** may even be blocked entirely, causing a **heart attack** or **stroke**. **Myocardial infarction** (**heart attack**) occurs when a block in the *flow* causes **muscle** damage from lack of **oxygen**, and this compromises the **heart's** ability to pump **blood**. **Strokes** occur when the **blood supply** to the **brain** is cut off or when a **blood vessel** in the **brain** bursts, spilling **blood** into the **brain** and causing damage to the **brain cells**.

Damage to the **heart** or **brain** can be reduced by breaking down the **clot** or **blockage**. *Laser* in on it and break it down, spin off any particles to *black wholes*, then facilitate **oxygen** and **nutrients** to go to **cells** that require repair through *white wholes*.

HYPERCHOLESTEROLEMIA

Cholesterol is a waxy substance that is found in the **body's cells**, in the **blood** and in some foods. It is carried in the **blood** by two kinds of **lipoproteins**, **low density lipoproteins** (**LDL**) what is considered "**bad cholesterol**" and **high density lipoproteins** (**HDL**) that are considered to protect against **LDLs**.

For more than a half a century people were told that ingesting foods like **red meat**, **eggs**, **bacon**, etc., raises **cholesterol** levels in their **blood** and causes **heart disease**. Newer studies that focus on the *effects* food have on **cholesterol** show that this Is not the case. The studies throughout the years have mostly been based on the assumption that **plaque** causes problems in the **veins** and **arteries.** If you change *perspective* then you can look at it as a **structural problem** where lack of *tension* and *elasticity* in the **veins** along with incompatible **density** of **blood** causes **twisting** and **pockets** to form that allow **plaque** to collect. You can strengthen the components to each other to avoid the damage. It is helpful to remember that **blood** does not *flow* in a straight line; it spirals through **veins** and **arteries** due to the **Coriolis effect**.

Blood pressure is the amount of **pressure** the **blood** exerts against the **blood vessel walls** as the **heart** pumps. Pressure increases when the heart *contracts* and pushes **blood** into the **vessels** and lowers when the heart *contracts* and *expands*. Symptoms of high **blood pressure** include headaches, nosebleeds, dizziness and lightheadedness. On a **physical** level excess **body weight**, **diet**, **lack** of **exercise** and **disease** all seem to be contributing factors. **Hypertension** is thought to be **genetic** because it runs in families; however, many times it is more of a *karmic space* of *rage* shared by **ancestors** and **descendants** alike. *EU ... KARMA, Pg. 302*

Blood pressure is measured with a **sphygmomanometer** that has a cuff which raps around the **upper arm** and is pumped up to create **pressure** on a large **artery** in the **arm**, stopping the **blood flow** for a moment. As the air is gradually let out of the cuff the flow of **blood** is released and it is measured. A **stethoscope** is used to hear the first **pulse** as the **blood** *flows* through. The **systolic pressure** is the measurement of the peak of every **heartbeat** represented by the higher number in a reading. The **diastolic pressure** is the measurement of the silence in-between the **beats** indicated by the lower number in a reading. A reading of 120–129/80–84 is considered normal in an adult, 130–139/85–89 is high-normal and anything above 140/90 considered high.

Interestingly, in a reading of 120/80, the difference between the two numbers is the same as 130/90 (a difference of 60 between the two). Anytime you are shifting energy for **blood pressure,** correct it to be one hundred percent potential for that specific person, regardless of the **numbers**. **Blood pressure** changes from minute to minute because it is **affected** by **activity**, **rest**, **body temperature**, **diet**, **emotional state**, **posture**, **medications**, and often by walking into a **medical clinic** or **hospital** and the actual **procedure** of having the **blood pressure** checked. Typically, it is *thought* that **blood pressure** is driven by two *forces*, one from the **heart** as it pumps **blood** into the **arteries** and through the **circulatory system,** and the other from the **arteries** as they resist the *flow*. A third factor that needs to be addressed is the **blood** itself and its **density**.

The **organs** most often *affected* by **blood pressure** are the **heart**, **brain**, **kidneys** and **eyes**. Make sure that all of the **structures** within these **organs** as well as the relationship between these **structures** are strong.

THE "GOOD NEWS" IS:

Your **physical intelligence** is directly linked to the back and forth *communication* from your **heart** to your **spine**. When they are in *sync* you are an irresistible *force* to be reckoned with!

THE "BAD NEWS" IS:

If you clear energy through the components of the **spine** and **CNS** without plugging into your *authentic desires* through your **heart**, you can clear *disappointing situations* to be **neutral**, but it does not correct the fundamental concern of whatever it was that made it *disappointing* in the first place. If the fundamental concern around *disappointment* is not solved, even in cases of substantial relief it is inevitable that more *disappointments* will follow.

NUGGET OF WIZDOM FROM THE VECTOR

IF YOUR BODY IS IN SYNC WITH YOUR HEART, THERE IS EXPANSION AND CONTRACTION THROUGHOUT THE ENTIRE BODY ALONG WITH EACH HEART BEAT. THIS SUPPORTS YOUR HEART'S ABILITY TO PUMP BLOOD EFFICIENTLY WITHOUT ANY UNNECESSARY EFFORT.

CNS (CENTRAL NERVOUS SYSTEM)

It Is beneficial to have a working knowledge of the **central nervous system (CNS)** in order to delete **physical** and *non-physical memories, karmas, collective fears* and *psychic energies* that are *affecting* the **body**, *soul* and *spirit*.

The **CNS** and **peripheral nervous system (PNS)** work together through a network of **nerves** to **hardwire** the **brain** to manage **systems, organs** and **structures** of the **physical body**, similar to the way electricity is structured in a house. **Hard wiring** means that you terminate equipment directly with cables and wires that come from an **electrical panel. Hardwiring** equipment requires a splice with the **insulated cord** and the **junction box**. If equipment is **not hardwired**, it comes with a **cord** and a **plugin** that you simply plug into the wall to make an **electrical connection**. It is easy to tell the difference. If equipment is **hardwired** it will not have a **plug**. If it is **not hardwired** it will have a **plug** at the end of the wires that you need to insert into an **electrical outlet** to connect it to **electricity**.

Your **CNS** is automatically **hardwired** into your **body functions** and is most powerful when it is also *consciously* plugged into the intelligence of your **heart**. The **CNS** is capable of *communication* with any part of the body without using **hardwiring** or a **physical network** of **nerves**. Just as you can call someone and *communicate* with your **cell phone** anywhere you go, your **CNS** is also capable of **communicating** with any part of your **body** without having to plug into a network.

The **CNS** is extremely *sensitive* and vulnerable to **physical traumas**, **infestations**, **poisons**, **toxins**, **calcifications**, **mineralizations**, **cellular waste** and **dead cells**. **Discomfort** and many **physical** *diseases* can be attributed to *stagnation* of the **CNS** not only from influences on the **physical** level but also from *emotional*, *mental*, *psychological*, *psychic* and *spiritual toxins* and *poisons*. Your own *memories* as well as those of your **ancestors, descendants** and *collective influences* are registered, documented, filed and stored in this **hard drive**. It even has an awareness of the **times** and **dates** when events occur and will respond weak to specific time elements. *EU ... DAILY ROUTINE, Pg. 159*

In this day and age, many people are not ingesting "real" food, clean air or water. **Pharmaceuticals**, **artificial food coloring**, **preservatives**, **heavy metals** and other **chemicals** are prevalent in our food supply. There are many unnatural *external forces* that the average person has to deal with. All of these are registered in the **hard drive** of the **CNS** and can have a detrimental *effect* as they *accumulate,* thereby creating *confusion* and *stagnation* in all the systems of the **body**.

When most people think of the **brain,** they automatically think of the **cranial brain**; however, the **spinal column** is actually a **torus** and collects information that is *encoded* by the **heart**. If you think of electricity in a house that is **hardwired** to the **junction** (**electrical panel**), each of the **fuses** in the **control panel** are connected to **specific outlets** in the **house** where we plug in appliances, heating and cooling systems, lighting, entertainment, etc., to a source of **electricity**. It is similar for the **systems** in the **human body** to be wired by the **CNS** and plugged into the **heart** as a *source of energy*.

THE SPINAL CORD

The **spinal cord** is situated within the **spinal canal** of the **spine**. It manages every one of the **bio-chemical** and **bio-logical** processes throughout your **body**, acting as an intermediary between the **PNS** and the **CNS** through a **network** of **nerves** that come in and out of it, similar to the **electrical panel** of a **house**. There are thirty one pairs of **spinal** nerves that branch off from the **spinal cord**, carrying **motor**, **sensory** and **autonomic** signals to the **body** that are part of the **peripheral nervous system**. *EU ... PNS (PERIPHERAL NERVOUS SYSTEM), Pg. 391*

TOP BRAIN

The top of the **spinal cord** and **spinal nerves** reach the bottom of the **brain stem** at **C1**. Here there are twelve pairs of **cranial nerves** that emerge directly from the **brain** and **brainstem** on either side of the **brain**; these **nerves** are part of the **PNS** except for the **optic nerve** which is part of the **CNS**. At **C3** (the lower part of the **neck**) to **T1** (upper part of the **chest**) is the **brachial plexus** that controls the functions of the **shoulders**, **arms**, **hands** and **fingers**. *EU ... PNS (PERIPHERAL NERVOUS SYSTEM), Pg. 391*

BOTTOM BRAIN

The **bottom brain** consists of the **sacral brain**, the **coccyx brain** and the **energetic tail**. The **sacral brain** can be located by tracing a path from where the **spinal cord** ends at **L4** (just below the **ribs**) extending down to the **sacral plexus** at **S2** where the **sacral dimple** is located (just above the top of the crack of the **buttocks**). From here the **nerves** branch off into the **ganglia** that are essential to the functions of the **lower limbs**.

The main function of the **coccyx brain**, commonly referred to as the **tailbone**, is to *eliminate* through the **rectum, anus, bladder** and **penile** *ejaculation.* As **embryos,** we have a **tail** that is absorbed by the **body** at around eight weeks gestation, when we become a **fetus**. Even though we cannot see this tail, we are aware of it. We can feel it energetically and use if for *balance* of the **body**, *soul* and *spirit*. *EU ... TAIL, Pg. 496*

Babies who are born with **spina bifida** have an open hole with or without skin tags and/or course hair growing out of the **canal** at the **sacral dimple**.

MENINGES

The **meninges** are three layers of protective **tissue** called **dura mater**, **arachnoid** and **pia mater**. The **meninges** of the **brain** and **spinal cord** are continuous and linked through the **foramen magnum** (a hole in the **skull** that the **spinal cord** passes through to reach the **brain**).

DURA MATER

Dura mater means "hard mother" in Latin. It is the **outermost** layer of the **meninges**. Tough and inflexible, it forms several structures to protect the brain from displacement. The **dura mater** also forms several vein-like **sinuses** that carry **nutrients** in the **blood** from the **brain** back to the **heart**.

ARACHNOID

The middle layer of the **meninges** is named after the spider because of the web-like appearance of the **blood vessels** within it. In some areas it projects into the **sinuses** formed by the **dura mater** which carry **cerebral spinal fluid** from the **ventricles** back into the **bloodstream**.

SUBARACHNOID SPACE

The **subarachnoid space** lies between the **arachnoid** and **pia mater**. It is filled with **cerebrospinal fluid**. All the **blood vessels** entering the **brain** as well as the **cranial nerves** pass through this *space*.

PIA MATER

The **pia mater** means "tender mother" in Latin. It is the **innermost** layer of the **meninges**. Unlike the other layers, it adheres closely to the **brain** and runs down the **sulci** (**fissures** in the **cortex** of the **brain**). It fuses with **ependymal** (the layers of **epithelial cells** lining the **ventricles**) that form **structures** called the **choroid plexus** that produce **cerebrospinal fluid**. The **capillaries** in the **pia mater** are responsible for *nourishing* the **brain**.

It is beneficial to strengthen the **structures** within the layers of the **meninges** to be strong within themselves and also in their interconnections. Check for *psychic energies* and *spiritual experiences* that are held in the layers of the **meninges**.

When **hemorrhaging** in the **brain** occurs, two potential *spaces* for **blood** to pool are the **epidural space** and the **subdural space**. The **epidural space** is between the **dura mater** and the **skull** (more common in adults). The **subdural space** is between the **dura mater** and **arachnoid** (more common in children).

CEREBRAL SPINAL FLUID (CSF)

Cerebral spinal fluid is a clear liquid produced within the **ventricles** of the **brain**, the **subarachnoid space** that surrounds the **brain** and **spinal cord**, and also in a *space* in the **spinal cord** called the **spinal canal**. It takes **nutrients** into the **brain** and **spinal cord** and also removes **waste** from the **system**. The quality of the **cerebral spinal fluid** is determined by its **clarity** and **density**. Any *stagnation* in the **CNS** has an effect on the **CSF** and vice-versa.

VENTRICLES

Although the **CSF** is manufactured in all the **ventricles** it circulates throughout the **system** in a specific pattern, *regenerating* **fluid** several times every twenty-four hours. There are four **ventricles** in the **brain** that connect with each other through the **central canal** of the **spinal cord** and the **subarachnoid space**. The **fluid** travels from the two **lateral ventricles** that extend across a large area of the **brain**, from the **frontal lobes** through the **parietal lobes** and into the **temporal lobes**. The **interventricular foramina** links up at the **third ventricle**.

The **third ventricle** lies between the **hypothalamus** and the **thalamus** and is connected by the **aqueduct of sylvius**. The **fluid** travels to the **fourth ventricle**, located between the **cerebellum** and the **pons**. It is then connected to the **subarachnoid space** through the **lateral foramen of luschka** and the **medial foramen** of **magendie** to be *reabsorbed* into the **bloodstream** at the **superior sagittal sinus**.

THE "GOOD NEWS" IS:

We are all capable of getting in touch with underlying weaknesses that are documented in the **CNS**, and able to delete them in a second or less.

THE "BAD NEWS" IS:

Many of the weaknesses held in the **CNS** *sabotage* every *aspect* of life. These "hidden thoughts" often revolve around **age** and *aging*.

NUGGET OF WIZDOM FROM THE VECTOR

NEW TECHNOLOGY IS AVAILABLE TO PRINT THIRD DIMENSIONAL OBJECTS FROM A PRINTER. MANIFESTATIONS OF THOUGHTS BROUGHT INTO EXISTENCE RIGHT BEFORE OUR EYES! IF YOUR THIRD DIMENSIONAL PRINTER IS NOT PRINTING, MAKE SURE IT IS PLUGGED INTO YOUR HEART AND YOUR CNS.

COLON FITNESS

The **large intestine (colon)** is the final segment of the **gastrointestinal tract**. It is an **elimination system**, whereas the **small intestine** is responsible for *assimilation* of **nutrients**. The **stomach** is simply responsible for *digestion*. Like the rest of the GI tract, there are four layers of tissues: the **mucosa**, **submucosa**, **muscularis** and **serosa**. *EU ... DIGESTIVE SYSTEM, Pg. 187*

Approximately five feet long, the colon is considered the **large intestine** even though in comparison it is much shorter than the **small intestine**, because it is much thicker. The **large intestine** is often included in medical literature as part of the **digestive system**; however its main responsibility is to convert digested food into **feces**, *absorbing* the last remnants of **vitamins** and **ions**, reclaimed from the **water** in the **feces** to be used in other *metabolic processes* for the **body**.

The **large intestine** is located in the **abdominal body cavity**. It is connected to a small **pouch** called the **cecum**, which is *attached* to the **ileum** of the **small intestine** at the **ileocecal sphincter**. A hollow tube known as the **ascending colon** climbs up to the top of the **abdomen**. It crosses over to the left side at a ninety-degree angle, just below the **diaphragm** at the **hepatic fixture**, where it becomes the **transcending colon**. On the left side of the body is the **splenic fixture**, where the tube takes another ninety-degree turn and continues down the left side of the **body** to become the **descending colon**. The **ascending colon**, **transverse colon** and **descending colon** are in the shape of an elongated, upside down U. At the end of the **descending colon** is the s-shaped **sigmoid colon** that straightens out into the **rectum**, an enlarged final **segment** of the **large intestine** that terminates at the **anus**.

Food (**chyme**) that has been *digested* by the **small intestine** enters the **cecum** where it is mixed with beneficial **bacteria** that colonize the **GI tract** over a person's lifetime. The majority of the **chyme** is slowly moved from one section of the **large intestine** to the other by slow waves of **peristalsis** over a period of several hours, and is sometimes emptied quickly by stronger waves of **mass peristalsis** after a large meal. The semi-solid **waste** that remains in the **large intestine** moves down to the **rectum** and is excreted during **bowel movements**.

Vitamin K, an important factor in **blood** *clotting,* as well as **vitamins B1**, **B2**, **B6**, **B12** and **biotin** is almost exclusively **produced** by **gut bacteria**. **Carbon monoxide** and **methane** are also *produced* along with other **gases** that can lead to **flatulence** passed through the **anus**. It is important that the **ascending colon, transverse colon** and **descending colon** are fit and operating as a team, and that the **transverse colon** in particular is receiving a steady supply of **oxygenated blood** via the **middle colic artery** and the **superior mesenteric artery**. *Fitness* of the **ileocecal sphincter** affects its ability to open and close properly, preventing the backwards *flow* of **waste** from the **large intestine** into the **small intestine**. *EU ... FITNESS, Pg. 250*

RECTAL AND ANAL REGIONS OF THE COLON

The **valve of houston** is a series of **folds**, typically three, and sometimes two or four that support the weight of **fecal matter**. The first is located near the commencement of the **rectum** on the right side, the second fold extends opposite the middle of the **sacrum**, the third projects backwards from the forepart of the **rectum,** and if there is a fourth, it is situated nearly 2.5 cm above the **anus** on the **posterior wall** of the tube.

"Houston, we have a problem!"

You can energetically tune in to count how many **folds** you have and strengthen any weaknesses for each **fold** to operate at maximum efficiency within itself and in harmony with the others. **Anal sphincter muscles** contract to prevent **stool** from leaving the **rectum**. **Rectal sensation** is the warning that a **bowel movement** is about to *occur*, and **rectal accommodation** allows the **rectum** to *stretch* and hold on to **stool**. It is important that all **systems** are strong within themselves and in conversation with each other and the **CNS**.

The **pudendal nerve** is responsible for function and control of **urination**, **defecation** and **orgasm**. It is located deep within the **pelvic region** and has three **branches**: one leading to the **rectum** and **anus**, one to the **perineum**, and the other to the **penis** or **clitoris**. The **pudendal nerve** can be damaged by the long-term use of sitting toilets for **defecation** because there is a significant difference in the shape of the **rectum** and **anal canal** in *sitting* and *squatting* postures. **Sitting** causes a sharp kink between the **rectum** and the **anal canal**, which leads to straining because a person is forced to hold his or her breath and push the **pelvic floor** downwards, whereas in the *squatting* **position** the **thighs** support the **colon**, straightening it out. The use of traditional Asian, African, Middle Eastern and Indian toilets prevents damage to the **pudendal nerve** because they require users to *squat* for **bodily functions**.

Many people concern themselves with what they put into their **body** without realizing the importance of *eliminating* the leftover **waste**, no matter what they eat. On a **physical** level, food that is alive as opposed to processed foods and dead flesh, has fewer **toxins** and **poisons** to *eliminate*, however if the *elimination process* is not efficient, even the purest foods will still have a detrimental *effect* on a person's *health*, *youthfulness* and ability to reduce **body mass** and **size**. *EU ... LOSING WEIGHT, Pg. 312*

It is not uncommon for **problems** in or with the **large intestine** and **rectum**, to be referred from the **mouth** and **esophagus** and vice-versa. Some common specific weaknesses occur between the **ascending**, **descending** and **transverse colon** with the **esophagus**. It is common for the **ileocecal sphincter** and the **epiglottis**, the **valve of Houston** and the **larynx**, the **rectum** and the **mouth**, the **anus** and the **lips** to refer weaknesses to each other. In general, the **reproductive system** is also intimately connected to the **elimination system** and vice-versa. *EU ... DEEP THROAT, Pg. 161*

Non-physical contributing factors often center around control issues on the *mental*, *emotional* and *psychological* level. **Anal people** have a tendency to have **anal problems**. **Constipation** at one end often leads to **constipation** at the other. If people feel that they are unable to verbally express themselves and are holding back words it often makes them **constipated**.

A common underlying weakness that causes **diarrhea** is often related to not being able to control the language that people use or feeling forced to put up with the language of others, being a "loud mouth," "explosive anger," "diarrhea of the mouth," "behaving like an asshole," and "putting up with assholes."

Often **diseases** are inadvertently named after the underlying energetic weaknesses and are *irritated* by the **diagnosis**; for example, **irritable bowel syndrome** (**IBS**) "I bull shit" is often connected to issues such as: Who's shit are you putting up with? Who is *irritating* you? Whom are you *irritating*? Are you full of it? Are you tired of putting up with shit, including the **diagnosis**? Did something **crappy** happen to you? Did you do something **crappy** to someone else? Is someone or something **cramping** your style?

Over the years I have provided many opportunities for people to attend free demos in hotels, bookstores, yoga centers, etc. When I am speaking, I am also automatically shifting energy and strengthening people to let go of what is bothering them. The **physical toxins**, **poisons**, **chemicals**, **minerals**, etc., need to leave the **body** as well as the *non-physical toxins* and the **colon** is the most efficient *exit portal*. *EU ... EXIT PORTALS, Pg. 220*

It is not uncommon for a large number of the people attending these events to use the restroom facilities at an accelerated rate. I always let people know that if the need arises to please just get up and go. It is confirmation that there is a lot of shift happening!

Also, before and during private sessions, people often will say "Can you just give me a couple of minutes, I just need to take a bathroom break" or they email me afterwards to say, "Holy crap! I am really letting it go!" Much of what people are letting go of through the **colon** in a **physical** way is *non-physical* at *root cause*.

THE "GOOD NEWS" IS:

Regular **bowel movements** are your best friend! Forgive them if they show up a little on the stinky side, in fact the stinkier the better! You are shifting … let the shift fly!

THE "BAD NEWS" IS:

Contrary to popular *belief*, having a bowel movement every few days is NOT efficient use of your ability to clear **waste** from your **system**. What goes in must come out, and for every *action*, there is an opposite and equal *re-action*. Basic science tells us that. Therefore, if the average person eats **three meals** a day, the average person should have at least three **bowel movements** a day. That would just account for the food that they put into their body. There is also *mental*, *emotional*, *psychological*, *psychic* and *spiritual crap* that people are *processing* … or not.

NUGGET OF WISDOM FROM THE VECTOR

"I LOVE MY TOILET. WE'VE BEEN THROUGH A LOT OF SHIFT TOGETHER!" TOILETS ARE THE MOST BENEFICIAL FIXTURE IN YOUR HOME OR BUSINESS. THIS IS WHY THEY ARE OFTEN REFERRED TO AS THE "THRONE." USE THEM REGULARLY! DELETE THE STIGMA OF CLEANING UP AFTER STOOLS, ESPECIALLY FROM CHILDHOOD EXPERIENCES OF "POTTY TRAINING," AS WELL AS FEARS OF SHIFTING ON PUBLIC TOILETS.

COMMON COLD AND FLU

There is a lot of misunderstanding around the **common cold** and the **flu**. The difference between the two, is that a **cold** comes on gradually, usually over a day or two with **sneezing**, **coughing** and a **runny nose**. If a person has a **fever**, it is generally just above normal. The symptoms of a **cold** usually last around three to four days, but it can take up to two weeks for the average person to regain energy levels and for all the symptoms to clear. The **common cold** and the **flu** are both caused by **viruses**, but the **flu** seems to hit without warning, knocking people off their feet with its intensity. People often experience a high **fever** with **chills**, **achy muscles** and **joints**, **headache** and/or **sore throat** that lasts three to five days. It often takes the average person two to three weeks to totally recover.

It is helpful to understand the difference between a **virus** and a **bacterial** *infection*. **Bacteria** have existed for *eons* and are able to survive in extreme **environments** in and outside of the **human body** because they can *reproduce* on their own. The vast majority of **bacteria** are not harmful, and some even destroy disease-causing **microbes** and provide essential **nutrients**. **Bacteria** are complex, **single cell organisms** with a thin, *flexible* **cellular membrane**. **Viruses**, on the other hand, are much smaller than **bacteria** and cannot survive without a **host**. They essentially are made up of **genetic material** coated with a thin layer of **protein**. They either attach themselves to **cell hosts** and reprogram the **cell** to replicate the **virus** by using the **structure** and **metabolism** of the **healthy cell** until it implodes and dies, or change **normal cells** into **malignant cells**, as in the case of cancer. Unlike **bacteria**, **viruses** are very specific in choosing the **cells** they attack; they even attack **bacteria**.

The discovery of **antibiotics** to cure **bacterial** *infections* is considered one of the most important breakthroughs in modern history. Unfortunately overuse and misuse of **antibiotics** in medicine and in the factory farming of animals has created "super bacteria" that are challenging to stop because they have become resistant to antibiotics. These are especially prevalent in **hospitals**, making the **hospital** one of the most dangerous **environments** for sick people. Adding insult to injury, every year the **flus** are named after one animal or another, like the swine flu, duck flu, equine flu, etc., and if the animals are not blamed, the Asians will do.

Since **colds** and **flus** are **viral**, **antibiotics** are not necessary unless there is a secondary *infection*, and they can have a detrimental *effect* on *healthy* **gut flora** in the **digestive tract** and throughout the **body**. Since the beginning of the twentieth century **vaccines** have been developed to fight **viral** *dis-ease*. The **vaccines** are often credited with drastically reducing the number of cases of **viral disease**; however, there is also mounting evidence that the decline in **disease** may coincide with access to clean water, improved hygiene, and with the advent of modern conveniences in developed countries.

Antiviral medications have also been *associated* with the development of drug-resistant **microbes**, and many **vaccines** are laden with highly **toxic ingredients**. The number of recommended childhood **vaccines** has increased to fourteen different **vaccines** and up to twenty-six injections for a one-year old baby, with most babies receiving multiple **vaccines** as early as two, four and six months. The **flu-vaccine** has been directly linked to the incidence of Guillain-Barre Syndrome, and other **vaccines** have been linked to **autism**, **ear** *infections* and high

infant mortality rate. This is a very sensitive issue for many people on the planet. It is important to recognize that when you educate yourself and consider the scientific evidence regarding these issues it is important to take into account whether or not the information is **peer reviewed**. This means that a board of scholarly reviewers in the subject area of the journal review materials they publish for quality of research and adherence to the editorial standards of the journal before articles are accepted for publication. Before you read any information, check into who is paying for the research, and for any weaknesses for conflict of interest as you read any **information**.

Pharmaceutical companies are protected by special laws giving them legal immunity if there is a problem with **vaccines**, so if you choose to **vaccinate** yourself or your children, educate yourself as to what you are injecting into your **body** or their **bodies**. Strengthen the benefits to one hundred percent optimum potential and spin out the **toxins** and **poisons** to *black wholes*. Do not put anything in your **body**, especially directly into your **blood stream** or your child's **bloodstream** unless you and they are strong to it on every level, *physical*, *mental*, *emotional*, *psychological*, *psychic* and *spiritual*.

The **medical establishment** and **pharmaceutical companies** approach the **cold** and **flu** as an unnatural event that needs to be eradicated or cured. Many of the **cells** in the **body** that are susceptible to **viruses** are the very **cells** that are already in the process of *degeneration* and often have excessive **waste products** that are weakening the *health* of the cell. To maintain *health* and *youthfulness* it is imperative that there is an *evenness* to your **cells** and the process of *regeneration* and *degeneration*. If you change your *perspective* to view the **cold** and **flu** as a natural event that purges the **body** of damaged old **cells**, the symptoms and by-products of a **cold** and **flu** can be seen as beneficial. Using over-the-counter medications to suppress the symptoms is counterproductive and adds more *congestion* to the **CNS**. The by-products and symptoms of a **cold** or **flu** may seem purely **physical**; however many of their *contagious* effects are really *non-physical.* Whenever there is *congestion* in the **sinuses**, always check for *unresolved grief* on the *emotional* and *psychological* level. For instance, typically the **flu season** hits right after the **holiday season** along with the **credit card bills**. Do not *underestimate* the underlying **financial** weaknesses and **corporate interests**. The **cold** and **flu** are **big business** and many of the over-the-counter **medications** are geared to keep people functioning in the work force rather than to benefit over-all *health*.

THE "GOOD NEWS" IS:

Just because you can view **colds** and **flu** as beneficial to your *health* doesn't mean you have to *suffer* with them. Once the underlying weaknesses are cleared many of the *symptoms* of a cold disappear immediately.

THE "BAD NEWS" IS:

Conventional medicine and the **pharmaceutical industry** encourage you to believe that you need to protect yourself against the **flu** with a **vaccine** and ease the *discomfort* of a **cold** with a variety of **medications** that suppress *symptoms* rather than solve the **root cause**.

NUGGET OF WIZDOM FROM THE VECTOR

IF THERE IS CONGESTION IN YOUR SINUSES THERE IS ALSO CONGESTION IN YOUR CNS AND CELLS. IDENTIFY THE UNDERLYING PHYSICAL AND NON-PHYSICAL WEAKNESSES TO SUPPORT HEALTH INSTEAD OF FIGHTING DIS-EASE AND DIS-COMFORT.

CONNECTION TO SOURCE

When people speak of "source" energy, they are often referring to their version of **God**, which is dependent on their *upbringing*, *cultural influences*, *religious* and *educational experiences*. For others, *source* is more literally, defined as the point of origin for a stream of *cosmic expansion*. The "God in the Sky," who is given human characteristics and personality and the "big bang theory" are not what I am referring to as "source" for the intent and purpose of this discussion. I am referring to the flow of the perfect structure of the fabric of the universe, the *holofractographic* nature of divine order that every human is connected with to *experience* co-creation, here on planet Earth.

Around the **age** of **three**, many people notice that they appear to be separate from *source energy*. A seemingly trivial event can trigger *accumulated traumas* on a *spiritual* level and on a larger scale if a baby *suffers traumatic experiences* that cause *fear* and distrust of the **mother** or **father**, **siblings**, **grandparents**, **aunts**, **uncles**, **cousins** or other trusted family **friends**. Many victims of **incest** and **molestation** disconnect from authority figures including **God** or *source energy*.

Accidents, crime, **natural disasters**, **wars**, etc., cause a shock to the **system** and a *disconnect* from *source*.

You can *reconnect* with *source* in an instant by strengthening the *authentic-self triad* of **body**, *soul* and *spirit* to be even with strong **boundaries** to *internal* and *external forces*. A more thorough connection can be made by systematically testing for *specific weaknesses* and *blocks in energy*. Start at the **brain** to the *mind*, activate the *crown chakra* and strengthen the *soul*, *all souls* and the *higher self* to each other and *highest existence*, defined as *God* or *Source*, back to the *higher self*, *souls, soul,* into the *mind* and **brain**, activating the **pineal gland**, **pituitary gland**, **hypothalamus**, the *seat of the soul*, the *third eye*. Strengthen **C1** and the **atlas**, *the throat chakra*, **cervical vertebrae**, **thoracic vertebrae** and activate the *heart chakra* at the **sternum**. Move down to the *solar plexus*, located at the **diaphragm**, and down to the base of the **spine** to activate **physical intelligence**.

Next, pull *macrocosmic energy* into the **intrinsic body**, through every **tissue**, every **organ**, going deeper into the **microcosmic**, the **cells**, **sub-cells** and **molecules** of the **body** deeper still to the **atoms, sub-atoms, nucleus, sub-nucleus** to the smallest **quantum particles**. Strengthen all the **structures** of any *empty spaces* within the **spine**, **organs** and **cavities** to the **macroscopic structure** of the **universe**. Pierce through the **earth's crust** with the *energetic tail* pushing deeper and deeper into the **earth's womb** to draw the energy up through the *root* and *sacral chakras*. Then spin out through the *black whole* any *elusive*, *hidden*, *deceiving*, *numbered*, *unnumbered*, *named*, *unnamed*, *known* and *unknown* **accumulations**, **frequencies**, *memories* of *traumas*, **poisons**, **toxins**, **chemicals**, *associated fears*, *limiting beliefs*, *frequencies*, *interferences, expectations* and/or *misinformation*. Strengthen *mental*, *emotional* and *psychological* issues and *delete* any *karmic*, *psychic* or *spiritual* need to *suffer*, *struggle* or to keep *paying the price* for self or others.

Weaknesses are held in the **inner** and **outer meninges**, the **cerebral spinal fluid** and the **spinal cord**. Test for **access points, holes, threads, cords, bonds, contracts** and/or **vows** that may be *recreating*, *birthing*, *cloning*, *seeding*, *repeating*, *recycling*, *spreading* or *repelling*. These energies may be from *outer* and *inner dimensions* and other *existences* in **space-time** from the *un-conscious* and *sub-conscious mind*, the *soul*, *true self*, *higher self*, *spiritual* and *dead influences*.

Many people have unresolved *life experiences* from *parallel* and *opposing universal forces*, **UFO** and *alien abduction experiences*, *multiple personalities* from the *past*, *present* and *future* with or without *spirit attachments* along with *environmental, cultural* and *religious experiences* as well as **peer, gender** and **linguistic influences**. Spin **oxygen, carbon, nitrogen** and **hydration**, even *production, distribution* and *transportation* of **hormones, digestion, absorption** and **assimilation** of **nutrients** in through the *white whole. Synchronize* the **heart** to the **beat** deep within the **womb of Earth.** Strengthen *Ka, meridians, acupuncture points, intuition, creativity,* **primordial cells** and projections of the **mind** and *spirit* through *astral travel, lucid dreaming, plant medicine* to *divine order, infinite potential* and **universal structure**.

Pull in the self-sustaining nature of the **earth** through the **quantum particles** of **matter** to *energy*, the **sub-nucleus, nucleus, sub-atomic, atomic** and into the **molecules**, the building blocks of the **physical body**. Strengthen the **sub-cells** and all *tori* at the **heart,** the base of the **spine** to the *crown* and the third dimensional world into the **sub-cells,** and **cells,** the **organ systems, organs, tissues** of the **physical body** up the **sacral components** of the **spine**, the **thoracic spine** and **cervical spine** into the **brain**, integrated with the *mind.*

Walking barefoot allows the middle of the **ball** of your **foot** (*acupuncture Kidney K1*) to transfer free **electrons** with powerful **antioxidants** from the **earth** to every *acupuncture meridian* in your **body**. This lowers *inflammation* throughout the **body**, regulates **heart rate**, the density of **blood** and **blood pressure**.

And don't' forget to strengthen **unconditional forgiveness** for self and others. As above, so below.

THE "GOOD NEWS" IS:

In any given moment you can let go of *fear* by putting *tension* into your **spine**, feeling your **heart beat**, connecting your *meridians* by placing your **tongue** on the **roof** of your **mouth** and going inward to connect yourself to *source energy*.

THE "BAD NEWS" IS:

When people feel *overwhelmed,* they have a tendency to hold their **breath**. *Inhaling* is your ability to receive *life force energy*. When you *exhale*, you let go of anything that hinders a full-hearted life. *Equilibrium* between the two is essential for **oxygenation** of every **system**, regardless of whether your breathing is deep or shallow.

NUGGET OF WIZDOM FROM THE VECTOR

YOUR PHYSICAL PRESENCE RESONATES STRONGLY WITH YOUR PERCEPTION OF THE PHYSICAL UNIVERSE. EVERY QUANTUM PARTICLE, ALL THE ATOMS, MOLECULES, CELLS, TISSUES, ORGANS, SYSTEMS AND ALL THE SYSTEMS WITHIN THE SYSTEMS, ARE TUNED INTO THE REALITY YOU CHOOSE. CHOOSE WISELY! HAVE FUN OUT THERE!

DAILY ROUTINE

Many aspects of a person's **daily routine** can have a detrimental energetic **effect** that they may not be aware of on the **conscious** level. People have weaknesses to time in **general** as well as **specific** weaknesses to **AM**, **PM**, **morning**, **afternoon**, **midnight,** etc. They can also energetically be weak to **specific times**, like **1:00**, **2:00**, **3:00**, etc., as well as to **military time** which often comes up from their **ancestors**' and **descendants**' warring experiences *past*, *present* and *future*; **13:00**, **14:00**, **15:00**, **dawn**, **morning**, **noon**, **afternoon**, **evening**, **dusk**, **late night**, etc., can all have hidden triggers creating issues that hinder people in their **daily routine**.

It is not uncommon for specific days to bother people because of *residual memories* of **traumas**, *deaths*, positive and *negative emotions* to **anniversaries**, **birthdays** etc. as well as the *collective influences'* effect on every individual. Terms people use to describe **days** of the **week** that go weak are "Manic Mondays," "Hump Day" (Wednesday), "Thank God It's Friday," "Day of Worship," (Sunday), etc. Many people are also inadvertently weakened by **specific months** or moving into and out of the seasons of **winter, spring, summer** and **fall** or **autumn**, and the *astrological effects* of these **months.** When you take into consideration the *cycles* of the **moon** and **sun** and their *effects* on each individual as well as on the **collective influence** as a *whole*, numerous factors create *underlying energies* that *sabotage effortless* success.

Often people are also *affected* by the **lack** of a **daily routine**, such as when they are out of work, on strike, about to take a holiday, children are out of school, etc. No matter how **challenging**, every day is a gift. Remember that **challenges** are disguised as **problems** just waiting to spin into **opportunities**. You are co-creating your reality along with the universe. Be aware of your *sub-conscious*, *un-conscious* and *conscious thoughts*. Strengthen congruency between all three by clearing any *psychic* and *spiritual energies*. Send *weak thoughts* out to a **black whole** and use your **mind** to strengthen your **physical intelligence**.

Many people have a tendency to let one "bad" event in their day ruin the entire day. If you get out of bed and stub your big toe, take the time to shift that energy; stubbing your big toe is often about **conflict** between your logical **intelligence** and your **intuition.** Set the **intention** for the day to be "this or better." You already know that you can handle "this" because you are surviving it in the **present**; strengthen yourself to "better" by letting go of **expectations** about how your day will be and allow the universe to spin unexpected, amazing events into your reality.

CASE STUDY:

A client came to me for a private session because, for over a decade, he had been experiencing major issues in his life, particularly with his **health**. He had gained weight, his body **ached** all over, he had **hearing** and **vision** loss and he was always **fatigued**. The leading weakness came up as **financial**. When I asked him what was going on in his life when he first noticed that he was not feeling **healthy**, he mentioned that at that time his business partner had defrauded him and many of their clients out of a huge amount of money. To protect his clients and his good name, he had chosen to take the financial hit, but he was still "paying the price" all these years later. As he was relating the story to me, his eyes filled with tears and he said, "I will never forget when I received that phone call … It was on Wednesday evening at eight o'clock."

This client was unaware on a **conscious** level that for well over a decade, every Wednesday at eight o'clock PM his **body**, **mind** and **spirit** were **re-acting** to the shock he had **experienced** when he received that call over ten years ago. The **accumulations** of those **sensations** and his **sensitivity** to them were weakening him in every **aspect** of his life every Wednesday. Now that this weakness has been cleared and he is aware of it, he can strengthen himself at that time every day instead of **un-consciously** weakening himself.

THE "GOOD NEWS" IS:

If you do even the smallest task, from the time you first wake up in the morning until the time you go to sleep, with the intention of taking immediate and consistent steps of **action** towards your goals, you are in the process of achieving them!

THE "BAD NEWS" IS:

If you are in the habit of using monumental *effort* to achieve anything that you have deemed important, your **daily routine** will be eroded by it. Consistently putting more *effort* than is necessary into any given activity depletes your *life force energy* and has a negative, draining *effect* on every *aspect* of life.

NUGGET OF WIZDOM FROM THE VECTOR

TAKE THE TIME EVERY MORNING, BEFORE GETTING OUT OF BED TO STRENGTHEN YOUR DAY BY PUTTING TENSION INTO YOUR SPINE AND FEELING YOUR HEARTBEAT. RECONNECT TO SOURCE. GET INTO THE FLOW WITH SPIRIT AND MAXIMIZE YOUR ABILITY TO ACCESS INFINITE POTENTIAL. IF THERE IS ANYTHING THAT HAS BEEN DEEMED IMPORTANT ON THE AGENDA FOR THE DAY, FEEL IT AND CLEAR ANY CONCERNS BEFORE YOU GET OUT OF BED AND YOUR FEET HIT THE FLOOR.

DEEP THROAT

The components of the **oral cavity** (**throat**) are intimately connected to the **pelvic cavity**, a container for the **reproductive organs** and parts of the **colon**. The **cervix, uterus** and **vagina** are continuous and often refer energetic weaknesses to and from the **head, mouth** and **shoulders**.

Along with your **genitals,** your **oral cavity** is one of the great pleasure centers of your **body**. They are both shaped like the **vesica piscis,** and their main function is to *give* and *receive* pleasure. You smile and kiss with your **lips**, sing and wrap your **tongue** around the finest delicacies that life has to offer. An understanding of the **inner structure** of the **mouth, reproductive system** and **pelvic cavity** can be very beneficial in increasing the benefit of those pleasures.

The **oral cavity** is a microcosm of the **cavities** throughout the rest of the **body**. The weaknesses are often referred from one **cavity** to another. If the **oral cavity** lacks *tension*, it is very likely that the rest of the **body**, also lacks *tension*, and this causes **structural problems**, dissipation in flow of energy and *aging*. You are made up of **atoms** and **atoms** are 99.9999% space. That includes the **cavities** of the **body**. When the **oral cavity** is *stable* and *balanced*, it centers the rest of the **cavities** in the **body**, creating evenness throughout. It is helpful to have a basic understanding of the anatomy of the **oral cavity** and **pelvic cavity** to facilitate energetic shifts.

ORAL CAVITY

The **mouth** (**oral cavity**) is a hollow **cavity** that is formed by the space between the **lips**, **cheeks**, **tongue**, **hard** and **soft palates** and the **throat**. It is also a container for several **organs**; the **teeth**, **tongue**, and the **ducts** of the **salivary glands**. The **oral cavity's** two main functions are **speech**, and to aid in *digestion*.

The **lips** are *flexible*, *elastic*, and made up of **collagen**, **elastin fibers** and **adipose tissue** that are covered by **squamous epithelium**, which is made up of flat thin **cells** that easily filter **molecules** through their **membranes**. The outside of **lips** and **cheeks** are covered by **keratinized epithelium** providing protection from dryness, while the inside is covered by **non-keratinized epithelium** that is hydrated by the **mucous membranes**. The **cheeks** are made up of layers of **skin**, **connective tissue**, **nerves** and **muscles**. The major **muscles** of the **cheeks** include the **buccinators**, **orbicularis oris** and **zygomaticus major**.

BUCCINATOR MUSCLE

The **buccinator muscle** is a major **facial muscle** holding the **cheek** to the **teeth** to prevent sagging. It is connected to the **facial nerve** (**CN VII**) and is one of the first **muscles** that a baby uses for the **sucking reflex**. **Smiling**, **chewing**, **whistling**, and **vocalization**, in particular *tone* and **echo**, are dependent upon this **muscle**. The **buccinator** facilitates **sounds** that require the **mouth** to open wide to produce the "I" and "E" sounds in *speech*.

ORBICULARIS ORIS

The **orbicularis oris muscle** (**the kissing muscle**) is a **sphincter muscle** that encircles the **mouth**, *extending* upward to the **nose** and down between the **lower lip** and **chin**; it allows the **lips** to close and pucker.

ZYGOMATICUS MAJOR

The **zygomaticus muscle** (**the smiling muscle**) controls *facial expression* and is also controlled by **CN VII**. It starts at the **cheekbone** and extends to the corners of the **mouth**, pulling the corners of the **mouth** up to smile and to create dimples.

HARD AND SOFT PALATES

The **hard palate** is located on the **roof** of the **mouth,** and is made up of the **maxilla** and **palatine bones**. The **soft palate** is a fleshy mass of **tissues** that ends in the **uvula** which hangs down into the **throat**. The **hard** and **soft palate** work together to separate the **mouth** from the **nasal cavity**.

The **maxilla bones** form the **upper jaw**, where the upper **teeth** are embedded, parts of the **eye sockets**, and the lower parts and sides of the **nasal cavity**. They are two irregularly shaped **bones** that join in the middle at the **inter-maxillary suture** to form the **hard palate**. There are four processes that the **maxilla bones** are responsible for. The **maxillary antrum** is the name of the air filled *space* that sits under the **cheekbones** and just above the **roof** of the **mouth**. The **anterior nasal spine** is the small amount of **bone** that protrudes from the **maxilla** at the lower end of the **nose**. The **zygomatic process** is the curved **bone** that forms part of the **cheekbones**, and the **alveolar process** are the **sockets** that the **upper teeth** sit in.

The **intra-orbital foramen** are two small openings below the **eye sockets** allowing passage of the **infraorbital artery**, **vein** and **nerve** that are branches to the **trigeminal nerve** (**CN V**). The **palatine bones** are a pair of **bones** located at the back of the **nasal cavity**, between the **maxilla** and the **sphenoid**, one of seven bones that make up the **orbit** (**eye socket**). It is part of three **cavities**: the floor and side of the **nasal cavity**, the **roof** of the **mouth** and the floor of the **orbit**. There are two important **foramina** (holes) in the **palatine bones**. The **greater palatine foramen** is located close to the **third mola**r in the **upper jaw** on either side, transmitting **nerves** and **blood vessels** to the **hard palate**, and the **lesser palatine foramen** transmits **nerves** and **blood vessels** to the **soft palate** and **tonsils**. Both **foramina** are part of the **pterygopalatine canal**, carrying **nerves** and **blood vessels** that descend from the **pterygopalatine fossa** to the **palate**.

GAG REFLEX

The **pharyngeal reflex** (**gag reflex**) is a **contraction** at the back of the **throat** caused by touching the **roof** of the **mouth**, back of the **tongue**, **tonsils** and back of the **throat**. People can learn to suppress it during the act of **fellatio** as well as instigate it to induce **vomiting**. The **pharyngeal reflex** occurs when there is *stimulation* of the **nerves** at the back of the throat. An **afferent nerve** receives the message and sends a response to the **motor neuron** to the **CNS** (**CN IX**) to stimulate a *reflex*. *Touching* the **soft palette** can also lead to a similar *response*, but that is instigated by **CN X**.

TONGUE

The **tongue's** main function is to move food around the **mouth** and to facilitate *speech* by controlling the *flow* of air to *produce* sound. It is an **organ** that is made up of **epithelium, skeletal muscles, nerves** and **connective tissues**. It contains small ridges called **papillae** that control the movement of food in the **mouth** and **taste buds** that detect **chemicals** found in food. **Saliva** moistens and softens dry food in the **oral cavity** to support *digestion* and the *swallowing* of food. It is mainly made up of **water** and two **enzymes**.

SALIVARY GLANDS

Amylase is an **enzyme** that breaks down **starches** in **carbohydrates**, transmuting their simple **sugars** into *energy sources*. **Lingual lipase** digests fat into **fatty acids** once it is activated by the acidity of the **stomach**.

There are three groups of **salivary glands** that secrete **saliva** into the **oral cavity**: the **parotid glands**, located on either side of the **jaw** just below the **ears**, and two sets of **submandibular glands**. The **parotid glands** secrete **saliva** into the **back** of the **mouth**. The first group of **submandibular glands**, located below the **jaw**, secrete into the **middle** of the **mouth**, and the second set of **submandibular glands**, secrete **saliva** just under the **tongue** into the **front** of the **mouth**.

TEMPOROMANDIBULAR JOINT (TMJ JOINT)

The **temporomandibular joint** (**TMJ**) connects the **mandible** (**lower jaw**) to the **temporal bone** of the **cranium**, allowing the opening and closing and side-to-side motion of the **mouth**. It also connects three surfaces: the **mandibular fossa**, the **articular tubercle**, and the head of the **mandible**. These three surfaces do not come in contact with each other because they are separated by an **articular disc** that serves as a cushion between the **bone surfaces**. The **articular disc** has no **nerve endings** or **blood vessels**, which makes it immune to **pain**. The **front** of it is attached to **pterygoid muscles** (for chewing) and in the **back** it becomes **retrodiscal tissue** that is fully supplied by **nerves** and **blood vessels**.

Three **ligaments** support the **TMJ** to keep it *centered, stable* and *balanced*. These are the **lateral ligament, sphenomandibular ligament**, and the **stylomandibular ligament**. The **lateral ligament**, running from the **articular tubule** to the **mandibular neck**, is responsible for preventing backwards dis-location of the **jaw**. The **sphenomandibular ligament** starts at the **sphenoid spine** and attaches to the **mandible**. The **stylomandibular ligament**, a thickening of the **fascia** of the **parotid gland**, cooperates with the **face muscles** to support the weight of the **jaw**.

TEMPOROMANDIBULAR DISORDER (TMD)

Temporomandibular disorder (**TMD**) describes a variety of conditions that affect the **temporomandibular joint**, **jaw muscles** and **facial nerves**.

The **mandible** is the only **bone** that moves when the **mouth** opens. Small movements only require a rotational movement of the **condyle** (the rounded part at the end of a **bone**) within the **socket**. For larger movements the **condyle** and the **disc** have to move forward and out of the **socket** down the **articular eminence**, a rounded **bone** located at the front of the **socket**. This movement is called **translation**.

The most common painful disorder of **TMJ** is **disc** displacement towards the front causing the sensitive, **retrodiscal tissue** that has **nerve** and **vascular tissue** to be pulled forward between the **bones**, where the **articular disc** normally rests. To fully open the **jaw** the **condyle** has to then jump over the back of the **articular disc** to be on its center, causing a clicking or popping sound. When the **jaw** closes, the **condyle** slides back out of the **disc**, once again clicking and popping back into place. This is **diagnosed** as "disc displacement with reduction."

In severe cases the clicking and popping disappears, but the opening of the **jaw** is limited because the **condyle** stays behind the **disc** the whole time and is unable to center itself. This is often **diagnosed** as "locked jaw" or "disc displacement without reduction." In most cases the condition resolves itself because the **retrodiscal tissue** adapts by becoming **scar tissue** and replaces the **disc** as a "**pseudo disc**."

TMD is not a **disease**; it is a **problem** with the **structure** and **function** of the **jaw**. Test if there is *balance* between the **mouth** when it is open or closed and the overall **structure** of the **mouth** from the **top** to the **bottom**, **front** to **back**, **side** to **side** and **inside** to **outside**. Many weaknesses in the **mouth** are referred from the **anus**, **pelvis**, **pelvic floor** and **genitals**.

THROAT

The **throat** or **pharynx** is a funnel shaped tube located in the back of the **mouth** that connects the **nasal cavity** and **mouth** to the **esophagus** and **larynx** in the **neck**. Food is swallowed into the **pharynx**, through the oropharynx region at the back of the mouth, and passed on to the laryngopharynx that connects to the esophagus and larynx (voice box).

The epiglottis, a flap of flexible fibers and cartilage, sits at the top of the larynx. It moves to cover the opening of the larynx during the *swallowing process*, thereby preventing choking by blocking the airway and directing food into the esophagus.

TONSILS

A ring of tonsils are formed where the mouth and nasal cavity meet, at the throat and palate. They are the body's first line of defense when they come in contact with germs, viruses and bacteria that enter through the nose and mouth. There are three types of tonsils; the palatine tonsils, adenoids and lingual tonsils. The palatine tonsils can be seen on either side when you open your mouth, the adenoids are situated on the roof of the throat, and the linguae's are at the base of the tongue. The tonsils and the adenoids, in particular, can become very enlarged, especially in children; this makes breathing challenging and causes a chronic runny nose. Cells that line the throat behind the tonsils can compensate for adenoids that have been surgically removed.

Weaknesses in the oral cavity are often referred from one cavity to another, in particular the pelvic cavity …

PELVIC CAVITY

The pelvic cavity is a container for the pelvic viscera (bladder rectum, genitals and the end of the urethra). The side-walls consist of the obturator internus and the piriformis muscles which also makes up the back wall of the pelvis. It is shaped differently in women than in men to accommodate the uterus during pregnancy and it has an extra orifice to accommodate the vagina.

PELVIC BRIM

The pelvic brim is the rim of the pelvic inlet, the circumference of a large rounded opening that is comprised of the upper inner surfaces of the lower pelvis, the sacrum at the base of the spine, and the wing shaped bones of the ilium and the pubis, and a pair of C-shaped bones that form the center of the lower pelvis. The pelvic brim slants down from the back to the front. It is met in the back by the front edge of the top of the sacrum (the tapered stacked bone of the lower spine). On either side the brim is formed by the inner edge of the **ilium**, named the **arcuate line** where the front of the **ilium bone** ends and the **lower torso** begins.

The lower border of the **pelvic brim** is formed by the upper edges of the **pubic bones,** known as the **superior ramus** of the **pubis**. Each of the **ramus** has a ridge known as the **pectineal line**; these are connected with each other by a flat, rectangle of **muscle** called the **pectineus muscle,** a strong **inner thigh muscle** responsible for *flexibility* of the **hip**. The **pubic bones** meet at a joint called the **pubic symphysis** that forms the lower border of the **pelvic brim**. There is a gap between the **perineal membrane** and the **pubic symphysis**.

PELVIC INLET

Several **tissues** pass through the **pelvic inlet** and are contained by the **pelvic brim,** including the **reproductive organs** of both sexes and some **elimination organs**, including the **urethra** and the **sigmoid (valve of Houston)**, **colon**, the **nerves** and **blood vessels** that supply them, and the **muscles** of the **pelvic floor**.

PELVIC FLOOR

The **pelvic floor (pelvic diaphragm)** separates the **pelvic cavity** above from the **perineum** below. It consists of the **levator ani muscles** and the **coccygeus muscle**, as well as the **fascia** covering them. The **perineal membrane** and the **deep perineal pouch** are considered by some, as part of the **pelvic floor**, and as being separate structures by others. The **pelvic floor** is a funnel shaped set of **structures** made up of several **muscles**. The **muscles** consist of various **fibers** that loop around the structures.

LEVATOR ANI MUSCLE

The function of the **levator ani muscle** is to support the **pelvic viscera**, keeping the **rectum** and **vagina** closed. It is a **sphincter** that resists rises in **intrapelvic pressure** during any straining such as coughing or heavy lifting to keep **urine** and **feces** from being expelled. The **levator ani muscle** has three main sets of **fibers**: the **pubococcygeus**, the **puborectalis** and the **iliococcygeus**.

The **pubococcygeus** attaches to the bony part of the **pubis**, extending back to the **coccyx**. The **fibers** at the front of the **pubococcygeus** loop around the **prostate** in **males** and the **vagina** in **females,** forming the **levator prostatae** or the **puboprostaticus**. In females it loops around the **vagina** forming the **pubovaginalis**.

The next part of the **levator ani muscle** is the **puborectalis muscle** that forms a sling around the **anus**, the **rectum**, around the **anorectal** end of the **gastrointestinal tract** and the **anorectal junction**. These **intermediate fibers** originate on the **pubis** and are responsible for maintaining the **anorectal angle** of **ninety degrees** that closes off the **anal canal**, forming a **valve** that stops the **rectum** from filling with **feces**.

When this **muscle** relaxes, it releases *tension* on the angle allowing flow of **feces** from the **rectum** into the **anal canal**. To **defecate** it is necessary to relax the **pelvic diaphragm muscles**, in particular the **puborectalis** portion of the **muscle**, to change the **anorectal angle** and prevent closure of the **anal canal**. The **levator ani** is innervated by branches **S2** and **S4** of the **PNS**. (S234 keep shit off the floor).

The **iliococcygeus** has thin **muscle fibers** that start at the front of the **ischial spines** and the back of the **tendinous arch**, attaching at the back of the **coccyx** and the **anococcygeal ligament**. The **levator ani muscles** are involved in support of the **fetal head** when the **cervix** dilates during childbirth. These are the **muscles** that are cut in an **episiotomy** in an effort to prevent ripping of the **perineum**. The **perineum** can be massaged to prepare it for stretching to avoid ripping or being cut. Test for any **structural** weaknesses as well as **physical fitness** of the **fibers** and **muscles** to withstand the **pressure**. Delete any *memories* of *birth traumas* up and down the family line from both the **mother** and the **baby** and *karma* with the **doctors**, the **midwives**, and at the other end with **dentists**.

COCCYGEUS MUSCLE

The **coccygeus** lies over the **sacrospinous ligament**, is connected to the **sacrum** and the **ischial spine,** and travels to the **sacrum** and **coccyx**, forming the back of the **pelvic floor**. Its main function is to support the **pelvic floor**. It is *innervated* by branches **S4** and **S5** of the **PNS**.

There is a **midline raft** called the **ligamentous midline** where the two halves of the **levator ani muscles** attach on the back surface of the **pubis** and also along the **fascia** of the **obturator internus muscle**. This is the location of the **rectal hiatus** where there is an aperture for the **anus** supported by a **ligament** called the **anococcygeal**. There is also a u-shaped gap called the **urogenital hiatus** that allows the **urethra** and **vagina**, in women, to pass through the **pelvic floor** into the **perineum** below.

Between the **urogenital hiatus** and the **anal canal** is a **fibromuscular connective tissue node** that joins the **perineum** and the **pelvic floor** with the **levator ani muscles**; this is called the **perineal membrane**. It is a thick **fascial** triangular shaped **structure** that attaches along the

pubic arch and the roots of the **external genitalia** with a border at the back that is not attached.

PERINEUM

Between the **pelvic diaphragm muscles** and the **perineal membrane** there is a **deep pouch**. The **deep perineal pouch** is a **fascial capsule** that contains various layers of **skeletal muscles** that are innervated by the **perineal branches** of the **pudendal nerve**. The **deep transverse perineal muscle** attaches laterally on the **ischiopubic ramus** in the **perineal body**, meeting at the **midline** with their counterpart from the opposite side. **The external urethral sphincter** surrounds the **urethra** in women, and the **membranous** part of the **urethra** in males.

Women have two extra muscles than men, the **compressor urethrae** originating from the sides of the **ischiopubic ramus** and looping back to meet at the **urethra**. This **muscle** aids the **external urethral sphincter** to close off the **urethra**. The **sphincter urethrovaginalis** forms around the opening of the **vagina** in the **perineal membrane** and in the **urethra** as well. Men have the **deep transverse perineal muscle** and the **external urethral sphincter** as well as **glands** called **bulbourethral glands** (**glands of cowper**) deep within the **perineal pouch**.

Problems in the **bones** shaping the **oral cavity**, **gums** and **jaw** are often referred to the **pelvic cavity** and **pelvic floor,** and vice versa. The **clitoris** is associated with the **frenulum**, the membrane that connects the **upper lip** to the **gums**. Using a **tongue** (yours or someone else's) to stimulate it will also *stimulate* lubrication of the **genitalia**.

Other common pairings are the **rectum** and **vulva** to the **mouth**, **outer labia** to outer **lips** and **anus**, **inner labia** to **mucosa** of the **mouth** and **anus**, **valve of houston** to the **larynx** and **cervix**, **esophagus** to the **colon** and **vagina**, **fallopian tubes** to the **eustachian tubes**, **temporomandibular joint** to the **hips**, and **ovaries** and **testicles** to the **eyes** and **ears**.

Psychosomatically, the **tongue** equals the **penis**; therefore everyone, male and female, has a **penis** (tongue). We all know how *attached* men are to their **penises!** It is cold out there! When you consider that for the vast majority of the time a **penis** is embraced by the warmth of the most desirable spaces, it is understandable that when a **penis** reaches out to explore, it is on the lookout for even more desirable places.

Judgments people place on sexual preferences between **consenting adults** are ridiculous when you realize how natural it is for **body parts** to be attracted to each other; **lip** to **lip** through **cunnilingus, analingus** and "**french kissing**," **tongue** to **penis** (**fellatio**), and all the combinations and variations of sexual intercourse.

THE "GOOD NEWS" IS:

If you are energetically strong to what you put into your **body**, **food**, **drink**, **smoke**, **tongues**, **penises** etc., you will be more likely to enjoy your favorite things without any *adverse effects*.

THE "BAD NEWS" IS:

If you are in the habit of biting back and *swallowing* words that are not palatable to you it can ruin all your fun! For instance **throat cancer** is often blamed on drinking **alcohol** and **smoking** and just recently Hollywood has highlighted **cunnilingus** as a dangerous sport. People have a tendency to *numb* themselves with these activities. The combination of *numbing* and relaxing creates a perfect **environment** for *anger*, *grief*, *shame*, etc., to fester as *dis-ease*.

NUGGET OF WIZDOM FROM THE VECTOR

IF YOU FIND YOURSELF IN THE UNFORTUNATE POSITION WHERE THE LEADING ACTOR IN YOUR LOVE LIFE, WHO HAS EARNED A REPUTATION FOR BEING A BOOZER, SMOKER AND PHILANDERER, IS BLAMING YOU FOR HIS THROAT CANCER DUE TO YOUR PREFERENCE FOR ORAL SEX, YOU HAVE ALREADY GONE DOWN … IT IS TIME TO GIVE THAT SILVER TONGUED DEVIL A PIECE … (OF YOUR MIND).

DENTAL

The hardest substance in the human body are the **teeth**. **Teeth** are made up of **enamel**, **dentin**, the **pulp**, **cementum**, **periodontal ligament** and the **gingival**.

ENAMEL

The **enamel**, the outer layer of the **tooth**, makes it shiny and white. It is mostly made up of **calcium phosphate** and covers the **crown**, which is what we see above the **gum line**.

DENTIN

Dentin forms the largest part of the **tooth** and is found under the **enamel**. It is made up of living **cells** that secrete a hard mineral substance.

PULP

The **pulp** is the softer, inner structure of the **tooth**. **Blood vessels** and **nerves** run through the **pulp**. It is this part of the **tooth** that feels a "tooth ache."

CEMENTUM

Cementum is a layer of **connective tissue** that binds the **root** of the **teeth** firmly to the **gums** and **jawbone**.

PERIODONTAL LIGAMENT

The **periodontal ligament** is within the **socket** of every **tooth** and allows slight movement of the **tooth** when chewing and grinding food.

GINGIVAL

The **gingival**, more commonly referred to as the **gums**, often has weaknesses that are referred from the **ovaries** and **testicles**. Receding of the **gums** is often caused by too much *relaxation* and not enough *tension* within the **mouth**, the **gums** and the **teeth**. Many people automatically assume that if there is *infection* in the **gums**, it stems from **bacteria**, however **candida** is also present in the **mouth**.

People who wear **dentures**, who have been taking **antibiotics**, are on **chemotherapy**, have been diagnosed with **diabetes** or **AIDS**, tend to have **yeast** in their **mouths**. Balance the **pH**, strengthen *positive ions* and *electromagnetic* charge to change the chemistry of the **micro-organisms** to support a *healthy* mouth. If a person is wearing **dentures**, strengthen the fit of the **dentures** to the **gum** to merge as one.

The main causes of **jawbone** deterioration are loss of **teeth** (a paradox as **jawbone** *dis-ease* often causes missing **teeth**), **trauma, developmental deformity** and **previous dental procedures**. **Bone tissue** needs to have stress or load exercise to maintain its **structure**. A missing **tooth** creates a **gap** and an unevenness in the **alveolar bone**, the portion of the **jawbone** that anchors **teeth** in the **mouth**. **Bone** is a dynamic **tissue** that is constantly breaking down and reabsorbed by **cells** known as **osteoclasts** and **osteoblasts**; these are formed in the **marrow** in a process called bone remodeling.

OSTEOCLASTS

Osteoclasts play a major role in liberating **minerals** and **molecules** within the **bone matrix**. Release of **calcium** plays an important role in *homeostasis* of the **bone tissue**.

OSTEOBLASTS

Osteoblasts are **cells** that are responsible for *regenerating* **bone tissue**. They are *associated* with **blood vessels** that produce the organic component of **bone** and are predominately made of **collagen**. As **osteoblasts** form new **tissue**, they may become embedded in the **bone matrix** and become **osteocytes**. Under high loading conditions, **osteoblasts** increase **bone mass**, and in low loading conditions, **osteoclasts** remove **bone tissue**. The interactions between the two are a delicate *balance* of *regeneration* and *degeneration*, a fifty/fifty proposition.

Biting and *chewing* stimulate the **root structure** of **teeth** that are embedded in the **bone tissue**. This is a natural ongoing process that maintains normal *healthy* **bone**. If **teeth** are missing or if there are *psychological* weaknesses around the *fear* of losing **teeth**, the **alveolar** deteriorates from a lack of need for it. Removing **upper back molars** creates air space in the **sinuses** that undermine the **maxilla** or **upper jaw**.

Clear *past, present* and future *grief* about life being "a grind," "chewing on problems," and "not being able to take a bite out of life," and *past life experiences* with **cannibalism**. When there is a **problem** with the **bite**, check if the weakness is biting into food or "feeling swallowed" by the food as a person takes a bite.

Delete fears from *past*, *present* and *future tooth loss*, *karma* with dentists, *accumulations* and *associations* with *traumas* and *tortures* of the **mouth** and **anus** as well as to the **pelvic floor** and **vagina**. Test if the person has *experienced* **sexual abuse** with weaknesses around **anal sex**, **oral sex** and **vaginal sex**.

Clear **traumas** and *karma* with **victims** and **perpetrators**. Issues with **survival** and the *root chakra* often are referred to the **roots** of **teeth**. Test for optimum **alkalinity** and for **parasites**, and clear all past *blunt force traumas* to the **head**.

People who grind their **teeth** at night do not necessarily have TMJ. Grinding of **teeth** is an attempt to *balance* the "daily grind" of life as the issues that arise in the **daily routine** are brought up by the ***sub-conscious mind*** and the ***un-conscious mind*** from **spiritual experiences** and **psychic energies** of other ***times, space*** and ***existences***. *Balance* all *aspects* of life and test for weaknesses to the ***false obligations*** of life.

CAVITIES

According to the American Dental Association, **tooth decay** is caused by foods containing **carbohydrates** (**sugars** and **starches**) being left on the **teeth**, and subsequently ***attracting*** **bacteria** that thrive on these foods to produce **acid** which wears away the **tooth enamel** resulting in **tooth decay**. There is growing evidence (Dr. Weston Price) that if the **minerals** and **fat soluble vitamins** (**A,D, E** and **K**) are not properly being ***assimilated*** and ***absorbed*** by the **body**, and there is a high level of **phytrates** (found in **grains, seeds, nuts** and **legumes**) the **blood chemistry** and ratio of **calcium** and **phosphorous** go out of *balance*, resulting in leaching from the **bones** and **teeth**.

It is true that **sugar** causes **tooth decay**, not only because it ***produces*** **acid** that ruins your **teeth**, but because it depletes **nutrients** from the **body**. It is also important that **nutrients** from foods such as coconut oil, grass-fed meats, seafood, bone broth and organic vegetables restore the ratio of **calcium** and **phosphorus** in the **blood** and enable ***minerals*** to bond to **teeth**.

Clear ***traumas*** and painful ***experiences*** of cutting teeth as a baby, wiggling loose **teeth** and losing milk teeth and any pain ***associated*** with it. **Cavities** in the **teeth** are often referred from **cavities** in the **body** and from trying to relax oneself out of **physical,** *mental* and *emotional* pain. Strengthen the **oral cavity** to other openings in the **physical body**, the **ears, nose, eyes, anus, vagina**, and to **organs** such as the **lungs, bladder, uterus, small** and **large intestine**.

DENTAL PROCEDURES

Celebrities frequently turn to cosmetic surgery to straighten, align and brighten their **teeth** for a megawatt smile. Now these procedures are more readily available for the general public. It was no different in the golden age of Hollywood when the all-powerful studios had a certain expectation of beauty that included hollow **cheeks** and slimmer faces. For instance, removing the **back molars** creates the illusion of striking **cheekbones**.

Over the years I have worked with several clients who were teenagers in the forties and fifties and suffered from the trickle-down effects of Hollywood when they were encouraged and in some cases forced to have all their **teeth** extracted so that they would have perfect **teeth** in the form of **dentures**. They often suffered severe *trauma*, *shock* and *horror* as a result.

Mercury is a powerful **neurotoxin** and at certain levels can cause **neurological** illnesses and *mental disorders*, yet it has been used for over one hundred and fifty years in **amalgam fillings** along with a combination of **silver**, **tin** and **copper**. Grinding **teeth**, chewing gum and drinking carbonated drinks can lead to increases of **mercury** levels within the **body**.

Clear any weaknesses to *unreliable information*, *tactics*, and *misrepresentation* of **information**. If you have **mercury fillings** strengthen yourself to it and other **metals** used in combination with each other. Spin out any *miasmas* of **heavy metals** from other *existences*, *time* and *space* to *black wholes*, *existences* and *dimensions in space-time*. Strengthen the *negative electro-magnetic charge* and *negative ions*. *EU ... TACTICS, Pg. 494*

Teeth are dynamic, living **organs** and share *associations* with other **organs** in the **body**. Check for any referred weaknesses to and from other **organs**, blocks in the **meridians**, the **endocrine system**, **vertebrae**, **muscles** and **nerves**.

The need for **crowns** often come up as "royal experiences" and *spiritual experiences* of wanting to "be crowned." Strengthen all **fillings**, **crowns**, **implants**, **bridges**, **root canals**, etc., to integrate with the natural components of the **teeth** and delete any weaknesses around **ETs**, **experimentation**, **heavy metals**, etc.

THE "GOOD NEWS" IS:

In **social media**, **advertisements**, etc., a beautiful smile is equated with sex appeal and perceived as a positive *emotion*; however, there are many cultures that *perceive* smiling as an unwelcome *negative expression*. Smiling can also be perceived as shallow, dishonest, contemptuous, invasive, or as a means of covering up pain or embarrassment.

THE "BAD NEWS" IS:

Teeth are an indicator of **financial *wealth*** and the ability to afford **dental work**, yet one of the leading causes for loss of teeth is previous **dental procedures**.

NUGGET OF WIZDOM FROM THE VECTOR

DENTISTS HAVE ONE OF THE HIGHEST RATES OF SUICIDE, NEXT TO DOCTORS AND VETERINARIANS. THEY TEND TO ATTRACT PATIENTS WHO HAVE KARMA WITH THEM. BEFORE AGREEING TO ANY DENTAL PROCEDURE MAKE SURE YOU ARE ENERGETICALLY STRONG TO IT AND HAVE CLEARED THE ACCUMULATED AND ASSOCIATED KARMA BETWEEN YOURSELF AND YOUR DENTIST, THE DENTIST'S OTHER PATIENTS, ASSISTANTS, RECEPTIONISTS, TECHNICIANS FOR YOURSELF, YOUR ANCESTORS AND DESCENDANTS.

DESIRE

Desire is an intense *feeling* of *wanting* or *wishing* for someone or for something to happen. The problem with having **wishes** is that it keeps people in the *wishing loop*. People **wish** for things that they don't have or they wouldn't be *wishing* for them, whereas **intent** is having an aim or **purpose** that a person plans to achieve.

Many people have a *desire* to enjoy the luxuries that life has to offer in our third dimensional world. It is natural for people to enjoy beautiful things and beautiful people, but this desire often becomes complicated by the *criticisms* about what beauty is, and *judgements* around the amount of beauty that any one individual *deserves*. Today's **society** encourages a **competitive environment** based on *accumulations* of material possessions where *wants* are encouraged to *stimulate* a **need** to compete for the spoils. *Authentic desires* are often left in the dust as people are hot in pursuit of prestigious **careers**, *relationships*, **homes**, **vehicles**, etc. This lack of authenticity creates an *imbalance* in people as they focus on the *false obligations* of life and completely ignore other *aspects* of their *whole being*. At the other extreme, some people *deny* their *desire* to be surrounded by beautiful things, as if *desire* is a dirty word and the *want* for material possessions, a selfish **need**.

You are a multifaceted being operating on multi-dimensional levels of *existences* in *parallel universes* and different *times* and *space*. Your **needs** are very simple and few on this third dimensional plane. You

need water, oxygen, basic nutrients, shelter and **warmth** to survive unless you are a breatharian in which case, **shelter** and **air** will do. It is natural for humans to have *wants* and **needs** that *expand* and *accelerate* along with the universe. It is only when the hunt for acquisition of "property" becomes more important than quality of life that the line between *wants* and **needs** becomes blurred. When you are *neutral*, you are better able to say yes to *authentic desires* and more likely to receive the best the universe has to offer. This is the *balance* of **give** and **take**. *EU ... GIVE AND TAKE, Pg. 266*

The vast majority of humanity consistently confuses *wants* with **needs** on a regular basis. For example, people don't **NEED** a cup of coffee, those designer jeans, those high heels, that vacation …these are all *wants*. When people make them a **need** they give them too much importance and instantly *sabotage* their chances of easily attracting them their way.

Common limiting situations are:

GETTING WHAT YOU *WANT* AND NOT *WANTING* IT

Many people have experienced this when they were duped by marketing, especially marketing geared for children to become consumers during the Christmas shopping season, romance for Valentine's Day and other holidays and birthdays. They get what they *wanted*, but it is not as much fun or as satisfying as the advertisements led a person to *believe*.

NOT GETTING WHAT YOU *WANT* AND STILL *WANTING* IT

Another variation of the *disappointment experienced* by children and the *anxiety* created for parents to give children what they *want* at all costs, no matter how high the price, is referred to as "helicopter parenting."

GETTING WHAT YOU *WANT* AND STILL *WANTING* IT

Sometimes people do get what they **want**, but then are unable to allow themselves to fully enjoy it because their *fear* of *losing* it, overrides their joy of having it.

NOT GETTING WHAT YOU *WANT* AND NOT *WANTING* IT

If this experience is *neutral*, it is a strong place to be; however, if people are *suppressing* underlying weaknesses and *lying* to themselves when they see others getting what they *want* and *denying* that they *want* it too, that can lead to a lot more of not getting what they really *want*.

Identify if you are weak to:

NEEDING WHAT YOU *WANT* AND NOT *WANTING* IT.

An example of this is the **need** to pass grade twelve to continue onto college, technical school or university, The student *wants* to move toward higher education; but is not strong to high school, so consequently sabotages the **far goal** by failing to show up for classes. When people fail to take consistent steps of *action* in the *present* for their *immediate future* (high school), they are unable to meet the requirements for their *intermediate future* (college, university, trade school, etc.) and *sabotage* their **ultimate goals** in the *far future*.

NEEDING WHAT YOU *WANT* AND *WANTING* IT BADLY

When people are not *neutral* to not getting what they **need** to move forward in their careers, purpose, health, fitness, education, that special relationship, etc., they may voice their *frustration* by saying, "I *want* it so badly!" The very importance they assign to the goal creates a **need** that becomes difficult to achieve because they have made it so important. In retrospect, when people say that they *want* something "badly," and they don't receive it, they actually do get what they asked for.

NOT **NEEDING** WHAT YOU *WANT* AND **NEEDING** IT ANYWAY

This is when people are putting their time, energy and effort where it is **not needed** because of their *wants*. An example of this would be using rent money to purchase "stuff," and ending up with nowhere to put the stuff because they have been evicted for not paying the rent.

THE "GOOD NEWS" IS:

Everything that is built or manufactured was once a *thought* that someone had a **desire** to bring into being on the third dimensional plane. Every individual can choose to support personal **desires** with his or her own energy to manifest *wants* and **needs**.

THE "BAD NEWS" IS:

Most people *sabotage* their *ability* to *produce* on the third dimensional plane because they are unaware that they are supporting undesirable situations and people in their lives with their own energy.

NUGGET OF WIZDOM FROM THE VECTOR

MANY "NEEDS" ARE "WANTS" THAT HAVE BEEN GIVEN TOO MUCH IMPORTANCE AND OFTEN ARISE FROM CULTURAL, RELIGIOUS AND ANCESTRAL THIRD PARTY NEEDS THAT HAVE NOTHING TO DO WITH A GIVEN INDIVIDUAL'S AUTHENTIC DESIRES. TO BE NEUTRAL TO WHAT YOU WANT AND NEED IS TO HAVE MASTERY OVER YOUR LIFE.

DETOX

The physical body files information in the **CNS** about everything that has ever happened to a person, including **pain**, real or imagined. As people go through life they *accumulate* **toxins, poisons, waste products**, etc. In this age where many people are eating **processed** and **genetically modified foods** laden with **dyes, pesticides, chemicals** and **poisons**, it is essential that all components of the **lymphatic system** are working at maximum efficiency to clear **waste** and prevent *stagnation* in the **CNS**. *EU ... LYMPHATIC SYSTEM, Pg. 320*

Although the **liver, kidneys, bladder** and **colon** are not officially considered part of the **lymphatic system** they play an integral role in *elimination* for the **body**. *EU ... COLON FITNESS, Pg. 149*

LIVER

The **liver** is a triangular shaped **organ** that is located across the **abdominal cavity**, just under the **diaphragm**, with the base of the triangle situated on the **right** side of the **body** just above the **right kidney**. The **liver** is encapsulated by **connective tissue** and supported by the **peritoneum** of the **abdominal cavity**.

The **coronary ligament** connects the upper center of the **liver,** and the **left** and **right triangular ligaments** connect the upper sides of the **left** and **right** lobes to the **diaphragm**. The **falciform ligament** runs below the **diaphragm** across the front of the **liver** to just below it to form the **round ligament** of the **liver** to the **umbilicus**, a portion of the **umbilical vein** left over from **fetal** development.

Four **lobes** make up the **liver**. The **right lobe** is five or six times larger in size than the **left lobe**, separated by the **falciform ligament**. The **caudate lobe** extends from the back of the **right lobe** to wrap around the **vena cava** that is situated just below it. The **quadrate lobe**, just below the **caudate lobe**, extends from the back of the **right lobe** to wrap around the **gallbladder**.

The **liver** plays an active role in the process of **digestion** through the production of **bile, metabolism, detoxification, storage** of **proteins, blood plasma** and **immunity**. It is also responsible for metabolizing **carbohydrates, lipids** and **proteins. Bile** is a mixture of water, bile salts, cholesterol and a pigment called **bilirubin. Bilirubin** is a product of the **liver's** digestion of deteriorating **red blood cells** and i**ron-containing cells** that cannot be recycled by the **body**. The **cells** are converted into the pigment **bilirubin**, which turns **bile** into a greenish color. Later in the process, **intestinal bacteria** process **bilirubin** into a brown pigment **stercobilin**, a **chemical** responsible for making **feces** brown in color.

METABOLISM

The **biliary tree** is a branched structure that carries **bile** through the **liver** and **gallbladder** to the **digestive system**. The tubes that transport the **bile** produced by **liver cells** are called **bile ducts**. They drain into microscopic **canals** called **bile canaliculi**, joining together to form the left and right **hepatic ducts** that carry bile from the **right** and **left lobes**, leading to the **common hepatic duct** and eventually the **common bile duct** that carries **bile** to the **duodenum** in the **small intestine**.

The **hepatic portal veins** collect **blood** from the **spleen, stomach, pancreas, gallbladder** and **intestines** via **capillaries** leading to the **liver**, and they distribute it where it is needed in the **body**. The **blood** that leaves the **liver** pools in **hepatic veins** leading to the **vena cava** to be returned to the **heart**.

There are approximately one hundred thousand small hexagonal shaped **lobules** inside the **liver**. Each has a **central vein** that is surrounded by six **hepatic portal veins** and six **hepatic arteries**. They are all connected by **sinusoids** that extend from the **portal veins** and **arteries** like spokes on a wheel.

Each **sinusoid** is made up of **Kupffer cells** and **hepatocytes. Kupffer cells** are **macrophages** responsible for breaking down **red blood cells** that are deteriorating and passing them on to the **hepatocytes. Kupffer cells** efficiently devour **bacteria, fungi, parasites,** dying **blood cells, cellular** and **parasitic waste. Hepatocytes** are **epithelial cells** that line the **sinusoids**. They are responsible for the majority of the **liver's** functions including **metabolism** of all the **blood** leaving the **digestive system** through the **hepatic portal vein**, storage and **bile** production. Tiny **vessels** called **canaliculi** run parallel to the **sinusoids** on the opposite side of the **hepatocytes** that drain into the **bile ducts**.

Once the **bile** is produced by the **hepatocytes**, it passes through the **bile ducts** to the **gallbladder**. When foods containing fats reach the **duodenum** it activates a **hormone** called **cholecystokinin** stimulating the **gallbladder** to release **bile**. The **bile** then travels to the **duodenum** to emulsify the **fat**, turning large clumps into smaller pieces that are easier to digest.

Hepatocytes also metabolize **hemoglobin**, a **red protein** that is responsible for transportation of **oxygen** and used as an energy source for the **body**.

DIGESTION

The **digestive system** breaks down **carbohydrates** into **monosaccharide glucose** that is a primary *energy source* for **cells**. The consistent *absorption* and *release* of **glucose** by the **hepatocytes** is an important function of **homeostasis** of the body. **Fatty acids** are also absorbed by **hepatocytes** and **metabolized** to produce *energy* in the form of **ATP**. Another **lipid** called **glycerol** is converted into **glucose** and other **lipids** such as **cholesterol**, **phospholipids** and **lipoproteins** are also produced by **hepatocytes**. **Hepatocytes** convert **amino acids** into **ammonia** and eventually **urea** to be excreted in **urine** as a waste product of **digestion**.

DETOXIFICATION

Enzymes in the **hepatocytes** are also responsible for monitoring the contents of **blood** for toxins such as **alcohol** and **pharmaceuticals** after the **blood** has passed through the **hepatic portal**. In addition they remove **hormones** produced by **glands** in the body that upset the delicate balance required for **homeostasis**.

STORAGE

The **liver** provides **storage** of many primary **nutrients**, **vitamins** and **minerals**. The **hormone insulin** stimulates **hepatocytes** to transport **glucose** and store it as **polysaccharides glycogen**. It also absorbs and stores **fatty acids** from **digested triglycerides**, **vitamins A**, **D**, **E**, **K** and **B12**, **copper** and **iron**. The storage of these **nutrients** provides consistency in the maintenance of **blood glucose**.

PRODUCTION

There are several crucial components of **protein** in **blood plasma**, including **prothrombin** and **fibrinogen** that are factors in **coagulation** and **blood clotting**, as well as **albumins** that are responsible for even **osmotic** pressure to support the **cells** in maintaining consistent levels of **water** within the **cells**, regardless of inconsistencies in other **body fluids**.

KIDNEYS

The **kidneys** are two bean shaped **organs**, each about the size of a **fist**, located in the **middle** of the **back** just below the **ribcage** on either side of the **spine** behind the wall of the **abdominal cavity**. **Kidneys** play a vital role in removing **waste**, regulating **blood composition** and **pressure**, the concentration of *ions*, **hydration**, **alkalinity** and *stimulating* red **blood cell** *production*. As much as one third of **blood** leaving the **heart** travels through the **kidneys** to be filtered before flowing to the rest of the **body**.

Three layers of **tissue** surround the **kidneys**: the **renal fascia, adipose capsule** and **renal capsule**. The **renal fascia** is the thin outer layer of **connective tissue** that fastens the **kidneys** and **adrenal gland** to the surrounding structures. In the middle is a layer of fat **tissue** called the **adipose capsule** that cushions the **kidneys**, and the innermost **membrane** called the **renal capsule** that protects them from *infection.*

The bean-shaped **kidneys** have a convex and concave surface. Inside each **kidney** there are three major areas, the **renal cortex**, the **renal medulla** and the **renal sinus**.

The **renal cortex** is the outer layer of the convex side. Next to it is the **renal medulla,** made up of **striped fibers** in cone-shaped regions called **renal pyramids**. **Renal papillae**, the peaks of these pyramids face inward towards the **renal sinus** and are lined up between **renal columns**. Next to the **renal medulla** is the **renal sinus,** a dip on the concave (inner) side where the **renal artery** enters and the **renal vein** and **ureter** exit, called the **renal hilum**.

The **renal artery** delivers a rich **blood supply** through a network of **segmental, interlobar** and **arcuate arteries** that become progressively smaller, like branches of a tree, passing between the **renal pyramids** and penetrating the **renal cortex** to enter the filtering mechanisms called **glomeruli** of the **nephrons**. **Blood** leaving the **nephrons** also follows the same path back to the **renal artery**.

Autonomic nerve fibers follow the network of arteries to regulate blood volume. Sympathetic nerve fibers constrict the arterioles located at the end of the arcuate arteries, decreasing the volume of urine output, while parasympathetic nerve fibers increase output of urine by dilating the arterioles.

In the renal cortex and renal medulla there are millions of tiny thin tubes called nephrons. Each tube is closed at one end with two twisted regions that have a hairpin loop between them called the loop of henie. The bowman's capsule is the closed end at the beginning of the nephron located in the renal cortex. The first twisted region after the bowman's capsule, called the proximal tubule leads to the loop of henie. The hairpin turn starts in the renal cortex, extends into the renal medulla and bends back down into the renal cortex to the second twisted region called the distal tubule leading to a straight portion at the open end of the nephron ending in a collecting duct.

The kidneys *filter* one fifth of the plasma and non-cellular waste from the blood inside the nephron, *reabsorb* nutrients from the inner tube of the nephron and *secrete* waste from the blood into the nephron. Strengthen the nephrons to the blood to facilitate *filtration*, *reabsorption* and *secretion* to optimum potential. To regulate the composition of the blood, strengthen *negative ions,* water volume and pH *regeneration* of the blood to consistency. Any fluid and *ions* that are not *reabsorbed* by the nephron is directed to the urine to be passed out of the body.

When a person has *memory problems* or other brain related disorders, it is often referred to the kidneys. Toxins that *accumulate* in the kidneys are not all physical. *Toxic thoughts* of *criticism*, *disappointment*, *failure* and *shame* tend to *accumulate* in the kidneys, leading to *dissatisfaction*.

BLADDER

Urine that is *produced* in the kidneys is passed through the ureters to the urinary bladder to be stored before passing to the urethra and exiting the body several times a day. The bladder is round in shape and its size depends on the person and circumstances. It is located in the pelvic cavity in front of the rectum and above the reproductive organs. The bladder is smaller in females because it shares space with the uterus.

The bladder is made up of several layers of tissue. The first layer, from the inside out is the mucosa. It is lined with transitional epithelial tissue that has many tiny wrinkles known as rugae which allow it to stretch and *accommodate* large amounts of urine. The second layer is called the submucosa. It is connective and nerve tissue with blood vessels that support the surrounding **tissues.** Next is a layer of **visceral muscles** called the **detrusor muscle** or **muscularis** that contracts during **urination** and also forms the **internal urethral sphincter**, a ring of **muscle** that surrounds the **urethral opening** that opens and closes to hold **urine** in and to expel it to the **urethra**. The **external urethral sphincter** *contracts* to help control and delay **urination**.

The outermost layer of the upper **bladder** is made of **serous membrane** that is part of the **membrane** of the **peritoneum** and **abdominopelvic cavity** which protects it from *friction* between the other **organs**. Next is the **adventitia**, a layer of **connective tissue** that has a loose connection with the surrounding **tissues** of the **pelvic cavity**.

It is important that the structures and functions of the **liver**, **kidneys**, **bladder** and **colon** are at optimum function within themselves and also in sync with each other and the **CNS**. **Waste** that exits the **body** is both **physical** and *non-physical*. *Accumulations* of **poisons**, **toxins**, **medications**, **chemicals**, **radiation** along with associated *fears*, *limiting beliefs*, *expectations*, *mental*, *emotional*, *psychological*, *karmic*, *psychic* and *spiritual toxins* are all released through the **physical body**. **EU … EXIT PORTALS, Pg. 220*

The **elimination systems** of the **intrinsic body** are also played out at the **microscopic** level within the **cells**. **EU … CELL-EBRATION, Pg. 111*

THE "GOOD NEWS" IS:

Black wholes/white wholes can be created throughout the **lymphatic system** to release harmful energies and spin in **oxygen**, **nutrition**, **trace carbon**, **nitrogen**, **hydrogen** and the perfect **structure** of the universe into the **cells** of your **body**.

THE "BAD NEWS" IS:

Common symptoms of **lymphatic blockage** and inefficiencies in the **elimination systems** are *aches*, **fever**, full body *dis-comfort* and multiple areas of **pain**. These are often blamed on the "flu." Unfortunately the so-called solutions for the "flu" often make the symptoms worse.

NUGGET OF WIZDOM FROM THE VECTOR

AVOID CONFUSION IN THE CNS THROUGH DETOXIFICATION OF THE ELIMINATION SYSTEMS OF THE BODY TO KEEP IT PAIN FREE.

DIABETES

Diabetes mellitus is a **disease** of the **metabolic** process causing **high blood glucose** (**sugar**) from inadequate **insulin** *production* or poor *utilization* of **insulin** in the **cells**. **Insulin** is a **hormone** *produced* in the **pancreas** from the **sugar** (**glucose**) in **carbohydrates**; it regulates **blood sugar** levels in the **body**. **Fruit, milk, potatoes, bread** and **rice** are the biggest source of **carbohydrates** in most diets. **Hyperglycemia** occurs when the **blood sugar** levels are too high, and **hypoglycemia** occurs when they are too low.

Normally, the **body** breaks down **carbohydrates** into **glucose** and converts it into energy for the **cells**. If the **insulin** levels are not working the **body** breaks down stored **fat** instead. The *metabolization* of **fat** raises **ketone** levels that can lead to a condition called **ketosis**. **Ketones** are made up of **acetone, acetoacetates** or **beta-hydroxybutyric acid**. Very high **ketone** levels can be toxic because they make the **blood acidic** which can damage the **kidneys** and **liver**. The **body** will do its best to lower **acetone** levels by *breathing* it out, which causes the **breath** to smell fruity and sweet and by passing it through **urine**.

Glucose cannot go directly into the **cells** unless **beta cells** in the **pancreas** release **insulin** into the **bloodstream**. If there is more **glucose** in the body than it needs, **insulin** helps to store it in the **liver** and releases it when **blood sugar** levels dip between meals and during **physical** *activity* to keep **blood sugar** levels even. Manufactured **insulin** given by syringe, an injection pen, insulin pump or tablets, is used to treat **diabetes**.

There are three types of **diabetes**: **type 1** which accounts for a small portion of **diabetes** cases, **type 2**, and **gestational diabetes** in pregnant women. In **Type 1 diabetes**, the **body** does not *produce* **insulin**, and the condition commonly *affects* people early in life, particularly during adolescence or in early adulthood. While there is no known cure for **type 1 diabetes**, **insulin injections** and **diet** can manage it. Clear any *miasmas, spiritual experiences* and *karmic spaces* of living a life of *struggle,* as well as issues with becoming a teenager or adult for the person dealing with **diabetes**, as well as **descendants** and **ancestors** up and down the family line.

Type 2 diabetes is the most common type of **diabetes**. It is a progressive **disease**, where the body is able to either *produce* **insulin**, but not enough for proper function, or the **cells** in the **body** have **insulin resistance** and do not react to it as they should. Overweight and obese people as well as people who have a lot of **visceral fat** are more at risk. Some people are able to control the symptoms of **type 2 diabetes** by losing weight, following a diet low in **sugars**, and getting enough exercise to regulate their **glucose** levels. If this is not effective, they usually end up taking **insulin** in tablet form. People over the age of forty or with a close relative who has had **type 2 diabetes** are more likely to develop the **disease**, as are people of Middle Eastern, African or South Asian descent. Low **testosterone** levels in men also increase risk.

There are often weaknesses of *self-sabotage* and "losing" *experiences* that have a *negative effect* on **absorption** and **assimilation** of life events. There must be enough *tension* throughout the **body** to keep all **systems** functioning with optimum *fitness*. Clear any *karmas* and other weaknesses of *past life* and *present life* events with Middle Eastern, African or South Asian countries. This can also be reflected on a global scale when countries are at war.

Gestational diabetes occurs during pregnancy and can cause complications, one of which is having an overly large baby. Generally women who are overweight or who gain an excessive amount of weight in the first trimester are more at risk, as are women who have a family history of **diabetes** or have had **gestational diabetes** in an earlier pregnancy. In most cases once the pregnancy ends, so does the **diabetes**; however, if the underlying weaknesses are not addressed, it leaves women more susceptible for contracting **diabetes** later in life.

To strengthen the *relationship* between the **mother** and **baby**, delete any weaknesses around past pregnancies and child birth and any *karmas* between the **baby**, **siblings** and extended **family**.

GUT FLORA AND DIABETES

There is a difference between the **intestinal bacteria** in slim people and in people who are overweight. Slim people tend to have higher amounts of **beneficial bacteria** and heavier people tend to have more **pathogenic bacteria** which causes *inflammation* and *storage* of **fat** in the **cells**.

Diabetics often have **staph bacteria** present in foot ulcers and in their **gut flora,** along with **E.coli bacteria** that *produce* lipopolysaccharides (**LPS**). Normally, **LPS** are cleared by the **liver**, unless they are amplified by **inflammatory cytokines**. **Cytokines** are small **proteins** that are released through **cell receptors** that affect the behavior of other **cells**, called **cell signaling**. The average person is exposed to factors that destroy **beneficial bacteria** through prescribed **antibiotics** and by eating animals that are routinely dosed with **antibiotics** to keep them alive in the **contaminated environment** of factory farming. Other factors that destroy beneficial **gut flora** are **antibacterial soaps, chlorinated water, agricultural chemicals**

and **pollution**. People with **diabetes** often experience intense thirst and hunger, increased urination, unusual weight loss, fatigue, tingling and *numbness* in the **hands** and **feet**, **cuts** and **bruises** that do not *heal* with ease and **impotence** in males. Badly managed **diabetes** can also lead to **problems** with the **eyes**, **feet**, **heart**, **high blood pressure**, **stroke**, **hearing loss**, **gum problems**, **kidney disease** and **coma**.

There are many factors to consider when you are energetically shifting people who have been diagnosed with **diabetes**. Shifting the **physical** components must be done frequently and consistently to maintain *homeostasis* of all the **systems** involved in the **body**. It is helpful if there is a cooperative *effort* from the person to coordinate diet and exercise and optimize the energetic shifts to strengthen the **physical** weaknesses.

To maximize *production* and *utilization* of **insulin,** strengthen the relationship of **glucose** and **carbohydrates**, **CNS**, **PNS**, **muscles**, **organs** and the **pancreas**. Delete any weaknesses between the **liver**, **pancreas**, **adrenal glands**, **alpha** and **beta cells**. Clear **dead cells**, **cellular waste**, *infections* and **parasitic** *infestations* to speed up *communication* between the **CNS** and the parts of the **body** that are involved. Strengthen the **islets of langerhans** in the **pancreas** to the **CNS**, **PNS**, **blood chemistry**, **bio-resonance**, **lymphatic system** and **circulatory system**. *EU ... ENDOCRINE GLANDS, Pg. 207

Strengthen the **gut flora** on a **cellular level** and clear any *karmas* with slavery of Africans in the production of **sugar cane**, *karmas* with **abused animals**, as well as with **pharmaceutical companies** and other **corporate institutions** that receive **financial** benefit from products used to control **diabetes**.

THE "GOOD NEWS" IS:

There are many ways that people can avoid **diabetes** and even turn it around by changes in life style such as exercise, avoiding **soft drinks** and other **sugary drinks**, as well as **factory farmed meat** that has been found to have a direct link to destroying beneficial bacteria in the gut.

THE "BAD NEWS" IS:

Most people assume that **diabetes** is a **problem** of ingestion of **sugar** and are not aware of the link to **beneficial bacteria** in the gut. They routinely wash with **antibiotic soaps** and ingest **factory-farmed meat** and **dairy products** laden with **antibiotics** and other drugs without being *aware* of the added risk to their *health*.

NUGGET OF WIZDOM FROM THE VECTOR

BESIDES THE PHYSICAL COMPLICATIONS, THERE ARE MANY UNDERLYING NON-PHYSICAL WEAKNESSES TO CONSIDER WHEN CLEARING DIABETES. ON AN EMOTIONAL LEVEL THERE ARE OFTEN WEAKNESSES TO THE SWEETNESS OF LIFE AS OPPOSED TO THE BITTERNESS OF EXISTENCE.

DIGESTIVE SYSTEM

The **digestive system** is a group of **organs** that work together to convert food and basic **nutrients** into energy to feed the whole **body**. The **digestive system** consists of several components in the **gastrointestinal tract**, sometimes referred to as the **alimentary canal**. **The gastrointestinal tract** (**GI**) is made up of the **oral cavity**, **pharynx**, **esophagus**, **stomach** and the **small intestines**. It is helpful to have an understanding of the physicality of the **digestive system** and an understanding of the eating process. *EU ... EATING, Pg. 202*

ESOPHAGUS

The **esophagus** is a muscular tube, about nine to ten inches long and one inch wide, starting at the **pharynx,** that travels through the **esophageal hiatus** of the **diaphragm** to the **stomach**. There are two **sphincters** at either end of the **esophagus**.

At the top of the **esophagus** is the **esophageal sphincter**, keeping it closed where it meets the **pharynx**, opening only in the process of *swallowing* to permit food to pass through. At the bottom end of the **esophagus**, the **lower esophageal sphincter** closes to prevent **chyme** (partially digested food) and **stomach acid** from coming back up the **esophagus**.

ACID REFLUX

Acid reflux is also known as **heartburn** and **acid indigestion**. If the **lower esophageal sphincter** is lacking the *fitness* to snap back into place, it allows some **chyme** to enter the **esophagus** causing a *burning pain* in the **chest**. On a **physical** level, strengthen the **CNS** to every **sphincter** involved in the eating process, the **orbicularis oris** (**the kissing muscle**), **esophageal sphincter, pyloric sphincter** and the **anus.** Many weaknesses in the **esophagus** are referred to the **large intestine** on a **physical** level and from *emotions* on a *non-physical* level. If a person feels he or she is "swallowing crap," "kissing ass," "putting up with shit," etc., there is a *suppression* of *anger* that can no longer be held down so the *bitterness* and *acidity* come up the **throat**.

STOMACH

The **stomach** is a rounded, hollow **organ** that is located on the left side of the **abdominal cavity** just under the **diaphragm**. Its main function is the **mechanical digestion** of food. The **stomach walls** and **chemical digestion** involve **molecules** that are divided into smaller **molecules**, Once a meal has been ingested the **stomach** stores the food for about one to two hours before turning the digested food into **chyme**, a process that is completed in the **small intestine, pancreas, gallbladder** and **liver**.

The **esophagus** connects to the **stomach** at the **cardia**, a narrow, tubular area that contains the **esophageal sphincter** and opens up to the body of the **stomach**. At the front is a dome-shaped region called the **fundus** and at the back a funnel shaped region called the **pylorus**. The **pylorus** connects the **stomach** to the **duodenum** and also contains the **pyloric sphincter**, which controls the flow of partially digested food out of the **stomach** into the **duodenum**. The inside of the **stomach** is lined with a layer of **gastric folds**, called **rugae** that grip and move food during digestion, allowing the **stomach** to *stretch* and *accommodate* large meals.

GASTROINTESTINAL TRACT

The walls of the **stomach** are made up of four layers of **tissue** that are consistent with the structure of the rest of the **gastrointestinal tract**.

MUCOSA

The innermost layer of the stomach is a **mucous** membrane called **mucosa**, made up of **epithelial tissue** with **microvilli** on its surface to improve the *absorption* of **nutrients** and to protect the **intestinal wall** from *friction* and acidic **chyme**. The **epithelial tissues** have **gastric pits** with many **exocrine cells** that secrete **digestive enzymes** and **hydrochloric acid** into the hollow region of the **stomach** called the **lumen. Hydrochloric acid** kills **pathogenic bacteria** that are naturally found in food. **Gastric lipase** splits **triglyceride fats** into **fatty acids** and **diglycerides**, and **pepsin** breaks **proteins** into smaller **amino acids**. The **mucous** protects the **stomach** from these **secretions** by producing **bicarbonate ions** that neutralize the **pH** of the **stomach acid**. **Glycoprotein** is an **intrinsic factor** that binds to **vitamin B12**, an essential nutrient for formation of **red blood cells**, allowing **vitamin B12** to be *absorbed* by the **small intestine**.

SUBMUCOSA

Surrounding the **mucosae**, is a layer of **connective tissue** with many **blood vessels** and **nerves** that support the other **tissue** layers and provides **nutrients** to the **stomach wall**.

MUSCULARIS

The **muscularis mucosae** is comprised of three layers of **smooth muscles** that move in three different directions. It surrounds the **mucosa**, allowing it to form folds to contact the contents of the **stomach**.

SEROSA

The outermost layer of the **stomach** is the **serosa** made up of a thin **serous membrane** of **squamous epithelial tissue** and **areolar connective tissue**, which together create a smooth, wet surface to protect the **stomach** from *friction* as it *expands* and *contracts*.

HORMONAL INFLUENCES

The **stomach** is under the influence of several **hormones** that regulate the *production* of **stomach acid** and the *release* of food into the **duodenum**.

GASTRIN

G-cells in the **gastric pits** *receive* signals form the **vagus nerve** and **amino acids** from digested **proteins** to release the **hormone gastrin** into the **bloodstream**. **Gastrin** stimulates stronger *contractions* of the **stomach** and causes the **pyloric sphincter** to open for food to enter the **duodenum**. It also binds to **receptor cells** in the **pancreas** and **gallbladder** to increase the secretion of **bile** and **gastric juice** for digestion.

CHOLECYSTOKININ (CCK)

Cholecystokinin (CCK) is produced by the **mucosa** of the **duodenum** and stimulates the **pyloric sphincter** to *contact* when food that is rich in **protein** and **fats** needs more time to be digested in the **stomach**. It also gives the **pancreas** and **gallbladder** time to release **enzymes** and **bile** into the **duodenum** to aid in digestion.

SECRETIN

Secretin is a **hormone** that is stimulated to protect the **intestines** from the acidity of **chyme**. It is released into the **bloodstream** via the **mucosa** of the **duodenum** to stimulate the **pancreas** to produce **bicarbonate ions** that neutralize the **acidity**.

GREHLIN

Grehlin Is a **peptide** that is produced by **grehlin cells** that act as a **neuropeptide** in the **CNS**. It is an important factor in regulating hunger and what many refer to as the **metabolism** (the distribution and rate of the use of energy). It is secreted when the **hypothalamus** is stimulated to register hunger caused by an empty **stomach**, thus creating hunger pangs. It also regulates "reward perception" through the **ventral tegmental area** of the **brain** that plays an important role in addiction.

LEPTIN

Leptin is a **protein** produced in the **adipose tissue** that you can think of as a *metabolic* **organ** which regulates **waste products** in the **body**. It is the **CEO** of **hormones** for weight and stress reduction. It is released from the **adipose tissue** through the **blood** to the **hypothalamus** and other parts of the **brain** for the purpose of regulating **appetite**, food **intake** and **stored** energy under a wide range of **environmental** conditions.

The amount released depends on how efficient the *metabolism* is, and the amount of **fuel** that is stored. The *sub-conscious mind* cannot tell how much fuel a person has, so it relies on the "leptin gauge" just as people rely on the gas gauge in their car without looking in the tank to see if the gas is really there.

The "full signal" controls the **body's** ability to manufacture **leptin** at high levels for a fast *metabolism*. Sometimes the **valve** is sticky, creating a need to eat compulsively because of mixed signals from the **environment**. The signals get crossed, thus creating panic because the **body** only knows that it is getting messages that it is "running on empty." If there is no food in sight, it is unaware that there will be a meal soon.

Put *tension* into your **spine** and flip the *energetic switch* for **leptin** to "on," with the intention of it being *distributed* exactly where it needs to go in your **brain** to *regulate* your **appetite** and quiet the battle of wills of what to eat and not to eat.

PYY

PYY is a hormone excreted as a **peptide** from the **ileum**, typically about twenty minutes after a person begins eating. Its purpose is to cause a person to feel full, thereby preventing over-eating.

SMALL INTESTINE

The **small intestine** has three major parts, the **duodenum**, **jejunum**, and the **ileum**. It is about ten feet long and extends from the **stomach** to the **large intestine**.

DUODENUM

The **duodenum** is a C-shaped part of the **small intestine** that is about twelve inches long, located below and to the right of the **stomach.** Once **chyme** passes through the **pyloric sphincter** it enters the **duodenum** and mixes with **bile** from the **gallbladder** and **liver**, as well as with **pancreatic juice** from the **pancreas** to neutralize the **acidity**, **emulsify lipids** and break the **chyme** into basic **nutrients**. A small amount of **nutrients** is *absorbed* through the walls of the **duodenum**, but most *absorption* occurs in the **jejunum**.

JEJUNUM

The **jejunum** is an approximately eight feet long section in the middle of the **small intestine**, located between the **duodenum** and the **ileum**. Once the **chyme** has been thoroughly digested by the **duodenum**, it is ready to be *absorbed* and *assimilated* by the **mucosa** of the **jejunum**. The vast majority of **nutrients** are absorbed into the **bloodstream** by the time it leaves the **jejunum**.

ILEUM

Upon reaching the **ileum**, the **chyme** is given one last sweep for any traces of **nutrients** or **pathogens** before passing through the **ileocecal sphincter** and entering the **cecum** where the **chyme** mixes with **bacterial flora** to become **feces**. This is where **digestion** ends and the important process of *elimination* begins. If there are **problems** moving the **bowels, toxins** back up via the **mesenteric veins** and through the **hepatic portal vein** that drains into the **liver**. *EU ... COLON FITNESS, Pg. 149*

Non-physical complications of the **liver** are often caused by repressed *anger, frustration, envy* and *resentment* that *stagnate* its main function of allowing energy (**Ka** or **Qi**) to **flow** through the **body** smoothly and with ease. The interaction between the **kidneys** (**essence**) and the **liver** (**storage of blood**) are intimately connected with the **reproductive system** because their energetic channels cross in many places. **Anger** is the gift that keeps on giving, and holding on to **fear** from the old stories causes disruption in the **flow**.

GALLBLADDER

The **gallbladder** is used to store and recycle excess **bile** from the **small intestine** to be reused for the **digestion** of the next meal.

Gall bladder attacks are usually caused by **congestion** from **gallbladder stones** that get stuck in the **neck** of the **gallbladder** or in a **bile duct**. Many people who have "silent gallstones" are unaware of them because they do not feel any **pain** and do not require treatment; however, **gallstones** can be broken down energetically and spun out to **black wholes**.

PANCREAS

The **pancreas** is a large **gland** located below and behind the **stomach**; it secretes **digestive enzymes** into the **small intestine** to complete the **chemical digestion** of food. *EU ... ENDOCRINE GLANDS, Pg. 207*

THE "GOOD NEWS" IS:

Once the weaknesses in the **digestive system** are sorted out, it strengthens the **digestion**, not only of food, but of life, allowing for the **assimilation** and **absorption** of **physical**, **spiritual** knowledge and pleasures, as well as for the growth of the **soul**.

THE "BAD NEWS" IS:

The anatomy of the **digestive system** is very **sensitive** and complicated. On a **physical** level, these **sensitivities** can be to **food**, **hormones**, **structural** weaknesses, etc.; however, many of them are referred from other **physical parts** and **systems**. The complications from the **non-physical** element are also reflected in the many loops and turns of the **intestines**.

NUGGET OF WIZDOM FROM THE VECTOR

ALTHOUGH THE DIGESTIVE AND ELIMINATION SYSTEMS ARE OFTEN CONSIDERED AS ONE SYSTEM BY THE MAINSTREAM

MEDICAL COMMUNITY, IT IS IMPORTANT TO RECOGNIZE THAT THEY HAVE TWO OPPOSITE FUNCTIONS.

DIS-EASE

Our **bodies** are composed of hundreds of different **systems**, each with a job to do and an ideal *frequency* of its own. They combine to create a harmonious **environment**; however, different **organs** *resonate* with different *frequencies* on the *macrocosmic* and *microcosmic* levels, sometimes causing misunderstandings and creating discord within the **body**. The laws of attraction dictate that we magnetically *attract frequencies* that *resonate* with *frequencies* similar to our own. When people fight **disease,** they are fighting with themselves and *attracting* more *dis-ease.* The human **body** is designed to return to *homeostasis* with ease. You can see this in the speed with which a small cut or wound heals.

When people are faced with a **diagnosis** of **serious disease**, **prognosis** and **treatment** options, they have a lot to **think** about. The reasons for **illness** are varied at *root cause* and are rarely **physical**. Insisting that **illness** is a *health problem* confuses the *mind* and the **systems**, and creates an ongoing dilemma. *Confused thoughts* are really contradictions between *conscious intent* and faulty *belief systems*. Even though people **think** they want to stay *healthy* and *believe* they will get better, they may be emitting muddled signals that *attract* more **illness** and less *health* to themselves.

When a person is **diagnosed** with a specific **disease** and told the reasons they have it, but their condition still does not change for the better after taking steps of *action* based on that **diagnosis**, it means that that particular **information** is not applicable to changing the situation. It is likely that there is an underlying weakness that has not been addressed, and that it is likely to be **non-physical** or **referred** from another **part** of the **body**. Once the **leading weakness** is **identified** and the **blocks** are *shifted* it clears the path for the **systems** to begin operating with ease to support *health* from every angle.

The **systems** of the **body** are built to work together with *ease* and *efficiency*. If you ask people to identify when they first noticed an **illness** or *dis-ease*, they often will tell you that at the time it seemed like everything in their lives were coming together and things were going "so well." Many people have an underlying weakness to things being *too easy*, and that triggers and *attracts experiences* of things being *difficult* and *uneasy*. Another assumption that people make is that if they are faced with **serious disease**, they automatically have the **desire** to live. On a *conscious* level this is often true but the *sub-conscious* and *un-conscious mind* may not be one hundred percent congruent. People often have *spiritual experiences* of **dying young** or **dying** at specific **ages**, unresolved *negative experiences* of **illnesses**, **plagues**, *accidents*, **homicidal** and **suicidal** *thoughts*, etc., that *attract* **illnesses** and *dis-ease* so that they can be resolved.

On an *un-conscious* level **patients** may be resolving *accumulated* and *associated karma* with their **doctors** or sometimes **doctors**, with their **patients**. Some babies, young children and their parents who are faced with **serious illness** and **death** at such a young **age** are resolving this *karma* and other *karmic spaces*.

THE "GOOD NEWS" IS:

Health is an expression of your infinite potential. When it appears that there is a lack of *health*, there are often underlying weaknesses around **finances**, **youthfulness**, *purpose* and *fitness* to *live well*. Once these blocks are removed and *homeostasis* is supported, it is easy to *live well*.

THE "BAD NEWS" IS:

When people give too much importance to certain *aspects* of life while ignoring others, the **unevenness** and lack of *balance* often causes **problems** in the **functions** and **systems** of the **physical body**. *Conventional thinking* that *health* is something that people need to strive for implies that it is difficult to have.

NUGGET OF WIZDOM FROM THE VECTOR

MAKING HEALTH YOUR NUMBER ONE PRIORITY DOES NOT MAKE YOU HEALTHY. MANY PROBLEMS THAT SEEM TO BE ABOUT HEALTH ARISE FROM UN-HEALTHY THOUGHTS IN OTHER ASPECTS OF LIFE THAT HAVE BEEN IGNORED IN THE PURSUIT OF PERFECT HEALTH.

DIVORCE

Although there are slight variances in **divorce** rates across the globe, Sweden, USA, Australia, the United Kingdom and Canada all share the highest divorce rates in the industrialized world. Using Canadian statistics as a baseline, one **marriage** out of every two **marriages** ends in **divorce**. This does not include the break-up of **common-law unions** despite the increase in the number of people who are cohabiting and operating as families without taking **marriage *vows***.

The lowest risk of **divorce** is during the first year of **marriage** but then the risk of **divorce** builds and peaks around the **fourth anniversary**. A substantial number of people are **divorced** before their **fifteenth wedding anniversary**. The vast majority of **divorces** are initiated by women, who cite reasons that the *relationship* "ran out of steam," "they fell out of love," "communication breakdown," "unreasonable behavior," infidelity (an increasing number of which are online affairs), "mid-life crisis" and "financial issues." Half of the women who file for **divorce** report *emotional*, *mental* and **physical** abuse.

There are many *internal* and *external forces* that compel a person to decide to marry. Women have a tendency to make important life decisions around **marriage** and **having children** in *seven-year cycles*. It is common for women to marry and/or become pregnant and separate from *relationships* at the **ages** of **twenty-one, twenty-eight, thirty-five, forty-two, forty-nine**, etc. Previous generations were more likely to **marry young** as their *choices* were limited by societal *perceptions* of what a woman was "supposed to do." The "seven year itch" can be attributed to a *cycle* of *spiritual experiences* that come to the forefront whether people are consciously aware of them or not. These *collective energies* can be hidden in **cultural** upbringing, **religious** training, *karmic* ties, **educational** weaknesses and manipulative **tactics**. Since women are enjoying more and more **financial** freedom and family law has been changed to make **divorce** easier, they have more *choice* regarding their **marital status**; however, there still are many **cultures** in many countries that still "marry off" their offspring.

Most people convince themselves that they are getting **married** for **love**; however quite often the reasons are about *timing* and *circumstance*. Often women who feel their *biological clock* ticking and who have a strong urge to have children, "settle" rather than settle down. In other words, they *choose* a **man** to **father** their **children**, but who is not necessarily good "marriage material." Too many women labour under the false assumption that the two automatically go hand in hand. **Unplanned pregnancy** is still a common reason for women who feel they "have to" get married even though in today's **society** the pregnancies are not as hidden.

First marriages have a **fifty percent** risk of ending in **divorce** and the risk becomes greater with each successive **marriage** – about **seventy percent** for the **second marriage** and **eighty-five percent** for the **third attempt**. **Men** are more likely to **re-marry** than **women**, perhaps because **seventy-five percent** of **divorces** are initiated by **women**, and many **men** report that they were "taken by surprise" and did not see it coming. As **age** increases the chances of **remarriage** for **women** become lower while the chances of **cohabitation** for both **men** and **women** who are **divorced** become higher. Logically it would seem that people would learn from the first **marriage,** and the **second** or **third marriage** would be easier because of *experience*. However, it is more likely that any underlying weaknesses that have not been resolved in the first **marriage** *accumulate* with each subsequent **marriage**.

Couples with children have a slightly lower rate of **divorce** than childless couples. While figures for joint custody are on the rise, joint custody does not mean that the child spends fifty percent of the time with each parent. It means that both parents have an equal right to make important decisions regarding their child. One year after **separation** or **divorce**, many children from **divorced families** have intermittent contact with their fathers or do not see them at all.

The **economic consequences** of a **divorce** tend to be more negative for women and children because most women continue to live together with their dependent biological children, while many men do not share a household with any or all of their biological children. The **daily routine** of raising children requires *energy* and *effort*, and for parents doing it alone it can be *exhausting* and *depleting*; however, energetically many parents are stronger to parenting alone rather than with someone they *perceive* to be inadequate. Delete all *collective influences, psychic, spiritual influences*, the "stigma" of being a "single parent" and any unreliable information that children of divorce are automatically damaged by it.

Weddings and **divorce** are **big business**. When a couple decides to **marry**, the **wedding** often takes on a life of its own, becoming the main focus, and often with a huge price tag. The **hotel industry, travel industry**, **wedding planners, clothing industry, clergy, government**, etc., all benefit **financially**. **Marriage** is a legal *contract*, and family law cases account for at least a third of all civil court cases and require more than one year to resolve. A vast majority of court cases that have been in the courts for four years or longer involve child custody disputes and support arrangements. The price tag for **divorce** is very high because of the *vulnerability* of the parties involved. *Emotions* are running high with *mixed* and *combined emotions*. Many **experts, lawyers, accountants, mediators**, etc., rely on **divorce** to earn their living. A high percentage of people involved in **divorce proceedings** are knocked off *balance* because they have not had any previous *experience* of going to court or being involved in court proceedings.

Do not underestimate the *greed* that feeds this machine. These **experts** are **not** your **friends**. They are comfortable with the process because this is what they do, day in and day out. It is part of their **daily routine**. Sever all *emotional attachments* to ensure that you hire the best possible **expert**. Clear any *karma* between any individuals involved with everyone up and down your **ancestral line** from all directions. There are often many *twists* and *turns*. Strengthen your **daily routine** from being disrupted by **paperwork**, **appointments** with **lawyers**, **accountants**, etc.

At **weddings** people often make *promises* to God in a church in front of witnesses; they *vow* to stay together "until death do us part," "in sickness and in health," etc. Test for *contracts, leases, vows, promises, bonds, cords* and *threads* that are still energetically *attaching* people to each other. Many people have a secret yearning for their *freedom*. Much of the *judgment* from others that newly **divorced** people *experience* actually comes from other people's *jealousy* of that *freedom*, although most people will try to convince themselves that it is the opposite. Many people have underlying weaknesses to signing any **contract,** especially a **marriage contract**. It is not uncommon for couples who have been living **common law** for several **years** to report a *negative shift* in their *relationship* after they decided to "tie the knot." The act of signing the **wedding contract** can bring up many *spiritual* and *psychic memories* of being sold into **slavery** and losing freedom in *past lives*. Breaking the **contract** also brings up many issues for both spouses. There is a saying that, "Hell hath no fury like a woman scorned!" Having worked on **divorce** with many women and men, I have found that it must have been a man who wrote this, as many men become extremely triggered when it comes time to divide assets because most men are considered the providers for the family even though women are also working outside the home and bearing the weight of domestic chores as well as raising children. **Society** has a tendency to negate the contributions that many women make when they choose to stay home and raise their families, without putting a true **financial** value on it.

As a result of my own personal *experience,* as well as from connecting with many men and women who are contemplating divorce, I have found that a kind of "honeymoon phase" sets in after both parties deal with the initial shock that the **marriage** is really coming to an end; at this point husbands and wives seem to be somewhat reasonable and there appears to be an *opportunity* for resolution. However, once **family** and **friends** become involved, and take sides, there are many more *external forces* to deal with along with the **lawyers**. When *property division* begins, there is sure to be more *conflict* as it brings up many *sentiments*, *emotions* and *fears* of **lack**. For most men and women, it is *challenging* to think of their spouse being intimate with another person; this brings up issues with *rejection* and being "replaced." Because women are taught as little girls to "be nice," many women tend to avoid conflict, and thus sabotage their window of *opportunity* to get a fair deal; this is particularly true of **women** with **children**, who are often the hardest hit because they usually end up caring for the day to day **needs** of their children, as well as their own **needs**. It is also common for many women to be paid less than men who are earning their living at the same **job** or **career**, and in many cases, women sacrifice their **careers** to stay home to raise children, and interrupt their **careers** to take maternity leave.

It is important to strengthen **both parties** to **each other** and the reasons they were attracted to each other in the first place so that both are strong to letting go of their partner with **love**. Delete *anger, regret, hostility*, feelings of *guilt* and the *external forces* that many people feel are bombarding them; especially those from **ancestors** and **descendants**, **church** and **family**. Test for any unresolved *karma*. There are often several layers of weaknesses, because when couples choose to marry they often have many *past life experiences* and issues to work through.

Delete the "need to be right" and the desire for **revenge**. Strengthen **both parties** to receive a **fair settlement**, and a "win" for both, especially when children are involved, so that it is also a "win" for the children.

RESULTS:

"I was going through a terrible divorce, my estranged husband was trying to force me to sell my home, that I paid for, he did not ... and wanted everything sold and split 50/50. Each time we would get to court, it would come time to go put money in the parking meters for our vehicles, and he would get into his, and drive off, postponing the proceedings again. This went on for four years. There was no negotiating with him, it was to be all his way, or no way. I was out of money, out of ideas and didn't know what to do. Then I thought of Colette and her energy work. I had received a free half hour session with Colette and decided to call her for any and all assistance she could render. I advised Colette that my lawyer had figured it would take four (4) days in court to go through all the paperwork and witnesses. Colette just laughed, did her thing and then informed me that I would be out of court by noon on that first day, I said, 'But Colette, court doesn't convene until 10:00 a.m. how can I be out 2 hours later?' Then I quickly said, 'You know what, I trust you, I trust in the Universe and so I will trust that it will work out.'

"Well, you could have blown my socks off. When we had everything all wrapped up, done, over, finished, I got a fair settlement, more than I had

hoped for, the house, contents, was paid back for all the money he had stolen from me and also a portion of his pension ... I was so very happy and ecstatic ... and I looked at my watch as I was walking out of the Court Building and it was five minutes to noon ...

"I had gone down that road 4 times before and the only difference was that Colette got me my divorce ... Thank you Colette, you will never know just how you saved me, my pets but mostly my life."

Love
Marion

THE "GOOD NEWS" IS:

Marriage is a "cultural universal," an **institution** common to all human **cultures** worldwide, and part of the **human condition**. There is pretty much a fifty/fifty split in **marriage** and **divorce**, so either way you are likely to **resonate** with half of the population at any given time. **Divorce** is one way to find out who your true friends are (and are not).

THE "BAD NEWS" IS:

Marriage and **divorce** are **false obligations** perpetuated by the vast majority of **cultures** around the world. Saying "I do" and then "I undo" uses a great deal of *time* and *energy* and often creates *imbalance* in the *aspects* of life.

NUGGET OF WIZDOM FROM THE VECTOR

WHEN A MARRIAGE DISINTEGRATES TO THE POINT WHERE IT ENDS IN SEPARATION AND DIVORCE, PEOPLE WILL OFTEN ASK, "WHY DID YOU GET DIVORCED?" A MORE PERTINENT QUESTION TO ASK IS, "WHY DID YOU GET MARRIED?"

DNA

DNA, or **deoxyribonucleic acid**, is a self-replication material present in nearly all **living organisms** as the main component of **chromosome's nucleic acid** containing the **genetic code**. Humans have trillions of **cells** and billions of miles of unraveled **DNA molecules** that take the shape of a twisted ladder in a **double helix**. **RNA**, or **ribonucleic acid**, is present in all living **cells**. Its role is to act as a *messenger* carrying instructions from **DNA** for the *synthesis* of **proteins**, except in the case of some **viruses** where the roles are reversed. **Proteins** are what make cells *replicate*. **Protein sleeves** need to detach from the **double helix** to allow **RNA** to read the exposed segment of **DNA**. What is the purpose of the **ninety** to **ninety five percent** of our **DNA** that is not used for **protein** *manufacture*? What scientists refer to as "**junk DNA?**" True, hereditary factors account for only five percent of *dis-ease*. The rest is **environmental**. We are walking **biographies** of our **ancestors**, the **air** they *breathed*, the **food** they *ate*, the **events** they *witnessed*, the **epigenetic** influences of **toxins, nutrition** – all that and *emotions* are all stored in our **DNA**. Our **conscious** *mind*, or **programming**, creates a **cellular** function. We trap **cellular** *memories* of **beliefs** and *experiences* from **un-conscious** conditions unless we change our *pilot wave* to play out our lives in new ways.

Human **DNA** is encoded with the **DNA** of all animals combined, and as such is the sum total of all the cumulative strands of organic creation containing the "digits" of all species. For example, **human DNA** is almost exactly the same as that of **chimpanzees**, we share a very high percentage of our **DNA** with **cats** and **cows**, and about half of our **DNA** is the same as that of the **fruit fly** and the **banana**. What came first, the **chicken** or the **egg**? Which is most important in the *cycle*? The answer is that you can't have an **egg** without a **chicken** or a **chicken** without an **egg**; they both are of equal importance. Many of us are aware of the story of the **caterpillar** that grows wings and transforms itself into a **butterfly**; however, most of us have not considered the **winged serpent** as the highest "digit" of **DNA** who then, loses its **wings** to become the lowly **snake** as a perfect representation of the **DNA strand**.

According to the story of **Adam** and **Eve**, the lowly **snake** is at the beginning of creation and just like the ancient Egyptian symbol, the **Ouroborus** (a tail devouring serpent or dragon) the **snake** is also at the end. If we consider **Adam** as a *vessel*, a passive *co-creator* with *God,* then the moment when the **snake** entices **Eve**, to explore her sexual nature can be considered the moment of *choice* and the first individual act of *creation* that resulted in the form of **Cain**, and then through the *sexual act* with **Adam**, in **Abel**. We can consider the *act* of *eating* the **forbidden fruit** from the **Tree of Knowledge** as the beginning of *self-awareness* and *duality*. Before the *act* of *eating*, mankind was self-sustaining and able to exist purely on the *essence* of the divinity of *God*. What goes in must come out! Taking sustenance in through food stimulated the *digestive* and *elimination process*, automatically presupposing **mortality** and **decay**. You may have noticed that the **excrement** that leaves the **body** is very **snake-like**, a reminder of humanities' "fall from grace" the moment humans became self-aware, separate from **God**, thereby altering their original **DNA**.

Lately, scientists have discovered that there is a sizable minority of women who have **y chromosome gene sequences** in their **blood**. The **cells** from the **fetus** reside in the **blood stream** and **organ** of every **pregnancy**, whether it ends in **miscarriage**, **abortion** or **live birth**. That explains why women who have had **male offspring** have **y chromosomes**, but what about the women who have not had **male offspring**? There are several common weaknesses that come up energetically. Number one is **abortion**, then **miscarriage**, a **vanished male twin**, and the potential for a woman to actually take on **male DNA** from **sexual intercourse**. Many people comfort themselves by using **condoms** to prevent **pregnancy** and **sexually transmitted disease**; however, if the multitude of **offspring** who were conceived through the failure of **condoms** are any indication, it is best to energetically shift any weaknesses around *dis-ease* and the *karma* between lovers and *unborn descendants*.

MIASMAS

Miasmas are *negative accumulated* **problems** from *past life experiences* that are *imprinted* on people in their *present* lives, *affecting* the **CNS**, **DNA**, **genes**, **chromosomes** and **cellular structures**. These can include **poisons** and **toxins** such as **petrol**, **chemicals**, **heavy metals**, **minerals** and **medications**, **diseases**, **parasites**, etc., as well as *emotional* and *psychological traumas*.

THE "GOOD NEWS" IS:

There is growing evidence in medical and scientific fields that training the *mind* or inducing certain modes of *consciousness* can have positive **health** benefits in the **physical body**.

THE "BAD NEWS" IS:

In order to *activate* and *attune* **DNA light codes**, our predominant **brain wave** state must be **theta** and **gamma**. Our **brain wave** is the flow of *electrical activity* measured in **hertz**. This requires a certain level of *awareness* that many people on planet **earth** do not enjoy.

NUGGET OF WIZDOM FROM THE VECTOR

THE COSMIC GRID OVERRIDES DNA AND GENETIC MAKEUP. IF THERE IS A WEAKNESS IN THE CONNECTION OF DNA, GENES

AND/OR CHROMOSOMES, THE WEAKNESS, NOT THE GENES, IS WHAT CHANGES THE GENES. NOT THE OTHER WAY AROUND.

EATING

The **physical *act*** of **eating** is something that most people take for granted unless they are in circumstances where food is not readily accessible; however, **eating** is a complicated process that can be broken down into **six steps**. If there are underlying weaknesses in any of the **six steps**, it can upset the delicate balance in the **digestive** and **elimination** process, *affecting health*, *fitness* and *youthfulness*, and creating **problems** in every *aspect* of life.

PREHENSION

Prehension is the process of delivering **food** to the **mouth**. This is a simple process for most people once they have survived infancy, and barring paralysis, infirmity, etc.; however, the **gathering** and **preparation** of **food** can have profound effects on the **digestive** process. In the old days people had to either **grow** their food, **gather** it, **hunt** for it and then invest large proportions of their time to **prepare** and **cook** it without the modern conveniences we enjoy today. Today, the vast majority of people do not **grow** their own **food**. Instead, they are becoming more and more removed from **food**, relying on **big business** to provide sustenance. The thrill of the **hunt** in wide open spaces has been replaced by *designated times* in *designated spaces* to "work out" before, during or after "work" on machines in **indoor environments**. Waiting for a turn in crowded lineups at **grocery store checkouts**, **take out places** and **fast food drive-throughs** or *waiting* to be *waited on* in **restaurants** has replaced the **physical gathering** of food supplied by nature in wide open spaces.

The reality for the vast majority of people is to wake up to an alarm clock, hurry to get themselves and their family ready to drive in the car, wait in traffic, drop children off at day-care, to get to work to pay for the car they are sitting in and the house that sits empty while they are at work, to pay for **processed**, **poisoned** and **packaged food** available at a **corporate store** nearby for their "convenience."

Allergies and other negative *re-actions* to food are often triggered by *emotional*, *psychological*, *spiritual* and *psychic* weaknesses which cause concerns around the process of *prehension* and *preparation* of food from the *past*, *present* and *future*. If the **gathering** and **preparation** of food is *perceived* as difficult it will continue to be difficult and the *struggle* experienced by our **ancestors** and the *collective influence* will create a *struggle* with **food**.

What are you afraid to "bite into?" Are you reluctant to open a "can of worms?" Is your **J.O.B. (journey of the broke)** getting to you while you *struggle* to get to it?

MASTICATION

In our **society**, friends and family gather round a table three times a day to **masticate**, **chewing** large portions of **food** and **conversation** into smaller more palatable pieces, **lubricating** and **impregnating** their food and words with their **saliva**. **Mastication**, or **chewing** is the first step in the breakdown of complex foodstuffs. It is mainly a *reflex* that inhibits the **muscles** in the **lower jaw**, causing them to relax and allow the **jaw** to drop as well as a *stretching reflex* that *contracts* **muscles** to close the **mouth**. Deficits in the chewing process can occur when the **upper** and **lower molars** do not *oppose* evenly and are common causes of *digestive dis-ease* in **ruminants** such as **horses** and **cows**.

At this time experts are recommending ingesting a vitamin-enriched diet through "smoothies" by grinding copious amounts of greens in specialized blenders that simulate the "chewing of cud." The *pre-digestive* benefits of the *interaction* of **saliva**, **food** and **water** are left out of the *mixing process*. Any disruption in the digestive process can create potential for weaknesses in the *pre-digestive process* on **physical** and *non-physical* levels. Test for any weaknesses in processing the **nutrients** if you are drinking smoothies on a regular basis, to ensure that the **nutrients** are being *absorbed* and *assimilated* at maximum potential.

Are any of these common *non-physical* dynamics *affecting* your **digestion**? Are you "chewing over"(worried about) a **problem** like a dog "chewing on a bone" and "burying your worry" underground only to dig it up to "re-bury it" and repeat the process over and over again? Has life become a "grind?"

DEGLUTITION

The last step in the **pre-gastric digestion** process is **deglutition** or **swallowing**, which is a complex process that can be broken down into **three steps**. The first step is a *voluntary action* of pressing **food** backwards into the **pharynx** by the **tongue**. This initiates a series of *reflexes* that push the food into the **esophagus** while squeezing the **larynx** shut, and shifting the **epiglottis** to cover the **larynx**. The third step occurs as the **tongue** presses backwards, beginning a **peristaltic** contraction in the **pharynx** through **involuntary *contractions*** that move food through the **digestive** process. *EU ... DEEP THROAT, Pg. 161*

What are you being "forced to swallow?" Are you "spitting mad?" Regurgitating your **problems** over and over again? Are you **choking back** words that express how you really feel? Do you feel unprepared to take in life?

DIGESTION

Once the food is **swallowed** and travels down the **trachea**, it lands in the **stomach** that has three mechanical tasks to perform: the **storage** and **mixture** of **food**, **liquid** and **digestive juices**, and the *release* of the contents into the **small intestine**. The **fat** and **protein** content as well as the nature of the **food**, the degree of **muscle *action*** when the **stomach** empties and the *readiness* of the **small intestine** to *receive* are all factors that *affect* the emptying of the **stomach**.

Are you having difficulty "stomaching life?" What are you having trouble "digesting?" Do you bring up the same **problem** over and over again? Do you feel like "puking?"

ASSIMILATION

The **small intestine** is where the final stages of **digestion** occur, taking in and *absorbing* the small food particles through **villi** and *assimilating* these forms to and from different **organs** through the **blood**. The **intestinal walls** also secrete and receive **enzymes** from the **pancreas** as a secondary role. It is not uncommon for underlying weaknesses on the *non-physical* level to have a *negative effect* on the **body's** ability to *assimilate* and *absorb* nutrients at the **cellular** level.

What is happening in your life that you are having trouble **assimilating**? Is it difficult for you to *absorb* life fully? Do you crave "comfort foods?"

DEFECATION

The final and most crucial step in the eating process is *defecation* or *elimination* of **waste products** in the form of **feces** discharged from the **anus** via the **large intestine**. *EU ... COLON FITNESS, Pg. 149*

Has the "shit hit the fan?" Are you tired of being "dumped on?" What or whom are you having trouble "letting go of?" Have you taken enough "crap" from people?

THE "GOOD NEWS" IS:

Negative re-actions in the **physical body** are often energetically weak on the **emotional** and *psychological* level. You can check to see if any of the **six steps** in the **eating** process are weak. Clearing the number one weakness in the process will often clear energetic weaknesses in the other steps, relieving the *negative effects* of any given **food**.

THE "BAD NEWS" IS:

Much of the **food** people ingest these days has been *modified*, *processed*, *poisoned* and *mis-treated*. Underlying energetic weaknesses can have more twists and turns than the **small intestine**. Generally the more "real" the **food** that you ingest, the fewer shifts in energy it takes to be strong to it.

NUGGET OF WIZDOM FROM THE VECTOR

YOU CAN FOLLOW THE WEAKNESSES TO SHIFT YOURSELF INTO BEING STRONG TO WHATEVER YOU PUT IN YOUR BODY SO THAT YOU GET THE BEST BENEFIT FROM IT. UNFORTUNATELY, THE BEST BENEFIT CAN BE VERY MINIMAL IN PROCESSED AND PACKAGED FOODS. IT IS MORE IMPORTANT TO CLEAR WHAT IS NOT BENEFICIAL THROUGH THE ELIMINATION SYSTEMS OF YOUR BODY, THE MOST EFFICIENT BEING THE COLON.

EMOTIONS

The words you choose to express yourself can have a big impact on the way you *feel*. Most people are unaware that they are out of *alignment* energetically to most of what they are saying and doing. For instance, it is common to hear people say, "I feel sad" or, "I feel happy." The fact is that you don't *feel* happy or sad; you are *re-acting* to the **sensations** that run through your **body** when you get in touch with the *thought* of those *emotions*.

When you combine *emotions* with too much *thinking*, it becomes very *challenging* to *feel* for answers that would improve your situation. In fact, one of the leading causes of **physical pain** is out-of-control *emotions*. Even when it is not the cause, a weak *re-action* to **pain** intensifies the reasons for the **pain** and the **pain** itself. *Feeling* is really an "off and on" switch. We either *feel* weak to energy or strong to it. We complicate **feeling** when we name it as an **emotion** or a combination of

emotions, confusing both the issue and the **CNS**. *Conflicting emotions* lead to *overwhelm* of both the **body** and the *mind*.

A "nervous breakdown" is aptly named because it is caused by the *overwhelm* of too many *sensations* running through the **body** concurrently over and over again. The "crossed wires" fray **nervous fiber** and etch **neurological pathways** from *thoughts* held in the *sub-conscious mind*, many of which come from *external forces* such as **ancestors**, **cultural**, **religious** and *collective limiting beliefs*. *Jealousy*, *frustration* and *rage* are examples of **accumulations** of *conflicting emotions*. Combining *thinking* with *mixed emotions* often triggers *feelings* of "being stuck" without hope of relief.

INTERESTING ANECDOTE

When I drive by or go into the **hospital** where my daughters were born the *memories* cause *sensations* that I associate with *joy*, **pain** and **contentment**. This is also where both of my parents made their transition in very unsatisfactory conditions, and that triggers sensations I *associate* with *anger*, *horror*, *dis-belief* and *hopelessness*. If I try to deal with all of these *re-actions* at the same time, I am likely to suppress the *feelings* and file them in the *memory bank* of my **CNS**, adding to the **pain** and *confusion*. Separating these *emotions* and *deleting* them one at a time allows me to control my *re-action* and take control of myself.

THE "GOOD NEWS" IS:

Many of the *emotions* that we *collectively* encounter in our interactions with ourselves and others revolve around the desire to be *touched,* and wanting to *touch* others. The quantum dichotomy is that nothing *touches*! Nothing has ever *touched* anything because everything is made up of **atoms** that are actually far apart. This knowledge can come in handy when you get in *touch* with that *relationship*, that in retrospect you wish you never had … technically you did not *touch*!

THE "BAD NEWS" IS:

People are searching for *approval*, *affection* and *acceptance*. They have good intentions, but they often *feel* under-appreciated and seek attention by creating unnecessary **drama** in their lives and for others. Many people who are prescribed **psychotropic drugs** or who self-medicate themselves with **recreational drugs**, **alcohol**, **over-work**, **shopping**, etc., are *numbing* themselves and *suppressing* communication from inner guidance systems that would provide answers to alleviate their doubts and quiet their *fears*.

NUGGET OF WIZDOM FROM THE VECTOR

SEPARATE YOUR FEELING AND EMOTIONAL RE-ACTIONS FROM YOUR THINKING. FEEL FOR ANSWERS AND ACT BEFORE YOU THINK.

ENDOCRINE GLANDS

The **endocrine system** includes all of the **glands** of the **body** and the **hormones** produced by those **glands** that have an intimate connection with each other and are directly controlled by *stimulation* of the **nervous system** and by **chemical receptors** in the **bloodstream**. The main **endocrine glands** consist of the **adrenals**, **hypothalamus**, **parathyroid**, **pituitary**, **pineal**, **thyroid**, **pancreas** and **gonads** (**ovaries** and **testes**). **The heart**, **kidneys**, **digestive system**, **adipose tissue** and **placenta** are also **hormone producing organs**.

ADRENAL GLANDS

The **suprarenal** or **adrenal glands** are a pair of **glands**, about one to two inches in length, that secrete three dozen **hormones** directly into the **bloodstream**. The **adrenals** are located just above the **kidneys**. Each **gland** can be divided into two distinct **organs**, the **adrenal medulla** and the **cortex**.

ADRENAL MEDULLA

The **adrenal medulla**, the smaller inner region of the **adrenal glands** is part of the **sympathetic nervous system** and is the **body's** first line of defense to adapt to **physical** and *emotional fear* and *anger*, secreting **epinephrine** (**adrenaline**) which raises **blood sugar**, affecting the "fight or flight" response, and **norepinephrine**, affecting **cardiac action**, **blood pressure** and controlling the *contraction* and *expansion* of **blood vessels** and **muscles**.

ADRENAL CORTEX

The outer region of the **adrenal glands**, the **adrenal cortex**, takes instruction from **ACTH** that is secreted by the **pituitary glands** and *affects* the way food is *utilized*, the **chemicals** in the **blood**, and characteristics such as **hairiness** and **body shape**. The **cortex** produces three types of hormones. **Mineral corticoids** such as **aldosterone** are responsible for regulating **minerals, electrolytes** and **fluid balance**. **Glucocorticoids** involved in **glucose metabolism** (metabolism of **carbohydrates** in the regulation of **blood sugar**). One of these, **hydrocortisone (cortisol)** is produced in response to **physical** or *mental* stress. **Estrogen** and **androgens** are *produced* by the **adrenal cortex**, supplementing those secreted by the **ovaries** and **testes**.

Addison's is a rare **endocrine disorder** caused by a chronically *under-active* **adrenal cortex** that produces insufficient **steroid hormones** causing fatigue, dizziness, **muscle** weakness, weight loss, difficulty in standing up, anxiety, diarrhea, headache, and sweating. **Cushing's** is the opposite **problem** – an *overactive* **adrenal cortex**, sometimes caused by a **tumor** in the **pituitary gland**. **Hyperadrenocorticism** is an **endocrine disorder** caused by high levels of **cortisol**. Under normal conditions **cortisol** helps to restore *homeostasis* by counteracting **insulin,** stimulating **gastric acid** *production* and *inhibiting* **sodium loss** because in order for **potassium** to move out of the **cell**, **cortisol** moves in and equals the number of **sodium ions.** Strengthen **pH** to the **kidneys** for *equilibrium* of **sodium** to **cortisol**.

Cortisol levels are *affected* by chronic "stress" from the **false obligations** of society, an *imbalance* in the *aspects* of life and **collective tactics**. Music and massage reduce *cortisol* levels whereas **caffeine,** worry over **sleep deprivation, commuting** and **anorexia nervosa** may be *associated* with higher **cortisol** levels. The **corticosteroids** that are commonly used for **non-endocrine diseases** such as **arthritis** and **asthma** cause the **adrenals** to shrink in size. These are powerful regulators that should be used with caution because medicinal doses are typically higher than what the **body** would naturally produce, therefore suppressing the **feedback loop**. They increase susceptibility to *infections*. Strengthen the benefits of the **medications** and spin out the detriments to *black wholes*. Also test for *associations past*, *present* and *future* with **tuberculosis**.

GONADS

The **gonads** consist of the **ovaries** in females and **testes** in males. Their main function is to produce **sex hormones** for the **body** that determine secondary sex characteristics of adults.

TESTES

The **testes** are a pair of **ellipsoid organs** found in the **scrotum** of males that produce **testosterone** after the start of puberty, **affecting** the development of **muscles**, **bones**, **sex organs** and **hair follicles**, including **pubic**, **chest** and **facial hair**. **Testosterone** increases strength and growth, in particular in the **long bones** during **adolescence**.

OVARIES

The **ovaries** are a pair of almond-shaped **glands** that are located in the **pelvis** above the **uterus** in females. They produce the female **sex hormones, progesterone** and **estrogen**. **Progesterone** is most active in females during **ovulation** and **pregnancy** while **estrogens** are a group of **hormones** that function as the main **primary sexual hormones**. **Estrogens** are released during **puberty** *stimulating* breast and **uterine** development, growth of **pubic hair**, and an increase in **long bone** growth.

HYPOTHALAMUS

The **pituitary** is often considered the "master gland," but the **hypothalamus** is the true power behind the throne because it plays a vital role in controlling many bodily functions including the release of **hormones** from the **pituitary gland**. The **hypothalamus** is located on the undersurface of the **brain**, lying just below the **thalamus** and above the **pituitary gland** to which it is attached by a **stalk**. This **gland** regulates **heart rate**, **blood pressure**, **body temperature**, **water balance**, **thirst**, **hunger**, **gastric reflexes**, influences *aggression*, *fear*, *memory*, *sexual behavior*, *maternal behavior* and *emotions*.

One of its major functions is to maintain **homeostasis** by responding to various signals from the **internal** and **external environment** of the **body**, including messages regarding **temperature, hunger, satiation** and **blood pressure**. The **hypothalamus** responds to the *emotional re-actions* from "stress" and controls the secretion of **melatonin** from the **pineal gland** while we are sleeping. It is also in charge of levels of **cortisol,** the "stress" **hormone**.

There are two sets of nerve cells in the **hypothalamus** that produce the **hormones**. One set sends **anti-diuretic hormone (ADH)** and **oxytocin** through the **pituitary stalk** to the **posterior lobe** of the **pituitary gland** and releases them directly into the **bloodstream**. ADH causes water re-absorption at the **kidneys**. **Oxytocin** stimulates *contraction* of the uterus during childbirth and **lactation**. The other set of **nerves** produce **hormones** that reach the **anterior lobe** of the **pituitary gland** via a network of **blood vessels** that run through the **stalk**. These **hormones** *stimulate* and *regulate* the **gonads**, the **thyroid (TRH)** and **adrenal cortex**, plus **human growth hormone**.

The **thyroid releasing hormone (TRH)** is the master regulator of **thyroid** growth and function by triggering the **thyroid** to produce more **thyroid hormone** secretions. If there is insufficient **thyrotropin-releasing hormone**, it causes **hypothyroidism** and under-activity of the **thyroid**.

Prolactin (PRH) regulates **lactation** and **orgasms**. Unusually high amounts are suspected to be a contributing factor for impotency and lack of **libido**. It also produces **cells** that are responsible for the formation of **myelin** coatings on **axons (nerve fibers)** and decreases **estrogen** in women and **testosterone** in men. **Prolactin** also contributes to **surfactant synthesis**, wetting agents that lower the surface tension of liquids, in the development of **fetal lungs**.

Dopamine is a **hormone** and **neurotransmitter** that helps to control the **brain's** reward and pleasure centers, and to regulate *emotional re-actions*. People who have low levels of **dopamine** are more prone to addiction, and it has been found to be a contributing factor to **Parkinson's disease**. Specific **dopamine receptors** are also *associated* with "risk taking" actions.

Somatostatin is a **hormone** produced by many **tissues** in the **body**, particularly in the **nervous** and **digestive systems**. It is a *regulator* of rapid reproduction of normal and **tumor cells** and a **neurotransmitter**. It also is produced in the **pancreas** and inhibits the secretion of other **pancreatic hormones** such as **insulin** and **glucagon**.

Gonadotropin-releasing hormone (GRH) stimulates the production of two more **hormones, follicle stimulating hormone** and **luteinizing hormone** that initiate and maintain the **reproductive** functions of the **ovaries** and **testicles** for the production of **sperm** in men and **ovulation** during the **menstrual cycle** of women. A deficiency of **GRH** in childhood prevents **puberty**. Any interruption in **follicle stimulating hormone** and **luteinizing hormone** can cause a lack of **menstruation** in women and loss of **sperm** *production* in men. They are controlled by the levels of **testosterone** in men and **progesterone** in women. As the levels of these **hormones** rise, the level of **gonadotropin-releasing hormone** decreases, and as they lower **GRH** increases.

The **pancreas** is a flat, pear-shaped **organ** that is located in the **abdomen**, behind the **stomach**, and is surrounded by the **small intestine, liver** and **spleen**. It has two main functions: **exocrine function** and **endocrine function**.

EXOCRINE FUNCTION

The **pancreas** contains **exocrine glands** that produce **enzymes** when food enters the **stomach**; these **enzymes** are essential to **digestion**, and are released into a series of **ducts** that gather in the **pancreatic duct**.

The **pancreatic duct** joins with the **common bile duct** which originates in the **liver** and the **gallbladder** to form the **ampulla of Vater**, located at the first portion of the **small intestine**, the **duodenum**. The **bile** is another vital **digestive juice** that combined with the **pancreatic juice** digests **fats, carbohydrates** and **proteins**.

ENDOCRINE FUNCTION

The **endocrine** function of the **pancreas** consists of islet **cells** called the **islets of langerhans** that create and release **hormones** directly into the **bloodstream**. One of the main **hormones** released is **insulin** which lowers **blood sugar**. **Hyperglycemia** occurs when the **blood sugar** levels are too high and **hypoglycemia** occurs when levels are too low. The other **hormone** is **glucagon** which raises **blood sugar**. Proper **blood sugar** levels are crucial for the function of **organs** such as the **brain, liver** and **kidneys**. Many of the issues causing **pancreatic** disorders revolve around *emotional* and **psychological** issues about the "sweetness" of life.

PINEAL GLAND

The **pineal gland**, also known as the **pineal body, epiphysis** and **third eye**, is a pea-sized, reddish gray **endocrine gland** located near the center of the **brain**, between the two **hemispheres**. It is tucked in a groove where the two rounded **thalamic bodies** join and is shaped like a **pinecone**.

The **pineal gland** is not isolated from the **body** by the **blood** to **brain barrier** as most of the rest of the **brain** is. It is activated by light, stimulating **nerves** in the **eyes** to produce **melatonin**, a **hormone** that affects wake/sleep and seasonal patterns along with various other **biorhythms** of the **body** such as **reproductive functions** by depressing the activity of the **gonads**. The **pineal gland** function changes drastically, falling off at **puberty**. It has an intimate connection with the **hypothalamus** as well as the **thymus**. **Pineal gland** function also affects the **thyroid** and **adrenal cortex**, is tied to the **circadian rhythms'** biological clock, and influences **pigmentation**. The **pineal gland** is often *calcified*, largely because of the intake of **fluoride** in **toothpaste** and **water**.

SEASONAL AFFECTIVE DISORDER (SAD)

People who are not energetically strong to seasonal changes produce too much **melatonin** causing a syndrome called **seasonal affective disorder** (**SAD**), *depression* and *exhaustion*, especially in the winter when there is less light.

Although the **pineal gland** was the last to be discovered in the **endocrine system** by the **medical community**, it has been held in high esteem by **mystics** and **esoteric** schools over the ages. It is considered the "portal" to **ethereal** energy, a bridge between **physical** and *spiritual* worlds. Activating the **pineal gland** awakens our *soul* to a higher level of consciousness and a level of resonance that communicates with our **primordial cells** allowing *vision* throughout all the *dimensions*, *planes* and *existences* of *space-time*, particularly *astral travel*, *astral projection*, *lucid dreaming* and *remote viewing*. Many people feel pressure at the base of their **spine** when the **pineal gland** is activated as it has a direct connection to **physical potential**. Research has shown that between the hours of one a.m. and four a.m., **chemicals** are released in the **brain** that inspires *oneness consciousness*. Governments around the world have been researching these *psychic* abilities and methods to control the *thoughts* and *actions* of people for many years now. The **pineal gland** has been honored by ancient societies in Rome, Egypt and around the world and by the Roman Catholic Church.

PITUITARY GLAND

The **pituitary gland** is a pea-sized gland located at the base of the skull between the **optic nerves**, and is connected to the **hypothalamus** by a stalk-like structure. It is sometimes referred to as the "master gland" because its **hormone** function controls **temperature**, the **thyroid**, childhood **growth**, **urine** and **testosterone**, **ovulation** and **estrogen** production. The **pituitary gland** is divided into two parts, the **anterior lobe** and **posterior lobe**.

ANTERIOR LOBE

The **anterior lobe** is made up of separate collections of individual **cells** that are like factories producing a regulatory **hormone messenger** or

factor. These **factors** are secreted in response to **external forces** that affect **internal boundaries** and cause *emotional re-actions*. The **hormones** produced in the individual **factors** are **cortisol**, **prolactin** and **gonadotropin** (**sex hormones**). The **hormones** travel via the **factors** through the **circulatory system** to stimulate their intended **gland**. **Thyroid stimulating hormone** (**TSH**) activates the **thyroid**, **adrenocorticotropic** (**ACTH**) stimulates the **adrenal cortex** and **gonadotropins** stimulate **testes** and **ovaries**.

POSTERIOR LOBE

The **posterior lobe** produces two **hormones**, **vasopressin** and **oxytocin**, that are synthesized by the **hypothalamus**. **Vasopressin** facilitates the reabsorption of water in the **blood** through the **collecting ducts** of the **kidneys**. **Oxytocin** stimulates the **uterus** at birth, orgasm, and in "letting" the milk down when a newborn begins to suckle. It bonds males and females after they have mated, bonds mothers to new-borns and increases trust in humans.

The **posterior lobe** is also the source of **human growth hormone** (**HGH**) that is of vital importance to a growing child because it affects **bone** and **cartilage**, **protein**, **fat** and **glucose metabolism**, **electrolyte balance** and **RNA** function. It also produces **endorphins,** belonging to the category of **chemicals** known as **opiates** that deaden **pain receptors**.

PROSTAGLANDINS

Prostaglandins are a group of **lipids** that differ from other **hormones** because they are not secreted from a **gland** and carried through the **bloodstream** to work on specific areas of the **body**. They are made up of **chemicals** at the site of **injury** or **illness** wherever and whenever they are needed.

There are different kinds of **prostaglandins** depending where the **organ** or **body** part is located. At the site of **tissue damage** or *inflammation*, they cause *infections*, **pain** and or **fever** as part of the *healing* process. **Thromboxane** and **prostacyclin** are types of **prostaglandins** that regulate **blood flow**. **Thromboxane** creates **blood clots** by contracting the **blood vessel** to prevent **blood loss** if **veins** and **arteries** are injured. **Prostacyclin** does the opposite by breaking down **clots** and *expanding* the **blood vessel**.

Prostaglandins also regulate *contraction* and *expansion* of the **muscles** in the **gut** and **airways** as well as the female **reproductive**

system inducing birth and controlling **ovulation**. They interact with **enzymes** called **cyclooxygenase** at specific **receptors** throughout the **body,** staying close to the site of injury, and are broken down very quickly by the **body**.

An overabundance of **prostaglandins** can lead to **heart attacks, strokes** and **menstrual cramps**. **Aspirin** is sometimes used to prevent production of **prostaglandin** when there is risk of **heart attack**, because its **molecules** enter the **cell** and **chemically** modify the **cyclooxygenase enzymes** rendering them useless. A deficiency may cause **high blood pressure** and **digestive** problems.

You can energetically send **prostaglandins** to *black wholes* when there are too many, or to sites throughout the **body** where they are **needed**. For example they can be used to induce **birth** and also to encourage **miscarriage** of an unwanted **pregnancy**. They treat stomach ulcers, glaucoma and congenital heart disease in newborn babies.

THYROID

The **thyroid** is a small butterfly-shaped **gland** just below the **adam's apple** that plays a very important role in controlling the **body's** *metabolism* and **oxygen** consumption by producing **hormones** that travel via the **bloodstream** to every part of the **body**. These **hormones** inform the **body** how to use energy with efficiency, and control **metabolism** for **physical** and *mental* alertness. They are responsible for the growth and maturity of **body tissues** and affect the **spleen's** ability to function at optimum potential.

The **thyroid** is different from other **endocrine glands** because it requires **iodine**, which comes from outside of the **body**, to produce **thyroxine** (**T4**) and **triiodothyronine** (**T3**). Its **cells** are the only ones in the entire **body** that are capable of absorbing **iodine** obtained through **food, iodized salt, supplements** and combining that **iodine** with the **amino acid, tyrosine** and converting it to **T3** and **T4**. **Problems** with the **thyroid** *affect* virtually all **metabolic** processes. If there is an excess of the **hormones**, it speeds the **metabolism** up too much; if there is not enough, it slows it down.

HYPOTHYROIDISM

An under-active **gland** causes the **body** to slow down causing symptoms of apathy, dislike of cold, hair loss, fatigue, constipation, muscle aches, heavy periods, weight gain, depression and a hoarse voice. Severe **hypothyroidism** can retard **physical** and *mental* growth in children, and can even lead to loss of ***consciousness***.

Thyroxine (**T4**) accounts for eighty percent of the **hormones** the **thyroid** produces. If there is too little it causes *mental confusion* and *sluggishness*, and if there is too much, it causes *anxiety*. triiodothyronine (**T3**) accounts for the other twenty percent of **hormone** production and **calcitonin** that helps regulate **calcium** levels in the **blood** to strengthen **bones**.

GRAVES' DISEASE

Graves' disease is a common form of **hypothyroidism.** In addition to the other symptoms, the patient manifests, a staring expression as one or both **eyes** bulge out of their **sockets**. This causes the loss of **eye muscle** control and **problems** with *vision*.

HYPERTHYROIDISM

Overproduction of **thyroxine** (**T4**) sends the body into "overdrive" causing tremors, palpitations, weight loss, increased appetite, anxiety, irritability, dislike of heat, sweating, and infrequent menstruation. The symptoms of severe **hyperthyroidism** are subtle, gradually creeping up on people, causing shortness of breath, chest pain and muscle weakness. In older people the typical symptoms are absent causing loss of weight, depression and eventually heart failure.

GOITER

Goiter refers to any swelling or overgrowth of the **thyroid gland** and can be caused by both too much and too little **thyroid hormones**. Benign **nodules** that cause *swelling* and overgrowth are normally treated with surgery and administration of **radioactive hormones** to shrink the **nodules**.

On the **physical** level it is important that the functions of the **CNS** to the **thyroid, hypothalamus** and **anterior pituitary gland** are strong. **Thyroid** issues occur most often in "middle aged" women. On the *emotional, mental* and *psychological* levels the **problems** of **hypothyroidism** are about "not being enough," and **hyperthyroidism** tends to be about "being too much." **Society** devalues women when they become a "certain age," which causes many women to question their worth. Many of the weaknesses around the **thyroid** are exacerbated by *actions* and *expectations* of what *actions* a woman is "supposed" to take.

On a *psychic* and *spiritual* level many of the weaknesses can be traced to experiences or *thoughts* of *beheading*, *hanging*, *slit neck*, "*cut throat behavior*," being *stabbed*, having *a broken neck* and *suffocation*.

PROBLEMS WITH SUPPLEMENTAL HORMONES

Using **supplemental hormones** over a long period of time precludes the manufacture of the corresponding **hormone** in the **body**. This causes the **gland** that would normally produce the **hormone** to atrophy.

THE "GOOD NEWS" IS:

If the weaknesses in the **endocrine system** are systematically addressed, an understanding of their functions throughout the **body** facilitate **youthfulness**, **longevity** and **vitality**.

THE "BAD NEWS" IS:

Hormone *production* and ***stimulation*** is influenced by so many factors and is so intimately entwined that at times it can seem ***overwhelming*** to track where the weaknesses are coming from.

NUGGET OF WIZDOM FROM THE VECTOR

THE INTRICACIES OF THE ENDOCRINE SYSTEM ARE COMPLICATED, ESPECIALLY IN THE CASE OF THE TESTES AND OVARIES WHERE PAST LIFE EXPERIENCES OF BEING A MAN OR A WOMAN OFTEN INFLUENCE THE BEHAVIOR OF THE GLANDS. IF ISSUES AROUND HAVING A UTERUS OR OTHER FEMALE PARTS COME UP IN A MAN IT IS BEST TO SILENTLY SHIFT IT; HOWEVER, MOST WOMEN DON'T MIND BEING TOLD THEY "HAVE BALLS."

ENERGETIC UPGRADE

You can use your **CNS** to deprogram ***errant energies*** that are held within the components of the **cranial brain, spine, heart** and the seven ***physical chakras aligned*** along the **vertical mid-line** from the **base** of the spine to the top of the **head**. An **energetic upgrade** occurs when you give yourself ***total permission*** to operate at one hundred percent potential. It is an automatic ***recalibration*** of your **power transmission,** encoding it with the ***authentic desires*** held in the ***universal heart field.*** The polar opposites of ***potential*** and **lack** merge to strengthen ***infinite*** *potential* and delete *negative influences* past the *zero-point* into *infinity* and *beyond*.

If you clear energy through the components of the **spine** and **CNS** without plugging into your *authentic desires* through your **heart**, you can clear *disappointing* situations to be *neutral*, but it does not correct the fundamental **concern** of whatever it was that made it *disappointing* in the first place. When you are plugged into your **heart's intelligence**, the energetic shifts delivered through the **neurons** of your **heart** fuse with those of your **spine** and are *encoded* to your *authentic desires*. To **build** the life you want instead of *adapting* to the life you are living, you have to plug into the *intelligence* of your **heart** to automatically *recalibrate* the **CNS** to the unified **heart field**.

RECALCULATION

Human beings often think they want their lives to be a certain way, but their energy is out of *alignment* with their *thoughts,* and that makes it challenging to bring **dreams** into *reality*. Letting go of *resistance* is often considered **anti-social** because **society** supports **conformity** and has a tendency to persecute individuals who allow themselves the *freedom* to climb out of the **box**. For example, consider a bucket of captured crabs. The ones at the bottom will grab on and hold back any who try to escape the *collective fate*.

We can energetically test the *percentage* to which a person is willing to **accept** change, and step full-heartedly into the *future*. We can also get a base-line for **resistance**, how much a person is willing to let go of the old story. When we bring these two into *alignment* at the **zero point** through our center we collapse the wave and *recalculate* our *perception*. **Resistance** to *change* is eliminated by letting go of the hidden "benefits" we think we receive by hanging on tightly to the old story.

It is not acceptable in today's **society** to take a day off from **work** unless you are **sick**. Many adults do "cheat" and take a "sick day" when they need down time; however children really pay the price because the only way they can have down-time from scheduled school days is to actually be **sick** or to add extra-curricular activities to their schedule. Being "sick" is often their only option when they choose to take time for themselves.

How long does it take for the *subconscious mind,* the *un-conscious mind* and the **conscious** *mind* to be congruent in order to *manifest* desired *change* or improvement? Some energetic weaknesses that are identified and eliminated bring obvious *changes* that are instantaneous and appear to be miraculous. Others have many layers that need to be peeled away before a person's *perception* catches up to the **change**. It is possible to test how long a person has been *affected* by a **specific issue** and the **time frame** when they are strongest to letting the issue go. Some issues are held down the **ancestral** line, and others are *soul experiences* that have been in play for **eons** or **centuries**. Others revolve around **decades** of *suffering*. The **goal** is to bring **conscious** belief into the **present** moment, and to take consistent steps of *action* to **effect** results in the *moment*; however, because we are dealing with the densities of the **third dimensional plane**, *patience* is required.

RECALIBRATION

Many people are using the terms "reset" and "reboot" to express the concept of **recalibration**; however, if you have ever been in the middle of a project on your computer and have had to **reboot** or **reset** your computer, you have felt the frustration of being held hostage by the powers-that-be in "computerland." Thankfully, it is not necessary to shut down to reroute the energy in human beings. When you *recalibrate,* you are free to spin *challenges* into *possibilities* by letting go of the *reverse perception* held by the vast majority. There are no *limitations*. There is no **box**. When you *recalibrate*, it opens you up as an individual to be complete and whole within yourself, and to give yourself *total permission* to dance your dance and participate in all of life's pleasures. If you are standing at the buffet of life, unwilling or unable to choose a new plate (canvas) and new cutlery (tools) then you are not able to enjoy the refinement of life and everything you *deserve* such as:

FULFILLMENT

Fulfillment is being in the act and/or the process of delivering the best version of self through accomplishments and achievements. True *fulfillment* is satisfaction on a grand scale. Many people in today's **society** search for *fulfillment* through **material possessions**, *fulfilling relationships*, etc., that are based on the **false obligations** of **society** rather than on their *authentic desires*.

HEART WIZDOM

Your **heart** transmits a huge *electromagnetic spectrum* that radiates and pulses throughout *space-time*, and is greater than that of the **brain**. It can be detected and measured several feet away from a person's **body** and between individuals who are in close proximity.

AUTHENTIC DESIRE

Many people dedicate their lives to the pursuit of **desires** that are dictated by **societal**, **cultural**, **religious** and *collective goals* and are based on the **third dimensional reality** rather than their *true essence* which encompasses their *whole being*. When every *aspect* of life is balanced, rather than focused on **false obligations** imposed by **society**, you live your *authentic desires*.

JOY

Joy is the ultimate expression of all that is, the feeling of *bliss* evoked at the prospect of possessing one's *authentic desires*. Many people strive for *happiness*; however, *happiness* is a lower *vibration* of *joy*.

CREATIVITY

True *creativity* is an expression of the *authentic self*. When all *energy centers* throughout the **body** are in *alignment*, you are able to access *creative solutions* to life's *challenges*, solutions that encompass every aspect of your being, and allow you to spin *challenges* into *possibilities* via the imagination and innovative ideas.

SENSUALITY

Sensuality is often confused with **sexuality**. Many people treat the maintenance of their **body** as if it is a **chore** rather than a *delight*. Your **body** is a special *gift*, honored throughout the universe and designed to **experience** **third dimensional life** through every *sense*. It is in your best interests to please your *senses* and to satisfy authentic appetites and passions of your **physical body**.

PURPOSE

Your *purpose* as a **conscious** being is to become a full expression of the *electro-magnetic spectrum* through the embodiment of life as a **human being**, here on planet **Earth**. This requires consistent steps of *action* towards an aim or *intention*.

SEXUALITY

Sexuality is the **orgasmic** expression of *joy*, the capacity of a person to express **sexual** habits and *authentic desires*. There are many versions of **sexuality** that abound the **earth**. **Sexuality** is often confused with **gender** and is often *sensationalized* and **expropriated** to "sell" material products on the **third dimensional plane**.

ABUNDANCE

Abundance is the dance of life, overflowing with a plentiful supply of *affluence*, *wealth*, *beauty* and *love*. *Abundance* of **finances** is more common in people who have round, firm **buttocks** that are able to do **a** "**bun**" **dance**.

FREEDOM

True *freedom* is stepping into the dance of life, totally uninhibited and *free* as an expression of "all that is." A state of **freedom** comes through discipline, inspiring *independence* and allowing everyone equal *opportunity* for life, liberty and the pursuit of *joy*.

THE "GOOD NEWS" IS:

When you eliminate the reasons for holding onto *past limitations* to below the zero point, and strengthen the possibilities for a brilliant future above one hundred percent, then you become strong to facilitating *change* for the better.

THE "BAD NEWS" IS:

There is often **resistance** to *change*, making it *challenging* to let go of old baggage because it becomes familiar and feels safe. People often **resist** *change* because of *past experiences* where things went from "bad to worse."

NUGGET OF WIZDOM FROM THE VECTOR

INFORMATION EQUALS ENERGY. AN ENERGETIC UPGRADE OCCURS WHEN YOU UTILIZE THE FLOW OF ENERGY TO BE THE ULTIMATE EXPRESSION OF YOUR AUTHENTIC SELF.

EXIT PORTALS

Your **body** is built to cleanse **toxins, poisons, minerals, cellular waste, parasites** and **parasitic waste**, etc., out of your **physical body** in the quickest way possible through the **elimination systems** including the **lymphatic system, colon** (**bowel movements**), expulsion of the contents of the **stomach** (**vomiting**), **bladder** (**urination**) and **genitals** (**orgasm** and **menstruation** for women). *EU ... LYMPHATIC SYSTEM, Pg. 320 ... COLON FITNESS, Pg. 149 ... DIGESTIVE SYSTEM, Pg. 187 ... REPRODUCTIVE SYSTEM, Pg. 445 ... MENSTRUATION, Pg. 327*

Although the **stool**, **vomit**, **ejaculate** and **urine** are very obvious in a **physical** sense the underlying causes are subtle because they are both **physical** and *non-physical*. *Toxic* and *poisonous thoughts* and *emotions*, *psychic energies*, *parasitic people* and *traumatic experiences* are also released through the **physical body**. Most people are familiar with the **physical** bodily functions of **elimination**, but there are also other ways of *eliminating* negative **physical** and *non-physical energies* through the *flow* of *Ka* (*Qi*). The *energies* can also be sent to *black wholes* that can be located inside and outside of the **physical body**. *EU ... BLACK WHOLE/WHITE WHOLE, Pg. 93*

It is helpful to have a basic understanding of the *exit portals* and their connection to the *meridians*, *channels* and *acupuncture points* throughout the **body** to facilitate the *release* of *weak energy* and to *spin strong energy* into it.

MERIDIANS AND ACUPUNCTURE POINTS

The *meridian system* supports life by providing *channels* to *transport* and *metabolize* the fundamental substances of *Ka* (*Qi*), **blood** and **body fluids**. The *flow* of *Ka* (*Qi*) in the *meridian system* concentrates at or injects small areas of the **skin's** surface called *acupoints*. These *acupoints* correspond to specific **organs** and **meridians**. There are also many **A-Shi Points** as well as **Extraordinary Points** that are not directly connected to the *meridians,* but still have therapeutic effects for treating *dis-ease*. Twelve *Principle Meridians* are connected to the **Yin** and **Yang organs** and eight *Extra Meridians* as well as *Luo Meridians* work in smaller networks.

SOURCE POINTS AND CONNECTING POINTS

Source Points refer to twelve points in the **wrists** and **ankles** where **Primordial Ka** (*Qi*) from the **organs** gathers to be distributed throughout the **body**. Weaknesses in the **ankles** are often referred from the **wrists** and vice-versa. Lack of support from *maternal energy* at a very young age can manifest as weaknesses in the **left ankle**, while lack of support from *paternal energy* weakens the **right ankle**. Weaknesses in both creates a feeling of "not having a leg to stand on." Unevenness in the right and **left ankle** causes *imbalance* through the entire **physical body**. Uneven *parenting styles* and *practices* can have a profound effect on *emotional*, *mental* and *psychological* well-being. Strengthen the *fitness* of all twelve **points,** the **wrists**, **ankles** and **organs** to clear **negative** *emotions* contained in the **organs**.

CONNECTING POINTS

There are fifteen **Connecting Points** where a *meridian* branches out into **Luo Pathways** throughout the **body**. These connections are responsible for **communication** between the **organs** and other *meridians*. Strengthen the *relationship* between *meridians*, *pathways* and **organs**.

THE FIVE TRANSPORT POINTS

The five transport **Shu Points** refer to five specific *points* named after the natural flow of water. These are *Well*, *Spring*, *Stream*, *River* and *Sea*. Each of the regular twelve *meridians* has a group of these *points* totaling *sixty points* (thirty *Yin* and thirty *Yang*) that *flow* to and from the tip of the four **limbs** and just below the **elbow** and **knee joint**. Their purpose is to facilitate *communication* between the **inner** and **outer** sides of the **body**.

The *Well Point* distributes *Yin* and *Yang energies* that travel through the **blood**. Check if there are any weaknesses blocking the *flow* of the *Well Point* after a person has *experienced* an unpleasant surprise or accident. People who are facing life and death choices in emergency situations can often be resuscitated when the *flow* of this fundamental *life force energy* is restored. The discomfort associated with *inflammation* can also have a profound effect on the *Well Points* and vice-versa.

The *Spring Point* is a concentrated, delicate *flow* that can be used to regulate temperature in the **body**. **Hot flashes**, **fevers** and **hypothermia** can all be rapidly adjusted by tapping into the *Spring Point*, **thymus** and **CNS** to correct the *flow*.

The *Stream Point* refers to *Ka* (*Qi*) that is flowing from shallow to deeper waters. Positive or negative *emotional excitement* "stirs the waters" to a boiling or bubbling point. Resistance to *agility* and *speed* within the system can *accumulate* within the **meridian** and create *blockage*, *congestion* and eventually *inflammation*, *infection* and a potentially *parasitic* environment. Clear the *Stream Points* of *emotional* debris and break down the **physical matter** to relieve painful **joints** from *stagnation* and *infestation*. In general, heaviness can often be attributed to **dampness**, as reflected in nature after heavy rains. Break excess water down to **ions** and out of the system. Strengthen **water**, **alkalinity**, *ions* and *electromagnetic charge* to be performing at optimum function within the **cells**.

The *River Point* refers to *Ka* (*Qi*) that is flowing smoothly in perfect harmony within and without all the systems. It is connected to the **heartbeat** of the **earth**, bringing relief from **disease** caused by **pathogens** and unnatural r**hythms** that result in **coughing** and **asthma**.

The *Sea Point* refers to the place where streams of *Meridian Ka* (*Qi*) come together and begin to infuse into the **organs**. Unnatural *flow* can cause symptoms of vomiting, dizziness and a heavy *sensation* in the **head**.

THE TWELVE MERIDIANS

The *Twelve Primary Ka* (*Qi*) *Channels* have *Yin* and *Yang* qualities that run sequential to each other, mirroring each other's function. The *Yang Channel* corresponds with the *Yin Organ* and is often used to treat *dis-orders* that originate from **problems** with *Yin*. *Yang Channels* are on the **external side** of the **limbs** while *Yin* travels on the **inside**. The **outside** of the **limbs** are generally tougher than the inside causing rough skin, padding and over-musculature. The **inside parts** of the **limbs** have softer **skin** and are *tender* to the *touch*. The *Yang* organs are divided into *Greater Yang*, *Lesser Yang* and *Yang Brightness.*

The **heart** (*Yin*) and the **small intestine** (*Yang*) are paired **organs** connected through *Greater Yang* (*Taiyang*), the **Small Intestine Channel of Hand**. The **small** and **large intestines** are located in the *Lower Dan Tian.* Proper circulation between *Original Essence* and the **small intestine** *Ka* (*Qi*) is essential for optimum performance.

Check for weaknesses of traveling to and from the **south**, living in the **south**, moving in and out of the **season** of **summer**, **heat** and the color **red**. The opening is in the **tongue** and will often involve **bitterness** in *taste*, *emotions* and **words**, the **smell** of **burning**, in particular *spiritual experiences* of **burning flesh** and weaknesses for *happiness* and the sound of *laughter*. *Balance tension* and *relaxation* in the **blood vessels** in sync to and from the **heart** for optimum performance. *Imbalances* of fire *energy* causing **heart burn** can be relieved by directing *Small Intestine Ka* (*Qi*) *channels* to cool **fire** in the **heart** and strengthening the upward *flow* of *Original Ka* (*Qi*).

The **kidneys** (*Yin*) and the **bladder** (*Yang*) are paired **organs** that are also connected through *Greater Yang* (*Taiyang*); the *Urinary Bladder Channel of Foot* opening, located at the **urethra**. They control **bone** development, **marrow** and the **brain**. Lack of performance between the two can be seen in the lack of *health*, particularly in *health* of **hair**. Check for weaknesses in the **bladder** to transform fluids into **urine** and effective **elimination** of **toxins**. Delete *experiences* of leaking *energy*, **body fluids**, *emotions*, etc. The emphasis is generally placed on the **kidneys** because they hold *Original Essence*; however, the importance of the connection between the **bladder** and **kidneys** should not be underestimated. Common weaknesses revolve around **water**, **winter** and **cold**, *fear* of things "going south" in a downward direction*, religious underground experiences* of "hell," *being buried* (*six feet under*), *darkness*, *black thoughts* or the color *black*, the *smell* of **decay**, the *taste* of **salt** and the *sound* of **groaning**.

The **lungs** (*Yin*) and the **large intestine** (*Yang*) are paired **organs** that are connected through *Yang Brightness* (*Yangming*) and the *Large Intestine Channel of Hand*. They govern **skin** and **hair** through the opening of the **nose**. Many **spleen** and **stomach** *dis-orders* are caused by *stagnation* of energy affecting the function of the **large intestine**, **small intestine** and the **respiratory system**. A strong lower **abdomen** provides space for *Dan Tian* where *Original Ka* (*Qi*) is stored. Regular **breathing** and proper *tension* from the back to support the **organs** in the **front** of the **body** eases the *flow* of *Ka* (*Qi*) through the **organs**. Check for *imbalances* from the *energies* of **metal**, weaknesses in traveling from and to the **west**, living in the **west**, moving in and out of the **season** of **autumn** or **fall**, *dryness*, lack of color, **albino** *experiences*, *being* **white**, *not being* **white**, *seeing* **white**, **strong odors**, **pungent** *tastes* and *emotional* weaknesses to *sadness* and the *sound* of **weeping**.

The **spleen** (*Yin*) and the **stomach** (*Yang*) are paired **organs** that are also connected to *Yang Brightness* (*Yangming*), the *Stomach Channel of Foot*. They govern **tissue** and **limbs** through the opening of the **mouth**. Bleeding **gums** and **bad breath** can often be relieved when weaknesses between the two are addressed. The **stomach** receives **nutrition** and moves it downward, while the **spleen** distributes the **nutrition** through upward movement. Strengthen the *flow* of both directions to empower this important connection, and clear any weaknesses for **dryness** in the **stomach** and dampness in the **spleen**. Most symptoms from **stomach** disorders originate in the **spleen** and are caused by excess. Too much *stomach fire* causes burning *sensations* in the **stomach**, ravenous appetite and constipation. *Emotionally* *repetitive re-actions* and persistent morbid *thoughts* are often responsible for many upsets in the **stomach**. Strengthen *feelings, intuition* and *sensitivity* to let go of *negative thoughts* and *limiting beliefs.* Check for weaknesses in the **solar plexus**, the color **yellow**, being forced to use **sweet words** and "lack of sweetness" in life, **fragrant odors**, **perfumes**, **essences** and the *sound* or *act* of **singing**.

The *Triple Burner* is connected to *Lesser Yang (Shaoyin)*, the *Triple Burner Channel Of Hand*. It is regarded in several ways as being formless (*Nan Jing*), as an **organ** coordinating the functions to metabolize water (*Nei Jing*), and also as a functional **system** in three separate zones of the **body**, the **upper**, **middle** and **lower burners**. The **head**, **neck**, **chest**, **heart** and **lungs** form mist in the **upper burner**. The area from the **chest** to the **navel** containing the **stomach, liver** and **spleen** form **foam** in the *middle burner,* and the *lower burner*, is equivalent to *swamp energy* settling in the lower **abdomen, kidneys** and **bladder**. Check if there are any weaknesses within the **three burners** and in their **connections** and *communications* with each other. The *flow* of energy through the **organs** needs to be fluid and smooth which can be achieved through perfect timing of *tension* and *relaxation* of **internal** and **external muscles** that support the **organs**. Strengthen any weaknesses for **reaching up** and **falling down, fast** and **slow** or *perceived* **success** and **failure**. Raising your **arms** above your **head** and slowly lowering them *stimulates* the *flow* of *Ka* (*Qi*).

The **liver** (*Yin*) and the **gall bladder** (*Yang*) are paired **organs** that are also connected to *Lesser Yang (Shaoyin)*, the *Gall Bladder Channel of Foot*. **Eyes** are the points of entry, controlling *fitness* of **muscles** and **joints**. Weaknesses show up as lack of *health* in the **fingernails** and **toenails**. Although the function of the **liver** is often considered more important, the **gall bladder** is responsible for the storage and excretion of **bile** produced by the **liver**. Any structural weaknesses affecting the flow of **bile** can lead to discomfort and pain in the **liver** and to the bloating and yellowing of the **skin**, **eyes**, **urine** and **tongue**. Check for weaknesses for traveling to and from the **east**, living in the **east**, **windy conditions**, the color of **green**, "feeling green," chewing or grinding **vegetation**, *re-actions* to *anger* and other "sour" *emotions*, **sour** *tastes*, the *sound* of **yelling**, weaknesses to **goats**, products from **goats** and their **odor**. Strengthen the **heart** to the **gallbladder** and vice-versa to clear *hesitations* in making strong *choices* and decisions.

The *Yin* organs are divided into *Greater Yin*, *Lesser Yin* and *Absolute Yin*. The **lungs** (*Yin*) and the **large intestine** (*Yang*) are paired **organs** connected through *Greater Yin* (*Taiyin*) and *the Large Intestine*

Channel of Hand. **Lungs** are considered to be the most delicate **organ**, sensitive to emotional outbursts of *anger*, *sadness* and *seasonal changes* especially when going from a **damp**, **hot summer** into a **dry**, **cool autumn**. People are often unaware of their **breathing** and don't notice that they spend much of their time *holding* their **breath**. Efficient breathing accelerates the *flow* of *life force energy* throughout the body, feeding all extremities including **hair** and **skin** by metabolizing liquid to hydrate the **skin**. **Deep breathing** diverts excess *Ka* (*Qi*) away from the **heart** to the **lungs** where it can be cooled to relieve **heart burn**.

The **spleen** (*Yin*) and the **stomach** (*Yang*) are paired **organs** that are also connected to **Greater Yin** (**Tailyn**), *The Spleen Channel of Foot*. The connection from the **spleen** to the **stomach** and vice-versa must be strong for the **spleen** to efficiently perform its function of *distributing* **nutrition** throughout the **body**. Weaknesses block the ability to *absorb* **nutrients**, which leads to fatigue, aches and a pale complexion. Lack of structure in the **upper cavity** of the **abdomen** causes deficiencies in the **spleen's** ability to carry **nutrients** upward, which often results in swelling and discomfort of the **abdomen**, diarrhea and cold **limbs**. The presence of **blood**, especially from the **digestive tract** or **uterus,** indicates that the **spleen** is compromised in its ability to control **blood** *flow*. **Cold** and **dampness** can also weaken the **spleen's** ability to transport and transform **nutrients**, and can lead to feelings of heaviness in the **chest**. Disturbances in *water metabolism* lead to production of **phlegm**. Shifting *emotional re-actions* from weather and lack of direction can be used to break **phlegm** down into **quantum particles** that can be eliminated through *black wholes*.

The **heart** (*Yin*) and the **small intestine** (*Yang*) are paired **organs** connected through *Lesser Yin* (*Shaoyin*), *the Heart Channel of Hand*. The **heart** is both a major component of the **circulatory system,** and also as a container for *spirit*. It is also considered the **organ** most connected to *thought process*. Its delicate balance is easily disrupted by *emotional distress*, causing symptoms such as dizziness, palpitations, shortness of breath and fatigue. Most disorders of the **heart** are considered to arise from deficiencies in the *flow* of *Ka* (*Qi*), *Yin*, *Yang* and **blood**. There are varied symptoms from weaknesses in each. **Panting**, **shallow breathing** and **sweating** often are attributed to weaknesses in the *flow* of *Ka* (*Qi*). Deficient *Heart Yang* often results in a swollen **face** with bluish and grayish undertones to the **skin** and **cold limbs**. Deficient *Heart Yin's* symptoms include flushed **palms**, **soles** and **face**, low-grade **fever** and **night sweating**. If the *flow* of **blood** is compromised the symptoms often manifest as restlessness, irritability, dizziness, absentmindedness and insomnia. Any weaknesses between the **heart** and **small intestine** create problems for the **small intestine** to maintain its role in *metabolism* and the management of **water** in the **body**. The **heart**, **mind** and **spirit** are all closely associated with the **solar plexus** as the container for *Fire Qi* that nourishes the **brain** and **spirit**. Generally, because the **heart** is a *Yin* organ, it is more vulnerable in the **summer** because **summer** is *Yang energy*.

The **kidneys** (*Yin*) and the **bladder** (*Yang*) are paired **organs** that are also connected through *Lesser Yin* (*Shaoyin*) the *Kidney Channel of Foot*. Your **inherent vitality** or *Original Essence, Yin* and *Yang*, is stored in the **kidneys**. *Ka* (**Qi**) is converted from **essence** to nourish your entire **body, brain** and **spirit** to support *growth, development* and the **reproductive system**. **Kidneys** are responsible for the control of **bodily fluids** and the *metabolism* of **water**. Weaknesses in the **kidneys** will often affect other **organs,** and involve deficiencies of *Yin* and *Yang* that often cause pain in the **lower back**, loss of **hearing** and ringing in the **ears**. Deficient *Kidney Yin* generates similar disorders in the **heart** and **liver** in both directions. Common symptoms are **dark circles** under the **eyes**, dizziness, thirst, **night sweats** and low-grade **fevers**. The **reproductive system** can also be compromised, causing **premature ejaculation** in men and lack of **menstruation** in women. When there is deficient *Kidney Yang*, the *soreness* in the **back** is often accompanied by feeling cold, fatigued, and weak in the **legs**, and by large amounts of clear **urine, incontinence** and **impotence** in men. Other organs that are commonly compromised are the **spleen** and **lungs**. Weaknesses between *Kidney Yang* and the **lungs** cause **breathing** difficulties such as wheezing, a faint voice, coughing, puffiness of the **face** and spontaneous **sweating**. Many weaknesses in the **kidneys** are amplified in the months of **winter**.

The **pericardium** (*Yin*) and the **triple burner** (*Yang*) are paired **organs** connected to *Absolute Yin* (*Jueyin*) the *Pericardium Channel of Hand*. *Ka* (**Qi**) is able to communicate with its surrounding environment to regulate its *flow* through **five gates** in the **body**. Two of these **gates** are called the *Laogong Cavities*, two are the *Younquan Cavities,* and the fifth is the **face**. The **face** will show any weaknesses in the flow of *Original Qi* because of this. The function of the **pericardium** is to regulate the *flow* of *Ka* (*Qi*) in the **heart**, dissipating any excess *Ka* (*Qi*) caused by illness, exercise, *emotional re-actions* and injuries that collect in the **pericardium**. The excess can be released through the *Laogong Cavities* in the center of the **palms**; this relieves delirium and high **fevers**.

The **liver** (*Yin*) and the **gall bladder** (*Yang*) are paired **organs** that also connect to *Lesser Yang* (*Shaoyin*), the *Liver Channel of Foot*. The main function of your **liver** is to transport and regulate *Ka* (**Qi**) throughout the entire **body,** and store **blood** when your **body** is at rest. Long term *frustration* and so-called **depression** are common *emotional* and *psychological* weaknesses that *stagnate* the ability of the **liver** to function; that can eventually *affect* the **stomach** and **spleen,** causing a change in the direction *of the flow*. *Rebellious Qi* is *Ka* (*Qi*) that **bucks** the *flow*, causing it to travel in the opposite direction. If the **stomach** *Qi* is compromised it **pushes up** instead of *flowing down*, which causes hiccoughing, vomiting, etc.; if the *Spleen QI* is compromised, it **descends**, causing diarrhea.

Overall *fitness* of the **abdomen** and in particular, women's **reproductive organs**, is dependent on strong **liver** function. Many weakening factors for the **liver** are instigated by the *mind* and cause *dis-orders* of the **menstrual cycle**, swollen and painful **breasts**, etc. If **blood** in the **liver** is compromised, the **liver** cannot handle its responsibilities to moisten the **body**, which leads to dry **skin** and **eyes**, blurred and weak vision, lack of flexibility, dizziness and spotty **menstrual bleeding**. The greater the deficiency, the more it causes *dis-order* in the **head** and **joints**. Normal circulation of the **liver** promotes a strong **gallbladder** and vice-versa.

QI JING BA MAI (The Eight Extra Meridians)

Qi Jing Ba Mai literally translates as enlightened *understanding* through the precious **essence** of life via the eight movements of the **meridians**. The *Eight Extra Meridians* are pathways of *energy* or (*Qi*) that run deep within our bodies, supplying the *twelve regular meridians* with *Ka* (*Qi*) and **blood**, and supporting **DNA** and **genetic heritage**. They do not have direct connections to the **organ system,** but with the exception of *Du Mai* (*Governing Vessel*) and *Ren Mai* (*Conceptual Vessel*), they share points with the twelve regular **meridians**.

The *Governing* and *Conceptual Vessels* are considered to be important *channels* because they contain *acupuncture points* that are independent of the *twelve regular meridians*. The *Conceptual Vessel* (*Ren Mai*) runs from the **perineum** along the middle of the **abdomen** and **chest**, passes through the **cheek** and enters under the **eye socket**. It is responsible for receiving and bearing the *Ka* (*Qi*) of the *Yin meridians* and the **birth process** of a child or creative idea. *Ren Mai* regulates the **uterus, menstruation, menopause, pregnancy**, etc. Energetic weaknesses affect the **lungs, chest** and **throat** and often cause **breathing imbalances** such as **childhood asthma**. The **Master Point** for **Ren Mai** is **Lung 7** on the **lung** *channel* that is coupled with **Kidney 6** on the **Yin Quai Mai Channel**. You can optimize the **Conceptual Vessel** by strengthening the connections of **Ren Mai**, **Yin Quai Mai**, **Kidneys**, **Lungs** and **Ka** (**Qi**) in all directions to each other.

The **Governing Vessel** (**Du Mai**) runs from the **tail** of the **spine** to the **crown** of the **head** and governs the *flow* of **Ka** (**Qi**) from all the **Yang** *meridians* of the **body**. It relates to *transformational cycles*, *survival issues* and being **grounded** to *manifest* in our third dimensional world. The **Master Point** for **Du Mai** is **Small Intestine 3** coupled with the **Yang Quai Mai Master Point of Bladder 62**. When these two *master points* are strong to each other it strengthens the entire **spine**, nourishes the **brain** and relieves **dizziness** and **tinnitus**.

The **Du Mai** governs the **Ka** (**Qi**) of all the **Yang Meridians**, regulating the inner **canthus** of the **eye**, where the **upper** and **lower eyelid**s meet. Drooping **upper lids** run in families who habitually protect their **hearts** from painful *sights*, and peek out from beneath the **hood** of their **upper eyelid** while hiding behind it. Weaknesses in **Du Mai** often cause stiffness in the **shoulders**, **neck** and **back**, as well as **problems** with independence and risk taking. You can optimize the **Governing Vessel** by strengthening the connections of **Du Mai**, **Yang Qiau Mai** with the **small intestine** and **bladder** in all directions to each other.

The **Penetrating Vessel** (**Chong Mai**) affects the **heart**, **chest** and **stomach**, regulating the vital passage of **Ka** (**Qi**) and **blood** in the *twelve regular meridians*. **Gynecological disorders**, **digestive** issues, **prolapses** and **problems** with the **heart** are common when **Chong Mai** is weak. The **Master Point** for **Chong Mai** is **Spleen 4** combined with **Pericardium 6** on the **Yin Wei Mai Chanel**. Energetic weaknesses in **Chong Mai** are often *spiritual*, *psychological*, *psychic* and *karmic*, relating to intergenerational patterns caused by abuse and **cellular memory** that negatively impact *self-acceptance* and *self-love*. You can optimize **Chong Mai** by strengthening the connections of **Chong Mai**, **Yin Wei Mai**, **Spleen**, **Pericardium** and **Ka** (**Qi**) in all directions to each other.

The **Linking Vessels**, **Yin and Yang Wei Mai** function to connect and network *vessels* and maintain the *balance* of the **body's Yin** and **Yang**. They relate to the *transitions* involved in the *aging process* and the accompanying *transformation* of **Yin** and **Yang energies**. The **Yin Wei Mai** is paired with the **Chong Mai** that permits energetic access to the **Inner Gate to the Self** (**Neiguan**). Energetic weaknesses are related to the meaning we draw from life and our ability to respond with clarity. The opening point of **Yang Wei Mai** is the **Triple Heater 5**. When coupled with the **Gall Bladder 41** on the **Dai Mai**, it dominates the exterior of the **body**. Strong connections provide relief from **chills** and **fever**. Weaknesses in these connections cause **problems** arising from a reliance on **outdated modes** of **behavior**, **old habits** and patterns from **psychic**, **spiritual** and **psychological energies** that prevent evolution and is often the last stage of defense before the **body** is invaded by **terminal pathogens** and **serious disease**, such as cancer and HIV.

The **Heel Vessel, Qiaos**, originates on the inside and outside of the **heel**, governing motion and increasing **agility** of the **body**, especially in the **lower limbs**. **Yin Qiao Mai** is paired with **Ren Mai**. Weaknesses in this connection cause imbalance of **left** to **right**, inversions of the **feet**, pain in the **eyes** and **stagnation** of the **systems**. Issues of **self-trust**, **abandonment**, **depression** and **feelings** of **unworthiness** on the **psychological** level are also common. **Yang Qaio Mai** is also paired with **Ren Mai**. Weaknesses between the two often cause the **sensation** of "walking on a slant," excessive **thinking** and **thoughts** of **overwhelm**, feeling out of control, insomnia, epilepsy, facial paralysis and Bell's Palsy.

The **Belt Meridian**, (**Dai Mai**) is the dumping ground for unexpressed **emotions** and **psychological** issues. The **Master Point** of the **Dai Mai** is **Gall Bladder 41** paired with **Triple Heater 5** on **Yin Wei Mai**. They impact the area behind the **ear**, the **cheeks** and **outer canthus** of the **eye**. Weaknesses can cause extreme **frustration**, **indecision** and **low self-esteem**.

THE BACK TRANSPORT POINTS AND ALARM POINTS

The **Back Transport Points** are in the back sections of the **bladder meridian**, and the **Alarm Points** are in the front of the **body**. They are close to the **internal organs** allowing **Ka** (**Qi**) to easily infuse into these **points**. They are helpful for evaluating the status of **internal organs** because **Ka** (**Qi**) easily infuses these **points**, directly regulating the functions of their corresponding **organ**. **Back Transport Points** are frequently used to treat **Yin Organ** disease in the **lungs**, **spleen**, **heart**, **liver** and **kidneys** as well as shifting **tissues** and **structural problems** that relate to these **organs**. Weaknesses in the **Alarm Points** frequently cause problems in **Yang** organs and **meridians** that affect the **stomach, gallbladder, bladder, large** and **small intestines**. If there is **Yin Organ dis-ease**, the **Back Transport** is usually the number one weakness with the **Alarm Point** referred, whereas in **Yang Organ dis-ease** it is usually the opposite, where the **Alarm Point** is often the leading weakness and the **Back Transport** is referred.

EIGHT INFLUENTIAL POINTS

There are **Eight Influential Points** where essence of the **Yin** and **Yang** **organs**, **Ka** (**Qi**), **blood, tendons, blood vessels, bones** and **marrow** **flow** and gather. You can optimize the **Eight Influential Points** by strengthening their connections in all directions to each other.

CLEFT POINTS

The **Cleft Points** are where **Ka** (**Qi**) gathers in the **elbows** and **knees**. Optimize the **Cleft Points** by strengthening their connections in all directions to each other. The **Yin Cleft Meridian** includes the **lungs, pericardium, heart, spleen, liver, kidneys, Yin Link Vessel** and **Yin Heel Vessel**. The **Yang Cleft Meridian** is made up of the **large intestine, triple burner, small intestine, Yang Link Vessel** and **Yin Heel Vessel**.

LOWER SEA POINTS

Lower Sea Points are where **Ka** (**Qi**) from the six **Yang organs**, the **stomach, small intestine, large intestine, gall bladder, triple burner** and **bladder**, travel downward to the six locations on the **Yang Meridians**, mainly in the region of the **knees**.

CROSSING POINTS

There are over one hundred **Crossing Points** all over the body where two or three **meridians** intersect. The majority of the **Yang meridians** are located in the **face**, **head** and **Yin** **meridians** of the **torso**.

THE "GOOD NEWS" IS:

The **meridians**, **channels** and **acupuncture points** move referred and related **physical** weaknesses, give clues as to what **body parts**, **actions, situations**, **seasons**, etc. may be **affecting** the **body part** in question and the **meridian** in general. A basic understanding of the inner workings of the flow of energy is similar to using a map to find your way from one destination to another.

THE "BAD NEWS" IS:

There is no downside. It may **seem** intimidating to attempt to understand the inner workings of **acupuncture points, meridians**, **channels** etc. however understanding the **flow** of **Ka** (**Qi**) is not that complicated when you recognize that every *point* runs on a *meridian* and every *meridian* *flows* with *Ka* (*Qi*) somewhat like the *flow* of traffic off highways onto smaller roads, avenues and crescents.

NUGGET OF WIZDOM FROM THE VECTOR

AS YOU BECOME MORE AWARE OF HOW ENERGY FLOWS, YOU INCREASE YOUR ABILITY TO ELIMINATE BOTH PHYSICAL AND NON-PHYSICAL WASTE THROUGH THE EXIT PORTALS IN THE PHYSICAL BODY AND TO SPIN BENEFICIAL ENERGY IN.

EXTERNAL FORCES

External forces are positive and negative life *experiences* that enter our **reality** and alter our *perception*. We can compare *external forces* to **snowflakes** in a **snowstorm** to better understand how they *affect* the *collective* as well as the **individual**.

Snowflakes, like people come in all shapes and sizes. Every flake is unique, yet all of them have **fundamental structures** in common because every snowflake has six sides. If you compare *external forces* to **snowflakes**, they seem insignificant on their own because anyone can put up with a **flake** or two; however, they gain **weight** as they *accumulate*. If they become too heavy for the roof, they can eventually weaken and collapse a person's house. Anyone who has survived winter on the prairies of Canada will be able to relate. Some people look forward to the first arrival of snow while others absolutely dread it. If you enjoy winter sports, the snow is equated with fun; however, if a person is focusing on icy roads, scary driving conditions, the trials and tribulations of dealing with extreme negative zero temperatures, wind chill factors, plugging in the car, being late for work because the car won't start, waiting for the tow truck, shoveling driveways, slippery walkways etc., they are in for a very long winter.

By the end of February everyone has pretty much had enough of winter. Even the people who enjoy snow get tired of stormy weather and bitter cold and begin to look forward to the melting of snow in spring. However, spring can be very elusive in Canada especially on the prairies. It is not uncommon to have major blizzards in March and still be waiting for spring to finally arrive in April and May. This is tedious for pretty much everyone. Eventually, the **body**, *soul* and *spirit* become weak and, just like a roof in a heavy snowstorm, the weight can become so heavy that the *authentic self triad* collapses under the burden of *doubt* and succumbs to *fear* from the *accumulated external forces*. People may not be aware of these *collective energies* because they are hidden in **cultural upbringing, religious training,** *karmic ties,* **educational weaknesses** and **manipulative tactics.** The *effects* of *external forces* can be subtle and leave a person wondering … What the E.F. happened? Strong **boundaries** empower you to recognize *negative energies* and have the *flexibility* to allow them to pass through you rather than *attaching* themselves to you.

Common *reality-altering flakes* that you are likely to encounter:

COLLECTIVE

In the same way that individual **cells** create the **organs** and **systems** of your **body,** your *consciousness* is similarly layered, and creates *collective consciousness* of your *experiences* as a *conscious* **being** in a **physical body.**

GOVERNMENT

Government is the means by which state policy is enforced through **institutions** that transcend an **individual's** *intentions* to mediate rules that govern living *behavior,* and thus government *affects* **human** *activity* in important ways.

EDUCATION

People encounter situations where they *see* themselves as less *intelligent* than others around them because they do not have a formal **education.** The truth is that the more **educated** a person is through **institutions,** the more *myopic* their *vision* becomes.

CULTURAL

There are **customary beliefs, social forms, material traits, rituals** and **traditions** that many follow with very little understanding of the history behind them.

RELIGION

Many **religions** have hi-jacked *spirituality* to justify *limiting beliefs* that are far from *spiritual.* An ever-present example is using religious beliefs to justify **war.** *Spiritual growth* is often devastated by the dictates of religious policies and corrupt leaders.

LINEAGE

Being born into a particular **family** in the third dimensional world does not limit you to that **family**; however, your upbringing within your **family** has a profound **effect** on your **perception** of **reality**. It is common for **ancestors** who have battled in **wars** to remain enemies even when they are in **spirit form**.

KARMA

Karma is not good or bad, positive or negative. It is **cause** and **effect**, the **result** of **actions** taken throughout **space-time**. For every **action** there is an equal re-action.

THE "GOOD NEWS" IS:

Being caught in the middle of **external forces** can seem **hopeless**; however, if people refuse to buy into an inaccurate version of history they can find **creative solutions** to life's **problems** by going inward for **intuitive answers**.

THE "BAD NEWS" IS:

If you feel caught **between** circumstances that leave you wondering what the **E.F.** is happening, you are probably the middleman, being controlled by **external forces**.

NUGGET OF WIZDOM FROM THE VECTOR

LET GO OF HISTORY. GOVERN YOURSELF, EDUCATE YOURSELF AND CELL-EBRATE YOURSELF! BE THE BEST VERSION OF YOUR SELF THAT YOU CAN BE.

EYES

Suppression of **thoughts** and **emotions** from **traumas**, **illnesses** and **negative emotions** can trigger weaknesses in **vision** because people avoid looking at certain **aspects** of their lives. To improve clarity of **vision** it is usually more productive to shift weaknesses in the **physical eyes** first and then correct **vision**. *EU ... VISION, Pg. 504*

First and foremost, you want to be sure that the **physical potential** for the **eyes** is connected to and operating at optimum potential from the **cranial brain** to the bottom of the **spine**. You also want to check that the

optic nerves at the back of the **eyes** are strong to functioning with the **optic brain**. This includes four **cranial nerves**: the **optic nerve**, **oculomotor nerve**, **trochlear nerve** and **abducens nerve**. Strengthen all *connections* on the **physical**, *mental*, *emotional* levels and **biochemical** *processes*. Strengthen **eyes** to be even with each other and the energy *circuitry* between the **eyes** to passively *receive* light. Correct the **axial length** (the linear distance from the front of the **cornea** to the back of the **retina**) to be optimal. Optimize the **muscles**, **internal mechanisms** and the shape of the **eyes** for the converging ability of each eye to work with each other to focus on a close object. Strengthen the **lens**, *position* of **lens** and the **shape** of the **eye** to be at optimum potential. Strengthen the **hypothalamus** to *homeostasis*.

The inter-relationships of the **brain** and the **CNS** must be integrated to the three layers of the **outer eye**, the **middle eye** and the **inner eye**. The **outer eye** consists of the **sclera**, **conjunctiva** and the **cornea**.

SCLERA

The **sclera** is the **white** of the **eyes** that gives the **eyeball** a **spherical shape**. It is made of tough opaque **tissue** that protects the **eye**. Six **muscles** connect to the **sclera**, around the **eye**. The **optic nerve** is *attached* at the back.

CONJUNCTIVA

The **conjunctiva** is a thin transparent covering on the **outer surface** of the **eye** and lining on **inner surface** of **eyelids**. It secretes **oils** and **mucous** to moisten and lubricate the **eye**.

CORNEA

The **cornea** is a dome shaped window covering the front of the **eye** (where a **contact lens** sits) that provides a major part of the **eye's** focusing power. It is extremely *sensitive* because there are more *nerve endings* in it than anywhere else in the **body**. The surface of the **cornea** is made up of a layer of **cells**, the **epithelium** that *regenerates* if the **eye** is injured. If **scarring** occurs there it can **affect** *vision*. The next layer is a tough **membrane**, called the **bowman** that protects the **cornea** from injury. Just under it is the **stroma**, made up of tiny **collagen fibers** that run parallel to each other that gives the **cornea** clarity. Lying between the final layer and give the **endothelium** and the **stroma** is the **descemet's membrane**. The **endothelium** is only one **cell** thick and is responsible for pumping **water** from the **cornea**. If it is damaged it does not *regenerate*, and the **cornea** loses *clarity*.

The **middle eye** consists of the **uvea**, the **pupil** and the **lens**. The **uvea** is made up of the **choroid, ciliary body, iris, pupil and lens**. The **choroid layer** of the **eye** consists of **blood vessels** and **connective tissue** between the **sclera** and the **retina**. It provides **oxygen** and **nutrients** to the outer layers of the **retina**.

CILIARY BODY

The **ciliary body** secretes transparent liquid within the **eye**. It also contains **muscles** that adjust the **lens** to focus **light** on the **retina**. When the **ciliary body** *contracts*, it allows the **lens** to thicken, thereby increasing the **eye's** ability to focus up close. When it *relaxes*, the **lens** becomes thinner and allows the **eye** to focus on distance. It must have *flexibility* and a strong *connection* to the **oculomotor nerve**.

The **iris** is the circular area of **fibers** that make up **eye color**. **Lighter colored eyes** tend to be more *sensitive* to both **light** and *emotions*. A **brown iris** shows warmth, openness and is less *sensitive* to **pain**. **Dark brown** and **black irises** show less *sensitivity* and more *passion*. **Hazel irises** show warmth and intellectual vigor, the **lighter** the **blue** of **blue irises**, the less *passion* and *compassion* is evident, while **green irises** show courage, daring and tend to belong to clever, *sensitive* individuals. People with **grey irises** have a tendency to be *emotionally guarded*.

The **pupil** is an opening in the center of the **iris**, is controlled by the **dilator** and **sphincter muscles** of the **iris**, and *narrows* or *widens* to let in **light**. The *lens* is a transparent **elastic body** that lies just behind the **iris**. Its purpose is to *focus* light onto the **retina**. It is important that it remains *flexible*.

The **inner eye** consists of the **retina, rods, cones, aqueous humor** and **vitreous humor**. The **retina** lines the **inside** of the back of the **eye**. It has millions of **photoreceptors** that *receive* light, converting it into images through *electrical impulses* that travel along the **optic nerve** to the **brain**. There are two types of **photoreceptors** in the **retina**: the **rods** and the **cones**. The **rods** detect *light intensity* and the ability to *see* in **dim light**. The **cones** are contained in the **macula**, a highly sensitive part of the **retina** that detects color and fine detail for tasks such as reading.

The **eyeball** is divided into two fluid-filled **cavities**, the **aqueous humor**, an anterior **cavity** in front of the **lens** that nourishes the **internal structures** of the **eye**; and the **vitreous chamber**, a posterior **cavity**, containing the **vitreous humor**, a **gelatin-like** substance on the front and sides of the **iris** that helps the **eye** to hold its shape. If the **vitreous humor** shrinks, it becomes stringy and separates from the **retina** causing floaters. The **eyeball** needs to be at optimum *density* to keep its ideal shape.

Strengthen the **connections** and **structure** of the **inner eye, outer eye** and **middle eye** to be strong to each other. For clear **vision**, all **components** of the **eyes** need to be strong to eliminate **cellular waste, parasites, parasitic waste, calcium** and other **minerals** through the **lymphatic system** and **black wholes**, and for **nutrients, oxygen** and **hydration** to spin in through **white-holes**. *EU … BLACK WHOLE/ WHITE WHOLE, Pg. 93*

Many weaknesses in the **eyes** are referred from other parts of the **body** that come in "two's." Strengthen the **eyes** to other **body parts** that come in **pairs** and **two's**, in particular the **ovaries** and **testicles**. Common words people use to describe the **sensations** they feel in their **eyes** are **dryness**, **itching**, **soreness**, **irritation**, **burning**, **irritation** and **pressure**. *EU … SENSATIONS, Pg. 456*

THE "GOOD NEWS" IS:

Your **eyes** are constantly changing because the **cells** are dying off and **restructuring** at an escalated rate. This is a plus because you can shift weaknesses as you feel them, and therefore you can consistently improve the **physical components** to work at optimum potential.

THE "BAD NEWS" IS:

Your **eyes** are **sensitive** and sophisticated **light receptors** that contain one billion working **parts** that are **physical** extensions of your **brain**. There are many reasons why you may not be **seeing** clearly, reasons that are both **physical** and **non-physical**. To maintain infinite potential, you must continuously and systematically shift many **components** on the **physical**, **emotional**, **psychological**, **spiritual** and **psychic** level.

NUGGET OF WIZDOM FROM THE VECTOR

SEEING IS NOT BELIEVING! IT IS BECAUSE YOU HAVE EYES THAT YOU CANNOT SEE. THE HUMAN EYE IS ONLY ABLE TO SEE FOUR PERCENT OF THE ELECTROMAGNETIC SPECTRUM. THAT LEAVES NINETY-SIX PERCENT UNSEEN, AND OF THE FOUR PERCENT THAT YOU CAN SEE, MUCH IS NOT PERCEIVED CORRECTLY.

FACIAL RE-ENGINEERING

There are many reasons why people **age**, and it tends to show in the **face** before anywhere else in the **physical body** because in most cultures the face is always on display. Every **chakra** in the **body** is also replicated in the **face,** and the **face** is a reflection of what is going on in the **body**. It is important to have evenness between the **body** and **face** to optimize *youthfulness* for both.

The underlying **bone structure** of the **face** is like the underlying form of a statue. The **tissues, muscles, ligaments** and **skin** are like clay that molds and flesh out the **face** to add *character* and individuality to it. It is important to maintain the **bone structure** and the **empty spaces** within the **face**. The **eyeball sockets**, the **sinuses**, the **ears** and the **oral cavity** must be strong in all directions, **up, down, front, back, left** to **right** and **right** to **left, inside, outside** and **in-between**.

Faces can be generalized into simple **shapes** and combinations of those **shapes** that share specific traits or tendencies. **Round faces** tend to belong to *easygoing* individuals, **oval faces** are *associated* with *sensitive* people with feminine traits, **square faces** generally reflect *practical* and down-to-earth people while **rectangular** faces typically belong to *idealistic* people, and **triangular** faces have a tendency to have exaggerated traits at the location of the widest and narrowest points. For example, a **wide forehead** and **refined jawline** indicate *mental intelligence* and *sensitivity*, whereas a person with a **narrow forehead** and **wide jawline** is likely to be more *close-minded* and *stubborn*.

The height of the **face** shows the capacity of the *mental*, *emotional*, and **physical bodies**. Keeping an *open mind* is essential. The **eyebrows** signify *emotional type* and the degree of understanding between the *mind* and the **heart**. Many women in particular, hide their *imagination*, *memory* and *observation* skills behind **bangs**, and men beneath the brim of **ball caps**.

The **shape** and **size** of the **eyes** represent the deeper inner feelings of an individual's *personality*. The **right eye** generally shows aspects of the **physical personality**, and the **left eye** reflects *spiritual* or *soul* quality. The distance between the **eyes** is ideally the length of one **eye**. **Eyes** that are closer together tend to belong to people who have a "narrower" *point of view*, whereas **eyes** that are further than an eye-width apart tend to belong to individuals who lack **focus**. **Eyes** that **slant upward** at the outer corners are indicative of *pride*. **Eyes** that **slant down** tend to belong to *generous* people who are more easily taken advantage of. As people **age**, their **eye sockets** and the **eyes** themselves typically shrink in **size**. Strengthen all the **cranial nerves** leading to the eyes (**numbered II, III, IV** and **VI**) to prevent shrinkage.

Reduce any **swelling** under the **eyes** by considering the **encapsulations** and **merging dead cells** and **tissues,** and maximizing the **lymphatic** *connections* to and from those areas. **Drooping** of the **eyelids** on the **outer corners** is often a *protection mechanism* to veil an open **heart**. Make sure the **eyelids** are strong to opening by connecting **eyelids** to the **CNS** and relieve pressure by improving **structure** of the socket behind the eyeball. The *Du Mai* governs the *Ka* (*Qi*) of all the **yang** *meridians,* regulating the **inner canthus** of the **eye** (where the **upper** and **lower eyelids** meet). Create *black wholes* in the back of the **eyes** to facilitate clearing of **physical**, *emotional*, *psychological* and *psychic* **toxins** and **waste**.

The **nose** is the *projector* of *personality*. It is the first part of the face to enter a room and make its presence known. The stronger and more dominant the **nose**, generally the stronger the personality. The **length** of the **nose** and the **firmness** and **fleshiness** at the **tip** are an indication of ability to *manifest*. The prominence at the **base** of the **nose** where it meets the **brow** can enhance or inhibit clarity between **left** and **right eyes** and **brain** *activity*. **Noses** that point down towards the **lips** generally belong to *sensuous, sexually* active individuals, while **noses** that slope up tend to belong to those who have *high ideals*. We take *life-force energy (Ka)* in through our **nostrils**, and the **size** and **shape** are often related to the ability to *manifest* and handle **finances**. **Noses** tend to widen with *age*. Decrease the **width** of the **nose** and increase the *regeneration* of the **cartilage** and **bone** to restore the **nose** to its optimum shape.

The **mouth** and **lips** have an intimate connection with the **genitalia**. **Large lips** tend to belong to more *emotional, sensitive* people. **Narrower lips** belong to more *critical, judgmental* people. A **large lower lip** indicates an ability to "give lip" (speak out). A **large upper lip** shows a high degree of **sexuality** and *sensuality*. The point of *sensitivity*, where the middle of the **top lip** meets the **lower lip** is comparable to the **clitoris** or **prostate**, the **lips** themselves to the **labia** and **scrotum** and the **tongue** to the **penis**. Strengthen **testosterone** in the underlying **structures** of the **lips** and the **muscles** that pull the **lips** up as well as **estrogen** to plump up the **lips** from the inside out.

The strength of the jaw, **chin** and **cheekbones** are an indication of an individual's **foundation, grounding** and *manifestation* capabilities on the **physical plane**. **Strong jawlines** and **chins** indicate an *adaptability* and *expression* through **physical** *manifestation* in the third-dimensional world. Weaknesses in the **jawline** are often referred to or from the **pelvic floor, pelvis** and **hips**. **Fleshy cheeks** show a kind-natured person with **exuberance** for life, whereas **flat, lean cheeks** generally belong to **logical** individuals who are well in **control** of their *emotions*.

Substantial differences between the **right** and **left** side of the **face** indicate division of the **male** and **female** *aspects* of an individual. The more balanced the face from **left** to **right** the calmer the individual tends to be. The **right side** (**left brain**) shows the more *analytical personality*, the **mind**, *yang* and **doing**, whereas **left side** (**right brain**) is *yin*, *creative*, *reactive* and *flexible*.

If you consider that information is *energy* and *thoughts* become **matter**, the many *thoughts* we have as we "face" life and face ourselves in the mirror have the ability to **physically** *change* the **shape** and **structures** of the **components** of the **face**, and they do so gradually over time. It is not uncommon for couples that live together over many years to begin to look more and more like each other because of their common *thoughts* and shared **space**.

Stiffness and *rigidity* of the **body** and *mind* contribute to **aging**. On the **physical** level these symptoms often originate from *stagnation* within the **systems** of the **body**. Proper *tension* throughout the **systems** and layers of **skin** are crucial to prevent and reverse **aging**. Strengthen the **buttocks** to the **face** and to the **CNS**. Proper *tension* in the **buttocks**, particularly for those who **sit** a lot, strengthens the components of the **face** to also have proper **tension**. Streamline all systems of the **face** to when you were younger by consciously *tensing* your **eyes**, **ears**, **nose**, **lips**, **inside of mouth**, **forehead**, etc., along with your **buttocks** and run the energy up your **spine**. Get into the habit of *conscious tension* on a regular basis throughout any given day and strengthen *tension* in the **face** before going to sleep at night.

The primary cause of **aging** in the **skin** is an *accumulation* of **waste products** within the **cells** and between the layers of the **skin**. Strengthen the branches of the **cranial nerve VIII** to the **nose** and the rest of the facial **muscles** and **bones** to the **cranial nerves** and all components of the **lymphatic system**. Check that basic **bio-chemistry**, **HGH** levels and **sexual hormones**, **oxygen** and **hydration** reach every layer of the **skin**. Strengthen resonance to youthful skin by increasing the **negative ions** and **electromagnetic charges** and **alkalinity**.

Instead of masking your feelings about chronological **age** and trying to **think** you are young, *feel* young. Do not *deny* and *suppress* your *feelings*; shift them. Throughout any given day, there will be thousands upon thousands of triggers that *affect* aging on a *conscious* and *subconscious* level. Don't take aging seriously – youthfulness is a game. Play to win by catching as many weaknesses as you can, and let the others go with a light heart.

THE "GOOD NEWS" IS:

You can sustain *youthfulness* by increasing *memories* of **youthfulness** and decreasing the *forgetfulness* of **aging**.

"Too much sitting" is the leading weakness for *aging* of the **face,** whereas **dancing** and other **circular movements** strengthen *youthfulness*.

THE "BAD NEWS" IS:

Many women struggle to rise to the unrealistic standards of the airbrushed, professionally made up models that are so prevalent in today's media. They are holding themselves to an unrealistic standard of beauty that is impossible to maintain on a daily basis. The models in the magazines have a team of hairdressers, makeup artists, photographers and lighting experts and can only capture the perfection for a split second in a photograph by photoshopping it.

NUGGET OF WIZDOM FROM THE VECTOR

ANYONE CAN HAVE A "BAD FACE DAY." WHEN YOU WAKE UP IN THE MORNING AND LOOK IN THE MIRROR AND DON'T LIKE WHAT YOU SEE. CLEAR THE SUB-CONSCIOUS AND UN-CONSCIOUS THOUGHTS THAT INVADED YOUR MIND THROUGHOUT THE NIGHT AND CONSCIOUSLY LOOK FOR QUALITIES IN YOUR FACE THAT YOU WANT TO REFLECT TO OTHERS.

FAMILY

When people think of **family**, they automatically think of the **family** they were **born into** and/or **adopted by**, as well as the **family** they may have created through **marriage**, **cohabitation** and **descendants**. As *multi-dimensional beings*, *family* is actually much more extensive than people realize. When a person is born into a specific **family**, the **ancestors** and **descendants** of every member of the **family** from both sides of their **parents**, **aunts**, **uncles**, **grandparents**, **great grandparents** etc., have an *effect* on them whether they are aware of the connections or not. It is very common these days for people to **marry**, **divorce** and **re-marry**, some more than once, thus creating even more interactions with **step-parents**, **step-siblings**, **step-grandparents**, etc. People who are **adopted** also have **biological parents**, **siblings** and all the extended **relatives** as well as **adoptive** family members to **deal** with.

The people we interact with in the first six to seven years of our lives have a significant influence on the formation of our *sub-conscious mind*. Even when we are raised in a **family unit,** each and every one of us has a different *relationship* with our **parents** than our **siblings** do because **birth order** and **gender** can have a profound effect on **family** *dynamics*. For instance, the **oldest born** child in a **family** is always the **eldest** as well as the **baby** until the next child comes along. When the **second child** is born, the **first child** remains the **eldest**, but relinquishes the role of **baby**, often with some *resistance* and *resentment*. If the **second child** is of a different **gender** than the first **sibling**, he or she automatically becomes the **oldest** of that **gender** as well as the **baby**. If the first **two siblings** are of the same **gender**, the **first** is the **eldest**, the **second** the **baby**.

If or when the **third child** comes along the **second sibling** now becomes the **middle child**, the **first** is the **eldest**, and the **third child** is now the **baby**, if they are all of the same **gender**. If the **third child** is also the **first child** born in the **family** of the **opposite gender**, he or she now becomes the **eldest** of that **gender**, as well as the **baby** of the **family**. The **first child** is still the **eldest**, the **second child** is now the **baby** of that **gender** and also takes on the role of the **middle child**.

There are so many *variations* of **order** of **birth** and **gender**. Each time another member is added to the **family**, it *affects* **parenting** and *family dynamics*. Most of the time people have *karma* with their **parents** and **siblings**, as well as with the **significant others** with whom they choose to have **children** and with whom their **children** *choose* to create a **family**. People also have *connections* with their *soul family*, who can appear to be complete *strangers* that they meet and *resonate* with so strongly that they feel more like **family** than the one into which they were born. These are *sisters* and *brothers* from other *mothers*. **Human beings** also have a familial connection with every other **human** on the planet and share **DNA** with **plants** and **animals**. As well, we are a *cosmic family resonating* with our *inter-and-intra galactic family* throughout the entire universe. It is essential to be strong to *family dynamics* by deleting the negative *effects* of **family** *now*, in the *past* and in the *future*.

THE "GOOD NEWS" IS:

Even on the days when we are feeling all alone and lonely we never truly are. We are always connected to *family*.

THE "BAD NEWS" IS:

The *relationships* between **family** members are complicated because of all the possible combinations of *inter-connectedness*. There can be many twists and turns making *karmic* connections challenging to unravel.

NUGGET OF WIZDOM FROM THE VECTOR

MOTHER–IN-LAW JOKES ARE POPULAR FOR A REASON! ANCESTORS WHO HAVE FOUGHT WARS WITH EACH OTHER OFTEN REMAIN ENEMIES EVEN ACROSS THE VEIL UNTIL THERE IS ENERGETIC RESOLUTION.

FEARS AND PHOBIAS

Fear is the most powerful and commonly *experienced emotion* that people face on a daily basis. It is caused by the interrelationship of a person's own experiences and those of others in the *past*, *present* and even the *future*. Seemingly insignificant occurrences during childhood can cause *fears* that have profound *effects* later in life. Conditions that contribute to *fears* and *phobias* often involve *relationships*, **money**, **finances**, **prosperity**, *health*, *self-criticism*, **occupation**, **illness**, *traumas*, **death** and even *fear* of *fear* itself. Having one *fear* often causes more *fears* and *phobias* in what can be a vicious cycle. *Fears* are reasonable because they are based on real life-time **problems**, whereas *phobias* are often *unreasonable*. For example, if a person lives in a high rise building on the top floor and *fears* injury from walking out the door if there is no balcony, it is a valid *fear*. If a person lives on the first floor and has the same *fear* of going out the door with no danger present, that is a *phobia*.

FEARS

Surprisingly, many people have *fears* of not having any **problems**, as well as the *fear* of not being able to solve **problems**. If they let go of their old **problems** and start feeling better, it triggers them because they feel "too good." Many people *fear change* because many of their *experiences* with *change* have been for the **worse** instead of the **better**. One would assume that people would have more *fear* of **failure**; however the vast majority are triggered when they begin to enjoy **success** because it brings up *memories* of **punishment** and *past* **failures**.

Common *fears* in *relationships* revolve around *commitment*, *rejection* and *abandonment*. Many people *sabotage* significant *relationships* because of a *fear* of intimacy, and/or of cohabiting for years, yet rarely do they take the time to look each other in the **eye**; then there are those who regularly expose themselves to *rejection*, **sexually transmitted disease** and other dating **traumas** in *fear* of never finding a suitable mate.

Financial success often fosters a *fear* of **losing money**. For some people the *fear* of being **homeless** and living in abject **poverty** is so great that they pacify themselves by *accumulating* and *hoarding* vast quantities of **merchandise** in an attempt to *feel* secure.

The *fear* of "getting old" and having to rely on others, being in an **accident**, being **disabled** or *suffering* with **disease** is more contagious than **disease** itself. Some people *fear* getting pregnant while others fear they will never become parents as their biological clock ticks away. Others, who *feel* they are not **grounded** have *fears* that come from *spiritual experiences* of being separated from *God* and fragmentation of the *soul* leading them to **churches** which instill even more *fear* through their teachings. These can add up to many life times of *accumulated fear* and lead to *phobias*.

PHOBIAS

Phobias are *re-actions* to *accumulated experiences* from the *past* that *project* unmanageable *fears* into the *future*. The *fears* often revolve around **starvation**, the inability to **breathe** and other **traumas** regarding **death** and **dying** that quite often lead to **panic** *attacks*. People who have *phobias* about computers and high-speed **technological equipment** often have weaknesses from *past life* situations of witnessing **technology** at its worst. Wide-open *spaces* such as the **sky** can trigger *fears* and *phobias* of seeing **spacecraft** and **alien abduction.** It is politically incorrect to call **ETs** "aliens," and the *fears* around **aliens** are often from sensationalized, inaccurate **information**. On the other hand **confined** and **crowded places** such as **elevators** often trigger *memories* of *imprisonment*, *fear* of **authority figures**, the spread of **germs** and **plagues**, etc., and *phobias* around **public toilets**.

Many people are weak to leaving their **homes**, causing *fears* of **public transportation**, **flying**, **trains** and **driving,** while others are triggered by being **home alone**. Almost everybody has an issue with **public speaking** that stems from *fears* of being *watched*, *initiating* **conversation**, taking **exams** and being **tested**, going on **dates**, attending **meetings** and **parties**, etc.

Past life situations of **war** and **natural disasters** can trigger *phobias* around **thunder**, **lightning** and *fear* of **storms**. *Fears* of **climbing** and **falling** can lead to *phobias* about **heights**. Most *phobias* with **animals** are caused by *past life* situations of abusing animals while *phobias* with **insects** revolve around *fear* of *infestation*.

Get a base line of how strong the *fear* is and test for *spiritual* and *psychic* experiences that perpetuate the fear. As the weaknesses are eliminated, the *fear* will dissipate and become a distant *memory*.

THE "GOOD NEWS" IS:

The more *fears* you face, the fewer *fears* you have. Many people shy away from taking **responsibility** out of *fear* that they will be blamed if there are **problems**. *Response-ability* is just that: a person's *ability* to *respond* to **problems**.

THE "BAD NEWS" IS:

Unresolved *fears* from the *past* negatively *affect* the *future*. Hiding from *fears* allows them to *accumulate* and gather importance until they become a recognizable force.

NUGGET OF WIZDOM FROM THE VECTOR

PEOPLE ARE ENCOURAGED TO WORRY, TO TAKE DIS-EASE SERIOUSLY AND TO AVOID WHAT THEY FEAR AT ALL COSTS. THE LAWS OF ATTRACTION AND REPULSION CREATE A MAGNET ON THE SUB-CONSCIOUS LEVEL FOR PEOPLE TO ATTRACT WHAT THEY TEND TO BE MOST PHOBIC ABOUT.

FIGHTING

When people want to make *change* happen, they often get into **fight** mode; yet **fighting** is rarely the best option, especially when people **fight disease, institutions, corporations**, etc. For instance when people are **diagnosed** and told that they have a **disease** like cancer that they need to take **seriously**, the very **seriousness** of the **diagnosis** is often the leading weakness for recovery. For years, people wouldn't even utter the word "cancer;" it was the dreaded "C" word. *EU … MEDICAL DIAGNOSIS AND PROCEDURES, Pg. 323*

When people "battle" **disease,** they are in a **fight** with a powerful *morphic field* that includes the *fears* of the *collective influence*, the economic **profits** created from the **disease**, and a minefield of tactics that I refer to as the "Dirty D's": **denial, disruption, degradation, deception, destruction, dissension** and **dissemination**. If people "run" for cancer, diabetes, MS, etc. or march against **corporations** and **institutions**, they are giving more power to the very thing they are **fighting**. Think of **diseases, institutions, corporations**, etc., as giant monsters with extremely huge appetites that need to be fed **thoughts** and **emotions** to survive. They are not fussy eaters; their **palate** is satisfied by both **negative** and **positive energy**. They will consume everything and anything to **survive**. Whether people are for or against it does not concern this beast. **Anger** and **fear** are its favorite delicacies.

THE "GOOD NEWS" IS:

If you become **neutral** to the **absolute best**, like a world free of **disease**, and the **absolute worst** like epidemic **suffering**, you are more likely to have **healthy** breasts, eat **organic food** and live free of any of these **problems**, because you have not made them a part of your life.

THE "BAD NEWS" IS:

The road to hell is paved with good intentions. When you "run" for cancer, "march" against a **corporation**, protest **governments** etc., you are feeding the monster.

NUGGET OF WIZDOM FROM THE VECTOR

DON'T FEED THE MONSTER! SOMETIMES EVEN WHEN IT SEEMS THAT YOU HAVE DODGED THE BEAST, YOU WILL FIND YOURSELF IN A PREDICAMENT WHERE YOU ARE FORCED TO FIGHT. IN THIS CASE, BRING YOUR OPPONENT DOWN IN ONE PUNCH OR ONE KICK. IF YOU ARE FORCED TO FIGHT, FIGHT TO WIN! AND THEN IMMEDIATELY CLEAR THE KARMA.

FINANCIAL STRATEGIES

When people (families) **struggle** with **finances** it weakens their **bodies** and **minds** as well as their **spirits** and consequently **affects** their **careers** and **purpose**. This **struggle** or **fight** can lead to **health** and **aging** issues, relationship **problems**, and lackluster performance in general. **Financial institutions** and the **global economy** are not built for the success of the average person, but for **corporate interests**. It is challenging for many people just to meet their daily **financial obligations**, and many are left **feeling** that they are unable to **invest** in their **future**, especially if they have not been raised in an **environment** where they learned how to handle **money** successfully. Navigating the up's and down's of the **stock market** and managing personal **finances** can be challenging, even for "the experts." Despite all the information they can access regarding the "economy" there are still losses.

Many weaknesses around **dealing** with and **handling money** are passed down from **ancestors** and are influenced by *collective fears* and inaccurate *perceptions* around **money**. When we clear the *karma* of our **ancestors** and **descendants** it is much easier to catch the wave and ride it rather than letting it pull you under and *struggling* to resurface. You can strengthen **money strategies** for **success** by resolving *emotional re-actions* to **money** and **finances**, and letting go of old patterns that are failing you. Create new, life-changing **strategies** that will benefit you and others by identifying the true weaknesses and *changing* your **strategy**.

There are common "mistakes" people make when they are dealing with **finances** and **handling money**. Some of these are:

AVERAGING OR LEVERAGING A LOSING POSITION

Many people will hold on to what does not work for them with a death grip because they don't want to admit that they may have made a **mistake**. If you don't label what is happening in your life as good or bad, negative or positive, and if instead you become *neutral* to what you are *experiencing*, it is much easier to "let go" and take steps of *action* towards improving the situation for the fulfillment of your *wants*, **needs** and *authentic desires* rather than other people's **desires**. *EU ... DESIRE, Pg. 175*

Just because a concept is valid does not mean it is complete. Money pits are similar to being **stuck** in the mud. If you are **stuck**, quit spinning your wheels and digging yourself into a deeper rut. Put your vehicle into **neutral** and push it **backwards** a bit, if need be. A slight *change* in your **steering** sets you on a new course.

EMOTIONAL STRATEGIES

It is important to separate *emotion* from **business** and become a *detached observer*. The *accumulations* of so many people spending so many hours of their day as a slave to "earning a living" creates a *collective negative impact*. The *energy* of **money** and **finances** is much like that of a **semi-truck** heading straight for you. If you are not strong to the *internal* and *external forces* and the dynamics of that *force*, and you habitually *attach emotion* to your **thinking**, the *flow* of your **money** and **finances** will reflect it. Eliminating triggers around **money** and **finances** from the *past*, *present* and *future* and the consequences of *choices* made by your **self**, your **ancestors**, your **descendants**, potential **descendants** and *collective influence*, will have a positive *effect* on your earning potential. You may want to pay attention to common triggers, which include phrases like:

"Bottom Line," "In the Red," "Loser," "Penny Pincher," "Loan Shark," "Top of the Heap," "Nickel and Dime," "Can't Rub Two Nickels Together," "Rich Bitch," "Money Makes The World Go Round," etc.

People who are on **spiritual journeys** or are recovering from **religious experiences** often have a weakness to this quote from the bible. *EU ... RELIGIOUS EXPERIENCES, Pg. 443*

"Again I tell you, it is easier for a camel to go through the eye of a needle than for a rich person to enter the kingdom of God." Matthew 19:24

If you feel yourself going weak to this **statement**, delete the *negative accounts* that are held in the "memory banks" of your **CNS**. Letting go of the *emotions* you *experience* around **finances** will have a *positive effect* on the **statements** you receive from your **bank**.

COLLECTIVE TRENDS

Trends come and go, this is true in fashion, home décor, technology, products, advertising, etc. It pays to be ahead of the game, riding the wave rather than swimming against it. When *change* occurs, many people fight the **current trend** instead of quickly *adapting* to get ahead of the game because they are waiting for things to return to "normal," whatever that is. *Nothing* stays the *same*. We can observe this in the fashion world where subtle differences in new styles make that jacket you purchased a few years ago obsolete because the new jackets have subtle changes in color, texture, length, etc. **Trends** change very rapidly because if one person has a *thought*, it is now part of the universal "soup." Often people are unaware that they are part of a **trend**. For example, take parents who are searching for a unique name for their baby. An original name pops into their mind, they don't share that name with anyone until the baby is born, and it is official. Their *connection* in the *unified field* becomes apparent, however, when their child attends pre-school and their son or daughter is one of five or six children in the class with the same name.

REVENGE STRATEGY

Many people use *anger* to *motivate* themselves to achieve **goals** with an "I'll show you" attitude. This strategy may seem successful for a time, but *motivation* generally only has a shelf life of around **three years**.

When the **excitement** wears off and the expiration date rolls around it is often impossible to maintain momentum because *anger* and *resentment* are **physically *exhausting***. *Motivation* is an underlying energetic factor for a vast majority of businesses that fail and become a statistic around the **three-year** mark.

"Trying to get even" strategies also have ramifications that create weaknesses in the **physical body**. **Kinesiology** shows that making a **fist** depletes our *energy*, yet many people who are attempting to cross the finish line first are sabotaging their efforts by running the race with closed *minds* and closed **fists**.

TRYING TO HIT THE HOME RUN STRATEGY

Often when a new movie or song is released or a new artist is introduced, they are deemed "an over-night success." We also see this in sports and dance when an athlete hits a home run, lands a triple axel, scores that touchdown, breaks records in races, etc. Those who appear to have **overnight success** most likely have been *investing* their **time** and *energy* in honing their *craft* for some **time**. On the flip side, if they have convinced themselves that fate alone determines great **success** through a combination of luck, good genes, *connections* to important people, etc., they are creating *limitations* for **themselves**, their **ancestors**, their **descendants**, and even their **unborn descendants**.

The vast majority of people limit themselves through their conviction that putting *effort* into something that they don't *believe* they can achieve is pointless, and/or that they don't *deserve* that much **success** in the first place. That is reserved for others who are more beautiful, smarter, sexier etc., so there is no use in "trying." Anytime someone uses the word "trying," there is a weakness. **Trying** is just another way of saying, "not doing." Anytime you hear yourself using the word "**trying**," go to your **spine**, delete the *limiting beliefs*, and strengthen yourself to **doing** by *feeling* your **heart**. As you eliminate *limiting beliefs* for **yourself** and **others**, you ensure your **success** and the **success** of those around **you**.

FAILURE TO LOOK AT THE BIG PICTURE

People do not lose money because they made a **mistake**. The "mistake" is not losing money; **losing money** is the **result** of not taking consistent steps of *action* towards the **goal** of **making money**. When people *re-act* to their own *limitations* and *limitations* from others around **money** instead of executing strong *choices* that are consistent with their **goals**, they are taking the long path to achieving **success**. Use your *feeling* to determine whether you are weak or strong to your **choices**, and strengthen yourself to consistent steps of **action** to follow through. If it is a clunker, it is a clunker. Appreciate what you have gained from the **experience** and move on!

THE "GOOD NEWS" IS:

Strong financial strategies improve our day-to-day quality of life and our spending power. We all come into this life wearing our birthday suits, **naked** of "things." If humanity woke up and **loved people** more than **things**, we could all spend more time *making* love and being **naked**.

THE "BAD NEWS" IS:

From the moment we wake up to the time we go to sleep, **society** emphasizes **loving things**, not **people**. They are operating under the premise that a better life equals **more things**. If suddenly **society** woke up and **loved people** more than **things** many **industries** would go out of **business**, and this would make **finances** worse in the short term.

NUGGET OF WIZDOM FROM THE VECTOR

THE UNIVERSE DEALS WITH INFINITY. IT DOES NOT CARE IF YOU TOOK A FINANCIAL LOSS! IT ACKNOWLEDGES GIVING AND RECEIVING. BE WILLING TO LET GO OF OUT-DATED FINANCIAL STRATEGIES THAT HOLD YOU BACK. USE YOUR FINANCIAL POWER TO VOTE WITH YOUR DOLLAR. VOTE FOR LOVE NOT WAR!

FITNESS

Many **problems** that are *perceived* as *health* issues are actually problems with *fitness*. When people *think* of *fitness,* they automatically *think* about **physical fitness**; however, *fitness affects* every *aspect* of peoples' lives. It can also be about being **fit to be** a parent, a sibling, an employee, an employer, a man, woman, etc. Many people have a weakness to being "fit to be" on the planet at this time. Increasing the *fitness* of your *soul*, *spirit* and **body** automatically improves your quality of life.

Physical fitness can be maximized by improved *economy* of *motion*. The *performanc*e demands on the average person can be satisfied through optimizing **physical potential** while carrying out daily activities. As wasted movements are **eliminated** and necessary movements are **refined**, the amount of **oxygen**, *strength* and *endurance* required to *effortlessly* accomplish any given task are maximized.

High intensity, **intermittent exercise** maximizes your **physical potential**. As you become *neutral* to the *sensations* of pushing your body to its **limits**, the *sensitivity* works in your favor by maximizing potential and minimizing injury. If your energy is not in *alignment* with the **exercises** you are performing you will not receive maximum benefit, and often *sabotage* your overall *fitness*. Many gadgets, equipment and weight training exercises are *inefficient* because they focus on specific **muscle groups** and only work with a small portion of overall **muscle mass**. Evenness throughout the **body** is more important than any one specific **body part**.

When people jog, they are actually teaching their **bodies** to "run slowly." They are better off to walk quickly and sprint for as long and fast as they can, to build *endurance* and *speed*. Running on a treadmill while *thinking* about errands, paying bills, picking the children up from daycare, etc., is teaching the **body** to "run on the spot" and not accomplish anything while **doing** it. Many people have *psychological* and *spiritual* weaknesses caused by *past life experiences* related to being forced to walk or forcing others to walk; that causes the *action* of *walking* itself to be weak. "Power walking" teaches the **body** to expend more *effort* than what is required to accomplish the simple task of walking.

Your **physical** movements are maximized when you take your *mind* and *spirit* out of the **body** and use your *instincts* like a wild animal so that *action* is supported by our **physical intelligence**.

For instance, if a jackrabbit sees a coyote, he *responds* by stopping for a split second and testing the energy to see if the coyote is *aware* of him. He then makes one of two choices: he either "freezes" in his tracks and halts all *motion* to make himself invisible, or he goes full out and runs for his life. He uses his *instinct* to make the *choice* and *commits* to either stay or run. He does not question whether or not he *deserves* to live, or which runners to wear. If he runs, he runs. If he stays, he stays. His *reflexes* kick in and he takes *action* through his *instinct*.

Physical pain in the **body** is often referred from other **body parts** in combination with *actions* and *positions*. Identify the **body parts** where the **pain** is actually coming from and strengthen those **body parts** to the *actions* and *positions* to prevent injury. Your overall level of *fitness* is a reflection of your *ability* to maximize all **components**, not only of the **physical body** but also in the *mind* and *emotions* to handle every **aspect** of life. The **components** of *fitness* are:

Power (strength in motion).

Balance for stability and equilibrium (having the ability to keep your feet underneath you).

Endurance is the length of time you are able to exert a specific force through a prolonged activity.

Timing by catching the moment (being in the right place at the right time).

Transition is the ability to use a set of skills in many different contexts and transfer those skills to be used with each other.

Flexibility is the ability to adapt, including elasticity of the joints, ligaments, skin and an ability to "go with the flow."

Coordination is the ability to synchronize motions.

Agility is economy of motion.

Speed is acceleration of motion.

Accuracy allows for precision under pressure (being able to hit the mark).

You can energetically identify the weakest **component**, the one that is holding you back the most from **optimum performance**, and *recalibrate* it with the other **components**. Continue to do so until all of the **components** are strong.

RESULTS:

"Running competitively has been difficult for the past four years or so. I have had many negative experiences with coaches, other athletes, and injuries which all had a major effect on me mentally, emotionally, and physically. Being a successful runner at a young age, and battling these negative experiences led to me having less confidence and constantly questioning my abilities in a competitive setting. I love running and competing, and I could never give up on myself. However, I lost the joy of running. I lost my edge and my competitive side, and I did not know how to get it back.

"Colette first worked on me this past Christmas. I immediately realized the difference in the way I thought about running. There were no negative feelings associated with running. I would go out for a run and enjoy myself; I would go to practice and be excited and ready to go! This is something I have not felt in years, and it felt amazing!

"I contacted Colette before every race during my indoor track season. I noticed that I was excited and positive before every race. From the first race to my last race I also noticed a major difference. I slowly saw my competitive edge coming back, which I have not had in over four years. I was more patient and confident during my race. I was able to separate my mind from my running, which allowed me to take chances that I typically would not have done. I did not view racing as a negative experience anymore. I was not afraid of racing, and I took each race as an opportunity to learn and gain more experiences.

"My indoor track season was a great success with the help of Colette! It is the first year that I fully completed an entire indoor season in a long time. I have compartment syndrome in my shins that has kept me off the track for nearly four years. Although it has taken several years, I now know how to manage the symptoms of my chronic injury. This indoor season I ended up breaking my university's 3000m record! Although it is not yet the fastest I have run, it gives me the confidence that I can run faster and even better than my personal best times from my past. Throughout the season I ran consistently well, which I view very positively. It is one thing to run a fast time once, but I was able to do this several times. My greatest achievement this indoor season was competing at my conference meet while being sick. Not feeling well made me question whether I should compete, but I decided that I did not want to give up on this opportunity. Not only did I work hard all season, but it would be another great learning experience. I actually ended up moving up in the rankings. My rankings going into my races would not have gotten points for my team's standings; however, after moving up in the rankings I actually earned some points for my team! Experiencing a sore throat, ear ache, headache, and chest congestion while running was agonizing but well worth it in the end! I know that there are only greater things to come!

"I finally enjoy and love running once again, and racing without fear feels amazing! Colette is brilliant and absolutely amazing! She is a very positive, supportive, and giving person. I appreciate the time Colette had spent with me, and impact she has had on my life. I am very fortunate and grateful to connect with her! Thank you very much!!"

Karissa Lepage, Regina

THE "GOOD NEWS" IS:

Your entire **body** is strongest when you are in tune with the ***rhythm*** of your **heart** and the ***rhythm*** of Earth. With every **beat**, your **heart *expands*** and *contracts* along with the **earth** and the entire **universe**. When you are in sync, movement feels ***effortless***.

THE "BAD NEWS" IS:

Many people are "relaxing themselves to death." ***Contraction*** and ***expansion*** need to be a fifty/fifty proposition in ***sync*** with the **heart**. If there is too much ***relaxation*** in the **physical body**, the *act* of *changing* **inertia** into ***action*** puts unnecessary strain on every **body function**.

NUGGET OF WIZDOM FROM THE VECTOR

LOOKING GOOD IS A BUSINESS DECISION. BE STRONG TO BEING AND PERFORMING ABOVE AVERAGE. EXERCISE YOUR FITNESS AND LOOK GREAT DOING IT!

FLUORIDE

At this time, water fluoridation has been banned in many countries, including China, Austria, Belgium, Finland, Germany, Denmark, Norway, Sweden, the Netherlands, Hungary and Japan; nearly all of Europe's water is **fluoride** free. Yet in North America, it is challenging to escape fluoridation because it is in the water supply, juice, soda, wine, coffee, soups, processed foods and baby formula.

Accumulations of **fluoride** build up over a lifetime because, while healthy adult **kidneys** excrete fifty to sixty percent of the **fluoride** ingested each day, the remaining **fluoride** sits in the **bones** and **pineal gland**. Formula-fed babies ingest the highest doses of **fluoride** because they are mainly on a liquid diet causing a much higher level of **fluoride** to accumulate in their **bones**. Later in life, **dental fluorosis** (mottling and staining of the **teeth**) is common in **babies** who have had too much exposure to **fluoride**. The staining and discoloration of the **teeth** is the effect we can see on the outside and is also an indication of what is occurring on the inside of the **body**.

Fluoride has been linked to damage of **sperm**, the **male reproductive system,** and an increase in **infertility**. It has also been linked to **lowered IQ** due to a buildup in the **brain**, which causes learning and behavioral **problems**. There is also an *association* between **pre-natal fluoride** and impaired ***visual-spacial organization*** and **fetal brain** damage. Since there is an intimate connection from the **reproductive system** to the **mouth**, test for any referred weaknesses and spin them out to ***black wholes***.

The **pineal gland** absorbs **fluoride** more than any other part of the **body**, which causes it to **calcify** and **atrophy**. This lowers **melatonin** *production* which contributes to a variety of *effects* in **humans**, in particular an *association* with early onset of **puberty**. Consumption of **fluoride** also has a negative impact on **thyroid** function, causing weight gain, muscle and joint pain, increased cholesterol levels and heart disease. Furthermore, fluoridation of water has also been linked to **bone damage**, causing arthritic-like symptoms and a higher rate of **bone fractures**, in particular **hip fractures** in the elderly.

Fluoride is the only **chemical** added to water for the purpose of **medical** treatment. There is no scientific link between adverse *health effects* and exposure to **fluoride** in drinking water levels that are below the maximum acceptable concentration. Unfortunately, the vast majority of people do not realize the risks and effects of **fluoride poisoning** because they are unaware of how much **fluoride** they are actually consuming. It is irresponsible to **mass medicate** entire communities without being able to control the individual dosage people are receiving, especially when the vast majority are unaware of the pros and cons of what they are ingesting. People from low income families are more likely to use tap water high in **fluoride** content, because of the prohibitive cost of **distilled** and **bottled** water. Some products that contain **fluoride** are de-boned meats, dental treatments, tea, vegetables and fruit laced with pesticide residues.

THE "GOOD NEWS" IS:

For those who live in a country where **fluoride** is banned from being used in the water supply it is comforting to know that **fluoride** is not an essential **nutrient**. Its only benefit is to reduce **cavities** in **teeth**. Statistically, North Americans who ingest **fluoridated water** do not have less **tooth decay** than European countries that are **fluoride-free**.

THE "BAD NEWS" IS:

The labels on **fluoridated toothpaste** are required to include a warning not to swallow the toothpaste, and to call a poison control center immediately if there is accidental **consumption** of more than a pea-sized amount of **toothpaste**. The amount of **fluoride** in a pea-sized portion of **toothpaste** is equal to the amount in an eight-ounce glass of fluoridated water.

NUGGET OF WIZDOM FROM THE VECTOR

FLUORIDE OCCURS NATURALLY IN WATER AND SOIL AROUND THE WORLD IN TRACE AMOUNTS. LOW FLUORIDE LEVELS CAN BENEFIT HUMAN HEALTH, BUT HIGH CONCENTRATIONS ARE TOXIC AND CAN LEAD TO SERIOUS DISEASE. DELETE ALL POISONING EXPERIENCES ON A PSYCHOLOGICAL, SPIRITUAL AND PSYCHIC LEVEL AND SPIN ACCUMULATIONS IN THE BODY OUT TO BLACK WHOLES.

FOWL BUSINESS

Billions of chickens and millions of turkeys are raised in North America alone, to meet the demand for chicken and turkey meat. The vast majority are raised in industrialized **farming operations** where they are totally removed from their natural habitat, unable to preen and clean themselves or to stretch and spread their wings. They are kept in extremely crowded conditions in giant sheds that are a breeding ground for **disease**. The **ammonia** from the **feces**, the dust and feathers choke the air, causing the birds to suffer from **respiratory disease** that occurs from poor husbandry and breeding programs.

BROILER CHICKENS

Chickens who are raised for their flesh are referred to in the **meat industry** as "broiler chickens." The **factory farms** who raise these chickens pack them into massive windowless sheds that hold thousands of birds. Chickens by nature have a pecking order in their **social structure**. Existing in crowded groups of **thousands** does not allow space for each hen and causes their **social structure** to collapse. The frustration leads them to resort to **cannibalistic** behavior as they peck at and inflict injury on each other.

There will always be a chicken at the bottom of the "pecking order." Rather than using good flock management, **commercial farms** prevent **cannibalism** and feather picking by "debeaking" the birds (**cutting off** a portion of their **beak** with a **heated blade** or through cauterization **without anesthetic**) to prevent them from injuring themselves and others as they react to the crowded, filthy conditions. The **beak** is a complex, **functional organ** with an *extensive* **nerve supply**. **Debeaking** causes **acute** and **chronic pain**, abnormal preening and an *inability* to forage for food. It is commonly used in **egg-laying hens** and **breeder hens** and less often **in broiler hens** because **broiler hens** reach **slaughter weight** on average at the age of **six weeks** due to the fact that they have been **genetically modified** and are regularly given **steroids** to *accelerate* their **weight gain** and **growth**. By the time the average "broilers" reach **six weeks** of age, they are **obese**, often **crippled** by their own **weight** and *suffering* from **heart** and **lung** collapse. They are pumped full of **antibiotics** to keep them alive long enough to reach **slaughter weight** in the filthy, stressful conditions they are raised in.

BREEDER CHICKENS

Just when you think that the lives of chickens could not get any worse, **concentrated breeding operations** rear their ugly heads. The **breeding birds** that give birth to the **billions** of **broiler chickens** in North America alone, live on average for a whole **year** instead of **six weeks**, under the *same* conditions, housed in a shed without access to sunlight or fresh air. They are **debeaked** at **one** to **ten days** of **age** and fed a **starvation diet** to keep them from gaining too much weight due to the **genetic manipulation** that causes **structural** *health* issues. The hungry birds are often denied *free access* to **water** to keep their manure drier and easier to clean.

MALE CHICKS

After *hatching* in the **incubators** the **chicks** of the **breeding chickens** are sent down a **conveyer belt** where workers sort out the **males** and toss them into a **chute** to be *ground up*, *alive* by a **meat grinder** or **macerator** because they don't lay eggs or grow fast enough to be sold for meat.

LAYING HENS

In **North America** it is common to store **eggs** in the refrigerator; most people would never store **eggs** at room temperature as is the common practice in **Europe** and other countries. **North American eggs** are routinely exposed to an **egg-washing process** that is **illegal** in **Europe** because it makes them more susceptible to **contamination** from **bacteria** such as **salmonella**.

Most **eggs** in **North America** come from industrialized, **concentrated feeding operations** where **thousands** of **egg-laying hens** are crammed into tiny **cages** with barely enough room to **stand** or spread their **wings**. The cages are stacked on top of each other allowing **feces** and other **contaminates** to drop and spread rampant **disease** and filth. **Eggs** from such large flocks are more likely to carry **antibiotic-resistant** strains due to the routine exposure to **pharmaceuticals** and **steroids**. Rather than reducing the size of the flocks and humanely raising the birds to ensure better sanitation and access to the outdoors, the solution for USA and Canada is to commercially scrub and **rinse** the **eggs** with a **chlorine mist**. It is impossible for the consumer to know the condition of the clean white eggs they purchase before they arrived at the grocery store. This **commercial process** compromises the protective **cuticle** of the **eggs** with **anti-microbial properties**, a natural barrier that comes from the hen and acts as a shield against **bacteria**. Some **eggs** are also treated with *vegetable* oil and **minerals** to ineffectively mimic this **protective shield**. The average **eggshell** has over seventy five hundred **pores**. Once the **cuticle** has been compromised, whatever comes into contact with the **egg** crosses the **permeable membrane** and is *absorbed* into its contents. If subsequent drying and storing conditions are not optimal, the trans-shell contamination increases the **risk** to consumers. In contrast, commercialized washing of **eggs** in **Europe** is largely **banned** to encourage good husbandry at the **farms**. It puts the onus on the **farmer** to **produce** the **cleanest eggs** possible because if the eggs are not clean, the **consumer** is unlikely to purchase them.

Refrigerating **eggs** became the *cultural* norm when mass production caused **eggs** to travel long distances and sit in **storage** for weeks before arriving at the grocery stores. The average **eggs** purchased from **grocery stores** are typically already **three weeks old**. The **date** the **egg** was actually laid can be many days prior to the **pack date**. The nutrient content is much higher in **organic free range** flocks and much less likely to contain dangerous **bacteria** such as **salmonella**. The **cleaning process** of **eggs** labeled **organic** must be non-synthetic and is often a gentle **dry brushing process**.

TURKEYS

The first thing that comes to *mind* when most **North Americans** think "turkey" are holiday centerpieces for the dinner table; however, they are **social**, **playful birds** that in the wild are able to fly up to speeds of fifty-five miles an hour and run at speeds of up to twenty-five miles an hour. The natural life span of a **turkey** is **ten years**, but the **turkeys** of today are **bred**, **drugged** and **genetically modified** to gain weight faster and are so obese that they cannot reproduce naturally. The vast majority of **turkeys** born in the **USA** are conceived through **artificial insemination** and their life span is on average **six months**.

THE SLAUGHTERHOUSE

Thousands of **fowl** are killed every hour at slaughterhouses.

The **fully**-**conscious** birds are **hung** by their **feet** from **shackles** on a moving rail. They are **stunned** by running them through **electrified water**, but many of the birds are still able to feel pain when their **throats** are **slashed** by **machines**. If they avoid the **blade** or their **throats** are **not properly slashed,** they are still **conscious** when they are **submerged** in the **scalding tank** to remove their feathers.

THE "GOOD NEWS" IS:

There is no upside to **factory farming**. There may appear to be monetary value in the efficiency of an industry that treats living beings as a commodity, however **money** is only one form of *energy*, an *expression* of *appreciation* for **service provided**. For every *action* there is a *re-action*. The cause of the **pain** and *suffering* of the birds has a profoundly *negative effect* on the entire planet and throughout the universe.

THE "BAD NEWS" IS:

Poultry are excluded from the Humane Slaughter Act in the USA, leaving the industry free to set the standards the birds are raised and slaughtered in. The *suffering* of the birds who are bred for consumption, *directly affects* the **eggs** and **meat** that are eaten on a daily basis whether the consumer is *aware* of it or not. Food is energy. Along with the *antibiotics*, *salmonella* and other **bacteria**, the *stress* and *fear* of the **abused birds** and the **cruelty** within the **industry** are energetically ingested with **every bite**.

NUGGET OF WIZDOM FROM THE VECTOR

BE AWARE OF WHAT YOU PUT INTO YOUR BODY. "YOU ARE WHAT YOU EAT." AS HORRIBLE AS THE PLIGHT OF THE BIRDS IS, THE PLIGHT OF PIGS ABUSED IN THE HOG INDUSTRY IS SO HORRENDOUS THAT THERE ARE NO WORDS TO EXPRESS THE MAGNITUDE OF THE HORROR.

FREEDOM

The vast majority of **humanity** is easily triggered by *thoughts* of losing their personal *freedom*. History is rampant with *collective experiences* of brutality, slavery, confinement, taxation, confiscation of property and many other inventive forms of *torture*. Nothing is sacred or safe. Governments are overturned, countries invaded, economies crumble, leaving victims scattered in their wake.

Many people *struggle* with the **false obligations society** impose on them to earn enough **money** to pay their rent or their mortgage, electricity, water, food, transportation costs, etc., and they just barely meet the basic necessities for *survival*. Even those who have a surplus of **money** to purchase the finer things in life, and who focus exclusively on third dimensional *wants* and **needs** create a **void** within themselves that cannot be filled by material possessions for balanced growth as *conscious beings*. **Money** cannot buy love; however, it has been useful over the ages to pay for the next best thing. **Sex**! Consequently, many people have underlying weaknesses around **prostitution** and **sexual slavery** from *past*, *present* and *future existences* in *space-time* that can be triggered when they enter partnerships and sign on the dotted line. These triggers can cause people to hang on tight to the *relationships*, **businesses**, **properties** and **situations** that no longer serve them and keep them tied to the hardships they are doing their best to avoid.

You hear a lot of people say that if you don't have *health,* you don't have anything. In today's world, many people do not have access to clean running water, let alone **health care**. Even in industrialized nations where there is a medical clinic or hospital around every corner, if you do not have the ability to pay for **health insurance**, it is highly unlikely that you can afford treatment. Many people are numbing themselves to the discrepancies between the **very rich,** the **rich**, the **middle class**, the **poor and** the **very poor**, discrepancies that are becoming more and more evident in industrialized nations as well as in "third world" countries around the globe. **Slavery** is alive and well. In this age of information it is next to impossible to be *unaware* of the *suffering* far away and close at hand, and yet people force themselves to carry on with "business as usual," suppressing both their own *accumulated memories* of **forced labor**, **enslavement** and **starvation** from their *spiritual experiences*, and those of their **ancestors**, as well as their concern for their **descendants**.

Throughout any given lifetime, it is normal to have up's and down's in different *aspects* of your lives and it is highly unlikely that every *aspect* is in perfect *balance* twenty-four hours a day, seven days a week. However, when the *aspects* of life are in *balance* you are *free* to have it all!

THE "GOOD NEWS" IS:

There is a certain **perfection** in *imperfection* because *imperfections* create a **need** or a *want* for a *better life*. The **problem** is that for many people, thinking of making their *lives better* activates hidden triggers of **sex**, **money** and **slavery**. As these triggers are *neutralized*, people are able to make better choices allowing **perfection** to take its place.

THE "BAD NEWS" IS:

There are times in life when a person can have **no money** but **great sex**, other times when they have **great sex** but **no money**, and, worst of all, there are times when they have **neither**. Every once in a while when the heavens are *aligned*, the two come together **perfectly**. It *feels* so **great** until the *fear* of "losing it" creeps in and people become **enslaved** by "hanging on to it" at all **costs**.

NUGGET OF WIZDOM FROM THE VECTOR

FREEDOM IS A STATE OF MIND. DISCIPLINE YOUR MIND AND FEEL FREE TO TAKE ACTION FROM YOUR HEART.

GENITAL MUTILATION

FEMALE

Female genital mutilation includes procedures that intentionally alter or cause injury to the female **genital organs** for non-medical reasons. Besides the obvious unnecessary **trauma**, these procedures cause severe bleeding, cysts, infections, infertility, complications in childbirth, increased risk of death for newborns, deaths and problems with urination. This violation of human rights is routinely carried out by traditional circumcisers on hundreds of millions of young girls between infancy and age fifteen in twenty nine countries in Africa and the Middle East.

There are three main types of procedures:

CLITORIDECTOMY

The partial or total removal of the **clitoris** and/or the **prepuce**, the fold of skin surrounding the **clitoris**.

EXCISION

Partial or total removal of the **clitoris**, the **labia minora** and sometimes also the **labia majora**.

INFIBULATION

Narrowing of the **vaginal opening** by forming a seal via cutting and repositioning the **inner** and **outer labia** with or without the removal of the **clitoris**. The **vaginal opening** is often cut open to *accommodate childbirth* and stitched back together after childbirth several times over a woman's lifetime. Other harmful procedures are **pricking**, **piercing**, **scraping** and **cauterizing** the **genitals**.

Female genital mutilation exists for a variety of **cultural**, **religious** and **social reasons** within **families** and **communities** who often considered it a necessary part of raising a girl properly. Motivated by *limiting beliefs* around proper sexual behavior, pre-marital virginity and the prevention of illicit sexual acts, **community leaders**, **religious leaders**, **circumcisers** and even some in the **medical community** uphold the tradition.

MALE

The practice of **circumcision** spread in the late nineteenth century in English speaking countries as a way to curb **masturbation** which was considered by the medical community at that time to have *harmful effects*. One of the greatest proponents of circumcision was Dr. John Harvey Kellogg, of the Kellogg's Cornflakes fame, who advised that a successful remedy for young boys who were caught **masturbating** was **circumcision** without **anesthetic** as *punishment*. He did not however advocate **routine circumcision** in infants.

Over eighty percent of men in the world are not **circumcised**. The vast majority of those who are **circumcised** are Jews and Muslims, and the reasons are **primarily religious**. The USA has the highest rate of **non-religious circumcision** in the world, peaking at eighty-five percent in the mid 1960's. **Circumcision** is the only widespread **surgery** in history that is advocated for reasons of **preventing disease**. In biblical times when soap and water were not readily available this may have been true; however, many babies are **circumcised** now so that the baby's **penis** looks like the father's.

Circumcision is *traumatic* and **painful**. It is not safe to put two day old babies under **anesthesia,** so it is performed without it. Even when local medication is used, it wears off before the **post-operative pain** does.

The baby is **strapped** spread-eagle to a board. A clamp is attached to the **penis**, the **foreskin** is pinched, and an instrument is inserted between the **foreskin** and the **glans** (**head** of the **penis**) tearing the attached structures apart, and one of the **most** *sensitive* **body parts** is **amputated**. It is not a "little snip" that babies do not *feel*.

The **foreskin** protects the **glans** of the **penis** throughout life from contamination, friction, drying and injury. The average male foreskin measures twelve square inches and consists of a movable double-layered **sleeve** that glides up and down the **penile shaft** reducing *friction* and retaining **vaginal secretions**. There are millions of **nerve endings** in the **foreskin** that enhance **sexual pleasure** for **men** and naturally **lubricate** the **penis,** making intercourse more pleasurable for both **men** and **women**, and making it easier for **women** to achieve **multiple orgasms**. Loss of the **foreskin** results in thickening and progressive *desensitization* of the outer layer of the **head** of the **penis**, particularly in older men. In cases of **erectile dysfunction** and **premature ejaculation,** delete *psychological* issues from *memories* of *trauma,* and energetically reconnect the **nerves**.

THE "GOOD NEWS" IS:

More and more people on the planet are questioning what has up until now been considered status quo, and they respect the rights of children to have their **genitalia** left intact. If, later in life, there are issues with the **genitalia** the medical system is able to provide **surgery** under **anesthesia**.

THE "BAD NEWS" IS:

Many men and women are horrified to discover that **innocent girls** on this planet, particularly in so-called **third world countries**, are being robbed of their God-given right to the ecstatic pleasure of **sexuality** and their *sensuality* through **mutilation** of their **genitalia** and **forced** "marriage" at a **tender age**. However, it is not surprising when you consider that many two day old **male babies**, in what are supposed to be the most **powerful nations** in the world, are routinely strapped to boards without their consent or an anesthetic and, with their **parent's permission**, have their **genitalia** mutilated in the name of cleanliness. What a welcome to the world!

RESPECT THE CREATION CENTERS OF ALL MALE AND FEMALE 0FF-SPRING. THESE SYSTEMS ARE PUT IN PLACE TO STIMULATE ACTIVE PARTICIPATION IN THE ECSTATIC PLEASURE OF HEAVEN ON EARTH. DO NOT MAKE ASSUMPTIONS THAT YOU OR ANYONE ELSE HAS THE RIGHT TO ALTER ANYONE WITHOUT THEIR INFORMED CONSENT.

GEOMETRIC SHAPES

Once you have a *feeling* for energetic *shifting*, you can speed the process up by energetically *shifting* more than one **body part**, **person** or *action* by using **geometric shapes** and *spinning* them into the **spine** and **heart**. The first **geometric shape** to emerge out of the **genesis pattern** is the **doughnut-shaped torus**. It is the **primary shape** existing in the universe and can be seen throughout nature and all life forms from the **atoms** all the way to the **galaxies**.

People have several *toruses* throughout their **bodies**. The **heart** is the first **organ** to develop in the **human body** forming a *torus*. The **brain** is another. The individual *chakras* throughout the **body** are also **toruses** located from the *base chakra* to the *crown* and at the *eighth chakra*. Every **body** forms a *torus* from the top of the **head** to the **soles** of the **feet**.

Toroidal forces rule throughout the universe. They are at play in many ways upon the **earth**. The *torus effect* is easily seen at the **equator** on planet **earth**. Everything is *holofractographic*, meaning that if something is occurring **inside** the **body**, it also is occurring in some way on the **outside** of the **body**.

It is best to start *shifting energies* one by one and as you gain confidence use the **vesica piscis** to speed up the process. Picture two **body parts**, **two people**, **two actions**, etc., one in each of **two circles** that intersect in the **middle**. In this case **one plus one** does not equal **two** because the *space* created in the **middle** creates a **third space** of *infinite potential*. For example, if you *perceive* a weakness between the **eyes** and the **ovaries**, you would place the **eyes** in one circle, and the **ovaries** in the other. The space created where they **overlap** is the *relationship* between the **two**. When you *spin* the **vesica piscis** into the **spine**, you are strengthening the **physical** *relationship* between the two in both directions – the **ovaries** to the **eyes** and the **eyes** back to the **ovaries**. At the same time a **torus** of *energy* is formed around the **vesica piscis** that is strengthening all the **physical** and *non-physical* weaknesses that may come up between the two pairs of **body parts**.

These often include *non-physical* weaknesses people have at the *thought* of **pairs** in general, **doubling up**, **coupling**, *past life experiences* of having **ovaries** and not having **ovaries**, **traumas** and **tortures** inflicted on the **eyes** and **ovaries**, *seeing* life through the **eyes** of a woman, seeing life through the **eyes** of a man, etc. This is why the intersecting *space* that is created in the **middle** has the potential to clear many energetic weaknesses in what seems to be one *shift*.

When you are comfortable clearing weaknesses in **two's**, you can start adding **triads** to your tool belt. The jump from *shifting* two things at once to **three** may seem like a small one; however if you take **three circles** that intersect in the **middle** to form a **triad**, you are really encompassing seven different *aspects* of the **problem** into one energetic *shift*. For example if you have a **mother**, **father** and a **baby**, one in each of the **circles**, each of those **circles** holds information regarding each individual from the *past*, *present* and *future*. This includes all *aspects* of that person. All the information intersects in the **middle** where a **triad** is formed amongst the **three**. There are also **three areas** that intersect between the **mother** to the **baby** and the **baby** back to the **mother**, the **father** to the **baby** and the **baby** back to the **father**, the **mother** to the **father** and the **father** back to the **mother**. When you add up the obvious *possibilities*, there are **seven**, however, when you consider all the information contained in each individual's circle, the potential for *shift* is **infinite**.

You can make **triads** between any **three subjects**, *actions*, **body parts**, **people**, **animals**, etc. It is essential that all parts of the **triad** are equal in all **directions** and **combinations**, and that all parts of the **triad** are able to **separate** and **integrate** as needed to effect change for better. One specific **circle** in a **triad** may stand out more than the other two. Train your **eyes** to notice the *leading weakness* first because once that **general** weakness is cleared, there is often significant *change* without going further. The goal is to create evenness within the **triad** so that it is working together as a **unit** as well as each **component** being strong to work **separately** and **independently** from one another.

Matters in life often come in **threes**, and there is a saying: "two's company, three's a crowd." You can often see this dynamic in play-groups with children, and on a more adult level, in the interactions between couples and other people who *affect* their *relationship*. Each part of the **triad** has to be strong within itself as well as strong to the other two **components** so that there is cooperation rather than antagonization among the **three**.

As you gain confidence in your ability to *shift* energy, you can use **squares**, **pentagons** and **hexagons** to *shift* energy in **four**, **five** and six directions. Every **geometric shape** is enhanced by the *torus* as you use your intention to *spin* it into the **spine** and **heart**.

THE "GOOD NEWS" IS:

Instant results are possible! Every energetic *shift* has the potential to *effect* profound *change* on many levels for every individual and every being in the universe. Many times the *perception* of those involved may take linear time to catch up to *perceive* the *change*. There is no need to be discouraged if it takes "time" for the *change* to be *perceived* and acknowledged.

THE "BAD NEWS" IS:

Most people are focusing on the four percent that they are able to *see* with the **naked eye**. Even when they *experience* profound *shift* and obvious **results**, they will often resist the *change* and sometimes reject the benefits.

NUGGET OF WIZDOM FROM THE VECTOR

DO NOT TAKE RESISTANCE TO CHANGE FROM OTHERS AS A PERSONAL AFFRONT. SHIFT AS MANY BLOCKS AS YOU CAN IN A GIVEN MOMENT. THE RESULTS WILL SPEAK FOR THEMSELVES.

GIVE AND TAKE

The laws of *physics* state that for every *action* there is an equal *re-action*, **cause** and *effect*, *give* and *take*. Keep in mind that If people have *limiting beliefs* in *general*, around the *acceptance* of the *give* and *take* in life, then the results they manifest once they do test strong to *giving*, *taking* and *receiving* will not be on the same scale as a person who had no weakness to *accepting* the *give* and *take* of life in the first place. For example, "Individual A" may test strong to *receiving* the benefits from *actions* he or she has taken to build a successful **career**; however when compared to "Individual B," the actual **physical results** of their *performance* can be very *different*, even though they have both applied themselves to the same **career**. The discrepancy in the **results** can be due to a weakness in the **concept** of *give* and *take* for "Individual A" in comparison to "Individual B." They are operating on a *different* scale because "Individual A" has a *limited perception* of the amount that can be *given* or *received*, whereas "individual B" has a higher standard for greater rewards.

When most people hear the word "give," they correlate it with *positive actions* of *compassion*, such as *giving* to *charity*; however, there are negative connotations to the word "give," such as "I give up" as in **submitting** to **authority**, "it is a given," implying that there are no **choices** available, or "give in," suggesting collapsing or **falling apart**. In the **metaphysical** community the word "take" is often replaced with "receive." **Take** is used in connection with the seizure of goods, physical capture, competition, copulation, theft, a redo or acceptance of a burden or consequences. **Receive** is a softer version of **take**, the **acceptance** of a gift, to act as a receptacle or to **receive** incoming radio waves as **perceptible** signals. If a person is weak to **giving**, **taking** and/or **receiving**, it is much more **challenging** to **manifest** abundance on the third-dimensional plane, and it can have a **negative effect** on all **aspects** of life. Delete **negative imprints** from the words themselves, as well as from the **perception** of lack, such as, "if I take it someone else loses," "if I don't take it, someone else will," "I can't take it anymore," and/or "I don't deserve to receive it."

There needs to be **balance** between **give** and **take** and **receiving** so that it is strong and even in all directions. People who **don't take** what belongs to them are **disappointed** or **angry** when someone else steps in and **takes** what they wanted; they often have the **perception** that is was **taken** from them. Others who participate in prayers, affirmations, meditations, vision boards, etc., to achieve or manifest **abundance** and sit at home waiting for the universe to knock on their door, are also setting themselves up for **disappointment**.

THE "GOOD NEWS" IS:

Once you **understand** the "rules" of a **give** and **take** world, you are better **able** to be in **balance** and give from your **heart**, to know that your gift is **received** with gratitude and to understand that there is always an even exchange in the greater picture because energy is reciprocal.

THE "BAD NEWS" IS:

Some people lament that they **give** and **give** of themselves and no one seems to notice or **appreciate** their efforts. **Giving** too much without **receiving** depletes energy and eventually leads to resentment in both the **giver** and the **receiver** of the "gift." This can lead to **health** issues.

NUGGET OF WIZDOM FROM THE VECTOR

IF WE GIVE TOO MUCH WE ARE GIVING AN EMPTY GIFT. IF WE ARE RECEIVING MORE THAN WE GIVE, WE ALSO RECEIVE AN EMPTY GIFT.

HANGOVER REMEDY

Over the years I have seen many miracles take place, but somehow few things are more impressive to a skeptical crowd than experiencing instant *relief* from a **hangover**, and if you have ever hugged the "porcelain throne" after a big night out, it is not hard to recognize why. There are many remedies out there but few of them work on all the various symptoms.

Some of these remedies are:

"Hair of the dog," or drinking **alcohol** first thing when you wake up. A Bloody Mary's (beer mixed with tomato juice) is one of the most commonly used "cures." It does temporarily alleviate the symptoms, but it also adds more **toxins** to the **system**, thus prolonging the agony.

Some people swear by **greasy breakfasts,** and for others **alkaseltzer** (sodium bicarbonate or baking soda) is the only thing they can keep down. It has been used as a **hangover remedy** for over **eighty years**, even though the other ingredients in it, namely **aspirin** and **citric acid** are more likely to *irritate* the stomach. **Problems** with **digestion** are often associated with *numbing experiences*. *EU ... DIGESTIVE SYSTEM, Pg. 187

There are several hang-over **pills** on the market, which help somewhat by alleviating a few of the symptoms, but they fail to provide full relief. The "side effects" from popping **Ibuprofen** and other **pain killers** can make matters worse by adding more **toxins** to the **systems** and causing **liver** damage.

Drinking coffee can be *stimulating*, which is beneficial if a person has things to do; however the **caffeine** will constrict **blood vessels** and boost **blood pressure** which increases the misery of a pounding **headache**. On the other hand, if regular coffee drinkers avoid their caffeine-fix because of an upset **stomach**, that can also cause **headaches** in addition to making them even more aware of their misery.

Conventional wisdom says that **dehydration** caused by heavy drinking is what makes people feel so sick the next day. In fact, many experts admit that they know very little about *cause* and *effect* of the symptoms of hangovers. **Dehydration** is just one of several factors on the **physical** level. Disrupted **biological** *rhythms*, **alcohol withdrawal**, **toxic substances** found in **alcohol**, especially in **dark liquors** such as **whiskey**, also have an *effect*. If a person is **dehydrated** and the fluids they are taking in are not getting to where they need to go, drinking large amounts of **water** and or **sports drinks** will not have the desired *effect*.

Some tee-totaling experts suggest hitting the **gym** and *sweating* it out, but they clearly have not *experienced* a hangover or they would know better than to suggest it. **Exercising** when people are not in *alignment* is a recipe for injuries, and **sweating** is a foul-smelling and inefficient method of clearing **toxins** from the **body**.

Sleep is an old reliable remedy for many reasons, if a person has the luxury of "sleeping it off." Lack of sleep can definitely escalate the symptoms. Much of the tiredness in the **eyes** is due to **dehydration** of the **eyeballs**. Create *black wholes* at the back of the **eye** to *spin out* waste and *spin* **in oxygen** and **hydration**. It is also possible to stretch the *effects* of time by shifting the energy with the intention that **ten minutes** equals **one hour** of sleep.

Alcohol is the product of a process in which **fruit**, **grains** or **vegetables** are *fermented*. **Yeast** or **bacteria** *react* with the **sugars** in the **food** to create **ethanol** and **carbon dioxide**. **Wine**, **cider** and some **liquors** are made from **fruit**. **Barley**, **rye** and other **cereals** are used to make **beer** and **spirits**. The **alcohol** content is dependent on the length of *fermentation* and the *distillation* process. Most people assume that when they are suffering from a hangover, they are *suffering* the *effects* of the chemical **ethanol**; however, there are many hidden ingredients in modern day **alcoholic beverages** that go unreported because **alcoholic beverages** are not monitored by the FDA and their brewers are not required to list ingredients. Common ingredients found in **beer** are GMO corn and corn syrup, high fructose corn syrup, fish bladder, propylene glycol, natural flavors, GMO sugars, caramel coloring, insect-based dye, animal by-products, carcinogens, and BPA, which is found in polycarbonate plastics and epoxy resins. Many people have issues with **corn**, **fish**, **sugars**, **food colorings** and **insects** for both **physical** or *non-physical* reasons. Test for any weaknesses to **ethanol** as well as any hidden ingredients. There are often *emotional attachments* when **allergies** are involved. *EU … ALLERGIES, Pg. 60*

A small percentage of the population *suffers* from an allergic reaction to **sulfites** that occur naturally in **wine**, or to **artificial sulfites** that are added to it. **Histamines** and **tannins** are also naturally occurring ingredients that cause **headaches** often *associated* with hangovers. The skin of the grapes are considered to be **amines**, along with chocolate, cheese and cured meats that are all high in **histamines** and can frequently trigger **migraine** headaches. **Tannins** are **flavonoids** that make wine bitter and prevent oxidation. They are also found in grape skins along with the stems and the seeds, causing high levels of **serotonin**. It is important to identify the leading **toxins** and **detox** them from the body. *EU … HEADACHES, Pg. 278 … DETOX, Pg. 178*

THE "GOOD NEWS" IS:

Hangovers are self-inflicted. They can resolve very quickly and a person will return to homeostasis once the **toxins** and the underlying energetic reasons are identified and cleared.

THE "BAD NEWS" IS:

Misery loves company! Family and friends who *suffer* together, stay together. Hangovers are often joked about, almost as a rite of passage.

NUGGET OF WIZDOM FROM THE VECTOR

HANGOVERS ARE NOT PUNISHMENT FOR HAVING HAD A "GOOD TIME." THEY ARE CAUSE AND EFFECT OF INGESTING SUBSTANCES INTO THE BODY THAT A PERSON IS NOT STRONG TO. ALTHOUGH THE EFFECTS OF A HANGOVER FEEL VERY PHYSICAL, MANY OF THOSE EFFECTS ARE CAUSED BY NON-PHYSICAL ISSUES.

HARD CORE SOFT DRINKS

When **soft drinks** were originally introduced to the public, they were **pharmaceutical concoctions**, elixirs containing some surprising ingredients. **Coca-Cola®** was invented in 1886 by Doctor John Pemberton, who was a **pharmacist** from Atlanta, Georgia. The **soft drink** was first marketed as a **tonic** to relieve headaches, hysteria, melancholy and morphine addiction; it contained extracts of **cocaine** and **caffeine** from the kola nut until 1905. In **Europe**, where prohibition was not a factor, the soda was called **Pemberton's French Wine Coca**; it contained **coca**, **caffeine** and **alcohol**, and became widely popular for its *effects*. Today it still contains **coca,** but the **psychotropic alkaloid** has been removed. Although the United States has an eradication policy encouraging Andean governments to eliminate coca as a medicinal crop, coca leaves, in their natural form are non-addictive, rich in essential nutrients, and have been chewed and consumed as a tea for thousands of years in the high Andes as a natural stimulant, a pain killer, and to relieve respiratory and digestive issues. It is **illegal** to **import** or **possess coca leaves** under **U.S. law** except for the **Coca-Cola®** **company** who are **exempt** from this **law**.

The lemon-lime flavored soda **7UP®**, invented by Charles Grigg of the Howdy Corporation in 1929, was introduced just before the **stock market crash** and also contained **lithium**, a **psychiatric medication** as one of its ingredients. It was originally named **Bib-Label Lithiated Lemon Soda** after the primary **medicinal ingredient lithium citrate** until 1936 when it was renamed. **Lithium citrate** continued to be one of the main ingredients until 1950 when it was removed after researchers discovered the potentially dangerous *side effects*.

Today, most sodas contain high **fructose syrup**, **chemical sugar substitutes**, **dyes**, **citric** and **phosphoric acids**, and **sodium benzoate**. Some top selling soft-drinks in America contain, **caffeine** and **yellow 5 dye**; some also have **brominated vegetable oil (BVO)** to contend with. **BVO** is *lethal* in its liquid and vaporous form, and at one time was used as a *sedative* before doctors realized that it caused *memory loss* in some patients. Over one hundred countries have banned **BVO** because it has been linked to *organ failure* and *birth defects*.

WHAT HAPPENS TO THE SYSTEMS OF THE BODY WHEN PEOPLE INGEST SOFT DRINKS?

Drinking a regular serving of today's sodas is equivalent to ingesting **ten teaspoons of sugar**; this causes a leap in **insulin levels** within twenty minutes, and stimulates the **liver** to convert the **sugar** into **fat**. After forty minutes the **caffeine** is fully ingested, **blood pressure** is raised, and then **dopamine** kicks in and *stimulates* the **brain pleasure centers** in a fashion similar to **heroin**. About an hour after drinking a soft drink, the **phosphoric acid** binds **calcium**, **magnesium** and **zinc** in the **gastro-intestinal tract**, creates a *diuretic effect*, and removes the **minerals** via the **urine**. In **diet sodas**, the **sugar** is replaced by **neurotoxic chemicals**, usually **aspartame**.

WHAT HAPPENS TO THE SYSTEMS OF THE BODY WHEN PEOPLE ENJOY A GLASS OF WINE?

The health benefits of **red wine** used in moderation, are greater than you might think. Per serving, **red wine** out-performs **commercial grape juice**, **raw blueberries** and **acai** in the amount of **antioxidants** such as **phenolics** and **polyphenols**, including **proanthocyanidin.** These powerful antioxidants stop **free radicals** from destroying **cells**, lower the risk of **diseases** such as **cancer** and **heart disease**, and promote *youthfulness*.

THE "GOOD NEWS" IS:

If you just purchased a case of soft drinks and now have no **desire** to drink it, all is not lost. It has successfully been used as a **cleaner** for **engines**, removing **rust** from **chrome**, **corrosion** from **batteries** and **stains** from **clothing** and **toilets**. It **unclogs plugged drains**, and in some countries it has proven to be an ***effective*, inexpensive pesticide**. Or you can donate it to your favorite police station for **cleaning blood** off the **roads** after *accidents*. Instead of your **soda,** you can enjoy a glass of **red wine**, but only if you are of **age**, due to **legislation** meant to **protect** our **young** and **vulnerable** from *ingesting* **harmful substances**.

THE "BAD NEWS" IS:

Soft drinks are consumed at the rate of more than **one billion drinks** per **day**. Left to their own devices, *accumulations* of **toxins**, **chemicals**, **dyes** and **acids** from these additives build up in the **body**, *stagnating* the **elimination *process*** on a **cellular** level and beyond. The vital flow of the **circulatory**, **lymphatic** and **energy systems** become *congested, inflamed* and *infected*, creating a perfect **environment** for *parasites* to thrive. **Obesity** and **diabetes** are *side-effects* of a build-up of **toxins**, **poisons**, **dyes**, etc., from overworked **elimination systems**.

NUGGET OF WIZDOM FROM THE VECTOR

IF YOU ENJOY SOFT DRINKS … REALLY ENJOY THEM! … GUILT FREE! WHEN YOU ARE AWARE OF THE EFFECTS OF WHAT YOU PUT IN YOUR BODY, YOU CAN DELETE PROBLEMATIC POISONS, TOXINS, ACIDS, ETC., FROM THE BODY SYSTEMS AS WELL AS THE ACCUMULATIONS OF THOUGHTS AND FEARS ON THE PSYCHOLOGICAL LEVEL. IF YOU ARE FEELING NEGATIVE EMOTIONS ABOUT INGESTING SODAS, YOU WILL NOT BE IN ALIGNMENT ON A PSYCHIC AND SPIRITUAL LEVEL TO NEGATE THE NEGATIVE EFFECTS FROM THE FEARS AND REGRETS OF THE COLLECTIVE CONSCIOUSNESS.

HARD MEN ARE GOOD TO FIND

Many conversations between women revolve around discussions of "a shortage of men." They search for answers as to why their *relationships* with their **significant others** begin with great promise, yet end in another *disappointing* version of the same old **dramas**. Over the years, working with thousands of women from around the world, I have heard many of them complain that "good men are hard to find." Common statements include:

"It is hard to find a good man who is also a great lover."

"There are more women out there than men. Statistics prove it!"

"Men prefer younger women."

Books are written about it, **movies** are based on it. Women who want to **settle down** often justify "settling" with a man with whom they are not energetically in *alignment* with because they want to start families and do not want to be alone.

BEING NICE

From the time they are little girls, women are taught that they are "sugar and spice and everything nice." In the same nursery rhyme little boys are told that they are "snips and snails and puppy dog tails." This gives them permission to "get dirty" once in a while! (Perhaps this is why some women refer to men as "dogs"). Can you imagine a world where men and women are the same? How boring would that be! The trouble is all the **unreliable information** out there that insists that there is a "battle of the sexes." The fact is that **many men** are **very capable** and **many women** underestimate the *primordial forces* that drive **human nature**. Most **men** are driven by the chase. *Actions* speak louder than **words**.

Growing up, the two most prized nuggets I received from my mom's very limited sexual education discourse are …

1. "Men have two heads. Their big head and their little head. They mostly think with their little head, so it is better not to upset them and hide the things you buy and gradually take them out of the closet," and (the other gem) …

2. "After a while, holding hands isn't enough."

My mom's intentions were good; she wanted me to take an easier path, but this is a synopsis of what I heard:

"Men are beasts. Scary, like two-headed monsters!"

"His thoughts are small."

"Don't upset him! He can't handle you."

"You are currency."

"Don't shine too bright; do it gradually so that you appear to "Be-Nice.""

N.I.C.E. (neurotic, insecure, confused, exhausted).

If you are trying to be everything for everyone, all the time, while looking your best doing it, you will fail in your mission. No matter how hard you try, you will not be able to maintain the illusion of the perfect photoshopped women you see in magazines and other media. Many people try to be what they think their partners want them to be. It is much more powerful to be the best version of yourself.

On the other hand, I have also worked with many men who **really** want to know, "What is it that women **want**?!" Many of them have dedicated **time** and *effort* into figuring this out. More often, unfortunately, both **men** and **women** feel compelled to "play the game" with no understanding of what the rules of the **game** are.

Playing games does not support true intimacy. The truth is that **men** and **women** are the same species. We all have **male** and **female** aspects, *masculine* and *feminine*, *yin* and *yang* that are *reflected* back to us by our **partners.** The next time you are feeling resentment towards your **partner**, go **inward** and ask yourself, what does this say about me? If your partner does not feel *desirable*, he or she will reflect *undesirability* and *disappointment* back to you. You in turn then reflect **undesirability** and *disappointment* back to him or her, and create a *vicious cycle*. When you love yourself, it gives your partner *total permission* to love you.

Many people find it challenging to talk about sexuality openly, largely due to their **social**, **cultural** and **religious** upbringing that conditions the **sub-conscious mind** to take a *natural event* and make it seem **unnatural**. There are also many *un-conscious* weaknesses from *spiritual* and *psychic experiences* that *affect* the *collective consciousness*. Delete any weaknesses that come up and strengthen yourself and others for strong *communication* and intimacy.

INCREASE SEXUAL POTENCY

To increase **sexual potency**, there must be an understanding of the female and male **anatomy** and how the **genitalia** work. Awareness of the *mind* can be used to strengthen the **CNS** to any particular **body part** to increase the function of the **genitalia** to the **CNS**. Many weaknesses in the **genitalia** are referred from weaknesses in the **oral cavity**. *EU ... REPRODUCTIVE SYSTEM, Pg. 445 ... DEEP THROAT, Pg. 161*

Men and women are triggered by the confusion of *mixed* messages of *respect* and *lack of respect* between the sexes. It is not uncommon for **women** to be *attracted* to **male strength** and yet be *afraid* of it at the same time. Many **men** do not understand *balanced aggression* and have *suppressed fears* and *fantasies* of injuring women. For both men and women there is often a lack of role models who show what a **fair** and **strong** *relationship* looks like. This weakens the *intuitive understanding* between men and women. **Religious dogma** and **society** have many rules regarding sexual activity that cause even more *confusion*. There is so much emphasis placed on virginity, "good girls" and "bad girls," "sluts" and "women you take home to mom." Many people have **negative associations** to their first **sexual experience**. "Giving it away" often triggers **past life** and **spiritual experiences** of **prostitution**.

MALE

Medical conditions such as high blood pressure, high cholesterol, atherosclerosis, heart disease, diabetes, neurological disease and problems with the **CNS** from stroke, MS and Parkinson's can lead to **erectile dysfunction**. Unfortunately the **pharmaceuticals** that are commonly used to treat these **problems** can also cause the **problem**. Men who are using **antidepressants** are caught in a catch twenty-two. **Erectile dysfunction** is **depressing** and the **antidepressants** cause **erectile dysfunction**. There also can be **problems** from **surgeries**, **radiations**, etc., for **prostate** and **rectal** cancer and problems with the **pituitary gland** that lead to excess **prolactin** and low levels of **testosterone**.

Erection is dependent on **mental** or **tactile sexual stimulation** that generates **electrical impulses** along the **nerves** leading to the **penis**. This leads to the release of **nitric oxide**, which then increases production of **cyclic GMP (cGMP)** in the **smooth muscle cells** of the **corpora cavernosa** to **relax** and allows **expansion** of the **penis** through rapid **blood flow** into the **corpora cavernosa**. The **pressure** from the expanding **penis** compresses the **veins** that drain **blood** out of the **penis** through the **tunica albuginea** which is made up mainly of **amino acids**. This, along with **buck's fascia**, the **fascia** which covers the **erectile bodies** of the **penis**, constricts the **deep dorsal vein** within the **penis** to sustain **erection** by trapping the **blood** in the **corpora cavernosa**. **Erection** is reversed when an **enzyme** called **phosphodiesterase type 5 (PDE5)** causes the **cGMP** levels in the **corpus cavernosa** to fall, stopping the **flow** of the **blood** by opening the **veins** to drain **blood** away from the **penis**.

You can calculate what percentage your sexual performance is at in comparison to a time when you feel it was optimal, **recalibrate** yourself to that time and strengthen yourself to that **experience** or to better performance. Many **sexual limitations** that people place on themselves are passed down the family line from their **ancestors** and **past life experiences** as well as from **collective humanities'** issues with sexual potency and survival.

Erectile dysfunction and **premature ejaculation** are opposite sides of the same coin. **Impotence** occurs when there is difficulty in achieving a hard, firm **erection**, and **premature ejaculation** is a lack of

neurological management in the act of **ejaculation**. Both are symptoms of **pressure** felt from not being in tune with a person's **higher self**. On a **psychological**, **mental** and **emotional** level, the **purpose** of **ejaculation** has changed significantly over history. **Ejaculation** is now, more than ever, an act of **release** rather than an act of **procreation**. Many times the energetic weaknesses revolve around **emotional re-actions** to **external forces**, **self-control**, **lack of self-control** and **control** of others. **Premature ejaculation** is often a weakness to **holding back**, especially in less experienced men who encounter **vaginas** for the first time. **Impotence** is generally a weakness to moving forward. Never underestimate the **power** of a real, live **vagina**!

There is a certain immaturity and recklessness in men, especially in younger men who are not careful with their **sperm** and where they are **depositing** it. The **risk** is part of the **thrill**. Young girls and younger women are often lulled into a sense of security by the **thrill** of being chased, and are inclined to experiment with the **power** they have over a man in the **physical** and **non-physical sense**; then they are slammed into reality when an unplanned **pregnancy** happens.

SIZE DOES MATTER

The answer to the age-old question, "Does size matter?" is, "Yes it does!" Having said that, there is not one perfect size for everyone. On average, most men can accommodate most women's needs; however, individual women have preferences for size, thickness, length, circumcised and uncircumcised **penises**. The **vagina** is able to **accommodate** a variety of objects, including **tampons**, **penises**, **babies**, etc. Generally if the **relationship** is a good fit, a woman is able to **physically** adjust her **vagina** to **accommodate** a man's **penis** to be the perfect fit.

It is possible to **enhance** the size of a **penis** from the inside out. The shifts are similar to **breast augmentation**, keeping in mind that the anatomy of the penis serves the dual purpose of **reproduction** and **urination,** it also relies on the **circulatory system**. *EU ... BREAST HEALTH AND AUGMENTATION, Pg. 102 ... CIRCULATORY SYSTEM, Pg. 137*

Men are either "growers" or "showers," meaning that some men do not display all their attributes unless they are aroused, while other men like to display their attributes twenty-four/seven. Men who have large **testicles** in comparison to their **penis** have a tendency to wander (think about **bulls** breaking through fences) compared to men who have smaller **testicles**.

WOMEN

Most **magazines** lead women to *believe* that they have to work hard to "get a man." The truth is that when women embrace their feminine divinity, they are irresistible *magnets* for men. Many women are unknowingly weak to receiving the benefits of their *feminine power* and give their **power** away to others, especially men too easily.

Sexual fantasies are abundant in **movies, romance novels, pornography**, etc., and have a profound effect on men and women. Women often attract what they *fear* because *sexual fantasies* in romance novels are about *submission* and *dominance* without the **physical** reality of **pain**.

Women are *magnetic* and men are *electric*. If there is a weakness in women to *receive* they have a tendency to *disassociate*. There is an old joke where after making love a husband asks his wife, "What are you thinking?" and she replies, "Beige, I think I will paint the ceiling beige."

When there is a lack of **desire** in women, it often is because the message from the **genitals**, *mind*, **CNS** and **PNS** are distorted and not getting through. You can energetically add **testosterone** to the **vagina** to make it more *aggressive*, which makes women less *vulnerable* and more willing to *accept* pleasure from a man. The interaction between men and women is really a **reflection** of the *masculine* and *feminine* traits that lie within each individual reflected by their **sexual partner**.

THE "GOOD NEWS" IS:

Hard men are good to find! When we are in *alignment* within ourselves, we bring the best out in others, men and women. What I have come to discover, after some experimentation, is that Mom was right … after a while holding hands isn't enough and **spice** is way more fun than **nice**!

THE "BAD NEWS" IS:

Significant others reflect their partners' greatest *fears* and their greatest *capacity* to **love**. Many people have *slavery* issues that hold them back from freely expressing their *authentic selves* and instead react to *sub-conscious* and *un-conscious thoughts*.

NUGGET OF WIZDOM FROM THE VECTOR

YOU AND YOUR PARTNER ARE A TEAM EFFORT! IN MOST CASES IT IS THE WOMAN WHO SETS THE STANDARD FOR GREAT

SEXUAL EXPERIENCES. IF YOU WANT TO BE TREATED LIKE A GODDESS, ACT LIKE ONE.

HEADACHES

Regardless of **gender** or **age**, many people will at some point in their lives will *experience* a **headache**, defined as a **pain** or *ache* in the **head**. Even though the **brain** does not contain **sensory nerves** that register the *sensation* of **pain**, it still can *ache* because it is full of *memories* and *residuals* of the effects of pain, and is often out of sync with the **cranium;** this causes *feelings* of **pressure**. **Headaches** seem to be caused directly by *over activity* or **problems** with **structures** in the **head** alone, or they can also accompany many **dis-eases** and **conditions**. The **medical community** has divided **headaches** into two basic types, **primary** and **secondary headaches**, characterized by common symptoms.

To facilitate energetic shifts it is best to think of **headaches** as a **pain** in the **head** that most of the time is referred from another location in the **body** or from a *non-physical* cause. Because The *non-physical* reasons for **headaches** have a lot of variables, it is advisable to check for multiple past *traumas* to the **head**, **face** and **neck** that trigger *emotional* and *psychological* *re-actions* to sights and sounds at specific events, held at specific times of the **year**, **month** or **season** as well as for *fears* and *phobias* that are triggered by *negative memories*.

When people feel *overwhelmed* and try to relax themselves out of "stress" and *pressure*, they often end up **relaxing** their *tail brain* and their *base chakra* instead, causing the *pressure* to rise to their **heads**. Squeezing their **buttocks** and putting *tension* into their **pelvic cavity** and **spine** relieves the *pressure* by pulling it down to be released.

Although it is not necessary to break **headaches** down into specific **types** to shift the energy, the **type** of **headache** and the words people use to describe it can give clues as to what the *issue* truly is.

PRIMARY HEADACHES

Primary headaches involve *pressure* and **structures** within the head such as **blood vessels**, **muscles**, **nerves** of the **head** and **neck**, as well as **chemical activity** in the **brain**. They are commonly caused by direct **physical stimuli** like **temperature** and **external pressure**, **epicranial pain** from the **scalp**, or **physical exertion**. **Primary headaches** are divided into **tension headaches**, **migraines** and **cluster headaches**.

The most common form of **primary headaches** are considered as **tension headaches**. People often describe the **pain** as if there is a tight band around the **head**, causing a constant dull *ache* felt on both sides of the **head** that often starts in the **neck** or spreads to the **neck**. Generally the **pain** begins slowly and gains momentum by mid-day. There are often unresolved *past life traumas* to the head, such as **scalping**, **being scalped** and, **scalping** others, as well as "dungeon" type *tortures* involving **vice-grips** on the **head**. **Tension headaches** are classified as **episodic** or **chronic**. **Episodic headaches** normally last a few hours or several days, whereas **chronic tension headaches** are continuous, lasting for two or three weeks in a month or for a few months at a time. There are many triggers that can weaken people to their **daily routine** or lack of it, weaknesses to *cycles*, in particular **menstrual cycles** and/or **specific weather**, **climates**, **barometric pressure**, **lighting**, etc.

The pain from **migraine headaches** is often described as *pulsing* and *throbbing* **pain** that occurs on both or just one side of the **head**, accompanied by **blurred vision**, **lightheadedness**, **nausea** and **sensory disturbance**. They can last for a few hours or for several days. Test for weaknesses between the **respiratory**, **reproductive** and **digestive systems** and even out the *pressure* between both sides of the **brain**.

Cluster headaches are the least common type of **headache**. People often describe the pain as *sharp* or *burning*, with **pain**, **redness** and **swelling** around one **eye**, causing drooping of the **eyelid** and *congestion* in the **nasal passages** of the *affected* side. They generally occur in **clusters** of four to eight weeks, one or more times at specific times of the day, striking quickly and lasting around an hour and a half.

Problems with the **sinus cavity** often revolve around *emotional* issues, in particular *grief*. There are often weaknesses to what a person would rather *not see*, is angry about *seeing* and other *emotional re-actions* to triggers that they may or may not be aware of. *Pressure* located on the **left** often revolves around **problems** of being a **woman**, while *pressure* on the **right** suggests **problems** of being a **man**.

SECONDARY HEADACHES

Secondary headaches are often caused by *external forces* that stimulate **pain-*sensitive*** nerves of the **head**. Many people have had the *experience* of "brain freeze" while they were ingesting a very cold drink or ice cream. Another example of **secondary headaches** are from alcohol induced hangovers. It is helpful to *detox* the outside substance from the **systems**

within the **body** and replace with **oxygen** and **hydration** by using *black wholes* and *white wholes*. *EU ... BLACK WHOLE/WHITE WHOLE, Pg. 93*

Internal forces involving the systems of the **physical body** can also cause blood clots, dehydration, glaucoma, tumors and stroke that often trigger **secondary headaches**. *External forces* such as **carbon monoxide poisoning**, unreliable information about **influenza** and **blows** to the **head** causing **concussion**, are common triggers. Excessive use of **headache medications** is the number one cause of **secondary headaches** that are referred to as **re-bound headaches**.

Delete any *memories*, *residuals* of *memories* or *remnants* of *memories* from *traumas* and *tortures* of **blunt force** to the **head**, **hangings**, **be-headings**, etc., as well as to **poisoning** and **gassing** *experiences*. Test for any *karma* with **pharmaceutical companies**, **doctors**, **scientific experimentations**, etc.

THE "GOOD NEWS" IS:

Many **headaches** can be relieved instantly by pushing *pressure* down the body and allowing it to be released through *exit portals* and *black wholes*. When the underlying causes for the *pressure* are addressed, common triggers no longer have the same *negative effect*.

THE "BAD NEWS" IS:

Stubborn **headaches** belong to people who stubbornly hold onto **physical** and *non-physical aspects* which cause their symptoms. Their frustration is like a toxic spill that seeps into every *aspect* of life, *negatively affecting* their **environment** and everyone else within that **environment**.

NUGGET OF WIZDOM FROM THE VECTOR

PEOPLE OFTEN FEAR CONTAGIOUS DISEASE BECAUSE THEY ARE UNAWARE THAT "CONTAGIOUS DIS-EASE" IS OFTEN NON-PHYSICAL. ONE OF THE MOST CONTAGIOUS DIS-EASES OF ALL IS HEADACHES. GENERALLY PEOPLE WHO HAVE A LOT OF HEADACHES, ARE A HEADACHE THEMSELVES, OR ARE PUTTING UP WITH A LOT OF OTHER PEOPLE WHO ARE A HEADACHE.

HEARING

Ears are responsible for detecting **sound** and delivering it to the **brain** for interpretation; they also play a major role in maintaining *balance* in the **body**. The anatomy of the **ear** can be divided into the **outer ear**, **middle ear** and **inner ear**.

OUTER EAR

The visible portion of the **outer ear** is made of rigid **cartilage** covered by **skin** referred to as the **auricle** or **pinna,** which is shaped somewhat like a radar dish to facilitate the collection of **sound**. The **sound** then passes through a tube-like pipeline, the **auditory canal** (**ear canal**) that connects to the outer layer of the **tympanic membrane** better known as the **eardrum**. The **earlobe** is the lower part of the **outer ear** that has **cartilage** and a large **blood supply** that helps to keep the **ears** warm.

The **size** and **position** of the **ears** on the **head** identify the intake of *mental*, *emotional* and **physical** data. In general, the larger the **ears** and the more zones they cover, the more information they take in. **Higher set ears** tend to belong to more **intellectual** people, while **low set ears** tend to belong to more **physical people**. **Ears** well **set back** on the **head** tend to indicate a more *intellectual* person, while **ears** that **stick out** belong to *seekers* who are extra *sensitive* to the people around them, often due to a challenging **upbringing**. **Ears** held **close** to the **head** are more likely to belong to people who *accept* conformity. **Large earlobes** indicate a more *sensitive* person and **small lobes** or **non-existent lobes** belong to people who tend to be more *emotionally* controlled.

MIDDLE EAR

After **sound** is captured by the **outer ear**, the **airwaves** travel through the **tympanic cavity** in the **middle ear**. This causes the **eardrum** to *vibrate*, which amplifies the **sound** and liquefies the waves. The **ossicles** are three tiny **bones** in the **middle ear** consisting of the **malleus** (**hammer**), a long handle that is attached to the **eardrum**, the **incus** (**anvil**) that bridges the **malleus**, and the **stapes** (**stirrup**) which is the smallest **bone** in the **body**. The **hammer** is first to feel the *vibrations* from the **eardrum**, and sends them to the **anvil**. The **anvil** then transfers the *vibration* to the **stirrup** and the **inner ear**.

INNER EAR

The **oval window** connects the **inner ear** to the **middle ear**. When the **stirrup** moves, it pushes the **oval window**, and *stimulates* the **cochlea**; this a spiral shaped **organ** that uses the *vibration* of **fluid** in the attached **semicircular ducts** to transform sound into **nerve impulses**. In the **cochlea** there are thousands of tiny **hairs** that transform **sound** *vibrations* into **electrical** *vibrations*. These **impulses** lead to and from the **vestibular** and **cochlear nerves** in the **cranial brain** to interpret the **sound** and **information**, and to *balance* the **head's position** in reference to the **brain** at the **atlas**.

The **Eustachian tube (auditory tube)** drains **fluid** from the **middle ear** to the **throat**. It also **maintains** and **equalizes** the **air pressure** on both sides of the **eardrum** for normal hearing. **Liquid** in the **inner ear** synchronizes with movement in the **body** and informs the **brain** of the movement.

PHYSICAL HEARING PROBLEMS

The **human ear** can hear, on average, between twenty and twenty thousand **hertz**. There are many causes of **deafness** and **loss** of **hearing**. Some are considered **hereditary** through flawed genes that cause malformations in the **inner ear**; others can be due to **prenatal exposure** to *dis-ease* or from **loud noises** and **trauma**. **Hearing loss**, or **deafness**, can be **conductive** or **nerve** related.

CONDUCTIVE DEAFNESS

Conductive deafness is caused when the **ossicles** in the **middle ear** fail to conduct **sound** to the **inner ear**, or when the **eardrum** fails to *vibrate* in response to **sound waves**. The **ear canal** secretes **cerumen**, a waxy substance that protects and lubricates the **tissues** of the **ear**. Too much **wax build-up**, **foreign objects**, **excess mucous**, **ear** *infections* and **medications** can affect the **ear canal** and block the **eustachian tubes**.

NERVE DEAFNESS

Nerve deafness can be caused by **disease** or *trauma* to the **cochlear nerve**; this makes it impossible for **electrical impulses** to reach the **brain**. In other cases, the **brain** is unable to translate the messages received by the **cochlear nerve**.

Earaches or **pain** in the **ear** can have many causes stemming from **middle ear** *inflammation* or, in the case of "swimmer's ear," an *infection* originating from a **skin** condition. **Tinnitus (ringing in the ears)** can happen in **one** or **both ears** and is usually due to damage from **loud noises**. A ruptured **eardrum** can also result from *sudden changes* in *air pressure, sudden changes* in lifestyle, and from **loud noises**. **Meniere's disease**, a malfunction of the **inner ear** on one side causes vertigo, tinnitus and hearing loss. *Infection* of the **mastoid bone** can occur from an uncontained **middle ear** *infection*.

Strengthen the *fitness* of all the components within the **inner, middle** and **outer ear** to be in strong communication within themselves, with each other and the **CNS**, *mind* and **brain**. Many weaknesses of the ears are referred to and from the **kidneys, mouth, eyes, nose, ovaries** and **testicles,** and it is common to find weaknesses between the **eustachian tubes** and **fallopian tubes**.

NON-PHYSICAL HEARING PROBLEMS

It is generally *believed* that **hearing** becomes less acute as people age because of *degeneration* of the **physical components** of the **ear** and **brain**; however, many times loss of hearing comes from *non-physical* causes and weaknesses *around* being heard and hearing others, as well as from hearing particular **tones** or **sounds**. If someone has **hearing problems**, it is helpful to ask what it is that they **do not want to hear** or what they would rather **hear**.

Many **hearing problems** are actually *listening* problems. Weaknesses in **hearing** of the **left ear** are often triggered by **negative experiences** of *listening* to or having to *listen* to significant **females, female** *experiences* and high-pitched *frequencies* and *tones*. When the **right ear** is *affected* it is often about *listening* to or having to *listen* to **males** and **male** *experiences*, **voices** and low *frequencies* and *tones*. As people age, they *accumulate negative experiences* of what was **said** to them and what they have **said** to others. There are often *memories* of **spiritual experiences** that amplify *negative* and *positive emotional re-actions*, in particular when there is **ringing** in the **ears**. Lack of *balance* in the **body** is often *associated* with lack of *balance* in the *aspects* of life, feeling under too much pressure to satisfy the **false obligations** of **society** at the expense of other *aspects*, or being taken by surprise. The *energetic tail* can be used as a **tripod** to *center* and *stabilize* the **body** to handle the speed at which the **earth** is traveling.

If a child that has been born deaf or has a tendency to ear *infections,* test for unresolved *karmas* with parents, siblings, other family members, the medical establishment and pharmaceutical companies. People often have *spiritual experiences* of *torture* and *traumas* that were heard and/or not wanting to hear them.

CASE STUDY:

At a live demo, there was a gentleman who had been unable to **hear** out of his **left ear** for many years. He stepped up somewhat reluctantly when his name was chosen. I was standing on his **right** side, and this gentleman was unable to **listen** to me as I spoke; yet he could clearly **hear** the man who was interning with me, and who was standing to his **left**, the sided of his supposedly "bad" **ear**.

The leading weakness for his **hearing** was actually a weakness to *listening* to the **higher pitched tones** of women in general and his **mother** in particular. As I was talking to him, *gophers* popped into my *mind*. I asked him if he had ever hunted **gophers** as a **child**. (**Gophers** are considered a hazard to livestock by farmers and ranchers on the prairies. **Children** are encouraged to kill as many as possible, and earn a bounty, by bringing the tails home as proof). He wept as he let go of a *suppressed memory* of **gopher hunting** with friends at the age of **twelve,** how he succumbed to peer pressure, and laughed with his friends as the **gophers screamed** in **pain** before they died.

The underlying *root cause* for his **loss** of **hearing** was a weakness to *spiritual experiences* of **listening** to women and children *screaming* in **pain** while men *roared* in **laughter**. His **hearing** was instantly restored when he connected with the *suppressed memory* and he forgave himself unconditionally.

THE "GOOD NEWS" IS:

Although **ear *infections*** are common in babies and young children, most clear up on their own. Identifying the underlying weaknesses can help alleviate **pain** and speed up **recovery**.

THE "BAD NEWS" IS:

Weaknesses to *listening* often cause **hearing problems** and *infections* of the **middle ear**. People have a tendency to **hear** what they want to **hear** and avoid *listening* to what is **painful** for them. If the underlying weaknesses are not addressed the **problems** with **hearing** often get worse before they get better.

NUGGET OF WIZDOM FROM THE VECTOR

VIBRATIONS OF SOUND ARE EXPERIENCED BOTH INTERNALLY AND EXTERNALLY AS A MECHANISM FOR CONNECTING PEOPLE MENTALLY, EMOTIONALLY AND PHYSICALLY TO THEIR PRESENT REALITY.

HOLY COW

In North America alone, millions of **cows** have become part of the **meat** and **dairy industry** every year. **Cows** are *gentle* by nature. They are *curious*, *clever*, *social* animals that form complex *relationships* with each other, much like **dogs** do in their pack.

BEEF CATTLE

When they are young, **cows** are routinely **branded** with **hot irons**, have their **testicles** cut off and have their **horns** gouged, cut out or burned off, all without **anesthetic**. In most cases, they are sent to massive **feedlots** to be fattened for slaughter as soon as possible.

Cows are **ruminants**. This means that they have a special type of **stomach**, called a **rumen**, that houses billions of **microbes** that can break down **grass** and **hay**. The **bacteria**, **fungi** and **protista** that provide **nutrients** so that the **cow** is able to *digest* **hay** and **grass**, also build up huge amounts of **methane gas**, particularly from the belching of the **cows**. **Ruminants** eat food, regurgitate it as **cud**, and eat it again. **Cows** are meant to consume and subsist on **cellulose roughage** in the form of **grasses** and **shrubs.** On average, they produce one hundred to one hundred fifty liters of **saliva** per **day** to provide the fluid, lubrication and alkalinity that buffers the **rumen**. After traveling through the **esophagus**, food, water and saliva are deposited in the **reticulorumen.** Heavier items such as stones, grains, etc., fall into the **reticulum**, while **grass** and **hay** travel straight to the **rumen** and divide into three zones, with **gas** *rising* to the top, **yesterday's feed** *sinking* to the bottom, and the **newly arrived roughage** *floating* in the middle.

Initially, **grazing areas** were a mixture of a variety of **grasses** and **flowers** that grew naturally. As small farms were bought out by **industrialized operations**, many of the pastures were seeded to **perennial rye grass** because, with the aid of **artificial fertilizers**, it grows very quickly and in huge quantities. Unfortunately, although it fills the cow, **rye grass** lacks the **nutritional value** of other grasses and prevents more nutritious plants from taking root in the **pastures**, which causes inhibited *digestion* and **sickly cattle.**

Most **cows** end up in **feedlots** and are unnaturally fattened up with **grains**, in particular **corn**, which disrupts the delicate *pH balance* and *temperature* in the **rumen,** making it very **acidic** and altering the perfect **anaerobic environment** in the **vat** that is necessary to keep **cows** *healthy*. The **rumen** produces huge amounts of **gas**, about thirty to fifty liters per hour in adult **cattle**, creating **methane emissions** that contribute to **greenhouse gas**. The effects on the **environment** are challenging to assess, as it is a study in progress.

DAIRY CATTLE

Like every other mammal, **cows lactate** because they have given *birth* to their **babies**. On most **dairy farms**, they are repeatedly **impregnated** through **artificial insemination**. Upon *giving birth*, they are *traumatically separated* from their **newborn calves**, usually within a **day**, and hooked up to **milking machines** several times a **day**. It is common for them to **bellow** for their **babies** for **days**. When their **bodies** wear out and they are no longer able to supply their **quota** of **milk**, they are sent to the **slaughterhouse**.

Cattle in the dairy industry are often given **BGH** (**Bovine Growth Hormone**) in the **USA**. In **Europe** and **Canada**, the practice has been banned due to health concerns for **human consumption**. Cows are **genetically modified** and **drugged** to produce on average **four** and a **half times** more **milk** than they would naturally produce to feed their calves. Many of the **cows** suffer from **mastitis,** an *infection* of the **udder** that results in painful *inflammation* and swelling of the **teat**; consequently they are injected with **antibiotics** to keep them alive.

A **cow's** natural life span is **twenty-five years,** but the average **dairy cow** lasts only about **four** or **five years** before it is sent to **slaughter**. Many of them are **lame** from **intense confinement**, the **filth**, and the **strain** of being **constantly pregnant** and giving **milk**. Their **meat** is mainly used for companion animals, low-grade hamburger, and soup because it is not deemed desirable for **human consumption**.

THE CALVES

Male calves are **by-products** of the **dairy industry**, and generally taken from their mothers at one **day old**. Many are **shipped** to **feedlots** to await **slaughter**. Others that are sold to the **veal industry** are immobilized in **small dark crates** to keep their flesh tender. They are fed a **liquid diet** low in iron and nutrient value so that their **meat is white** until they are **slaughtered** a **few months later**. Many of them *suffer* from **anemia, diarrhea** and **pneumonia**. The **female calves** are raised to replace the **milk herd**.

TRANSPORT AND THE SLAUGHTERHOUSE

Cattle that survive **feedlots**, **dairy sheds** and **veal farms** are eventually crammed into trucks where they typically go **without food**, **water** or **rest** for the duration of a journey which can sometimes last for **days**. Many of them collapse in the hot weather or sometimes freeze to the side of trucks until they are pried off with crowbars. On arrival at the **slaughterhouse**, many are not *healthy* enough to **walk**. These are known in the cattle industry as "downers" and have to be dragged off the truck by ropes or chains. *Traumatized* and *confused* by their journey, many of the **cattle** that are able, do not want to leave the truck. They are routinely **beaten** and **prodded** in their **faces** and **rectums** to make them co-operate. The **cows** are then forced through a chute and shot in the head with a captive-bolt gun that is meant to **stun** them; however, the lines move very quickly and the workers at the **slaughterhouse** are often undertrained so many of the animals are still *conscious* when their **throats** are **slit** and the **butchering** process begins.

THE "GOOD NEWS" IS:

In **Hindu tradition**, the **cow** is considered a **sacred symbol** of the **earth** as the maternal, gentle provider and sustenance of life. The **cow** magically transforms **water** and **grass** into **milk** and *freely* **nurtures humanity** in the same way that a *liberated soul* shares *spiritual knowledge*.

"One can measure the greatness of a nation and its moral progress by the way it treats its animals. Cow protection to me, is not mere protection of the cow. It means protection of all that lives and is helpless and weak in the world. The cow means the entire subhuman world." Mahatma Ghandi

THE "BAD NEWS" IS:

People are busy! No one really wants to think about where the **meat** or the **milk** on their dinner table is coming from. People go to the air conditioned/heated **grocery stores** to routinely choose their neatly packaged **cuts** of **meat**, grab a gallon of **milk,** and rush home to feed their families at the dinner table that night before heading off to soccer practice, movies, concerts, etc. However, in this day and age of information, **ignorance** is no longer a plausible **excuse** for *allowing* the **cruelty** these animals endure to *suffer* in **silence**.

HOMEOSTASIS

Homeostasis is the ability and tendency of any **organism** or **cell** to maintain **equilibrium** by adjusting to the **effect** that **external** and **internal forces** have on **physiological** processes. There are three main ways that the **body** adjusts to **inner** and **outer stimuli**: **responses**, **reflexes** and *re-actions*.

RESPONSE

The behavioral **response** of a living **organism** is triggered by **external** or **internal stimuli**, often referred to as "fight or flight" reaction or "stress response." The **nervous system** initiates, coordinates and directs specific changes in the functions of the **body** to prepare it to deal with a **perceived** threat.

REFLEX

A **reflex** is a **response** to a **negative stimulus** that **acts** to return your body to **homeostasis** (**natural order**). This is a **physiological reaction**, not to be confused with **re-actions** that are a **voluntary response** to a **stimulus** from the **environment**.

Simple *reflexes* require a minimum of **two neurons**: a **sensory neuron** (**input**) and a **motor neuron** (**output**). More complex *reflexes* involve the **spinal cord**, **brainstem**, **cerebrum**, **spinal fluid** and the other components of the **spine**. The **neural pathway** that a **nerve impulse** follows typically consists of five components: the **receptor**, **sensory neurons**, **integration center**, **motor neuron** and **effector**.

The **receptor** is at the end of a **sensory neuron**. **Sensory neurons** are also called **afferent neurons**. They conduct **nerve impulses** towards the components of the **spine** (**CNS**) and **blood** towards the **heart** from the **organ system** it is supplying. The **integration center** consists of one or more **synapses** in the **CNS**, while the **motor neuron** conducts a **nerve impulse** away from the **integration center** to an **effector**. **Motor neurons** are also referred to as **efferent neurons**. The **effector** responds to the different **impulses** by *contracting* if the **effector** is a **muscle fiber**, and by *secreting* a **product** if the **effector** is a **gland**.

RE-ACTION

A *re-action* is a *mental* or *emotional dis-order* forming an individual's **response** to his or her life situation. This is a process that involves change in the **atomic nuclei**. **Re-actions** require a high level of *neural processing* and, because of this, they can be influenced by a variety of factors such as "*emotional distress*."

RESULTS:

"I had been experiencing debilitating pain from my pelvis to my neck over a span of 6 years prior to discovering Colette. In a determined effort to bring my body back into a healthy, pain-free state I sought the care and professional guidance of many medical doctors, TCM doctors, chiropractors, acupuncturists, RMTs, physiotherapists, sports therapists, and osteopaths. While each specialist seemed to temporarily relieve the pain, nothing lasted. All the while I kept up a moderated regular yoga and strength training practice, swam often and practiced meditation to help with pain management. However, as the pain lingered on and on in my life I started to feel intuitively that the source was very deep, just as the pain had launched itself very deeply into my muscles, tissues, and fascia and was not releasing, despite the continuous efforts I was making to gain a state of homeostasis back in my body. Enter Colette. In just one session Colette quickly and effectively identified the root causes of such lengthy pain in my body and immediately cleared 90% of it away. Her highly attuned intuitive gifts zoomed in on long standing blocks in my psyche, allowing for an incredible scope and breadth of healing. I hope more people discover and choose Colette first in their journey of healing, rather than after years and years of unnecessary pain, frustration, and cost, as was my experience. We are all meant to live our lives in wholeness. Anything short of that is denying ourselves our birthright. Thanks Colette, for sharing your extraordinary healing skills with us all."

Lila

THE "GOOD NEWS" IS:

It is natural for the body to automatically return to *homeostasis* if we just get out of the way.

THE "BAD NEWS" IS:

As conscious beings, we are constantly being bombarded by *external* and *internal forces* that have a negative *effect* on the **body**, *soul* and *spirit*. The **physical body** generally takes the hardest hit.

NUGGET OF WIZDOM FROM THE VECTOR

TRAIN YOUR MIND TO AUTOMATICALLY NOTICE THE DIFFERENCE BETWEEN EMOTIONAL RE-ACTIONS, RESPONSES AND REFLEXES.

HYSTERECTOMY

Hysterectomy has become a popular, routine "solution" to relieve **heavy bleeding**, **bloating**, and other **menstrual** discomfort and, in more serious cases, it is a means to deal with **malignancy**. The premise is that the **uterus's** main function is for pregnancy, and that it is no longer necessary once a woman is not bearing children. There is mounting evidence, however, that the **vast majority** of **hysterectomies** performed are avoidable through other approaches that have fewer complications and a shorter recovery period.

Women who have exploratory surgery or removal of the **uterus**, **fallopian tubes** or **ovaries,** often experience common side-effects beyond the risk of *infection*, **hemorrhage**, **blood clots**, adhesion and damage to other **organs**. Regardless of whether a **partial** or **full hysterectomy** is performed, the broad bands of **ligaments**, bundles of **nerves** and **blood supply** attached to a network of **arteries** and **veins** that attach to the **uterus** are severed. Usually the **cervix** is removed as well. When the **nerves** that attach the **uterus** are severed, loss of *sensation* is not limited to the **pelvic floor,** but also *affects* the **vagina**, **clitoris**, **labia** and **nipples**. When the **ligaments** are severed, many women also *experience* an unnatural shifting of the **bones** and **organs** in the **pelvis**, which *affects* the **hips**, **lower back** and **skeletal structure,** and causes compression in the **spine** that eventually leads to drooping of the **rib cage** towards **the hip bones** and leads to major thickening of the **waist**.

The *relationship* between the **respiratory**, **reproductive** and **digestive** **systems** is an intimate connection. Removing an **organ** from the **reproductive system** will affect the **respiratory** and **digestive** **systems**. Weakened **pelvic floor muscles**, along with the loss of feeling from the severing of the **pelvic nerves** commonly cause **bladder** and **urinary** problems such as an inability to control the flow of **urine** and **stool** and/or **constipation** due to the **bowel** moving down into the space that the **uterus** normally occupies. Without the support from the **uterus,** the **bowel** *expands* like a balloon, pressing directly against the **bladder**.

Many women also report a searing **pain** that radiates down from the **waist** to the back of the **knees,** and a **cyclical pain** in the **vagina** when they sit or walk. That can often be relieved when *accumulations* from *past*, *present* and *future tortures* of **hot irons** being forced into the **vagina** as punishment for "witch" crimes are cleared energetically. Unfortunately, women are still abused by this form of torture in some countries today.

For many women who undergo **hysterectomies**, sexual *sensation* is diminished **substantially** or **entirely**, particularly for women who can no longer connect to *sensations* that occur during **uterine orgasm**. A small number of women can still *experience* slight **vaginal wall** *contractions*, although most report a total loss of *sexual feeling*. Severing the *flow* of **blood** to the **uterus** also limits **blood** *flow* from the **pelvis** to the **external genitalia**, **ovaries**, **vagina**, **labia** and **clitoris,** as well as to extremities in the **lower torso**.

One of the many functions of the **uterus** and the **ovaries** is **cardiovascular** protection. Women who have their **uterus** removed are **three times** more likely to experience **cardiovascular disease**. Seventy five percent of women who have **hysterectomies** also undergo **castration** of their **gonads** (**ovaries**). This leads to a **seven times** greater risk of **heart disease**. Even when **ovaries** are not removed surgically, damage to the **blood supply** from the removal of the **uterus** often causes a dramatic loss of function in the **ovaries** which is similar to **castration**.

In a **vaginal hysterectomy**, the surgeon cuts around the **cervix** removing it and the **uterus** through the **vagina**. The **vagina** is shortened when the **opening** is sutured closed and attached to one or more of the **severed ligaments**. Many women *experience* prolapse of the **vagina** through the **vaginal opening**, like a pocket that has turned inside out due to the sutures giving way. In an **abdominal hysterectomy** a horizontal **incision** is made above the **pubic bone** and then, depending on its size, the **uterus** is pulled out through the **vagina** or through the **incision**.

The most consistent **problems** women *experience* after **hysterectomy** are a loss of *sexual feeling*, loss of *vitality*, **joint pain**, profound **fatigue** and *major personality changes affecting* every *aspect* of life, particularly, *youthfulness*, **finances**, **career** and **purpose**.

UTERUS

The **uterus** is a powerful **muscle** located in the **lower pelvis**. It supports the **bladder** which sits just in **front** of it, and the **bowel** directly **behind** it. It is a **hormone responsive sex organ** that provides many functions, pregnancy being just one of them.

OVARIES

A woman's ovaries are her **gonads**, comparable to **testicles** in men, and they produce **hormones** throughout her lifetime. On the **physical** level, it is important to reconnect the *vital flow* through the **circulatory**, **nervous** and **lymphatic systems** of the **reproductive**, **respiratory** and **digestive systems**. Make sure that all **systems** within **systems** are functioning at optimal levels and that the "empty space" the **organs** used to occupy, maintain **structure** to support other **organs** and **body** processes. Clear all *direct karma* with the **medical establishment,** the **surgeons**, as well as the "need to be cut." *EU ... PSYCHIC SURGERY AND TRANSPLANT, Pg. 425*

CASE STUDY:

I worked with a fifty-seven year old woman who was experiencing heavy vaginal bleeding for several years, before and after menopause. She had a grapefruit sized fibroid tumor in her uterus that the doctors were reluctant to remove without a total hysterectomy because of concerns of uterine and cervical malignancy. She was reluctant to undergo the surgery because she did not want to sacrifice her sexual pleasure, specifically uterine orgasm. We worked on her letting go of non-physical concerns and weaknesses regarding the surgery as well as the physical aspects of maintaining the connections between the CNS, PNS, reproductive, respiratory and digestive systems. We also worked on strengthening the structure of the empty space of the removed organs.

She is happy to report that she has not lost any function, and was able to achieve orgasm within two and half weeks of the surgery.

THE "GOOD NEWS" IS:

If the **uterus**, **ovaries**, **cervix** have been removed, it is possible to energetically *rejuvenate* and improve function in the **body** by clearing *accumulations* of *non-physical trauma*, **torture**, **castration**, **rape** and other *negative life experiences* in the *past*, *present* and *future*. Pay particular attention to *religious experiences*. *EU … RELIGIOUS EXPERIENCES, Pg. 443*

THE "BAD NEWS" IS:

A woman's ability to *experience* the ecstatic orgasmic pleasure of life is drastically reduced and most often severed following a **hysterectomy** if the energetic weaknesses are not addressed.

NUGGET OF WIZDOM FROM THE VECTOR

DESPITE POPULAR BELIEF FROM A PATRIARCHAL MEDICAL COMMUNITY, THERE IS NEVER AN AGE OR A TIME IN A WOMAN'S LIFE THAT HER UTERUS AND HER OVARIES ARE NOT ESSENTIAL TO HER HEALTH AND WELLBEING. AVOID UNNECESSARY REMOVAL.

INSIGHT

The key to *insight* is using *sensitivity* to FEEL, and fine-tuning *thoughts* for clear *perception*. Many people *feel* that they are too **sensitive**; however it is more likely that **institutions** and others around them are not **sensitive** enough. **Sensitivity** works against people when they become "over-sensitive" and "over think" *challenges*, thereby impairing their **ability** to *feel* for the optimum *choice* through their *intuition*. People can hone their *intuitive ability* by using **sensitivity** to *feel* energetic weaknesses held in the **CNS**. *Feeling* is an "on and off switch." Many people confuse **feeling** with **emotions**. If they don't *re-act emotionally* to the **sensations** that they **experience**, their *perception* becomes fine-tuned to their *intuition*. The *thought* can then be used to **deprogram** the *negative effects* from their **CNS** and encode their *authentic desires* from their **heart** to find *creative soul-utions* that are in *alignment* with their *purpose*.

It doesn't matter how brilliant a person's **intellect** is: expecting a **logical answer** to a **logical question** will just lead to another **question**. **Logical questions** require *intuitive answers*. Instead of getting an **answer** to the original **question**, people end up with more **questions** and more **answers**. It is then challenging to discern which **answer** is the right one for the original **question**. Making a life-time habit of asking **question** after **question** leads to an *accumulation* of **thousands** of **unanswered questions** and **answers**, tumbling about with no clear *purpose* or apparent connection with the *applicable answer*.

You access your *intuition* through your *thoughts* and *feeling*. If you get into the practice of going inward to notice the *sensations* that run through your **body** as you encounter *challenges*, you are better able to pinpoint the energetic weaknesses and clear them without *judgment*. When you are in *alignment*, you can automatically *feel* strong to *external* and *internal forces* that are weakening you and your situations.

What does being in *alignment* with your energy mean? It is similar to the *sensation* you get when you meet a "stranger" and instantly *feel* connected on a deep level. The ways people meet their "soul mates" and "soul family" are diverse, "bumping" into them at the most likely and unlikely of times. You can set your "auto pilot" to *attract* **people**, **places** and **situations** just like a magnet attracts metal filings. When you are bothered by something, honor yourself by taking the time to ask yourself the **question**, "What is this really about?" **Think** about one specific **question**. Then stop **thinking** and go inside to **feel** for the answer while *connecting* to your **heart**. Take consistent steps of *action* based on the **answer** you receive in this way.

RESULTS:

"Hello Colette, Thank you for the wonderful, insightful session that I had with you a couple weeks ago. It really moved me forward and boosted my respect for myself. Thank you for your kindness, wisdom, and compassion. I admire you greatly. Warm regards"

Marie Holmes, Paris

THE "GOOD NEWS" IS:

Every **problem** has an **answer**. You want to strengthen yourself to the most *applicable answer* for your specific **question** at a given moment. You are unique, so even if someone else seems to have the same **problem** as you do, the best **answer** for them is not necessarily the best **answer** for you. When you remain *neutral*, your *perception* of the **problem** and the **answer** will be accurate.

THE "BAD NEWS" IS:

In this age of technology, **information** is available at the click of a mouse. Our ability to access more and more **information** with ease allows us to *expand* and *accelerate* with the universe in a way humanity, as we know it, has not *experienced* until now. The many benefits are sometimes outweighed by the *anxiety* of being faced with too many **answers** and confused by **inaccurate information**.

NUGGET OF WIZDOM FROM THE VECTOR

THOUGHTS ARE INSPIRATIONS FROM THE MIND. THESE INSPIRATIONS CAN CAUSE EMOTIONAL RE-ACTIONS JUST FROM THE THOUGHT OF HAVING EXPERIENCED AN EMOTION CONNECTED TO THAT THOUGHT. YOUR SENSITIVITY TO FEEL AND YOUR ABILITY TO PERCEIVE EXPANDING DIMENSIONS COMES FROM THE INTUITION OF YOUR HEART'S INTELLIGENCE AND THE CNS.

INTEGRATION OF THE BODY

Anatomical *relationships* are *emotional,* **physical** and **behavioral.** *Stagnation* results in a breakdown of *anatomy* and *emotional* organization, which then results in an equivalent breakdown in **behavior.** This leaves the **physical body** vulnerable to *internal* and *external forces. Self-awareness suffers* when the connection between **body,** *soul* and *spirit* are not in *balance.* When people are distracted by **false obligations** and deny other *aspects* of their *authentic selves,* there is a corresponding *imbalance* which manifests as **physical disease** in the **body,** as *emotional* and *mental disease* in the *mind,* and as a loss of life *purpose* and direction in the *spirit.*

Problems in the **physical body** can be caused by *traumas,* **illnesses,** *limitations, phobias* and *fears* occurring from the *past, present* or even the *future.* Every **part** of the **body** is in *communication* with any other specific **part** of the **body.** For example, a **thumb** can have a *specific effect* on a **big toe.** At the same time any **given part** that you happen to select is also *communicating* with all the **other parts** in the **body.** Poor *communication* between **several parts** can randomly weaken any **other part** of the **body,** causing a lack of *integration* in the **entire body** and *rejection* between the **body parts.** You can strengthen the *communication* between every **part** of your **body** in **general,** and also reverse the *rejection* of any one **body part** that is not efficiently **communicating** with your *mind* and the rest of your **body.** The many weaknesses that create the **problem** can be **physical,** *non-physical* or **both.** For example, if the **lungs** relate weakly to the **hands,** using the **hands** has a weakening influence on the **lungs** and can eventually lead to serious **breathing problems.** It is important that the *relationship* between every part of the **body** is strong to the **CNS,** because that is where **pain** and *pleasure* originate, and because we *feel* with our **CNS**. *Synchronicity*, *acceptance* and clear *communication* facilitates integration between the *mind* and **body** and is enhanced by clear conversation between the two. If we use the example of the **lungs** to the **hands**, the **lungs** are not just in conversation with the **hands**; they are also conversing with the *mind*, **systems**, **organs**, **glands**, etc. Clear *communication* between the **lungs** and the **hands** enhances the whole **body**.

It is easiest to test and strengthen the top three weaknesses in each of the **systems** and then the strength of each **system** to each other. The **digestive system**, **reproductive system** and **respiratory system** are intimately connected and often refer weaknesses to each other. There are also the **urinary system**, **endocrine system**, **elimination system**, **CNS and PNS**, **skeletal structure** as well as the **circulatory system** to consider. It is possible to strengthen the top three weaknesses of each **body part** to all the *internal* **organs** and back to each other so that each **organ** and **gland** is strong to working with the others in all directions. *Eliminate* any *dead cells* and **tissues** at the location within the **CNS** that manages a particular **organ**. You can use *relationship circles* to strengthen the **organs**, **body parts** and **systems** to each other. *EU ... RELATIONSHIP INSURANCE, Pg. 437*

At times **specific parts** of the **body** need to be integrated directly to the *mind* and the *mind* to that **part** of the **body**. This includes the **brain** to the *mind* and the *mind* back to the **brain**. If a **body part** is weak to the **CNS** and **PNS** as well as to the *mind,* it will require strengthening from the *mind* to the **nervous system** as well as the **nervous system** back to the *mind* and **body part**. For example, if there is a **problem** with the **big toe** (**body part**), there can be a weakness to the *mind*, the **circulatory system** and specifically the **heart** (**organ**). Or the weakness may be from the *mind,* the **brain,** the **big toe** (**body part**) along with the **circulatory system** and specifically the **heart** (**organ**). It could also be from the *mind* to the **CNS**, the **big toe** (**body part**), **circulatory system** and specifically to the **heart** (**organ**). Or it could be the *mind* to the **CNS**, the **brain**, the **big toe** (**body part**) the **circulatory system** and specifically the **heart** (**organ**).

THE "GOOD NEWS"IS:

Maintaining strong connections between the **body parts**, the components of those **parts** and the **heart/***mind* connection in a three way conversation empowers general well-being, strengthens the body to *homeostasis*, stops the process of **disease**, and promotes *rejuvenation*.

THE "BAD NEWS" IS:

Poor **communication** leads to weak **relationships** and a lack of **recognition**, which results in **rejection** and lack of **integration** throughout the entire **body**. Slight variations in the **CNS** can cause extremely varied symptoms due to its complexity and **sensitivity**.

NUGGET OF WIZDOM FROM THE VECTOR

IT DOES NOT MATTER WHICH BODY PART IS BOTHERING YOU. THE WEAKNESS CAN BE TURNED INTO A STRENGTH BY PLACING THE THOUGHT OF THE BODY PART(S) INVOLVED ON THE CNS (SPINE), PARTICULARLY ON THE SPINAL CORD, FOR LESS THAN A SECOND AND ALIGNING THEM TO BE STRONG WITHIN THE SYSTEMS, WITH EACH OTHER AND THE CNS AND IN SYNC WITH THE RHYTHM OF YOUR HEART BEAT.

INTERNAL FORCES

People have stories based on **memories** held in their **sub-conscious** and **un-conscious mind**s that they repeat to themselves and others. These stories keep them needlessly **re-enacting** different versions of the same old **problem** until they recognize the underlying **internal forces** that are holding them back from achieving their potential. **Internal forces** are what keep people awake at night feeling like their **mind** has them on an exercise wheel like a hamster in a cage. They are **stagnant, recycled, positive** and **negative thoughts** from the tales told about their story. **Accumulations** of these stories gather over **space-time**, gaining momentum every time people indulge in the untruths of their lives, until they have the potential to **implode** the **body**, **soul** and **spirit** triad, blowing it apart from the inside out. Once **internal forces** work for people rather than against them, they can **align** themselves with **authentic desires** from **heart consciousness** and choose better options based on results rather than on the "What I.F.s."

Neutrality is the key to calming **internal forces** that stir up the "What I.F.s." Some common "What I.F.s" are: **what** will happen **if** I do or don't do the right or wrong thing and **if** I do, **who** will suffer or benefit? **When** will it change, **if** it ever does? **Where** will I end up **if** I can't find the solution? **If** this continues, **how** will I make ends meet? **If** I can't solve this, **why** not?

Many of the stories that people tell themselves are based on their **ancestor's limitations** that have been passed down and imposed on the family line. **Cultural influences**, **religious** and *spiritual experiences*, *traumas* and familial *tragedies* all play a role. These *internal forces* are held in the **CNS**, the **cells** and the **quantum particles** of our being. Once they are identified and released all the way at the **atomic** level, people are able to transcend the concerns and create a better reality instead of reacting to the old stories.

People often go weak at the **molecular** level because **molecules** are the building blocks of everything that appears solid in our **third dimensional world**. It is helpful to have a basic understanding of what **molecules** are made of and **how quantum particles** work.

MOLECULES

Molecules are made up of **atoms** that are held together by **chemical bonds**.

ATOMS

Atoms are the smallest part of **matter**, invisible to the naked eye. They represent **elements** and are made up of **neutrons**, **protons** and **electrons**.

SUB-ATOMS

For a long time the **atom** was thought to be the smallest part of **matter** that could exist. Now we understand that **atoms** are made up of even smaller particles called **sub-atoms**. The three main **sub-atomic** particles that form an **atom** are **neutrons**, **protons**, and **electrons**.

NUCLEI

At the center of the **atom** is the **nucleus** or **nuclei (plural for nucleus)**. It consists of **neutrons** and **protons** that are bound together. **Electrons** are **negatively** charged **particles** that spin in circles around the **nucleus**, changing energy levels as they travel.

SUB-NUCLEI

Protons are **positively charged particles** that reside in the **atomic nucleus**. The number of **protons** in the **nucleus** determines the **atomic number of elements** in the **periodic table** of **elements**. Neutrons also reside within the **nucleus,** but they have no **electrical charge**. They are said to be the glue that holds the **protons** together. Every **proton** and every **neutron** is identical; however, the number of **neutrons** within each **nucleus** determines the specific characteristics of the **atom** and the **element**. The number of **protons** remains the same. Like charges repel each other, and unlike charges attract each other.

Isotopes are **nuclei** with identical numbers of **protons** and varying numbers of **neutrons**. **Isotopic** means uniformity in all directions.

QUANTUM PARTICLES

All particles can spin, just like the earth does on its axis. This spin can be **up** and **down**, **left** and **right**. **Fermions** are particles of matter that follow a set of laws called **Fermi-Dirac Statistics** that were written by Enrico Fermi and Paul Dirac in 1926. They possess a **half-integer** spin.

There are two types of **matter** particles:

In standard theory, **quarks** are elementary particles that are fundamental constituents of **matter.** There are six **quarks** that are grouped in three sets of two, with each subsequent group a heavier version of each other. The six **quarks** are named **Up**, **Down**, **Charmed**, **Strange**, **Top** and **Bottom**. In *holofractographic theory*, they are the **singularity structure** at the center of the *black whole* **proton**.

Leptons are particles that are grouped into "flavours," also in three sets of two with each subsequent group a heavier version of each other. These are the **Electron**, **Electron Neutrino**, **Muon**, **Muon Neutrino**, **Tau** and **Tau Neutrino**. The **Electron**, **Muon** and **Tau** have +1 charges while all the **neutrinos** are neutral.

Hadrons are the result of placing **quarks** into groups. If a group has two **quarks** it is considered a **meson**, while particles with three **quarks** are called **bosons**. **Mesons** are **subatomic particles** that transmit a strong interaction binding the **nucleons** together in the **nucleus** of the **atom**. **Bosons** are **subatomic particles** that have **zero** or **integral spin**.

When you delete old patterns held in the **CNS**, your **cells molecules**, **atoms**, **sub-atoms**, **nuclei** and **sub-nuclei** all the way down to your **quantum particles**, peel away layers of **limiting beliefs** which allows you to move on to "better."

THE "GOOD NEWS" IS:

If you think outside the box, like Einstein, you are able to use your **logical mind** to ask a **question** and allow the *intuitive answer* to flow to you via the **H.S.N** (**Higher Self Network**) instead of getting caught up in the "What I.F.s."

THE "BAD NEWS" IS:

The "What I.F.s" can be very sneaky and cause **doubts** that are dredged up and hidden in the tiniest particles of a person's being. The more they are **suppressed**, the more damage they are capable of.

NUGGET OF WIZDOM FROM THE VECTOR

YOUR EXPECTATIONS OF HOW YOU WILL ACHIEVE GOALS PLACE LIMITATIONS ON YOUR TRUE GREATNESS. WHEN YOU LET GO OF THE "WHAT I.F.S" AND ALLOW THE UNIVERSE TO PROVIDE FOR YOU, YOU CAN ALWAYS EXPECT GOOD THINGS!

INTUITION

Intuition comes from the part of our *soul* that contains our *mind*, *will* and *emotional reactions*. It is the expression of the perfection of *spirit* that has **human attributes** and links with the **human experience** through *feeling* rather than **thinking**. **Human beings** are connected to *multidimensional selves* through *feeling*. Many people don't want to *accept response-ability* for the "ugly" *choices* they have made because there are *aspects* of their **identity** that are *challenging* to *accept*. It does not matter how great people's *intentions* are; if they are not backed by *intuition,* progress through *intention* will be hit and miss. People cannot rely on *intuition* or *intention* alone. **Intuition** without *action* makes people feel stuck despite their *intentions*. When people hone their ability to *feel* in *alignment* with their *actions*, their *perception expands* and gives them access to **answers** that are unavailable without *intuition*. When they first begin to connect with their *intuition*, people are often *overwhelmed* by the vast *choices* that are now available. It may seem that those *choices* were not there before; however it is more likely that their *perception* was *limited*, and this led them to *believe* they had *limited choices*.

You want to be sure that your *intuition* is strong to **answers** and results in order to *manifest* the best outcome available in the moment. The **answers** presented to you are neither right or wrong, positive or negative. They are *choices* that are available to you now – *choices* you were unaware of before. It is up to you to *allow* the **answer** that is most *applicable* to your **situation** to come to you through your *intuition* rather than by chasing after it with your **logical**, **linear** *mind*.

When people *re-act* to their *emotional* cues rather than look for **answers** within, even the most *positive emotions* can have a *negative* *effect* on the outcome. It is not about having a pat answer to solve anyone's **problem** at any time. It is about being able to choose the best **answer**, most *applicable* in the moment and take *action* on it. People are not bothered on the *emotional* and *mental* level unless there is an energetic weakness that causes them to *misinterpret* the **situation** or **people** they are interacting with. Many people are so bothered when they resolve a long-standing issue, that they insist it is still bothering them even when it is not.

As you *allow* yourself to take *action* on your *intuitive insight,* it is important to have strong *external* and *internal boundaries* within your *authentic self* in order to sift through your own baggage and the *re-actions* of others.

THE "GOOD NEWS" IS:

Your **baggage** does belong to you. The "stuff" that gets in your way reveals unknown *treasures* that you would have missed had you not gone deeper.

THE "BAD NEWS" IS:

Your **baggage** comes up for a reason. As tempting as it can be to sweep it under the rug, eventually it will show up in an unrecognizable form and usually at a most inconvenient time.

NUGGET OF WIZDOM FROM THE VECTOR

WHEN YOU USE YOUR INTUITION TO RECEIVE ANSWERS TO LIFE'S PROBLEMS, YOU ARE SIMPLY ALLOWING YOURSELF TO EXPAND YOUR PERCEPTION TO FIND ANSWERS FOR CREATIVE SOLUTIONS THAT ARE NOT AVAILABLE WITHOUT INTUITIVE INSIGHT.

KARMA

Karma is not punishment; it is just the way the universe works. It is not good or bad, positive or negative, but a matter of *cause* and *effect*, a debt from *acts* of transgression, causing **death** to other living things. *Karma* can be *directly* caused by a person through *accumulations* of interactions within the world and with other people. It can also be *indirectly* caused by others through *associations* with **ancestors**, **descendants**, *cultural influences*, *collective consciousness*, etc., or it can be caused by *karmic spaces*.

Accumulated Karma is *karma* that people have directly brought to themselves or that is *directly* caused by them. **Associated Karma** is the *effect* of *karma* that does not directly belong to a person. It is *associated* with **family members**, **friends**, **co-workers**, *cultural influences*, *the collective consciousness*, etc. When *karma* intensifies, it transforms into *curses* and creates additional *karma* and *karmic spaces*. *Karmic spaces* are *karmas* that do not involve *personalities*, but *attitudes* to *personalities*.

Ma Jaya Sati Bhagavati is a Brooklyn-born spiritual teacher, mystic, and visionary who invested her lifetime in learning and teaching about *karma*. Her teachings embody radical acceptance, unconditional love and selfless service. The eleven karmic spaces identified by Ma Jaya Sati Bhagavati are *jealousy*, *anger*, *pride*, *indifference*, *ego*, *lack of awareness*, *intent*, *worldly desires*, *abuse of power*, *desire to be right* and *attachment*.

Most people come into their current lifetime with more than one *karmic space*, and some come with all of them. As you read about the *karmic spaces* below, the ones that stand out for you the most are the ones that you want to focus on clearing. As one *karmic space* is cleared, you will begin to notice that others also stand out. If certain **people** pop into your *mind* as you go through the *karmic spaces*, take the time to clear the energy between **yourself** and that **person**. It is very common to have *karma* between **families** that are tied to each other through **ascendants** and **descendants** even if they did not know each other in this lifetime.

JEALOUSY – Blindness To Your Own Beauty

Jealousy makes people dwell on their losses instead of taking consistent steps of *action* to improve their future. People often *judge* themselves because they want what others have. It is even possible to be *jealous* of yourself by *comparing* yourself to who you *have been*, with who you *are now* and who you *might become*. It is easy to get stuck in the *past* when people convince themselves that their "best days are behind them," or by "putting off" *changes* that could empower them because they are waiting for that "perfect career," "losing weight," or meeting "that perfect someone."

ANGER – Forgetting Your True Nature

Anger is "the gift that keeps on giving," passed down from generation to generation, awakening *feelings* of *shame* and *unworthiness* that are learned in childhood. The *combined emotions* of *anger* and *shame* can cause *reverse perception*, where the slightest *criticism* leads to *feelings* of *unworthiness* and a need to constantly *apologize* for no reason.

The *mixed emotions* of *fear* and *anger* foster *paranoia*, putting people in "attack mode" in an effort to avoid being attacked. Children and animals often bear the brunt of *suppressed anger* between adults when they "let off steam." As *anger accumulates*, it builds into *rage* and literally can make people's "blood boil;" this can cause many *health problems* such as high blood pressure, arthritis and cancer to run in families. Others use *religious beliefs*, **war** and **prejudice**, to justify their *anger* and *need* to seek **revenge**.

PRIDE – Fear of Rejection

Many people who are weak to the extremes of being **everything** and being **nothing** alternate between *arrogance* and *unworthiness*. They appear to be *confident*, but deep down they *fear* that people will discover that they are *unworthy* of love. Consequently, they often hide behind *arrogance* and their **desire** to be right to avoid *rejection*. Often the two extremes meet in a pretense of *spirituality*.

INDIFFERENCE – Dimming Your Light

It can be **painful** to witness the *overwhelming* images and stories from the media and internet that people are inundated with on a daily basis. Many people are *feeling hopeless* and *exhausted* by the *challenges* of their own daily lives and don't feel they have the energy to care about the *suffering* of others; this creates a lack of *compassion* that is rampant in many **industries**, **medical institutions**, **factory farms**, etc. The magnitude of it all causes many people to dim their own light by *choosing* not to take steps of **action** to ease the *suffering* in the world. They hide from the **pain** through assumed *righteousness*, by showing *intolerance* for others and by hurting others for the sake of an idea. *Compassion* is often misplaced, causing people to lower their vibration and become part of the **problem** rather than the **solution**. That is not true *compassion*.

EGO – Believing Your Own Press

When people are unable to let the *past* go and continue to wallow in the "same old story," they tend to *over re-act* and *over-indulge* in their *self-thoughts*. Repeatedly revisiting an unpleasant or painful *past* event and all its ramifications is to indulge in *anger*, *fear* and other *negative emotions*. This only creates destructive **thinking patterns**. Chaos is created in the *mind* when people continuously create positive and negative **stories** about **others** that revolve around **self**; this can quickly cause a "poor me" attitude that leads to **complaining,** and begs the question, "Why me?" If you consider the many ways people **suffer** and **struggle** around the world, people might ask instead, "Why not me?"

LACK OF AWARENESS – Letting Opportunities Pass

Opportunities are often hidden in **challenges**. Many people go through life oblivious to the fact that they are creating more **karma** for themselves and others because they are torn between their desire for **comfort** and **oblivion**. Lack of **awareness** in how **actions** affect others creates **confusion** and more **karma** of being **unaware**, and results in missed **opportunities** for positive **change** through addictive **behaviors**. When people habitually suppress the **sensations** of **discomfort**, they can become **desensitized** to the point of automatically indulging in **repetitive actions** which limit their ability to progress in every area of their lives; that creates **inertia** and eventually **oblivion**.

INTENT – The Road To Hell Is Paved With Good Intentions

Procrastination is a form of **self**-**deception** wherein people tell themselves the lie that they will get around to working on their dreams **tomorrow**. As they watch the days go by with unfulfilled **intentions**, the broken promises eventually build up, becoming heavier and heavier, until they crush the joy of creation and lead to an **acceptance** of **mediocrity**.

"Would have," "could have," "should have," **inaction** results from the **conflict** between the **desire** to take **action** to **improve**, and the **desire** to "stay the same." The disruption of the natural **flow** between the two states eventually leads to the **sadness** of a life full of **past** **regrets**, stale **promises**, and "almost doing."

WORLDLY DESIRES – All or Nothing

Many people live a life dictated by gathering material **possessions** and obsessing over the newest toy, which only succeeds in distracting them from their true **purpose**. Others take the opposite approach by dedicating themselves to the **renunciation** of the pleasures of life and the basic tools required to **expand** and **attract** abundance. Both focusing on fulfilling **material desires** and denying oneself **comforts** and **pleasures**, are **limiting choices**. There is nothing wrong with prosperity, wealth, pleasure or sex. **Wealth** is not a guarantee of happiness, but neither is **poverty**.

Hunger for **worldly desires** begins when people, as infants, commit to sustaining the life of their **bodies** as they search for their mother's breast, and this continues throughout the rest of their lives. This is natural; however, when people confuse their *wants* with their **needs**, it tends to lead to **greed**. **Instant gratification** is never *satisfying* because if people are enjoying one bite of life while **thinking** about acquiring the next, they are not enjoying what they already have. You cannot take it with you, yet many people cling to their **material possessions** as if they were more important than life itself. Whether people are caught up with devoting their energy to **getting** what they *want*, or in *self-denial* by **denying** what they want, the lower *mind* will constantly demand their attention and rule their lives.

ABUSE OF POWER – Love Is True Power

Most people have *experienced* abuse of **power** in **government**, **business** and **religion,** as well as on a personal level. Abuse of **power** has the most *negative effect* on self and others because feeling powerless and out of control allows others to take advantage of a person over and over again. This creates more *karma* for them and the abuser.

People can *want power* so badly that they are *attracted* to **powerful people** in order to feel **power** through *association* without regard for the consequences. Abuse of **power** can become a vicious cycle, especially in **families** where the abuse trickles down from the **grandparents**, **parents**, **siblings** and **extended family**. **Power** is not abusive in itself; it is how **power** is used that makes it abusive. The true nature of *power* is the same as the *power* of the universe: *unconditional love*. Anytime **power** of the *mind* is placed ahead of the *power* of *love*, it is **power** for the sake of **power** alone.

DESIRE TO BE RIGHT – Love Is Clarity Itself

When people are concerned and have *self-judgement,* it tends to lead to the **need** to be **right** because they **think** that being **wrong** confirms their *limitations* and *unworthiness*. People who are forced to defend themselves as children may grow into *defensive* adults out of habit. When people are committed to "having the last word" and promoting their point of view, it often leads to conflicts in intimate *relationships*, **career**, **friendships**, etc. The **need** to be **right** can lead to a very lonely place, the loneliest of all, and it will create **isolation** from others.

Placing an exaggerated importance on **mental clarity** becomes an enemy of love because the *mind* will tell you that love is not real.

Attachment to being **right** can take precedence over love itself, which inevitably leads to bigotry and intolerance. **Desire** to be **right** mixed with **religion** is a powerful cocktail that historically has led people to do terrible things to each other. *True religion* is the *religion* of *kindness*.

ATTACHMENT – The Consummation Of Your Life

Attachment is the *master karma* with all the others rolled into one. Everything *changes* and *loss* comes to all of us, but the more we hold on to the *loss*, the greater the **pain** of that *loss*. Letting go of *attachment* leaves you *free* to love and *free* to live. Clinging to the small **ego** and its **dramas** is an *attachment* to *emotion*. Deep-rooted *emotional* habits are the building blocks of *karma*. It is not possible to possess the *divine* by clinging tightly to it.

Confusing *love* and *personal power* with *attachments* leads to issues with **possession,** especially of significant others. Children and lovers are not **possessions**. They are loaned to you with *love*. When praise or blame have **power** over you, it means you are giving in to *attachment*. Being *attached* to outcomes leads to *expectations*. *Expectations* create *limitations* and *disappointment*. If you are not *attached* to the outcomes in the form of *expectations*, you will not be *disappointed* by how things turn out. People can also get caught up in *psychic ability* by becoming *attached* to certain states of *consciousness*.

KARMIC ISSUES

To effectively clear *karma*, it is crucial that the debt is paid in full, with no **need** for anyone to *suffer* or *struggle* with it, and no **need** to learn from the *karma* any longer by repeating the *experience*. When people are really bothered by something someone else does, it is likely that at some point they have also "been there, done that, and have the t-shirt." You must test strong to no longer **needing** to "pay the price" or owing anything anymore, as well as *unconditional forgiveness* for yourself and others.

It is common to have *karma* with **significant others**, meaning **spouses, parents, grandparents, siblings, children, in-laws**, etc., as well as with random people who come into your life, like **employers, employees, doctors, lawyers, dentists, bankers, fellow students, teachers**, etc. The interconnections of *karma* often have many twists and turns. People also have *karma* with members of their *soul family* who are more often than not, exclusive from their **genetic family.** It is very common for people to *feel* they have met their "soul mate." The problem is that many **think** that "soul mates" have to be **significant**

others because of **false obligations** that **society** places on that **relationship** above all others. Either way**, soul mates** have a tendency to share a lot of **karma**. Once the **karma** is cleared, there often is no longer a reason to stay with each other, and this realization can cause a lot of **confusion** and **disappointment**.

Past lives often come up when clearing **karma**. A person does not have to **believe** in **past lives** to have **past life karma** because there are enough people on the planet who do **believe** in **past lives**, and so it has become part of the c*ollective consciousness.* In fact, **past lives** are actually **variances** in the **vector** of *space-time,* not **linear time** as we **perceive** it here on **earth**.

Clearing **karma** is removing the **effect**, not only from living people, but also from **spirits** who have been on the **receiving** end of **karma** from others and their **ancestors**. Once their **experiences** are resolved and the **karma** is cleared, everyone can move on from the **karma**, up and down the family line. As each and every one of us clears **karma**, it makes the world a better place because "outer peace" is only possible through the "inner peace" of every individual.

Common **karmas** that people have are, **owing** a **debt** or someone **owing** them a **debt**, paying off someone else's **karma**, including **spirit attachments** and **revenge**. People often have **karmas** of causing someone else to be **ill**, or becoming **ill** because of someone else. We can even have **karma** of causing others to **create karma** for themselves or **in-between** life **karmas**.

THE "GOOD NEWS" IS:

Attracting **situations** and **people** with whom you have **karma** is common. It is an opportunity not only to clear the **karma**, but also to make your life and the lives of others **better**.

THE "BAD NEWS" IS:

To be able to clear **karma** you need to **acknowledge** that there is such a thing. Once you **acknowledge** that there is **karma**, you **need** to get past the erroneous **teachings** that people are **supposed** to **suffer** with **karma** by **re-living** *it* instead of *resolving it*.

NUGGET OF WIZDOM FROM THE VECTOR

KARMA IS THE KEY TO UNIVERSAL TRUTH. IT IS NOT MEANT TO BE RE-LIVED – IT IS MEANT TO BE RESOLVED. THE COSMIC JOKE IS THAT WE COME HERE TO CLEAR KARMA BUT CAN'T

REMEMBER WHAT THAT KARMA IS AND WHO IT IS WITH ONCE WE ARRIVE ON EARTH.

LEARNING DIS-ABILITIES

Many **students** today face a prognosis of **learning disabilities**. Being **labeled** ADD, ADHD, OCD, autistic etc., can create a stigma at a very early age that demoralizes the self-image of a child for his or her entire life, and leads to a matrix of *expectations* and *limiting beliefs* regarding the child's *future* and the *future* of the entire family unit. Children are often diagnosed with several **dis-abilities**. If this is the case, check to see which **label** is the weakest and clear that one first.

The **seriousness** of the situation can often be resolved with *creative solutions* by finding the leading underlying weakness. Many children who have been labeled with **learning dis-abilities** have an issue with their "line of sight" and the mechanisms of their **eyes**. For instance, if it is *uncomfortable* to look **down,** the **physical** *action* of **reading** is often also *uncomfortable.* It is particularly *challenging* to *begin* **reading** if a person has a weakness to **looking down** and to the **left,** while a weakness to **looking down** and to the **right** causes **problems** with *remembering* the **material**. Many times this is actually due to *sensitive* children using their "built-in radar" for **inaccurate** and **unreliable information**.

Some children have an underlying weakness to **leaving** the **house, going** to **school, being** at **school, leaving school** and/or **coming home** from **school**. These weaknesses often come up when the *internal* and *external boundaries* are weak to subtle and major *differences* in the dynamics at **home, school** and **business** for the **student,** the **parents,** the other **siblings** as well as extended **family**. Energetic weaknesses to the **building,** the **classroom(s), teachers** and other faculty from the **janitor** to the **principal, peers, siblings, sounds, smells, lighting,** etc., can all *accumulate* to have a negative impact on a person's ability to learn.

For some **students**, there can also be challenges around learning specific **subjects** that often test weak on the *psychic* and *spiritual* level. Many people have weaknesses to **testing others**, being **tested** and **exams** in general. These weaknesses often transpire from *feeling* weighed, examined and compared from birth onward. **Parents** generally have many concerns regarding their children and the **perception** of whether or not their **parenting** measures up to that of **peers, family** and **authority figures**. Parents' *concerns* and *fears* for their children can be triggered by unresolved *negative life experiences* stemming from their own **educational** *experiences* at particular **ages** and moving into and out of specific **grades**. Many children will have more of a weakness with one **parent** than the other, and this can create a **comparison** between he or she and their **siblings**. There is often one child in the family who *acts* these weaknesses out for the **parents** as well as for their **siblings**. An "only child" can also **compare** himself or herself to the *unborn potential descendants* of their **parents**.

It is important that the *physical intelligence* (coming from the **brain**, not the *mind*) and **physical environment** support **physical presence** for every **student**. Being forced to **sit** for extended periods at **cubicles** and **desks** is a weakness for many individuals in **schools** and **businesses**. Many **parents** have learned to *suppress* this *discomfort* at **work**. Trying to **relax** oneself out of the *discomfort* of **sitting** still creates a lack of *tension* at the **base** of the **spine** and in the **buttocks**, which creates pressure in the **head** and weaknesses throughout the entire **spine**, and ultimately slows down **systems** that are conducive to *manifestation* on the **physical plane**.

It is not uncommon for **students** to have a weakness to **textbooks** because of **outdated**, **inaccurate logic** and insignificant *intuitive information.* During the time they are written, printed, bound and distributed, the **logical information** contained within **textbooks** is already obsolete. Throughout history, many people have kept the benefits of **information** exclusively to themselves or restricted **information** to an elite group in order to give themselves a distinct advantage in the paradigm of "survival of the fittest." It is common for **descendants** to have many weaknesses about **education** as a result of the *negative experiences* of **maternal** and **paternal ancestors** and the *collective consciousness*, and as a consequence of **ancestors** who have prevented others from learning, or who were themselves prevented from learning.

Poor **penmanship** can be the result of a lack of *coordination* from the **brain** to the **arm** and **hand** or the opposite, a **localized** issue from the **arm** and **hand** back to the **brain**. If it is **localized** in the **arm** and **hand**, check for weaknesses from the **ancestors'** *negative life experiences* of *trauma* and *tortures* to the **hands** and **feet** that are passed on down the family line; it can also stem from the person's own personal *spiritual experiences*. It is common for weaknesses in the **upper limbs** to be referred from weaknesses in the **lower limbs** and vice-versa. Check for the **structural integrity** of the **bones** and **joints** of the **shoulders**, **biceps**, **triceps**, **forearms**, **wrists**, **hands** and **fingers**, as well as the **hips**, **quadriceps**, **glutes**, **calves**, **ankles**, **feet** and **toes**.

Common *expectations* of **gender** specific *understanding* places *limitations* on the ease of **learning**. Examples of common **limiting**

thoughts that children take on include **girls** are not supposed to be "good at math," it is awkward "to run like a girl," and **boys** "have trouble sitting still."

Difficulty with *organizational skills* often begins in the **home**. *Learning*, *focusing*, *retaining*, *retrieving* and *recalling* information can all have weaknesses and are often a result of **physical environment**. **Clutter** in the **home**, especially in the **bedrooms**, creates **clutter** in the *mind*. Strengthen the ability to *organize* words, put *ideas* into words and to *writing* words on paper for optimum expression. **Words** that are used to describe **math** can weaken people's ability to perform certain functions because of their *emotional re-actions*; for example, **words** such as **problem**, **division**, **percentage**, **equations**, **addition**, **fraction**, **multiplication**, **minus,** etc., can create *confusion* and block *understanding*. **Math** has a **language** of its own. Strengthen understanding of the "language of math" to be comprehensive. *Fear* of making mistakes can come from a weakness to making others "a-count-able" for their mistakes and/or from a weakness regarding *traumas* of *past* mistakes where a person was held **accountable**. Resistance to completing **assignments** and **projects** on time can be as simple as having a weakness to *finishing* and *starting*, *beginning* and *ending* tasks. Once you *accept* that there is no **beginning** and there is no **end**, the rest is easy. Many people have underlying resistance to the **Gregorian calendar** because they are in tune with a more natural rhythm. If the information in any given **subject** comes too easily and a person does not have to **study**, it can bother them because **study** is supposed to be **difficult** according to the vast majority of the *collective influence*.

Surveys show that a large *percentage* of **adults** say they would "rather die than speak in public" because of the *fear* of being *humiliated*. A lot of the **fear** rises from the *sub-conscious mind* due to *negative experiences* of being called up to *speak* in front of the **class**, being *berated* for **incorrect answers**, chosen last for **teams**, **bullied**, **teased**, etc., in early *educational experiences*. Weaknesses from the *un-conscious mind* are also very common from *accumulations* of lifetimes of *experiences* of being "tarred, feathered and run out of town," "burnt at the stake," and many other barbaric forms of **public** *humiliation* and *torture*.

Some people have a weakness to **hearing** the **printed word** because of a *fear* of **judgments** being handed down from the **courts**, being **interrogated**, **interrogating others**, etc. If there are **problems** with **speaking,** also check for underlying issues of being *seen*, *heard*, *not seen* and *not heard*. Strengthen *external boundaries* in the *authentic self-triad* so that people in the **audience** who *feel discomfort* at the *thought* of **speaking** in public, don't *affect* the **speaker**. **EU ...* PURPOSEFUL COMMUNICATION, Pg. 429

Although Attention Deficit Disorder (ADD), Attention Deficit Hyperactive Disorder (ADHD) and Obsessive Compulsive Disorder (OCD) appear to be **behavioral** issues, they are more often a **problem** with the **physical intelligence** of the **brain** and the **CNS**, and conflict with the *mind*.

ADD AND ADHD

Hyperactivity is often the result of **impulsive reactions** in the **CNS** and/or **PNS** that come from a **need** to *feel* more *alert*. This is temporarily satisfied by the *re-actions* from the **adults** and **peers** around the **child**. *Past life* explosive *traumas*, such as **bombings**, **radiation**, **microwaves**, etc., that are held in the *memory* of the **cells**, create a resistance to *expansion*, and weaken the *internal* and *external boundaries* of the **body**, *soul* and *spirit*.

On the **physical** level, check for **oxygen** flooding the **brain** at **birth**. In some people this can also shut down the connection of the **brain** to the **respiratory system**, thereby creating an unevenness in a person's **inhalation** and **exhalation** that *affects* the *receiving* and *giving* of information.

OCD

In the case of **OCD**, *thoughts* of not having a **system** or a **protocol** to follow can create a **need** to *systemize* everything down to the tiniest detail. Instead of following a natural rhythm and cycling into "off" and "on," the body's functions get stuck in the middle of a process which creates an ongoing running tape of *criticism*. High *expectations* from the **individual** as well as from the entire **family** can create too much emphasis on *societal obligations*, which causes *imbalance*. Strengthen the ability to be *spontaneous*.

THE "GOOD NEWS" IS:

Many times when the damaging *imprints* of *past* failures are *deprogrammed* from the *memory* of the **body**, *soul* and *spirit* and when *confidence* is *reprogrammed* into the **CNS**, a child will immediately *choose* to tap into more of their potential to become a better **student** and progress very rapidly.

THE "BAD NEWS" IS:

Most **educational systems** are not geared for *creativity* and **learning**. Many have become a babysitting service for parents who go to work, and are geared to *produce* adults who are able to function as "good employees."

THE EDUCATIONAL SYSTEM IS A SYSTEM. SYSTEMS ARE CREATED TO BENEFIT THE MAJORITY OF PEOPLE WHO USE THEM. UNFORTUNATELY, THE VAST MAJORITY OF PEOPLE USE LESS THAN FOUR PERCENT OF THEIR POTENTIAL. THE BRAVE FEW WHO HAVE DARED TO THINK OUTSIDE OF THE BOX, STAND OUT NOW AS THE GREATEST MINDS IN THE HISTORY OF OUR PLANET YET, THEY HAVE ALL BEEN RIDICULED OR PERSECUTED FOR THEIR GENIUS.

LOSING WEIGHT

When people say they "want to lose weight," they are immediately **sabotaging** their **efforts** because they are not properly defining their **goal**. What most people really mean to say, is that they want to decrease their **body mass** and **size**. **Body mass** is not just **weight**; it is also **size**. Most women **think** they are concerned about their **weight**, but they are really more concerned about fitting into their "skinny jeans."

The word "lose" is a trigger for most people because of previous **experiences** of **losing money**, **pets**, **loved ones**, **homes**, **businesses**, etc. A person's first instinct when they **lose** something is to **try** to **find** it. **Weight loss** is no different; that is why many people "yo-yo" diet, **losing weight** and then **finding** it, only to **lose** it and **find** it, over and over, again and again.

There are many other technical and non-technical terms for **weight** issues that are also used to describe the reduction of **body mass**. When incorrect words are used, it triggers the **body** into slowing down. Common expressions that trigger people are "starvation diet," "eat like a pig," "pot belly," "fatty," and all the variations thereof, "getting heavy," "thunder thighs," etc. People also talk about the weight "creeping up on them." These are all triggers around **body mass** and **size**, not just **weight**.

The fluctuation of the needle on a **scale** that is **wavering** between **desirable** and **undesirable numbers** seems to be an insignificant event; however, it can trigger numerous **experiences** of being **undesirable**, **measuring** up or not, **wavering** between diet food or food people really want, **fluctuations** in **weight** and **never** attaining the "perfect weight." Numerous people **sabotage** themselves when they do succeed in releasing weight quickly because it triggers **memories** of "wasting away" while sick and dying. It is important to be strong to both extremes, **obesity** and **anorexia**, and to be comfortable at any **weight** **in-between**.

Being **overweight** is not a *health* problem! It is a *fitness* problem. Implying that eating is a **social disease** rather than a *choice* makes it more *challenging* to overcome compulsive eating. People tend to *attract experiences* that bother them so that they are able to **resolve** issues that rise up from the *past*, and as **unresolved** issues pile up, so does the **weight**. It is important to be strong to everything you **put** and **don't put** into your **body** along with all the processes of **eating**. *EU … EATING, Pg. 202*

Energetically connect to any *experiences* of **starvation**; watching others **starve**, being **starved**, **starving** others and, on the other end, **overeating, binging** and **gorging**. You are less likely to *sabotage* yourself by *losing self-control* and *over-eating* if you are strong to changing the **amount** you eat and the **speed** at which you **eat** at any given **meal**, or even "not eating" at all.

Information about **nutrition**, what is "good and bad" to eat, can weaken people to the **food** they put in their **body** regardless of whether it is **nutritional, organic food, junk food** and everything *in-between*. Whether they **eat** low calorie **organic salads** and they *feel* they are *denying* themselves, or they **eat** high calorie **junk food** and *feel guilt* with every bite, there will be **resistance** to the *digestion* of that **food** on the **physical** and *non-physical* levels.

Many cravings and/or allergies to **food** are caused by *negative experiences* in the **harvest** or **preparation** of food by **self** and **ancestors**. *Thoughts* around **hunting, butchering, growing, harvesting,** and the **cooking** of **food** are common weaknesses for many people, which causes a *negative re-action* to what they are putting into their **bodies**. If people *believe* that **food** makes them **gain weight**, it is much more likely that it will. **Weight gain** is not only about **over-eating**; it is also about slowing **body** functions down while **processing** food. **Over-eating** is often a *re-action* to **not eating**. Insisting that **weight gain** is caused by **eating**, rather than by *processing* food and the lack of *elimination,* causes the **body** to slow down and this makes it more likely that people will gain weight.

Many people have difficulty reducing **body mass** in spite of controlling food and nutritional supplementary intake. It clearly indicates that conventional protocols for "losing weight" are not working for most people. *Emotional, mental* and *psychological* issues play a significant role in getting to and maintaining *desirable* **weight**. Another misperception regarding **weight loss** and **gain** is the latest trend where people force themselves to drink at least eight glasses of **water** a day regardless of whether they are thirsty or not. **Water** is very **heavy**, which quickly becomes apparent, if you have ever attempted to move a fish tank or carry a bucket of **water** for any distance. When people consume more **water** than **needed**, it *swells* their **cells**, like overfilled **water balloons,** *expanding* and **weighing** down the **bones, muscle** and **tissues.** Your **body** has built-in mechanisms to indicate your **need** for **hydration.** Make yourself *aware* of the signals your **body** sends before you become **dehydrated.** *Feel* them and **act** on them. It is not "too late" to drink water once you are thirsty. *Not listening* to their **bodies** is the number one weakness to **gaining weight** for many people.

It is important that all the systems in the **body** are operating at optimum potential to distribute **water** evenly throughout the **systems,** to exactly where it **needs** to go. The **body** is mostly made up of **water.** If you add more to it than it **needs,** it is like pouring a glass of **water** to top up the ocean. If it is not getting enough **water,** it is like drying out a piece of beef jerky in the desert.

Tea, coffee, juice, beer, wine etc. are **fluids;** therefore consider them as if they were **colored water** because any fluid contributes to the *expansion* of the **cells.** Most **bottled water** is sold through **soft drink companies.** Litter from the **plastic bottles** and **bottle caps** are quickly becoming an **environmental disaster** and some **chemicals** used in producing **plastic bottles** have been linked to many **diseases. Glass containers** are a much stronger option. Clear any *karma associated* with the **water industry** and **big business.** *EU ... HARD CORE SOFT DRINKS, Pg. 270*

Excessive **deep breathing** also stretches the **abdominal cavity.** Strengthen **oxygen** to go exactly where it needs to go in the **body,** through adequate *tension* of the **systems,** regardless of whether **breathing** is **deep** or **shallow.** The **respiratory, digestive** and **elimination systems** are intimately connected and need to be *synchronistic* in processing **nutrients, water** and **oxygen.**

Elimination is more important than *intake.* Strengthen the **large intestine** to the **CNS** to speed **digestion** and **elimination** of **waste.** There are one hundred trillion **cells** in your **body** that are also **eliminating** on the **microcosmic** scale. Strengthen the **tension** and **flexibility** of the **cellular membrane** to optimum potential for allowing **nutrients, oxygen** and **water** in and **cellular waste** out.

Glucose *metabolizes* in the **mitochondria** of the **cells** and is important for **elimination.** Excess **glucose** trapped in the **cells** causes them to **ferment** and **swell.** When the internal **actions** of the **body** are strong, **glucose** gets *metabolized* through the **lymphatic** and **circulatory systems.** If there is *stagnation* in those **systems** and the **CNS,** the **glucose** becomes a **waste product** rather than a *metabolizer.* *EU ... MITOCHONDRIA REGENERATION, Pg. 342*

Dieting is a huge **industry,** particularly in North America. Unfortunately, most weight loss schemes revolving around particular **diets, diet pills,**

supplements, etc., are *ineffective* and *contradictory*. There are many **tactics** used to promote a particular diet, and a lot of confusing information regarding **dieting**. The **diet industry** is over-complicating a very simple fact. If a person's **intake** exceeds his or her **capacity** for **elimination**, is likely that **weight** and **size** will increase. The most efficient **system** for **elimination** is the **large intestine** or **colon**. Although the **diet industry** makes it seem complicated, the **equation** is really very **simple**.

1 meal + 1 bowel movement = maintenance of body mass.
3 meals - 1 bowel movement = gaining body mass.
3 bowel movements - 1 meal = reduction of body mass.

What people refer to as "fat" is really an *accumulation* of **waste products**. **Purging** and **bowel movements** are the most **efficient** method for clearing **body waste**, as well as *accumulations* of *non-physical waste*. **Physical weight** gain is the result of a buildup of **overpopulated, enlarged, fermented, calcified** and **encapsulated toxic tissues** and **cells**.

Free radicals are **atoms** or groups of *atoms* with an odd (unpaired) number of **electrons** and can be formed when **oxygen** interacts with certain **molecules**. Once formed, these highly **reactive radicals** can start a *chain reaction*. **Antioxidants** are **molecules** that can safely interact with **free radicals** and **terminate** the *chain reaction.* **Free radicals** are mainly made up of **decomposition, dead cells** and **cellular waste**. The principle **antioxidants** are **vitamins E** and **C, beta-carotene** and **selenium**. Strengthen the **antioxidants** to the **cells** throughout the **body** and support the **cells** to be **slender, empty, streamlined, vertical** and "perfectly lined up" with no **bulging**. **Evenness** throughout the **body** promotes a decrease in **size** and increases the body's ability to break down **toxins, scar tissue, encapsulations**, excessive **connective tissue** and **minerals** that are constantly birthing into their various forms.

Parasites are a major contributing factor to **weight gain**. They can imitate **tissues** and **cells**. The more **parasites** a person *accumulates*, the heavier the **physical body** becomes. **Parasites** are everywhere in the **body** and in all ecosystems of the universe. To prevent *infestation,* increase *negative ions* and *negative electro-magnetic* charge throughout the **systems** of the **body** to effectively curb **parasitic activity**.

Putting excess **minerals** in the **body** is like pouring cement into it. Surplus **minerals** block the *detox* process and **prevent** *penetration* of **oxygen** across **cellular membranes**.

SPOT REDUCTIONS AND CELLULITE ELIMINATION

Instead of trying to reduce the size and mass of specific spots in the **body** through **exercise**, use *fitness* of the area of the **body** to **reduce** it. Strengthen **tissues** to break down into **cells** that can be eliminated through the **lymphatic system**, and to being reduced to **molecules** and **atoms** all the way to the **quantum field.** Check for coming into this lifetime with a *miasma* of **fatty acids, heavy metals** and **petrochemicals** that are held in the **CNS**. Strengthen **testosterone** levels in the **thighs** to prevent and control **cellulite**.

Exercise for spot reduction of "fat" usually does not work and often leads to gaining of **weight**, especially for those who are not strong to **exercise**. **Abdominal exercises** or **crunches** can put stress on the lower back and trap **muscular waste products** in the **muscles**, causing more **stiffness** and **retention** of **waste products** in the **lower back** and **abdominal** areas. **Effortless action** of **muscles** through fluid, circular motions using the lower **torso** are much more *effective*. Test for *negative associations* with **physical exertion** from *past lifetimes* of **forced labour** and **slavery.**

SWELLING OF THE GUT

Swelling of the **gut** is caused by **encapsulations** within the **peritoneum,** a smooth **membrane** consisting of a thin layer of **cells** that *secrete* **fluid** which fills **body cavities**, the layers of the **abdominal muscles** and the **skin**. On a deeper scale, the **cells** of the **large intestine** are also enlarged. **Body cavities** are enlarged from excess, enlarged **cells**, foreign **cells** from other parts of the **body** and **space-time**. These **cavities** can be strengthened from the **microcosmic** level to the **macrocosmic** level, reflecting the perfect **structure** of the universe. *Relaxed space* between the **structures** can be invaded by **encapsulations** with *mis-matched* and *merging* **cells** and **tissues**. Strengthen *tension* within each **layer** as well as *tension* in-between layers. Bypass the **liver** and **kidneys** for large amounts of **waste products** to go directly to the **colon,** and create *black wholes* to instantly laser in on **waste** and relieve the **systems** of an overworked **lymphatic system**.

Your **body** is always moving towards *rejuvenation* or in the opposing direction towards *degeneration* and **aging**. *Rejuvenation* of **cells** and **tissues, adequate human growth hormone** and a strong **endocrine system** result in a release of **body weight. Body size** can swell when people attempt to *expand* their *spiritual awareness* and contain it in their **physical body**. Strengthen your **body** to be a **streamlined, light container** and allow your *spirit* to be *external* from it. Any time a person over-guards and over-protects anything or anyone, it causes them to puff up to make themselves *feel* bigger, much as animals do when they feel threatened. The *thought* of *judgments* from *spiritual experiences* causes many people to try to **relax**, causing more *space* to *accumulate* between **cells**. It also reminds people of **death** and **dying**, **dead people** and **dead things**, which slows down all the *processes* of the **body**.

Humanity as a whole, has many issues with **starvation** that arise from **indoctrination**, *fear* of not enough supply for demand, running out of sustenance for **future generations**, **self-starvation**, etc. These underlying issues are major triggers that *sabotage efforts* to release **body mass**. **Information** on the **internet** and in the **media** is readily available and when **humanity** is *aware* that there are **starving babies**, **children** and **adults** in the world, yet *chooses* to ignore it, a part of every one of them is also **starving**. In addition, when people treat **animals** with *disrespect* and **cruelty** in the name of **sustenance**, they also *disrespect* themselves and **food** becomes their **enemy**.

ANOREXIA AND OBESITY

Anorexia and **obesity** are two different sides of the same coin, with varying results that depend on the underlying **agenda**. **Information** equals **energy**. Many people surrender their "lives" to **false obligations** at the expense of a more *balanced* version of themselves, and they desperately search for **control** of their **physical environment** through **control** of **input** into their **body**. Strengthen yourself to the *lightness* of *humanity* rather than the **burden** of being **human**. Shift any weaknesses around **starvation**, **starving others**, **being starved** of **food**, *attention*, *love*, *acceptance*, *creative pursuits* and **gluttony**.

It is not uncommon to hear random comments regarding people's **weight**. There is a fine line between the definition of "skinny" and "slim," "fat," and "pleasantly plump." Delete all programs of being "too much" or "not enough" that *attract judgments* and *criticisms* from **self** and **others**. Check for issues of **control**, **self-control** and **control** of others.

Many people *sub-consciously* and *un-consciously* add **armor** to their **bodies** in the form of excessive **connective** and **adipose tissue** to protect themselves from the *attention* of the opposite sex. **People** who *fear* intimacy with **others** often protect themselves with extra padding on the **hips**, **thighs** and **buttocks** to avoid being touched. **Connective tissue** also tends to *accumulate* on the **back, waist** and **shoulders**. People who have *fears* about being **middle-aged** tend to add **waste** to their "waist," and those who have had "a belly full" tend to add **weight** to their **belly**. These issues commonly run up and down the family line, particularly on the **maternal side**.

Typically, in the *past* and at **present**, much of **meal** and **food preparation** as well as many if not most **domestic chores** are commonly the responsibility of **wives** and **mothers**. Many women **resent** having to shop for and *prepare* **meals** that they otherwise would not eat if they did not have a family to feed. They find themselves "eating like a man," even when they, themselves are not hungry. It is common for **resentment** to be held in their **flesh** and their *thoughts* while they are *preparing* and *planning* **meals** and going about **domestic chores**. Many are serving *resentment* with every **meal** and spreading *anger* when they are "cleaning" their **homes**.

When people fill their *minds* they also fill their **bodies**. Full **bodies** are **heavier** and more **massive**. *Energy converts* to **matter** and fills up the *empty spaces* within their **bodies**. Trapped *emotional re-actions* to their *thoughts expand* their **bodies** and create more *space* to be filled. It is natural for human beings to want to *expand* and *accelerate* along with the universe. People have an inherent program to increase **body size** when the main focus in life is to expand their **finances**. When they focus on the **false obligations** of **society**, they tend to lose *balance*, fall short of **goals**, and kick into high gear **weight gain**.

Shift **finances**, *relationships* and *spiritual experiences* to be strong with each other for yourself, your **ancestors** and **descendants**. Delete sabotage from the *mind* to decrease *frustration* from not getting what is **needed** to *feel safe*. When people have **needs** it is more challenging to master their **body** and **physical presence**. *Negative emotions* come up when they **think** about **losing** or *not losing* weight, **gaining** or **not gaining** weight. **Overeating** is often blamed on *depression*. It is more likely that *stagnant thoughts* are creating *stagnation* in the **body**, which ultimately leads to **weight gain**.

Many times when people have experienced the same *emotion attached* to the same *thought* over and over again, the *accumulative effects* create hidden **benefits**. Test if there are more **benefits** to **keeping** the weight on as opposed "to letting it go." Common weaknesses that contribute to carrying excess **weight** include, "being able to throw weight around" and "pulling one's own weight." **Eliminate** the **benefits** of **being heavy** and strengthen to *lightness* of *being*.

Misery loves **company!** There is often *fear* of leaving **family members** behind when it comes to "losing weight." Strengthen members of a **family** to *resonate* with **slimmer members** by shifting "weighty issues" that keeps the **family** linked together through **problems** rather than *creative solutions*.

"Diet dogma" often encourages people to lose weight so that they can be **fit**. "Get fit" first and the release of **weight** will follow. Issues of *fitness* are not only **physical,** but also revolve around being "fit to succeed" or being "fit" to be a **family member**, **spouse**, **sibling**, **parent**, **son** or **daughter**. *EU ... FITNESS, Pg. 250

RESULTS:

"I hope you had a great Christmas! I am really enjoying your tele-seminar! Unfortunately I wasn't able to listen last week live and won't be able to listen tomorrow but I am getting some serious results and I love listening to the recordings. Even though I haven't been on the calls live for two weeks I am definitely experiencing the shift regardless. I swear Colette! It is blowing my mind! I've noticed my body tighter and firmer and I haven't put on any weight over the holidays yet! I have been eating what is in front of me. LOL! There are times where I have just stopped getting dressed and thought, 'why is my body feeling so good!' and then I giggle and think to myself 'its Colette's teleseminar!' So grateful to have found you! I hope you continue these sessions in the future! Thanks Again!"

DP, Canada

THE "GOOD NEWS" IS:

Once the many underlying issues around reducing **body mass** are resolved, excess weight *melts* away.

THE "BAD NEWS" IS:

The many issues around **excess weight** have as many layers as the **tissues** that they are held in. Many of these issues are **deep-rooted** and revolve around **sexuality**, *fitness*, **finances**, *significant relationships*, etc. These can be *challenging* to face and people easily become *discouraged*, and *sabotage* their success.

NUGGET OF WIZDOM FROM THE VECTOR

MOST PEOPLE BELIEVE THAT AGING INEVITABLY LEADS TO WEIGHT GAIN. IT IS MORE LIKELY THAT WEIGHT GAIN IS AN EFFECT CAUSED BY THE ACCUMULATION OF WASTE PRODUCTS

OVER TIME, CAUSING THE PHYSICAL BODY TO DEGENERATE AND AGE.

LYMPHATIC SYSTEM

The **lymphatic system** is a subsidiary of the **circulatory system** built from a network of **tissues** and **organs** consisting of **lymph vessels**, **lymph nodes** and **lymph fluid**. The **tonsils, adenoids**, **spleen** and **thymus** are considered to be **organs** of the **lymphatic system**. The **lymph** does not flow in cycles like **blood** in the **circulatory system**. It runs from the **body tissues** through **lymphatic vessels** toward the **heart**.

The **lymphatic system** has three primary functions. It is responsible for returning excess **intestinal fluid** to the **blood**. About ninety percent of this **extracellular fluid** is returned to the **capillaries** while the other ten percent surrounds **tissue cells**. It is common for small **protein molecules** to leak through the wall of the **capillaries** which increases the **osmotic pressure** of the **intestinal fluid** causing *accumulation* in the **tissue**. Over time **blood volume** and **pressure** suffer a significant decrease, which leads to swelling of the **tissues**. **Lymph capillaries** pick up the excess **fluid** and **proteins,** and return them to the **veins**.

The second function of the **lymphatic system** is absorption of **fat** and **fat-soluble vitamins** from the **digestive system** to the **blood**. **Blood capillaries** absorb most **nutrients**, but **fat-soluble nutrients** are absorbed by **lymph capillaries**, called **lacteals**, located in the center of hair like projections found in the **villi** of the **mucous lining** of the **small intestine**.

The third function of the **lymphatic system** is what most people are most familiar with – the transport of **lymph fluid, which** contains the **white blood cells** that empower the **body** to eliminate **toxins, poisons, excessive cellular waste, parasitic waste**, etc., and destroy invading **organisms** with **lymphocytes** contained in **lymphatic organs**.

LYMPH

The **interstitial fluid** that travels through the **lymph system** is called **lymph. Interstitial fluid** is the main component of **extracellular fluid** that surrounds the **cells** in **tissue spaces**. **Lymph** is mainly made up of **water** as well as **proteins, cellular waste, dissolved gases**, and **hormones**, but it may also contain **bacterial cells, diseased tissue**, and **white blood cells** if there are **pathogens** involved. The **lymph** from the **digestive**

system, called **chyle**, is not clear like the rest of the **fluid**. It has a milky color to it because of **triglycerides** that are formed from the **intestinal villi**.

LYMPH VESSELS

Lymphatic vessels are very similar to **veins** in structure, except that the **lymph fluid** travels into progressively larger **lymphatic vessels** called **lymphatic trunks** as they approach the **heart**. The **lymph** is moved through the **vessels** by **skeletal muscle** *contractions* that constrict the **vessels** to push the **fluid** forward, and by **valves** to prevent it from backing up into the **lymphatic capillaries**.

There are two major **lymphatic vessels** that merge with the **blood vessels** at the **subclavian vein,** which is an extension of the **auxiliary vein** located on the outside of the **first rib**. These divide into the **left** and **right subclavian veins**. The two main **lymphatic vessels** are called **collecting ducts**.

LYMPH DUCTS

The **lymphatic vessels** carry the **lymph** to the two major **collecting ducts**, the **thoracic duct**, and the **right lymphatic duct**, to return the **lymph** back to the **venous blood** that is circulated as **plasma**. The **thoracic duct** empties into the **left subclavian vein**, draining **lymph** from the **legs**, **abdomen**, **left arm**, the **left side** of the **head**, **neck** and **thorax**. The **right lymphatic duct** empties into the **right subclavian vein** from the **right arm**, **right thorax** and the **right side** of the **head**.

LYMPH NODES

There are several hundred **lymph nodes** in the **body**, most of which are located in the **thorax** and **abdomen**, with high concentrations in the **armpits** and **groin**. **Lymph nodes** are small kidney-shaped **organs** that filter **lymph** coming from the **lymph vessels**. The exterior of each **lymph node** is made up of **fibrous connective tissue**. The inside is made of a net-like **tissue** that is full of **lymphocytes**, which are small **white blood cells**. The **tissue** also has **macrophages**, large specialized **cells** that target and destroy damaged or dead **cells**. Once the **lymph** has been cleared of **microbes** it carries on to the **lymphatic ducts**.

LYMPH NODULES

Lymphatic nodules exist outside the **lymphatic vessels** and **lymph nodes**, and outside the lining of **mucous membranes** throughout the body that are *associated* with open **cavities** (the **digestive system**, the **urinary system**, the **respiratory system** and the **reproductive system**). The **tonsils** and **adenoids** are the first line of defense against *infection* of the **throat**. *EU ... DEEP THROAT, Pg. 161*

Peyer's patches are masses of **lymphatic tissue** that are located in the **ileum** of the **small intestine**. They contain **T** and **B cells** that detect and attack **antigens** from **pathogens** to prevent *infection*.

SPLEEN

The **spleen** is an **organ** about the size of a **fist**, located on the **left** side under the **rib cage**. It mostly consists of regions of dense **fibrous connective tissue** called **red** and **white pulp**. The largest region (**red pulp**) has many **cavities** to filter damaged **red blood cells** from the **blood**, and **macrophages** that *attack* and recycle **hemoglobin**. The **red pulp** also stores **platelets** in case of **blood loss**. **White pulp** is made of **lymphatic tissue** that surrounds the **arterioles** of the **spleen**. It has **T** and **B cells** plus **macrophages** to fight off *infection*. Although it is possible to live without a **spleen**, ancient civilizations consider the **etheric spleen** to be responsible for *absorbing*, *assimilating* and *distributing Ka* (*prana*) to be *digested* by the **body**.

THYMUS

The **thymus** is a small **organ** made of **glandular epithelium** and **stem cell connective tissue**; it is located in front of the **heart** and behind the **sternum**. **T cells** are produced in the **thymus** during fetal development and throughout childhood until **puberty**, by which time the **macrophages** have destroyed the vast majority of them. Eventually the **thymus** is replaced by **adipose tissue**.

Test for accumulations of pathogens and waste in the **lymph**. The fluid should be clear unless it is the **chyle** from the **digestive system**. Keep in mind that the fluid travels in one direction from the body to the **lymph trunks** and **subclavian veins**. The **lymph vessels** need to have optimum *fitness* with enough *tension* to move the **fluid** with ease. Strengthen the **density** of the **lymph** to the **density** of the **blood,** strengthen the **lymphatic duct** function on both the **left** and **right** side of the **body** and strengthen the optimum ratio of **white blood cells** to **macrophages** in the **lymph nodes**. Use the **lymph nodes** that are strong to clear the weak ones. Strengthen any weaknesses in the structures of the **lymph system**, **digestive system** and **circulatory system** and communication to and from each other and the **CNS,** the **Peyer's patches**, **spleen** and **thymus**. Also strengthen other

organs and **systems** of **elimination** such as the **liver**, **kidneys**, **bowel** and **bladder** to the components of the **lymphatic system**. *EU ... DETOX, Pg. 178*

THE "GOOD NEWS" IS:

A basic knowledge of the **lymphatic system, digestive system** and **circulatory system** is helpful to identify weaknesses within each system and their communication with each other as well as the **CNS** to optimize *health*.

THE "BAD NEWS" IS:

Quite often, when people are faced with serious *dis-ease* such as cancer, and the **lymphatic system** is performing its function, the **lymph nodes** are the first to be sacrificed, radiated and cut out.

NUGGET OF WIZDOM FROM THE VECTOR

THE LYMPHATIC SYSTEM MAINTAINS A DELICATE BALANCE OF PRESSURE AND CHECK POINTS, DENSITY AND FLOW OF LYMPH WHILE ALSO BALANCING THE WHITE BLOOD CELLS AND MACROPHAGES IN SYNC WITH TISSUES AND OTHER SYSTEMS. YOUR BODY MUST BE STRONG TO THE TOXINS IT IS ELIMINATING TO OPTIMIZE THIS DELICATE BALANCING ACT.

MEDICAL DIAGNOSIS AND PROCEDURES

It is not uncommon for the **diagnosis** of a "deadly disease" to be the leading weakness, preventing a person from returning to *homeostasis*. The very seriousness of **labeling** someone with a **disease**, listing the **symptoms**, **treatment**, and in some cases a prediction of **death** in a specific **time frame**, can all contribute to difficulty in resolving the *dis-ease*. For many people the *experience* of going through **procedures**, such as having blood taken, transfusions, intravenous, catheters, being medicated, etc., all bring up *accumulated negative life experiences* and *traumas* from the *past*, *present* and *future* and, unfortunately at times, the "practice of medicine," which is just that, practicing. *EU ... THE PRACTICE OF MEDICINE, Pg. 498*

On an energetic level, it is possible to track common threads of how a person contracted a **disease**; however, the underlying weaknesses and order of events leading to **disease** are as individual as a person's fingerprints. This is why some **procedures**, **treatments** and **medications** work for some people and not for others.

After being diagnosed, many people wonder what they did to **deserve** this **disease**, and ask "**Why** me, and **why** did I get it?" They would be better off asking, "**Why** not me, and **why** did I **choose** this?" This may sound harsh, but people are making **choices** on the **sub-conscious** level that their **conscious mind** is unaware of. When **spiritual experiences** are added to that mix, along with the **fears** of their **ancestors, descendants** and the **collective influence**, plus the **karma** they may have with **doctors**, **nurses**, **pharmaceutical companies** and other **patients**, there are a lot of **non-physical** reasons **why** a person may end up with any given **dis-ease**.

RESULTS:

"I am a fifty-one year old woman with a medical history of scoliosis surgery at age 13 and stomach problems from years of anti-inflammatory medications. I was having minor problems on and off as far back as 2010 and was on a high dose of prescription acid reducers.

"In the fall of 2013, I was admitted to the Emergency department of the hospital for very bad nausea, vomiting, stomach spasms, heart palpitations, shivering, shaking, anxiety and exhaustion. My minor problems became major ones with numerous all night Emergency room visits, vast amounts of medications at various dosages, ranging from high to exceptionally high, a thirty pound weight loss, leaving me at a whopping 105 pounds. I was pricked with needles, scanned, x-rayed, probed with cameras and underwent countless procedures, blood tests and lab work. After exhausting myself with the medical system, I was still very sick, and yet, had no answers as to why or what was wrong or how I could feel better.

"I started having sessions with Colette in the summer of 2014, and so ended my emergency room visits. I am happy to report that I am off all medications and manage to keep everything I eat down. My energy is coming back and I have even started to gain a little weight. I am looking forward to continued improvements to my health and vitality. Thank you so much for being there for me when everyone else was saying, 'Sorry, we can't do anything more for you.' "

Cindy Leigh Yelland,
Kelowna, BC

THE "GOOD NEWS" IS:

Technology and science are advancing at a rapid rate allowing for a higher success rate for recovery. If you use your **intuition** to **perceive** the underlying **non-physical** weaknesses, you can eliminate **cause** and **effect** and strengthen individuals to get the optimum result from any **procedure**, **treatment** and/or **medication**.

THE "BAD NEWS" IS:

Even if a person has undergone a series of **tests** and **procedures**, yet has not been **diagnosed** with a particular **disease**, the lack of a resolution of the **symptoms** will have a **negative effect** on that person's ability to **heal**. If a person insists that the source of his or her **discomfort** and **pain** is not the true weakness, it is likely that the symptoms will intensify, because now both the original **discomfort** on the **physical** level as well as the **discomfort** of being unable to resolve it must be dealt with or tolerated.

NUGGET OF WIZDOM FROM THE VECTOR

THE REASONS FOR DISCOMFORT OR PAIN ON THE PHYSICAL LEVEL ARE RARELY PHYSICAL AT ROOT CAUSE. IF THE UNDERLYING NON-PHYSICAL WEAKNESSES ARE PINPOINTED AND CLEARED, IT CAN BRING INSTANT RELIEF.

MEMORY

The thought of someone losing the capacity to remember, or noticing others who are losing their **memory**, particularly their **ancestors**, is a common **fear** in the **collective consciousness** that can weaken the ability to **remember**. People remember the **effects** of an **experience** more than the **experience** itself. For instance, **memories** of "calling others names" and "being called names" can bring up **emotions** that **affect** their ability to **remember** names. Repeating things over and over in an attempt to memorize information can create a need to repeat things over and over to be able to "get it."

Memory loss is often caused by upsetting **thoughts** that people don't want to **remember**. Many of these **thoughts** come from **past life memories** or **unknown influences** from **external forces**. This can create a **want** to forget. Habitual forgetting in the form of **suppression** is a dangerous practice, as it can lead to serious **health** issues that are held in the **tissues** of the **body** and disrupt cognitive skills in the **brain**. Many times when people can't recall or recover information, it is **diagnosed** as a learning disorder; however, a cluttered **home**, **school** and **work environment** can have a disruptive **effect** on people's ability to create order to their **thoughts** and is often the leading weakness. If people get in the habit of having a place for everything, then everything is more likely to be put back in its place along with unorganized *thoughts*.

Trying to *remember* "important" information makes it more challenging to *remember* because of the *fear* of *forgetting* it. Any time people give too much importance to something, they tend to put more *effort* than necessary into it, thereby creating even more *challenges*. *Negative memories* from early **education** have a profound *effect* on children, one that tends to follow them into adulthood. The weaknesses from being ridiculed in front of the class, being called on and not having the answer, failed tests, etc., can be shifted if you go back to specific **grades**, **subjects**, **teachers**, **classmates**, etc., and clear the *accumulative effects*.

People **think** that a poor *memory* can come from a lack of **focus**. In fact, anytime people **focus** on anything for more than a second, they are holding onto that *thought* and not moving forward to the next one. This creates the *perception* that they are "focusing," but unless they consistently move on to the next **thought**, they are actually **stuck** on the preceding one, making it more *challenging* to resolve situations or **problems** with *creative solutions*.

Expectations create *limitations*. If a person expects *memory loss* to come with age it is likely that it will. **Society** encourages dementia and senility through common statements such as, "you can't teach an old dog new tricks," "over the hill," etc., and by diagnosing loss of *memory* as a *mental* and **physical illness** without considering the underlying energetic weaknesses.

THE "GOOD NEWS" IS:

You are always in connection with the entire universe and taking in information on the **sub-conscious** and **un-conscious** level whether you are *aware* of it or not. It is similar to downloading information on the **hard drive** of a **computer**.

THE "BAD NEWS" IS:

"Too much information" often leads to *overwhelm*. Unorganized information is more *challenging* to access, especially when *emotions* are mixed with **thinking**, because it causes *resistance* to the information, which slows down the **thinking** *process*.

NUGGET OF WIZDOM FROM THE VECTOR

INFORMATION IS FILED IN THE CNS JUST LIKE DATA IS FILED ON THE HARD DRIVE OF ANY COMPUTER. YOU HAVE ACCESS TO EVERY

FILE. COMPUTERS DO NOT REFUSE TO GIVE YOU INFORMATION BECAUSE YOU DON'T DESERVE IT OR UNDERSTAND IT. YOU ASK FOR THE FILE AND RECEIVE IT, UNLESS YOUR COMPUTER IS SLOW IN WHICH CASE, YOU CLEAN IT AND GET IT UP TO SPEED.

MENSTRUATION

Menstruation, or **menses,** is the monthly shedding of the **lining** of a woman's **uterus** (**womb**). **Menstrual blood** is actually part **blood** and part **tissue** that flows out of the **body** from the **lining** inside the **uterus** through the **cervix** and the **vagina. Menstrual cycle** is a term that is used to describe the sequence of events that occur as a woman's **body** prepares for **pregnancy** each month. Cycles range from **twenty-one days** to **thirty-five days**, with the average being **twenty-eight days**. The rise and fall of **chemicals** called **hormones** via the **pituitary gland** and the **ovaries**, trigger the **reproductive system** to respond in phases during a cycle.

MENSES

Menses, when the **lining** of the **uterus**, the **endometrium**, is actually shed typically lasts from the **first day** to **day five** if **pregnancy** has not occurred. Most women bleed anywhere from **two** to **seven days**.

FOLLICULAR

When the levels of **estrogen** rise, typically between **day six** to **fourteen**, the **endometrium** begins to grow and thicken. **Follicle stimulating hormone** is also released between **day ten** to **fourteen** causing **follicles** to grow. One of these will form a mature **ovum** (**egg**).

OVULATION

Ovulation occurs between days **fourteen** to **twenty-eight** when the **luteinizing hormone** causes the **ovary** to release the **ovum**.

LUTEAL

From day **fifteen** to **twenty-eight**, after the **ovum** has been released, it travels through the **fallopian tube** to the **uterus**. Another **hormone** called **progesterone** rises to prepare the **uterine lining** for pregnancy. If the **ovum** is fertilized by **sperm** and attaches itself to the **uterine wall**, the woman becomes **pregnant**. If not, **estrogen** and **progesterone** levels drop and the thickened **lining** is shed.

MENARCHE

Menarche, a girl's first **menstrual cycle**, is the accepted benchmark to define the transition from a **girlhood** to **womanhood**; however, it is a process that takes place over several years, beginning with **breast-budding**, **armpit hair**, a huge **growth spurt**, **pubic hair**, and mature **breasts** that eventually leads to **menarche**. The **age** at which girls begin **menstruation** varies and is dependent upon **body type**, **race**, **culture**, **diet**, **ancestral norms**, etc. In North America, the average **age** of a girl's first **period** has dropped from **sixteen** to **twelve** within a **century**, and it is common for **breasts** to bud by age **seven**.

It is important that a woman is strong to all *phases* of the *cycle* and also strong to the *astrological effects* of the **moon** and its *phases*. Women who live in the same household or work closely together have a tendency to instinctually follow the same rhythm, similar to pack animals in heat, and once underlying issues are cleared, they often follow the *cycles* of the **moon**.

CULTURAL AND RELIGIOUS CONSEQUENCES

Any real conversation about **menstruation** is still largely taboo; people continue to make jokes or apologize for it as if it is a "dirty little secret." Many **cultures** still view it as a *curse* from the days of inquisition that caused much **fear**, particularly in **men**. Fewer **cultures** still adhere to ancient traditions that revered **menses**, recognizing **menstrual blood** as the nectar of the **holy grail** (**womb**) and respecting the creative power a woman harnesses, particularly in the **first days** of her *cycle*. Shamanic tradition honors a woman who is "on her moon" as a *natural purification process*. Comparing a woman's *cycle* to the *cycles* of the **moon** brings a better understanding of how powerful the energy of her **cycle** is.

As a woman **ovulates**, she is harnessing the *power* of *creation* with the potential of bringing life into being, similar to the waxing of the **full moon**. If the **egg** is not **fertilized**, her **uterus** begins the *process* of shedding the **egg** through **menstruation**. The **first day** of **menstruation** is comparable to the *waning* of a **new moon**, causing a lot of women to *experience* a lull in energy that begins to build again towards rebirth. A woman's *power* and *energy* is being recharged through the cleansing. It is so strong that it pulls the energy towards earth and affects the ability of shamans to clearly see visions in **sacred ceremonies**. This is why tradition dictates that women do not participate in **ceremony** at this time.

THE FEMININE HYGIENE BUSINESS

There is a huge **industry** of **feminine hygiene products** sold to the unaware buyer, through ridiculous, insipid **marketing** techniques. The products range from pads, tampons and panty liners, to deodorants, etc. Most of the products are made from inferior ingredients such as **rayon**, **viscose** and **wood pulp** whose **fibers** can easily break down and stick to the **vaginal wall**. Instead of using **organic cotton**, many are bleached with **chlorine** and laced with **dioxin**, a by-product of **pollution** from **incinerators** and **pesticide spraying**, to give them that pure white feel. Even the **applicators** can be **toxic** as they often are coated with **phthalates** so that they glide into the **vagina** more easily. **Phthalates** can disrupt the delicate balance within the **endocrine system**.

PRE-MENSTRUAL SYNDROME

Pre-menstrual syndrome is a combination of *emotional*, *psychological* and **physical** disturbances that occur after a woman **ovulates**, and typically builds until the onset of **menstrual flow**.

Cultural, **religious**, **ancestral**, *psychic* and *spiritual* weaknesses cause many *re-actions* of being *cursed*, being a *curse* and *cursing* others. Many women "pay the price" *collectively* by *denying* themselves the **wisdom** of this **natural** monthly *detox* that has the potential to *rejuvenate* their **bodies**, *souls* and *spirits*. Women are encouraged to think of **menstruation** as a **medical condition**, treatable with **pharmaceuticals** such as **diuretics**, **painkillers**, **oral contraceptives**, **drugs** *for* **suppression** of **ovulation**, and **anti-depressants**. *Emotional, mental* and *psychological* weaknesses abound, creating many of the **problems** and horror stories *associated* with **PMS**, where **men** are held hostage by the unreasonable requests of a **woman** "gone mad." It is not uncommon for **women** who force themselves to behave like men in a masculine role to be "mad." The *collective accumulated anger* can easily escalate into *rage*, causing many **women** to be plagued with **heavy periods**, **bloating** and **severe cramping**, etc., because they *suppress* the *emotional* and *psychological* issues instead of shedding everything that has occurred between **moons** along with the **uterine lining**.

Toxic and *poisonous thoughts*, *emotions*, **products**, etc., *accumulate* and cause increasingly noticeable symptoms that are passed down from **generation** to **generation**. Women who fight their "feminine side" tend to be pulled in two directions which causes **physical cramps, circumstances** and **situations** in which their "style gets cramped" because of their **period**. Once these weaknesses are *eliminated,* the symptoms often subside or disappear altogether. **Cramping** can be alleviated by *tensing* the **brain** and clearing *memories* from the **body**, *soul* and *spirit* of past **pregnancies**, being **born** and **giving birth**.

A young **girl** is vulnerable as she makes the transition to **womanhood**, facing both her own *re-actions* and those of her **parents**, extended **family**, **peers**, **social media** etc. It often becomes uncomfortable for **fathers** to show affection for "daddy's little girl," making it taboo to give her a hug when she needs it most. **Mothers** are often in competition with their **daughters** for **men's** attention, whether they are aware of it or not on a *conscious* level. Clear *karma* in all directions and also with **pharmaceutical companies**, **medical systems**, **doctors**, **nurses**, etc., and boost the potential for all **women** up and down the family line.

PERI-MENOPAUSAL SYNDROME

Peri-menopause is considered to be the "time frame" **before** a woman reaches **menopause**. Women notice many symptoms as early as their late **thirties** and **forties**; however, these are actually a *continuation* of unresolved **problems** that occurred during their **adolescence** and **twenties**, **problems** that were formerly labeled as **PMS**.

MENOPAUSE

A woman is considered to be in **menopause** when she has not had a **menstruation cycle** in **twelve months**.

POST-MENOPAUSAL SYNDROME

A woman is considered to be in **post-menopause** after **twelve consecutive months** without **menstruation** until **death**. **Post-menopause** comes about naturally from **hormonal** changes, but can also be induced or triggered by **illness** or **surgery**. The following are "symptoms" of **pre-menstrual syndrome** as well as **peri-menopause**, **meno-pause** and **post-menopause**:

1. **Absent** or **irregular periods** that are **shorter**, **longer**, **heavier** and **lighter** as well as "spotting." This is often due to "stress" levels a woman is experiencing at any given time in her day to day life. **EU ... DAILY ROUTINE, Pg. 159*

2. Weakened libido, that results in a loss of **sexual drive** *without a loss* of sexual function. **EU ... HARD MEN ARE GOOD TO FIND, Pg. 273*

3. *Emotional thoughts* and *feelings* that behave like a roller-coaster. **EU ... EMOTIONS, Pg. 205*

4. Ongoing and persistent *feelings* of **tiredness**, **low** *energy* **levels**, *irritability* and *fatigue*, causing *mental* blocks, lack of *concentration*, *memory* lapses and a decreased *attention span*. *EU ... LEARNING DIS-ABILITIES, Pg. 308*

5. Waking up many times during the night, tossing and turning, **insomnia** and other **sleep** *dis-orders*. *EU ... SLEEP, Pg. 474*

6. Weight gain, specifically a thickening around the **waist** or **middle**, accompanied by appetite *changes* and food *cravings*. *EU ... LOSING WEIGHT, Pg. 312*

7. A swollen **belly** with a *feeling* of *tightness* and *discomfort* or **pain** in the **stomach** area along with **bloating**, **digestive issues** and excessive **intestinal gas**. *EU ... EATING, Pg. 202*

8. Bouts of *sadness* are normal for everyone; however millions of women are diagnosed with clinical *depression* when they feel "stress and anxiety," of any sort, leading to "oversensitivity," *irritability*, and in extreme cases, *panic attacks*. *EU ... SENSATIONS, Pg. 456*

9. Palpitations and bouts of *pounding* or rapid **heartbeat** from an overstimulated **CNS**, **circulatory system** and other irregularities of the **heart**. *EU ... CNS (CENTRAL NERVOUS SYSTEM), Pg. 145*

10. A generalized *dis-comfort* or **pain** *associated* with *touching*, putting **pressure** on the **breasts**, preceding or accompanying **menstrual periods** or in **pregnancy**, **post-partum** or **menopause**. *EU ... BREAST HEALTH AND AUGMENTATION, Pg.102*

11. Many women with regular **menstrual periods** get **headaches** and **migraines** just before their **period** starts and before **ovulation,** as do many women who "no longer" **menstruate**. *EU ... HEADACHES, Pg. 278*

12. Muscle strains and *aches*, particularly in the **neck**, **shoulders** and **back** are common when people are overloaded by too much of the "stress" **hormone**, **cortisol**. Many of these symptoms originate from *non-physical* weaknesses, and the **physical** issues are often referred from the **respiratory** and **digestive system** or from a **hormonal** *imbalance*. *EU ... ENDOCRINE GLANDS, Pg. 207*

Information regarding **pre-menstrual syndrome, peri-menopausal syndrome, men-o-pause** and **peri-menopause** may easily lead a woman to believe that her best days were prior to reaching **puberty** and that it is all "downhill" from **menarche** on. The symptoms tend to revolve around *accumulated anger* and *disappointment* within themselves and their inter-reactions with men. Many women harbor *accumulated resentment* from years of putting family needs before their own while working outside the home and trying to rise to *expectations* to perform like men and "look good doing it." Some of the "symptoms" women are told to also expect during **peri-menopause, menopause** and **post-menopause** are:

1. Hot flashes, which are sudden transient **sensations** of warmth throughout the **body** that are most noticeable on the **face** and **upper body**. Many of these can be traced to the "burning rage" many women feel towards men and a patriarchal system. When **hot flashes** occur during **sleep,** they are often accompanied by intense bouts of **sweating** along with **odor** issues. There is often **stagnation** between the **base chakra** and **sacral chakra** energies creating fears regarding **financial** survival as an "old woman" who is "used up" and feels like "life stinks."

2. Vaginal dryness, thinning hair and **brittle nails** can be blamed partly on fluctuating **hormones**; however **itchy, irritating, uncomfortable sex** and lack of **lubrication** are often **associated** with a general **feeling** of "drying up," "falling between the cracks," and a general lack of **hydration** and **nutrients** getting to where they are most needed.

3. Some women also suffer from "burning mouth syndrome," a **burning pain** on the **tongue, lips** and entire **mouth**, along with "bad breath" and a "bad taste" in the **mouth**. This is not surprising, because energetically the **mouth** and **vagina** are very intimately connected. Women who are in the habit of suppressing what they really want to say to be "nice" are more likely to **experience** this.

4. Bleeding or tender **gums** are common in **peri-menopausal, menopausal** and **post-menopausal** women. They are also common in **men, younger women** and during **pregnancy**, as well as in people who are not hygienic or in some cases over-hygienic regarding the care of their **teeth**. The underlying weakness is generally the same in most cases, a lack of **tension** and **structure** within the **mouth**. *EU ... DENTAL, Pg. 170*

5. Disturbances in the **nervous system** cause misfiring of the **neurons** and affect the **hypothalamus**, which in turn causes a **feeling** of electricity in the **head** and between the layers of the **skin**. Itchy "crawly" skin and tingling in the outer extremities of the **body** are often linked to the **fitness** of the **skin** and **collagen** levels as well as **experiences** of parasitic **infestation** and **parasitic people** from the **past**, **present** and **future**.

6. Osteoporosis is a **degenerative** bone disorder causing the thinning and weakening of **bones** and a lack of **density** and **bone mass** from an unevenness in the **regeneration** and **degeneration** of **bone** cells. This is often related to low **estrogen** levels; however, high deposits of **calcium** that **stagnate** the **CNS** and their connection to the **bones** is generally the primary weakness. It is not uncommon for **karmic** weaknesses to come up when the **bones** are involved.

7. Allergies, in particular hay fever, dermatitis and asthma are also said to be **effects** of **menopause**; however, they are **often re-actions** to **sensations** labeled as **emotions,** particularly **sadness** and **grief**. The dizziness and spinning **sensations** that some women **experience** are generally from lack of **balance** in **aspects** of life that **accumulate** over decades.*EU ... ALLERGIES, Pg. 60*

8. Some women report unexplained **soreness** and **inflammation** in their **joints**. These symptoms are often related to **trauma** or lack of **exercise**, and lead to a **diagnosis** of **arthritis**. The **non-physical** weaknesses are often caused by **accumulated experiences** of **suppressing anger** from doing what was **expected** of them rather than what they **wanted** to do.

9. Accidental release of **urine** while coughing, laughing, sneezing or over-exerting themselves can also occur when **sensations** of a full **bladder** are not acknowledged by the **PNS** and **CNS**. Women who are "pissed off" are more likely to have a tendency to "piss themselves."

ENDOMETRIOSIS

Endometriosis occurs when the **endometrial tissue** escapes the **uterus** and the **pelvic cavity**, spreading to the **abdomen**, **ovaries**, **fallopian tubes**, **perineum**, **bladder**, **bowel**, **vagina**, **cervix**, **vulva**, and in rare cases, to other **tissues** in the **lungs**, **arms** and other locations. Misplaced **tissue** develops into **growths** or **lesions** that behave in typical **endometrial** fashion, by causing **internal bleeding** because there is no way for the **tissue** to leave the **body**. **Inflammation**, **pain** and **infertility** builds up just like snow on the streets, **stagnating** the **CNS** and its connection to the **reproductive system**. This is often due to a lack of **structure** and **tension** in the **uterus** and other parts of the **reproductive system**; it is also a consequence of women **trying** to **relax** themselves out of their **problems**.

Non-physical issues often revolve around "explosive anger" **accumulated** from **past life** and **ancestral** issues such as "blowing things out of proportion," being blown up and blowing up others. Test for **mis-matched body parts** on the **psychic** level. *EU ... PSYCHIC CLEANSE, Pg. 419*

THE "GOOD NEWS" IS:

Men-o-Pause, as much as it is "supposed" to be **feared** and **dreaded,** is really just the moment in time when a woman has not **menstruated**

for a full **twelve months**. All it takes is one period within that time frame to prolong **menses** according to the medical definition. The ***non-physical*** reality is that many women who have issues while in **men-o-pause** are weak to their own masculine energy, causing them to want to take a "pause from men" and the ***anger*** that they feel towards them.

THE "BAD NEWS" IS:

Information regarding **men-o-pause** is often presented with statements such as "the condition all women dread!" Negative verbiage is also common regarding all the other phases of **menstruation**. For instance, the end of your "period" is horrific unless you compare it to the beginning, when you get "the curse" and "start on your rag." Women are told not to expect "relief" when they reach **post-menopause** because the "symptoms" will most likely continue, just like when "periods cramped their style" in-between the times they were "knocked-up."

NUGGET OF WIZDOM FROM THE VECTOR

THE ONLY BLOOD THAT SHOULD BE SHED ON THE GROUND OF EARTH IS SACRED BLOOD. WOMEN AND MEN ARE BOTH RE-AWAKENING TO THE ROLE MENSTRUATION PLAYS AS A PART OF DIVINE FEMININE WIZDOM.

MENTAL ILLNESS

Mental illness refers to a wide range of ***mental health*** conditions, including depression, anxiety disorders, schizophrenia, bi-polar disorders, dementia, etc. Each of these conditions drastically ***affects*** **mood** and **behavior**, and has ***negative effects*** on the lives of people who are suffering, as well as on the lives of the people they rely on and who rely on them.

Most people at one time or another in their lives will have concerns due to ***mental*** "stress." Red flags are raised when ongoing problems ***affect*** a person's ability to function in regular **society**; however it is often ***overwhelm*** from the pressure to satisfy **false obligations** imposed by **society** that cause many people to succumb to "mental illness." "Experts" in the field are now coming to the conclusion that **mental illness** is a result of biological predisposition (genetic), and environmental stressors during pregnancy and infancy that ***affect*** the neurological development of the **brain**. **Environmental factors** in early childhood and adolescence can either lessen or increase the expression of neurological defects. A combination of **biological**, ***psychological*** and **socio-economic environment** plus **culture** all play a significant role in *mental health*. The field of epigenetics is now proving that significant change can occur in the **DNA** when *thoughts*, *emotional re-actions* and **behaviors** change; the *effect* is both *mental* and **physical**.

When people suffer from "mental illness," they often end up being prescribed a cocktail of **psychotropic drugs** used by **psychiatrists** and **psychologists**. These drugs can be broken down into several categories: **antipsychotics**, **antidepressants**, **stimulants**, **anti-anxiety medications**, and **mood stabilizers**.

Antipsychotics affect a person's *metabolism* and often cause significant **weight gain**, an increase in diabetes, tremors, muscle spasms, restlessness and a permanent and irreversible condition called **dyskinesia**, which is involuntary movements of the **tongue, lips, mouth**, **arms** and **legs**. Most "antidepressants" that are used to treat depressive disorders are selective **serotonin re-uptake inhibitors (SSRIs)** that *affect* serotonin levels in the **brain**. Other **antidepressants** affect **norepinephrine** and **dopamine** levels in the **brain**. There are also older versions of **monoamine oxidase inhibitors (MAOIs)** that have more **physical** side *effects*, such as dry mouth, constipation and reactions to foods. **Antidepressants** cause an increased risk in **suicidal thinking** and **behavior** in children, adolescents and young adults, as well as sleep disturbances, agitation, appetite changes and sexual dysfunction.

Stimulants are the most commonly prescribed drugs for children who are diagnosed with ADHD. They are used to increase the level of **dopamine**. Sometimes, **anti-stimulants** are also prescribed. The most common "side-effects" are sleep problems and decreased appetite. "Anti-anxiety medications" are often used for abnormal levels of "anxiety" in patients who are **diagnosed** with anxiety disorder, obsessive-compulsive disorder, panic attacks, social anxiety and post-traumatic stress disorder. **Benzodiazepines** are also commonly **prescribed** for "anxiety disorders" that target a specific **receptor** in the **brain** called **GABA**. Common "side-effects" are drowsiness, blurred vision, nightmares and other sleep disturbances. **Lithium** and other **mood stabilizers** as well as seizure medications are commonly **prescribed** for people who are **diagnosed** with **bipolar disorder** and **manic depression**. Side-effects include **suicidal** *thoughts*, **thyroid** problems and weight gain.

It is important that when people are taking **prescribed pharmaceuticals** that any benefits from the medication(s) are strengthened to optimum potential for *desired effects* and that the many "side effects" are deleted. Check for *karma* with the **medical** and **psychiatric establishment**, **pharmaceutical companies** and *past life* issues of being *committed*, or to having had others **committed** to **mental facilities**.

ALZHEIMER'S

Alzheimer's is the most commonly **diagnosed** form of **dementia**, but there is a difference. **Dementia** is a *dis-ease* caused by the progressive loss of **nerve cells** (**neurons**) in the **brain**. As **brain cells** die, they are not replaced and eventually cause the **brain** to shrink. Common symptoms of **dementia** include *memory loss*, impaired *cognition* and loss of **physical co-ordination**, depending on the area of the **brain** that is *affected*.

Alzheimer's is not a "normal part of aging," although the major risk factor is **age**. The majority of people who suffer from **Alzheimer's** are **sixty-five years** of **age** or older, although symptoms of early onset **Alzheimer's** can begin in the forties and fifties. When people are approaching **sixty-five years** of **age**, they are inundated with *external forces* from the *collective consciousness* because that is the age that most people are expected to retire. *EU ... DAILY ROUTINE, Pg. 159*

The most common symptom of **Alzheimer's** is difficulty in *remembering* new information because **Alzheimer's** *affects* the **cortex** of the **brain**, causing it to shrivel, and damaging **thinking**, **planning** and *remembering* skills. Shrinkage of the **hippocampus**, an area in the **cortex**, causes **problems** with the formation of new *memories* and the **ventricles** of the **brain** to swell and become larger. As **Alzheimer's** advances, it leads to increasingly severe symptoms, including disorientation, **mood** and **behavior** *changes*, **confusion**, **suspicion** about **caregivers** and **family members**, difficulty **speaking**, **swallowing** and **walking**, the most common *non-physical* symptoms of "not wanting to move forward."

Microscopic changes in the **brain** cause **plaque** and **tangles** to occur in the **cortex**, long before symptoms of **Alzheimer's** are noticeable. **Plaques** are deposits of **protein fragments** called **beta-amyloids** that crowd the spaces in between the **neurons**. **Tangles** are twisted **fibers** of **tau,** another **protein** that builds up inside the **cells**. Healthy **cells** are organized in orderly parallel **strands** or **tracks**, with **nutrients** running up and down the **tracks**. The **tau** is responsible for order and keeping the **tracks** straight. When these **tracks** are "tangled," they are unable to retain order, fall apart, disintegrate, and leave the **cells** to die.

Cells are always in the process of *degenerating*, *regenerating* and every stage in-between, so at any given time **plaques** and **tangles** will be seen in the average **brain**. People who are **diagnosed** with **Alzheimer's**, however, generally develop **plaques** and **tangles** in the areas that are responsible for **memory**; they then spread to other areas of the **brain** at an accelerated rate. Strengthen the **cells** to return to perfect order.

People who suffer from **Alzheimer's** have a tendency to have *limiting beliefs* about **aging** and weakness to **retiring.** Often they are in *denial* of what they are *experiencing*, and *numb* themselves to what is happening and has happened in their lives to the point where it leads to **complete system shutdown**. *EU … SENSATIONS, Pg. 456*

SCHIZOPHRENIA

Schizophrenia is a long-term *mental* disorder that most often appears in late adolescence or early adulthood, and causes inconsistent and contradictory *thoughts*, *emotions* and **behaviors** that lead to *mental* fragmentation, *personality* dis-orders and paranoia. People who are **diagnosed** with **schizophrenia** have a tendency to *re-act* to delusions, most commonly voices that encourage them to *act* out with inappropriate *actions*.

The *personality* **problems** associated with **schizophrenia** that are considered to be genetic are often triggered by **ancestral** influences; as such, they impact **parenting** and early **environmental factors** that are passed down the family line. Babies who are born in the **winter months** are more susceptible to **schizophrenia** than babies born in other **seasons**. These energetic weaknesses are often *accumulative*, and come from the *collective consciousness*.

In **utero** and during the early formative years, **child** and **adolescent brains** are much more *sensitive* to chronic "stress" and frequent periods of moderate "stress" than the **brains** of **adults** are. What may seem moderate "stress" to **adults** can be *traumatic* for **children,** making them more susceptible to the risk of *future* **mental illness** that is often re-triggered in **adolescence**.

Multiple personalities that quite often have *entities* with conflicting agendas attached, can come into being when people are exposed to *trauma*. **Paranoia** is often caused by weaknesses from *spiritual experiences* of stalking others and being stalked. *EU … PSYCHIC CLEANSE, Pg. 419*

DEPRESSION

The **medical community** considers **depression** or **mood dis-orders** to be one of the most common **mental illnesses** in the general population. People often *experience sadness* and *grief* when they *re-act* to *traumatic* life events such as challenging and abusive *relationships*, **divorce, career challenges, bankruptcy, prejudice, workplace "stress," death, grieving, disability, chronic medical conditions**, and

substance abuse; however, underlying **physical** factors can also contribute to extended periods of *grief* and *sadness*.

Major depressive disorder is characterized by periods of time lasting over two weeks during which a person is debilitated to the point where *emotional*, **social** and **professional** repercussions occur. Often so-called "stress" is the trigger for an initial episode of **depression** that can lead to several recurrences. **Women** and **children** who have *suffered* from **abuse**, **neglect** and **family violence** are more likely to suffer from **depression** than men.

People will often say they "feel sad;" however, they don't really *feel sad* – they are *experiencing* an *emotional re-action* to the *thought* of *sadness*. Many times when people are "feeling sad" they are really energetically weak to the *thought* of *feeling sad*, *not feeling sad*, *feeling happy* and *not feeling happy*. Identify and clear weaknesses to all of the above because any one of these will *attract experiences* of "sadness."

Feelings of *guilt*, *shame*, *worthlessness*, *helplessness* and *hopelessness* are often triggered by *emotional re-actions* to *deserving*, *feeling hopeful* and *helpful*. It is very common for people to *experience hopelessness* when they become *hopeful* and *helplessness* when they become *helpful*. Check for underlying weaknesses to both. People also experience seasonal depression that comes on in the fall and is relieved in the spring. This is often blamed on the loss of daylight, but can actually be caused by underlying *traumas* that occurred on specific dates.

Postpartum depression follows the birth of a child and is often blamed on a rapid shift in **hormone levels**. This is sometimes the case; however, there are often many *non-physical* weaknesses between the **mother** and **baby**, *karmas, memories* of *traumas* from **child birth**, etc., that are better cleared during **pregnancy**. *EU ... PREGNANCY, Pg. 398*

Bereavement at the loss of a loved one is also a major factor in depression. The *process* of *grieving* a significant loss can take days, weeks, months and even years. Clear any underlying weaknesses in the *relationship* between people to speed up the *process*. The **need** to *grieve* for a long time often comes from the *perception* that it is "disrespectful" to get over a loss too quickly.

Sorrow and **grief** often manifest as **upper respiratory issues** and *congestion* in the **sinuses**. *Psychological phobias* to **success** are also common as are *mixed emotions* about **prosperity** and *healthy relationships*. Delete any *internal forces* around *discouragement* and *frustration*.

THE "GOOD NEWS" IS:

Mental illness can be viewed from another **perspective:** as a dysfunction in **systems** that can be **recalibrated** and **reset** by clearing the weaknesses and strengthening connections from the **CNS** to the *mind* and **heart**. A **printer** does not work if you don't plug it in, and neither does the **brain**.

THE "BAD NEWS" IS:

Psychiatry is the **study** and **treatment** of **mental illness** and "abnormal behavior." Its most fundamental tenet is that virtually all problems of **thinking**, *feeling* and **behavior** are **illnesses** that **need** to be "treated" from a **medical** *perspective*. "Normal" **behavior**, **thinking** and *feeling* is an **arbitrary assumption** and the "solution" is often an **experimental** cocktail of **psychotropic drugs**, increasingly used on **children**, particularly **children** who are **victims** of **social dis-ease**.

NUGGET OF WIZDOM FROM THE VECTOR

AN IMPORTANT QUESTION TO ASK … SINCE WHEN DID IT BECOME REASONABLE TO PRESCRIBE MEDICATIONS FOR DEPRESSION THAT LIST "WORSENING OF DEPRESSION" OR "MAY CAUSE ANXIETY AND SUICIDAL THOUGHTS" IN THE SMALL PRINT OF THE INFORMATION ACCOMPANYING THE MEDICATION?

MERGING THE MASCULINE AND FEMININE

Yin and *Yang* energies are a concept derived from **Taoism** of polar energies inherent throughout nature and within our **physical** and *spiritual* **bodies**. When there is *balance* and *harmony* between these polar forces within ourselves, it results in order of the **body**, *soul* and *spirit*.

The *Yin-Yang* **symbol** is an image that consists of a **circle** divided into two teardrop shaped **halves**. One is **white** and one is **black**, and within each **half** there is a smaller **circle** of the **opposite color**. The **circle** represents all of creation because it has no **beginning** and no **end,** and the swirls of the **tear-dropped shapes** represent the constant *change* of all **matter** that makes up the universe. One cannot exist without the other because **day** becomes **night** and **night** becomes **day**, **birth** becomes **death** and **death** *regenerates* birth. The smaller **circles** within the **tear-dropped shape** show that there is always a **seed** of the *opposite energy* within each **polarity**.

The **white** area is referred to as *Yang* and represents **solar** qualities of **light**. It is masculine, active, analytical, dominant, aggressive and controlled by the **left brain**. Its effects are mainly seen on the **right** side of the **body**. The **black** area is called *Yin*, representing **lunar** aspects and qualities of the **dark**. It is feminine, passive, intuitive, submissive and controlled by the **right brain**. Its *effects* are mainly seen on the **left** side of the **body**.

The duality of **physical structure** begins with the **brain** that is split into **left** and **right hemispheres**. The **CNS** seems to direct the **left** and **right** sides differently, guided by the **body**, *mind* and *spirit*. *Internal* and *external re-actions* reflect this. The **right** side and **back** of the **body** tends to have *masculine*, *yang* (**male**) characteristics dominated by *mental* influences, structured actions and determination. The **left** side and **front** of the **body** has more flexible *feminine*, *yin* (**female**) characteristics that *re-act* to *emotional* influences stimulated through creativity. When one side relates strongly to the other there are no **problems**; however, just as it is in our most intimate *relationships*, shift happens that can disrupt the *flow* and cause one side to become out of touch with the other. Unevenness from one side to the other creates weaknesses in *balance* and **structure,** and is one of the leading causes of serious **disease** in the **physical body** and *dis-ease* of the *mind*.

If we consider our true nature as *conscious beings* traveling in a **human body**, our *consciousness* contains both of these *opposing energies* without the *association* of **gender** that is attributed to *feminine* and *masculine* energies from the superficial *perspective* of **humans**. *Balance* in the polarities of *yin-yang* is key to **mental** and **physical** *health*. History is full of examples of the serious consequences inflicted on the earth when these energies are thrown out of *balance* and either one dominates the other's presence. *Suffering* and **chaos** are generally the result.

The importance of *harmony* between the proportions of these energies within our *consciousness* is called the **hermetic principle,** and was delivered by the messenger of the Greek gods himself, Hermes: "As above, so below," and "As within, so without." Many people search for answers **outside** of themselves and would be better off going **inward**. These sayings remind us that we co-exist in a reality that we co-create with God. If there is *harmony within*, there will be **harmony without**. If there is *chaos within*, there will be **chaos without**. Our *thoughts affect* our **physical environment** and our **physical environment** *affects* our *thoughts*.

Letting go of the false division between **male** and **female** and embracing the merging of the *masculine* and *feminine* is a reunion on many levels within the **biological body** through heightened *insight*. The *masculine* states, "I understand, I am creative." And the *feminine* replies, "I understand how to create." One plus one equals infinite possibilities for creation. As men and women shed their *self-limiting beliefs* and **ancestral**, **cultural** and **religious** *beliefs*, they are more able to co-create a better *future* for themselves and their **descendants** and for **society** as a whole.

THE "GOOD NEWS" IS:

Every part of your **body** is capable of communicating freely with every other **part** of your **body**, even if you have had **organs** removed or **limbs** amputated. When they are reunited, they are like long lost lovers who finally meet again and have a deep appreciation of the renewed connection.

THE "BAD NEWS" IS:

If the communication between the **left** and the **right** side of your **body** is breaking down, you are headed for separation and even "divorce." If you are vested on insisting that the miscommunication is caused by only one side or the other, even the best experts are not going to be able resolve the argument.

NUGGET OF WIZDOM FROM THE VECTOR

GOD IS NOT SEXIST! THERE IS NO NEED TO LOOK FOR AN EXPERT OUTSIDE OF YOURSELF TO MEDIATE BETWEEN THE TWO SIDES OF YOUR BODY. YOUR CNS AND YOUR MIND ARE THE PERFECT MEDIATORS TO RESOLVE ANY REJECTION BETWEEN THE LEFT AND RIGHT, FRONT AND BACK, AND EASING THE CONNECTION TO THE ELECTRO-MAGNETIC FIELD AND YOUR HEART.

MITOCHONDRIA REGENERATION

Cells are the structural and functional units of all living **organisms**. Some **organisms** such as **bacteria** are **uni-cellular**, consisting of only one **cell**. Other **organisms** such as **humans** are **multi-cellular**. Each **cell** has the capability to take in **nutrients**, convert the **nutrients** into energy, carry out specialized functions, and reproduce. Every **cell** also stores its own set of instructions for carrying out each of these activities. There are two general categories of cells: **prokaryotic cells** and **eukaryotic cells**.

PROKARYOTIC ORGANISMS

Bacteria are **prokaryotic cells**. Some **bacteria** grow in filaments or masses of **cells**, but each **cell** in the colony is identical and capable of independent existence. There is no continuity or communication between the **cells**. **Prokaryotes** are capable of inhabiting almost every space on the earth, including the surface of our **bodies**.

EUKARYOTIC ORGANISMS

Eukaryotic organisms include fungi, animals and plants as well as some unicellular organisms. **Eukaryotes** are about ten times the size of a **prokaryote** and can be one thousand times the volume. **Eukaryotic cells** contain membrane-bound compartments in which specific metabolic activities take place. The most important of these is the **nucleus** that houses the **DNA**. **Eukaryotic organisms** also have other specialized structures called **organelles**, which are small structures within **cells** that perform dedicated functions. These can be thought of as tiny **organs**. The **mitochondria organelles** contain **DNA** and are referred to as "cellular power plants."

Mitochondria are complex **organelles** that convert *energy* from **food** into a form that the **cell** can use. They have their own genetic material, separate from the **DNA** in the **nucleus**, and they can make copies of themselves. **Mitochondria** have two functionally distinct **membrane systems** separated by a space: the **outer membrane** houses the whole **organelle**, and the **inner membrane** has folds or shelves that project inward called **cristae**. The number and shape of the **cristae** in **mitochondria** differ, depending on the **tissue** and the **organism**. It is their job to increase the surface area of the **membrane**.

Mitochondria play a vital role in generating *energy* in the **eukaryotic** cell through a number of complex pathways. Some of the best energy-supplying foods that we eat contain **complex sugars**. These complex sugars can be broken down to a less complex **sugar molecule** called **glucose**.

GLUCOSE

Glucose enters the **cell** through special **molecules** found in the **membrane** called **glucose transporters**. Once inside the cell, **glucose** is broken down to make **adenosine triphosphate** (**ATP**) via two different pathways: **glycolysis** and the **Krebs cycle**.

Glycolysis (**anaerobic metabolism**) does not require **oxygen** and occurs in the **cytoplasm** outside the **mitochondria**. During **glycolysis**, **glucose**

is broken down into a **molecule** called **pyruvate**. This reaction produces **hydrogen ions** that make four energy packets of **ATP** per **molecule**.

THE KREBS CYCLE

The **Krebs cycle** (**citric acid cycle**) occurs inside the **mitochondria** and is capable of generating enough **ATP** to run all of the **cell's** functions. The process begins with a **glucose molecule** that has been stripped of some of its **hydrogen atoms** and transforms the **glucose** into two **molecules** of **pyruvic acid**. The **pyruvic acid** is altered by the removal of a **carbon** and two **oxygen molecules** that go on to form **carbon dioxide**. The **carbon dioxide** is then removed converting a **molecule** called **NAD+** into a higher *energy* form called **NADH**. **Coenzyme A** (**CoA**) then attaches to the remaining **acetyl unit** forming **acetyl CoA**. The **acetyl CoA** enters the **Krebs cycle** by joining to a **four-carbon molecule** called **oxaloacetate**. These two **molecules** join to make a **six-carbon molecule** called **citric acid**. While the **citric acid** is being broken down, **hydrogen ions** and **carbon molecules** are released. The **carbon molecules** make more **carbon dioxide**. Then the **hydrogen ions** are picked up by **NAD** and another **molecule** called **flavin-adenine dinucleotide** (**FAD**). This process produces the **four-carbon oxaloacetate** again and repeats the cycle.

The **Krebs cycle** is capable of producing from twenty-four to twenty-eight **ATP** from just one **molecule** of **glucose** converted to **pyruvate**. If your **mitochondria** are working at infinite potential with enough **oxygen**, you can create a vast amount of *energy* from one **molecule** of **glucose**. **Mitochondria** are also involved in other processes such as **signaling**, **cellular differentiation**, **cell death** as well as the control of the **cell cycle** and **cell growth**.

REPLICATION AND INHERITANCE

In **single-celled eukaryotes**, growth and division of **mitochondria** is connected to the **cell cycle**. In mammals the **mitochondria** can replicate their **DNA** and divide mainly in response to the energy needs of the **cell**. When the needs are high, the **mitochondria** grow and divide. When the needs are low, the **mitochondria** are destroyed or become inactive.

An individual's **mitochondrial genes** are not inherited by the same mechanism as **nuclear genes** are. When an **egg cell** is fertilized by a **sperm**, the **egg nucleus** and **sperm nucleus** each contribute equally to the genetic make-up of the **zygote nucleus**. The **mitochondria DNA** usually comes from only the **egg**. The **sperm's mitochondria** enter the egg, but do not contribute **genetic information** to the **embryo**. Instead, **paternal mitochondria** are marked with **ubiquitin** to select them for destruction later when they are in the **embryo**. The **mitochondria** that survive, divide to populate the **cells** of the **adult organism. Mitochondria** are therefore inherited from the **female line**, known as **maternal inheritance**.

DYSFUNCTION OF MITOCHONDRIA

Mitochondria disorders often present as **neurological dysfunction**, but can also manifest as **myopathy (muscular** weakness), diabetes, multiple endocrinopathy (**hormone** *disorders*) and a variety of other **system** *disorders*. **Diseases** that are thought to be caused by mutation of the **mtDNA** of the **mitochondria**, include Kearns-Sayre syndrome, the onset of which is generally before the age of twenty; it paralyzes the **eye muscles** and degenerates the **retina**. MELAS syndrome causes **brain** dysfunction, seizures, headaches and **muscle disease** from **lactic acidosis** of the **blood**. Leber's hereditary optic neuropathy causes a loss of **central vision** and is inherited from the **mother**.

Environmental influences may interact with **hereditary pre-dispositions** and cause **mitochondrial disease**; for example, **pesticide exposure** may cause the later onset of Parkinson's disease. Other suspected pathologies involving **mitochondrial dysfunction** include schizophrenia, bipolar disorder, dementia, Alzheimer's disease, epilepsy, stroke, cardiovascular disease, pigmentosa reticularis and diabetes mellitus. The common denominator among these seemingly unrelated illnesses is **cellular damage** causing **oxidative stress**, which is toxic imbalance from an inability to produce **reactive oxygen species**.

MITOCHONDRIA AND LESS AGING

The role of **mitochondria** as the cell's powerhouse can be compromised when there is leakage of the high-energy **electrons** in the **respiratory chain** that forms **reactive oxygen species**. This can result in significant **oxidative stress** in the **mitochondria** with high mutation rates of **mitochondrial DNA**. A vicious cycle can occur as **oxidative stress** leads to more mutations that lead to **enzymatic abnormalities** and further **oxidative stress**.

Test for any weaknesses between the **structures**, **organs**, **systems**, **cells** and **tissue** at the **quantum level**. Ensure that **oxygen** *production* and *distribution* is optimum. Check for weaknesses up and down the **maternal line**.

THE "GOOD NEWS" IS:

Healthy **mitochondria** support *regeneration* and *degeneration* of **cells** for healthy **systems**, **youthfulness** and vitality.

THE "BAD NEWS" IS:

A number of *changes* occur in the **mitochondria** during the **aging process** leading to **oxidative stress**.

NUGGET OF WIZDOM FROM THE VECTOR

THERE IS MUCH DEBATE OVER WHETHER MITOCHONDRIAL CHANGES ARE CAUSES OF AGING OR MERELY CHARACTERISTICS OF AGING. A BASIC UNDERSTANDING OF THE KREBS CYCLE AND HOW MITOCHONDRIA FUNCTION CAN BE BENEFICIAL IN SUPPORTING YOUTHFULNESS.

NERVOUS SYSTEM STRUCTURES & REGENERATION

The **nervous system** is the **body's** information **gatherer**, **storage center** and **control system**. Its overall function is to gather information about the **body's external** and **internal** status, transfer this information to the **brain**, analyze it and send impulses out to initiate appropriate **motor** *responses* to meet the **body's** needs. More than ten thousand million **nerve cells** and their **fibers** or **axons** make up the **nervous system**. The **system** is comprised of specialized **cells** called **neurons** that communicate with each other and with other **cells** in the **body**. There are over one hundred billion **neurons** in the **brain** alone. The key functions of a **neuron cell** are to facilitate *processing* and *storage* of **information** for **short term**, **medium term** and **long term** *memory* for the survival and function of the **cell**.

The **axons** are grouped together in chunks of **nerves** that contain **sensory fibers** conducting information from the **sensory organs** to the **CNS**, and **motor fibers** in the **body** that carry information to the **CNS**. The **nerve fibers** that carry information quickly are enclosed in a **sheath** made of a fatty-substance called **myelin,** and are called **myelinated nerve fibers**. The **myelin sheath** has regular indentations along its length called the **nodes of Ranvier**. Non-myelinated **nerve fibers** that carry information are grouped together and are enclosed in a single sheath.

The anatomy of the **nerve** includes the **cell body** called the **soma**, **dendrites** and **axons**. The **soma** is composed of the **cytoplasm**, mitochondria, **organelles** and the **cell nucleus** that contains information controlling the activity of the **neuron. Dendrites** are outgrowths of the **cell body** that conduct **impulses** to and from the **neuron**. The fatty **myelin sheath** is the insulated coat that separates the **axon** in a **nerve bundle**. The **epineurium** is the outermost **fibrous sheath** made up of dense irregular **connective tissue** that surrounds a **peripheral nerve** as well as the **blood vessels** that supply the **nerve**. The **perineurium** is a **connective tissue sheath** that surrounds the **fascicle**, a bundle of **nerve fibers** within a **nerve**. The **endoneurium**, also called the **endoneurial channel**, is a layer of delicate **connective tissue** around the **myelin sheath** of each **myelinated nerve fiber**.

AXONS (NERVE FIBERS)

The **axons** are extended **fibers** of the **nerve cell** that carry **impulses** to and from the **soma**. **Nerve fibers** are usually less than a millimeter long, but some have axons that are several centimeters in length. For instance, **sensory neurons** whose **dendrites** are in the **skin** of the **feet**, have **cell bodies** near the **spinal cord** and **terminal buttons** near the **base** of the **brain**.

Axons conduct "outgoing" signals emitted by the **neuron** away from the **cell body**. They are not only the **physical strand** that appears to connect **neurons** to each other, they are also the **center** of its *memory*. Within the enclosed **microtubules** are hundreds of thousands of **tubulin dimers**.

MICROTUBULES

Principal information storage and processing **structures** are called **microtubules**; they are **fibrous**, hollow rods that function primarily to help support and shape the **cell**, and also function as routes along which **organelles** can move. They play a huge role in the *action* within a **cell** and form the **spindle fibers** that manipulate and separate **cells** during **mitosis** (cell division). There are large clusters of **microtubules** in a **neuron** that store information where *memory* and *thought* occurs.

TUBULIN DIMERS

Tubulin dimers are one of several members of a family of **globular proteins** that are made up of six distinct families: **alpha**, **beta**, **gamma**, **delta**, **epsilon-tubulins** and **zeta-tubulins**. The most common members of the **tubulin family** are the **proteins** that make up **microtubules**, **a-tubulin** and **b-tubulin**.

A-tubulin and **b-tubulin** bind to **guanosine triphosphate** (**GTP**) and convert into **guanosine diphosphate** (**GDP**) as **molecular switches** that are involved in transmitting signals from stimulus outside to the inside of a **cell**. **B-tubulin** is exposed on the **plus** end of the **microtubule**, and **a-tubulin** is on the **minus** end. When they bind to **GTP**, they are "on" and tend to assemble into **microtubules**; when they bind to **GDP**, they are "off" and tend to fall apart, affecting the stability of the **microtubule**.

Neuron cells constantly switch polarity at the end of the **axons** from positive to negative by using **potassium** and **sodium ions**.

In the resting state, the **nerve membrane** is electrically polarized, being approximately 70 mv more negative on the inside than on the outside. This polarization is due to **ion** pumps in the **cellular membrane** that distribute **ions** across the **membrane**. Unequal *distribution* creates leaks that decrease the potential of the **membrane**. The **sodium channel** is responsible for the polarization of the **membrane**, while **potassium channels** are responsible for re-polarizing the **membrane**.

NEUROTRANSMITTERS

The specific purpose of **neurotransmitters** is to communicate with each other. They are stored in tiny breakable balls at the end of **axon terminals** and are released on command by **hormones**.

The two classes of **neurotransmitters** are **peptides** that degrade and wilt after usage, and **classical** that are recycled and reused.

Upon the arrival of certain **hormones** to the **neuron cell**, appropriate **neurotransmitters** are automatically released. Depending on the way **axon terminals** are arranged, **hormones** will cause one of two things to happen: **stimulation** or **suppression**. A strong **hormone release** stimulates a strong **transmitter release** causing the **neurons** to fire up, whereas a weak **hormone release** causes *suppression* and a weak **transmitter release** that freezes **muscles** into a state of *fear*. **Transmitters** are at both ends of the **microtubules**. One end is designed to start or slow a program, and the other end kicks the program to another **cell**.

SOMATOSENSORY RECEPTORS

Somatosensory receptors stimulate the **nervous system** in the form of our five senses, **touch** (**pain**), **vision**, **taste**, **smell** and **hearing**. **Somatic senses** recognize **pain**, **temperature** and **pressure**. **Sensory receptors** are classified according to the type of energy they detect and respond to.

Mechanosensors *affect* hearing and **balance**, **photoreceptors** detect **light**, **chemoreceptors** allow **smell** and **taste** and also *affect* the **digestive** and **circulatory systems**. **Thermoreceptors** detect changes in **temperature**, and **electroreceptors** detect electrical currents in the surrounding environment. The process is first **chemical**, then **electrical**, and causes the *reactions* of **hormones** (**neuro-peptides**) and the release of **electrons**, and ultimately stimulates the **neurotransmitters**. When the **neurotransmitters** and **electrons** combine over many **neurons**, it completes what we call a **thought**.

AXON TERMINAL BUTTONS

There are two methods that **neurons** use to extend their **axon terminals** sufficiently closely enough to communicate with each other: either at one of the **receptor sites** around the main body of another **neuron cell,** or at an **axon terminal** located at a **node** on a **dendrite** of another **neuron cell**.

MYELIN

Myelin acts as an **insulator** and speeds **impulse** transmission. The **Schwann cell nucleus** is the mechanism responsible for the production and maintenance of the **myelin sheath** and the **nodes of Ranvier**, constrictions in the **myelin sheath**. Typically, any given **neuron** is connected to many thousands of other **neurons**.

SYNAPSE

The **junction** between a **nerve** and another **cell** sends messages that are passed to and from the **brain**. They take the form of electrical **impulses** that are produced by a **chemical** change that progresses along the **axon**. The exact moment an **axon** of one **cell** and a **dendrite** of another **cell** connect, is called a **synapse**. **Calcium channels** occur in especially high concentrations at the **synapse**, and **neurotransmitter release** is triggered through these **channels**. At the **synapse,** the **impulse** causes the release of **neurotransmitters,** and this in turn drives the **impulse** to the next **neuron**. These **impulses** travel very quickly – up to two hundred and fifty miles per hour. The **synapse** is not actually a connection, but a **gap**. If the **gap** is somehow clogged at the **transmission sites**, or **receptor sites**, the **neuron** to **neuron** connections will not work properly.

SYNAPTIC CLEFT

The space between the two **cells** is called a **synaptic cleft**. The **nerve cells** are generally created in groups within the **brain** and the **spinal cord**. The **neurons** are called **nuclei** and constitute the **gray matter** of the **brain** and **spinal cord**, while the groups outside of the **brain** and **spinal cord** are called **ganglia**. The remaining areas of the **nervous system** are tracts of **axons** called **white matter**. **Tracts** carrying information of a specific type, such as **pain** or *vision*, generally have specific names.

NERVE JUNCTIONS

Pain exists in the many **nerves** and **nerve junctions** that run from the **brain** to the **head** and **face**. It is important to *regenerate* the **myelin sheath** to infinite potential in order to shift **neuro-junction pain**. Check for disconnections from **neurological functions** to the **muscles**, **arteries**, **veins**, **fascia**, **bone**, **cartilage**, **connective tissue**, **skin**, **organs**, **glands** and **lymphatic system**, and strengthen the *energy channels* in all directions to be strong to integration. As well, ensure that the **neuro-fibers, neurotransmitters, neuro-junctions,** and **neuro chemicals** have a strong *relationship* with each other for optimum **myelin sheath integrity** and *regeneration*.

If you think of the **synapse** as a pitcher throwing a ball to a catcher, the **neurotransmitter** would the pitcher, the **impulse** would be the ball, the **synaptic cleft** would be the distance between the pitcher and the **nerve junction**, which would function as the catcher. Both the pitcher and catcher must be fit to have perfect *coordination* between the two, for the ball to reach the catcher's mitt or the batter (*disease*) will knock the ball out of the park.

The **diagnosis** of those serious **diseases** that are associated with **nerve structures** and *regeneration* are almost never **physical** at root cause. Many of the **problems** come from people trying to **relax** themselves out of **problems**, slowing down and *stagnating* the *fitness* of the **CNS**. It is important to maintain proper *tension* throughout the **body**, particularly the components that make up the **spine** and **CNS** to avoid a build up of **toxins**, **poisons**, **cellular waste**, etc. All the **systems**, **parts** and **functions** need to be in strong communication with the **CNS** and **PNS**.

EPILEPSY

Epilepsy is a **neurological** disorder characterized by recurring **seizures** that can vary from brief and barely detectable episodes to long periods of vigorous shaking and freezing of **muscles**. **Seizures** that occur due to a specific cause are not considered to be **epileptic seizures**.

Seizures take many forms and are generally categorized into two major groups, **primary generalized seizures** and **partial seizures**. **Primary generalized seizures** begin with widespread electrical discharges that involve **both sides** of the **brain** at the same time. These are considered to be hereditary in many cases.

Partial seizures begin in a **limited** area of the **brain**. They can be caused by many factors such as head injury, brain infection, stroke, tumors or in some cases, they are formed in the womb as a *miasma*, *affecting* areas of the **brain** causing **cortical dysplasias**. On a **physical** level, strengthen any weaknesses in the **cranium** and alertness of the **brain** by evening out the **brain cells** with the **spinal cord cells**. On a *non-physical* level there are many factors that can contribute to **seizures**. The most common weakness is from *external forces* that weaken the **physical intelligence** of the **body** due to excessive *re-actions* to stimuli from the **physical environment**, and from *spiritual* and *psychic* energies. When a person feels an energy drop from these forces, it can weaken the **body**, *soul*, *spirit* triad. In an attempt to keep the energy up some people react with a **seizure**. It is important that the **CNS**, **brain**, **spinal cord** and **tail** are all in a strong *relationship* with each other.

What many consider to be **hereditary** issues are often issues that have not been resolved by the **ancestors**, and are being played out by their **descendants**. Once the underlying, *non-physical* issues are resolved, many people automatically are relieved of the symptoms. *Emotional*, *mental* and *psychological* influences often revolve around a lack of self-love and *struggling* with life. The lack of trust in self, and a disconnection from others and the world manifest as a **disconnect** in the **synapse**. Delete *expectations* of **punishment** and **punishing** others.

MULTIPLE SCLEROSIS

Multiple sclerosis or **MS** is a dis-ease that *affects* the **brain, spinal cord** and the **optic nerves,** which causes problems with balance and muscle control, and limits basic bodily functions. The fatty material of the **myelin** is affected, causing scar tissue that blocks signals from the **brain** to the **body** and back. Symptoms include having trouble walking, feeling tired, muscle weakness or spasms, blurred and double vision, numbness and tingling, sexual problems, poor bladder and bowel control, pain, depression and problems with focus and memory. Generally, these symptoms begin between the **ages** of **twenty** and **forty.** Most people who are diagnosed with **MS** have attacks called **relapses** when the symptoms escalate, followed by times of **recovery** when symptoms improve. For others, the ***negative effects*** of the ***dis-ease*** are a steady progression over the course of years. It is important to test for **referred** weaknesses between the **body parts**, and to strengthen the person to **specific positions** or ***actions*** that ***stimulate*** the area. Go back to the **age** when the condition was first noticed to track underlying ***emotional***, ***mental***, ***psychological***, ***psychic*** and ***spiritual*** issues.

Body heat is a major factor that is problematic with **MS**, but many people notice that their symptoms decrease if they receive more **vitamin D** by living in sunnier climates. It is possible to lower **body temperature** by picturing a **thermostat** and turning the dial down a degree or two and focusing that intention on the **spine**. Also test for underlying weaknesses of ***trauma*** from **plagues**, **viruses** and other ***infections***.

Many people who have been diagnosed with **MS** have ***un-conscious*** weaknesses on the ***psychological*** level of being on the planet with no escape in sight. There are often ***spiritual experiences,*** both their own and those of their **ancestors,** of being **blown up** or **blowing others up**, being **shot** and **shooting** others, being **cut** and **cutting others,** as well as weaknesses to **natural catastrophes** such as **earthquakes, tsunamis, hurricanes**, etc.

Finally, ***anger*** is the underlying ***emotion*** that tends to ***affect*** people diagnosed with **MS**, causing ***acidity***, ***inflammation*** and ***infection*** in the **CNS**. There are often issues of **incest** and **sexual abuse** up and down the family line.

PARKINSON'S

Parkinson's is a diagnosis of **neurodegenerative disease** that has no known definitive tests to confirm the **diagnosis**. It ***affects*** movement that is normally controlled by **dopamine**, a **chemical** that is responsible for ***sending*** and ***receiving*** signals in the **brain.** The symptoms are tremors, stiffness, impaired balance, rigidity of the muscles, trouble speaking and writing, stooped posture, sleep disturbances and constipation. The progression of the **disease** on a **physical** level is basically due to ***stagnation*** and lack of ***tension*** in the components of the **CNS**. The lack of definitive information regarding the **disease**, the **diagnosis** and the **prognosis** is a major limiting factor for recovery.

THE "GOOD NEWS" IS:

The connections between the **CNS**, the *mind* and other **body parts** can be strengthened energetically to be in better communication with each other simply by putting *tension* into the **spine** and the **body parts** to speed up the communication.

THE "BAD NEWS" IS:

When too much emphasis is put on *relaxing*, it causes *stagnation*, and too much **relaxation** in the **CNS** creates problems in communication between the **neurons**.

NUGGET OF WIZDOM FROM THE VECTOR

MANY PEOPLE ARE TRYING TO RELAX THEMSELVES OUT OF THEIR PROBLEMS AND UNKNOWINGLY CAUSE EVEN MORE PROBLEMS BECAUSE THEY ARE TOO RELAXED. TENSION IS ALL THAT! PUT TENSION INTO YOUR BODY AS YOU SIT, STAND OR LIE DOWN AND WHEN YOU GET UP. THIS WILL IMPROVE PHYSICAL INTELLIGENCE BETWEEN THE CNS AND THE COMPONENTS OF YOUR BODY.

NEUTRALITY

When people are in a place of *neutrality*, they suspend *judgment*, *criticism* or *urgency* because **time** does not exist in that moment, and they are able to *perceive* different *choices* without *fear*. When people become *neutral,* others often *perceive* it as *indifference* because many people talk about "thinking and being positive." The difference is: when people are *neutral* they are less likely to attract outcomes that do not appeal to them and more likely to make better *choices* to attract what they *want*. When people are *indifferent*, it means that they don't care about the consequences of their *actions*, or the outcome for themselves and the *effect* it has on others.

Everything and everyone, is made up of **atoms**, and **atoms** are made up of **electrons** that have a *negative charge*, of **protons** that have a *positive charge*, and of **neutrons** that remain *neutral*. It is not **physically** possible to turn a "negative" into a "positive." Many things in life are *perceived* to be *negative*. When people become *neutral* to any given **problem** rather than attempt to convince themselves that a *negative* is a *positive,* they are much more open to *creative solutions*.

Questions that many people get caught up in include: What will happen? What will I do if it does? I wonder which way it will go? and on and on ... When you are *neutral* you are better able to handle *external forces*, reduce *re-actions* to the words and *actions* of others, and clear deep programming that is limiting your ability to *change* with *ease*.

OPPOSING FORCES

You may have heard the saying that "opposites attract," and asked yourself, **why**? Generally, people have a tendency to attract **situations**, **people** and **events** to themselves in an effort to *re-solve* concerns they have had from the time their *sub-conscious mind*s were being molded, as well as concerns from *un-conscious thoughts* resulting from *spiritual experiences*. Re-living the same or the exact opposite scenarios from childhood over and over again in different **relationships**, **careers**, **parenting**, etc., in an attempt to "get it right" is common. The connection is often challenging to see because people tend to *act out* dramas with people they have *karma* with. *EU ... KARMA, Pg. 302*

Once your *karmic ties* are released, you are free to expand your horizons by going *inward* towards *balance* rather than playing out the same old unbalanced scenarios with people in your life. It is a natural state of order for human beings to want to *expand* and *accelerate* as co-creators with the universe. Everything comes together and *balances* out through its opposite. When you are *neutral* to both the "absolute best" and the "absolute worst" outcome, you become *neutral* to all *possibilities* held *in-between*. This aligns your energy with your heart's desires.

Logically it would seem that most people would be stronger to the **absolute best** outcome. This is a *limiting belief*. People are more likely to get triggered when they get in touch with their **absolute best** because it takes them out of their comfort zone. People who dare to think outside of the box lead the way to unlimited potential. **Leadership** means that you are no longer one of the crowd and standing out for most people is extremely uncomfortable.

The *transition* to *neutrality* occurs in a **split second** when *opposing forces* spin into *coherence*. *Coherence* happens when you give yourself *total permission* to dive into your *future* with whole-hearted abandon, *willing*, *ready* and *able* to let go of the **problem**. In that **split second** of *neutrality*, when you let go and give yourself *total permission* to live your dreams, you become consistent with your *authentic desires, committed* and *neutral* to your *future*. When your *thoughts* are *encoded* with your *heart energy,* all **problems** have the potential to spin into perfect order in alignment with the universe.

THE "GOOD NEWS" IS:

The "absolute best" is the best place to be! When your **CNS** is *aligned* with your **heart,** you are able to ride the wave of your infinite potential rather than being caught in the undertow.

THE "BAD NEWS" IS:

When people full-heartedly embrace their unique qualities, it triggers everyone around them. This often causes *misperception* and *frustration* for people who are taking consistent steps of *action* to reach their **goals**, which causes them to feel as though they are going backwards.

NUGGET OF WIZDOM FROM THE VECTOR

THE MORE YOU SHINE YOUR LIGHT, THE DARKER YOUR SHADOW. IF YOU ARE IN A TUG-OF-WAR BETWEEN TWO EXTREMES, LET GO OF THE ROPE! ALLOW THE PROBLEM TO FALL AWAY. ALIGN YOUR ENERGY WITH WHAT MAKES YOUR HEART SING.

NEW YEAR'S DAY

Almost half of North Americans make New Year's **resolutions** and very few are successful in keeping them. Some of the most popular **resolutions** are:

1. **Lose weight.** (Most people are not in *alignment* with losing anything, and have a tendency to **try** to find what they have **lost** when they do, including **weight**. This is called "dieting"). *EU ... LOSING WEIGHT, Pg. 312*

2. **Get organized**. (You already are part of the perfect organization of the *unified field*).

3. **Spend less, save more**. ("Save yourself" by **investing** in **yourself** more; **spend** less *energy* searching for answers outside of you).

4. **Enjoy life to the fullest**. (**What** does this mean? **Define** "full" so that you can put a plan of *action* into place to get to where you *want* to go).

5. **Staying or getting fit to be healthy**. (*Health* is a *given* when all of your **systems** are *fit*). *EU ... FITNESS, Pg. 250*

6. **Learn something exciting**. (Hang out with **babies**! They will show you **how**)!

7. **Quit smoking.** (Many people have difficulty "quitting" because they have *limiting beliefs* that **quitting** makes them a "loser"). **EU … ADDICTION, Pg. 47*

8. **Help others fulfill their dreams**. (*Empower* yourself to **fulfill** your dreams and **lead** by example).

9. **Fall in love**. (**Fall** and **fail** are only one letter apart. It is amazing the difference one "l" can make … **Live** in *love*, don't **fall** or **fail** in it).

10. **Spend more time with family**. (*Invest* time in your **family**; don't "do time" with them).

Whether you make New Year's **resolutions** or not, the *collective influence* of **failing** to keep them has an *effect* on every one, every year. If you have *mental*, *emotional* and **physical** *fitness*, you will be in *alignment* with your goals and able to move forward with **ease**. If you are not in *alignment*, you are more likely to **fail** along with the vast majority of humanity.

THE "GOOD NEWS" IS:

Many **cultures** do not follow the **Gregorian calendar** and celebrate the beginning of the year following the **Julian calendar** on **January thirteenth**. **Chinese New Year** is one of several **cultures** that celebrate sometime between **January twentieth** and **February twentieth**, following the **lunar/solar calendar**. Other **cultures** celebrate following the **Sikh calendar** on **March fourteenth**, the **Hindu calendar**, generally on **April thirteenth** or **fourteenth,** or the **vernal equinox**, which is generally on **March twenty-first**, and in **Ethiopia** they follow their own **ancient calendar** with the new year falling on **September eleventh** or **twelfth** at the end of the summer season. If you make a **resolution** on **January one** and it doesn't work out, all is not lost; you can always adopt other *traditions* and have a second, third, fourth or fifth go at it.

THE "BAD NEWS" IS:

Psychic memories and other *errant energies* from other *existences*, *parallel dimensions* and *planes* in *space-time* in the *past*, *present* and *future*, and along with **cultural**, **religious** and *collective influences*, have the potential to trigger *suppressed memories*. The many strengths and weaknesses around these dates that go unrecognized result in missed *opportunities* to delete disadvantages and take advantage of the *collective influence* in moving towards your goals.

NUGGET OF WIZDOM FROM THE VECTOR

EVERY TIME YOU FALL ASLEEP AND AWAKEN, IT IS A NEW DAY IN A NEW YEAR BECAUSE EVEN SEEMINGLY SMALL CHOICES CAN STEER YOU IN A COMPLETELY NEW DIRECTION AND ALTER YOUR REALITY IN A MATTER OF SECONDS.

NUMERICAL PROFILING

"Everything is numbers and to know numbers is to know thyself."
Pythagoras (approximately 569 BC-495 BC)

Pythagoras was a Greek mathematician who lived from approximately 569-470 BCE, and is considered by many to be the originator of modern numerology which has its roots in Babylonia, Alexandria, Christian mysticism, the Gnostics, the Hebrew Kabbalah, Hindu Vedas, and in Chinese and Egyptian teachings. The universe is composed of **mathematical patterns** and everything within the world can be expressed and understood in this format. *Energy* can be described as *vibration* and *vibration* can be described as *frequency*. **Frequency** can be expressed through numbers that are organized into **shapes**, **patterns** and **forms** to show the amazing order that exists throughout nature.

Numerology is the "study of numbers" and how they *affect* character and aptitude as a part of the *cosmic plan*. Every **letter** has a **numeric value**, and the combinations of the **letters** *vibrate* or "resonate" with a specific *frequency*. The **sum** of the **numbers** in people's **birth dates** and the **letters** in their **names** have an influence on the course their lives take, or in some cases, don't take. There are specific **numbers** or *cycles* of **numbers** that have a tendency to *affect* the **collective population**, as well as more specific weaknesses in every i**ndividual**. In this book I have listed the **numbers one** to **nine** to empower you to get a general *feeling* for what these **numbers** mean in relation to *sacred geometry* and *universal coherence*.

Most people can find a solution to a simple **problem** that only concerns **themselves**. However, as soon as you add another **person** or another **problem** to the **equation,** it becomes more complicated very quickly. As the number of **people** or **problems** rise in any given situation, it is common for people to *feel overwhelmed* because they lump the **problems** and **people** together instead of breaking it down into smaller, manageable components that can be addressed one at a time. It is most efficient to address the **weakest component** first, as once the number one weakness is addressed, many of the other issues fall away.

For the vast majority of people, energetic weaknesses come in 3's, 5's, 6's, 8's and cycles of 18 and 36. One of the most common *negative effects* **numbers** have on people is when they reach certain **ages**. It is common for **toddlers** to come to the realization that they are separate beings between **two** and **three**, at the **age** of **five** children officially start **school**, the *sub-conscious mind* is formed by the **age** of **six** or **seven**, etc. The *accumulations* of *negative experiences* that people have at these **ages** are held in the *sub-conscious mind* and become more bothersome as they add up over the years. For instance, a person may not be aware that he or she has a weakness to an *experience* that occurred at the **age** of **three**. If that *experience* is not resolved, by the **age** of **six** the issue has escalated to double the **problem**. By the **age** of **nine** it has tripled and so on.

Every individual is *affected* in this way whether they are *conscious* of it or not, and most people may have several *cycles* of weaknesses occurring simultaneously. To complicate matters even further, the *experiences* of our **ancestors**, the *collective influence*, and **cultural** and **religious** **experiences** are all *imprinted* on the *sub-conscious mind*. These *external forces* weaken the *internal forces* of many individuals without them being aware of where the impact is coming from.

The following numbers are free from the cyclical influences of 3, 5, 6 and 8:

1, 2, 4, 7, 11, 13, 14, 17, 19, 22, 23, 26, 28, 29, 31, 34. 37, 38, 41, 43, 44, 46, 47, 49, 51, 52, 53, 56, 58, 59, 61, 62, 67, 68, 71, 73, 74, 76, 77, 79, 82, 83, 86, 89, 91, 92, 97, 98,101,103

However there are also underlying weaknesses around the **number seven** and **number two**.

In the Bible, there are references to the "sins of the fathers" being part of a **seven year** *cycle*. Many people have weaknesses in combinations of **sevens** on a *spiritual* level. It is possible to heal the **ancestral** line and your **descendants** by going back and forth **seven generations** when you find a weakness in yourself, and clear it in both directions. It is also common for some people to have weaknesses to **twos** and **pairs**. Weaknesses around being the "other half" of a pair, "being paired up," "coupling," and "being a couple," often have a *negative effect* on intimate *relationships* between people, as well as on **body parts** that come in **twos**. For example, weaknesses from **two eyes** can be referred to the **two ovaries**, or **two ears** to the **two lungs**, etc.

THE "GOOD NEWS" IS:

When people recognize that they are being triggered by *cyclic* and **numerical** weaknesses, they are much better equipped to handle them with grace and ease.

THE "BAD NEWS" IS:

There are various ways that people can be *affected* by numbers. It is challenging to catch them all, especially when people are not aware of the power numbers hold over them.

NUGGET OF WIZDOM FROM THE VECTOR

MANY PEOPLE ARE TRIGGERED BY THEIR CHRONOLOGICAL AGE. AGE IS NOT "JUST A NUMBER." DO NOT UNDERESTIMATE THE NUMBER OF TOXIC THOUGHTS HELD BY THE COLLECTIVE CONSCIOUSNESS AND THEIR EFFECTS ON THE HUMAN BODY. LIFE IS EASIER WHEN YOU ARE STRONG TO YOUR AGE.

NUMBER ONE

The qualities of **number one** are reflected in the **circle**. The circle is the "master symbol" in geometry, symbolizing the cosmic womb, the unlimited possibilities and potential from which all uniform **shapes** and **patterns** are birthed. Many of the great masters have spoken of "singularity" in ancient texts over the ages because we all "come from one." This can be seen in **physics** and through the language of **sacred geometry**.

The **circle** appears to be an **isolated system** bounded by its form, but it is actually connected to an **infinite** amount of **information**, making it endlessly **circular**. There is **no beginning** and there is **no end**. The **circle** represents all **time** and all **space**, the **past**, the *present* and the *future*. The most fundamental *relationship* within the **circle** is the *relationship* between the **diameter** and the **circumference**. While the **diameter** has a **finite** number value, the number value of the **circumference** is **infinite**. If you think of a **circle** as a **dot**, you can see discreetness or structure in it. The *relationship* between the **circumference** and the **diameter** of a **circle** (**dot**) is named after the sixteenth letter of the Greek alphabet, **pi**, and numerically as 1:3.141. Three **primary shapes**, the **triangle**, the **square**, and the **pentagon**, are birthed from uniform divisions of the **circle** through **pi**. The dynamics generated within the **three primary shapes** are the building blocks of **nature**, made up of the **five platonic solids**. If you take a **circle**, add a **triad** in the **center** and **polarize** it (one **triad** facing **up** and one **triad** facing **down**) you create new **isolated boundaries**. Every **boundary** is a new *perspective* of new **information** that is part of the greater **whole**.

Information equals *energy*. More *energy* is created with each **point** and each **point** grows inside to create more **points**, on and on to **infinity**. Yet it would never exceed that **first boundary**. As you keep an open *mind,* you *expand* your **boundaries** and enter a *new dimension*. Size matters! When **physicists** speak of **dimensions,** they are referring to **expanding boundaries**.

NUGGET OF WIZDOM FROM THE VECTOR

ONE IS ALL AND ALL IS ONE. LIFE FORCE ENERGY.

NUMBER TWO

On the first day of Genesis, the **sphere** divided in order to reflect and *experience* its mirror image, just as humans were made in the image of *God*. *God* said, "Let there be light," and there was light! It was *God's* **spoken word** that created the *vibration* of *conscious thought* to *manifest* the **world**.

Two **circles** represent **polar opposites**. One **circle**, the **female,** is the *receptor* of *consciousness* (*magnetic*), and the other is **male**, the **conductor** of the **expression** of *consciousness* (*electric*). When the two intersect they birth a **third space** in the **center** that creates the *electro-magnetic spectrum* of *light* itself, the "Holy Trinity," the **Vesica Piscis**. In this case, one plus one does not equal three; it creates a **third space** *of infinite potential*, representing *life force energy* and the **power** of **creation**.

You can find the shape of the **Vesica Piscis** throughout the pleasure **centers** of your **body**. Life sustenance in the form of **food** is taken in via your **mouth**. The vagina (**Yoni**) is an inter-dimensional portal you cross through when you make the transition from *spirit* to **physical form**. Music, communication and the songs of nature are heard through your **ears** and uplift your **heart**, the first organ to develop as a **fetus**. It is also the same shape as the **eyes**, the **brain, hypothalamus** and **pineal gland**.

Your **pineal gland** is a pinecone-shaped **gland** that secretes **DMT** (the nectar of lucid dreaming). There are many monuments around the world, honoring the **pineal gland** represented by the **pinecone**. One of them is a gilt bronze Roman fountain dating from first or second century AD in the

Cortile della Pigna, (Courtyard of the Pine Cone) at the Vatican Museum. The shape of the **Vesica Piscis** is also the shape of the **Eye of Horus**, an ancient Egyptian symbol of **protection**, **royal power** and *health.*

NUGGET OF WIZDOM FROM THE VECTOR

TWO EQUALS DOUBLE THE FUN! 1 + 1 = INFINITY! BOTH MALE AND FEMALE ARE BIRTHED THROUGH THE VESICA PISCIS. YOU CANNOT HAVE EVIL WITHOUT GOOD, NEGATIVE WITHOUT POSITIVE OR LIGHT WITHOUT DARK.

NUMBER THREE

On the second day of Genesis, after conception has taken place, **cell division** begins and a **third sphere** is created in exact likeness to form a two-dimensional **tetrahedron**. The blueprint for light is based on the geometry of the **triangle**. It is a fundamental **structure** of *creation* throughout the universe.

NUGGET OF WIZDOM FROM THE VECTOR

THE HOLY TRINITY IS THE POWER OF ALL THAT IS ONE, DIVIDING INTO POLARITY BEFORE IT MANIFESTS AS PHYSICAL MATTER THROUGH EXPANSION AND ACCELERATION.

NUMBER FOUR

On the third day of Genesis a fourth **sphere** created the inner most **circle** emanating from original *creation*. The **square** is an ancient symbol representing the **four corners** of the **earth**, providing a safe, secure, **solid foundation** on which to build our lives while living on this planet we call home.

The **square** has **horizontal** and **vertical** lines at **right angles** to each other. The **four corners** define **physical space** through the directions of **north**, **south**, **east** and **west**, as well as the **seasons, spring** (birth), **summer** (growth), **fall** (pruning) and **winter** (death). This gives people an objective *perception* for the *manifestation* of **matter** – to plant the **seed** of a *thought*, to nurture its growth, to reap the harvest, and then to re-seed.

NUGGET OF WIZDOM FROM THE VECTOR

FOUR IS THE KEY TO CONSCIOUSLY BRINGING THOUGHT INTO PHYSICAL MATTER IN OUR THIRD DIMENSIONAL WORLD.

NUMBER FIVE

On the fourth day of Genesis the growth evolves to **five** complete **spheres**. The **geometry** of the **five**, represented by the **pentagon**, is the *vibration* of infinite evolution through pro-creation expressed as the **Phi Ratio** or "Golden Ratio" which is seen throughout all of nature and the entire universe.

Current **physics** dictate that things go to further **dis-order** because **theories** at this time are based on the **entropic behavior** of **conservation laws**, which describe the natural tendency of the universe to **fall apart** into **disorder**. A simple example demonstrating this theory is housekeeping. People need to **work** constantly at keeping a room **clean** and well-arranged because if they don't keep up with the routine, the room will gradually return to a **messy state**. Any parent who has hosted a birthday party for toddlers understands that a **lack** of **order** means that there must have been **order** before. It is amazing how a room full of excited children can create **dis-order** from **order**, and yet no matter how hopeless it may seem, soon after the party, **order** can be quickly **restored**.

The incredible **organization** of **nature** is not **random**! We live in the perfect organization of a *holofractographic*, non-linear, universal structure, and **organization** is the ultimate **hard drive**. The **Golden Ratio** is **nature's** way of **counting**. The name of this sequence is traditionally called the **Fibonacci Series**. **Nature** begins **counting** the same as we do, with 1. It then **repeats** itself 1+1 = 2. Presently at 2, **nature** reaches **back** into the *past* and adds the *past* to the *present* to make the *future* 2+1 = 3 and continues this process, ad infinitum …

1+1= 2, 2+1 = 3, 3+2=5, 5+3 =8 and so on … 13, 21, 34, 55, 89, 144, 233, 377, 610, 987, 1597, 2584 …

Even though many of us prefer not to go **backwards**, it is a part of nature on this planet. Its power can be seen in the petals of fruit blossoms, lilies and buttercups that use the **geometry** of **light** to *photosynthesize* light into **matter**. Most **seed heads** are produced at the **center** and then extend outward and up to one hundred forty four **spirals** to match a **Fibonacci** number. The **bracts** on **pinecones** are also arranged in a **pair** of **spirals** in **opposing directions**. Tree branches, root systems, lungs (the bronchioles and alveoli) begin as **one trunk** and **branch** off to two **growth points**. One of the new **stems** will branch into **two** while **one** remains **dormant**.

The **geometry** of the **golden rectangle** is a nesting process that can be repeated into infinity. The **ratio** of **both sides** are expressed in the form of a **spiral** called the **logarithmic spiral**. The **golden numbers** are converted to **length** so that each line measures approximately 1.618 times longer than the preceding one. In the next stage the **lines** are **squared** into areas and organized around another **square** the same size as the first **square**. Each **square** contains a number of universal dynamics that include **inter-angular** *relationships*, points of *contraction* and *expansion*, **lines** and **radials** of force. When this trajectory is continued through the other squares, a **Fibonacci spiral** is *generated*, known as the **Golden Spiral**, which is a universal archetype that is the **organizing principle** of a multitude of forms found throughout **nature**.

Spirals show up in **galaxies** and **hurricanes**. The **Milky Way** has several **spiral arms**, each at an **angle** of **twelve degrees**. **Spiraling patterns** are also evident in pineapples and cauliflower. If you cut an apple in half, the seed pattern replicates that of a **pentagon**. The **distance** between the **mouth** and **nose**, the **eyes** and the bottom of the **chin,** and even the size of **teeth** follow **phi** in the faces of **humans** and many **animals**. The **human body** is full of examples of proportions from the **length** of the **joints** or the **fingers**, to the **hand**, to the **wrist** to the **forearm**, **upper arm** to **shoulder,** and from the **joints** of the **toes** to the **foot**, from the **ankle** to the **knee**, **knee** to the **hip**, etc. The **proportions** from the **top** of **head** to the **navel** and the **navel** to the **feet** also follow the **Golden Ratio**, as do the proportions of **dolphins**, **starfish**, **sand dollars** and **urchins**. In **honeybee** colonies, the **females** outnumber the **males** very closely to the 1.618 **ratio**. (Males have one female parent and females have a male and female parent). In fact, the **hive** itself follows the **pattern** of the **Golden Spiral**.

A **DNA molecule** measures 34 angstroms long by 21 angstroms wide in the cycle of the **double helix spiral**. Their numbers with their ratio of 1.6190476 are very close to the ratio of 1.6180339 of **phi**. The form of the **pentagram star** nestled in the womb of the **pentagram** is also created by the **phi ratio**. The secrets of divine creation are held in the **four elements**: **earth**, **fire**, **water** and **air**, plus **ether**, the divine essence within us all that gives free will to every individual.

NUGGET OF WIZDOM FROM THE VECTOR

THE THREE PRIMARY SHAPES ARE KEYS THAT CAN BE USED TO UNLOCK THE SECRETS OF CREATION; HOWEVER, THE PENTAGON IS CONSIDERED THE MASTER KEY. PEOPLE COME OUT OF PEOPLE.

THIS REMINDS US OF DIVINE ORDER. WE ARE SPIRALING INTO CONTROL, NOT SPINNING OUT OF IT.

NUMBER SIX

The geometrical form of the six-sided **hexagon** is built on internal form, the **Star of David**, and represents the concept that our **material world** is a reflection of unseen *spiritual reality*. The upward pointing **triangle** represents the *cosmic source* of the *divine*, and the downward pointing **triangle** symbolizes the birthplace of **material form**. When you acquire a perfect *balance* between the *divine* and the **human**, you become co-creators *balancing spirituality* and **matter**, the *eternal* and the **transitory**, through discrimination between the **male** and the **female**, the **left brain** (logic) and the **right brain** (creativity), the **upper heart** (logic) and the **lower heart** (creativity).

Hexagons illustrate the *balance* between opposite and complimentary components of positive and negative *thoughts* held in the *conscious*, **sub-conscious** and **un-conscious mind. Birth, absorption** and **growth** oppose the forces of **death, metamorphosis** and **decay** to create the perfect **balance** of fifty/fifty *regeneration* and *degeneration*. The **geometry** of the **six** shows us that people can be totally **unique individuals** and also be a *holofractographic* representation of the **universe**. Individual **snowflakes** all have **six** sides and together create **snowstorms**, yet, just like human fingerprints, no two are exactly alike.

NUGGET OF WIZDOM FROM THE VECTOR

AS ABOVE, SO BELOW. THERE MUST BE EQUALIZATION OF THE UNION OF OPPOSITES IN ALL DIRECTIONS TO PERCEIVE THE WORLD AS IT REALLY IS, RATHER THAN HOW IT APPEARS TO BE.

NUMBER SEVEN

By the seventh day of Genesis, the seventh **sphere** has completed the process of replication, and emerges as the **Seed of Life** to remind humanity that there is nothing that cannot be **re-created** or **re-directed**. We are born again in every minute and able to build the life we *want* or *do not want*, as the case may be. *God* can now rest and reflect on the seventh day because **third dimensional matter** is *manifesting* from the **conscious mind** and spinning into existence.

Seven is the number of **magic**, holding space for intuitive creativity from the void at the center of the universe where everything spins into **form**.

The rhythms of the **seven** relate to the **seven days** of the **week** and the **stages** of human **development**. At **seven** children lose their baby teeth, at **fourteen** adolescents face the trials and tribulations of puberty, at **twenty one** people are considered to officially be an adult, and so on. Many people make important life decisions around marriage, divorce, having children, career changes, moving, etc., in *cycles* of **seven**, at the ages of **twenty-one**, **twenty-eight**, **thirty-five**, **forty-two**, **forty-nine**, etc. There also are **seven** main *chakras* that take a person through **sensory experiences** corresponding with the **seven visible spectrums** of **color**, in the **rainbow** of **light**.

The first **geometric shape** to emerge out of the **genesis pattern** is the doughnut-shaped **torus** that is revealed throughout **nature** and in all **life forms**, **atoms**, **planets**, **stars** and **galaxies**. It is the **primary shape** in existence in the universe, and the heart with its **seven muscles** is the first **organ** to develop in the **human body** forming a **torus**. **Toroidal forces** rule throughout the universe. They are at play in many ways upon our earth. The **torus effect** is easily seen at the **equator** and at the *eighth chakra* in the **human body**. The power of **spin** is the foundation of "why." **Why** does the universe work the way it does? **Why** do we **spin**? Everything is **spinning**, **spiraling** and **curling** throughout the universe. Yet, mainstream educational institutions are still teaching that the earth and other planets are rotating around the sun in **neat circles**. First of all, this implies that people constantly have to relive their *past* as each year revolves into the other in the same old groove, and secondly, it does not take into account that all the planets are constantly in motion, **spiraling**, **spinning** and **curling** into **space-time**, each on its own **individual path** as a smaller part of the **whole**. *Change* is happening every second of every minute of every day. You cannot relive the *past*, but you can adjust it. Any time people box themselves in with a given set of data, they automatically limit their *perception* because any new **information** coming in has to fit into the box of that **isolated system**.

Nassim Haramein has applied the **power** of spin to **Einstein's field equations**, factoring in the **curl** of **space-time** itself to find *creative solutions* for the *challenges* humanity faces in a complete view.

"We are at the point in our evolution in humanity where we have to transcend our current understanding of the physics of the universe and reach a unified level of physics where we have a whole-istic view of the physics that include the fundamental forces of nature instead of fighting it." Nassim Haramein

NUGGET OF WIZDOM FROM THE VECTOR

MAGICAL SEVENS HAVE THE POWER OF SPIN. THEY CHANGE THE VIBRATION OF SOUND INTO THE LANGUAGE OF LIGHT, SPINNING UNSEEN PORTALS OPEN TO TAP INTO THE INFINITE POSSIBILITIES OF THE HEAVENS. CONTRARY TO THE LIMITING BELIEF THAT "MONEY MAKES THE WORLD GO ROUND," IT IS REALLY TORQUE THAT DOES IT!

NUMBER EIGHT

The **figure eight** represents the *flow* of *energy* between two **polar opposites** that unite and then go off in their own direction. The **loops** represent the ability to *give* and *receive* in a continuous cycle of **cause** and *effect*, *action* and *re-action*. The number **eight** grounds us in our **third dimensional world** through the **laws** of **gravity** and *karma*.

The **Ouroboros**, an ancient symbol that is seen in many **cultures** as a **dragon** or **serpent** biting its own tail, represents **time**, **life**, **continuity**, **completion**, **repetition**, **self-sufficiency** and **re-birth**. Ancient texts also speak of a **serpent** of **light** resting in the heavens at the mouth of the **galactic center**. Astronomers have recently discovered two enormous **gamma ray** emitting **structures** bubbling out of the **center** of the **galaxy**.

Infinite potential is equated with *infinite change*. The opposing **loops** gain momentum and **combust** into sudden *change* when people are forced to face hidden *aspects* to get to the truth of a particular situation through the **confrontation** of **established authority**. The **crossing-point** is the point of *neutrality*, empty of *judgment* and brimming with *possibility*.

Many people are aware of the *seven chakras*, few are aware of the *eighth chakra*, a few inches from the *heart chakra*. It completes the expression of *personality* as *conscious beings*. Some people may refer to this as the completion of the **ego**.

The eighth octave completes the Solfege scale ...

DO-RE-MI-FA-SOL-LA-TI ... DO!

It feels awkward if you do not complete the scale because of the missing key. The *eighth chakra*, or the *Universal Heart*, unlocks your higher trans-personal awareness to express your individual **heart**, *mind* and *will* by accessing the higher octaves of our *soul's awareness*. The *eighth chakra* also allows for *expanded vision*. If you are lost on a city street and cannot find your way, entering a building and taking an elevator to the highest floor to look out over the city will *expand* your *vision* to include the **bigger picture**. When you are able to see much more of the surrounding landscape, it is much easier to find your way.

NUGGET OF WIZDOM FROM THE VECTOR

INFINITE POTENTIAL IS INFINITE CHANGE. THE CROSSING POINT HORIZON APPEARS AS DARK OR LIGHT DEPENDING ON WHETHER YOU ARE ON THE INSIDE OR THE OUTSIDE OF THE BLACK WHOLE. IF YOU ARE ON THE INSIDE OF THE LOOP, YOU APPEAR TO FACE DARKNESS, AND IF YOU ARE ON THE OUTSIDE OF THE LOOP YOU APPEAR TO FACE LIGHT. THE CROSSPOINT IS THE PLACE OF NEUTRALITY AT WHICH YOU CAN TAKE RESPONSE–ABILITY FOR YOUR ACTIONS AND THE REALITY YOU ARE CREATING.

NUMBER NINE

Nine is the final **single digit** that completes the **root essence** family and the *cycle* of *experience*. After **nine**, is **ten**, which when reduced to one digit (10 … 1 + 0 = 1) creates a new *cycle*. There is no **beginning** and there is no **end**. The **nine** *resonates* with **wisdom**, **idealism**, **completion** and **enlightenment** through **knowledge**. In the Mayan culture, the number **nine** is an expression of the *cycles* and movements of the **sun**, emphasizing **evolution** and **ascension**.

"If you only knew the magnificence of the three, six and nine, then you would have the key to the universe." Nikola Tesla

The **Solfeggio *Frequencies*** are a collection of powerful **tones** that have echoed throughout history. **Solfeggio *frequencies*** appeared on the scene around 1999. Leonard Horowitz spoke of them as an integral factor in the composition of **Gregorian** and **Sanskrit** chants. These *frequencies* are the keys to accessing genetic markers in our **DNA**. The **scale** used to produce the **sound** of **chant** is; UT-RE-MI-FA-SO-LA. This is not to be confused with the **Solfege scale**, DO-RE-MI-FA-SO-LA-TI-DO which is a version imposed by the Roman Catholic Church during the days of inquisition and still used to this day.

Leonard Horowitz identified the *frequency* of the **heart** when it is connected to the universe (love) to be 528 Hz, and considers it to be the **chord** that was lost to **humanity** due to the influences of the church. The numerical values of the *Solfeggio frequencies* start with 174 + 111 added to the previous lower *frequency*. The final *frequency* + 111 = 174, is a continuous equation to complete the circle and start anew. The frequencies of the Lost Chords are defined here:

OI	→	174 Hz
O2	→	285 Hz
UT	→	396 Hz ... Freedom from Guilt and Fear
RE	→	417 Hz ... Undoing Situations and Facilitating Change
MI	→	528 Hz ... Transformation and Miracles
FA	→	639 Hz ... Connecting Relationships
SO	→	741 Hz ... Expression and Solutions
LA	→	852 Hz ... Awakening Intuition
09	→	963 Hz

Sound is **matter** whose *vibration* can be visualized through **Cymatics**, which is the study of wave phenomena; the term itself was first coined by Dr. Hans Jenny, a pioneer in this field. Even as you **speak**, you create **infrared light** that can be measured and expressed in an image.

In 2012, **Douglas G. Preston** discovered the ancient *Solfeggio frequencies* within the **Gregorian chant** that he applied to a mathematical scale. If you use the **Pythagorean** method of reduction, every single one of the *frequencies* in the scale (eighty-one in all) represent a perfect set of thirds (3s, 6s, 9s). Every single frequency is a **three**, a **six** or a **nine**.

For example:

753: 7 + 5 + 3 = 12 ... 1 + 2 = 3 ... 3
861: 8 + 6 + 1 = 15 ... 1 + 5 = 6 ... 6
693: 6 + 9 + 3 = 18 ... 1 + 8 = 9 ... 9

The **Solfeggio** *Frequencies* are *cyclic* variations of the numbers 369, 147 and 258.

174: The Sound Of Creation

174, 147, 714 Hz 7 + 1 + 4 = 12 ... 1 + 2 = 3 ... 3

258: The Sound Of Silence Plus The Sound Of The Heart

258, 528, 825 Hz 2 + 8 + 5 = 15 ... 1 + 5 = 6 ... 6

The tone of 528 allows for **DNA** strands to be manipulated without causing damage to outlying pieces in a lab.

396: Relationship To The World And Sovereignty Of The Spirit

396, 693, 963 Hz 3 + 9 + 6 = 18... 1 + 8 = 9 ... 9

The key to the universe is a simple equation:

Creation + Heart = Harmony

Creation is: the bridge between *will* and **physical matter**, and the harmony of the **sound** of **silence** in between each **heartbeat** that is connected to an **ethical world** and *sovereignty* of the *spirit*.

Nassim Haramein's published paper, The "**Schwarzschild Proton**," lays down the foundation for what could be fundamental **change** in our current understanding of **physics** and *consciousness*. With the collaboration of **Dr. Rauscher**, he wrote a **scaling law** for **organized matter** of *frequency* versus **radius**. On the scale are the *frequencies* of **objects** in **hertz** (cycles per second). The *energy* of the **object** is described by its *frequency*. **Haramein** and **Rauscher** placed the **data points** from the universal *frequency* of **quasars**, the **galactic oscillation rate** and **radius, solar dynamics, stellar dynamics** and all the way down across the boundary of **quantum theory** to the tiniest measurement science has, the **plank's length**, which is the **time** that it takes for a **proton** to go across its **radius** or **diameter**, which is the smallest oscillation of the structure of the electro-magnetic field that can occur. Remarkably, the **points** line up all the way from the **quasars** to the **planck's length**, with the **biological resolution** being almost in the **middle**, a little bit closer to the **stars**. This is a huge scale! In the **standard** model of the **scaling law**, everything should have been **random**. The odds of these **points** lining up in a **non-organized universe**, are extremely low, yet they do! If we lived in a **random universe**, the **data points** would be all over the place! Also, the distance between the **data points** are divided with each other yielding a very close approximation to the **Phi Ratio** and its inverse.

At the center of the **geometric properties** of the **torus**, we find **singularity** or **zero volume**, often referred to as the "zero point," where **space-time** structure *balances* to create a perfect **vacuum** through the convergence of a minimum amount of **vectors**. In the twelve lines of the **cuboctahedron**, all forces *balance* out evenly in a complete **equilibrium** of stillness and absolute **zero degrees**. This is a perfectly stable, super conductive, super-fluid medium with infinite *energy potential* connected to every **point** in the universe. **Infinity** is everywhere and exists in a state of perfect *balance* and *equilibrium*. The **geometry** of the **vacuum** repeats in the form of **embedded vector equilibriums**, and as a **cuboctahedron** it can be divided into smaller and smaller parts without ever losing *balance*. This state of *balance* can be described mathematically as a **tetrahedral fractal**. **Tetrahedrons** contain the smallest possible **geometric volume** for minimum *energy consumption* with optimal **structural stability**.

The **geometry** of **space** takes the form of a three dimensional **sixty-four tetrahedral vector matrix**, creating repeating **vector** *equilibriums*, which are **cuboctahedrons** that repeat in harmonic intervals that follow the **Golden Ratio (Phi)**. The **vector** *equilibrium* has the ability to **collapse** when forced into **rotation**, and this creates **expansion** and **contraction** of infinite potential in differentiated form, driving the **toroidal** dynamics of all space regardless of size. The more we go inwards, the denser it gets, and the farther out, the less dense, regardless if it is an **atom** with **electrons**, **neutrons** and **protons** or **galaxies** with **stars** and **planets**.

"The vector equilibrium is the zero point for happenings or non-happenings. It is the empty theatre and empty circus and empty universe ready to accommodate any act and any audience." **Buckminster Fuller**

Adding **eight tetrahedrons** to the **cuboctahedron** and then eight more in layers creates a **sixty-four tetrahedron grid**, the very first **octave** of one **space-time** within another. In the **unified field** we are all connected though the infinite vacuum medium of the fractal geometry of **space-time**.

You are not an insignificant little dot. You are an *infinite being*, swimming in *infinite potential*.

NUGGET OF WIZDOM FROM THE VECTOR

NINE IS THE ROOT ESSENCE OF COMPLETION. WHEN YOU WERE SIXTY-FOUR CELLS OLD, YOUR PHYSICAL EXISTENCE MATCHED THE GEOMETRY OF A THIRD DIMENSIONAL FLOWER OF LIFE, EXPRESSED AS A SIXTY-FOUR TETRAHEDRON GRID. YOU ARE THE CENTER OF YOUR UNIVERSE AND SO IS EVERYONE ELSE.

PAIN

When people *experience* **pain**, it *feels* **physical**; however the root cause for **pain** is never purely **physical**. The source of **pain** is similar for everyone, but the sequences and causes of **pain** are very individual. When people *experience* **pain**, they can most efficiently arrive at resolution by asking first and foremost, "**What** is the **pain** really about?" "Is it **physical** or *non-physical*?" **Physical** *aspects* of **pain** are **biochemical**, **biological** and **systemic** whereas *non-physical* **pain** stems from *mental*, *emotional*, *psychological*, *psychic* and *spiritual* weaknesses. Insisting that **pain** is coming from a source that is not based in truth makes it more difficult to resolve and often makes it worse. For instance, **pain** can appear to be a **physical** issue when it really is the result of *mental* "stress" caused by a lack of **money**. Until the underlying weaknesses causing the lack of **money** are addressed, the **pain** will remain. Unsuccessfully spending **money** in an attempt to resolve the **pain** becomes **painful** in itself, and now the person has two major issues that are not resolved: less **money** and more **physical pain**.

NON-PHYSICAL

Clues to the source of the *non-physical* components of **pain** are hidden in the words that people use to describe the **pain**. Every word *vibrates* at a different *frequency* and **painful words** held in the *memory* are often the cause of **physical pain** resulting from *emotional*, *mental* and **psychological traumas**. When people have *limiting beliefs* that **pain** is only **physical**, they often invent *experiences* and **thoughts** to explain the **pain**, causing more *limitations* and more *painful thoughts* that in turn cause even more **pain**. It is necessary to look at the complete picture to reduce and eliminate **painful situations**. *EU ... SENSATIONS, Pg. 456

PHYSICAL

People have a tendency to try to *relax* themselves out of **pain** and discomfort because they avoid *feeling* it by **thinking** about it. The vast majority of the time, they are *suppressing* the **pain** and *relaxing* the systems of the **body** to the point where the **systems** lose their *fitness*, which causes a build-up of **toxins** in the **CNS** and *inflammation* in the **muscles** and **joints** of the **body**. This becomes a vicious *cycle* of more **pain** from the built up *stagnation*, and more *relaxation* to get out of the **pain**. If, for example, a person has **pain** in the **right knee** and it does **feel** weak as a **physical problem**, it is unlikely that the discomfort or **pain** is actually coming from the **knee**. Most of the time it is **referred** from another **body part** or from several other **body parts**.

Think of the **right knee** and scan the person's **body** with the intention of *feeling* for the next weakest **body part**. Your *thought* will go to the **body part** or one of the **body parts** that is *affecting* that **knee**. Clear both **body parts** on the **CNS**. This can be accomplished by focusing on the **whole spine** or the **specific location** of the **spine** where **peripheral nerves** are located. Continuing with the example of the **knee**, the person may only *experience* the **pain** when in a certain **position** or while taking a specific *action*. Assume that it only "hurts" going **down stairs**, not going **up stairs** or while **standing up** from a **squatting position**. In that case *scan* the **body** to see if there is another **body part** that is weakening the **knee**. Shift the **knee** and any other **body part** as well as the *action* of "going **down** the **stairs**" or **standing** up from a **squatting position** and clear it on the **CNS**.

Physical pain can be divided into two major categories: **nociceptive pain**, which is **somatic** and **visceral pain,** and **non-nociceptive pain**, which is divided into **neuropathic** and **sympathetic pain**.

NOCICEPTIVE PAIN

Most **physical pain** in the **arms**, **legs** and **back** is **nociceptive pain**. When specific **pain receptors** are stimulated by temperature, vibration, flexibility and chemical stimuli the result is **nociceptive pain**. **Skin** that has been cut or a **bone** that has been broken, are examples of **nociceptive pain** caused by signals in the pathways of the **brain** to and from the **PNS** via the **spinal cord**.

Somatic pain affects the **tissues** of the **skin**, **muscles**, **joints, bones** and **ligaments**. It is **musculoskeletal pain** that many people describe as "cramps," or sharp, **localized pain** that is extremely *sensitive* to *touch* and *movement*. The **pain** is activated by specific **receptors** that react to heat, cold, flexibility of the **muscles**, inflammation or **oxygen** and **nitrogen** deprivation.

Visceral pain comes from the three main **body cavities**: the **thorax** containing the **heart** and **lungs**, the **abdomen** containing the **liver**, **kidneys**, **spleen** and **bowels**, and the **pelvic cavity**, containing the **bladder**, **uterus** and **ovaries**. Specific **receptors** *affect flexibility*, cause *inflammation* and limit **oxygenation** due to a lack of **blood** supply to the **organs**. **Visceral pain** is often **referred** between **body parts**. Common weaknesses are between the **pelvic cavity** to the **lower back**, **abdominal pain** to the **mid-back**, **thoracic pain** to the **upper back**, and vice-versa. People often describe the **pain** as a "deep ache" that is vague in nature.

NON-NOCICEPTIVE PAIN

Non-nociceptive pain originates in the **CNS** and **PNS**, and is caused by **nerve cell dysfunction**. It can be further divided into **neuropathic** and **sympathetic pain**.

Neuropathic pain can originate from the **PNS** in the **nerves** between the **tissues** and the **spinal cord**, or from the **CNS** in the **nerves** between the **spinal cord** and the **brain**. It is often referred to as a "pinched nerve" and can be caused by *degeneration* from *dis-ease*, **stroke**, **brain hemorrhage**, **oxygen starvation**, *inflammation* from a slipped **disc**, or

viral infections. The injured **nerve** malfunctions and communication with other **systems** becomes unreliable which causes *hypersensitivity* to *touch*, *vibration* and *temperature*, **tingling**, **numbness**, and weakness of the **extremities** that the **brain** interprets as **pain**. People often use the words **shooting**, **burning** and **stabbing** to describe *hypersensitivity* of the **nerves**.

Sympathetic pain is often caused by lack of communication between the mechanisms of the **PNS** and the **CNS**, and that causes hyperactivity in the **sympathetic nervous system**. Fractures, soft tissue injuries and traumas to small **peripheral nerves** result in the loss of **blood** *flow* to the **tissues**, creating *stagnation* that *affects* the *communication*, *responsiveness* and **speed** of the **PNS**. The **skin** around the injury loses its ability to control temperature, and that can cause abnormalities in **sweating** which permeates throughout the **limbs**. The **pain** can be so intense that a person could lose the use of a **limb** as a consequence of **muscle wasting** and issues with the **joints** and **bones**.

CASE STUDY:

In 2010 on a flight from Vancouver, BC to Penticton, BC a young man struggled down the aisle on crutches, and sat in the seat in front of me. I was sitting next to a doctor who was on his way home from a pain symposium that he had attended regarding pain management. He asked me what I did for a living and I told him that I taught seminars on how to eliminate pain. The young man overheard our conversation and asked if we could help him out. His foot had been run over in a motorbike accident a few years earlier, and he had been on crutches ever since. He said that he had been on many pain medications, yet was unable to get relief from the pain or to put any weight on the foot.

The doctor said, "Ask her, I just relieve pain. She says she can eliminate it." The young man replied, "No, offense but I would rather talk to him." I told him no offense was taken, but suggested that he attend the free demonstration of energetic work that I and my colleague, Phil Free were giving that evening.

There were about fifty people attending the demonstration that evening, and he came in on crutches just as we were about to begin. I immediately called him up to the front and we got to work. Within five minutes, the pain was drastically reduced, and within twenty minutes, he was walking for the first time in years without crutches. It was very emotional for him and the audience who witnessed him letting go of the pain and walking out of the building, carrying his crutches.

The pain was actually referred from his right index finger, his "trigger finger." He was wearing army camouflage pants and said that he had always drawn to "army clothing" but didn't feel like he was "that kind of guy." Once the underlying past life issues regarding his battlefield experiences were cleared, we worked on the physical issues, and as he let go of the emotional and psychological traumas that had been triggered when the accident happened he was able to use his foot again.

THE "GOOD NEWS" IS:

It is possible not only to relieve **pain**, but to **eliminate** it when the underlying concerns or issues are resolved on all levels of existence. This does not have to take a lot of time. It can happen instantaneously.

THE "BAD NEWS" IS:

The main problem that **doctors** and **patients** face when it comes to **pain**, and **back pain** in particular, is that even with all the modern technology and advances in medicine, arriving at an **exact diagnosis** only happens rarely because the focus is on the **physical aspects**, and the underlying factors are ignored.

NUGGET OF WIZDOM FROM THE VECTOR

PAIN IS NOT PUNISHMENT. IT IS THE BODY'S WAY TO CALL ATTENTION TO AN UNHEALTHY STATE OF THE BODY, SOUL AND SPIRIT. OUR BODY IS DESIGNED TO EFFICIENTLY AND EFFORTLESSLY RETURN TO HOMEOSTASIS.

PERCEPTION

Perception is usually defined as the process of simple *sensory stimuli* of *sight*, *taste*, *smell*, *sound* and *touch* evolving into meaningful *experiences* through complex constructs of *association*. The vast majority of people give the most credence to **visual** and **tactile** *perceptions associated* with the third-dimensional plane. Objects appear to be solid; however, they are actually very fluid because they are made up of **atoms** that are constantly in motion. Humans are inclined to *experience* objects through **identifying patterns**. For instance, when people see familiar **objects** such as a chair, they observe the chair as they have always known it to exist.

Perception is influenced by the *expectations*, **needs** and *values* that are held in the *sub-conscious* and *un-conscious minds*, as well as by what people **consciously perceive**. Stimuli or absence of stimuli results in different **percepts** depending on a person's **upbringing**, **cultural** and **religious experiences**, etc. This can be better understood by looking at a situation such as the robbing of a bank. The bank robbers, customers in the line-up of the bank, the tellers, the guards and the police who arrive on the scene after the robbery has taken place will have similarities in their description of the events as they occurred, yet specific details of the height, weight, color and race of the individuals involved are often very different. This is because every person in the situation is **physically viewing** the situation from a different **angle** depending on their **location** in the building and whether they are farthest or closest to the perpetrators. Their own height and weight influence their **perception** of what tall, skinny, fat, etc. mean and all are open to their **interpretation** of what they **observe**. Furthermore, the **emotional re-actions** to what each person witnesses have many **variations** and also play a significant role in what is **perceived**. While the police officers and guards have been trained to **observe** details under challenging circumstances, and the bank personnel have been educated in how to behave in the case of a robbery, many of the clients are innocent bystanders with no reference as to how to act under duress of this kind. Finally, **past life** or **death memories** and **traumas** held in the **CNS** from **spiritual**, **psychic**, **ancestral** and **collective experiences** of **war**, **natural disaster** and **destruction** held in the **sub-conscious** and **un-conscious mind** will also have an **indirect effect** on what each person **perceives**.

When people are under duress, they have a tendency to "see what they want to see" and "hear what they want to hear." There is a search for **informational cues** and **instant categorization** of what they are witnessing. The less reliable the information that they can access, the more room is left for **misinterpretation** and **misrepresentation** of the **sensory stimuli** that they are **experiencing**. Once a **perception** is categorized, most people will actively ignore and distort any information that violates the **initial categorization** which causes **perception** to become more **selective** and **less objective**.

Your **reality** is formed by your **perception** of how the world works. If you **perceive** it to be a difficult place, it will prove to be difficult. If you **perceive** it to be full of **possibility** with a "price to be paid" for every **possibility**, every **possibility** will come with a **price tag**. Your **perception** of the universe as a place where **expansion** and **acceleration** are the **natural** state of order, as opposed to **entropy** and **disorder**, will automatically empower you to find "things in order." If people only solve the **peripheral** concerns and ignore the **fundamental** underlying concern, that initial **problem** becomes a **vortex** with a force all of its own, gains momentum with every turn as it **spirals** out of control, and creates more and more *peripheral* concerns to contend with.

REVERSE PERCEPTION

Every **problem** has a "story" and many of the tales we tell ourselves about the **story** of our lives are inaccurate accounts from the point of view of our *sub-conscious* and *un-conscious minds*. A vast majority of the time what we **think** the **problem** is, is completely **opposite** to the **truth** of our situation. Our thoughts about **what** happened, **who** was involved, **when** and **where** it happened, **why** it happened, and **how** it was or can be resolved, are unlikely to be true. It is much more productive to *feel* the story and identify the un-truths, and then clear them energetically to arrive at *creative solutions* by spinning *reverse perception* into *true perception*.

SCOTOMA

Scotoma (**blind spot**) is a dissimulation of the visual field located where the **optic nerves** exit the **retina**, a location called the **optic disc**. A lack of light-detecting **photoreceptor cells** on the **disc**, creates a region of reduced information within the **visual field**. This is similar to a "blind spot" in the visual field of a poorly designed automobile. Most people do not have direct *conscious awareness* of **visual scotoma** because the **brain** compensates by filling the information in with the **unaffected eye** to prevent *perception* of an **incomplete image**. People who have **scotoma** describe the *effect* on their *vision* as "things disappearing on them."

While not everyone is affected by **visual scotoma**, everyone is *affected* by *psychological scotoma*, which is a dissimulation in the field of *perception* that prohibits an individual's ability to *perceive personality traits* in themselves that are obvious to others. The five major *personality traits* identified by many *psychologists* are **neuroticism**, **extraversion**, **openness** to *experience*, **agreeability** and **conscientiousness**. These are actually a *continuous succession* of *traits* with some more pronounced than others. Test for weaknesses of the five major *personality traits*, strengthen them individually and as a whole for strong *communication*, *integration* and *recognition* of and between *traits*.

THE "GOOD NEWS" IS:

Strong *perception* connected to your *feeling* will provide you with complete and instant *insight*.

THE "BAD NEWS" IS:

Many times people will *repeat* and *recycle* the same old **patterns** because of *past perceptions* they are not aware of, conflicting *personality traits* and/or because they have *reverse perception*.

NUGGET OF WIZDOM FROM THE VECTOR

THE "WHAT I.F.'S" AND THE "WHAT THE E.F.'S" CAN TIP THE SCALES TO DISORDER IN AN INSTANT. NEUTRALITY IS THE KEY TO STRONG PERCEPTION. WHEN YOU ARE NEUTRAL TO THE QUESTION AND THE ANSWER, IT IS EASY TO FIND CREATIVE SOLUTIONS TO ANY PROBLEM.

PERFORMANCE

A lot of people complain that it is challenging to keep up with the constant pressure of today's fast-paced world despite the fact that they have historically **unprecedented access** to **information. Information** equals *energy*, yet the vast majority of people are falling far short of using their optimum potential, and still *perceive* themselves to be working beyond their limits. The "stress" people *feel* as a **human race** is a result of living in the confines of a **closed system**. What people *perceive* to be optimal performance is very deceptive when one considers that the **naked eye** is only capable of seeing four percent of what is possible in the *electromagnetic spectrum*. It is essential to gain an understanding of oneself to tap into the *infinite possibilities* of the *unseen*, and to open the doors to true potential.

Many people limit their performance because they are on "auto pilot" doing things the same old way through habit, working harder **physically** and spending long hours solving **problems** without considering the unknown influences that are blocking their true potential. Identifying and clearing these specific weaknesses allows maximum performance to become a reality through **structured, consistent steps** of *action* and **efficient** use of **time** and *energy*. For example, many families *struggle* with their morning routine, getting themselves ready for work, their children ready for school, making breakfast, etc. It is challenging to perform at optimum potential in your **career** if you are **physically** exhausted and *feeling* defeated before you even get out the door, yet many people take for granted that "this is just the way it is." It is important to be strong to **leaving home, transportation** to and from **work** or **school, leaving work** or **school** and **arriving home**. Breaking down the components of these daily mundane tasks allows them to be performed with more efficiency. **Optimum performance** is achieved through the *balance* of the **body**, *soul* and *spirit*. There are often weaknesses in the **physical environment** at **work** and at **home**, particularly in the **bedrooms** because a **cluttered home** leads to a *cluttered mind*, weakening **performance**.

Better **performance** is not a gift that is given to a few chosen people. Some people are born into families that are genetically superior or have financial advantages; however, if the individuals in those families don't use those benefits to improve their **performance**, those advantages can become a detriment rather than a gift. In contrast, others are born into families that appear to be at a disadvantage and yet they **perform** at exceedingly high levels. Every **activity** you participate in has the potential to increase or decrease productivity. If you are operating at optimal performance in one *aspect* of your life, you can use that *experience* to strengthen every other *aspect* of your life and thus increase your **performance**. For instance, professional athletes train for years and *transfer* their skills to other *aspects* of their lives by applying the same **principles** to achieving their goals in education, business, and life in general. Successful performance builds on one successful performance after another.

Too many people go to work every day with the attitude that they will "never get ahead" and consequently they don't put real effort into *effecting change*. There are underlying energetic weaknesses that come from **ancestors** who have *suffered* and *struggled* to survive, or on the other end of the spectrum, **ancestors** who have sacrificed everything to ensure their **descendants' success** by working long hours in what they considered to be "dead-end jobs." Many of these weaknesses come from *feeling hopeful* that **help** is arriving, which leads to *experiences* of *hopelessness* when **help** doesn't "arrive." *Past life experiences* of **abuse** of **power** can also be at the root of the **problem**.

It is empowering to think in terms of **career** rather than **J.O.B.** (journey of the broke). Every **career** has *aspects* or **jobs** that are more or less pleasurable to perform, but if those jobs are performed with the purpose of improving performance and achieving long-term goals, it is easier to recognize *opportunities* that are hidden in the *challenges*.

RESULTS:

"Before I started working with Colette I couldn't move out of a dance level called Novice and the dance Slip Jig was the problem. I couldn't get a first place in that dance. I had gone to many dance compositions but I

couldn't do it and when I did it I didn't feel alive my energy was low and I wasn't enjoying myself, then my mom introduced me to Colette on a phone conversation. As the session went on I started feeling a some what of a 'click' also my body was basically telling me this is what is going to help. I also felt many changes in my body, also I could connect myself to my body.

"A day after the phone session I had a dance competition and dancing the Slip Jig felt amazing. My body just felt like it knew what to do, I felt energized and I felt like I had danced my dance which is an amazing feeling which is so great that it's to hard explain. Well that day I got first in the Slip Jig. And then a couple months later I went to the Mid Atlantic Regional championships. I dance in the traditional set (a dance). And the moment I stepped on that stage I got a feeling that I get when I know something good is going to happen, and something good did happen I made no mistakes and out of sixty girls I won!

"Colette has changed my life problems and my dancing in many more ways by Colette."

Shea Betten (11 years old), New York

THE "GOOD NEWS" IS:

The average person uses, at best, four to five percent of his or her potential. If you tap into just a little more of your potential you can easily become a **stronger version** of yourself and excel at anything.

THE "BAD NEWS" IS:

Many people rely on **motivation** to achieve their goals. If **motivation** is their driving force, then when the **motivation** runs out they will be left with *struggle*, and *struggle* inevitably leads to more *struggle*.

NUGGET OF WIZDOM FROM THE VECTOR

IF YOU EXHAUST YOURSELF BY TRYING TO ACHIEVE SUCCESS IN A CONFINED SYSTEM, YOU WILL ONLY ACHIEVE MORE EXHAUSTION. THERE IS NO BOX! EVERY MOMENT IS A P.R. MOMENT BECAUSE THE UNIVERSE RECOGNIZES ACTION CONNECTED TO GOALS.

PETS

Every **species** throughout the universe feels the ramifications of the actions of **humans**. **Wild animals** have fewer obvious issues than **pets** because **pets** live more intimately with **humans**. That said, many **problems** that appear to be the **pet's problem** actually stem from *associations* with their owners and their attitudes about life. Many **physical** issues are the result of discord in the **homes** they live in and poor *relationships* with the **people** and other **pets** they live with because they are very *sensitive* to the *psychological* state of **humans** and the stimuli from their **physical environment**. The *emotional* state of animals is varied because they are *sensitive* and easily detect **illness** and **injury** in other **animals** and in **humans**. When problems arise, always check for weaknesses in the *relationship* between the **owner** and other **people** or **animals** in the **pet's environment**. The *memories* of *mental*, *emotional* and *psychological traumas* can be triggered instantly by **smells, sounds**, **physical** *sensations* and **events**, and this can cause the animal to panic. For instance, after any fireworks display you will often see notices for lost pets that panicked and ran because they were **overstimulated** by the *sights*, *sounds* and **smells** of the **fireworks** and **crowds**.

When **animals** connect with **people** telepathically, they most often do so by flashing **pictures** or short "movies;" this is why it is easiest to communicate with them when people do the same thing. Due to their shorter life span, animals often have numerous *psychic attachments* to **alive** and **dead** **bodies,** *mismatched body parts,* and *multiple personalities* that merge into their present lives. *EU ... PSYCHIC CLEANSE, Pg. 419*

There is a lot of argument as to whether or not **animals** have *souls*. They do have a *mind*, *will* and *personality traits*, and they are *affected* by *spiritual* issues and **events** revolving around **humans** because they are in *service*. For instance, many **horses** have *traumas* of being used for war and will bravely go into battle, with their owners, but they do not have *karma* with other **horses, soldiers**, etc. because when they are in battle they are in *service* to the **people** who own them.

People often give animals **human** *personality traits,* but **animals** are *innocent* by nature and *suffer* from *past life traumas* without accumulating *karma*. They can, however, get caught in *karmic loops* by returning in different forms to **specific people** and **families** in a series of lifetimes.

BEHAVIORAL ISSUES

If a **pet** has unexplained **patterns** of *inappropriate behavior*, it is advisable to check for *past life experiences*; they may have been another **species** or in some cases another **breed** within a **species**. *Associated* **behaviors** can be perceived as both positive and negative, depending on the situation. For example, a **dog** can have *memories* of having been in the **body** of a **bull**, **lion**, **wolf**, **fox**, **bear**, **rabbit**, etc., **memories** that are *imprinted* on its personality. Some dogs are "butt headed," always bumping into and knocking over things; people and other pets in their enthusiasm, while others are as shy and skittish as a rabbit and can be habitual diggers from *past life experiences* of having lived underground. A **guard dog** that **roars** like a **lion** is an asset, whereas other dogs that love to **howl** like **wolves** or **yip** like **foxes** as a preferred method of *communication* can cause disturbances in a residential neighborhood. *Past life memories* can cause seemingly unexplainable **behaviors**.

Many **pets** have weaknesses to being **trapped** and suffer from **separation anxiety** and *panic* when they are forced to be in enclosed spaces. *Memories* of **mutilation** can result in *hyperactive* and *aggressive* **behavior**. It is common for the **paws**, **feet** and **claws** to have previous *traumas* of **steel traps**, **injuries**, **ingrown nails** and **hooves** that can cause *desperate* **behavior** when their **nails**, **hooves** or **claws** are trimmed or touched. **Dogs** that have had **dewclaws** removed, **cats** that are **declawed** and **birds** that have had their **wings clipped** often have *imprints* of *traumas*, which cause many **behavioral problems**. **Animals** who have had their **tails docked** often have weaknesses that refer to the **cranial brain** and the rest of the **CNS**, and that *affects* them in a **physical** and *non-physical* way. **Genital** and **reproductive** *traumas* are common for **pets** and **livestock** because many have been **neutered** in cruel ways. **Chaining** animals leaves them exposed to the **elements** and **dangers** that they are unable to fend off, and often triggers previous *hanging experiences*. Many **pets** have weaknesses to having been previously **eaten** or **cooked**.

Character traits are purposely bred into specific breeds and, depending on the circumstances, can be viewed as positive or negative attributes. Large dogs can have past life *memories* of having been "lap dogs" and "lap dogs" can have *memories* of having been "guard dogs" which clearly leads to **behavioral** issues. **Scent hounds** follow their **noses** and can be oblivious to **sound**, **touch** or **sight** when they are hot on a trail; this makes them challenging to train. **Sight hounds** get nervous if they are "stared at" because that is how they hunt. Many **dogs** that are bred to **swim** are challenging to keep away from **water**, **retrievers** are "high energy dogs" and can be compulsive about **retrieving**, while **herding dogs** will "herd" anything if you let them and even when you would prefer they didn't. For example, many people consider **pit bulls** to be dangerous as a breed because they have been bred to "fight until death." Their **physical structure**, **musculature**, and *aggression* have been **genetically** manipulated to create a "fighting machine." When they are triggered, they can be extremely *aggressive* and quickly inflict damage with their powerful jaws. However, many **pit bulls** that are raised to be *gentle* would not "hurt a fly." Even **dogs** that are rescued from fighting "careers" **prefer** to be *gentle* and have no desire to fight or injure others, even though they have been severely abused and trained to fight for the entertainment of **abusive people**.

HEALTH ISSUES

Many *health* issues that **pets** *suffer* from are similar to and a consequence of *resonating* with their owners who are ill or have a *fear* of **illness**. When owners are **sick** or *fear* their **pet** is **sick**, the *re-action* to *negative emotions* can perpetuate the **illness**. To energetically strengthen **animals**, it is helpful to remember that, because most animals have a **horizontal spine** rather than a **vertical spine**, they bear the weight of their **body** differently than **humans** who are upright. This can cause a lot more confusion between the **upper** and **lower torso** and their **extremities**. **Animals** who are **leashed** or **chained** often have **neck** issues that **refer** to their **hips** and **patellas**.

You can strengthen your **pet** by running the *energy* all the way from the **skull** to the **tip** of the **tail** to delete all possible weaknesses in a general way, and then be more specific by testing the **systems, organs, bones** and **tissues** for any weaknesses. *Scan* their entire **bodies** for **physical** and *non-physical traumas* including **poisons, toxins, chemicals, medications** from this and previous lifetimes. **Animals** are easily *affected* by **poisons** and **toxins** because their systems are very *sensitive*. Strengthen them to being an **independent species** and energetically separate them from their **owner's** *limiting beliefs*.

THE "GOOD NEWS" IS:

We receive a lot of benefit from the **pets** in our lives. A **purring cat** or the **wag** of a **dog's tail** *vibrates* at twenty to one hundred and forty **megahertz**, lowering "stress," **blood pressure**, risk of **heart attack**, healing **tendons, muscles,** *infections*, **swelling**, shortness of **breath** and improving **bone** *health*. **Cats** typically will sit and lay on locations where there are "negative energy grids" in the home and on peoples' bodies to clear weak energy; they will often place their paws on the exact spot where they feel a weakness. Even the lowly **insect**, will only sting or bite a person where they detect an energetic weakness, which is why some people attract mosquitoes and others do not.

THE "BAD NEWS" IS:

Many **animals** on this planet are being **tortured** and **abused** by **humans**. The vast majority of **people** simply accept that it is happening, while at the same time they shower love and affection on **specific animals**, generally **pets**. It is not energetically possible to separate the extreme **abuse** from the *acts* of **love**, and every **animal** on the planet, including **humans**, *suffers* because of it.

NUGGET OF WIZDOM FROM THE VECTOR

AS WITH HUMANS, INJURIES AND PAIN IN ANIMALS HAVE A BASIS IN A PRE-EXISTING WEAKNESS. MANY TIMES THE WEAKNESS IS AN EXTERNAL FORCE COMING FROM THEIR OWNERS. DOGS IN PARTICULAR ARE VERY LOYAL AND WILL DUTIFULLY TAKE ON THEIR OWNERS' ISSUES, WHEREAS CATS WILL ONLY TAKE ON PROBLEMS IF THEY ARE IN THE MOOD.

pH REGENERATION

The **pH** of an **aqueous solution** is a measure of its **acidity** or *basicity*. The "**p**" stands for **power percentage** or **potential**. The "**H**" stands for **hydrogen**. **Hydrogen** is the lightest and most abundant **chemical element**, constituting roughly seventy percent of the universe's **chemical mass**. **Stars** are mainly composed of **hydrogen** in its plasma state, but naturally occurring **elemental hydrogen** is relatively rare on earth.

An **aqueous solution** is a **solution** in which the **solvent** is **water**. A **solvent** is a **liquid, solid** or **gas** that dissolves another **solid**. Solutions with a **pH less** than **seven** are said to be **acidic** and those with a **pH above seven** are considered **base** or **alkaline**. **Seven** is considered to be **neutral**.

Some **molecules** are *repelled* by water and some are *attracted* to it. **Hydrophobes** are considered "water fearing" because they have the **physical** properties of a **molecule** that are **repelled** by a mass of **water**. **Hydrophiles** are considered "water loving" and tend to be *dissolved* by **water**.

ACIDS

Acids can be identified by taste (sour) and by their reaction with **metals** and other **bases**. The three common types of acid are **acetic**, **sulfuric** and **tartaric**. **Acetic acid** (vinegar) is an **organic compound**. Organic compounds are **molecules** that contain **carbon**. **Sulfuric acid** (car batteries) is an **inorganic compound**. Inorganic compounds are **molecules**

containing **minerals**. All **mineral acids** release **hydrogen ions** when they are dissolved in **water**. Finally, **tartaric acids** (baking, food and wine preservation) are **organic compounds** with **acidic properties**. **Organic acids** are weak **acids** that can penetrate the **cellular membrane** of **bacteria**. They do not dissolve completely in **water**, but are very soluble in **organic solvents**.

BASES

Bases are the chemical opposites of **acids** that are able to accept **hydrogen ions**. **Ions** are **atoms** or **molecules** in which the total number of **electrons** are not equal to the total number of **protons,** giving them a net *positive* or *negative* **electrical charge**. **Electrons** carry a *negative* charge while **protons** carry a *positive* charge. **Anions** are **ions** with more **electrons** than **protons** giving them a net *negative* charge. **Cations** are **ions** with fewer **electrons** than **protons**, and therefore they have a *positive* charge.

Neutrons are **sub-atomic particles** composed of the **nucleus** and **atoms**. **Neutrons** have a *neutral* charge. There are two kinds of **neutrons: Elementary particles** that are the basic building blocks of the universe, and **composite particles** that are made up of two or more **elementary particles**.

pH SCALE

The **pH scale** (0 – 14) is the full set of **pH numbers** that indicate the *concentration* of H+ and OH **ions** in **water**. Each **pH** value below 7 is 10 times more **acidic** than the next higher value and each **value** above 7 is 10 times more **base** (alkaline).

Some examples of products, showing their approximate **pH value** on a **pH scale** are: 0 = hydrochloric acid

1 = upset stomach acid
2 = normal stomach acid
3 = sodas, vinegar, lemons
4 = orange juice, acidic soil
5 = tomatoes, bananas, coffee
6 = bread, salmon, potatoes, normal rain
7 = pure water, milk, human saliva, blood
8 = seawater, eggs
9 = baking soda, phosphate detergents
10 = borax, antacids

11 = milk of magnesia
12 = ammonia, non-phosphate detergents
13 = bleach
14 = sodium hydroxide

H+ (hydrogen)ion concentration and pH relate inversely. OH (hydroxide – one hydrogen atom plus one oxygen atom) ion concentration and pH relate directly. Both H+ and OH ions are always present in any solution. A solution is acidic if the H+ are in excess and basic if the OH ions are in excess.

Pure water has a pH around seven, varying with temperature. When an acid dissolves in water, the pH will be less than seven, and when a base dissolves in water the pH will be greater than seven. pH levels may be obtained by using a pH indicator, (a substance that changes color around a particular pH value) Litmus paper is a water-soluble mixture of different dyes extracted from lichens. Blue litmus paper turns red under acidic conditions and red litmus paper turns blue under basic conditions. Neutral litmus paper is purple.

The kidneys and lungs are responsible for maintaining the proper balance of acids and bases in the body. If this delicate *balance* is not ideal, there are several problems that can occur:

ACIDOSIS

Acidosis is a condition in which there is excessive acid in the body fluids.

METABOLIC ACIDOSIS

Metabolic acidosis is a condition in which the acidity of the blood (usually referring to the acidity of the blood plasma) is increased because of an inability of the kidneys to excrete acid. This causes the lungs to compensate in an attempt to reduce the metabolic acid that can lead to respiratory acidosis.

RESPIRATORY ACIDOSIS

Respiratory acidosis is caused by a build-up of carbon-dioxide in the blood due to poor ventilation (the rate that gas enters and leaves the lungs). Acidosis affects the CNS, causing headaches, sleepiness, confusion, loss of consciousness and even coma. The muscles are affected by seizures and weakness, the intestines and gastric systems by diarrhea, nausea and vomiting, and the respiratory system by shortness of breath and coughing. Arrhythmia of the heart and increased **heart rate** are also common. Test the interconnections between these **systems** for weaknesses within themselves and with each other. Strengthen them in all directions.

ALKALOSIS

Alkalosis is a condition in which the **body fluids** have excess **base** (alkali).

METABOLIC ALKALOSIS

Metabolic alkalosis is caused by too many **bicarbonates** in the **blood**. **Bicarbonates** are a vital component of the **pH buffering system** to regulate **acids** and **bases** in the **metabolic system**.

HYPOCHLOREMIC ALKALOSIS

Hypochloremic alkalosis is caused by extreme lack or loss of **chloride,** a **chemical compound** in which one or more **chlorine atoms** are bonded to each other. It may occur along with prolonged vomiting.

HYPOKALEMIC ALKALOSIS

Hypokalemic alkalosis is caused by extreme lack or loss of **potassium** that can occur when people are on **diuretic medications**. **Potassium** occurs in nature only as an ionic salt and is found in dissolved salt water. It is necessary for the function of all living **cells**, present in all **animals**, **plants**, and is especially high in concentrations of **fruit**. **Potassium dysfunctions** result in **neurological** disorders.

COMPENSATED ALKALOSIS

Compensated alkalosis occurs when the **body** returns the **acid/base** *balance* to normal but the **bicarbonate** and **carbon dioxide** levels remain abnormal. **Respiratory alkalosis** is a condition of **low** levels of **carbon dioxide** and too much **oxygen** in the **blood** due to excessive **breathing**. **Physical** causes can be fever, high altitudes, lack of oxygen, liver disease, lung disorders and **salicylate** poisoning.

Salicylates are derivatives of **salicylic acids** that occur naturally in **plants** and are found in many **medications**, **perfumes** and **preservatives**. **Salicylate** *sensitivity* is considered to be a **pharmaceutical** *re-action*, not an **allergy**. **Aspirin** is a common **salicylate drug**. On the *emotional* and **psychological** levels "stress and anxiety," *depression, anger* and *fear* can lead to **hyperventilation**. **Hyperventilation** is a common symptom of

panic attacks along with belching, bloating, chest pain, confusion, dizziness, dry mouth, light headedness, muscle spasms in the feet and hands, numbness and tingling in arms or around the mouth, palpitations, shortness of breath and sleep disturbances. **Hyperventilation** can also be a symptom of **bleeding**, **heart** or **lung** disorder or *infection*. Test for weaknesses in the **CNS**, **muscles**, **circulatory system** and **intestines**. Strengthen the **systems** within themselves and with each other.

The **pH** levels throughout the **body** vary. **Blood** is generally slightly **alkaline** with a **pH** between 7.35 and 7.45 and is unlikely to be changed by the food you eat. Your **stomach** is very *acidic* with a **pH** of 3.5 or below so that it is able to break down **food**. Your **urine** changes with what you ingest, but only for a short time.

THE "GOOD NEWS" IS:

Studies have shown that a **pH** slightly above 7.4 (alkaline) cause **cancer cells** to become dormant and a **pH** of over 8.5 causes **cancer cells** to **die** while *healthy* cells thrive. **Alkaline environments** also discourage **parasitic** *infestation*.

THE "BAD NEWS" IS:

There is much controversy regarding **alkalinity** and **acidity** in the **body** and whether eating **alkaline** plant based foods rather than **acidic** meat based diets improves *health*, vibrancy and the **body's** ability to *absorb* **minerals**. Energetically, people who tend to be *angry* with "acidic thoughts" tend to be more **acidic**.

NUGGET OF WIZDOM FROM THE VECTOR

ACIDIC THOUGHTS, PARASITIC PEOPLE AND SITUATIONS ARE ALL ASSIMILATED, ABSORBED AND DIGESTED THROUGHOUT THE BODY. TEST FOR THE OPTIMUM pH FOR ANY GIVEN INDIVIDUAL BODY PART IN RELATION TO THE REST OF THE BODY AND BALANCE OUT ANY WEAKNESSES. THE VAST MAJORITY OF PEOPLE TEND TO TEST WEAK TO ACIDITY RATHER THAN ALKALINITY.

PHYSICAL ENVIRONMENT

Your **physical environment** consists of the **home(s)** you live in, the **town**, **city**, **village**, **state**, **country** and **continent**, the **school(s)** you attend, the **buildings** you work in, the **vehicles** you use for transportation, the **restaurants** you eat in, etc. The more your **physical environment** supports you, the easier and more effortless life is. If there are very different dynamics **between** the **home** and **school** or **business**, it makes life much more challenging, especially for children. When your **physical environment** supports your **body**, *soul* and *spirit,* you are able to become a stronger version of yourself in every *aspect* of life. There are often underlying energetic weaknesses that people may or may not be aware of, in their **daily routine** or **lack** of **routine** that hinder their ability to produce in the third-dimensional world.

You don't always have total control over many **elements** regarding your **environment,** but in general you can strengthen your life by influencing your **environment** in a strong way to the best of your ability. One of the easiest ways to shift your **environment** for the better is to remove all **televisions**, or at the very least have a **designated room** for **television** rather than one in every room, and to make strong *choices* as to what you watch.

Balanced **Feng Shui** can make substantial improvements for members of a **family** and for a **business** because it attracts **people** and **clients** into people's lives. These are commonly referred to as the **elements** of **fire**, **air**, **earth**, **water** and **ether**. When the **elements** in a **home** are out of *balance*, the energy can be changed using **color**, **furniture**, **light fixtures**, **textures**, **plants,** etc. For example, excess **water** (**blues**) causes *grief* and *sadness* that can be counteracted by adding **earth**, **rocks**, **crystals** and **wood** to draw the **water** out. Excess **fire** (**reds and oranges**) causes **fiery responses**, leading to *aggression*, *hostility* and an increase in **appetite**. Adding **water elements** calms the **fire**. **Plants**, **earth**, **rocks** and **crystals** also add life to a room that is too fiery. Too much **wood** causes **procrastination**, **stubbornness**, and a lack of **initiative** to get things done. **Metal** will block and prevent the growth of **wood**. Lighting a room with **candles** also automatically usurps the **power** of **wood**. Excess **metal** (**grey**) causes a lack of **focus** in direction. **Rock** can dull a sharp **blade** and **water** will erode it. It is unlikely that there is too much **earth** in any given home, but if that is the case, it is important to realize that **earth** creates **isolation** and **reclusiveness**. **Wood** (**plants**) will draw the **earth** out and **metal** will move the **earth**.

It is also possible to **imprint** positive *energies* into everyday **items** in your **physical environment** so that every time you use, see or touch them, they automatically strengthen you. If the **bedrooms** and children's **rooms** are **uncluttered**, they are more likely to promote the calmness of **water**, **earth** and **rock**. If the goal in the **master bedroom** is to create *excitement* the element of **fire** works best.

When people want to improve *energy* in themselves, it is very common for them to spontaneously feel the urge to clean their **physical**

environment, and often they end up **organizing**, **de-cluttering** and cleaning their **homes, garages, basements, yards, file cabinet**, etc. It is possible to clean the *energy* in any room you enter by taking the time to *feel* for any weaknesses; support your **physical potential** in that room by going to the base of your **spine** and clearing whatever it is that is bothering you. Push **your energy** from the **feet up** and picture the **ceiling** opening up to let the **negative molecules** of *energy* go. You can also perform an "energetic sweep" of a room by creating **vortexes** of strong *energy* spinning through the **room**, clearing "energetic cobwebs" and trapped *thoughts*. Don't forget to include the corners! Do the same for the mattress you are sleeping on.

THE "GOOD NEWS" IS:

Challenges are *possibilities* disguised as **problems**. People are more likely to grow in *challenging circumstances* when they take response-ability for where they are at any given time, including their **physical environment**. Even if it is not possible to **physically** move to another **location**, it is always possible to strengthen yourself to the **location** you are in.

THE "BAD NEWS" IS:

At times *external forces* will overcome a person's *equilibrium* by shaking things up a bit (or a lot) to keep *action* happening. History is full of stories of immigrants who escape a **country** and flee to another for a better life. Many times weaknesses to a city or country actually come from their long lost **ancestors**.

NUGGET OF WIZDOM FROM THE VECTOR

IN THE CASE OF EARTHQUAKES AND OTHER NATURAL DISASTERS, WAR, RELIGION AND OTHER MANMADE DISASTERS, THE EFFECT IS FELT IMMEDIATELY. MORE OFTEN, THE EFFECTS OF A NEGATIVE ENVIRONMENT ARE SUBTLE AND PROGRESSIVE, LIKE A DEFLATED BALLOON RUNNING OUT OF AIR.

PHYSICAL POTENTIAL

Physical potential is a combination of **structural integration, physical intelligence** and *fitness*. Strong *internal action* of all your **quantum particles**, **atoms** and **molecules** create energy through connection to the energy of the **universe**. The **universe** does not need to consume

food to *manifest* energy. Relying on **food** as your only source of energy limits your ability to increase your **physical potential**.

It is important that your **structure** is **integrated** from the **bottom** to the **top**, **top** to the **bottom**, even from **left** to **right** and **right** to **left**, **front** to **back**, **back** to **front**, from the **inside out**, **outside in** and everything **in-between** *spaces*. The **upper** and **lower torsos** need to be strong within themselves and strong to each other. The **rib cage** needs to support the **lungs** so that **inhalation** and **exhalation** is even from both **lungs**. If you view the **brain** and divide it into **right** and **left hemispheres,** it appears as a **double torus**, each *balanced* in **polarity**, *receiving* and *transmitting* information from the **unified field**. Finally, remember that your **heart** was formed before your **CNS**, and its energetic field can be measured several feet away from your **body**. Tuning into your **heartbeat** calms the **CNS**. Just as a **mother's heartbeat** can *synchronize* with her **baby's heart** to sooth her **infant** from any distance, so too can *synchronization* with the *heartbeat* of the **earth** sooth all of **humanity**.

THE SEAT OF THE SOUL

The seat of the soul is the "seat of authority," and the center of the government of your *soul* is accessed through the *mind*, *will* and *emotional* function or dis-function, and is stimulated by the **CNS**, via *responses*, *re-flexes* and *reactions*. It is important that there is a strong connection from the **third eye** to the **sacrum** and **thymus** in all directions.

THIRD EYE

The *Ajna center* sits one finger's breadth above and between the **eyebrows**. The "third eye" is also often referred to as the Eye of Siva, Wisdom Eye, Divine Eye and All-Seeing Eye. *EU ... CHAKRAS, Pg. 118*

SACRUM

A "seat" is something on which the **base** of an object **rests**. The **sacrum** is the **seat** of the **brain**. People literally are sitting on their **physical intelligence** and need to keep it strong to *manifest* in the **third-dimensional plane** through the use of their **physical intelligence**.

THYMUS

The **thymus** is a pinkish grey **gland** composed of two **lobes**. It is located between the **heart** and the **sternum**. Its main function seems to be the *production* of **t-cells**. The **thymus** is most active during neo-natal and pre-adolescent periods. By early teens, the **thymus** begins to atrophy and **thymic stroma** is replaced by **adipose tissue**. The shrinking of the **thymus** is linked to susceptibility to cancer and *infection* in the **elderly**, and is adversely *affected* by "stress" which causes it to shrink and *produce* fewer **lymphocytes**. HIV and AIDS is an acquired **t-cell** immunodeficiency syndrome that specifically kills **CD-4+ t-cells**.

The **thymus** is part of what many refer to as the "seat of the soul." In the **physical body**, it links the **pineal gland** to **physical intelligence** and *intent* from the **heart** with and to the "language of dreams," connecting *insights* from the dream world with **physical reality**. One way to *activate* the **heart chakra** and the **thymus** is to lightly tap the **sternum** with your last three **fingers**. The **middle finger** (*spiritual finger*) is the "mediator" containing *Qi* from the **pericardium meridian**, sometimes referred to as the *heart governor* and/or the gateway to the *heart chakra*. It is part of the *yin* system in the **body**. The **fourth finger** (**ring finger**) is intellect, self-expression and the pathway of the *san jian channel* that is thought to control the *yang* energies as well as being the avenue for original *Qi*. The **left ring finger** is closest to the **physical heart**, signifying the bond of love, which is why in many **societies** it is the chosen **finger** for a **wedding ring**. The **right ring finger** is closer to the *spiritual heart*, and the **baby finger** stimulates communication with the **heart meridians**.

UNIVERSAL HEART FIELD

When you are plugged into the *cosmic heart*, your **physical manifestations** are in sync with the **earth** and with your **heart beat**. Your connection to the **heart field** truly is from the "bottom of your heart," opening portals to the *eighth chakra*, the *unified heart field*.

EGG OF LIFE

Primordial cells are the first *original eight cells* of life. All **cells** in the **body** are constantly being replaced over a lifetime, except the *first eight primordial cells* that remain *immortal*. It is *possible* to go back to the *original blueprint* and access pertinent information from the *primordial cells*. They sit within the **body** just above the **perineum** and *root chakra*, remaining in place until the *soul* leaves the **body**. In the first few hours after the **fusion** of an **egg** and **sperm**, the **pro-nucleus** of each forms the **vesica piscis** and continues to evolve into the **zygote**. The **zygote** then divides into **two, four** and **eight** *primordial cells*, referred to by ancients as the "Egg of Life." The *primordial cells* continue to develop into **sixteen**, **thirty two**, **sixty four** and so on, eventually forming a **torus**.

THE "GOOD NEWS" IS:

When the **universal heart field,** the **seat of the soul** and the **egg of life** are in sync with each other they support **physical potential** and strengthen the **relationship** of the components of the **body** to each other.

THE "BAD NEWS" IS:

There are many **physical**, **emotional**, **psychological**, **psychic** and **spiritual** factors that can influence **physical potential**. Much of the **problem** on a **physical** level is a lack of **tension**, causing **stagnation** throughout the **body**, **soul** and **spirit**, as **people** **try** to **relax** themselves out of **problems** instead of connecting with **creative solutions**.

NUGGET OF WIZDOM FROM THE VECTOR

ANYTHING MADE OF CELLS IS PERFECTED TO OBSERVE THE ENTIRE SYSTEM FROM LARGE TO SMALL AS A FEEDBACK MECHANISM. THIS ALLOWS HUMANS TO BECOME THE BEST VERSION OF THEMSELVES. EVERYONE CONTRIBUTES TO THE EVOLUTION OF EVERYTHING. ENERGETIC BLOCKS ARE RELEASED AND REPLACED WITH PERFECT BALANCE OF THE BODY, SOUL AND MIND.

PNS (PERIPHERAL NERVOUS SYSTEM)

The **peripheral nervous system** (**PNS**) consists of twelve pairs of **cranial nerves** and thirty-one pairs of **spinal nerves** that are tied into the **brain** and **spinal cord,** which connects with various **limbs** and **organs**. If we think of ourselves as a **binary computer**, then the **CNS** would be the **hard drive** and the **PNS** would be the software. The **spinal nerves** take impulses to and from the **spinal cord**. They are divided into two categories, the **autonomic** and the **somatic**.

SOMATIC NERVOUS SYSTEM (SONS)

The **somatic nervous system** handles voluntary control of **body movements**, and contains all the **neurons** connected to the **skeletal muscles** and the **skin**, thereby connecting external **sensory organs** through the **brain** to the **muscles**. It is composed of **sensory receptors** in the **skin** that send sensory information through the **dorsal root ganglia** of the **spine** to the **synapses** on **inter-neurons**; they in turn charge the **motor neurons** projecting out of the **ventral root ganglion**. This activates **muscle movement** to simple circuits such as the **patellar reflex** (the *reflex* that happens automatically when the **patella** is tapped on the **knee**) and withdrawal *reflexes*, such as removing your finger from a hot stove.

More complicated **motor *behavior*** is achieved through a central circuit involving millions of **neurons**. Sensory information arriving at the **spine** ascends through the **medulla, pons, mid-brain** and **thalamus** to the **somatosensory cortex** (the basis of intentional **voluntary *action***) where it is relayed to the **motor cortex**, back through the **thalamus, mid-brain, pons, medulla, spine** and to the **muscles**.

AUTONOMIC NERVOUS SYSTEM (ANS)

The **autonomic nervous system (ANS)** is a ***non-conscious*** involuntary control system that connects the **brain, spinal cord, organs** and **glands**. It regulates **heart rate, digestion, respiratory rate, salivation, perspiration, papillary dilation, energy utilization, temperature** and **sexual arousal**. The **ANS** sets the *balance* between *relaxation* and *tension* in the **body** to meet environmental demands through ongoing *behaviors* such as foraging for food, reproduction, and "emergency" reactions/responses for survival. It can be further divided into three more categories: the **sympathetic**, the **parasympathetic** and the **enteric nervous systems**.

SYMPATHETIC NERVOUS SYSTEM (SNS)

The **sympathetic nervous system (SNS)** stems from the **thoracic** and **lumbar** regions of the **spinal cord**. The **SNS** mobilizes resources for short-lived **survival *behaviors*,** such as predator avoidance and **reproduction,** by acting upon the **organs** and **glands**. It modifies **digestion, salivation, heart rate, blood pressure** and **oxygen *assimilation*** by directing **blood** towards the **lungs** and **muscles**.

PARASYMPATHETIC NERVOUS SYSTEM (PSNS)

The **parasympathetic nervous system (PSNS)** stems from the **cranial nerves** and the **sacral spinal cord**. It is responsible for maintaining and stabilizing bodily functions in everyday situations by managing the *acquisition, storage, digestion* and *assimilation* of energy in a balanced fashion.

THE ENDOCRINE GLANDS

The **endocrine glands** are a collection of involuntary **organs** that are regulated by the **ANS**, control the **hormone** levels of the **brain**, and the activity levels across a range of **organs** and **neurons**. The **endocrine glands** include the **hypothalamus**, **pituitary**, **parathyroid**, **pineal**, **thyroid**, **adrenals**, **pancreas**, **ovaries** and **testes**. *EU ... ENDOCRINE GLANDS, Pg. 207*

Smooth muscles are an involuntary **muscle group** that are controlled by the **ANS**, and which regulate **pupil dilation**, **uterine contractions**, **respiratory tract breath rate**, and **heart rate**.

Spinal injury in the **ANS** causes abnormalities in **autonomic** regulations that are not as obvious as when the **somatic nervous system** is injured. These irregularities include **temperature fluctuation**, poor **fluid retention** and distribution due to compromised **thirst signals,** loss of **bladder** and **bowels function**, irregular **breathing**, and fluctuation in the **heart rate** due to uneven **blood** *distribution*. These irregularities can be *permanent* or *transient*, but they can also *rebalance* systems to find a new *equilibrium*.

SOMATOTOPY

Somatotopy is the point-for-point correspondence of an area of the **body** to a specific point on the **CNS**. A point on the **primary somatosensory cortex**, the main sensory receptive area for sense of *touch*, corresponds to the **post-central gyrus**, a prominent structure in the **parietal lobe** of the **brain**. Areas that require fine control, **fingers**, **toes**, **feet**, **hands**, **penis**, **face**, etc., have larger portions of the **somatosensory cortex** than the more course control movements such as the rotation of the **trunk** of the **body**.

Skeletal muscles are **voluntary muscles** that are controlled by **the SNS**. They are one of the three major **muscle groups**, composed of **cells** that are attached to the **bones** by **tendon fibers**. Each of the **muscle groups** is arranged in opposing groups, such as the **biceps** and **triceps**, where the *activation* of each **muscle** is *balanced* by another **muscle** to ensure fluid movement.

When you are energetically strengthening the **PNS**, check whether or not a particular **nerve** *feels* weak compared to the others; if so, follow that weakness. Otherwise, start from the **bottom** of the **spine** and work your way up, strengthening and innervating all vital **organs**, **glands** and **systems** in the **body**, particularly the **lymphatic** and **vascular systems**. Strengthen the **pathways**, **biological** and **biochemical** *processes* between the specific **body parts**, the **PNS** and the **CNS**. Make sure it is strong in all three directions. Start at the **bottom** because if the foundation is weak, just as in a building, it causes the rest of the **structure** to compensate for those weaknesses. Strengthen the neuromuscular, **neurolymphatic**, **neurovascular**, **neuro-skeletal**, and **neuroendocrine systems** to the **lymphatic system**, and vice-versa. Elongate and expand *space* between the discs of the **vertebrae, top, bottom, left, right, front, back** in all directions. Clear **poisons, toxins, chemicals, petrols, medications, minerals, calcifications** from all parts of the **spine** and **spinal cord**. **Physical** *traumas* that are commonly held in the **spine** stem from **surgeries, birth, dentistry, chemicals, repetitive impact** and **strain**. *Traumas* can also be *psychological, mental, emotional, psychic* and *spiritual*. These can *affect* the entire body or specific systems such as the **nervous, skeletal, muscular, reproductive, urinary, respiratory, digestive** and **endocrine systems**. Remove the *memories, residuals* and *errant energies* that are creating blocks for the **body**, *soul* and *spirit*.

S1, S2, S3, S4, S5, SACRUM Hip Bones/ Buttocks

L5 LUMBAR Lower legs/ Ankles/ Feet
L4 LUMBAR Prostate Gland/ Lower Back Muscles/ Sciatic Nerve
L3 LUMBAR Sex Organs/ Uterus/ Bladder/ Knees
L2 LUMBAR Appendix, Abdomen, Upper Leg
L1 LUMBAR Large Intestine, Inguinal Rings
T12 THORACIC Small Intestine, Lymph Circulation
T11 THORACIC Kidneys, Uterus
T10 THORACIC Kidneys
T9 THORACIC Adrenal and Supra Renal Glands
T8 THORACIC Spleen
T7 THORACIC Pancreas/ Duodenum
T6 THORACIC Stomach
T5 THORACIC Liver/ Solar Plexus/ Blood
T4 THORACIC Gall Bladder, Common Duct
T3 THORACIC Lungs/ Bronchial Tubes/ Pleura/ Chest/ Breast
T2 THORACIC Heart/ Heart Valves & Coverings/ Coronary Arteries
T1 THORACIC Forearms/ Hands/ Wrists/ Fingers/ Esophagus/ Trachea
C7 CERVICAL Thyroid Gland, Bursae In Shoulder/ Elbows
C6 CERVICAL Neck Muscles/ Shoulders/ Toenails
C5 CERVICAL Vocal Cords/ Neck Glands/ Pharynx
C4 CERVICAL Nose/ Lips/ Mouth/ Eustachian Tube
C3 CERVICAL Cheeks/ Outer Ear/ Face Bones/ Teeth/ Tri-Facial Nerve
C2 CERVICAL Eyes/ Optic Nerves/ Auditory Nerves/ Sinus/ Mastoid Bones/ Tongue/ Forehead
C1 CERVICAL Blood to Head/ Pituitary Gland/ Scalp/ Facial Bones/ Brain/ Inner & Middle Ear

TWELVE PAIRS OF CRANIAL NERVES

The **cranial nerve ganglia** originates in the **CNS**, but the twelve **cranial nerve axons** extend beyond the **brain** as part of the **PNS**, with the exception of **cranial nerve II**, the **optic nerve**, which is a tract of the **diencephalon**. The **cranial nerves** transmit information from the **sense organs** to the **brain**. Some of the **nerves** control **muscles** while others are connected to the **glands** or **internal organs**. The **cranial nerves** are listed in **medical books** with r**oman numerals**.

Cranial nerves are classified a **sensory, motor** and **mixed nerves.** The **sensory nerves** are **I, II, VIII. Motor nerves** stimulate **muscle** and also contain **fibers** of **proprioception**, which is the *non-conscious perception* of movement and spatial orientation; their numbers are **III, IV, VI, XI, XII. Mixed nerves** are a combination of both **sensory** and **motor nerves**, and they are identified as **V, VII, IX, X.** Interestingly, their **sensory functions** are often unrelated to their **motor functions**.

I OLFACTORY NERVE (**Sensory**)

– controls the sense of smell
– stems from the **telencephalon (Limbic brain)**

II OPTIC NERVE (**Sensory**)

– provides visual impulses to the **retina**
– stems from the **diencephalon (Limbic brain)**

III OCULOMOTOR NERVE (**Motor**)

– controls **muscles** that raise the **eyelids,** move **eyes**, regulates the size of **pupils** and **focus** of the **lens** in the **eye**
– stems from the **mid-brain**

IV TROCHLEAR NERVE (**Motor**)

– innervates the **superior oblique muscles** to turn **eyeballs** down and laterally, and to **proprioception** (*non-conscious perception* of movement and spatial orientation)
– stems from the **mid-brain**

V TRIGEMINAL NERVE (**Mixed**)

– supplies **sensory fibers** to the **forehead, skin** of the **cheeks**, **chewing movements and muscle sense**
– stems from the **pons**

VI ABDUCENS NERVE (**Motor**)

– controls the **external rectus eye muscles** that move the **eye** and **eyelid** laterally
– stems from the posterior of the **pons**

VII FACIAL NERVE (**Mixed**)

– controls **facial expression,** *sensation* of **taste** at the **tip** of the **tongue, saliva***, secretion* of **tears, muscles** of the **neck**
– stems from the **pons** and runs lateral to the **vestibulocochlear nerve**

VIII VESTIBULOCOCHLEAR NERVE (**Sensory**)

– controls **hearing** and *balance*
– stems from the **pons** and runs lateral to the **facial nerve**

IX GLOSSOPHARYNGEAL NERVE (**Mixed**)

– controls the **carotid sinus, taste** and other *sensations* of the **tongue** and **soft palette,** *reflex* control of the **heart**, aids in *reflex* control of **blood pressure**
– stems from the **Medulla**

X VAGUS NERVE (**Mixed**)

– controls **swallowing, speaking, secretions** from the **glands** of the stomach, senses **aortic blood pressure**, slows **heart rate**

– stems from the **Medulla**

XI SPINAL ACCESSORY NERVE (**Motor**)

– controls the movement of **muscles** in the **shoulders, head, larynx** and **pharynx, swallowing** movements and **voice** *production*.
– stems from the side of the **Medulla**

XII HYPOGLOSSAL NERVE (**Motor**)

– controls movement of the **tongue**
– stems from the **Medulla**
This is a fun mnemonic (memory device) to empower you to remember which nerves are **sensory**, **motor** or **mixed**.

S = SENSORY NERVES
M = MOTOR NERVES
B = BOTH (MIXED)

SOME SAY MORE MONEY BUT MY BROTHER SAYS BIG BOOBS MATTER MORE

I Olfactory – **Some** – Sensory
II Optic – **Say** – Sensory
III Oculomotor – **More** – Motor
IV Trochlear – **Money** – Motor
V Trigeminal – **But** – Mixed
VI Abducens – **My** – Motor
VII Facial – **Brother** – Mixed
VIII Auditory/ Vestibulocochlear – **Says** – Sensory
IX Glossopharyngeal – **Big** – Mixed
X Vagus – **Boobs** – Mixed
XI Spinal Accessory – **Matter** – Motor
XII Hypoglossal – **More** – Motor

I find it helpful to picture the **PNS** as if it were a **tree**: the **branches** of the **tree** are the **cranial nerves,** the **roots** of the **tree** are the **ganglia** at the **sacrum**, and the **CNS** and **components** of the **spine** are the **trunk.** It is important to recognize that just as the **branches** and **roots** of a **tree** *nourish* each other, so do the **cranial nerves** and **PNS**. A weak **CNS** and **spine** are like a weak **trunk** on a **tree** that is more susceptible to the "winds of change." Always check for weaknesses between the three as they are intimately connected.

THE "GOOD NEWS" IS:

Everything that has ever happened to any one individual is documented and recorded in the **CNS** and **PNS**. If you follow the weaknesses from the weakest to the strongest, you can track down the root causes of **problems** in the **hard drive** and **soft-ware** of your **binary computer**.

THE "BAD NEWS" IS:

The complex nature and sensitivity of the **peripheral nervous system** makes it susceptible to even the slightest variation causing extremely varied symptoms. If people insist that the problems within the **PNS** are all **physical**, and therefore do not address the *non-physical* issues, then any **problems** within the **PNS** are more challenging to reverse.

NUGGET OF WIZDOM FROM THE VECTOR

FOLLOW THE WEAKNESSES AS THEY COME UP. THE REASONS WHY PARTICULAR NERVES ARE COMPROMISED ARE SIMILAR, BUT WHEN YOU TAKE INTO CONSIDERATION ALL THE PHYSICAL AND NON-PHYSICAL WEAKNESSES AS WELL AS THE ORDER IN WHICH THEY OCCURRED, EVERY PERSON HAS HIS OR HER OWN PATH AS TO HOW THEY ARRIVED AT THE STATE THEY ARE IN. IT BECOMES CLEAR THAT THE CONDITION OF EACH PERSON IS UNIQUE.

PREGNANCY

Pregnancy is divided into three sections of development called **trimesters**. The development of the **baby** is tracked by **gestational** age (ten months) and **fetal development** (nine months). A basic understanding of what is occurring for most **babies** and **mothers** at any particular stage of development during a **pregnancy** is helpful in establishing a baseline. The information provided in this book is referring to **gestational age**, as that is what most people are familiar with. If there are **twins** or multiple **babies**, shift the energy for each one individually and then expand the shifts to include the **mother**, the **father**, **grandparents**, **siblings**, extended family, as well as their *relationships* with each other.

THE PLACENTA

The **placenta** is an **organ** that develops in the **uterus** during pregnancy, attaching to the top or the side of its wall and connecting to the baby's **umbilical cord**. It provides **oxygen** and **nutrients** to the baby, while also removing **waste** from the baby's **blood**.

Conditions that **affect** the **placenta** can cause heavy **bleeding** in the mother and/or lack of **nutrition** and **oxygen** to the baby. **Placental abruption**, is when the **placenta** partially or fully separates from the **uterus** before delivery. **Placenta previa**, is a condition where the **placenta** partially or completely covers the **cervix**, most commonly in early pregnancy. It often resolves itself as the **uterus** grows. **Placenta accreta**, occurs when the **blood vessels** of the **placenta** grow too deeply into the **uterine wall**, which causes **vaginal bleeding** in the third trimester and severe **blood loss** after delivery.

The **placenta** is usually delivered within thirty to sixty minutes after the **baby**. Sometimes it gets trapped behind a partially closed **cervix** or does not detach from the **uterine wall**. This is called a **retained placenta**.

Strengthen the *relationship* of the **placenta** to the **uterus**, the **uterus** to the **placenta**, the **umbilical cord** to the **placenta** and the **placenta** to the **umbilical cord** for optimum *fitness*.

FIRST TRIMESTER

In the **first trimester** the building blocks of the **baby's structure** and **body systems** are formed. This is a delicate process, and **miscarriages** are more likely to occur in this **trimester** if there are underlying **physical** and *non-physical* weaknesses that are not being addressed.

WEEK ONE

The first week of **pregnancy** is considered to begin before you even conceive, on the first day of your last **menstrual period**. *EU ... MENSTRUATION, Pg. 327*

WEEK TWO

Most women begin the process of **ovulation** two weeks after the first day of their **menstrual cycle**, when **follicle-stimulating hormone** (**FSH**) begins **ovum** (**egg**) *production*. Two other **hormones**, **estrogen** and **luteinizing hormone** are also *produced*. The **uterine lining** thickens as the **egg** matures and is about to be released into the **fallopian tubes**. **Fertilization** occurs and **gender** is determined in the moment when the **sperm** penetrates the **egg**. There are forty-six **chromosomes** in the **genetic** formula, two of which are responsible for determining the **gender** of the baby. The **mother** only has **X chromosomes**, whereas the **father** has **X** and **Y chromosomes**. If the **sperm** that fertilizes the **egg** is an **X** the **baby** will be **female**, and if it is **Y** he will be **male**.

FERTILIZATION

The **sperm** is released during **ejaculation** and swims through the **vagina** and **uterus** to the **fallopian tubes** to hook up with an **oocyte** (**egg cell**). **Enzymes** in the **acrosome**, at the head of the **sperm** penetrate two layers of the **oocyte**, the **outer corona radiata** and **zona** pellucida. The **nuclei** of what is a **haploid cell** fuses together to form a **diploid cell** known as a **zygote** that stimulates **cell** division to produce an **embryo**. Recently it was discovered that some **women** have **Y chromosome** gene sequences in their **blood**. This is understandable if it is a **woman** who has given birth to a **son** in the *past*, however, many of these **women** have not. The **physical** and *non-physical* causes of **microchimerism** occurs when **cells** from the **fetuses** of previous **pregnancies** remain in the **blood** and **organs** of a **woman's body**, including those of **pregnancies** that end in **abortion** and **miscarriage**, from *known* and *unknown pregnancies*, vanished **male twins** and also through the act of **sexual intercourse** alone, because of the potential for unborn **descendants**.

Clear any *karmic* ties beginning with the **mother** to the **baby** and the **baby** back to the **mother**, **baby** to the **father** and **father** back to the **baby**, then a triad between the three, expanding out to **grandparents**, **great-grandparents**, **siblings** and **descendants** up and down both family lines. It is much more efficient to clear the *limiting effects* before the **baby** is conceived, but this is rarely the case.

WEEK THREE

The **zygote** begins to transform into a **cluster** called a **blastocyst** by dividing and redividing into a ball of **cells** the size of a grain of sand. It travels from the **fallopian tube** to the **uterus**. Some women are aware of **implantation bleeding**, which occurs **six** to **fourteen** days after **conception** when the **blastocyst** attaches to the **uterine wall**. **Women** who notice this *experience* commonly have spotting or sensations of what feels like a full-on period. At this point many **women** also *experience* a rise in **body temperature**, **food cravings** and **nausea**, often referred to as "morning sickness," caused by a rise in **estrogen** and **progesterone**. The "sense of smell" is heightened along with concerns of "survival" from a stimulated **base chakra**. Clear any *emotional* and *psychological* weaknesses of having another being inside of the **mother** by strengthening the *internal* and *external boundaries*.

WEEK FOUR

Once the **blastocyst** attaches to the **uterus**, the cluster of **cells** divides into two parts, an **embryo** and a **placenta**, and begins to develop an **amniotic sac** around it. At this stage the **embryo** appears to be made up of three layers. The innermost layer is the **endoderm** that eventually becomes the

digestive system, liver and **lungs**, and the outer layer, the **ectoderm**, makes up the **nervous system, skin, hair** and **eyes**. The layer in-between, the **mesoderm**, includes the **heart, sex organs, bones, kidneys** and **muscles**. The **placenta** encapsulates the **embryo**, delivering **nutrients** and eliminating **waste** products. At this point most women have skipped a period and become "in doctor-inated" through **pregnancy tests**.

WEEK FIVE

In the fifth week the **heart** begins to beat and the **circulatory system, spinal cord** and **tail** begin to develop. The **umbilical cord** and **placenta** are actively providing **nutrition** and clearing **waste** from the **embryo**. It is at about this time that the **pregnancy** becomes *consciously* accepted by the **mother** and sometimes by the **father**. **Women** tend to be more aware of the implications of **pregnancy** on the *conscious* level because of the *changes* taking place in their **physical body**.

Clear any *fears* of survival from the *sub-conscious mind* around **finances, career, purpose** and *karmas* with **employers, employees, medical** and **government institutions**, etc., as well as from the *spiritual consequences* of giving birth to a **baby** held in the *un-conscious mind*.

WEEK SIX

By now the **circulatory system** is fully functioning with a **heart beat** pulsing at one hundred to one hundred sixty beats per minute. **Buds** are developing that will eventually grow into **arms** and **legs** and the **pituitary gland** is functioning to aid in the formation of the **brain, muscles** and **bones**. The **eyes, nose, mouth** and **ears** are starting to form, and the **embryo** is about a quarter of an inch in length.

WEEK SEVEN

The **brain** is now rapidly developing along with the **heart**, the **kidneys**, the **tongue**, and the continued development of the **arms** and **legs**. Even though the **embryo** is only about a half an inch in length, many women experience pressure on their **bladder** due to the expansion of the **uterus** and **hormonal** influences, in particular of **chorionic gonadotropin (hCG)** that stimulates **blood flow** to the **pelvis** and strengthens the **placenta**.

WEEK EIGHT

The **embryo** is now almost three quarters of an inch in length. Webbed **fingers** and **toes**, as well as **eyelids**, the tip of the **nose** and the **upper**

lip are forming along with an increase in **brain cells** that are beginning to route **neural pathways** and the airways of the **respiratory system**.

Many moms experience worry regarding their **pregnancy** as monitoring of the progress of the **pregnancy** begins in earnest now. They often attend their first **pre-natal checkup** at this time or within the next couple of weeks. Concerns about **fetal development** increase. Childhood **illnesses** become a concern and in large part are instigated by mothers who buy into the *limiting beliefs* of the *negative aspects* of raising children instead of using their *intuition* to resolve **problems** in a natural progression.

Continue to resolve *karmas* with any **medical personnel** and test for weaknesses that arise with each and every appointment with the **doctors**. Take into consideration the **receptionists, nurses, mid-wives**, other **patients, specialists** and **lab technicians**. Also check for weaknesses with **medical procedures**.

WEEK NINE

By the ninth week the **embryo** is considered a **fetus**. The **tail** is no longer physically present; however, energetically, it has a major *effect* on the baby's **physical potential** that continues throughout its entire life. The **eyes** are fully formed but the **eyelids** will remain fused until the twenty-seventh week. The **heart** has four distinct **chambers**, and **teeth** and **external reproductive organs** are beginning to form.

At this time **pregnancy hormones** *affect* women's **breasts** by causing rapid growth and increased *sensitivity*. Many women experience heightened **desire** for sexual activity due to stimulation from the **breasts** and increased **blood flow** to the **pelvis**, while other women *experience* the exact opposite. Strengthen both **partners** to be strong to the **changes** occurring in the woman's **body**.

WEEK TEN

Week ten is considered the first week of the baby's **fetal development**. The **tissues** and **organs** are rapidly developing along with the **arms, legs, hands, feet** and **joints**. **Nail-beds** are developing and **fingers** and **toes** are no longer webbed. Development of the **frontal lobe** of the **brain** is apparent. There is a lot of movement from the **fetus** that typically is not yet noticed by the mother. Many women also *experience* more episodes of "morning sickness." Strengthen the mother to her **daily routine**, the *changes* that are occurring in her **body**, and clear *negative* *associations* and concerns with vomit and vomiting. Purging is actually a very efficient way to release weaknesses of both the **physical** and *non-physical energies*. *EU ... DAILY ROUTINE, Pg. 159*

WEEK ELEVEN

At this point, the **fetus** is very active and busy exercising its limbs, although mothers are usually not aware of it yet. The **nasal passages** and **diaphragm** are taking shape and the **bones** and **gums** are getting stronger.

WEEK TWELVE

The **fetus** is now about two inches long and moves up from the **pelvis** into the **lower abdomen**. The **digestive system**, **kidneys** and **bladder** are functional and the baby is preparing for eating by making sucking motions. The **pituitary gland** is producing **hormones** and the **bone marrow is** beginning to make **white blood cells**.

WEEK THIRTEEN

In the thirteenth week the **fetus** develops **vocal chords** and **veins**.

SECOND TRIMESTER

In the **second trimester** the chances of **miscarriage** drop, and many women begin to feel some relief from the **nausea** and **exhaustion** because the development of the **placenta** is complete and requires less energy from the woman's **body**. It is not uncommon for mothers to now *experience* **acid reflux** due to **hormones** that *relax* the **esophageal sphincter** and the pressure from the growing **uterus** on the **stomach**. *EU ... EATING, Pg. 202*

In the **second** and **third trimesters** it becomes increasingly apparent that a woman is **pregnant**, as the average woman gains approximately one pound per week in the **second** and **third trimesters** as opposed to the three to five pounds she gained during the entire **first trimester**. The words **fetus** and **baby** become somewhat interchangeable in the **second trimester**, depending on the point of view of the people involved.

WEEK FOURTEEN

The **fetus** is now making **facial expressions** and the **palates** of the **roof** of the **mouth** are fully formed. The **kidneys** and **liver** are producing **bile** and **urine,** the **spleen is** forming **red blood cells**, and the **meconium** (**first stool**) is forming in the **large intestine**.

WEEK FIFTEEN

Many women will *experience* flutters as the **skeleton** matures and the **fetus** has **longer limbs**. The **hairline**, **eyebrows** and a fine layer of very soft hair called **lanugo** protects the skin and provides insulation. The **auditory bones** are beginning to develop, although the **fetus** cannot **hear** yet.

There are many referred weaknesses from the **oral cavity** to the **pelvic cavity** and, combined with **hormonal** changes from the **pregnancy**, that can cause *inflammation* in the **gums** of the mother. Strengthen the **gums** to the **ovaries** of the mom and also to the **ovaries** (**testicles**) of the **fetus** and vice-versa. Check for unresolved *karma* with **dentists**.

WEEK SIXTEEN

At sixteen weeks most **fetuses** are about four and a half inches long and a period of rapid growth is about to begin during which they double in size within the next four weeks. The **heart** is pumping about twenty-five quarts of **blood**, and the **face** is taking on its individual characteristics. There is now about fifty percent more **blood** being *cycled* through the **circulatory system** between the **mother** and the **fetus**.

WEEK SEVENTEEN

The **cartilage** that makes up the **skeleton** is now hardening into **bone**, and the **auditory bones** are now mature enough for the **fetus** to **hear**. The **fetus** is also gaining **adipose tissue** that is fleshing out the **body**. The **sinus cavity** and the **bone structure** of the **face** is beginning to make up its features and the mother is often feeling congestion in her **nasal passages** as a result of **pregnancy hormones** that cause *inflammation*.

WEEK EIGHTEEN

The **fetus** is now about six inches in length. The **myelin** of the **nervous system** is being formed along with the **reproductive organs** and **genitalia**. Many women *experience* dizziness from the rapid increase of **blood flow,** and may notice **lower back pain** as the physical center of gravity shifts to accommodate the growing **uterus,** and **pregnancy hormones** cause the **joints** in the **body** to become looser to prepare the **hips** for **delivery**.

WEEK NINETEEN

The **skin** of the **fetus** is now developing a **waxy substance** called **vernix caseosa** to protect the delicate **skin** from the **amniotic fluid**. The **ligaments** surrounding the **uterus** are beginning to stretch causing "round ligament pain" for many mothers in the **groin**, **pelvic area** and lower **abdomen**.

WEEK TWENTY

Many women experience *cramping* in the **legs** around the twentieth week for many reasons, such as the increasing weight of the **baby** and **amniotic fluid**, changes in **blood circulation** due to the high increase in **blood**, and too much *relaxation* from the combined *changes* of all the **systems** which puts pressure on the **nerves** and **blood vessels** of the **legs**.

Strengthen the **upper** and **lower torsos** to be even from **bottom** to **top** and **top** to **bottom**. Also strengthen the **structure** throughout the **body** to be *centered*, *stable* and *balanced* in all directions. *Cramping* can be alleviated by tensing the **brain**, **legs** and **spine** to speed up the **CNS**. On an *emotional* and *psychological* level, many mothers may be feeling a lot of *pressure* from *relationships* at **work** and at **home** regarding **financial concerns** from both the **parents**, **employers** and **fellow workers** regarding her **pregnant body** and **maternity leave**. Strengthen her to the "lightness of being" and clear any *negative associations* with her **mother**, **mother-in-law**, being a **mother**, **mothering**, etc.

WEEK TWENTY-ONE

During the first half of the **pregnancy**, the many internal *changes* in a woman's **body** occur to accommodate the growth of the baby and the **placenta**. In the **last half** of the **pregnancy** the *changes* are externally noticeable and the reality of the **baby** becomes very apparent to the **mother** and to those around her. Some women experience **stretch marks** from the rapid growth, **varicose veins,** and dark patches from excessive **pigment** called **melasma** on the **face** and on other parts of the **body** that have been exposed to the **sun**. Many of these issues are considered to be **genetic**; however it is much more likely they are **ancestral**, meaning that the *fears* and *concerns* about the *negative effects* of **pregnancy** on the **physical body** held by the **woman** and her **partner** are shared by **both** their **ancestors** and then passed down to her. The human **body** is very resilient and will easily return to **homeostasis** once these *concerns* are resolved.

WEEK TWENTY-TWO

By the twenty-second week of **pregnancy**, the baby's **face** is almost fully formed with **lips, eyebrows** and **eyes**, although the **color** of the **eyes** is not apparent yet. The **lanugo** that protects the baby's **skin** is now thicker. **Hormones** and **cortisone** also appear to thicken the hair on the **mother's head** because there is less **hair loss** during **pregnancy**. This also *affects* **facial hair** and **hair** on the **arms** and **legs** until about **six months** after *delivery* of the **baby**.

WEEK TWENTY-THREE

At this point the baby's **hearing** is fully functional. Listening to **music** and **dancing** can *stimulate* the **baby** as well as *soothe* it. The **face** is almost fully formed, as are the **genitals**; if it is a **girl**, she already has **eggs** of her own in place.

Since many women retain excess water in their **ankles** and **feet**, strengthen evenness of the **circulatory system** from the **lower** to the **upper torso**, and strengthen the **density** and **bio-chemistry** of the **blood** to be at optimum potential to support the **hearts** of both the **mother** and the **baby**.

WEEK TWENTY-FOUR

Most babies are about twelve inches long and gain about six ounces a week at this time. The **alveoli** in the **lungs** are maturing in preparation for the baby's first **breath**. It is common for many women to experience *burning*, *itching*, *sensitivity* to **light**, *excessive tearing*, etc., due to **hormones**. Strengthen *tension* in the **eyes** for optimum **hydration** and **oxygenation**.

WEEK TWENTY-FIVE

Capillaries in the **lungs** and throughout the **baby's body** are forming, and the **nostrils** are opening in preparation for the first breath outside of the **womb**. Many mothers are beginning to feel restrictions in their own **breathing** due to the mounting pressure on the **diaphragm**, particularly when they are lying down and sleeping. It is normal to notice a faster heart rate due to the excess **blood** being pumped through the **body**. Sleeping on the **left side** eases the strain on the **liver** and **kidneys** and stimulates **blood flow** to the **uterus**.

WEEK TWENTY-SIX

The baby is now testing out the *coordination* of its rapidly developing **nervous system** by moving a lot, especially the **arms** and **legs**. The **eyelids** are still fused, but the baby can *perceive* light and dark through the mother's belly.

WEEK TWENTY-SEVEN

On average, the baby now weighs about two pounds and is practicing breathing by taking in small amounts of **amniotic fluid** to develop its **lungs**. The baby is also establishing the beginnings of a **sleep** *cycle* by drifting off to **sleep** and waking up at regular intervals.

THIRD TRIMESTER

In the **third trimester** the baby is very close to full development and is basically gaining weight and fine-tuning the **systems** of the **body**.

WEEK TWENTY-EIGHT

At the beginning of the **last trimester**, most babies are approximately two and a half pounds and, because of their rapidly advancing **brain**, are now able to dream. Many women experience **hemorrhoids** and **lower back pain** along with **sciatica** due to a combination of increased **blood flow**, **hormones** and the increased pressure on the **sciatic nerves** as the **uterus expands**. On a *non-physical* level women are often weak to "bending over backwards" to please people.

WEEK TWENTY-NINE

The baby's **skeleton** is getting stronger and the **skull** is increasing in size to accommodate advanced **brain** development.

WEEK THIRTY

Although the **baby** is only on average about three pounds now, the combination of the added weight of the growing **uterus**, the **amniotic fluid** and the **weight gain** of the mother herself, can cause stress on the **lower torso**. Use the **energetic tail** to strengthen *balance*, creating a tripod to balance the weight. **EU ... TAIL, Pg. 496*

It is common for women to *experience* **foot pain** and some women even need to increase the size of their footwear because of the *expansion* of the metatarsals. This is due to carrying extra **weight** while under the influence of the **hormones** that soften **joints** and **ligaments** to prepare the **pelvis** for **birth**.

Strengthen any weaknesses in the **structure** of the **toes**, **feet**, **ankles** and any referred weaknesses from and to the **fingers**, **hands**, **wrists** in the mother and in the baby. Strengthen both to the *speed* the **earth** is traveling at and the **earth** to the *speed* that they are at.

WEEK THIRTY-ONE

It is common for women to feel *contractions* of the **uterus** called **Braxton Hicks contractions** during the **last trimester** of **pregnancy**. These *contractions* are nature's way of preparing the **mother** and the **baby** for **birth**, and are opportunities to train the *mind* and **body** to support *ease* in **birth** and **delivery**. Many women have *fears* that are passed down from their **mothers,** and the *collective fear* of **mothers** in **general** around the **pain** of childbirth. Women *sabotage* each other with stories that they are all too happy to share regarding the **pain** and *traumas* of childbirth. Most women are unaware that a good proportion of women actually achieve **orgasm** during **birth**. The *misrepresentation* of information regarding "labour and delivery" and the trend towards treating birth as a **disease** rather than a natural process that requires *fitness*, causes a lot of unnecessary *fear*. Laying a woman flat on her **back** with her **legs** up in the air defies the laws of gravity and is actually for the convenience of the **medical community**. **Squatting** is the natural position that *accommodates* an *easy* **birth**. Women are better off if they consider the **birth** as a "sporting event" they are **physically** training for, just as they would if they were going to run a marathon. A common weakness for **birth** is not wanting to *feel* "out of control." Clear *karmas*, *miasmas* and *negative emotions* that stem from the **mother**, **father**, **baby**, **grandparents** and the **medical community** regarding **birth**.

WEEK THIRTY-TWO

By the thirty-second week, the baby is almost fully developed and is busy fine-tuning its **swallowing**, **sucking** and **breathing skills**. The baby weighs approximately four pounds now, and is about sixteen inches in length.

WEEK THIRTY-THREE

The baby's **bones** are becoming less *flexible* with the exception of the **palates** of the **skull** that remain unfused to *accommodate* travel through the **birth canal**. Around this time the **uterus** shifts and puts even more pressure on the **diaphragm**. It is common for women to compensate when they feel shortness of breath by using the **chest** and **neck muscles**. Strengthen evenness of structure **front** to **back**, **side** to **side**, and **top** to **bottom** to alleviate stress on the **upper torso**.

WEEK THIRTY-FOUR

Babies born between the thirty-fourth and thirty-seventh week are considered **premature**; however, they most often are perfectly *healthy*. The woman's **breasts** are now producing **colostrum** in preparation for breastfeeding.

WEEK THIRTY-FIVE

The baby's **kidneys** are now fully mature and, if the baby is a **male**, his **testicles** are descending into the **scrotum**.

WEEK THIRTY-SIX

The average baby at thirty-six weeks weighs about six pounds and is shedding the **vernix caseosa** from the **skin**. Babies often begin turning their head towards the **birth canal** in preparation for **birth**. If the baby does not turn on its own, health providers try to coax the baby into position using a procedure called **external cephalic version** (**ECV**). This is much more successful if underlying energetic weaknesses are addressed. There may still be residual weaknesses to giving **birth** for the **baby** and the **mother**, *fears* about **caesarian section**, *karma* with the **medical system**, weaknesses to "head first" positions, etc. Strengthen the **placenta** to the **uterine wall** before and after an attempt to turn the **baby**.

WEEK THIRTY-SEVEN

At week thirty-seven the **pregnancy** is considered full term and delivery is imminent. A **pregnancy** is not considered to be overdue until the forty-second week.

At one point, an **episiotomy**, a **procedure** where the **skin** and **tissues** between the **anus** and **vagina** are cut in an attempt to prevent tearing and ripping, was performed by doctors on a regular basis in **vaginal births**. Recent studies now show that the **procedure** causes increased **tearing**, **sphincter dysfunction**, **painful sex** and **incontinence**. Strengthen *fitness* of the **perineum**, in particular the *flexibility* of the **sphincter muscles**.

Clear any **need** to be **cut**, **cutting** others and being **cut** by others and any *karma* with the *medical establishment* as well as *anger* for and from **men**. Perineal

massage at this time, can be very beneficial in preparing the **skin, muscles** and **tissues** of the **perineum** to stretch and *accommodate* the **baby**.

WEEKS THIRTY-EIGHT TO FORTY

The baby now has very little room to move in utero and **delivery** is imminent. One of the first signs of preparation for **delivery** is a woman's exaggerated *want* to "nest." Cleaning and organizing house is almost always a sign that a woman is ready for *change*, and especially so when she is **pregnant**.

There is a **mucous plug** that prevents **pathogens** from invading the **uterus**. When the **plug** lets go, it is often referred to as "bloody show" and can happen weeks before the actual **delivery**, as the **cervix** begins to thin in preparation for **birth**. Some women do not notice when the **plug** releases and for others it is very apparent. A more obvious sign that **delivery** is very near is when the **amniotic sac** breaks and lets go of the **amniotic fluid** leaving no doubt that the **birthing** *process* has begun. There are many factors that come into play regarding the **time, date** and **location** of a **baby's birth**. It is not uncommon for babies to be born sooner or later than their "due date" because of *astrological* and *numerical influences*. It is also very common for babies to be **conceived** on specific significant **dates** that pertain to the **mother** and **father**, such as **birthdays**.

TRYING TO GET PREGNANT

Many people take for granted that at some point they will get married and raise a family, but then they find themselves "trying to get pregnant" without success. The *vibration* attracts the outcome. *Fear* of getting pregnant *attracts unwanted* pregnancy. *Fear* of not being able to get **pregnant** leads to **problems** with **fertility**. It is a not an uncommon occurrence for couples that **try** and **try** to get pregnant to conceive only after they decide to **quit trying**. This is because *neutrality* breeds success.

There can be many *non-physical* underlying weaknesses that can cause obstacles to "getting pregnant." Using the word "trying" automatically weakens the situation. Anytime you are **trying** to do something, you are **not doing it**. People who are *struggling* to get **pregnant** are generally *struggling* with *fear* and **desire**: they *consciously believe* that they have a **desire** to have a **baby**, but *fears* that are held in their *sub-conscious* and *un-conscious mind* are not in *alignment* with the **goal**. Women who have **miscarriages** and/or **abortions** are strong to "getting pregnant," but are not strong to "having a baby." Strengthen them to both **goals**. There are often *associated* and *accumulated karmas* and weaknesses to "labour and delivery" from *spiritually*, *psychically*, *emotionally* and *mentally limiting beliefs* around **birth** and **dying**.

Some women are only able to successfully bring either **girls** or **boys** into the world, but not both. Many have weaknesses to **men** in general, and therefore bringing more **men** into the world feeds into their *fears* of **sons** having to go to battle and being killed in wars, etc. Other women may be members of **cultures, religions** and **societies** that devalue the worth of females; throughout history women have been persecuted and even sentenced to death for producing **girls** instead of boys.

Women and men often confuse "marriage material" with "father or mother material," and make the assumption that both always go together in a neat package. **Couples** can be strong to being together as **husband** and **wife**, **common-law partners**, etc., but no matter how beautiful the *relationship* seems to be, it does not mean that they are strong to having children together. Generally when a man has *balanced* fairness, self-respect and respect for others, a woman will feel safe to co-create babies with him.

On a physical level there are often slight **twists** or **tilts** to the **pelvis** and **uterus**. Correct any **structural** weaknesses in the **uterus** and **pelvic floor** as well as the *relationship* of the fertilized **egg** to the **uterine wall**. Clear any **toxins**, **poisons, chemicals, medications, parasites**, *traumas*, etc. held in the **DNA** up and down the family line. If **inter-uterine insemination (IUI)**, **sperm donation** or **surrogates** are involved, be sure to clear any weaknesses or *karmas* with the **biological parents** and their **ancestors** and other **descendants**, the **doctors, lab technicians**, *processes*, **procedures**, etc.; as well, strengthen the benefit of **fertility drugs** and spin so-called *side-effects* out to *black wholes*.

RESULTS:

"My twin pregnancy was diagnosed as monoamniotic monochorionic around 12 weeks. This is a very high risk pregnancy with a 50% chance of survival until the babies reach viability. This diagnosis was completely devastating for my husband and me.

"Colette worked on the babies, on me, and on my husband. She made the babies and me stronger to each other, made me strong to my new role as a mother, and, most importantly, taught me not to worry about the pregnancy. One of the most powerful things she said to me was, "If a mother cannot see a bright future for her children, then who can?"

"My husband had lost the use of his right arm due to a work accident that occurred in 2005. He was extremely worried about not being able to hold his little girls. After one session, he was able to remove his brace and move his fingers. By the time the girls were born a month later, he had gone from wearing a brace all the time to not needing it at all. He is now able to workout on a regular basis and can carry both girls at the same time! His doctor cannot explain why or how the arm started working again, but he told my husband to keep doing what he was doing because it's working.

"Colette continued to work on our family throughout the pregnancy. They were born at 32 weeks and 5 days gestation. The doctors had prepared us for 3 pound babies who may have a great deal of trouble breathing and feeding. The babies who came out were 4lbs, 3oz and 4lbs, 9oz; they needed oxygen for only a few days and have always been very enthusiastic eaters. Our neonatologist had gone to great lengths preparing himself and his staff for all the complications that small premature twins can have; he did not prepare anyone for my big, noisy babies! The nurses commented more than once that these girls didn't have any of the troubles that they were expected to have. I very much believe that without the energy work, they would not have been as strong and healthy as they are. We have had no complications from their prematurity and it has in no way slowed them down. At every checkup with their pediatrician, we had to remind her that they are premature; when they had their one-year checkup, she said she doesn't even consider them preemies anymore. They are big, active babies who are engaged, happy and interested in everything. They are currently working on walking and enjoy learning sign language with mommy, wagon rides, and cuddling their stuffed bears."

Laura Mack, Regina

THE "GOOD NEWS" IS:

Babies can be energetically shifted in the **womb**, eliminating many problems prior to their entrance into the world by checking for **physical** and ***non-physical*** weaknesses, and energetically ***re-aligning*** them to optimum potential.

THE "BAD NEWS" IS:

Many **babies** who make their entrance into the third-dimensional world have major challenges to overcome, challenges that could have been cleared prior to their arrival. Most people focus on **nutrition**. **Structure** is more important than **bio-chemistry** because without *balanced* **structure** the **systems** cannot distribute **nutrients** efficiently.

NUGGET OF WIZDOM FROM THE VECTOR

THE PRIMARY WEAKNESS FOR CHILDREN IS A MOTHER'S WORRY. IF A MOTHER CANNOT SEE HER CHILDREN WITH A BRILLIANT FUTURE, WHO WILL?

PROCRASTINATION

Many people think about **procrastination** as an inability to make *choices* about important **goals**. However, **procrastination** is a *choice*. It is a *choice* to not take *action* on "important projects" while participating in other **projects** or *activities* that are less crucial but more appealing. **Procrastination** can also be defined as **inefficient time management** between when a person *commits* to a project and intends to complete it and when they actually get around to doing it.

There are several reasons why a person is inclined to **procrastinate**. If you tune into each reason separately instead of clumping them all together, you can pinpoint the main weakness and eliminate the *emotional re-actions* to the triggers. Many of the reasons for **procrastination** come from *mixed* and *combined emotions* in the *sub-conscious mind* as witnesses to how **parents** and **grandparents behaved** when faced with unpleasant tasks and their style of parenting to get their children to do chores, etc.

A common excuse for putting things off is the *feeling* of not being *ready* to perform something **perfectly**. Many people tell themselves that they need to "get ready" before they **start**. The **problem** is that their sense of what they *want* to **do** is so removed from the **end product** that they are discouraged from **starting**. A lot of people who *believe* they have a weakness to **beginning** something are really weak to **ending** something and vice-versa. Some people like the *excitement* of **starting** a new project, but it already *feels* old once they have given it any real *thought*, so they are already "bored" before they **begin**. To complete **projects** with ease, it is necessary to be strong to consistent steps of *action* to see the project through, and to avoid *overwhelm*. It is empowering to break the project down into manageable portions that also have a **beginning**, **center** and **end**.

Procrastinators are often **perfectionists** in disguise who have the *attitude* that "if you cannot do something perfectly don't do it at all." This **all** or **nothing** *attitude* is a *karmic space* that many people have along with "the need to be right." **Past**, **present** and **future** stories of **success** and **failure** need to be strong to the task at hand and to increments of improvement.

Many people rely on a **list** of **affirmations** to **motivate** themselves without realizing that a list is in itself is a very powerful **affirmation**, especially once everything that is written on it is crossed off. When **affirmations** and **actions** are in conflict, **action** will be the determining factor for **success** and completion of **goals**.

Another common problem that many people share is rating work performance according to how much **effort** and **struggle** they put into it rather than how efficiently they get the "job" done. Many of the underlying weaknesses come from excessive **emotional re-actions** to **limiting beliefs** that achievement is **challenging** and never **easy**, and from the **attitude** of "If it is not worth **suffering** for it is not worth doing." This **attitude** erodes every minute of the **daily routine**. When you are strong to your **daily routine**, the **job** is done with **purpose**. It is accomplished efficiently and quickly, leaving more time for **play**.

THE "GOOD NEWS" IS:

Many **procrastination** issues come from a **fear** of achieving great **success**. The reasons for **procrastination** are usually **external forces** that weaken their **internal boundaries**. **Multiple personalities** are often involved. When these **psychic energies** are cleared, you are much more likely to step into your **authentic self** and achieve your **authentic desires**.

THE "BAD NEWS" IS:

Procrastination does not just weaken **careers**, it limits **fulfilling** exploration in all **aspects** of a person's life.

NUGGET OF WIZDOM FROM THE VECTOR

YOU ARE NOT EFFECTIVE IF IT IS NECESSARY TO HAVE A BOARD MEETING WITH YOURSELF TO MAKE A DECISION. DON'T PROCRASTINATE … SEND ERRANT ENERGIES ON THEIR WAY!

PROSPERITY

Society and **collective influences** have created a minefield of **limiting beliefs** and **expectations** around **money**. Many **limiting beliefs** held by individuals do not arise from their own personal **experiences**, but from inaccurate **perceptions** and **fears** regarding their **ancestors'** and **descendants' financial** *struggles* in the *past*, *present* and *future*. **Fears** of retribution for non-compliance with **authority figures**, not playing by the **rules**, *judgement* and *criticism* from **educational experiences** and "measuring up" to the standards of the *collective consciousness* are common weaknesses that diminish **finances**. The old paradigm of "survival of the fittest" creates a competitive atmosphere where *abundance* is something that has to be created rather than accessed. The *perception* is that there is not enough to "go around" and that if someone has something another person *wants*, they have to compete for it.

If you *perceive* money as if it were an ocean, then the **money** *flows* in with every **wave** and the *action* of sending **money** out automatically *stimulates* bringing **money** in. The *energy* is **always** there. It is a matter of tapping into the *energy* of **money** and allowing yourself to "let it go." Holding onto money with a "death grip" kills this *energy*. Universal "law" dictates that what you **lose** will be balanced out by what you **gain**. When you are strong to "losing everything," you are strong to "gaining everything." It becomes a *choice*. Strengthen yourself when you *feel* weak to **money** triggers **before** you take *action*, so that you make the best **financial** *choices* in the moment.

There is no such thing as "lost money;" just as each wave is made up of different drops of **water**, so is each wave of money made up of different **dollars**. If you **lose money** in one situation, you can always replenish it through another. Insisting that every time you invest **money** it has to return to you in the exact same **dollars** that you put out is like requiring the ocean to create waves from the exact same drops of **water**. The easiest way to generate **finances** is by providing benefit to others. The more you benefit others, the more that benefit is returned to you as long as you are strong to *receiving* it. *EU ... GIVE AND TAKE, Pg. 266*

Although the ocean **loses** water through evaporation, the evaporation generates clouds that produce more water through precipitation. It is a useless waste of energy to try to control the **financial** weather; it is much more productive to take *action* by providing **products**, **services** and **information** that benefits others. **Trying** to control the *flow* of **finances** is like expecting the weather patterns to revolve around your schedule. The universe is not "conspiring against people" any more than the weather conspires against a person if it rains while a person is on holiday. If the weather is being altered (perhaps by **chemtrails**) that is a **man-made** condition that has been built in to the **system** to benefit **specific** people at the **exclusion** of others. Delete any *karma* of causing other people to have instability in their **finances** and *negative life experiences* of being **enslaved** by or **enslaving** others. *EU ... KARMA, Pg. 302*

Many **problems** that appear to be about **money** are actually about weaknesses around *relationships*. Strengthen all *relationships* with **clients** and **businesses** you are in competition with by deleting *karma* of **stealing**, being **stolen** from, relying on others for **money** and others relying on you for **money**. Strengthen partnerships for **yourself**, your **ancestors** and **descendants**. In particular, clear issues around **marriage** and **divorce** that create disharmony in all *relationships*, especially for **finances**. *EU ... DIVORCE, Pg. 194*

The *relationship* that most influences your **finances** is your **relationship** with **money**. Think back to your first *experience* with **money**. Was it positive or negative, good or bad? The first *experience* you remember about **money** and your **emotional re-actions** to that *memory* can hold many clues as to root causes and *limiting beliefs* that may limit your potential for *attracting* money.

As you read the following **words**, notice if your energy drops and, if it does drop on a particular word, **delete** the weaknesses on your **CNS** and strengthen yourself to your **heart**.

Limiting beliefs and *expectations* around the **amount** of **money** you *deserve* to *receive*, **earn, keep, give, win** or **make** are common, as are **specific amounts** and **numbers** that you *allow* yourself to have. As you probably have noticed, the impact of adding one **zero** to your **assets** can have a profound effect on your **bank** statement. A lot of *anxiety* can be created over something that is supposed to be **nothing**! The threshold for the amount of **money** people are *willing* to handle is very low, with many people going weak at earning more than **two hundred thousand dollars** annually. Notice your *re-actions* as you think about adding **zeros** to your bottom line and increasing your annual income. You can test the **numbers** by counting in increments of **$10,000**, **$20,000**, **$30,000**, etc., up to **$100,000**, **$200,000**, etc., and on to **one million dollars**, **one billion dollars**, etc.

What will you do with more **money when** you *receive* it? Strengthen *awareness* of **what** you *want* and **where** and **how finances** will be used by being very **specific** about **what** you will **invest** your **money** in (the best **investment** is in **yourself**). **Visualize** it, **write** it down, go to your **heart** and **feel** exactly what you want to *manifest* to the tiniest detail, and then strengthen yourself to **this** or **better**! Let it go and allow the universe to provide it for you.

Women, in particular often have had *experiences* and continue to have *experiences* where they are not *allowed* to take *action*. Strengthen the weaknesses and delete the *accumulative effects* of the *past* and *present* where there was or is inequality between **men** and **women** and *choice* to make connections that translate into *opportunities* for stronger **finances**.

Many people talk about wanting more **money**, winning the **lottery**, etc., however, their energy does not support it. The thought of having more **money** often triggers concerns over having to **count** it, **what** to do with it, "being accountable" for it, having to deal with and rely on **accountants** and other "experts." Are you **organized** with the **money** that you currently have? Do you leave coins lying around the house, avoid looking at your **bank accounts**, with no idea where you are **financially**? Do you avoid **paper work** and **book work** like the plague? The more **organized** your **finances** are, the more the universe will view you as *worthy* of more **assets**. An organized **physical environment** strengthens your potential to create more **assets** and *abundance*.

Banks are also called **trusts**. Do you **trust** your **bank**? The word "trust" often triggers memories of "mistrust." If you hold the view that **savings accounts** are "save me accounts" you are more likely to draw situations to you where you **need financial** rescuing. People who work as **tellers** in **banks**, **cashiers**, **government** employees, etc., often have issues around **counting**, **handling** and **wasting** other people's **money**; this creates an inability to handle their own funds. Delete the *effects* of your own lies and accusations regarding **spending** as well as the lies and accusations of others.

What frame of *mind* are you in when you are paying your **bills**? Notice if you *feel resentment* as you **spend money** to pay for **utilities**, **rent**, **mortgages**, **taxes**, **car payments**, **repairs** and other common **expenses** that are a part of life. Get *neutral* by realizing that paying **bills** is just a way to show *appreciation* for **services** rendered. Do you have *memories* of being told that **money** is **dirty**? "Get that money out of your mouth," "wash your hands, money is filthy," and other such scoldings have been *experienced* by many people at a tender age. Delete all *negative life experiences* on the *spiritual* and *psychic* levels and strengthen one hundred percent infinite potential by clearing any weaknesses to handling **money** with all the *senses*: *taste*, *touch*, *sound*, *smell* and *sight*.

Many entrepreneurs who have *chosen* to build their own businesses and organizations have become so *attached* to their creation that they often refer to it as "their baby." Combining *emotion* with business often leads to a situation where the **business** takes on a life of its own with the *creator* working for the **business**, rather than the **business** working for the *creator*.

The *mixed* and *combined emotions* people face in this situation are similar to those *experienced* by parents who limit the potential of their child by hanging on too tight once they have matured and are ready to leave home. **Family businesses** that are passed down from generation to generation often create more weaknesses than strengths for those who are *expected* to inherit them.

Winning **money** or making *easy* **money** often alarms **ancestors** who are in the here and now as well as those on the other side of the veil because of their *experiences* of *struggling* to "make ends meet," especially for those who endured the "dirty thirties," the hardships of immigrants, being enslaved in a new country or by invaders of their homeland, *traumas* from a "rape, pillage and plunder" mentality, and other *negative war experiences*.

Psychosomatically many of these triggers are apparent and held in the **genetics** of the family line. People with **strong noses** and **large nostrils** have a tendency to be able to take life in more fully. If the **nostrils** are very noticeable when viewing someone from the front it is an indication of a "love to gamble," whereas people whose noses point downwards at their "assets," indicate a **strong sex drive** and love of the "finer things in life." *Abundance* can also be thought of as "a-bun-dance of the ass(ets)." It is no accident that in this day and age many people find round, firm, plentiful **buttocks** extremely attractive and refer to them as "nice buns," and "booty." Flat, flaccid, lifeless **buttocks** are an indication of an inability to produce **assets** in the **physical world**.

Often times there will be one sibling in the family who either reaps the majority of the benefits of past **ancestral** *abundance* or is designated to be excluded from that *abundance*. Choices to have only one child or being an only child often are made because of weaknesses around sharing *abundance* and *fears* that there is "not enough to go around."

The word "work" triggers many people. Having to "work for a living," being "out of work," "working hard," things "not working out," and "working out," are common weaknesses for most people; they bring up *negative experiences* of **forced labor** or of causing others to **labor** for your benefit and providing benefit to others at the exclusion of yourself.

Are you on a "journey of the broke," treading water financially, with your J.O.B. keeping you just above broke? Many people are unaware that they have weaknesses around deserving to pay their **bills** and having "money to spare." Set your *intention* to have more than enough and be willing to share the benefit of that *abundance* with others. Deprogram the need for a **job** by strengthening the *internal* and *external boundaries* of the *mind*, **body** and *spirit* to *internal* and *external effects* from your **work** place, **living** space and **sleeping** space. Get in touch with the **sensations** that you feel in your **body** when you think of a **job** that you didn't like, were fired from, etc. Strengthen yourself to those sensations so that they work for you instead of against you to inspire *creative solutions* to your **money** issues.

Life is more fun when your **purpose** is strong to your **career** and your **career** is strong to your **purpose** because your **daily routine** is in *alignment* with your *authentic desires*. There are many jobs within a **career** that many people find tedious or unpleasant. When you accomplish small **jobs** with **purpose**, it strengthens your **purpose** to your **career**. *EU … DAILY ROUTINE, Pg. 159*

THE "GOOD NEWS" IS:

It is your *God-given* right to tap into *abundance* and reap the benefits. Everywhere in nature you can see *abundance* at work and play. Your **reality** is formed by your *thoughts*. Once underlying weaknesses are deleted it is natural to connect with *abundance* and steer your **reality** to be in *alignment* with your **heart's** path.

THE "BAD NEWS" IS:

Even though it is a *God-given* right to tap into *abundance*, many *hidden*, *deceptive*, *recurring energies* that are held in the *sub-conscious* and *un-conscious mind* that can limit a person's ability to *receive* it. It is extremely challenging to rise to infinite potential if people do not have access to resources that allow full expression in the third dimensional world.

NUGGET OF WIZDOM FROM THE VECTOR

CATCH THE WAVE AND RIDE THE TIDE OF ABUNDANCE. LET GO OF ANY EMOTIONAL, PSYCHOLOGICAL, SPIRITUAL OR KARMIC NEED TO EXPERIENCE POVERTY. IT IS YOUR NATURAL STATE TO EXPAND AND ACCELERATE ALONG WITH NATURE AND THE UNIVERSE. IF YOU RECEIVE TOO MUCH ABUNDANCE, YOU CAN ALWAYS GIVE SOME OF THAT ABUNDANCE AWAY.

PSYCHIC CLEANSE

Many people who hear the word "psychic" automatically think of a gypsy with a crystal ball. Some people are born with very highly evolved "psychic abilities" that allow them to read other people's *thoughts*, *see* things that are *unseen* by others, *hear* and *feel* **sounds** and *frequencies* that others are unable to *hear*, *tele-transport* to other **locations**, etc. These **psychic abilities**, however, are not reliable or consistent when *intuition* and *perception* are not used along with them. Everyone has the ability to connect on the *psychic* and *spiritual* level to access **information**, but if they don't use their *insight*, that **information** can be very confusing. Energies from the *psychic* and *spiritual* planes include:

PSYCHIC ATTACK

A psychic attack is when someone is intentionally or unintentionally invading your inner sanctum in the form of *thoughts*, **programs**, *implants*, *mind* **control**, *curses* and *spells*. *Curses* and *spells* are energy patterns transported from *space-time*; they are directed towards an individual or a *collective consciousness*, and they may or may not be intentional. *Curses* are always *negative* and can be as simple as a light curse, like "damn you," or they can be elaborate schemes involving more than one individual and calculated to disrupt other people's *equilibrium* and ability to make strong *choices*. *Spells,* on the other hand, are more like "recipes" that are concocted to stir up both good and bad outcomes for the individuals they are cast upon.

SPIRIT ATTACHMENTS

Spirit attachments are **earth-bound** *spirits*, commonly referred to as "ghosts," who are trapped on the third dimensional plane for various reasons. When they *attach* to another person, it is generally because they have some form of *karmic debt* with that person.

DARK FORCE ENTITIES

Dark force entities have a desire to dominate and victimize others for personal gain at the expense of the universe. They are often vengeful **victims** who use the very same **tactics** of **denial**, **disruption**, **degradation**, **deception**, **destruction**, **dissension** and **dissemination** that were used on them.

SOUL FRAGMENTS

Soul fragments are *mismatched body parts* from other *times* and *space* that *merge* into a person's present **body**. **Body parts** from the person's previous life or from other "dead people" *merge* in the form of **quantum particles**, **atoms**, **molecules**, **cells**, or they can take over the whole **body** of a person. If *mismatched* and *merging* **body parts** are energetically weak, ask the following questions: **what** part? **whose** is it? **where** from? **When** did it *attach*?

Chances are that people who feel as though they have "two left feet," when they dance actually do, on an energetic level. Once *mismatched* **body parts** are integrated with the rest of the **body**, *coordination* and other qualities of *fitness* vastly improve. Unfortunately, many people are not aware that they are not fully integrated and unnecessarily go through life feeling awkward and out of step.

EXTRA TERRESTRIAL ENERGIES

E.T.s are alternate beings traveling from *universal*, *galactic*, *inter-galactic* and *intra-galactic times* and *space*. It is politically incorrect to refer to them as "aliens."

ALIEN IMPLANTS

When *alien implants* come up as a weakness, they need to be *eliminated* because they take up room and interfere with *frequencies* that have an effect on the **body**, *soul* and *spirit*. If you detect energetic weaknesses around "alien" **abduction** or **experimentation**, it does not necessarily mean that it actually **physically** occurred in this lifetime. You can detect where *spaces* in the **physical body** are weak from being taken up by **implants** and *frequency interference* from **lasers, surgical implants, fillings, root canals, crowns** in teeth, and **radiation** *experiences*, and you can detect whether they come from the *past*, the *present* or the *future* by sending them and their **problems** to *black wholes*, and by correcting the *collective fear* around having them or not having them.

ELEMENTAL ENERGIES

Elemental energies, commonly referred to as **fairies, gnomes, divas,** etc., are **alternate beings** from other *dimensions* and *planes* of *existence* that inhabit the **earth**.

MULTIPLE PERSONALITIES

Multiple personalities are *aspects* of the **self** that are conceived along with an individual, but they do not have a **physical presence**. You can view *multiple personalities* as the "different hats" you put on for *different* **jobs**. People do not **behave** in the same way when they head a board meeting as they do when they talk to their toddler or go out with their friends. They adjust their **behavior** to the situation. It is possible for the skills and talents of *multiple personalities* to enhance a person if the "dominant personality" is appropriate for the "right job" in the correct context. **Multiple personalities** can also cause problems if they are not *integrated* and if the "wrong personality" is dominating at the "wrong time."

Personalities that have outgrown a person eventually create a fuss and hinder a person's success. If *multiple personalities* are creating havoc in a person's life, they are like bored teenagers who are tired of hanging out with their parents. It is time to cut the apron strings and let them strike out on their own.

Test if problematic *personalities* are strong to leaving and if the *whole being* is strong to letting them go. Strengthen *personalities* to function at optimum potential while integrated as a *whole being*, and strengthen the *whole being* to allow them to leave when they are no longer beneficial.

FETAL DEBRIS

When we are conceived, multiple conceptions occur that also create **fetal debris** because human beings are multi-dimensional beings who conceive concurrently in different *dimensions*, *existences* and *space-time*. The *remnants* of this **debris** can *accumulate* and *stagnate* **systems** in the **physical body**, particularly in the **CNS**.

CASE STUDY:

A client began having serious health problems and mental issues right after her mother made her transition She had been diagnosed with COPD, chronic obstructive pulmonary disease, a breathing disorder that is often accredited to smoking, and instead of her breathing becoming better once she was hooked up to an oxygen tank, there was very little improvement. She believed her breathing was challenged because the damage to her lungs from smoking for a good part of her life. That, however, was not the leading weakness. The leading weakness on the physical level came from her digestive system, not her respiratory system as most people would assume. She also had an emotional weakness which created an inability to "digest life;" in addition there were underlying weaknesses on the psychological, spiritual and psychic levels. She never had a strong connection with her mother and had suffered a cold and cruel upbringing. Being hooked up to an unfeeling oxygen tank triggered memories of never feeling nourished in her mother's womb.

My client's mother had been born with two sets of reproductive organs including ovaries, fallopian tubes and two uteruses, and there were traces of an umbilical cord in her mouth at her birth. The leading weakness for my client was that she had developed as a fetus in the uterus of the absorbed twin, rather than in the womb of her mother, which caused a disconnect between herself and her mother from the moment she, as a cytoplast, attached to the wall of the "wrong" uterus.

Errant energies can be deprogramed and deleted when they are having a **negative effect** on the **authentic self**. Identify where the **energies** are being held in the **physical body**, and **release** them.

MEMORIES

Everything that has ever happened in the *past*, *present* or *future* is documented and filed in the **CNS** of a person, including *memories* in the **sub-conscious mind** of a person's upbringing, *memories* in the **unconscious mind** of **religious**, *psychic* and *spiritual experiences*, as well as *memories* of **ancestors** and the *collective consciousness*.

FRAGMENTS

Some *memories* are "left over energies" that are not complete, like insignificant *fragments* of **material** left over from a **sewing project** that are stitched together to make a **quilt**.

RESIDUALS

Residuals are like "whiffs of smoke" that hang in the air after someone has smoked in another person's home. Once the house is aired out the smell of smoke seems to be gone, but after leaving home and returning, there is still a "hint" of the *smell*.

IMPRINTS

Specific *memories* can be *imprinted* in a **physical body** and on a **physical space**. People can *feel* this when they hold a piece of jewelry or sit in a particular chair, walk into a room, etc.

HESITATIONS

A person can have **emotional**, **psychological** and **religious** *imprints* that cause *hesitation* on the **physical** level, and weaken the **body's** ability to *heal*. Statements such as, "healing takes time," "suffering is required," "only

God can heal," "illness is a result of sin," etc., cause **hesitation** in the **physical body** to heal quickly. *Non-physical hesitations* can create havoc for people in their **daily routines**, **careers** and **family** lives.

SENTIMENTS

Energies can be held over life-times and shared in families through **ancestral** *experiences*, and they can create a *sentimental sadness* when they leave. People have a tendency to hang on to *negative energies* because they *fear change*, just as they stay in undesirable *relationships* with people because they *feel* familiar. Many people *cry* and or *laugh* as they let go of *sentimental sadness*.

ATTACHMENTS

People can become *attached* to the energy of a favorite **dress**, a favorite **city**, a favorite **food**, etc., and *energies* can also become *attached* to people. *Dark energies* and **dark matter** are *traumas*, *tortures* and **illnesses** that are *deceptive* and *elusive* because they are *hidden* in *cords*, *bonds*, *vows*, *contracts*, *ties*, *access points*, *holes* and *threads* that are *birthing*, *cloning* and *seeding*, and come from *frequencies*, *interferences* and *fears* from the *collective experiences* of other *dimensions*, *parallel universes, existences time* and *space* which may or may not be **named**, **numbered** or **known**. They can cause *re-actions* that **repeat**, **repel**, **recycle** and **spread**.

"It's cold in here! Must be something in the atmosphere!"
A line from the cheerleading movie, Bring It On.

It is common to feel a cool breeze or an entire room grow cold when *errant energies* are coming or going. "Goose bumps" and "hair standing on end" are indications that there are *unseen energies* around. You can *intuitively* connect with these *energies* and ask them specifically **where** they are from, **why** they are here, **what** they want, **how** and **when** they arrived, and **where** they *want* to go. At times there are too many to communicate with individually in which case you can send them away with the *intention* that they will get to **where** they **need** to go, recycled in light. Once these *energies* are *removed*, it is important that the *spaces* they were occupying are *replaced*, *restored* and *integrated* back to *homeostasis*.

THE "GOOD NEWS" IS:

If your *body*, *soul* and *spirit* triad is intact, your *authentic self* will easily recognize *errant energies* and *release* them to where they belong in the perfect structure of the fabric of the universe.

THE "BAD NEWS" IS:

It is easy for *errant energies* to *attach* to people who are not **consciously** aware of them. These *energies* are attracted to people who practice *unawareness* on a daily basis through mundane every day commitments and **false obligations** imposed by **society**. A vast majority of the most *unaware* people *relax* themselves into oblivion through their **television sets**. People who are more aware of these *energies*, and who do not know what to do with them, tend to go to **nightclubs, bars,** etc., to *numb* themselves to the *psychic effects* with **drugs** and **alcohol**.

NUGGET OF WIZDOM FROM THE VECTOR

ERRANT ENERGIES ARE LIKE NARCISSISTIC CHEERLEADERS. IT'S ALL ABOUT THEM! THEY HAVE NO LIMITING BELIEFS ABOUT WINNING AND WILL MERCILESSLY SLAUGHTER YOU AND YOUR ENTIRE TEAM TO WIN. IF THEY DON'T SUCCEED, THEIR MOTHERS WILL!

PSYCHIC SURGERY AND TRANSPLANT

If a person has had **organs**, **limbs** or other **body parts** removed or damaged through **amputation, accidents** and other *traumas*, it is possible to energetically reconnect that **body part** to the existing **physical body** to relieve "phantom pain," and in some cases to repair **nerve damage** and **circulation** of a damaged **body part**. After amputation, the **brain** continues to receive signals from the missing **organ** or **body part**, signals that are often *misinterpreted* as **pain**. The **medical establishment** focuses on the **physical** *aspects* of this **pain** trying to eradicate it through **heat application, biofeedback, relaxation techniques, massage, removal** of **scar tissue, physical therapy, neuro-stimulation, medications** and **anti-depressants** with limited results. If the **pain** persists, there are underlying energetic weaknesses that are the leading cause of that **pain**. Many of these are not **physical** and usually come from *experiences* on the *spiritual* and *psychic* levels from *past life traumas* of **war** and battlefield *experiences* that were inflicted on the person, or that the person has inflicted on others. The **problem** can also be *associated* with *traumas*

inflicted by or **suffered** by **ancestors,** or with **fears** of **trauma** for **descendants** in the *future. Mismatched body parts* are often involved.
EU ... PSYCHIC CLEANSE, Pg. 419

If the reasons why the **body part** or **organ** *experienced trauma* in the first place are not addressed for the sake of the *whole being*, relief from the situation will not be one hundred percent. It is necessary to clear the *non-physical* reasons why a person *attracted* an **accident** or **illness** on the **sub-conscious** or **un-conscious** level that would create a situation where removal of the **body part** was the solution. The one thing that all **body parts** and **organs** have in common is that they are made up of **atoms** and **atoms** are **99.9999% space**. The perfect **structure** of *space* is what every **body part** and **organ** has in common. It is important that if an **organ** or **body part** is damaged or removed, the integrity of the *space* is maintained as if that organ were actually in place. Every part of our **body** is in communication with every other **body part** and with the **CNS**. Usually the underlying *non-physical* reasons and *memories* of *traumas* are the weakest. Once they are deleted, the **physical** issues can be addressed by reconnecting the **nerves, circulation, muscles** and **ligaments** and strengthening the *relationship* of that **body part** to be integrated with other **body parts** on a **cellular** level.

Clear any *karmic spaces* of a "need to be cut" that attract surgeries and any **karma** with **doctors, surgeons, pharmaceutical companies** and the rest of the **medical community**.

RESULTS:

"When I first met Colette, I was dealing with a nerve injury that caused me to lose the use of and feeling in most of my right hand. Initially, I thought she was absolutely crazy and did not believe that someone could energetically heal my hand. Dozens of doctors had told me that this would be a lifelong injury and that I would forever suffer from chronic regional pain syndrome. Colette began to work on me and cleared energetic blocks; our first session felt more like a visit with an old friend than an appointment to fix my hand. By the end of that first hour, I felt tingling in my fingers. Colette continued to work on me, and shortly before the birth of my twin daughters I regained the full use of my hand. I cannot imagine how it would feel to not be able to hold my baby girls, and thanks to Colette I don't have to. Colette's work gave me my life back: I can now do things that I never thought were possible."

Mike B.

THE "GOOD NEWS" IS:

Even when it seems that there is no hope for recovery, if the underlying **non-physical** weaknesses are identified and **eliminated**, it is possible for the **physical body** to follow.

THE "BAD NEWS" IS:

When people **experience accidents** and seemingly "hopeless" situations, they often are not aware of the underlying weaknesses that **attracted** the situation or **accident** on a **sub-conscious** and **un-conscious** level, and so they **consciously** give in to the **hopelessnes**s of the situation.

NUGGET OF WIZDOM FROM THE VECTOR

YOU ARE MORE THAN PHYSICAL MATTER! THE PHYSICAL BODY IS OFTEN THE VICTIM OF UNDERLYING NON-PHYSICAL ENERGETIC WEAKNESSES THAT HIGHLIGHT THOSE WEAKNESSES IN PHYSICAL DRAMAS.

PURPOSE

People often complain that they **feel** desperate to "know" what their **purpose** is. Much of the confusion around **purpose** is caused by whether people **perceive purpose** as a **verb** or a **noun**. Many people consider **purpose** to be a **verb**, something they must **do** with **intention** to attain an **object** or **objective**, something that requires **motivation** and a **reason** or **justification** to **exist**; if, however, you consider **purpose** to be a **noun**, then it is the reason for which something is **designed** or is **created** to **exist**.

You do not have to **justify** your **existence**. The **purpose** of your **existence** is a given because you already do **exist**. It does not require energy to have **purpose**, but it does require **action** to **align** your **existence** to your **infinite potential**. People often focus on the **answer** to a **question** rather than on the **question** they are **asking**. A valuable **answer** to any **question** requires a pertinent **question**. Rather than asking, "What is my **purpose**?" you could ask, "What do I **choose** to do with my **existence**?"

A lot of the confusion comes from living with the **limiting belief** that a world of **suffering** and **struggle** is **acceptable** because there is **scarcity** and **lack**. The principles for living that most people adopt are based on a **collective** delusion that only works for a few, not for the masses. Most people live their lives in this distorted **reality** in which they are surrounded by **abundance** and **wealth**, yet **choose** to live by principles that cause *suffering* and **lack**. Many people also **try** to turn **negative situations** into **positive situations** through "positive thinking." **Trying** to turn a **negative** into a **positive** paralyzes people from moving forward because they are making *choices* based on *emotions* rather than on facts. The fact is that it is impossible to turn **negatives** into **positives,** especially on the third dimensional plane, because the **third dimension** is made up of **atoms**. The **nucleus** of an **atom** is made of **protons** that have a **positive electrical charge** and **neutrons** that are **neutral**. They are surrounded by a cloud of **electrons** with a **negative charge** that *balances* out the **positive charge** of **protons** to make the atom *neutral*. When you are *neutral* to the **best** and **worst** case scenario of a **problem**, you are able to make *choices* that *neutralize* the **positives** and **negatives**, and therefore give **structure** to the life you want to lead through your **purpose**.

If people do not make a *choice,* the universe **will** choose for them and generally that *choice* will *resonate* with their **greatest fears** and **negative thinking**. Most people blindly follow the dictates of **government** and other **institutions** instead of taking *response-ability* for themselves. When people *accept* that they are in an *abundant* universe, their capabilities and interests lead them to their **purpose**. Each and every one of us has *unique abilities* that give flavour to the universal soup. When you are strong to the *give* and *take* of the universal plan, it is easier to connect with your **purpose** to *attract* **careers** that support your direction in life as a *whole being* rather than *fragmented* pieces of what you should be or do.

THE "GOOD NEWS" IS:

If you do the smallest tasks with *purpose*, from the time you wake up until the time you go to sleep, you are **aligned** to your **purpose** and moving towards your **goals**.

THE "BAD NEWS" IS:

Most people are so focused on the **false obligations** of **society** that they ignore other *aspects* of their *whole being*. People who are out of *balance* within their *authentic selves* require monumental *effort* just to get out of bed to start their day, and they are often exhausted before their feet hit the floor.

NUGGET OF WIZDOM FROM THE VECTOR

YOU ARE A CONSCIOUS BEING WITH INFINITE POTENTIAL, WHO IS TRAVELING IN A HUMAN BODY. YOUR PURPOSE IS TO BE THE BEST VERSION OF YOURSELF. IF YOU ARE CONNECTED TO UNIVERSAL INTELLIGENCE AND TAKE CONSISTENT STEPS OF ACTION TO GIVE AND RECEIVE, YOU ARE AUTOMATICALLY IN ALIGNMENT WITH YOUR PURPOSE.

PURPOSEFUL COMMUNICATION

The most efficient way to solve **problems** with others is to use **purposeful *communication*** that is geared towards *creative solutions*. *Efficiency* of **words**, the *spaces in-between* **words**, *tone* of **voice** and congruent **body language** are all important aspects of communication. Every **problem** has three parts: an **issue**, a *trigger*, and a *choice*.

ISSUES

It is important to identify what the **issue** is before people deal with a **problem** and discuss it. When people consider a truth's validity, they are facing an **issue** that is a matter of controversy or uncertainty. One way they can *accept* or *reject* the truth of an **issue** is through **argument**, which means breaking down and examining the facts to find **resolution**; it does not mean the kind of *argument* that many people are reduced to where they get louder and louder to prove their point.

People often confuse **fact** with *opinion*. An **opinion** is a personal claim that someone *believes*, and that **claim** is *stated* as an *opinion*. **Claims** can be *subjective*, and are dependent on a person's *tastes*, *preferences* or **objectives**. It is obvious when people make **claims**, because their sentences will be peppered with words such as "and," "or," "but," "if," and "then" to logically connect the information between **claims**; however, the word "but" always **negates** the information **preceding** it. Make sure you are strong to *hearing*, *being heard*, **listening**, being **listened *to***, **speaking** and being **spoken** to. Test for any other weaknesses in the connective **words** you use and you hear others use.

People often give credibility to the **claims** of others when they *perceive* them to be **experts** in a given field. There are several factors to consider about "expert" opinion. Is the **claim** related to the person's field of **expertise**? Just because someone has a lot of letters after their name does not mean they are an **expert** in anything or everything. The less initial plausibility a **claim** has, or the more extraordinary the **claim** is, the more important it is to pay attention to whether you are **weak** or **strong** to it. Just because the **claim** conflicts with the **claims** made by other **experts** in a given field does not necessarily mean it is incorrect. **Claims** made by several, or even the majority of **experts**, are not necessarily correct and are often incorrect or biased, due to **corporate** and "special interests groups." It has been a common practice throughout the ages to ridicule forward thinkers and persecute them for *voicing* a *different opinion* from the *accepted opinions* of others in their field. Do not feel obligated, socially or otherwise, to accept public or expert opinion and do not be afraid to taking a different point of view.

TRIGGERS

People often *accept* or *reject* claims or have more *confidence* in a **claim** because of irrelevant considerations based on *emotional re-actions* such as *fear*, *compassion*, *pride*, *loyalty*, etc. There are many ways that people fool themselves and others into *accepting* or *rejecting* a **claim** or *opinion* that has no basis in truth. In some instances the claim may appeal to a personal *belief system*, and in other cases *peer pressure* from **friends**, **families** and **associates** allow people to justify **acceptance** of the claim on the grounds that "everyone" believes it, too. Another way people will deceive themselves is by "jumping on the bandwagon" to support a **position**, a **candidate** or a **policy** that is most likely to **win**. This *wishful thinking* is often based on their **desire** for it to be true, or because their ego has been massaged. In addition, **scare tactics** and **appeals** for pity that are not relevant to the **issue** are also commonly used to support a **false claim**. People will also put up a "smokescreen," by bringing in an irrelevant topic to draw attention away from the topic at hand or to assert that the **claim** is true for one person but not for another. When *anger*, *indignation* and *sarcastic remarks* are directed at another individual, it is often designed to deflect **negative** attention away from themselves, or to serve as a **revenge tactic**. These **tactics** are not only used by individuals, but also on a larger scale, by **corporations**, **governments**, **political parties**, the **media**, **church**, etc.
EU ... TACTICS, Pg. 494

The *mind* can also fool us into *accepting* or *rejecting* a **claim** that resembles a legitimate **argument** but is not based on sound **reason**. One common **tactic** used to confuse an **argument** is to personally attack an individual's **character**, **personal history**, **situation**, **job** or **special circumstances** instead of addressing the **claim** or **argument**. Other tactics involve **poisoning** the **argument** with innuendos about a person before she or he has a chance to make a **claim**, **behaving** in a manner that disregards the **authenticity** of a person, or **denying** a **claim** because of its origins with a specific **group**, **political party**, **organization**, **race**, etc. Each of these methods puts the "burden of proof" on the "wrong" side of the **argument** and results in a distortion or an exaggerated version of the **facts**.

There can be many solutions to any given **problem**. **Perfectionists** tend to allow only two alternatives by adopting a policy that will solve a **problem** "perfectly" or "not at all." This requires a precise line to be drawn on a scale or continuum when it is often impossible to draw that line. **Creative solutions** are hard to come by when people refuse to take the first step to solve a **problem** by insisting that doing so will sabotage **efforts** "down the road," and that the remaining steps will be **erroneous**. On the flip side, taking steps based on the first step that continues to make the **problem** worse is also a "slippery slope." Never assume that a **claim** is true or false. Test it!

At times a **claim** is based on both an **argument** and an **explanation**. These are two separate functions. **Explanations** are designed to show **how** or **why** something **is** or **will** be, whereas **arguments** are used to show that something **is**, **was**, **should**, or **will** be. Explaining **how** an event happened is a **justification** and does not make a **relevant argument**. There are **physical** explanations for phenomena based on *cause* and *effect*, and **behavioral** explanations based on the *psychological effects* from **social**, **economic**, **political** and **historical** events. Alternatively, a person can place the event in context to create a **functional claim** or **argument**. Test for weaknesses in **relevance** and **reliability**.

Certain **words** can be used in an attempt to define specific people in terms of their **race**, **culture**, **religion**, **gender**, etc. The intent is to **manipulate** them and others into **compliance** by describing them as the "worst possible" thing they can be, and thus rendering their **accomplishments** or **concerns** invalid. For example, many **cultures** restrict the sexuality of women to conform to a **patriarchal**, pre-approved vision of *femininity* and **restraint**; any deviation from the vision is considered "slutty" **behavior**. Other cultures label a women's conduct as "bitchy" if she exhibits *aggressive* or *assertive* **behavior**, like a man might. Women's *intuitive* **behavior** has been labeled "crazy" and "hysterical" throughout history because the medical field was an exclusively male profession until the middle of the nineteenth century. The word, "hysterical" is derived from the Greek word "hystera" which means **uterus**. Defining the "symptoms" of **menstruation** as a "medical issue" allowed men to diminish women's concerns or **issues** as invalid. *EU ... MENSTRUATION, Pg. 327*

CHOICES

It can be challenging to wade through the subtle nuances of **claims** and **arguments**; however, when you are aware of these common pitfalls in *communication* and the motives behind **words** and *actions*, you can perceive those *challenges* as *possibilities*. Clear understanding allows for strong *choices* based on *creative solutions*.

THE "GOOD NEWS" IS:

When you are contemplating the validity of an **argument** or *action,* be it your own or someone else's, you can test whether it is *weak* by *feeling* for the truth.

THE "BAD NEWS" IS:

Most of the "bad news" comes from the **media**, and is frequently based on **pseudo-reasoning**, **half-truths**, *fear* and *sensationalism*, all or much of which is intended to confuse the **issue** rather than to solve it.

NUGGET OF WIZDOM FROM THE VECTOR

DON'T REACH YOUR CONCLUSIONS ABOUT THE TRUTH BY THINKING ABOUT WHAT YOU OR OTHERS SAY OR DO. FEEL FOR WHAT IS WEAK AND TAKE STRONG ACTION BASED ON THE TRUTH IN THAT MOMENT. NON-VERBAL, INTUITIVE COMMUNICATION IS THE BEST COMMUNICATION BECAUSE THERE IS NO ROOM FOR ARGUMENT.

QI

Ancient Chinese philosophy states that *Qi* is the most fundamental substance in the world and in the **human body** for the maintenance of life's activities. The Chinese character for *Qi* is the same character that is used to symbolize **air** or **gas**. Just as **gas** is used to create heat, *Qi* warms the **body** and keeps it at a constant temperature for regular physiological functions to take place. *Imbalances* in the *distribution* and *absorption* of *Qi* can lead to a lowered body temperature, intolerance for cold, as well as cold **hands** and **feet**.

Qi coordinates the **body's** substances and retains the **body's organs** to keep **blood** flowing through the **veins**. At the same time it controls and adjusts bodily excretions such as **sweat**, **saliva** and **urine**. It also *coordinates* the storage of **sperm** to prevent *premature ejaculation*, maintains the integrity of all the **organs**, and prevents them from dropping into positions where they are unable to function at optimum potential. There is a fine *balance* between the secretion and distribution of the fluid substances within our **body fluids** that *coordinate* the functions necessary for promotion and consolidation of optimum **blood circulation**, and the *metabolism* of **water**. *Regeneration* and *degeneration* must be fifty/fifty to maintain one hundred percent potential.

Qi must be able to travel **up**, **down**, **outward** and **inward**. Any stagnation of the *flow* in any direction will have a weakening effect on life force energy, which will lead to **illness,** and ultimately to the end of life. *Qi* is a quality that is attributed to *Yang* because it is warm, mobile, and its function is to move. **Blood** and **body fluids** are attributed to **Y**in (*Yin Fluids*) because they function to nourish and hydrate the **body**. *Qi* vaporizes the functional substances in **food** to transform them into **food** *essences* that are *metabolized* in the **blood**. **Indigestible food** and **waste** are processed as **urine** and **stool**.

Each **organ** has specialized movements that contribute to the whole with all of the systems within the systems operating in *coordination* for optimum potential. For instance, the movement of *Spleen QI* is up, transforming the pure parts of **digested food** from the stomach into *nutritional essence*, while *Stomach QI* pushes **food** down in order to remove impurities. *Lung Qi* performs in all **four directions** with every breath we take: **In** when we **inhale**, **out** when we **exhale**, **up** to provide **nutritional** *essence,* and **down** to move li**quid waste** through the **kidneys**. Any weaknesses that obstruct effortless *flow* of *Qi* in any direction can have a profound effect on the *fitness* of the **body**, *soul* and *spirit*, and influence the **physical**, *mental*, *emotional* and *psychological* well-being of an individual. **Structural integrity** is essential for the transmutation of *spiritual* and *psychic* dynamics to prevent blocks in the *flow*. It is very beneficial for people to be strong to their *perceptions* of the direction their lives are taking. When you are strong to the "ins and outs" of life, your *instinct* and *reflexes* are intact, and allow you to take the "ups and downs" you *experience* in the **economy, businesses, friendships, romance** etc., in stride; this makes the *experiences* of "climbing to the top," things "going downhill," and "going down," both *figuratively* and **physically** *neutrally satisfying*.

There are four kinds of *Qi*. They are *Inborn*, *Pectoral*, *Nutritive* and *Protective*.

Inborn Qi is the most essential and vital type found in the **human body**, because it possesses original prenatal and congenital properties of "Congenital Essence," which is a vital substance inherited from **parents** after **conception**. It is stored in your **kidneys** and supported by "Acquired Essence" from the **spleen** and **stomach** through the *assimilation* and *absorption* of **food essence** in the *digestive process*.

Strengthen connections **to** and **from** the *Vital Gate* and "Congenital Essence" through both **kidneys** via the **Triple Burner**, the **organs** of your **body**, **muscles**, **skin** and the *meridians* in all directions.

Pectoral Qi supports **breathing** and the **volume** of your **voice** through the function of strong **lungs**, the **heart**, and the entire **circulatory system**. It is stored in the **chest** and is a *combination* of **air inhaled** by the **lungs** and *food essence* from the **spleen** and the **stomach**. Optimum *flow* through the **blood vessels** and the **heart** are integral to regulating your **heartbeat** and supporting the circulation of other *meridians*, types of *Qi* and **blood**. It is also a factor for temperature control, as it keeps the **body** warm and influences activity in the outer **limbs**.

Strengthen **air** to your **lungs**, and f*ood essence* via your **spleen** and **stomach** to **blood vessels** and **heart** for optimum *fitness* of the **body**, *soul* and *spirit.*

Nutritive Qi supplies nourishment to the **body** and its **organs** through your **blood** which is sometimes referred to as "Nutritive Blood." It has *Yin* properties and is able to provide some of the necessary substances needed for the *production* of new **blood**.

Strengthen *flow* to and from the **Middle Burner** to the **lungs**, the **heart**, the rest of your **circulatory system**, as well as to the structure of every **organ** and its *relationship* with the other **organs** in your **body**.

Protective Qi has the qualities of *Yang* energy. It originates from the same source as *Nutritive Qi*, but flows separately from it outside of the **circulatory system**. *Protective Qi* provides **nutrients** for healthy **hair**, **skin** and **muscles**, and it regulates **sweat glands** and **pores**. In some ways it can be considered to be similar to what most people refer to as the "immune system," guarding against *dis-ease* and **Evils**. The **Evils** are seven environmental factors that may or may not contribute to **illness** and wellbeing: *Wind*, *Summer*, *Heat*, *Dampness*, *Dryness*, *Cold* and *Fire*. Weaknesses to any one or more of these **environmental** factors are often mistaken for *health* issues.

Strengthen the internal path of *Food Essence* from the **spleen** and **stomach** to the **circulatory system**, the **diaphragm**, the **chest**, **chest wall** and **abdominal cavities**. Strengthen the external path of *Food Essence* from the **spleen** and **stomach** to **skin**, **hair** and muscles.

Life force energy flows effortlessly when Inborn, Pectoral, Nutritive and Protective Qi are connected to *Source* and operating with optimum *fitness* in a *coordinated* effort.

YIN AND YANG ORGANS

Organs are functional units within your **body** that have important *Yin* and *Yang* properties in *relationship* with and to each other. Chinese medicine considers the **liver, heart, spleen, lungs, kidneys,** and sometimes the **pericardium,** as *Yin* or *Fu* interior **organs**. Their function is to *produce, transform, regulate* and *store Qi,* **blood** and **body fluids**.

The *Yang* or *Zang* exterior **organs** include the **gall bladder, stomach, small intestine, bladder** and the **Triple Burner** which is considered more as a functional unit because it does not have an actual **physical structure**. The *Yang Organs* are mainly responsible for digesting **food** and transmitting **nutrients** to the **body**, but they do have **empty cavities**. It is important that **empty cavities** maintain the perfect structure found throughout the entire universe by strengthening any **structural weaknesses** in all **directions**.

You can simplify the strengthening of the many combinations between *Yin* and *Yang Organs* and their **inner** and **outer** *aspects* to the intrinsic body **in-**between by shifting them with **geometric symbols**, in this case as a **pentagon**. *EU ... GEOMETRIC SHAPES, Pg. 264*

Although **lungs** govern *Qi,* the *Qi* from the **lungs** must merge with *essence* from the **kidneys** to produce *Original Qi.* The **kidneys** provide the basis for *Qi* and the **liver** spreads it. *Cooperation* between the **heart** (**fire**) and the **kidneys** (**water**) is crucial because they are dependent on each other to provide *spirit* and *essence* in order to maintain human *consciousness*.

THE "GOOD NEWS" IS:

When *Yin* and *Yang* qualities are in *alignment*, they create a tremendous force field in the *center* of the **body** that allows you to proceed at your greatest potential in every *aspect* of life and on all levels of influence.

THE "BAD NEWS" IS:

Any underlying weaknesses in the *flow* of *Qi* will have a detrimental *effect* on a person's **physical**, *emotional*, *mental* and *psychological* wellbeing. This can sabotage the ability to *manifest* with *authentic desires* for **careers, finances, relationships, youthfulness,** and other **false obligations** imposed by **society**.

NUGGET OF WIZDOM FROM THE VECTOR

YOU ARE AN INFINITE BEING CONNECTED TO INFINITE ENERGY OR INFORMATION. IF THERE IS A KINK IN THE HOSE THAT IS OBSTRUCTING THE FLOW OF QI, YOU CAN UNKINK IT AND TAP INTO THAT SOURCE ENERGY. THIS ALLOWS YOU TO BE A STRONGER VERSION OF YOURSELF IN EVERY ASPECT OF LIFE TO IMPROVE YOUR HEALTH, WEALTH AND HAPPINESS WITHOUT STRUGGLE.

REALITY

Nothing is solid in the unified field. **Reality** changes in the flash of a second, highlighting different *aspects* of life that flash in and out of being over and over again to create **objects** that can be *experienced* on the **physical plane**.

On a movie reel, within one second there are twenty-four still-frames with a *space* in-between each **frame**. The speed at which one picture succeeds another gives the impression that the pictures are actually moving which is why movies are often referred to as "motion pictures." You *perceive* your **reality** through your five **physical senses**, and each of these senses, has a specific spectrum or range that is a unique filter for every individual. Any weaknesses in *touch*, *sight*, *sound*, *smell* or *taste* may or may not be compensated for by extra strength in another of the senses; this creates a unique interpretation of every *experience* for every individual, and a general *experience* for the *collective whole*.

Everything you *experience* in the **physical** third-dimensional plane is made up of fluid *thoughts* expressed as **solid matter**. Your *thoughts* determine how the energy *manifests*, frame by frame, and they shift the unseen into the seen on a **particle** by **particle** basis.

THE "GOOD NEWS" IS:

Your *thoughts* are an *observation* of **reality**, reflected back to you, second by second through the truth of your *experience*. NOTHING *exists* in your **reality** independent of your *observation*.

THE "BAD NEWS" IS:

Interpretations of reality are based on incomplete and often inaccurate *collective life experiences* that limit people from *receiving* the "whole story" in its entirety.

NUGGET OF WIZDOM FROM THE VECTOR

PATIENCE IS A GOOD QUALITY TO HAVE WHEN YOU ARE STEERING REALITY. ALTHOUGH SOME THINGS MANIFEST INSTANTLY, IT IS MORE COMMON THAT THE DIFFERENT VARIATIONS NEED TO FALL INTO PLACE BEFORE YOU REALIZE YOUR GOAL IN THIRD DIMENSIONAL FORM.

RELATIONSHIP INSURANCE

Relationships are the **foundation** for **success** in personal and professional lives. Most people feel compelled to purchase **life insurance**, **car insurance**, **home insurance**, **business insurance**, **medical insurance**, etc. Purchasing "ease of mind" through **insurance** has become a huge **industry**, but in reality the best "insurance" you can have is strong *relationships*. When you are at your most vulnerable and confronting the most difficult *challenges*, the strength of your personal and professional *relationships* will significantly determine your ability to navigate the difficulties you encounter along the way. When your "pilot wave," the energy from the *electromagnetic frequency* of your **heart**, is strong to *attracting* people who are beneficial to your *authentic self*, it functions like a magnet that *attracts* metal filings. The **magnet** does not have to do anything but be in the presence of **metal**. Too often, however, people have *reverse perception* and **think** the reverse is true because they feel the **need** to adhere to the **false obligations** imposed by **society**, rather than to the **needs** and *authentic* desires of the *soul*. The **needs** of the *soul* are often very different from the **needs** of the third dimensional world. It is not uncommon for people to *attract relationships* into their lives that seem to be of benefit on the third dimensional plane but limit the growth of their *souls*; yet often it is the people who seem to be the "enemy" who are most beneficial to the *soul*. This can create a lot of confusion. When people recognize themselves as *conscious* beings rather than as **human** beings, it is much easier to tap into infinite potential.

GENERAL RELATIONSHIPS

Check for weaknesses in the *relationships* that are instigated by *negative re-actions* to *emotions*. These *re-actions* may be *perceived* as negative, positive or a combination of both positive and negative, and can include various *emotions*. *EU ... EMOTIONS, Pg. 205*

Often, *emotions* that weaken *relationships* revolve around *receiving* and *giving* attention to **self** and **others**, seeking **inner** and **outer** *approval*, *accepting* and *rejecting appreciation*, *self-affection* plus *affection* from and for **others**. The vast majority of energetic blocks in *relationships* arise from a lack of integration of *sub-conscious memories* stored as a child, *un-conscious memories* of *spiritual experiences,* as well as from the *conscious experiences* encountered on a person's journey. Ensure that your *relationships* are strong to *attracting abundance* and mutual *respect*, *acceptance*, *recognition* and integration of *actions* and "points of view" by being on similar wavelengths.

ROMANTIC RELATIONSHIPS

1 + 1 = INFINITY

Female energy is *magnetic* and **male** energy is *electric*. When the two intersect, they create an *electromagnetic* spectrum of light. In this case "one plus one" does not equal two because it creates a third *space* of *infinite potential* by joining *life force energy* and the power of *co-creation*. This is represented by the **vesica piscis**, a geometric symbol that can be found throughout the *pleasure centers* of the **physical body**.

Many "love at first sight" *attractions* are initiated by *karma* and end in *disappointment*. The greatest irony is that the main purpose of *relationships* is to resolve *accumulated*, *associated karma* and *karmic spaces* for **self**, **ancestors** and **descendants**, yet people tend to have "amnesia" of the *past*, including the exact nature of the *karma*, which makes it challenging to resolve. *EU ... KARMA, Pg. 302*

The single most important *relationship* you have is with your *authentic self*. All *relationships* are dependent on your *relationship* with yourself, are a reflection of your *personalities* in *action*, and are mirrored back to you by **others**. Many of us use "love" to mask our **problems**, which is, of course, an illusion that many people "fall for" when they "fall in love." For most people*, falling* implies a loss of control. *Feeling* out of control is not a solid foundation on which to solve anything. It is often a diversion **tactic** that has been romanticized by **social media** through **romance novels**, **movies**, **television**, etc., and is a huge **money** maker for many **industries**. Love sells, and advertising is geared to play on people's *emotions* to make **money** for **big business**. "Single's Awareness Day" (better known as **Valentine's Day**) is my busiest time of the year next to **Christmas**. *Pressure* mounts when on a designated day people are *expected* to prove to **themselves** and to **others** that they are "in love" with their significant other by purchasing flowers, chocolates, candy, cards, romantic dinners, jewelry, etc. Every year the bar is raised and the **pressure** is amped, whether people actively participate or not. Even people who see this as a **marketing event**, often underestimate the powerful undercurrents of this energy.

If you have a **problem** and you mask it by focusing on anyone or anything outside yourself, it is unlikely that you will solve anything and, in fact, you are more likely to confuse the **issue**. Clearing the **problem** first and strengthening the **situation** before *choosing* to involve **others**, allows for stronger *relationships* that strengthen mutual *respect*, *acceptance*, *recognition* and *integration* of **actions**, points of view and similar wavelengths in all **relationships**, whether they are personal or professional. The **reasons** for people's weaknesses in **romantic** *relationships* are many, and often the underlying weaknesses are both complicated and subtle, making them *challenging* to resolve. There are many accumulative *psychic forces* and *spiritual experiences* held by the *collective consciousness* that most people are unaware of, and that commonly weaken the average person. These include *hatred* of people, disconnections to *source energy*, **self-destructive** tendencies, **suicidal experiences**, seeking **revenge**, *traumas* of **radiation**, **cannibalism**, and *demonic* and *evil forces* throughout the ages.

Check for **vows** of **poverty, chastity, marriage** and **revenge** from **self, partners, ancestors, descendants** and **potential descendants**. Strengthen them to forgive unconditionally. Many other weaknesses in *relationships manifest* because of weaknesses in the **physical environment** at **home**, at **work**, and from **educational** *experiences* that do not support a loving, peaceful **environment**.

Misunderstandings in *relationships* frequently arise from inadequate communication. People are often weak to *hearing*, being *heard* or not being *heard*, *listening* or *not listening* or being *listened* to, and they confuse weaknesses to **being seen** or **seeing others** with weaknesses that are *hearing, listening, speaking* and *being spoken* to. *Purposeful communication* comes from the *efficiency* of **words**, the *spaces* in-between **words**, and from **body language**. Every **problem** has a trigger causing an *issue* that is in **reality** an *opportunity* in disguise. It is important to identify what the **issue** is before it can be resolved. *Non-verbal, intuitive communication* is the most powerful. By *speaking* less about the **problem** and focusing on the *solution*, you can utilize your *intuition* to better understand what other people truly **need** without having to *verbalize* it. *EU ... PURPOSEFUL COMMUNICATION, Pg. 429*

You can test how strong the **foundation** of a *relationship* with significant others is by testing whether **both** parties are strong to **loving** each other and **liking** each other. Just because people **love** each other does not necessarily mean that they **like** each other and vice-versa. You can also test energetically whether **both** parties are strong to *wanting* "things to work out," and strengthen both of them to be *neutral* to the outcome. There are often weaknesses to "being together" as a couple that bring up survival issues emanating from weaknesses in the *root chakra*. Incorrect assumptions about a "mate" are frequently influences from *past relationships*, many of which are not even from the people in the *relationship,* but from the **ancestors** and the *collective consciousness.*

RELATIONSHIP CIRCLES

You can check *relationships* from one **person** to another **person**, one **person** to a **group**, or one **group** to another **group**, **business** to **clients**, etc., by using *relationship circles*. People have *relationships* with everyone and everything and are able to strengthen partnerships **between lovers**, **family**, **co-workers**, **employees**, **employers**, **clients**, our **physical spaces**, **body parts**, **organs**, etc. The strongest **geometric shape** to use for **relationships** between two **people**, **things** or **places** is the **circle**. This is how to use a **relationship circle** to get strong to any *relationship*:

Draw two intersecting **circles** that meet halfway between the two. Write an "**A**" in one **circle** to represent yourself and in the other **circle** write a "**B**" to represent the **person, place** or **thing** you want to be strong to. Once you named yourself "**A**" and the other "**B**," from that point on do not use your **name** or the **name** of the other **person, place** or **thing** because it is much easier to remain *neutral*.

Is "**A**" strong to "**B**"? If not, strengthen "**A**" to "**B**" by running energy up and down your **spine** for yourself and the other person; if "**B**" is a **place** or **thing**, give it an imaginary **spine**. Once "**A**" is strong to "**B**," test if "**B**" is strong to "**A**." If "**B**" is not strong to "**A**," strengthen it. Once "**B**" is strong to "**A**" it is not uncommon for "**A**" to go weak to "**B**" because *internal* and *external forces* between the two have changed. Double-check that both "**A**" and "**B**" are strong to each other. Once they are, check whether *internal* and *external boundaries* of each of the **circles** are strong to *internal* and **external forces** from the "What I.F.'s" and the "What the *E.F.'s.*" *EU ... EXTERNAL FORCES, Pg. 232 ... INTERNAL FORCES, Pg. 297*

The *space* where the circles intersect represents "the relationship" that has a life of its own, because many times *relationships* with significant others takes the form of **marriage**, **live-in arrangements**, **co-parenting**, **business partnerships**, etc. Many of these **institutions** may have *hidden* **contracts** of **chastity** and **poverty** due to *karmic ties* and *psychic energies* that become a *living force* which is *served* by the **partnership** itself, rather than *serving* the **needs** of the individuals in the *relationship*.

As more **people**, **places** and **things** are involved, you can add another **circle**, creating a **triad**, with all three **circles** intersecting in the center. If the *relationship* involves a **place** or **thing**, give the **place** or **object** an imaginary **spine**. You can envision the **relationship circle** spinning into the **spines** of the **people**, **place** or **object** involved, somewhat like a Frisbee.

Relationship circles are very effective in clearing the dynamics between **parents** and a **child** because all three are being taken into consideration at once. An example of this is:

A = mother, B = father, C = child

The *relationship* between the **mother** and **father** is "**A**" to "**B**" and "**B**" to "**A**." The *relationship* between the **father** and **child** is "**B**" to "**C**" and "**C**" to "**B**." The *relationship* between the **mother** and **child** is "**A**" to "**C**" and "**C**" to "**A**." The intersecting area of the **circles** represents the *relationship* among the three of them.

Relationship circles are also very effective in clearing *internal* and *external forces* between the *relationships* of **organs**, **systems** and **body parts**. An example of this is:

A = respiratory system, B = reproductive system, C = digestive system

The *relationship* between the **respiratory system** and the **reproductive system** is "**A**" to "**B**" and "**B**" to "**A**." The *relationship* between the **reproductive system** and the **digestive system** is "**B**" to "**C**" and "**C**" to "**B**." The **relationship** between the **respiratory system** and the **digestive system** is "**A**" to "**C**" and "**C**" to "**A**." The intersecting area of the **circles** represents the *communication* of these three **systems** with each other.

Using more than three **circles** becomes very complicated because within **relationship circles** involving **two circles**, there is **one intersecting area** and **three dynamics** involved in the *relationship*, "**A**" and "**B**" plus the **intersecting area**. When you add a **third person, place** or **thing**, you now have "**A**," "**B**," and "**C**," plus the **intersecting areas** between "**A**" and "**B**," "**B**" and "**C**," plus "**A**" and "**C**" to consider as well as the **intersecting** area in the **center** where all **three** meet. That adds up to *seven dynamics* among **three relationships** that are being cleared at once.

ATTITUDE

Every **situation** and encounter with **people** is just an *experience* you are going through. If there is no *judgment*, you can become *neutral* and choose to be *innocent* in that situation. Often **people** confuse **innocence** with **naivety**. **Innocence** is a *choice* to "make space" for **people** and **situations** to *change* "for the better" despite appearances that may suggest the contrary. **Naivety** is about hiding from the **problem** and ignoring the **solution** to the detriment of others and oneself.

RESULTS:

"Hi Colette, I just wanted to say thank you for an incredible weekend! The shifts I experienced are beyond words! Not only do I feel NO emotional charge about my past relationship. I think I've dropped like 5 lbs since Saturday. I put on a skirt I bought a week ago and it's loose in the waist now! I was carrying a lot of stuff from that relationship and I FINALLY feel free. I've done so much healing work over the past two years and none of it compares to the instant shift I experienced this weekend.

"You are a great teacher and I appreciate you sharing yourself wholeheartedly with us all weekend!"

Andrea Dupuis, Leader to Luminary Training Inc., Vancouver

THE "GOOD NEWS" IS:

Choice is *freedom* to *experience* life at its finest, here on planet earth. **Perception** is greatly influenced by your *relationship* with **yourself**, the rest of **humanity**, the **planet** and all **universal beings**. It is possible to strengthen your wavelength to *attract* beneficial **people** and **situations**.

THE "BAD NEWS" IS:

For many people, *purposeful communication* is limited because they **re-*act*** to *experiences* and encounters instead of perceiving them as a full expression of their infinite potential. The reasons why people *re-act* have many **hidden** and *deceptive* aspects that are influenced greatly by *spiritual*, **religious**, *collective*, **cultural**, *karmic*, *astrological* and *psychic* energies of which the average person remains unaware of.

NUGGET OF WIZDOM FROM THE VECTOR

LOVE IS EVERYTHING, YET IT ALONE DOES NOT CONQUER ALL! IF IT DID, THERE WOULD BE NO STARVING AND ABUSED PEOPLE AND ANIMALS IN THE WORLD. UNCONDITIONAL LOVE REQUIRES ACTION.

RELIGIOUS EXPERIENCES

When confronted with this question ... "Does *God* cry?" My first response was, "Of course not! *God* is all-powerful!. Why would *God* cry?" Now that I have a better understanding of my universal connection with everything and everyone, I understand that a part of *God* does cry along with each and every one of us, but *God* only cries because we do.

People around the world are raised in many **religions**, each with its own separate set of **rules**, **obligations** and **promises**. The one thing every **religion** has in common is that it **divides**. It **divides family** members who *choose* to strictly follow **religious** *beliefs* as opposed to those who wish they could "believe" in a **religion** that was worthy of followers. On a greater scale it **divides** sections of **cities**, sections of **countries** and even pits **continent** against **continent**. On the other hand, **religion unites** people with **common interests**, **goals** and *celebrates* their **accomplishments**.

Space is the common **divider**. **Nothing** *touches*. **Nothing** ever does, because people are made of **atoms** as is everything a person *perceives*, yet the **atoms** themselves don't ever *touch*; there is always *space* between them. **Try** as people may to live the *belief systems* of **religion** in an attempt to perfect themselves, it is a *concept*. Even if a *concept* seems strong because so many people *believe* in it, that does not mean the **concept** is **valid**. Many **religions** have been fashioned to benefit a select few while the masses *suffer* the consequences of weak *belief* systems.

Women, **girls**, **homosexuals** and **people** of **color** have been discriminated against far too long through a twisted interpretation of the "word of God" by "cherry-picking" priests and clerics who carefully selected a few **bible verses** and quoted them out of **context**. For example, they, not *God*, **claimed** that **Eve** was second to **Adam** and that it was she alone who was responsible for the **original sin**. The *belief* that women are somehow inferior to men, ordained to be subservient to their husbands, has prevented women from taking on an equal role in many **faiths** and **religions**, and has prohibited them from service as **high priests**, **deacons**, **pastors**, **chaplains** etc. Unfortunately, the justification for the subjugation of women inside **churches**, **synagogues**, **mosques** and **temples** contaminated every *aspect* of our lives. It has been used as a leading **excuse** for **authoritarians** to deprive women of **control** over their own **bodies**. Obvious examples of this include **genital mutilation**, **unacceptable risks** in **pregnancy** and **child birth**, laws that do not consider **rape** a crime, and **courts** that punish the **victim** because "she asked for it." The *denial* of and unequal access to **education** and **employment** has *affected* women's economic welfare and *health* by forcing many into prostitution. In the same **scriptures** there are many passages in which **women**

are revered as **pre-eminent leaders,** and it wasn't until the fourth century that dominant male Christian leaders distorted the **Holy Scriptures** to perpetuate their ascendant positions within the **religious hierarchy**.

Many **people** in the "west" are dismayed by the images of women who are forced to cover up, their faces and bodies, **denied** access to equal *opportunities* and who are expected to work as **slaves** on the other side of the globe. Their dismay stems from their failure to recognize that the images they see are a reflection of themselves because discrimination in the west, although subtle, is definitely present. For instance, the **celebration** of Christmas, the birth of the savior for Christians, has become a "religious event." **Events** require **time**, **money**, **energy** and **effort**, as anyone who has ever been responsible for organizing an event understands. The vast majority of the responsibility to create the "magic of Christmas" in most **homes** is delegated to the **women,** along with **childcare** and **housekeeping**. If you take a situation in an **office** where there are **ten people** working together, **seven men** and **three women**, **society** deems it to be acceptable (and somehow cute) for the **men** in the **office** to rush out at the last minute to grab gifts just before the stores close on Christmas Eve, while their **wives** and/or **girlfriends** are busy "doing Christmas." Meanwhile, the **three women** in the **office** have been juggling the extra responsibility for the **event** of Christmas, in-between their responsibilities at the **office** and at **home**. *Productivity* for women is clearly **divided**, and the **men** are clearly at an **advantage**, getting ahead while the **women** fall more and more behind.

It is common for **men** and **women** to have weaknesses to **religious** *experiences*, weaknesses that stem from their **current lives** as well as from *past lives* as victimized **women** or as domineering **men** who ruled over them. Common *negative experiences* include being **burnt** at the **stake**, **crushed**, **whipped**, **flogged**, **stoned**, **buried alive**, **tarred** and **feathered**, **hung**, **tortured**, **enslaved**, **sacrificed**, **raped**, **pillaged** and **plundered**. Delete *negative patterns* caused by each *experience* as it arises and cut all **cords**, **ties**, **bonds**, **contracts** and **vows** to the **church** as **suffrage**.

THE "GOOD NEWS" IS:

More and more **women** and **men** around the planet are waking to the truth of who they are, and are honoring themselves by embracing the *divine feminine* and the *divine masculine* within themselves.

THE "BAD NEWS" IS:

The discriminatory **thinking** and the outdated **attitudes** and **traditions** that exclude specific **members** of **society** from the *freedom* to contribute equally are self-defeating and a violation of the teachings of the founders of all great **religions** who call for proper and equitable treatment for every **man**, **woman** and **child**.

NUGGET OF WIZDOM FROM THE VECTOR

NO MATTER HOW SHINY A BOX LOOKS, IT IS STILL A BOX. IF YOU FEEL "HOLIER THAN THOU," YOU SERIOUSLY NEED TO DEVELOP A SENSE OF HUMOR. IF THE POPE CAN QUIT, SO CAN YOU. YOU HAVE A DIRECT LINE TO GOD, USE IT!

REPRODUCTIVE SYSTEM

The **reproductive system** might be better defined as a "re-creation center" if you consider the percentage of time it is used as a *center of pleasure* rather than for the purpose of **reproduction**. It is helpful to have a basic working knowledge of how **female** and **male genitals** work together for both purposes.

FEMALE

The **female reproductive system** is described in most **medical texts** as having seven parts, listed as the **uterus, cervix, vagina, two fallopian tubes** and **two ovaries**. They go on to say that the **reproductive system** is designed to carry out several functions, listing **pregnancy** and **birth** of offspring as the most important.

The blatant omission of the **clitoris** and the **prepuce** can be compared to the **glans (head)** of the **penis** and **foreskin** being left out of discussions of the **male reproductive system** because the **embryonic cells** that become the head of the **penis** in **male babies** are the same **cells** that make up the **clitoris** in **female babies**. The difference is that the **nerves** are packed into a much smaller area, making the **clitoris** very sensitive. The patriarchal **medical system** also neglects to note that the vast majority of women use their **reproductive systems** to house **babies** for a comparatively short time of their lives, and some do not use it for this purpose at all. This explains why so many **women** are advised to avoid the "hardships" of **menstruation** by having a **hysterectomy** when their childbearing years are over. **EU ... HYSTERECTOMY, Pg. 290*

The **female reproductive system** is designed to carry out several functions that stimulate *mental* and *emotional* wellbeing through *orgasmic* pleasure. It also is responsible for *producing* eggs for *reproduction*, and transfers them through the *fallopian tubes* for **fertilization** and *attachment* to the wall of the **uterus**. Visible to the naked eye are the large, fleshy lips of the **labia majora** that protect **internal genitals** from *infection* or **injury**. Nestled inside the **labia majora** are the **labia minora**, a smaller set of lips that surround the opening to the **vagina** and **urethra,** and meet at the **clitoris**. The **clitoris** is a small, very sensitive protrusion that becomes erect when it is stimulated. It is covered by a small fold of **skin** called the **prepuce**, similar to the **foreskin** in **males**. On either side of the **vaginal** opening are two small **glands** about the size of a pea that secrete **mucous** to lubricate the **vagina**; these are called the **Bartholin glands**.

The **vagina** or **birth canal** joins the vaginal opening to the **cervix** which is located at the bottom of a pear shaped **organ** called the **uterus**. The uterus itself can be divided into two parts, the **cervix** and the main body or **corpus**. The **corpus**, or **womb**, is capable of expanding to accommodate a developing baby. A channel within the **cervix** allows **semen** in and **menstrual blood** out. The lining of the **uterus** thickens in anticipation of **pregnancy** and, if **pregnancy** does not occur, the average woman sheds the excess **lining** and **blood** every twenty-eight days. **Fallopian tubes** are attached to the upper end of the **uterus**, and serve as a tunnel for the **ovum** (**egg**) that comes from the **ovaries** on its journey to the **uterine wall**. The **ovaries** themselves are small oval shaped **glands** that are located on either side of the **uterus**. They are responsible for producing **hormones** that are essential for *vitality* as well as for supplying **eggs**.

There is a lot of controversy around another part of a woman's anatomy that is not listed in **medical texts** as part of the **female reproductive system** because of a lack of evidence as to its existence. Although the existence of the **G-Spot** is questioned by the **medical community**, the *effects* of its stimulation have successfully been captured on film by the porn industry for years. The **Gräfenberg spot**, or **G-Spot**, is a sensitive area just behind the front wall of the **vagina**, between the back of the **pubic bone** and the **cervix**. When it is stimulated through **penetration** via the fingers in **masturbation**, the **penis**, **sexual toys**, etc., many women have an **orgasm** accompanied by **ejaculate** from the **Skene glands**. These **glands** have highly variable **anatomy** and in some women seem to be absent entirely, which may explain in part the controversy of women's ability to **ejaculate**. Many **women** who do **ejaculate** seek medical attention in the mistaken belief that they are **urinating** when in fact they are expressing **fluid** that has a composition very similar to the fluid generated in **males** via the **prostate gland**.

MALE

Unlike the **female anatomy**, the majority of the **male reproductive system** makes its presence known, or not, externally. Typically, the anatomical illustrations of the **male reproductive system** are shown at half-mast, unsure of which direction to go or how to get there. Viewing these **illustrations** of their equipment in this semi-erect state "testes" weak on the **psychological** and **psychic** level for many **men** who are concerned about their sexual performance. Any time you are working energetically on the **male reproductive system**, keep in mind that it is also a major *pleasure center*. I recommend viewing it in its full glory, **erect** and **fully functional**.

The **scrotum** is made up of two pockets of **skin** and **smooth muscles**, each protecting a **testicle** located side by side under the **penis**. **Testes** are the male **gonads** responsible for the production of **testosterone** and **sperm**. Each **testicle** is attached to the **abdomen** by the **cremaster muscles** and a **spermatic cord**. The **cremaster muscles** *expand* and *contract* along with the **scrotum** to automatically change the distance of the **testes** from the **body** according to ideal temperature for *production* of **sperm**. The inside of the **testes** is divided into small compartments called **lobules**. Each **lobule** contains a **tubule** that *produces* and conveys **semen**, and is lined with **epithelial cells** containing many **stem cells** which divide and form **sperm cells** through a process called **spermatogenesis**. **Spermatogenesis** does not occur before **puberty**. It begins when the **luteinizing hormone** (**LH**) triggers the *production* of **testosterone**, and the **follicle stimulating hormone** (**FSH**) triggers the maturation of **germ cells** in order to stimulate **stem cells** in the **testes**; these germ cells are called **spermatocytes**, and their function is to develop the **sperm head** and become **spermatozoa**.

The **epididymis** wraps around the upper, back edge of the **testes**. It is comprised of several feet of long, thin **tubules** that are coiled tightly into a small mass, designed to delay the release of immature **sperm** until it is ready to be released through the **reproductive organs**. The **spermatic cord** is a bundle of **fibers** and **tissues** that form a "cord-like" structure running through the **abdominal** region and pairs off to each to attach to a **testicle**. The cord has **nerves**, **veins**, **arteries** and **lymphatic vessels** that support the function of the **testes**, and facilitates the passage of **semen** as one of its many functions; it may also contribute to **impotence** when damaged.

The **vas deferens** is a muscular tube that is part of the **spermatic cord**. It travels from the **epididymis** through a passage in the **abdominal wall** called the **inguinal canal,** enters the **abdominal cavity** over the **pelvic brim,** and extends back to the **pelvic cavity** ending just behind the **urinary bladder**. It transports mature **sperm** to the **urethra**, a tube that carries **urine** or **sperm** to the outside of the **body** in preparation for ejaculation. The **spermatic cord** itself is protected by **fibrous tissue** to prevent *trauma* such as **testicular torsion**. It becomes dilated into a portion called the **ampulla** at the base of the **bladder** on the back wall. Just above the **prostate gland** the tube becomes slimmer and unites with a **seminal vesicle**.

The **seminal vesicles** are a pair of **glands** that *store* and *produce* some of the liquid in the **seminal fluid**. They are about two inches in length, located at the back of the **bladder** and at the front of the **rectum**. The liquid that is produced by the **seminal vesicles** contains **proteins**, **mucous** and **fructose** that feed the **sperm**. It has **alkaline pH** to empower the **sperm** to combat the **acidic** environment of the **vagina** long enough to fertilize the **oocyte**. The **vas deferens** passes through the **prostate**, and joins with the **urethra** at the **ejaculatory duct** that opens and expels **sperm** along with the secretions from the **seminal vesicles**. The **urethra** is a muscular tube, approximately eight to ten inches long. It passes through the **prostate** and ends at the **external urethral orifice**, located at the tip of the **penis**. **Semen** exits the body from the **ejaculatory duct**, and **urine** from the **urinary bladder** via the **urethra**. The **prostate** is a walnut sized gland that surrounds the **urethra** and ends at the back of the **urinary bladder**. It produces most of the fluid that makes up **semen**. The **prostate** has **smooth muscle tissue** that constricts to prevent the flow of **urine** and **semen**. Finally, **Cowper's glands** (**bulbourethral glands**) are a pair of pea-sized **glands** located at the back of the **prostate** and in front of the **anus**. They secrete the **alkaline fluid** that lubricates the **urethra** to neutralize **acid** from **urine** following **urination**, and prepares the **urethra** for the flow of **semen**.

PROSTATE PROBLEMS

A lot of men *experience* a problem with their **prostate** at one time or another in their lives. On a **physical** level, *stagnation* in the system builds up causing *inflammation* of the **prostate** that can eventually lead to *infection*, *infestation* and *complete system shut down*. The *stagnation* in the system manifests on the **physical** level, but often there are various *non-physical* weaknesses coming from *emotions, thoughts* and *psychic* energy. Most of the **problems** stem from a lack of use of the equipment for various reasons. *Fear* of a **diagnosis** of cancer is a common reason for the **prostate** becoming too *relaxed* and open to **problems**. As men *relax* themselves out of the information, the **prostate** becomes relaxed, not unlike the *relationship* between breast cancer and how **women** regard or relate to their **breasts**.

BPH (benign prostatic hyperplasia) means that the **prostate** is enlarged, is putting pressure on the **urethra**, and is therefore causing problems with **urination**. It is common in men **fifty** and **older**. To strengthen the **prostate**, break down the existing excess **tissue** and pinpoint **physical** and **non-physical** weaknesses that are *stagnating* the system. **Chronic pelvic pain syndrome** (**CPPS**) is common in younger men; it causes **pain** in the lower **back, groin,** in the tip of the **penis,** and is accompanied by painful **ejaculation,** *inflamed* **testicles** and *burning* **pain** when **urinating**. The *burning* **pain** is similar to what **women** *experience* when they want to "take a pause" from men, causing symptoms of **men-o-pause**. The common denominator is built-up *anger* that leads to **hot flashes, sweats** etc. Once the underlying weaknesses are deleted and the equipment is put into use again, there is usually relief and rapid improvement.

Acute bacterial prostatitis is a **bacterial** *infection* causing fever, chills, pain when **urinating**, and sometimes **blood** in the **urine**. **Chronic prostatitis** is a recurring *infection* over a long period of time. On a **physical** level and *non-physical* level, check for *infections* and weaknesses to **sexually transmitted** *dis-ease,* especially **chlamydia**. Strengthen the **lymphatic system** to the **pelvic cavity** and **oral cavity**. It is important to have at least **three bowel movements** a day to prevent extra pressure on the **prostate**.

The **penis** is the external sexual organ located at the front of the **scrotum** and below the **umbilicus**. It has two main **physical** functions: to deliver **semen** into the **vagina** through **sexual intercourse**, and to pass **urine**. It contains the **urethra** and the **urethral orifice** as well as large pockets of **erectile tissue** that allow it to fill with **blood** and become erect. The **erection** causes the **penis** to swell and increase in size. Although the **female** and **male** repro**ductive systems** appear to be very different, in some ways they are very similar in their functions. Some **female** to male **counterparts** that are similar are ...

labia majora to the **scrotum**
labia minora to the **spongy urethra**
prepuce to the **foreskin**
clitoris to the **penis head (glans)**
Bartholin glands to the **bulbourethral glands**
g-spot (the Grafenberg spot) and **Skenes glands** to the **prostate**
appendix testes to the **fallopian tubes**
prostatic utricle to the **vagina**

THE "GOOD NEWS" IS:

A healthy **reproductive system**, along with strong *lower chakras* naturally provides pleasure and enhances *relationships*.

THE "BAD NEWS" IS:

The fact that the **medical community** considers the main function of the **genitals** as a **system** for **reproduction** explains why so many **medications** that are systematically prescribed for various conditions have so called "side-effects" which are casually dismissed when they compromise the ability of the **genitals** to perform and provide *pleasure*.

NUGGET OF WIZDOM FROM THE VECTOR

IT IS HELPFUL TO UNDERSTAND THE "INS AND OUTS" OF THE PHYSICAL REPRODUCTIVE SYSTEM. EMOTIONAL RE-ACTIONS PLAY A HUGE ROLE IN THE ENJOYMENT OR LACK OF ENJOYMENT AND PERFORMANCE OF GENITALS.

RESPIRATORY SYSTEM

The **respiratory system** is basically an **oxygen** delivery system that works through the exchange of **gases**. Its primary function is to supply **oxygen** to all parts of the body via **oxygenated blood**, and to pump **carbon dioxide** out. When people breathe, they *inhale* oxygen and *exhale* carbon dioxide through the **mouth, nose, trachea, lungs** and **diaphragm. Oxygen** enters the **respiratory system** via the **nose** and **mouth**, passes through the **larynx** (where sound is produced) into the **trachea,** a tube that enters the **chest cavity**. There it splits into two smaller tubes called the **bronchi** which also further divide into smaller tubes called **bronchial tubes**. The **bronchial tubes** lead directly into the **lungs** and divide into millions of spongy, air-filled sacs called the **alveoli**; these are surrounded by the **capillaries** which lead to the **arterial blood vessels**, thus supplying **oxygen** to the **body**. This is often referred to as the **tracheobronchial tree** because the branches of the **alveoli** follow the phi ratio that is also replicated in the branches of a **tree**.

Oxygen from the *inhaled* air passes through the **alveoli walls** and into the **bloodstream**, and leaves the **lungs** to be carried to the **heart**. At the same time, **carbon dioxide** is released into the **alveoli** through the **veins**, and is then exhausted through the **lungs**. **Venous blood (de-oxygenated blood**) is returned to the **right** side of the **heart** and then pumped out by the **pulmonary artery** that is divided into two branches, one for each **lung**. **Red blood cells** pass through the tiny **capillaries**, one at a time, exchanging **gases** with the **air** from the **alveoli**. The **capillaries** eventually join together to form the **pulmonary veins** that carry the **blood** back to the **left** side of the **heart** in a continuous cycle.

The **cells** in your body need a constant supply of **oxygen** to produce *energy* (***Ka or Qi***). As *energy* is utilized, **waste products** are produced in the form of a **gas** called **carbon dioxide**. When the delicate *balance* between the two is not even, **cellular function** is impaired, causing damage and even **cellular death**.

BREATHING

Respiration (**breathing**) is accomplished by **cause** and *effect*, *expansion* and *contraction*, *inhaling* and *exhaling*. It occurs between twelve to twenty times per minute. The breathing process is facilitated by the **diaphragm**, a large dome-shaped **muscle** that sits under the **lungs**. The **diaphragm** is actually a sheet of **muscles** that lies across the bottom of the **chest cavity** where it is attached to the **lower ribs**, **lumbar spine** and **sternum**. It facilitates **oxygen** to enter the **lungs** and expels **carbon dioxide** out of the **lungs**.

INHALATION

When you **breathe in**, the **diaphragm contracts** (*tenses*) in a **downward** motion, creating a vacuum that *causes* a rush of air to enter the **lungs**.

EXHALATION

The **diaphragm** *expands* (*relaxes*) as you **breathe out**; as the **diaphragm** moves up, it pushes on the **lungs** and causes them to deflate. Breathing is controlled by the **autonomic nervous system** in a coordinated effort from the **brain stem**, the **medulla oblongata** and the **pons**. **Neurons** in the **dorsal respiratory group**, located in the **medulla** are responsible for normal **resting** *inhalation* and **passive** *exhalation*. The **ventral respiratory group** is only used when there is **forced** *exhalation*, for instance when a person is **vocalizing**. The **pneumotaxic area** is located in the **pons** and regulates the amount of **air** taken in with each **breath**. When there is a need to breathe faster or deeper, it lets the **dorsal respiratory group** know that it needs to adjust. Higher concentrations of **carbon dioxide** in the **blood** and **exercise** increase the rate of **breathing**. These **neurons** in **infants** are very vulnerable and are easily damaged, as in the case of **shaken baby syndrome**.

LUNGS

The **right lung** has three **lobes**: the **right superior**, **right middle** and **right inferior**. It is shorter and broader than the **left lung** because of the location of the **liver**. The **left lung** has two **lobes**, the **left superior** and **left inferior lobes**, and a **cardiac notch** that accommodates the **pericardium**.

For the **lungs** to perform at optimum potential the airways need to be open and free of *inflammation*, *swelling* and excess **mucous**. It is preferable for air to enter through your **nose** as opposed to your **mouth**, because the **cilia** (small hairs in your nose and air passages) sweep out particles and keep the lungs clean. **Cells** in the **trachea** and **bronchial tubes** produce **mucous** to keep **air passages** moist and to help stop allergens, viruses, bacteria and dust from entering the **lungs**. Impurities are coughed up or swallowed along with the **mucus**.

PERICARDIUM

The **pericardium** (**pericardial sac**) is a conically shaped sac of **fibrous tissue** that surrounds the **heart** and **major blood vessels**. The **pericardium** has an **inner** and an **outer coat**. The tough **outer coat** is attached to the back of the **sternum**, the center of the **diaphragm**, and loosely encloses the **heart**. The **inner coat** is made up of two layers that have a small amount of **pericardial fluid** in the *space* in-between. If the **pericardium** becomes *inflamed* from **injury**, *dis-ease* or *trauma* from **surgery** or **medical procedures**, it can lead to a condition known as **pericardial effusion**. Too much **fluid** in the **pericardium** causes expansion that presses inward; this can result in poor **heart function**, cause the **chambers** of the **heart** to collapse, and ultimately lead to a condition called **tamponade**.

It is helpful to have a basic understanding of how the **respiratory system** works. You can ensure that all the working parts are operating at optimum potential within themselves, with each other and with the **CNS** including the **structure** and *balance* of the **rib cage**, and the **abdominal** and **chest cavities**.

COUGHING, SNEEZING AND HICCUPS

Coughing and **sneezing** are reflexes caused by the *irritation* of the **nerves** within the **nasal passages** or **airways**. The purpose is to expel irritants that are collected by mucous.

Cough receptors are located on the back wall of the **trachea**, the **pharynx**, and at the **carina of trachea**, where the **trachea** branches into the main **bronchi**. When the **receptors** are stimulated, impulses travel via the

internal laryngeal nerve, stemming from **CN X** to the **medulla**. People tend to be easily triggered by **coughing**. It is usually assumed that **coughing** is an indication of *infection* in the **lungs**, but energetically it often comes up as a **problem** with the **timing** of the **swallowing reflex**. If people feel very *irritated*, "swallowing their words" and suppressing what they really want to say, they will eventually start to "cough up" *anger* and "choke on their words."

Sneezing and **congestion** of the **sinuses** is often energetically connected to suppressed *grief* and *fear* of *rejection*, or *rejecting* others and **information**. If you connect with what you were **thinking** the moment before you **sneeze**, you can easily find the trigger.

Hiccups are caused by a sudden involuntary *contraction* of the **diaphragm** and the **larynx** that causes a total closure of the **glottis** (**vocal cords**), thus blocking **air** intake.

The **respiratory system, digestive system**, **reproductive system and colon** are intimately connected, and if there is a weakness in one, the weakness is often **referred** from one or both of the other **systems**.

BRONCHITIS

People who are diagnosed with **bronchitis** have a chronic **cough** and *inflammation* of the **airways** which causes the production of too much **mucous** that is frequently *associated* with **viral** or **bacterial** *infections*. It is not uncommon for people who are diagnosed with **COPD** and **bronchitis** to be **smokers**; therefore both are often called "smoker's cough."

If you are a **smoker**, ensure you are strong to **smoking**, and clear any weaknesses to **information** regarding **smoking**, *karma* with the **tobacco companies**, **medical institutions**, and **pharmaceutical companies**. Strengthen the **smoke** to go through the **throat** and **lungs** without sticking.

PNEUMONIA

Bronchial pneumonia is an infection of one or both of the **lungs**, whereas **lobar pneumonia** affects one of the **lobes**. It is caused mainly by **respiratory viruses** that enter the **lungs**, *inflaming* the **alveoli** and causing them to fill with fluid. **Pneumonia** can be **bacterial** and/or **viral**, and can also be caused by **mycoplasmas** that are the smallest free-living agents with traits of both.

Viral pneumonia is caused by a **virus** invading the **lungs**, and multiplying. Most cases of **viral pneumonia** are short-lived with few **physical** symptoms to indicate that the **lung tissue** is filling with fluid; however, they can become severe, particularly in people with pre-existing **heart** and **lung**

disease and in pregnant women. If **bacteria** enter the picture, it can complicate matters, and lead to **bacterial pneumonia**.

There are many **germs**, **organisms** and **fungi** that contribute to **bacterial pneumonia**. It can develop after a "cold or flu," after **surgery**, after **viral** *infections,* in people with **respiratory** *dis-ease* or from *inhalation* of **food**, **liquid**, **gases**, **dust**, etc. There are also many **emotional**, **mental** and *psychological* "germs" that also cause *inflammation* and *infection* in the **lungs**.

COPD

Chronic Obstructive Pulmonary Disease (**COPD**) is a progressive *dis-ease* of the **alveoli**. Shortness of breath is the main symptom along with **wheezing**, **chest tightness** and a **chronic cough**.

EMPHYSEMA

Emphysema is a *dis-ease* in the **lungs** where the *inhale* is weaker than the *exhale*. This causes damage and death to the **alveoli**, leaving empty *space* or **holes** in the **lungs** that become lost **tissue**.

CYSTIC FIBROSIS

Cystic fibrosis is considered a genetic disease passed on by both parents; it primarily *affects* the **lungs** and **digestive system**. The defective **gene** produces a **protein** that controls the flow of **salt** and **water** outside of the **organs**, mainly the **pancreas** and **lungs**. This results in a thicker and stickier **mucous** that is difficult to cough up and can lead to severe **lung** *infections*. The **mucous** also interferes with the **pancreas**, preventing **enzymes** from breaking down **food**, and **nutrients** from being *absorbed* and *assimilated*.

Clear any *karma* between the **parents** and **children** up and down the family line, and also the *karmic space* of a need to *suffer* or *struggle* in life. Test the density of the **mucous** and make sure that the **cells** are not *expanded* from too much **water**.

THE "GOOD NEWS" IS:

"Clearing the air" and *speaking* your **truth** can be like a "breath of fresh air" for everyone involved.

THE "BAD NEWS" IS:

People often worry about the quality of the air they breathe due to **pollutants**, **dust mites**, etc., yet they remain unaware of the weaknesses they have to the *emotional* **garbage** they are dumping into their **physical body**.

NUGGET OF WIZDOM FROM THE VECTOR

WEAKNESSES OF THE RESPIRATORY SYSTEM AND BREATHING OFTEN INDICATE PROBLEMS WITH THE GIVE AND TAKE IN LIFE, AND A RELUCTANCE TO ABSORB AND ASSIMILATE LIFE-FORCE ENERGY.

SCANNING FOR WEAKNESSES

It is great idea to incorporate a habit of *scanning* your **body**, another person's body, a crowded room, a building, documents, symbols, etc., to feel the weakest link and have it stand out. Generally, any **situation** in any given moment can always be made stronger. If not, it is *neutral* and does not need to be *shifted*. *Recalibrate* by closing your **eyes** and taking a moment to strengthen your **eyes** and *vision* to "seeing" from your **heart's** *perspective*. Set an *intention* that once you open your **eyes**, wherever or whatever your **eyes** are drawn to **first** is the **number one weakness.** It is common for more than **one weakness** to stand out, but it is most efficient to *shift* the weakest link first because, once that is *shifted,* it often automatically *shifts* other **weaknesses**, saving you **time** and *energy*.

A reading with **tarot cards** works in the same way. **Cards**, **words** and **symbols** can be energetically *shifted* so that the weakest one stands out the most. The person who is reading can choose the cards for someone else or can have the person "being read" *choose* the **cards**. Once they are connected they tell a story that can be interpreted through *intuitive* deduction.

To identify and clear a weakness, it is possible to quickly *scan* for **weaknesses** in the **Feng Shui** of **rooms, buildings, gardens, businesses, cities, countries**, etc., or for a weak **word** in a **sentence** or **paragraph** in **documents, emails, advertisements**, etc. People are often triggered if **pain** *leaves* and then seems to *return*. Once something has *shifted*, it is not uncommon for it to appear to come back because the **human body** only has so many **body parts** to indicate the multitude of **physical** and *non-physical* energies from **false obligations**, *internal* and *external forces*, *karmas*, *psychic* energies etc., that the **body** is exposed to. If you strengthen people to *feel* the **pain** for just a second, they are able to *perceive* that it is *different*. The acknowledgment that *change* has taken place, opens the **heart** and the *mind* to more *possibilities* of healing

THE "GOOD NEWS" IS:

Scanning is an efficient, powerful **tool** that becomes automatic once you put it into practice.

THE "BAD NEWS" IS:

The biggest challenge for optimum accuracy when you are *scanning* is to let go of all **thinking** and *feel* for the **weakness** rather than look for it. It seems simple enough, but can be challenging to put into practice.

NUGGET OF WIZDOM FROM THE VECTOR

FINDING A WEAKNESS IS SIMPLY A COMPARISON, NOT A JUDGMENT. IT IS GENERALLY MOST BENEFICIAL TO SCAN FOR WEAKNESSES RATHER THAN STRENGTHS BECAUSE WHEN SOMETHING IS STRONG IT DOES NOT REQUIRE SHIFTING.

SENSATIONS

Your **physical body** *experiences* many *sensations* on in any given day. These *sensations* can be triggered by *external* or *internal forces* that you may or may not be aware of on a *conscious* level. If you are *neutral* to what you are *experiencing* with no *emotional re-action*, it allows you to understand the underlying reasons why you are **experiencing** these particular *sensations* and move through the **pain** and *discomfort* quickly.

People *experience* their world through five main **senses**: **touch**, **taste**, **smell**, **sight** and **sound**. Besides the five obvious senses, others include **hunger** and **thirst** as well as those *senses* that many people do not consciously acknowledge. These are **equilbrioception, proprioception, thermoception** and **nociception**.

EQUILIBRIOCEPTION

This is better known as the **sense** of **balance**, *perceived* through the **fluid** in the **inner ear**.

PROPRIOCEPTION

This is *perception* of one's body *space* and **position**.

THERMOCEPTION

Perception of **temperature** is not reliant on **touch**. For instance, a person can feel the **heat** of **flames** in a **fire** without **touching** it.

NOCICEPTION

Perception of the *sensation* of **pain** is not reliant on **touch**. Different **receptors** *perceive* **pain** differently on the **skin**, **joints**, **bones** and **organs** in the **body**. The **words** people use to describe what they are feeling are clues to track the underlying energetic weaknesses causing the *sensations*. Common words that people use to describe *sensations* are:

DISCOMFORT

Discomfort is a gift, a gentle nudge from the universe. If people pay attention and take consistent steps of *action* that are energetically in *alignment* with their **goals**, they can avoid the "frying pan treatment," If "the frying pan" treatment is too subtle and they still need convincing to move out of an *old paradigm*, the frying pan is gentle compared to the "two-by-four" treatment.

PAIN

Pain is an indication that something is not in *alignment*. This quite often will *manifest* in the **physical body**, but the **pain** may be originating from many sources: *emotional*, *mental*, *psychological*, *spiritual* as well as **physical**.

ACHING

Aching is often *associated* with a person who is *aching* to make a **career** change, to travel to a specific **country**, to do something or be with a particular **person**, etc. At times people can identify the exact **body part** that is expressing the *ache* by naming it, as in a **headache**, **heartache**, a **toothache**, etc.

BURNING

People may have had encounters with others who boil over with *anger* and *resentment*; at the least provocation they react with *explosive anger*. They are often described as having a "short fuse," being "in a volcanic rage," or "doing a 360." On a **physical** level, *health* problems *associated* with *anger* often present as **heartburn** (**acid reflux**); this is common when people get in the habit of *suppressing angry* words and *actions* until they are no longer able to control the eruption. The expression, "that makes my blood boil," is not far from the **truth** and will often present as the **high blood pressure** and **inflammation** in the **physical body** that many people *experience* due to *accumulations* of *anger*.

HURTING

There is an expression, "my feelings were hurt." In fact it is *impossible* to hurt *feelings*. People feel different *sensations* as they connect with the **words** others use, and they react or respond to what they are *feeling*. Who do they want to *hurt*? Who wants to *hurt* them? The answers to these questions are clues to the underlying reasons people express the *sensation* of **pain** as *hurt*.

HYPERSENSITIVITY

People are often accused of being "hypersensitive," however, energetically the weakness almost always comes up as a weakness to the people around them for not being *sensitive* enough. If a *sensation* is bothering a person, it is a clue that there is a deeper message that the universe is sharing with them. Use your *sensitivity* to work for you rather than against you. *Balance* the **histamine** and **anti-histamine** ratio and delete *traumas* from *negative life experiences*, *past*, *present* and *future*.

IRRITATION

When people find themselves in *irritating* **situations** or communicating, working with, living with *irritating* people, or if they themselves are *irritating* other **people** and **situations**, it is more likely that **pain** and *discomfort* will be expressed as *irritating*. On a **physical** level this often *manifests* as annoying **skin** conditions that are more *irritating* than **painful**. Irritable Bowel Syndrome (I.B.S.) is aptly named. When people are "talking bull shit" or putting up with "bull shit" from others, or **speaking** or **thinking** about "crappy situations," it often does *irritate* the **bowel** and other **elimination systems** in the **body**.

NUMBNESS

Numbness and *numbing* are often *re-actions* to not wanting to *feel*. Not wanting to **feel** certain **body parts, events, situations,** specific *emotions*, etc., can lead to a lack of *feeling* in certain areas of the **body** often described as "pins and needles." The **effect** of suppressing these

sensations often presents as **stomach** and **sexual** issues. Addiction to **medications** and **substances** are also common forms of *numbing*. **Hands** and **feet** and other extremities that go *numb* often are affected by the extremes of *wanting* to and **not wanting** to *feel*. It is common for **mismatched body parts** to be involved.

PRESSURE

When people describe **pain** or *discomfort* as **pressure**, it often is coming from an *accumulation* of many sources and a feeling of *overwhelm* from the **pressures** of life.

STABBING

Stabbing or a "knifing pain" is often related to past *knifing experiences* such as **surgeries, battles, slaughtering**, etc. The experience of being "stabbed in the back" or "stabbing others in the back" through gossip and other malicious activities often brings on *stabbing* **pain**. People who are *unconsciously* resolving issues of having "been cut" or cutting up others are more likely to *experience stabbing* **pain**. Check if the pain is coming from the *past* or the *future*. If it is coming from the *present* ... run! (just kidding, shift it).

STRUGGLING

Wrestling with **problems** and *struggling* to resolve them brings up painful *memories* of not being able to resolve hardships with ease. These *memories* are stored in the **physical body** and often lead to stiffness or an inability to be *flexible* in **body**, *soul* and *spirit*. It is common for people struggling to rise from a prone or a sitting **position** to feel stiff and awkward about facing life's *challenges*.

SUFFERING

When people describe the *sensations* they feel as *suffering*, they are often creating unnecessary *suffering* for themselves and others on an *unconscious* level.

TENDERNESS

At times people will use the word *tender* to describe a **body part** that is in **pain**. Recycled *emotional* and *psychological* **pain** that has gone unresolved for many years is likely to be at the root. Often it will arise when a person feels the need for **tenderness** from a specific person, or simply wants to be more **tender** with others.

The word "tender" can also mean an offer of **payment** to stop a **foreclosure** on a **mortgage** or to enter into a **contract**. People who feel that they are in a **financial** predicament will often transfer the **pain** of facing their **finances** into their **body**.

THROBBING

Throbbing **pain** is generally about **experiences** of **pounding** others and "being pounded" both **physically** and figuratively. The **pounding sensation** is like a beat of a drum and amplifies the **feeling** of being beaten and beating others down.

ITCHING

When people have an "itch to scratch," it is often about the **discomfort** of "feeling stuck," "itching to do something," or "itching to be with someone." Being **itchy** often triggers past **situations** of **infestations** in the **body** and in the **home**.

SHOOTING

Shooting **pain** is often a **collective fear** of being **shot** or **shot** at in the **past**, **present** and the **future**. The words people use when they are preparing for an **argument** are often referred to as "ammunition," and losing an **argument** or being **rejected** is frequently described as being "shot down." **Behaving** like a "big shot" or **feeling** **victimized** by others who are "taking a shot at you" can trigger painful **shooting experiences**.

DRYNESS

People will often use the word **dryness** to describe the **sensations** they are feeling in their **eyes** and **vagina**. The **reproductive system** and the **eyes** are intimately connected, and weaknesses are often referred from one to the other. **Memories** of nomadic lifetimes of living in **dry**, **hot**, **windy**, **sandy** **deserts** often trigger **sensations** of **dryness**. At the time of this writing, there are twenty-nine countries in Africa and in the Middle East where millions of babies and children are subjected to the **torture** of **female genital mutilation** for cultural and traditional reasons. **Thoughts** and **memories** of **procedures** that cause intercourse to be **painful** often trigger **dryness** in **women** and **men** alike. *EU ... GENITAL MUTILATION, Pg. 261*

THE "GOOD NEWS" IS:

The **sensations** you **feel** in your **body** are not just an indication of what is happening on a **physical** level, but also on every other level of your existence. They can work in your favor to resolve **underlying energetic issues** before they become major **physical issues**.

THE "BAD NEWS" IS:

People are tempted to ignore the more subtle "negative" **sensations** they **feel** because they are taught that those **sensations** are "bad news" that people would rather not **receive**. Subtle **sensations** begin as a whisper; if people don't listen to the whisper, **sensations** become louder until eventually people **receive** the "frying pan treatment." If they still refuse to listen, the "two-by-four" treatment is sure to follow.

NUGGET OF WIZDOM FROM THE VECTOR

BE SENSATIONAL! IF YOU FEEL THAT YOU ARE TOO SENSITIVE, DON'T PANIC. CHECK FIRST TO SEE IF YOU ARE HANGING OUT WITH INSENSITIVE, REPRESSED ASSHOLES ...

SHIFT HAPPENS

To use a computer, all that is required is a basic understanding of how to make the programs work. You do not need to be a computer programmer, to go **online**, send an **email**, use **word document**, **excel**, **copy** and **print**, etc. You may be familiar with the frustration of working with a computer that is "running slow" because of corrupt **files** or a slow **internet** connection. It is even more frustrating if your **bio-computer** is not fit to rise to the **challenges** of everyday life here on planet earth. Similarly, it is essential that your **CNS** is operating at the highest **speed** and is plugged into a reliable source of **energy**, your **heart**, to **effect** immediate **change**. A **shift** in energy is a flip of a switch in the **frequency** of the bandwidth of the **brain** and the **CNS** resulting in a **change** to the data **speed** or **rate** measured in **bits per second** or in **hertz (cycles per second)**. You can **speed** up your results by deprogramming or deleting **files** that are slowing you down and reprogram your "hard drive" to be at optimum **efficiency** and **speed**. The "corrupt files" do not just **affect** your **physical potential**, but the potential of your **authentic self** and your **whole being**.

Information equals **energy**. **Negative effects** are the consequences of inaccurate **information** that slow down the processes of a person's **bio-**

computer. These energies are held in the stories people tell themselves about who they are, and in the *memories* in which they become enmeshed, and to which they consequently become *attached.* If they tell themselves a story often enough, it becomes their reality and can be imprinted on their **body**, *soul* and *spirt.* *Accumulated thoughts associated* with "the story" cause *re-active* **behavior**. The ramifications of weak **behavior** have a direct *effect* on people's **physical existence** by throwing them "off balance." Every choice made has a *parallel effect* felt through all *dimensions* and *vectors* of *space-time*. These *choices* indirectly *affect* every single individual in the entire universe.

As we become more aware of the undercurrents of energy, we peel away layers of long-held **untruths** that were based on *limiting beliefs*; *intuitive answers* are then revealed in a flash of brilliance that opens **portals** to *infinite potential* and **outcomes**. It is amazing how tenacious *limiting beliefs* can be. Just when a person thinks an issue has been resolved, it appears to rear its ugly head once more because there are still persistent *remnants* and *residual* energies that need to be cleared. *Remnants* are like scraps of fabric. They can be thrown out or used to make a beautiful quilt. The scraps seem insignificant on their own, but when you stitch them together they become transformed into a quilt. *Residuals*, on the other hand, are similar to when someone smokes in your house. You can air the house out until you are satisfied that the smell is gone; however, when you leave and re-enter your home, your *perception* changes and you may still detect a hint of smoke.

Energetic upgrades are executed by plugging into your **heart** and using your *insight* to log on to the **Higher Self Network** (**H**.**S**.**N**.). The *shift* occurs from placing your *thought* on the components of your **spine** and **CNS** for a millisecond. It is possible to communicate with individuals or groups that are located in the same **physical** *space*, connect by **phone** or **internet**, or *remotely shift* the energy with *intuitive communication* alone. The energetic *shifts* have one hundred percent potential to take you to infinity and beyond, inspiring *creative solutions* to **problems**. Generally "shift happens" by focusing on the entire **spine**, and at other times a particular location on the **spine** will stand out for a specific *shift*. Strengthen your *intention* that any *general energetic shift* you facilitate will be **specific** enough to effect infinite *possibilities* for *change*.

GENERAL AND SPECIFIC WEAKNESSES

If everything we think about has the potential to manifest as a third dimensional reality, what happens to the *thoughts* that get away from us? Fundamentally, most people share *collective thoughts* that satisfy the need to fit in with others in a topsy-turvy world. These are generalities that we use to adapt to the ever-increasing pace of keeping up in today's world. Think of non-productive *thoughts* as helium-filled balloons; it is possible to jump up and grab hold of the strings of many *thoughts*/balloons at once to *eliminate* them, but it is also inevitable that some will escape and become part of the *collective whole*. Some of these *thoughts* are **light** and some are **dark**. When your *thought* is focused, you are able to burst the balloons of *limiting thoughts* in a split second and combust *challenges* into *opportunities*. As you strengthen yourself to the fundamental weaknesses humanity faces, you are better able to maximize your potential through every *aspect* of life. The odd balloon will get away; however, once you address the *fundamental challenges*, fewer balloons escape your attention and become peripheral annoyances that you can jump up and grab one at a time to address **specifically**.

Each energetic *shift* builds upon the others, boosting your potential and your ability to *effect positive change*. The **question** is just as important as the **answer**. Complicated, long, drawn-out stories and **questions** lead to **confusion**, whereas one-word **questions** lead to specific one-word **answers**.

THE "GOOD NEWS" IS:

You don't need to rely on fate for your life to improve. You can upgrade your high tech equipment on a regular basis to make sure it is **consistent** and up to **speed**.

THE "BAD NEWS" IS:

The more *aware* people become, the more they realize how *unaware* they really are. This is actually "good news" when people remind themselves that the whole point of becoming *aware* is to expand their *minds*.

NUGGET OF WIZDOM FROM THE VECTOR

SHIFT HAPPENS IN MILLISECONDS BEYOND THE LIMITATIONS OF THE BODY, SOUL AND SPIRIT, AND IS REINFORCED BY THE HEART'S INTELLIGENCE AND THE EXPANSION AND CONTRACTION OF THE UNIVERSAL HEART BEAT. PHYSICAL LIMITATIONS ARE A DISTORTION OF THE INFINITE POTENTIAL OF THE UNIVERSE.

SKIN

Skin is a work in progress, always changing because of its many specialized **cells** and **structures**. It provides the **body** with a protective barrier as the first line of defense against potentially harmful substances from the **external environment**, it helps to maintain **body temperature**, and it is a *sensory* feedback mechanism. The **skin** is made up of three main structures or layers: the **subcutaneous**, the **dermis**, and the **epidermis**, which is the outermost layer.

SUBCUTANEOUS TISSUE

The deepest layer of **tissue** is the **subcutaneous tissue**, also referred to as the **hypodermis**. It is a layer of **adipose** and **connective tissue** that protects the **bones** and **organs**, helps to regulate **body temperature** and plays a role in **pigmentation**. The majority of the **subcutaneous layer** is made up of **adipose tissue** as well as **fibers**, **nerves** and **hair follicle roots**. There are also large **blood vessels** and **sweat glands** that cool overheated bodies. Some **medications** are injected directly into the **subcutaneous layer** because its limited **blood flow** is capable of not only of storing "fat," but also of slowly releasing **drugs** so as to introduce them gradually into the **system**.

DERMIS

The **dermis** is the second or middle layer of the **skin**, containing **collagen** and **elastin fibers** that form a mesh made up of **fibroblast cells**; these play an important role in the overall *health* of the **skin**. Small **blood vessels** called **capillaries, lymph nodes, sebaceous glands, hair follicles, sweat glands, apocrine glands** and **nerves** are all contained in the **dermis**. This layer is thicker than the **epidermis**, gives the **skin** its **elasticity** and **firmness**, helps to maintain **temperature**, and synthesizes **collagen**, **elastin** and **reticular fibers** to support the **structure** of the **skin**. The thickness of the **dermis** varies depending on the **location** of the **skin**; for instance, the average thickness on the **eyelids** is .3mm, but on the upper back it is 3.0 mm.

There are two layers within the **dermis**, the **reticular layer** and the **papillary layer**. The **reticular layer**, closest to the **subcutaneous tissue**, is made up of thick **collagen fibers** that are arranged parallel to the **skin**. The **papillary layer** is made up of thinner **collagen fibers**, closer to the **epidermis**. The **capillaries** nourish the **skin** and provide **oxygen** while the **lymph nodes** clear the **skin** of **cellular waste**, **parasites** and **parasitic waste, toxins, poisons**, etc. The **sebaceous glands** produce an oily substance called **sebum** that provides waterproofing and lubricates the **skin** and **hair**. **Nerves** transmit *sensations* of **pain**, *itching* and **temperature**. Specialized **nerve cells** called **Meissner's** and **Vater-pacini corpuscles** are contained within the **dermis**, and are responsible for transmitting *sensations* of **touch** and *pressure*.

Many of the anti-wrinkle creams that are applied to the surface of the **skin** are ineffective because **wrinkles** develop in the **dermis** and the creams are not able to penetrate through the **epidermis**. This is why energetic *shifts* are much more effective for *youthfulness*, because they can be applied from the inside out to strengthen *utilization* of **collagen** and **elastin**.

EPIDERMIS

The **epidermis** is the waterproof outer layer of the **skin** that provides a tough barrier to protect the **body** from the **external environment**. It is quite thin on some areas of the body such as the **eyelids**, and thickest on the **palms** of the **hands** and the **soles** of the **feet**. It may or may not have **hair follicles**, **nails**, **sweat** and **sebaceous glands**, depending on where it is in the **body**. The **epidermis** is primarily composed of **keratinocytes**, **cells** that are made up of tough **proteins** called **keratins**. It is continually renewing itself and repairing damage to the **skin** by *regenerating* new **cells** and shedding the **squamous cells** that have already died. The lower layers of the **epidermis** are alive and active, while the surface is mostly made up of **dead cells** that are being shed. The **epidermis** is made up of five **epithelium layers**; from the inside out, they are the **stratum basal**, **stratum spinosum**, **stratum granulosum**, **stratum lucidum**, and **stratum corneum**. The bottom layer, the **stratum basal**, has **cells** that are shaped in columns and divide and push mature cells into the highest layer. As they reach the top layers they flatten out and die. The next layer is the **stratum spinosum** that is also referred to as the "prickle layer" because of the spinous look of its **cells**. Its main purpose is to protect against foreign **materials** and to *produce* and *retain* **moisture**. The primary function of the third layer, the **stratum granulosum,** is to prevent **fluid** loss. This layer is made up of thicker **cells** called **lipids** and **keratin** that protect the dense **cells** lying underneath. The **stratum granulosum** is the transition from **living cells** to completely **dead cells** on the outermost layer of the **epidermis**.

The next layer is the **stratum lucidum** which is a thin, translucent layer of **dead skin cells** in the **epidermis**; it is only readily seen by microscope in areas of thick **skin** such as the **palms** of the **hands** and **soles** of the **feet**. The **keratinocytes** that are located in the **stratum lucidum** produce a type of oily substance made from **lysosome** *degeneration*. This is responsible for creating **enzymes** that *degenerate* old **cells** and *regenerate* new **tissue**. **Keratin** is made up of granules of **keratinocyte proteins** that are also found in **fingernails**, **toenails** and **hair**, as well as in **hooves**, **horns** and **claws** in animals.

The outer-most layer of the **epidermis** is called the **stratum corneum**. It was commonly assumed that the **stratum corneum** was biologically inert, acting like a thin sheet of plastic that protected the **epidermis** from exposure to **external elements**. It is now known that there is more than meets the eye regarding the intricate systems of the **stratum corneum**.

YOUTHFUL SKIN

As in all parts and **organs** of the **body**, **structure** equals **function**. Understanding the **structure** of the layers of the **skin** and their function is beneficial in facilitating a *shift* in the improvement of **skin**. The **stratum corneum** has a major *effect* on the **appearance**, *youthfulness*, *fitness* and *health* of the **skin**.

The structure of the **cells** in the **stratum corneum** are similar to the alignment of bricks and mortar. By way of analogy, a **protein** complex made up of threads of **keratin** called **corneocytes** functions as **bricks** do, while **water** is like the **mortar** that holds the **bricks** together. It is important to recognize that **cells** are most alive in the basement of the **foundation** that the **skin** is built on, and they are pushed up through the layers as they mature to eventually die and be shed from the **epidermis**. Any **supplements** that are taken to improve **skin**, **hair** and **nails** must be strengthened to get to where they are required from the **inside out**. Existing conditions in the **nutrition** of the **skin** can be improved by checking to make sure **nutrients** are getting through to all of the layers.

Lamellar is formed in the **keratinocytes** of the **stratum spinosum** and the **stratum granulosom**. As the **cells** mature and reach the **stratus corneum**, **enzymes** degrade the outer envelope of the **lamellar bodies**, releasing **lipids**, **free fatty acids** and **ceramides** that form a continuous layer, This is referred to as a **lamellar lipid bilayer** because it is formed by two layers of the tiny threads of **corneocytes**. Each **corneocyte** is surrounded by an insoluble **structure**, made up of **protein** called the **cell envelope** which is comprised of mostly **loricin** and **involucrin**. The **cell envelopes** are considered to be either "rigid" or "fragile" in the study of dermatology, depending on the interaction from the **lamellar bilayer**. There is a layer of **ceramide lipids** attached to the **cell envelopes**. These **lipids** repel **water** between the **cell envelope lipids** and the **lipid bilayer**, thus maintaining the *balance* of the **stratum corneum** by facilitating **hydration** from the trapped **water molecules** held between them, and preventing them from migrating to the lower layers of the

epidermis. Strengthen the *relationship* between the **water molecules, ceramide lipids** and the **cell envelope** in all directions.

Specialized **structures** made of **protein**, called **corneodesmosomes** also play an important role in holding the **corneocytes** together in order to facilitate shedding of the **skin** in a process called **desquamation.** Strengthen activation of the exfoliation process by ensuring the energetic connections between the **enzymes**, the **water molecules** and **alkalinity** are structurally sound and working at optimum potential with each other in all directions.

The *absorption* of water from the external atmosphere combines with water from the internal dynamics of the **stratum corneum** to be dispersed to its outermost layers. These natural **moisturizing factors** are easily leached from **cells** when the **skin** comes in contact with **water**, which is why excessive contact with **water** actually makes the **skin** drier.

MELANOCYTES

Melanocytes are **cells** containing **melanin** that produce **pigment** in the **hair** and **skin**. They are buried below the surface of the **skin**, **hair**, **brain**, **inner ear**, **heart** and **eyes**. Environmental factors, such as exposure to **ultraviolet radiation**, **chemicals**, **herbicides**, etc., cause **physical** and **non-physical** *re-actions* that influence the color of **skin** and **hair**. **Melanin** is released from the **melanocytes** of the lower levels of the **skin**, and eventually travels to the surface of the **tissue** to replenish it. Unevenness of the **cells** causes changes in **pigmentation** because of the impact on the **melanocytes** and their ability to consistently *produce* and *distribute* **melanin**. The more a person is exposed to **ultraviolet radiation**, the more active the **cells** become, not just in the **skin**, but also in the **brain**, most specifically in an area of the **brain** called the **substantia nigra** that stores high levels of **melanin**. Limited **melanin** *production* in the **brain** *affects* the **brain's** ability to synthesize **chemicals** which in turn *affects* the **neurotransmitters**.

Freckles, moles, birthmarks, stretch marks and so-called "**liver spots**" are patches of **melanin** that have accumulated in one area because the **cells** in one or all of the layers of the **epidermis, dermis** and **subcutaneous tissues** are uneven. This can be caused by **bacteria, pigment granules, cellular waste, parasites** and **parasitic waste** that is trapped in between the layers. **Skin problems** are the result of the layers within the **epidermis, dermis** and **subcutaneous layers** not removing and flushing out basic **waste products** such as cellular waste and dead cells. This leads to acne, eczema, psoriasis, dermatitis and other skin problems.

Identify where the weakness is coming from in each layer of skin and send accumulations of waste products, parasitic waste, toxins, poisons, etc., out to black wholes. Strengthen nutrients, water, oxygen, etc., to go to where they are needed in each layer via white holes. If you think of the layers of skin as if they were a building, and picture each floor with its own power, water and sewage system, it is easy to see that every floor needs to be clean for the entire building to be clean. Optimum cooperation between the floors is essential to maintain cleanliness in the building from the foundation to the top floor.

Emotional and psychological issues are often a factor in irritations and outbreaks of the skin, as are psychic and spiritual experiences that are held in the sub-conscious and un-conscious mind. The location of blemishes and other skin problems on the face and body are often connected to both physical and non-physical issues regarding specific organs and other body parts. For instance, skin problems on the forehead are often linked to the digestive system and an inability to absorb and assimilate what is taking place in a person's life. Weaknesses in the liver often show up between the eyebrows, while dehydration and weaknesses in the kidneys present around the eyes as dark circles and as skin problems at the temples. Clogged pores on the nose are often connected to the heart, and to issues with a person's purpose and identity being in sync with their heart. Weaknesses in the respiratory system often show up in the cheeks as overheating and overly acidic skin.

If hormonal fluctuations are causing problems, they will usually appear on the upper chin and below the lower lip. If a woman is ovulating, the ovary that is releasing the egg will often cause the problem on the same side of the body. The chin, jawline and neck often are affected by the stomach and adrenal glands. When people are feeling overwhelmed and vulnerable, the skin on their shoulders is affected along with keratosis (rough goose bumps) on the back of the arms. When upper legs, thighs, lower back and buttocks are involved, it is quite often a reaction to products such as lotions, detergents, skin softeners etc. It is not uncommon for people to have a thickening or padding of tissue on the upper back, back of arms, front of thighs, etc., if they are feeling vulnerable about a certain body part or are suppressing emotions from specific ages. The words people use to describe specific problems often give clues as to what underlying issues are bothering them. *EU ... SENSATIONS, Pg. 456

It is also common for people to become "allergic" to products that are connected to a **job** or **career** that they wish to leave, but feel trapped in for reasons involving **finances**, **family obligations**, **societal** *expectations*, and *spiritual experiences* from *past lives*. These are not necessarily from people's own lives, but can come from **ancestors**, **descendants**, **co-workers** etc. For example, many **rashes** and **skin outbreaks** happen in **bakers** who become allergic to **flour**, **sugar** and **oils**, in **hair stylists** who develop sensitivities to **hair products**, in **exterminators** who can no longer tolerate the **chemicals** in **sprays** and **insecticides**, in **gardeners** who *react* to **plants**, in **medical practitioners** who become allergic to **latex gloves**, etc. Clear *past life* triggers that involve the present occupation or activity which brought them in contact with the **chemicals** or **products**.

Skin care is a huge industry. Test for any *karmic* issues with any people involved in the **beauty industry**, **magazines** and other **media**, **scientists** involved in **animal abuse** for **testing**, **dermatologists**, **allergy specialists**, etc.

TISSUES

There are four major types of **tissues** that are found throughout the body in different **organs**. They are **connective tissue**, **muscular tissue**, **nervous tissue and epithelial tissue**. **Connective tissue** makes up the vast majority of the **tissues** in the **body**. There is loose **connective tissue** that many refer to as **fat tissue**, and dense **connective tissues** that make up **cartilage**, **bone**, **blood** and the **lymph system**.

There are three types of **muscle tissue**. **Skeletal muscle**, allows **muscles** to *contract*, **smooth muscle** that is found in the walls of **internal organs** and **blood vessels**, and **cardiac muscle** found exclusively in the walls of the **heart**. **Nerve tissue** is made up of string-like **neurons** (**nerve cells**) that *receive* and *conduct* impulses to and from all parts of the **body**.

The **epithelial tissue** is the outermost layer of **tissue** that is made up of many types throughout the **body**. **Simple squamous epithelium cells** are located in the **air sacs** of the **lungs**, the lining of the **heart**, in the **blood** and in the **lymphatic vessels**. They secrete a lubricating **substance** and filter foreign **matter**. **Simple cuboidal epithelium cells** are found in **ducts**, **glands** and **kidney tubules**. They also secrete a lubricating **substance** and absorb **matter**. **Ciliated tissue** is **tissue** that has **cilia** (**small hairs**). **Simple columnar epithelium cells** are also responsible for the absorption and secretion of **mucous** and **enzymes**, mainly in the **tissues** of the **uterus**, **bladder**, **bronchi** and **digestive tract**. **Pseudo-stratified columnar epithelium cells** are also **ciliated** and can be located in the esophagus and **respiratory tract**. Lastly, **stratified squamous epithelium cells** line the **mouth**, the **esophagus** and the **vagina** to protect them against abrasion and **transitional epithelium cells** allow for the *contraction* and expansion of the **bladder**.

HAIR

The **hair root** is similar to the root system of a plant. It is contained in a tubular structure with the **hair follicle** underneath the **scalp**. As new **cells** are birthed in the **hair root**, they enlarge and divide to be pushed through the **scalp**, causing visible **hair growth**. The **hair** that is visible is actually **dead tissue**, as are the tips of the **fingernails** and **toenails**.

A basic understanding of the anatomy of a **strand** of **hair** can be very beneficial to improve **shine** and **manageability**. Every **strand** of **hair** is made up of the **hair shaft** and the **hair root**. The **hair strand** can be divided into three layers. The outer layer called the **cuticle**, is made up of hard, transparent **cells** similar to the **scales** of a fish. Uniformity of the **scales** of the **cuticle** determine the **shine** and **resilience** of the **hair**. The middle layer is called the **cortex** and consists of "rope-like" **fibers** that depend on the **cuticle** for protection. Any inconsistencies that damage the **cuticle** causes **split ends** because of moisture loss in the **cortex**. The innermost layer of **hair** is called the **medulla**. It has the least apparent effect on the *health* and **shine** of the **hair**.

The three stages of **hair growth** are promoted by **stem cells.** Hair has **three stages** of growth, the **anagen** or **growth** phase, the **categan** or **transitional** phase and the **telogen** or **resting** phase. The average rate of **hair growth** is about one hundredth of an inch because in the **anagen** phase there is very rapid *production* of a **protein** called **keratin**. During the second phase, the *production* of **keratin** falls off over a period of a few weeks and causes the hair to **shrink** and *contract*. The final stage, the **telogen** phase, generally lasts three to four months. Now the hair rests in the **follicle** until it is physically dislodged by brushing, combing, washing, massaging, etc., to be replaced by a new hair in the **follicle**.

At any given time the average **head** of **hair** has about ten to fifteen percent of its hair in the **telogen** phase, while eighty-five to ninety percent is in the **anagen** phase. Hair loss occurs when the **telogen** phase and the **anagen** phase are not *synchronized*.

THE FOLLICLE

It seems that people are rarely satisfied with their **hair**. If it is **curly**, they wish it was **straight**, if it is **fine** they want it to be **thicker**. It is either too **dry** or too **oily** or both, and can always be enhanced by **dying** it to change its **color**. **Hair** also seems to have a tendency to **grow** on the **body** where people don't want it and not grow on the **head** where people do want it! Understanding the anatomy of the **hair follicle** is helpful to energetically **encourage** and **discourage** hair growth in different areas of the **body**.

The **color** of **hair** is determined by the **pigment cells** producing **melanin** in the **hair follicle**. As people age, **pigment cells die** and **hair** turns **grey** while **skin** develops unwanted **dark spots**. Strengthen the **melanocyte cells** that are causing unwanted **pigment** in the **cells** of the **skin** to go to the **hair follicle**.

The *health* of the **hair** is dependent on the **health** of the **hair follicle** and the funnel shaped **infundibulum** where the **follicle** sits. The **papilla** is a large **structure** made up of **connective tissue** at the base of the **follicle**. The **papilla** is usually oval or pear-shaped and encased by the **hair matrix** except for the **root sheath** that is connected to the surrounding **connective tissue**. The **hair matrix** is one of the fastest growing **cell populations** in the **body**, and is constructed of **epithelial cells** and some **melanocytes** that produce **pigment**. **Cell division** is rare in the **papilla**. People suffer temporary **hair loss** from **chemotherapy** and **radiation** because the **dividing cells** are killed so rapidly.

The **bulb** contains several types of **stem cells** that supply new **cell growth** to the **follicle**; it is located at the insertion point of the **arrector pili muscle**. This **muscle** is responsible for making **hair** stand on end, by causing "goose bumps." **Sebaceous** glands are also attached to the **follicle,** and produce **oil** at the **scalp**. There are more **sebaceous glands** in **fine hair** because there are more hair **follicles** than in **thick hair**.

Hirsutism is an extreme condition in which **women** develop **male hair patterns** such as a **beard** and a **mustache** and other unwanted **facial hair**. Test for weaknesses they have regarding their **gender**, *past*, *present* and *future*. On a **physical** level, there are often weaknesses in the **endocrine glands** causing excessive **testosterone**. Send the excess **testosterone** to the **genitals** and **thighs** to increase **libido** and decrease **cellulite**.

Male pattern baldness is the most common form of **hair loss** in **men**; the **hairline recedes** and there is **hair loss** on the **crown**, or both.

Female pattern baldness generally does not escalate at the same rate as it does in men. The **hairline** is typically preserved and the **crown** usually does not *suffer* as much of a loss. *Anger* is often an underlying weakness in a person who is **losing hair**.

Shock and *grief* can instantly make a person "go grey" or make **straight** hair **curly** or **curly** hair **straight**. Issues around **scalping**, **skinning people alive**, **trapping animals** for fur and other *associated traumas* and **tortures** can accumulate within the **DNA** of a family, causing problems such as **trichotillomania**; this is a *psychological dis-order* that causes a person to feel the compulsion to **pull** out his or her own **hair**. It differs from **alopecia**, which is a condition where round patches of **hair** fall out at the **scalp**.

Fungal infections such as **tinea capitis** (**ringworm**) causes loss of hair in **ring shaped** and **round patches**. There is no actual worm involved, unlike in the case of head *lice infestations* where the **insects** actually live on the **scalp** and live off human **blood**.

Telogen effluvium is usually a temporary condition that causes the **hair** to fall out about two months after a **physical shock** to the **system**, such as giving birth to a child, or at times of high *emotional* and *psychological* "stress." *Inflammation* of **hair follicles** also leads to *infections* that are often caused by *emotional* and *psychological* distress, especially from *suppressed anger*. Each **hair** on your head is like an **antennae** that is constantly feeling the undercurrents of your **environment** and sending those messages to your **body**. People who attract **parasites** on the **outside** often attract **parasites** on the **inside** as well. **Dandruff** (**seborrheic dermatitis**) is also caused by *inflammation* of the **scalp**, and is characterized by *itchiness* and **flakes**. Underlying *emotional* and *psychological* weaknesses are common, particularly from *memories* of **fleas**, **flies** and **tick** *infestations* which resulted in the spread of *dis-ease* and **plagues**.

For optimum growth of **hair** on the **head,** strengthen **progesterone** to go to the **melanocyte cells** of the **hair follicle**, and strengthen *regeneration* of the **mitochondria** of the **cells**.

Permanent **hair** removal is possible through **electrolysis** and **laser therapy**. **Electrolysis** is a procedure in which a very thin needle is inserted into the individual **hair follicles**, one at a time to apply an **electrical current**; in **laser therapy**, the **laser** is aimed at several **hair follicles** at once. Both destroy the hair **follicle** by cutting off **blood supply**. **Laser** therapy is much more **cost effective** and less *painful* than **electrolysis**, and has the highest success rate for **dark hair**;

however, it is unlikely to work on **blonde, red** or **grey** hair because the **laser** searches for **pigment** in the **root**. That said, it is possible to enhance the **effects** on **lighter hair** by applying an energetic **laser** to cut off **blood supply** to the **hair follicle**, thereby slowing down **hair growth** in areas where it is not wanted.

FINGERNAILS AND TOENAILS

Fingernails and **toenails** are made up of **living cells** that are mostly hardened **protein** called **keratin**. There are five parts to nails, the **nail plate**, the **nail bed**, the **cuticle**, the **nail folds** and the **lunula**. The **nail plate** is the part of the **nail** that can be **seen**, the **nail bed** is the **flesh** underneath the **nail plate**, the **nail folds** are the **skin** that **supports** the **sides** of the **nail plate**, the **cuticle** is a thin layer of **skin** that rims the base of the **nail plate**. The **lunula** is the half-moon at the **base** of the **nail plate**.

Older, **living cells** are constantly being replaced by new **cells**. **Fingernails** grow faster than **toenails**, and all **nails** on the dominant side of the **body** grow faster than on the other side. To have strong nails It is important that there is an **evenness** in the **nails** from **left** to **right**, **top** to **bottom** and every other angle.

THE "GOOD NEWS" IS:

The **cells** in the **skin**, **hair** and **nails** are a reflection of the *health* of every **cell** in the **body**. If you pay attention to what they show you, it is possible to use that information to shift all the **cells** of the **body**.

THE "BAD NEWS" IS:

The **skin**, **hair** and **nails** are complicated structures with many functions. When any of the **structures** are not operating at optimum potential within themselves and with the others as a whole, it causes damage and **aging** to the **skin**.

NUGGET OF WIZDOM FROM THE VECTOR

YOUR SKIN, HAIR AND NAILS SEEM VERY ALIVE, YET BY THE TIME THEY ARE VISIBLE TO THE NAKED EYE, THEY HAVE ALREADY LIVED AND ARE MAKING THEIR TRANSITION. THE SAME IS TRUE FOR MANY PEOPLE WHO HAVE A PESSIMISTIC ATTITUDE. THAT IS WHY SOME PEOPLE CANNOT STAND TO LIVE IN THEIR OWN SKIN.

SLEEP

Sleep is an altered state of consciousness that we all need for **homeostasis**. This is obvious when we tune into animals on the planet. Mammals, birds, reptiles, aquatic animals and even insects all require **sleep**, and do so with their **systems** in a heightened **anabolic** state that uses *energy* to build the **molecules** in **organs** and **tissues** through **metabolic pathways**; these are an elaborate series of **metabolic** *reactions* that happen within the **cells**. They are fired by **catabolism**, the **chemical reactions** that break down **molecules** into smaller units. The balance between **anabolism** and **catabolism** is regulated by **circadian rhythms**. **Circadian rhythms** follow approximately, a twenty-four hour cycle that responds primarily to **light** and **dark**, which causes **physical**, *mental* and *emotional* changes. There are a group of **molecules** in the **cells** that interact throughout the **body** and are driven by the **biological clock**.

Thousands of **nerve cells** in the brain coordinate all the **systems** so that they are in *sync* with each other. This occurs in an area of the **brain** called the **suprachiasmatic nucleus** (**SCN**), which is located in the **hypothalamus**. The **circadian rhythms** are triggered by factors in the **physical body** as well as by the **physical environment**. The amount of light that a person receives switches **genes** off and on to control the *internal* clocks influencing **sleep-wake cycles**, **hormones**, **body temperature** and other important bodily functions. These rhythms have been linked to insomnia and other sleep dis-orders, to diabetes, depression, bipolar **dis-order** and seasonal affective **dis-order**. The **SCN** is responsible for the production of **melatonin,** a **hormone** that causes sleepiness when there is less **light**.

Strengthen the *fitness* of **metabolic pathways** and optimum *balance* between **anabolism** and **catabolism**, as well as the relationship between the **SCN**, the **hypothalamus**, the **optic nerves**, and **melatonin** *production* to be strong within themselves and each other.

Most people concern themselves with why they cannot **sleep**, without considering why it is difficult to **wake** up. When you are excited about the next day it is hard to **sleep**. You can hardly wait to get up because you cannot wait to start your **day**. However, it is challenging to be inspired to **wake** up in the morning if you are getting up to go to a **J.O.B.** (**journey of the broke**) that you totally dis-like, and yet the vast majority of people in industrialized nations spend most of their time doing just that. Not surprisingly perhaps, **insomnia** and **prescriptions** for **sleeping pills** and other **medications** are at **epidemic** levels in the developed world. **Sleep deprivation** is often referred to as "sleep debt" because **sleeping** has become **big business**, and the fight against **insomnia** has largely been left to **drug companies** and **commercial sleep centers**.

Many people cannot **sleep** because of **depression** and *anxiety*, which in turn aggravates **depression** and *anxiety* precisely because they cannot **sleep**. **Women** are twice as likely to have **insomnia** than **men**. Many report having more difficulty sleeping when they have their **menstrual cycle** or are in "men-o-pause." **Older** people, in general, sleep less than the **young**, especially **young adults** and **teenagers**. Some **insomniacs** can't **sleep** because they are on **medications** that keep them awake. Others are taking **medications** to help them sleep because they are concerned about getting to work, or have other **financial** concerns. However, those patients whose **insomnia** is caused by an excess or lack of *neurotransmitters* are least likely to respond to common treatments and **medications** for sleep deprivation.

Much of the **information** about **sleep** is operating under the **assumption** that when people **sleep** they are **resting**. If, however, **sleep** is viewed as a time when people access other *dimensions* and **realities** that are occurring at the same **time** as their own **reality** before they fall **asleep**, it only makes sense that those **realities** are also *productive* and possibly as challenging or even more challenging than the reality on the **third dimensional plane**. Another consideration to contemplate is that *consciousness* does not rest or go to sleep along with you; it just applies itself to a different direction because *consciousness* is made up of **body**, *soul* and *spirit*. When you are asleep, your *sub-conscious* and *un-conscious minds* are hard at work, processing what occurred during your day, and what you plan to accomplish the next day. Many people try to *relax* themselves into **sleep,** and end up relaxing their **bodies** to the point that it creates *stagnation* in all the **systems**. It is much more beneficial to *tense* your **body** to meet the pressure of the surface you are sleeping on so that every **system** in your **body** has the *fitness* to operate at full potential. Proper *tension* in the **body** also allows the *conscious mind* to remember dreams and other beneficial **information** that is accessed in the state of **sleep**. Longer periods of **sleep** encourage a division between the **conscious, sub-conscious** and **un-conscious** mind. It is important to clear energies from the **mattress** you are sleeping on before and after sleep. A **cluttered bedroom** inspires a **cluttered mind**. It is not beneficial to **sleep** with **televisions, laptops, phones** and other **electronic devices** that influence the *sub-conscious* and *un-conscious mind*.

It is also important to ensure you are strong to anyone who shares your **sleeping space**. **Snoring** is a consequence of being too *relaxed* while in the state of **sleep**, particularly in the **mouth** and **throat**. When **snoring** is involved, there are often underlying *non-physical* weaknesses of "getting even" between couples. Partners keep each other awake all **night** because it is a more acceptable option than "speaking their truth" throughout the **day**.

Many people would have better quality of **sleep** and would be more *productive* if they were strong to **sleeping** for shorter periods of time in *intervals* rather than accepting the *limiting belief* that it is necessary to keep their **bodies** in a **stagnate** state for long blocks of time. In many **cultures** afternoon siestas compensate for less sleep at night; they **nap** during the hottest time of day when **physical** *productivity* is lowest because of the **heat**. Sadly, as modern technology creeps into these **cultures,** many people now use this time to "get caught up" on the **false obligations** of **society** rather than using the time to optimize their **physical potential**.

The division between **light** and **dark** has become blurry since the introduction of **electricity**. Many people who have difficulty **sleeping**, especially those who choose to work "graveyard shifts," often have weaknesses to **death** and **dying**. Going to sleep can trigger *memories* of being *in-between* life and **death** and **experiences** of **euthanasia**. It is interesting that the party after a person is interred is called a "wake."

Many people **jar** themselves **awake** with **alarming noises** from "alarm clocks." (What an unfortunate word!) If you have ever lived with a **cat**, you may have noticed that they do not come equipped with a **snooze button**, nor do they follow the dictates of the **Gregorian calendar** or "daylight savings time." If you are using your **snooze button** to catch a little bit more **sleep**, you can also let go of the **linear** nature of **time** by *shifting* the "ten-minute snooze" to *feel* like an **hour** on a *non-physical* level; then upon *re-awakening*, be like your **cat** – take the time to stretch your **body** and your *mind*, and to strengthen your **daily routine** before you get out of bed.

JET LAG

It is assumed that people suffer from **jet lag** because they have crossed **time zones**. In fact, the leading weakness for most people is not the length of **time** they are in the **air**, but what is required to get into the **air**. Going through **x-ray machines**, **metal detectors** at **security**, having **uniformed officials** search through **private belongings**, having **passports stamped** and being **herded** like animals in a **chute** going off to their **deaths** – all this triggers **fears** of being **imprisoned**, **experimentation**, **radiation**, **explosive disasters**, **war**, etc., in most people. Another major weakness is the reason for flying. If you reflect on a time when you were "catching a flight" to **somewhere** or **something** that was *exciting*, like a **holiday** or a visit with **someone** that you *miss*, it is rare that you *miss* **sleep**. Many people, however, are flying to **business meetings, funerals** and other **family events** that they are not in *alignment* with. There are often *emotional, mental* and *psychological* triggers of **packing**, leaving **others behind** and **being** left **behind**, and weaknesses of **entering** and **exiting cities, countries** and **continents**. Many people also have weaknesses to being confined on the **plane** with **strangers**, not having **control** of being the **pilot** of the plane, *fears* of **take-off** and **landing**, *sensitivities* to the *barometric pressure*, **weather patterns**, the **climate** within the **plane** and *electromagnetic frequencies*.

Clear all **karma** with **travel agents, airlines, cab drivers, shuttles**, other **passengers, luggage handlers, customs officials**, the **pilot** and **flight attendants**. Strengthen yourself to make strong choices before you **book** the **flight**, while you are **traveling**, and after you have **arrived** at your **destination**.

THE "GOOD NEWS" IS:

Human beings are naturally *productive* when their *authentic* **triad** is strong and they are tuned into their *heart intelligence*.

THE "BAD NEWS" IS:

There is a lot of concern about **sleep** and **sleep deprivation** these days. The purposes and mechanisms of **sleep** are not fully clear, and the bottom line is that most "expert information" regarding **sleep** is centered around **productivity**. **Productivity** is usually judged by the **false obligations** of **society**. The concern is that without enough **sleep**, people are not as *productive*.

NUGGET OF WIZDOM FROM THE VECTOR

WE CAN LEARN A LOT FROM ANIMALS WHO SLEEP WHEN THEY ARE TIRED, SLEEP FOR SHORTER PERIODS AND WHO UPON AWAKENING, GRADUALLY EASE THEMSELVES INTO WAKEFULNESS BY STRETCHING THEIR ENTIRE BODIES, UNLESS THEY ARE STARTLED OR IN DANGER.

"SPIRITUAL" MEN

Many **women** who believe they are searching for a **spiritual man** are actually searching for an *intuitive man*, and confusing that with a man who is on a **spiritual journey**. **Women** are often excited when **men** show up to participate in new age, metaphysical workshops and spiritual gatherings. I often hear comments such as, "Wow! there are actually real live men here!" and the funniest comment ever, "I am going to nab me one of those before darshan! Shake up the celibacy rules around here!" The **problem** is that just because **men** show up for these events does not necessarily mean they are *intuitive*. **Men** and **women** who are on *spiritual journeys* give more importance to *spirit* than to the **body** or the *mind*, and quite often are ineffective in *producing* in the third dimensional world. *Intuitive men* and **women**, on the other hand, are *balanced* and able to operate at optimum potential in the **body**, *mind* and *spirit*.

THE "GOOD NEWS" IF YOU ARE A MAN IS:

Just **showing up** at a "spiritual event," regardless of your motives, will exponentially improve your chances with **women**. There is definitely something sexy about a *spiritual man*; however, when "spiritual insights" do not *manifest* into anything **solid** on the third dimensional plane, *disappointment* eventually creeps in.

"Eighty percent of success is showing up."
Woody Allen

THE "BAD NEWS" IF YOU ARE A MAN IS:

You are walking a very fine line. Many of the **women** you meet at "spiritual events" *want* you to have the **answers**, and can also "read you like a book" even when they *pretend* they can't. You have been *graced* with a small window of *opportunity* because **women** *want* to *believe* in you. It is definitely sexy to have all the **answers** and "walk your talk!"

"I walk the line, because you're mine."
Johnny Cash

THE "GOOD NEWS" IF YOU ARE A WOMAN IS:

If you happen to be with a man that you **thought** was *intuitive*, but who turns out to be on a *spiritual journey*, all is not lost. This is the perfect opportunity to discover exactly what you do *not want* and who *you are not*. It is just an *experience* you are having; there is no **need** to *judge*

him or **yourself**, or to take it personally once you **understand** that most **women**, from a young age, are taught to look for "the one" and men are taught to "be the one," for the **moment**, until they find "the one." *Next!*

"It's raining men, Hallelujah! It's raining men, Amen!"
Paul Shaffer

THE "BAD NEWS" IF YOU ARE A WOMAN IS:

The vast majority of **men** who are capable of *producing* in "big business" often apply themselves almost entirely to the pursuit of third dimensional gains. A **man** who is *balanced* in **body**, *soul* and *spirit* is truly a *treasure*, a valuable **asset** for any **woman,** "spiritual or not." The demand exceeds the supply, which creates "cut-throat competition," which can lead to **thyroid** issues. *EU … ENDOCRINE GLANDS, Pg. 207*

(I was unable to find a quote where women actually take responsibility for their relationship instead of blaming it on men or other women).

NUGGET OF WIZDOM FROM THE VECTOR:

CLEARING KARMA IMPROVES RELATIONSHIPS. IF THE KARMA IS CLEARED AND THE RELATIONSHIP IS STILL RESISTANT TO CHANGE FOR THE BETTER, KEEP IT SHORT AND SWEET. NO NEED TO BEAT YOURSELVES UP. FACE THOSE ASPECTS OF YOURSELF THAT YOU REALLY DON'T LIKE AND THAT ARE BEING REFLECTED BACK TO YOU THROUGH THE OTHER PERSON, AND THEN MUTUALLY MOVE ON (TO BETTER), ASAP!

STRUCTURAL INTEGRITY

The **spine** supports the **upper body**, providing **stability** and *balance*. It allows for *movement* and *flexibility* while protecting the **spinal cord** and the **CNS**, just as your **skull** protects your **brain**. The **spine** is also referred to as the **vertebral column** or **spinal column**, and runs down the *midline* of the body from the **base** of the **skull** to the **coccyx**. It consists of thirty-three **vertebrae** that are divided into **regions**, and numbered according to their location: **cervical (C1-C7)**, **thoracic (T1-T12)**, **lumbar (L1-L5)** and **sacral (S1-S5)**.

CERVICAL

The seven **cervical vertebrae** in the **neck** are the thinnest and most delicate to allow flexibility to the **neck**. The **atlas (C1)** is the first **vertebra** and supports the **skull**, just as Atlas, the Greek God, supported the **world** on his **shoulders**. It sits on the **axis (C2)** and *rotates* around the **odontoid process** to form a pivotal **joint** called the **atlanto-axial joint** which connects the **skull** to the **spine**. This **joint** allows the **head** to turn from side to side and to nod up and down. The upper limit of the **dural canal** is the **foramen magnum**, the larger hole where the **spinal column** enters the headspace at **CI**. The **atlas** is a small two-ounce bone, yet it is responsible for supporting the head that weighs, on average, between five and eleven pounds. If the **atlas** is out of *balance*, the entire **spine** and **body** twist and shift causing *imbalance* to **muscles**, **blood supply**, confusion in the messages of the **nerves**, and **organ** dysfunction.

THORACIC

The twelve **thoracic vertebrae** that are located in the **chest region** are larger and stronger than the **cervical vertebrae** and are much less *flexible*. Each of the **thoracic vertebrae** form **joints** with a pair of **ribs** that make up the **rib cage** to protect the **organs** contained in the **chest**.

LUMBAR

The five **lumbar vertebrae** that are located in the **lower back** are larger, stronger and more *flexible* than the **thoracic vertebrae** because they are not attached to the **rib cage**. This region of the **back** is more susceptible to **problems** that cause **back pain** because they support **upper body weight**.

SACRAL

The **sacral region** of the **spine** is formed by the five smaller **vertebrae**. At adolescence, they begin to fuse together with the three to five vertebrae of the **coccyx**; this fusion is complete by the age of twenty-six to thirty. The **sacrum** has a flat and triangular shape and supports the **base** of the **spinal column**, locking the **hipbones** together at the **back** and forming the **rigid pelvis** with the **sacroiliac joints** on the **sides**. It protects the **nerves** of the **cauda equina** as they pass through the **sacrum** from the **vertebral foramen** of the **lumbar vertebrae**, branching out through four pairs of holes of the end of the **sacral foramina**. The **gluteus maximus, iliacus** and **piriformis** are **muscles** from the **hip joint** that originate on the surface of the **sacrum** and allow the movement of the **legs**.

COCCYX

The **coccyx**, or **tailbone**, is in the **coccygeal** region and provides points of attachment for **muscles** in the **pelvic** and **gluteal** regions. On average, it is made up of four fused **vertebrae**; however, some people have three and others have five. The length of the **coccyx** has no apparent *effect* on the **body**, but a longer **tailbone** has been associated with advanced **psychic** abilities. When people **sit**, the **coccyx** bears their weight.

The **spine** has normal **curves** when you observe it in profile, but it should be **straight** from **left** to **right**. Normal **kyphosis** is a slight **forward curvature** that occurs in the **thoracic spine**. **Lordosis** is a slight **backwards curvature** that is normal in the **cervical** and **lumbar spine**. **Hyperkyphosis** is an exaggerated **concave curvature** in the **thoracic** region of the **spine**; it is also referred to as a "humpback" or "dowager's hump," and is frequently blamed on **osteoporosis** and **aging**. Energetically it is often the result of the *fear* of **aging** and "going backwards" in life. The *alignment* of the **head** on the **body** is also significant. Many "go-getters" who are constantly focused on reaching their goals, have a tendency to "stick their necks out." Their **heads** are so far ahead of their **bodies** that they leave their **bodies** behind and wonder why it is so difficult to get things done in the **physical** world. The excess **tissue** in the area is often a solid mass-like "armour" developed by people who do not acknowledge their accomplishments by giving themselves a "pat on the back."

Lumbar hyperlordosis is an exaggeration of the **convex curvature** of the **lumbar spine**. Many people have **lower back problems** from "bending over backwards" to meet **society's** *expectations* and **false obligations**, causing a "sway back." It is also typical for people to have their **tailbone** tucked under just as you see in dogs when they are frightened; this results in an unnatural **curvature** of the **spine** and a lack of *rotation* in the **pelvis**. Weaknesses in the **sternum** are often referred to the **lower back** and vice-versa.

Scoliosis is an abnormal **curvature** causing **S** or **C** shaped **curves** and **twisting** that can be seen when observing the **spine** from the **back**. It is often blamed for twisting the **ribcage**; however, it is more likely that the **ribcage**, is twisting the **spine**, or the **atlas** is out of *balance*. Check that the **ribs** themselves are in alignment and support optimum performance of the **lungs**. Also test for *pulling* towards and *pushing* away from *masculine* and *feminine* energy.

Each **vertebra** is made up of the **body, transverse process, spinous process** and the **vertebral foramen**. The bulk of the bone mass bearing the weight in a **vertebra** is called the **body**. The **transverse processes** are thin bones that point out to the left and right sides of the **body**, and the **spinous process** extends from the ends of the **transverse process** at the back. They enclose the **vertebral canal** made of the **vertebral foramen** creating a hollow space between the adjacent **vertebrae** to give the **spinal cord** and **meninges** passage.

INTERVERTEBRAL FORAMEN

The **intervertebral foramen** is the actual *space* through which **nerves** leave the **spine** and extend to other parts of the **body**. In the **spinal column**, stacking occurs around the **front** part of the bones (**the bodies**). Behind the **body** of the **vertebrae** is a **ring** of **bone**. Looking at a **vertebra** from either side, the **body** and **ring** combine to make an arch-like shape. A **hole** is created by the meeting of the **pillars** of the **arch** with the **bone** below. This opening is called the **intervertebral foramen**.

INTERVERTEBRAL DISCS

Between the **vertebrae** of the **spine** are thin regions of **cartilage** that are known as the **intervertebral discs**. They are made up of an outer shell called the **annulus fibrosis**, and a soft inner region known as the **nucleus pulposus**. The **annulus fibrosis** is comprised of numerous thick bundles of **collagen fibers** that bind the **vertebrae** together while allowing them to be *flexible* and able to move. The **nucleus pulposus** is the inner core of the **vertebral disc**, made up of a jelly-like material that consists mainly of water, as well as a loose network of **collagen fibers**. They act as "shock absorbers" to protect the **vertebrae** from colliding with each other from the forces of **compression** and **torsion** as they support the **body's weight**.

ALIGNING STRUCTURE

The **skeleton** is like the **scaffolding** of a **building** that supports the **structure** within different **rooms** and *spaces*, each with their own function. The **spine** is the **foundation** of the **building**. If the **foundation** of the **building** is not *stable* and *balanced,* the integrity of the entire **building** and every **room** within it will be compromised. The **atlas** and the **base** of your **spine** need to be *balanced* with each other for both to operate at optimum potential. It is important that the **physical structure** of the **body** and all of the **organs** and **systems** are *integrated* and even in all directions **up**, **down**, **forward**, **backward**, **diagonal left** and **right**. The **upper torso** and **lower torso** support and complement each other when they are *even* and have perfect *fitness*.

Systematically *scan* your **body** from the **feet** up to the **head** and back down again. Test percentages for any comparative weaknesses. For instance you can test your **upper torso** to your **lower torso** to ensure that they are equally strong and operating at "fifty/fifty." Train yourself to notice anything that stands out or feels different from the rest of the **body**.

It is most beneficial to **start** energetic *shifts* at the **feet** and work your way to the **top** of the **head,** because the **feet** meet the **ground** like the **foundation** of a **building**, and bear its entire **weight**. It is also important to recognize that the **atlas** (**C1**) is the superstructure that carries the **weight** of your **head**, similar to a **tower** on a **skyscraper**. Once you have *shifted energy* from the **feet** to the **top** of the **head**, work your way back down the **spine** to be sure that the **head** is in *alignment* with the rest of the **body**.

The **right side** expresses *masculine energy*, **logical** and ready to move **forward**, focused on the *future*. The **left side** deals with the *past*, and embodies *feminine energies* of *creativity* and *imagination*.

If you compare **feet** to the **wheels** on a car, you can easily see why it is important they be in *alignment*. Turning **feet in** or **out** while **walking** or **running** will quickly *exhaust energy*. The motion of **walking** or **running** should be *initiated* from the **hips**, *followed through* with the **knees**, and ending on the **balls** of the **feet**; this provides bounce and lift to a person's **step** and cushions the **body**. Many people jar their **spine** with every **step** because, when they **walk** or **run**, their **heel** strikes the ground first. Every **step** you take on this planet is a challenge to love fully as you walk through the *fear* of being in a **physical**, **biological body**. Your **toes** are the *antennae* that reach out to *feel* the **earth**. The different sizes and lengths of the **toes** act as **points** of **distribution** and *reception* of *energy*. The **soles** of your feet are the *soul experiencing* its **physical presence**, *absorbing* solid female *yin* energies from the **earth** to integrate with the *yang* energies received from the **sun**. When you are in sync with the rhythm of the **earth**, you are better able to meet the *challenges* you face, because the earth's pulse calms *fear*. Check if both the **left** and the **right foot** are evenly distributing the **weight** from the rest of your **body**, and within each **foot**.

The **ankles** are intimately connected to the **wrists**, the **feet** to the **hands**, and the **fingers** to the **toes**. It is common that weaknesses in one area are referred **from** or **to** the **other**. **Ankles** indicate the **support** or **lack** of **support** that a child *received* from **parents, family** and **culture** from the moment of **conception**. Much of what occurs during the first **seven years** of life is reflected in the structure of the **calves**, and in the *alignment* from the **ankles** to the **knees**. Many people who have had to "stand their ground" and "dig their heels in" to survive their upbringing, get in the habit of "locking" their **knees** in an attempt to steady themselves. The **lack** of *flexibility stagnates* energy and is quite often referred **to** or **from** the **forearms** and the **elbows**. It also creates a weakness from the **front** to the **back** and **back** to the **front** of the **upper** and **lower torsos**.

As you work our way up from the **knees** to the **hips** and the **pelvic floor**, much of the *energy* from *experiences* during the **teen years** is held in the **thighs**. The *space* or lack of space between the *thighs* is reflective of **religious** upbringing that encourages women to "keep their legs together," and abstain from **sexual** *activities*, as well as other **cultural** *experiences* and *expectations* that **adolescents** endure as they go through **puberty**. This is a **problem** area for many **women** because *non-physical waste* as well as **physical waste** encapsulates and is stored as **cellulite**. The **hips** and the **pelvic floor** are intimately connected to the **jaw** and **chin**. If there is a **problem** with one, it usually is referred back and forth to the other, as well as to the **upper arms** and **shoulders**. Check for any unevenness from the **left** to the **right**. The main weakness in the **arms** and **legs** is not due to a lack of **exercise**; therefore, check that **hydration, oxygenation** and **nitrogen** are at strong levels where they are needed, and that the **glucose** is feeding the **mitochondria** of the **cells**.

The **spine** is protected by the **rib cage** towards the **top**, and by the **pelvis** at the **bottom**, but the middle of the **spine** is un-protected by **skeletal structures**. This is to allow for free movement of the **organs** involved in the **digestive, elimination** and **endocrine systems**. Excess **weight** from **waste** and excessive **connective tissue** often settles in the **waist**, particularly when people reach "mid-life" or have had a "belly full" of life's *challenges*.

As you move up the **body** to strengthen the **spine**, the *alignment* of each **vertebra** in relation to the one above it and below it is crucial for **structural integrity**. Check for any weaknesses in *alignment* from the **front** to the **back**, and from **side** to **side** that cause **lipping, spurring, fusion** and **spinal nerve impingement**. It is important that the **discs** between the **vertebrae** have elasticity and are properly **hydrated** and **oxygenated**. **Elongate** and open any *spaces* between the **discs** and the **vertebrae**. *EU ... PNS (PERIPHERAL NERVOUS SYSTEM), Pg. 391*

Test for *rotation* of the **spinal column** from **left** to **right**, **right** to **left** and the **upper torso** to the **lower torso,** as well as for **tilting** at the **tailbone**. Moving up the **spine**, check for **tilting** or **problems** with *rotation* of the **ribcage**. People who have a tendency to **hold** their **breath** or to take **shallow breaths** tend to have collapsed **rib cages** and **chest walls**. Strengthen them to **deep breathing** and *expansion* of the **rib cage**. Test each **vertebra** for **calcification**, and for the **facets** on the **left** and **right**. Strengthen the *relationship* between the **lymphatic system** and each **vertebra** to each other to eliminate excess **waste, parasites**, etc. If there is a **herniated disc**, delete "exploding" *traumas* from *past*, *present* and *future*.

The **shoulders** from **left** to **right** and **right** to **left** should be **even**. People who feel that they are "shouldering a heavy burden," or who have "a chip on their shoulder," tend to carry one **shoulder** lower or higher than the other. Often **one** or **both shoulders** will be *rotated* back when people are *angry* and "holding back punches." **Shoulders** that are *rotated* forward cause issues with the **chest**, the **ribs** and the **sternum**, and there are often *non-physical* issues around protecting the *heart*. **Shoulders** that are pulled up around the **neck** indicate that a person is *anxious*, like a **turtle** that is afraid to come out of its **shell**.

Stiffness in the **neck** and **pain** on a **physical** level can be caused by a **combination** of parts that make up the **physical structure** of the **head** and **neck**, including the **bones**, the **nervous system**, the **fascia**, the **circulatory system** and the **lymphatic system**. On a *non-physical* level, it is common for people to have *emotional* and *psychological* issues. Many people who appear to have their **head** attached to their **body**, do not on an energetic level. It is common for those who are *traumatized* by **hanging** and **beheading** *experiences* to *feel* a sense of separation of their **heads** from their **bodies**. It is also common for people who do not *feel* that they belong on **earth** to have their "head in the clouds." A lack of *flexibility* to *rotate* the **neck** to turn **left** or **right**, **up** or **down** often comes from weaknesses in "taking direction," or "taking a direction." When the **range** of *motion* towards the **left** is limited, it often comes up as a weakness to looking at the *past*; and if turning to the **right** is challenging, looking towards the *future* is weak. It is common to have *emotional*, *psychological* and *psychic* weaknesses underlying the **symptoms** of **neck pain**.

People who have **back surgeries** often have more than one because the success rate is so low. There are often *emotional* weaknesses and a lack of *flexibility* in **rigid situations**. If **metal** was used in the **back surgery**, its particles often drift and settle in the **feet**, which causes *stagnation* in the main *exit portals* and an inability to *feel* the energy from the earth.

Muscles work in co-ordinated **groups**. The *relaxation* of one **muscle** group allows the opposite **group** to *contract*, while the remaining **muscles** act to *stabilize* the rest of the **body** as the **bones** are moving. Test for *balance* of the **muscles** from **front** to **back** and **left** to **right**. The **muscles** are *balanced* when the **skeletal structure** is *balanced*, and vice-versa.

Disease of the **spine** can be congenital. **Spina bifida**, for example, is a disease that causes a baby to be born with abnormalities arising from defective closures of the **vertebral arch**; this allows the **spinal cord** and the **meninges** to protrude. It is important to connect with **fetuses** during **pregnancy** to check on the development of the **skeletal structures**, the **organs** and the **cavities** on a regular basis, and to clear underlying *karmic*, *psychic*, *spiritual*, *emotional*, *psychological* as well as **physical** weaknesses to prevent **birth defects**. *EU ... PREGNANCY, Pg. 398*

Other diseases of the **spine** can be *trauma* related; **spinal disc herniation**, commonly referred to as a "slipped disc," is a good example of this. It is caused by a tear in the **annulus fibrosus** or the **intervertebral disc**, which allows the jelly-like material from the **nucleus pulposus** to bulge out in a **hernia** due to weaknesses in the **structure**. Clear any *associated* and *accumulated karmas* and *spiritual experiences* of **blowing** others *up* and on an *emotional* level of **blowing** things *out* of proportion.

Spinal stenosis, more commonly referred to as "pinched nerves" or **sciatica**, is an abnormal narrowing at the **vertebral canal** in the **foramen**. The consequent impingement of the **nerves**, generally in the **lumbar spine**, puts pressure on the **cauda equina**, and causes **pain** in the lower extremities or in the **cervical** structure of the **neck**, which is more dangerous because it involves the **spinal cord**, and *affects* major **organs**. It can also cause *numbness* that may involve the **perineum** and the **bladder**. *EU ... PNS (PERIPHERAL NERVOUS SYSTEM), Pg. 391*

Osteoporosis, a thinning of the **bones**, is more common in **females** and is considered a consequence of **aging**, especially in low-weight **women**. People are commonly advised to take **calcium supplements** for prevention and treatment. It is important to consider that **aging** could also be a consequence of thinning of the bones developed from lack of *tension* and *stagnation*, in part from a build-up of **minerals** in the **spine** and **CNS**. If you are taking **calcium supplements**, strengthen them to go where it is useful; otherwise it is like pouring **cement** into your **body**.

To maintain **health** and **experience rejuvenation**, it is vital that every **organ** in the body is operating at maximum efficiency. The most important **organs** are the **heart, lungs, kidneys, liver, large intestine, small intestine, stomach, gall bladder** and **spleen.** Each **organ** needs to be strong within its own **structure** and strong to working in harmony with all the other **organs** and the **CNS** for proper **biochemistry, bio-resonance, waste removal** and **absorption** of essential **nutrients**. The **organs** require **structural support** from the **thoracic, abdominal, cranial, oral, sinus** and **pelvic cavities.** Some of the **organs** themselves create **cavities** on a regular basis when they empty, such as the **lungs, bladder, gallbladder** and **uterus.** It is also important to remember that **space** is not empty. It has perfect universal **structure** under ideal circumstances. Energetically optimizing these **spaces** from the **bottom** to the **top, side** to **side, forward** and **backward** strengthens the entire **body structure**.

RESULTS:

"Thank you Sheila for introducing me to Colette. I received more than one marvelous healing from this call tonight. I am a 3rd generation meta physician, my mentors are notable and many over the years. I have trained and have enough certifications to wall-paper a pretty good sized wall. I have had great success in facilitating healing for others however until tonight I have never experienced an instantaneous healing for myself.

"For the first time in my life I am able to stand, sit and walk straight. I hesitated to write even so until today, 2 days later and after visiting my Chiropractor to share my joy and yes, to have him verify that my body has indeed changed physically. I have tried to keep this to as few words as possible, I could go on and on with great gobs of joy and do so with everyone I encounter but words cannot explain what I am feeling ,knowing and being now. Please feel free to use this testimonial in all or part. In Love, light, grace, ease, joy and unlimited gratitude."

Liza

THE "GOOD NEWS" IS:

Energetic **shifts** move **structure** because **body structure** is not fixed in **space**. Finding comparative structural weaknesses and **re-aligning** them allows the **body** to re-pattern itself according to its original **blueprint**. If there is a **miasma** that a person came in with, it can also be shifted to re-pattern itself after another person who represents ideal **structure** as a point of reference.

THE "BAD NEWS" IS:

Symptoms are caused by *dis-order* of the **muscular-skeletal structures**, and is rarely **physical** at root cause; however, most people try, unsuccessfully, to change it by addressing the **pain** as a **physical** problem.

NUGGET OF WIZDOM FROM THE VECTOR

IT IS IMPORTANT THAT THE BODY STRUCTURES ARE EVEN. THOUGHTS AND EMOTIONS HAVE A SIGNIFICANT IMPACT ON BODY FUNCTIONS. EVENNESS IS CREATIVE ENERGY AND INTUITION IN MOTION. YOU CAN CHOOSE TO DRIFT FROM DRAMA TO DRAMA, FIGHTING THE WINDS OF CHANGE, OR YOU CAN TAKE RESPONSIBILITY AND STEER AN EVEN OUTCOME.

SUBTLE ENERGIES

Surrounding the **physical body** are seven layers of *subtle bodies* that many refer to as the *aura*. The *seven bodies* can be divided into **three bodies** on the **physical plane**, **three** on the *spiritual plane*, and the *astral body* that is the bridge in-between. Within each layer of the *aura* are *seven chakras* that *vibrate* at progressively higher *frequencies*. The **subtle bodies** become more and more **dense** as they come closer to the core of the **physical body**. *Subtle bodies* are a *reflection* of the **collective whole**. Every body is made up of **atoms** that are within **cells** in the **body**, within the layers of the **skin** and on to the layers of the *subtle bodies*. The seven *subtle bodies* are the *etheric body*, *emotional body*, *mental body*, *astral body*, *etheric template*, *celestial body* and *causal body*. For most "intuitives," the **colors** and **patterns** of the *subtle bodies* are *perceived* as specific **colors**.

ETHERIC BODY (stores the blueprint)

The *etheric body vibrates* closest to the **physical body,** extending up to about **two inches** and pulsating at 15 – 20 cycles per minute. It is responsible for *receiving*, *assimilating* and *transmitting* "*Ka*" or "*Qi*" to the **physical body** via **receptors** connected to the *emotional body*. The *etheric body* stores the **blueprint** when people incarnate on this dimensional plane, and it holds clues to the *past life traumas* that shape their *health* in the current lifetime. It is *perceived* in a **grayish blue color**.

EMOTIONAL BODY (feeling)

The *emotional body* is *associated* with *feeling*. It is more fluid in nature, extending out about **three inches**, but it does not strictly follow the contours of the **physical body**. The *emotional body* changes **colors** as *emotional re-actions* occur; for example, brighter **rainbow colors** are *associated* with *happy emotions* and **gray** with *unhappy emotions*, similar to "mood rings." The *emotional body* has the most impact on the *etheric* and *mental bodies*.

MENTAL BODY (thoughts and mental processes)

The *mental body* holds *thoughts* and *mental processes*. Many people see it as a **vibrant yellow** in **color** when a person is processing *thoughts*, and it blends with the **colors** of the *emotional body* when there is *emotion* attached to the *thought*.

ASTRAL BODY (insight)

The *astral body* is connected closely to the *heart chakra*. It is the bridge between **physical** and **spiritual bodies** through *insight*, and functions as a *portal* to the *astral plane*. It extends out about **six inches** from the **physical body** with "clouds" of **rainbow colors** and **pinks**.

ETHERIC TEMPLATE (template of blueprint)

The *etheric template* is the *blueprint* of the *etheric body* before it *manifests* into **physical form**. It extends **one** to **one** and a **half feet** from the **physical body**, often appearing dark blue in color; however, because it contains all forms of the **physical world**, its **color** can vary.

CELESTIAL BODY (ecstasy of divine love)

This is a *plane* of *ecstasy* that connects the *whole being* through *divine love*. It allows *communication* with those in the *spiritual realm* to unite the **heart** with **humanity** and **nature**. Most people describe it as "shimmering" **pastel colors**.

CAUSAL BODY (gateway to cosmic bodies)

The *causal body* is an expression of the *mental experiences* on the *spiritual plane*. It extends out to **three** and a **half feet** from the **body** and surrounds all the other layers. Often **seen** and *experienced* in the shape of a **silvery-gold egg** vibrating at a very high *frequency*, it contains the *kundalini force* as a key to entering the *cosmic plane* via the *universal heart field*.

The light body is what the Egyptians call "*Ka*." It is the highest *subtle body* on the **astral plane**, and is the farthest from the dense **physical body**. "*Ka*" refers to reaching a very high level of s*uper consciousness* where the dense **physical body** is no longer needed.

THE "GOOD NEWS" IS:

A basic understanding of the *subtle bodies* and *chakras* as seen through *auras* leads to a deeper understanding of **physical**, *emotional* and *spiritual health*.

THE "BAD NEWS" IS:

Children often *sense auras*, but are discouraged by **adults** and the **educational** *system* from exploring that knowledge. Eventually the *intuitive ability* to **see** and *feel* the *vibrations* from *auras* fades as **logic** takes its place.

NUGGET OF WIZDOM FROM THE VECTOR

THE PHYSICAL BODY, MIND AND INTELLECT ARE PART OF A GREAT ILLUSION. OUR TRUE ESSENCE AS CONSCIOUS BEINGS COMES FROM KNOWLEDGE OF THE SUBTLE BODIES AND OUR TRUE NATURE COMES THROUGH ASPECTS OF OUR SOUL.

SUCCESS

Upon meeting someone for the first time, it is always acceptable to ask, "What do you do?" Most people answer with their occupation … "I am" a … (fill in the blank). Achieving **wealth**, **respect** and **fame** is accepted as the **foundation** for **success**, yet the true definition of **success** is much more individual and personal. We can compare two brilliant scientists to illustrate this point. The light bulb, the phonograph and moving pictures are considered to be **Thomas Edison's** most important inventions; however, several other scientists were already working on similar technologies. At the same time, **Nikola Tesla** was working on alternating-current electrical power transmission, a much more efficient system than the direct-current system **Edison** was working on, and he truly electrified the world with his first-of-a-kind power plant at **Niagara Falls**. **Tesla** was also working on a mass communication system to wirelessly transmit voices, images and moving pictures; he is considered by many as the "true genius" behind radio, telephone, cell phones and television. In the end, many people consider **Thomas Edison** more successful than **Nikola Tesla** because he held over a thousand patents, and was a master of building modern innovative factories and achieving financial support for them. In contrast, even though **Nikola Tesla** was the more forward thinker, he faded into obscurity and was destitute when he died. Judging according to **society's** standards, most people would deem **Edison** to have been the more successful scientist; however, they are not acknowledging the underlying currents that were taking place in the **financial world** at the time, and the corruption that was directing the flow on the material plane. **Success** on the **physical plane** does not necessarily reflect *success* of the *whole being*.

Innovators are **entrepreneurs** improve their lives and inspire others to do the same. Like them, when you are "breaking ground," you must take *actions* and *risks*. Life is a game, and it is much more fun when you "play to win" and have others win along with you. To achieve true *success*, you must define what **success** means to you, and then go after it with consistent, concrete steps of *action*.

Many people focus on success from the standpoint of satisfying **needs** and *wants*. Many of these *perceived* needs are really **false obligations** that **society** imposes on people, when, in fact, you are a *conscious being* traveling in a **human body**. There are many *aspects* to true *success*. Those who practice single-minded purpose around **career**, **family**, **education** and *health* often *experience* acute *disappointment* even when they achieve their **goal**, because it was to the detriment of other important *aspects* of life.

You can train yourself to *feel* for the **answer** that is most *applicable* to your **situation** in any given moment and make it work. It may not be the "right" **answer** for others, so don't always expect them to happily follow your lead. People teach others how to treat them. When a person *chooses* to make *changes* in the way he or she wants to be treated, it is not always met with *joy* and *appreciation*. In fact, it is very common to be met with **resistance** from the closest family members who were enjoying the "status quo." As you **consistently** *feel* for **answers** and clear blocks that limit the future, your progress will *expand* and *accelerate* at a much faster rate. This often triggers many weaknesses on an **emotional**, **psychological** and *psychic* level in others as they recognize how quickly you have changed, while they have not. Your *body*, *soul* and *spirit* must have strong *boundaries* to handle *external forces* that are up front and right "in your face." Many people have negative *spiritual experiences* of "leaving others behind" and/or "being left behind." You do not want to take in other people's *perceived* **failures** to slow yourself down, so that they can catch up to you. Strengthen others around you to "come along for the ride," if they *resonate*, and then let go of the *expectations* of the time it will take. Everyone is on an individual journey, with different priorities at any given time in their life. If you suspend *judgment*, it is much easier to be in the *flow*.

It is better to have a "sloppy success" than a "perfect failure." The biggest **failures** occur because of **trying**. When you are **trying**, you are not **doing**. *Doubt* does not feed **success** and *fulfillment*. Life is a game, acknowledge the game, and get strong to your worst **failure** being better than your last **success**.

THE "GOOD NEWS" IS:

You can become **successful** by conducting and living your life *successfully*.

THE "BAD NEWS" IS:

Becoming **successful** usually involves some *perceived* **failure**. People who don't take risks rarely *experience* **failure**, nor do they **lead**.

NUGGET OF WIZDOM FROM THE VECTOR

THERE IS NO FAILURE WITHOUT SUCCESS AND NO SUCCESS WITHOUT FAILURE. SUCCESS IS NOT A NOUN, IT IS A VERB … A WORK IN PROGRESS.

SUPPRESSION

Often people will be amazed when they become *neutral* and realize that the cause of their *discomfort* and **pain** is far from what they thought it was. The **body** and *soul* have many **imprints** from diverse *vectors* throughout *space-time* which present as weaknesses on the *psychological*, *psychic* and **physical** levels. As those weaknesses are peeled away, the *authentic self* emerges for all to witness. Many people find it challenging to face these *experiences* and therefore shy away from them; instead, they *suppress* and hold them in the **hard drive** of their **CNS**. This causes *limitations* in every *aspect* of life and often leads to **physical pain**.

There is a specific **order** to the "lack of order" in *suppression*. It is easy to understand the stages of *suppression* if you compare them to the scenario of a traffic pile-up: First, a car **stalls** and **blocks** one lane of **traffic**. Next, the *congestion* causes the **traffic** to back up as people search for an **alternate route**. Then, the **confusion** causes an **accident**, which blocks another **lane**, and leads to people becoming *impatient*, blowing their own **horns**, and *inflaming* the **situation**. The energy around the traffic jam becomes more and more *acidic* as people become increasingly *angry* and *frustrated* because they need to make *alternate* **arrangements** to compensate for arriving late to work, picking their children up from daycare, etc. In a similar way, the process of *suppression* can be tracked in specific areas of the human **body**. For instance:

STALL (*suppression*)

In the beginning stages it is common for people to *experience pressure* in the **head** that gradually shifts down the **body**.

TRAFFIC JAM (*denial*)

The suppression leads to *denial* that often presents in the **physical body** from the **head** to the bottom of the **trunk**. Some people describe *denial* as, "having your head up your ass." They are accurate in that assessment, and it explains why *denial* is so **painful**.

BLOCKAGE (*lying*)

The weight of the blockage becomes heavier and moves down into the **trunk** of the **body**.

INFLAMMATION (*numbing*)

Inflammation sets in as people begin to *re-act* to the *suppression* of "lying to themselves" and to others. This leads to the *numbing* of the **body** and *mind*, often beginning in the **digestive system**, **elimination system** and **reproductive system**. When people *lie* to themselves, they often feel the **need** to "blow their own horn" or "beat themselves up" through **addictive behaviors** and an "eat, drink and be merry" **attitude**.

CONTAMINATION (*infection*)

Energy becomes increasingly **contaminated** from the "build-up" of the *suppressed emotional re-actions* of the people caught in the jam; it now moves down the **hips**, into the **legs** and **feet** of the **body**.

EXPLOITATION (*parasitic*)

For some people, the after-effects of the jam continue for a long time as they are forced to deal with **authority figures**, **insurance companies**, etc. If you are attracting **parasites** from the **outside** of the **body**, it is highly likely that you are also attracting them on the **inside**. When people feel **exploited**, they tend to practice *forgetting* which can lead to many weaknesses in their **cognitive function**.

CALLING IN THE TOW TRUCK *(complete system shut down)*

When people have **problems** in their **feet**, particularly in their **soles**, the *suppression* is often a concern of the *soul*. The **soles** of the **feet** and the **palms** of the **hands** are major *exit portals* for the **body**. The *feeling* of helplessness from an inability to deal with *multiple emotions* and *sensations* can lead to a *complete system shut down* of the **body** and *soul*.

THE "GOOD NEWS" IS:

There really is no upside to *suppression* itself, but recognizing *suppression* is very *productive*. Many people who believe they have cleared the energy of a **situation** are often surprised when they unexpectedly encounter an "amplified version" of the same **problem** they thought they had **resolved** years earlier. This is because they had "forgotten" about it, not **solved** it.

THE "BAD NEWS" IS:

Suppression is a fact of life because people are not able to control it while they sleep. Every morning, the new **information** that has been gathered in their **sleep** from their *sub-conscious* and *un-conscious mind accumulates* and merges with the *suppression* they have not released from the previous days.

NUGGET OF WIZDOM FROM THE VECTOR

SUPPRESSION AND FORGETTING ARE VERY DANGEROUS ACTIVITIES. MANY OF US HAVE BEEN TOLD TO "FORGIVE AND FORGET." FORGIVENESS IS A GIFT THAT YOU GIVE YOURSELF; CHOOSING FORGETFULNESS IS NEVER PRODUCTIVE.

TACTICS

Edward Snowden is an American computer specialist, a former employee of the **Central Intelligence Agency** (**CIA**) and former contractor for the **National Security Agency** (**NSA**). He came to international attention as the whistleblower who leaked thousands of classified documents that outlined global surveillance programs run by the **NSA**, **UK**, **Canada**, **Australia** and **New Zealand** with the cooperation of several **European businesses** and **governments**. Some of the leaked documents share **tactics** employed by the **NSA** that are calculated to destroy people's **reputations**, influence the **media**, and **manipulate** the population. These **tactics**, which I refer to as the "Dirty D's," are responsible for much of the *anxiety* shared by the *collective whole*.

DENIAL

Denial is making a **statement** that is not true, or asserting that an allegation is false in order to avoid a **confrontation** with others and oneself.

DISRUPTION

Disruption is purposefully **preventing** a **system**, **process** or **event** to proceed as usual by creating a **disturbance**.

DEGRADATION

Many people with extraordinary **talent** have been intentionally subjected to **degradation** through **ridicule**, **humiliation** and other **demeaning tactics** to lower their status in **society** by the "powers that be."

DECEPTION

Deception is an **act** or **statement** intended to **dupe**, **cheat** and **deceive** people into *believing* something that is not true.

DESTRUCTION

Destruction is the ultimate **goal** of those who take action to annihilate something or to destroy the reputation of a person or a group beyond **repair** or **restoration**.

DISSENSION

Infiltrating groups and causing **conflict** and **dissension** amongst the members so as to hinder them from accomplishing their **goals** is a common **tactic**.

DISSEMINATION

Dissemination is broadcasting **information** through the **media**, **advertising**, **public announcements** and **speeches** to persuade or influence people in one-way communication with no clarification.

THE "GOOD NEWS" IS:

Now that you are aware of the **Dirty D's** and their *negative effects* on you and your loved ones, it is easy to prevent the rhetoric from seeping into your home in one easy step. Get rid of your **television set**! Or at the very least be selective about the quality of the **programming** that you allow into your inner sanctum.

THE "BAD NEWS" IS:

While **Edward Snowden** has been busy informing people how little privacy they really have and the potential **negative effects**, the vast majority of people are still busy whistling this tune … "Hi, ho, Hi ho, it's off to work we go," and don't take the time to be *aware* of what is really taking place around them.

NUGGET OF WIZDOM FROM THE VECTOR

ARE YOU BEING SNOWED? NEVER UNDERESTIMATE THE POWER OF WILLFUL IGNORANCE.

TAIL

The **coccyx** (**tailbone**) is a **remnant** of a **tail** that all mammals have at one point in their development. In humans it is present for **four weeks** and is most prominent when an **embryo** is **thirty-one** to **thirty-five** days old; after that it is absorbed by the **embryo**. Although this **tail** is **physically** *absorbed*, energetically it is still there as a source of *strength* and to aid in *stability* and *balance*. The **nerves** from the **spinal cord** ending in the **brain** of the *phantom tail* have a strong influence on **physical intelligence**.

Some people have odd *re-actions* when you first tell them that they have an *energetic tail*, but once you tune into its **power** and play around with it a bit, you quickly recognize its **strength**. For some people it is really challenging to get in touch with their *tail* because it is detached, bent or kinked from a fall or some other *trauma*. Once you clear energetic weaknesses of *shock*, *karma*, **cultural** and **religious** *experiences* of separation from family, most people begin to *sense* its presence.

It is fun to give your *tail* **color**(**s**) and picture it as if it were long and sleek like a cat's tail, strong and muscular like that of a dragon's, athletic like a monkey's, etc., and/or give all of these qualities to your *tail*, depending on your mood and the circumstance. People who have **problems** with *balance* or **walking** can use their *tail* like a kangaroo does, as a **rudder** for *balance*. On an airplane you can wrap your tail around yourself and slap people with it to discourage infringement of your *space*.

INTERESTING ANECDOTE

A very left–brained woman who attended a seminar had a strong resistance to the information about the **phantom tail**. On the morning of the second day, she shared an *experience* she had upon leaving the seminar the night before. While walking, she was startled by a man who came up behind her. She turned to him and angrily berated him, "How dare you step on my tail!!" Even as she spoke, she realized how shocked she was by her own words and by his immediate response, "I am SO sorry ma'am, it will never happen again." He *instinctively* knew that he had infringed on her *space* and was genuinely sorry that he had, even though on a **logical** level he was not aware of how he had offended her.

The universe is **holofractographic**, so it is not surprising that recently **NASA** has discovered that our **solar system** also has a **tail**, called the **heliotail**. The **heliotail** is a huge bullet-shaped **comet** with a clover-leafed shape at the end. The discovery was made using data collected by the **Interstellar Boundary Explorer** (**IBEX**) using measurements of **neutral atoms**.

THE "GOOD NEWS" IS:

Although the thought of having a *phantom tail* may seem a bit surprising, once you accept that it is there and you start using it for your benefit, you will find many uses for it.

THE "BAD NEWS" IS:

Many people who are told they have a *phantom tail* automatically resist the idea. It is not unlikely that if you inform people that they have a *phantom tail*, you will be ridiculed.

NUGGET OF WIZDOM FROM THE VECTOR

"GETTING TAIL" HAS A WHOLE NEW MEANING ONCE YOU BECOME AWARE OF YOUR ENERGETIC TAIL! REGARDLESS OF WHETHER YOU OR OTHERS AROUND YOU BELIEVE THERE IS A PHANTOM TAIL, ENERGETICALLY IT IS STILL THERE. IT IS VERY BENEFICIAL FOR PEOPLE TO CONNECT WITH THEIR BRAIN AT THE SACRUM TO IMPROVE THEIR PHYSICAL INTELLIGENCE.

THE PRACTICE OF MEDICINE

If you ask the vast majority of people what the leading cause of death is for North Americans, most will repeat the statistics that we are fed by the **medical** and **pharmaceutical community** through the **media**: **heart disease** and **cancer**. However, the prestigious **Journal of the American Medical Association** published a study in 2000 by **Dr. Barbara Starfield**, a **medical doctor** with a master's degree in **public health**. The most shocking revelation of her report is that **iatrogenetic damage**, a fancy word for a state of **ill health** or **adverse effects** resulting from **medical treatment**, is the **third** leading cause of **death** in the U.S. after **heart disease** and **cancer**. This means that the **combined effects** of **errors** and **adverse effects**, including **deaths** from **unnecessary surgeries**, **medication** and other **errors** in **hospitals**, **infections** and **non-error**, **adverse effects** of **medications**, are responsible for more **deaths** than cerebrovascular disease, respiratory disease, accidents, diabetes, Alzheimer's and pneumonia. Since then, other studies have supported this statistic and they even suggest that **Iatrogenic deaths** and **damage** are much higher; yet the vast majority of the public remains ignorant of the truth unless they, or a loved one have had an extended stay in a hospital.

THE "GOOD NEWS" IS:

If you have survived a prolonged hospital stay with no **ill effects**, congratulations! You have beaten the statistics! If deep down you have always wanted to go on an exotic adventure in faraway places, but have not been able to muster the courage to go due to *health concerns* from dangerous **parasites**, not being able to speak the **language**, poor **accommodation**, etc., you have already survived the worst. Go ahead and book it!

THE "BAD NEWS" IS:

If you have been in an accident or have a medical emergency, **go to the hospital** to stop the **bleeding**, restart your **heart**, put together broken **bones**, etc. There are many **talented**, **caring**, **qualified doctors**, **nurses**, **surgeons**, and **technicians**, who are dedicated to putting you back together and to facilitate your recovery. Unfortunately, your chances of full recovery are dramatically reduced the longer you stay in the hospital.

NUGGET OF WIZDOM FROM THE VECTOR

MANY UNDERLYING ENERGETIC WEAKNESSES ON THE SPIRITUAL AND PSYCHIC LEVELS, PARTICULARLY UNRESOLVED KARMA,

AFFECT A PERSON'S RECOVERY IN THE HOSPITAL. CLEARING KARMA BETWEEN THE PATIENT, ALL MEDICAL PERSONNEL, THE EMERGENCY RESPONDERS, DOCTORS, SURGEONS, NURSES, TECHNICIANS, JANITORS, OTHER PATIENTS, ETC., WILL FACILITATE A QUICK RECOVERY.

TRAUMAS

There are five fundamental *traumas* that are most *often re-enacted* throughout peoples' lives. These are **abandonment**, **abuse**, **betrayal**, **denial** and **rejection**.

ABANDONMENT

Many people have *associations* that link **abandonment** to "giving up on themselves" and on others. Often the **abandonment** is involuntary because of dangerous conditions such as **war** and **natural disasters** that are not in the control of an individual. It is not uncommon for people who are in the process of bettering themselves to become triggered or to trigger others because of *past*, *present* and *future* **concerns** and **worries** that revolve around "leaving others behind," "being left behind," "climbing over others," to get to the top, etc., that originate from **self**, **ancestors**, **descendants**, *psychic energies* and *spiritual experiences.* They *un-consciously* sabotage themselves and their efforts just as they are about to achieve their **goals** because they are not aware of the real reasons for their *feelings* of *worthlessness*.

ABUSE

Abuse comes in many forms and variations from excessive mis-use of **power** and corruption in **government**, **families**, **customs**, **religion**, etc. **Abuse** can be **physical**, *mental*, *emotional* and *psychological*; it can also come from the *collective consciousness.* They may or may not be actual *traumas* an individual is *experiencing* or has *experienced* in this lifetime or other lifetimes, or they can be triggered from *resonating* with the *fears* of the *collective whole*.

Many **physical** *traumas* come from *fetal memories* and weaknesses in the **birthing process**. Other *traumas* that are common weaknesses for people include **surgeries**, **dental traumas**, **beatings**, **amputation**, **electrocution**, **suffocation**, **drowning**, **strangling**, **animal attacks**, **car/plane/train crashes**, **burnings**, **stabbings**, **shootings**, **molestations**, **poisoning**, **public humiliation**, **rape**, **sodomy**, **suicide**, **choking**, **kidnapping**, etc.

BETRAYAL

People can **betray** themselves by "giving in" to that piece of chocolate cake they **promised** themselves they wouldn't have, and then "add insult to injury" by not enjoying it. They can also **betray** or be **betrayed** by **parents**, **siblings**, **extended friends** and **family**, **children**, **grandparents**, **institutions**, the **educational system** and the **media**. **Governments** fighting **treason** with **treason**, **politicians** and other "leaders" who **lie** and **cheat** their **constituents**, a wife **cheating** on her husband, a "best friend" who is having **sex** with a **friend's wife** behind his back – these are some examples of common **betrayals**. Other examples of **betrayal** that *affect* a huge part of the population are **corporate greed**, the **banking system**, **thieves**, **commercials**, **corrupt police** and **soldiers, pedophilic priests**, **fathers** who abandon their **families, doctored news** from the **media**, *experimentation* by **pharmaceutical companies**, the **medical system** and the **government** … and the list goes on. At times it may seem that people possess an endless capacity for **betrayal** of both others and themselves.

DENIAL

People usually think of **denial** as the refusal of a reasonable request that could easily be *fulfilled*. **Denial**, however, can also be the refusal to admit, acknowledge, or recognize the **true** cause of *health*, *fitness*, **financial**, *relationship* and/or **career problems** by assigning blame to something or someone **else**. In cases of **organ transplant**, **denial** is a *rejection* of the **donor organ**.

REJECTION

Many people "sell themselves short" to avoid facing **rejection**. This is one of the reasons many people list public speaking as their greatest *fear*, greater even than **death**. *Fears* of **rejection** stem from *experiences* of "discarding another person," "dropping communication," "shaking people off," "creating unnecessary distance," "pushing people away," and "throwing someone aside." Other forms of **rejection** are "blackballing" others by **excluding** them from a "select group," or "blacklisting them from clubs," "disinheriting someone in a will," "abruptly terminating an employee or a lover," "ending a performance," "giving someone the "cold shoulder," "blowing" or "brushing someone off," etc.

Traumas from *space-time* are often **re-opened** by **experiences** with *internal* and *external forces*. *Trauma* is not necessarily *trauma* that people have *experienced* from someone else. It can also bring up *residual memories* of *traumatizing* others, of witnessing *traumatic scenarios*, and even of encouraging someone else to *traumatize* you. There have been many creative forms of *trauma* inflicted by **torture** throughout history; these can *re-open* "a can of worms" through seemingly *insignificant events*, such as a **smell**, a **siren**, a visit to the **doctor** or **dentist**, **accountant**, **lawyer**, **principal**, being stopped for a traffic violation by a **police officer**, etc. Even watching television broadcasts of **natural disasters** such as **tornados**, **hurricanes**, **tsunamis**, **earthquakes**, etc., as well as **man-made disasters** where people are regularly **blown up**, **attacked**, **crashed into**, **molested**, **raped**, **buried alive**, **hung**, **knifed**, **drowned**, **shot**, etc. via the "**news**," **movies**, **commercials**, etc., can trigger deep, long-held *traumas* to rise to the surface.

THE "GOOD NEWS" IS:

When people recognize that they are being triggered by *traumas* that they may not be aware of on a *conscious* level, there is no need to relive the *trauma*. Acknowledging the true source for a split second is all that is necessary to clear *traumas* one layer at a time.

THE "BAD NEWS" IS:

People often **assume** that no one wants *trauma*. That is not the truth. Many **institutions** and **individuals** thrive on the *traumatization* of others. Some of the *traumatization* is **intentional** and some of it is *un-conscious*.

NUGGET OF WIZDOM FROM THE VECTOR

THE SAYING, "STICKS AND STONES WILL BREAK MY BONES BUT WORDS WILL NEVER HURT ME," IS ONE OF THE BIGGEST UNTRUTHS OUT THERE. THE EFFECTS OF PHYSICAL TRAUMA ARE SHORT-LIVED COMPARED TO VERBAL ABUSE. WORDS CAN INJURE A PERSON FOR AN ENTIRE LIFETIME AND ARE CARRIED INTO THE NEXT GENERATION.

TRUTH

Many people are searching for the **truth**, the **whole truth** and nothing but the **truth**, but what if the **truth** is different for everybody? **Truth**, like beauty, is "in the eyes of the beholder," and often *beliefs* are *perceived* as **truths**. *Perception* of **truth** is often based on what people *want* to be **true**. It is common for people to make their *belief systems* fit their **reality**, and to shape their *experiences* of the world to *reflect* that

reality by surrounding themselves with "other believers" who also reinforce the **truth** of that **reality**.

History is rife with examples of the ability of humans to live their lives based upon "truths" that are later found to be *false beliefs*. What was accepted to be **true** in the *past* is often found to be **untrue** in the *future*. People will say that they "know it to be true," yet **ignorance** is the only common state for everyone because there is always something that people don't **know** or do not *want* to *accept*, and human understanding of the world and each other is constantly evolving. For example, at one time the world was thought to be flat and there was a lot of **resistance** to *accepting* the *possibility* that this was not **true**.

People say, "when I see it, I will believe it;" however, *belief* is not necessarily **truth**. *Beliefs* are often *limiting*. It is best to have no *beliefs* to get to the **truth** because **truth** has its own energy. If you don't *believe* in **anything**, then you can *believe* in **everything**, including **yourself** and your *ability* to *feel weaknesses* to get to the **truth** of any **problem**. **Philosophers** love to explore **truth** and have several **theories** about it.

CORRESPONDENCE THEORY

The **correspondence theory** is based on the *belief* that **truth** is that which "corresponds with reality," and that **truth** does not *change* because **reality** agrees with it. For example, if you see **flowers** in a **vase**, then **flowers** are in the **vase**. The **problem** is that when people see **flowers** in the **vase**, it is based on their *perception* of "**seeing** the **flowers**" in the **vase**, but they are unable to see the **atoms** that make up the **vase** and the **flowers**. **Aristotle** was referring to the **correspondence theory** of **truth** when he said, "To say that something is when it is, is true. To say that something is when it is not, is false."

COHERENCE THEORY

The **coherence theory** is the result of "thinking inside the box." Certain **propositions** may have no connection with **reality**, but they are **internally consistent** within a **closed system**. The reasoning may seem **valid,** and as a **system**, it is **coherent** with one **proposition** leading to another; however, it can all be **based** on **untruths** because the **analysis** is **based** on an **isolated system**. We are all **connected**. There are no **isolated systems**.

PRAGMATIC THEORY

Pragmatic theory evolves from *judging* something to be **true** because it works for the **purpose** that is **needed** in **matters** of **practicality**. It is

contingent on the *observation* of the **circumstances** in which it is used, and could be **invalidated** if there were any **true** *effort* to do so. An example of **pragmatic theory** in the present day study of the **quantum field** is when an **infinite energy density** in the **vacuum** is "renormalized" to delete the *effects* of "nasty infinities" that crop up in **mathematic equations** and **conceptual physics** in order to **validate** the **theory**. **Renormalization** is also what **society** tries to do when they drug children who are **labeled** with ADHD, ADD, autism, etc.

All this **thinking** about **truth** is **problematic** because **reality** is not dependent on the **language** used to describe it. **Truth is subjective** because everyone is on his or her own journey. It is both **rigid** and *flexible* at the same time. A person's **opinion** on **truth** can change as that person becomes more **mature** or more **educated** through *life experiences*.

It is also **problematic** when people rely on **trust** to get to the **truth**. Blindly **trusting** yourself or others to get to the **truth** can lead to **situations** of *attracting* **untruths** because many of the **tales** we tell ourselves about the "story of our lives" are inaccurate accounts from our *sub-conscious* and *un-conscious minds*.

What people **think** is happening, **who** they **think** it involved, **when** they **think** it happened, **where** they **think** it happened, **how** they **think** they can resolve it, and **why** they **think** it is happening are unlikely to be **true** because as **humans** they are **multi-faceted** and operating on so many levels. It is much more *productive* to *feel* the **story** and identify the *un-truths* in order to clear them energetically. **Problems** are really made up of **unanswered questions**. If you break the **problem** down into **questions** and find the appropriate **answers**, you will get to the **truth** rather than to the **assumptions** of what the **truth** is.

THE "GOOD NEWS" IS:

The **truth** is **funny**! Many people roar with **laughter** when they hit the **truth** and realize that they may be participating in a giant cosmic joke by taking their **problems** too **seriously**.

THE "BAD NEWS" IS:

There are many versions of the **truth** and many inaccurate **answers**. If the **situation** does not *change* for the better, you have more work to do to get to the **truth** of the **situation**.

NUGGET OF WIZDOM FROM THE VECTOR

TRUTH RESONATES. IT IS BEST TO FEEL FOR THE TRUTH WITH YOUR INTUITION RATHER THAN THINK ABOUT IT. TRUTH CAN BE CAPTURED IN A MOMENT IN SPACE-TIME TO RESOLVE ISSUES AROUND ANY PROBLEM, AND IT CAN EFFECT CHANGE IN MILLISECONDS. TRUTH IS EVIDENT IN RESULTS, AND RESULTS SPEAK FOR THEMSELVES.

VISION

Generally it is more beneficial to work on the **physical eyes** before shifting the weaknesses in *vision*. Test which is weaker, the **eye** or the *vision*, and start from there. *EU ... EYES, Pg. 234*

Contrary to popular *belief*, conventional **vision care** is not designed to **treat** or *heal vision*, but to mask the **symptoms**. The **symptoms** are **signals** to the **body** that something in the **body** and/or *mind* is out of *balance* and requires attention; however, many people accept that the solution to their *vision* **problems** is using progressively stronger **corrective lenses** that are **prescribed** by **optometrists**.

To correct *vision*, it is helpful to understand what **vision acuity** means. **Vision acuity** is measured by a person's ability to identify letters of a predetermined size at a standard distance of **twenty feet**. **Twenty feet** was the distance chosen because **light rays** that enter the **eyes** are roughly **parallel** at **twenty feet**. Looking at an object from **twenty feet** away is considered to be equivalent to looking at an object **miles** or even **light years** away.

Normal vision is defined as being **20/20**. The **first number** is the "testing distance," and the **second number** is the **distance** at which a person with **20/20 vision** can **read** a **letter**. According to optometrists, a person with normal vision should be able to read the smallest letters on the eye chart from a distance of **twenty feet**, and thus is considered to have **20/20 vision**. As **visual acuity** worsens, the **first number** stays the same because the person is always "tested" from a **distance** of **twenty feet**. The **second number** rises because it means the **smallest letter** that a person can identify is what someone with **20/20 vision** can **identify** at a greater **distance**. For example, **20/200 vision** indicates that the **smallest letter** that a person is able to **identify** could be **identified** by an individual with **20/20 vision** from **200 feet** away. The standard for all **lens prescriptions** was developed by **Dr. Herman**

Snellen in 1862, and was based on the **vision** of an assistant who he *thought* had good **vision**.

Corrective lenses are prescribed in **diopters** which are measurements of **lens power**. The **smallest** unit is a **quarter diopter** or **0.25**. The **higher** the **number**, the **stronger** the **lens**. **Concave lenses** are used to **correct near-sightedness** of **+0.25 diopters** and **up**, whereas **convex lenses** are used to correct **far-sightedness** of **-0.25** and down. A **combination** of both **plus** and **minus diopters** are used to correct **astigmatism**. The **eye** is considered to have a **refractive error** when the **eye**, in a state of **rest**, is unable to **focus** the image of **distant objects** upon the **retina**; however, **eyes** in their natural state are NEVER in a **state** of **rest**, not even when people are asleep.

During an **eye exam,** the **physical** definition of **vision** is based on both **subjective** and **objective** approaches. In the **subjective** approach, **visual clarity** is based on the patient's *perception* of the letters on eye charts. The **objective** approach is a **mechanical** one. First, the ability of the **eyes** to **focus** is temporarily paralyzed either through the use of **eye drops**, or by *blurring vision* with a lens. Then **retinoscopy** is used to measure each **eye's** ability to **focus** by beaming a light on the **retina** as if it were a **camera lens**. The *focusing* power of the **eye** is *equalized* with a series of **optical lenses**.

The **eyes** use **central vision** to *perceive* details and **colors** by using **central focus**. **Central vision** is most *active* during the **day** and works best under **illuminated** conditions. **Peripheral vision** is **always** *active*. It is the primary source of *perception* in **dark** and **low light** conditions. The **mind's eye** uses **central vision** to **analyze** the **details** of a person's **world,** whereas **peripheral vision** *feels* the world from a larger perspective. **Peripheral vision** is significantly reduced while wearing **glasses** because the full **prescription** is located at the **center** of the **lens**. The **eyes**, therefore, respond by repeatedly returning to the **center**, because unless a person is looking **straight** ahead while wearing **glasses,** *vision* becomes *distorted*.

Eye examinations are based on **central vision** and take place in **unnatural** conditions in **dark rooms**. **Glasses** are a **feed-back tool** that **train** the **eyes** to remain in **one** *position* and eventually **stay** there. The part of *vision* that focuses **straight ahead** only knows how to **analyze** and **discriminate**. Consequently, the more people wear **glasses**, the more they learn to *judge* their world rather than *feel* it. When people **focus** intently on something, their **vision** *blurs* and their **visual field** closes in. *Mental* strain of any kind produces *sub-conscious strain*, causing a person to use too much *effort* to **see**. Using the **same long-**

distance focus for all *activities* trains the **eyes** to **limit** their *ability* to *adapt* to every new **situation**.

The *visual sense* of the **eyes** has three components that can be strengthened to each other. The **sensory component** receives information, the **integrative component** compares visual input with *past experiences*, and the **motor component** determines the final outcome through *speech*, *movements*, and *actions*. Improvement of *vision* is possible by removing **lenses** and **glasses**, including **sunglasses**, or by using **glasses** with a reduced **prescription**. When people remove **corrective lenses**, they are challenged by *sensations* and *emotions* that they did not "want to see." This avoidance caused them to "need glasses" in the first place. People can **identify** the underlying *non-physical* weaknesses and clear them until the **eyes** are strong to the *sensations* they *experience* when they are being **exposed** to life without **glasses**.

It is helpful to ask **what** happened to a person **prior** to the **deterioration** of sight. Many people avert their **eyes** so that they don't have to see **painful** scenes. Invariably young children can clearly describe the *negative emotions* that precipitated the **deterioration** of their **sight**. To avoid these experiences, it is common for people to create *multiple personalities* that hinder **sight**. *Vision* also directly or indirectly *affects* **posture** through a person's t**houghts**, *feelings* and *actions*. Strong **posture** strengthens *vision,* and vice-versa. It is helpful to practice "soft focus" and to avoid **staring** with the **eyes** "wide open," as people have a tendency to do when they are "day dreaming," because it **trains** the **eyes** to "not see."

PROGRESSIVE MYOPIA (NEARSIGHTEDNESS)

Generally when people are **nearsighted**, the **cornea** and **lens** focus the **light rays** short of the **retina,** causing *blurring* of **objects** that are **far** away. Less often the **cones** and **lens** are too powerful, also causing **nearsightedness**.

On a **physical** level the **shape** of the **eye** is t**oo long** from the **front** to the **back**, which causes the **focus** to be in **front** of the **retina**. On the *non-physical* level, there are issues about being *neutral* to "seeing the big picture." The weaknesses often come from *limiting beliefs* held in the *sub-conscious* and *un-conscious mind* from **ancestors**, **descendants**, *spiritual experiences* and the *collective consciousness*.

HYPEROPIA (FARSIGHTEDNESS)

When people *experience* **far-sightedness,** the **cornea** and **lens** focus the **light rays** behind the **retina** causing *blurring* of objects that are **close up**. Less often the power of the **lens** and **cones** are too strong. People who are diagnosed with **far-sightedness** are generally born with it.

On a **physical** level, the **shape** of the **eye** is **too short** from the **front** to the **back**, which causes the focus to be **behind** the **retina**. This can be adjusted by strengthening the **ciliary muscle** to be thicker and stronger. On the *non-physical* level, there are often issues about being *neutral* to **details** and reading "small print."

ASTIGMATISM

Astigmatism is a combination of both **myopia** and **hyperopia** that is usually caused by an irregularly curved **cornea** (the **front surface** of the **eye**) which in turn causes **light rays** to focus incorrectly on the **retina**. It can also be caused by an irregularly-shaped **lens**.

PRESBYOPIA ("OLD-AGE VISION")

With **age**, the **lens** of the **eye** has a tendency to **harden**, and that leads to an inability to see **up close**. This typically happens around the age of **forty**, and continues until age **sixty-five** when **accommodation** of the **eyes** is considered to cease. Strengthen the *fitness* of the **eyes** and **accommodation** to be at optimum potential. Many *non-physical* issues are *limiting beliefs* about **aging** that are held by the ***collective consciousness***.

You can lessen your reliance on **glasses** by gradually wearing **reduced prescriptions** and going for periods of time without wearing glasses at all. (Do not do this while driving). Delete **financial** issues of **paying** for **glasses** and **corrective lenses** that are no longer needed, and any *karma* with **optometrists, doctors, eye wear businesses**, etc.

COMMON DIAGNOSES OF EYE DIS-EASE

COLOR BLINDNESS

"Color blindness" is better defined as a **deficiency** in the *ability* to discern **color**. There are often underlying ancestral weaknesses that usually originate from the **maternal line**. Common triggers are the **primary colors** (**red**, **blue** and **yellow**) and "stop and go" colors (**red** and **green**).

Strengthen **light** *sensitivity* to the **cones**. The **macul**a is the part of the **retina** that is responsible for **color** and detailed **up-close** *vision*.

ATROPHIC OR INVOLUTIONAL MACULAR DEGENERATION

Many of the weaknesses come from *accumulations* of **minerals, cellular waste, parasitic waste, mimicking cells**, etc., and a from a lack of *fitness* in the **eye** itself, which causes **thinning** and **breaking** of **macula tissue.** Strengthen *absorption* of **anti-oxidants, vitamins, lutein** and **zinc** to the **eyes**.

EXUDATIVE MACULAR DEGENERATION

Lack of *tension* in the **eye** and the **blood vessels** of the **eye** cause **scar tissue** to develop from **small blood vessels** that **break** and **bleed** under the **retina** in a continuous cycle. A strong **lymphatic system** is essential to break down **cellular waste** and can be complemented by creating **black wholes** in the **eye**. Strengthen **nutrients** and **oxygen** to reach all areas of the **eye**.

DRY EYE

On a **physical** level, the **outer lipid layer**, the **oily film** that seals **tears** and keeps them from evaporating, is *affected* as well as the **lacrimal apparatus,** and **nasolacrimal duct**, and the **mucous** coating on the **cornea**. Strengthen all **ducts** within the body. Many of the underlying weaknesses causing **dry eyes** come from *psychic* and *spiritual* issues such as *mis-matched body parts*, *multiple personalities, spirit attachments*, *past* and *present life experiences* of living in the **desert**, etc. Dryness of the **eyes** is a reflection of the "grit in life" and weaknesses to foreign *sensations* in the **body**. *Karma* with **optometrists** and **surgeons** and any weaknesses to **lasers**, if someone has had **LASIK surgery**, should also be tested. **Burning** in the **eyes** is often an *emotional re-action* of *anger* about what a person has **seen**, is **seeing** or can't **see**.

THE "GOOD NEWS" IS:

Many **learning disabilities** are caused by an inability to **read** or look at **printed words**, and by weaknesses in the **line** of **sight**. When *vision* is strengthened, many **learning disabilities** are lessened or resolved.

THE "BAD NEWS" IS:

The more **educated** you are, the more likely you are to be **myopic**. A very small percentage of people are born **myopic**, yet by the time **students** have graduated from **college**, a very high percentage are **near-sighted**.

NUGGET OF WIZDOM FROM THE VECTOR

WHAT YOU SEE IS NOT ALWAYS WHAT YOU GET! YOUR ENERGY INDICATES THE RANGE AND QUALITY OF YOUR PERCEPTION. VISION FLUCTUATES ALONG WITH EMOTIONAL RE-ACTIONS TO SENSATIONS. A CHRONICALLY COLLAPSED FIELD OF VISION IS OFTEN THE RESULT OF REACTIONS TO "FEAR OF LIFE."

WATER

Advertising for the **bottled water industry** has been systematically undermining people's faith in **public water** in Canada and in the United States despite the fact that North Americans have access to one of the best public drinking water systems in the world. The irony is that many people are now paying for **bottled water,** and a high percentage of the water that is **bottled** comes from **public** water sources that are **free**. At this time, the **Environmental Protection Agency (EPA)** is responsible for the regulation of **tap water**. **Tap water** is routinely tested for **E-coli** and is required to provide source and quality reports. **Bottled water**, on the other hand, is controlled by the **Food and Drug Administration (FDA)** and does not need to meet the same stringent standards.

The production of **plastic bottles** uses **millions** of **barrels** of **oil** a year, and each **plastic bottle** requires **three times** the **water** it holds to make **one bottle**. A very small percentage **of plastic bottles** make it to **recycling depots**. The rest end up in **landfills** and **litter** the landscape, or are **incinerated**. In addition, the **environmental** impact on **groundwater**, **glaciers**, **lakes**, **rivers** and **streams**, plus the energy required to transport and distribute water from the **bottled water industry**, which happens to have major ties to the **soft drink industry**, are underestimated by most people. **Filtration systems** and **reusable glass containers** are a much stronger option. *EU … HARD CORE SOFT DRINKS, Pg. 270*

Clean water is a **basic right**, and should be guaranteed to **all life** on the **planet** regardless of their ability to **pay** for it, their **geographic location** or, in the case of **babies**, **plants**, **trees aquatic life** and **animals**, their ability to demand that **this basic right** be **honored**. **Water** is a resource belonging to the **earth** and shared with **all life** that **inhabits** the **earth**; it is not a commodity to be **prostituted** for **corporate interests**.

The amount of **water** ranges from **fifty** to **sixty-five percent** of **body mass** in **adults** and approximately **seventy-five** to **seventy-eight** percent in **infants**. The average **adult male** is made up of about **sixty** percent **water**, while **women** are about **fifty-five** percent **water** because they naturally have more **adipose tissue** than **men**. Overweight **men** and **women** generally have **higher** percentages of **water** in their **bodies** than **lean** people. Many people buy into the *limiting belief* that in order to lose **weight** and be *healthy*, they must drink **eight glasses** of water a day **regardless** of whether they are **thirsty** or not. Please note that, if you consume more water than your body needs at any given time, it swells your **cells** like overfilled water balloons, and it expands the **bones**, the **muscles**, the **tissues**, and overall **body mass**. It is not "too late" to drink water once your **body** indicates to you that it is **thirsty**. Take notice of the **signals** your **body** sends, don't **ignore** its subtle messages, and strengthen the **systems** in your **body** to operate at optimum potential to *distribute* **water** to exactly where it needs to go. Drink the best quality of **water** available. Take advantage of technology that provides excellent **filtration systems** to clean, **alkalized** and **ionized tap water**.

People have good reason to be concerned about the **pollution** of the **waters** of the **earth** and the *negative effects* on all life on the **planet**. The levels of **pollution** in the **body** are directly *affected* by the **pollution** in the **water** on **earth**. *As within*, *so without*.

CRYSTAL CLEANSE OF THE WATERS

Crystals can be **programmed** to **detoxify** the **waters** of the **earth**, as well as the **water** that makes up the **body**. This clearing is an *opportunity* to take *action*, to delete the *fear*, and to become part of the **solution**. **Crystals** and **minerals** have *healing properties* through their own *consciousness*, a *resonance* or *vibration* as unique as our own **DNA**. They *capture light* to *reflect* back to us that which is needed to gently push us along our journey. **Crystal** *healing* uses the *subtle energies* of **crystals** and **gemstones** to heal and **protect** other **organisms**. When a **crystal** is applied to a **body's** *electromagnetic system*, it *transfers* the energy of its particular *vibration* or *frequency* to restore *balance*, **clarity**, and the *natural energies* that have been compromised or depleted in an *energetic field*; in short, it releases the blocks that impede potential. By definition, each **mineral** has its own **crystalline structure** composed of specific **atoms** and **chemical bonds**. Every **chemical** has characteristic, transferable, **vibrational** and **rotational**

frequencies; these can be measured by using **spectrophotometers** to translate the *vibrations* and *rotational band frequencies*.

Although **crystal *healing*** at this time is considered an "alternative medicine," it has been used for **centuries**. Its roots are in ancient **Egypt**, but **China** and **India** have also used the **properties** of **crystals** for healing purposes for over **five thousand years**. Changes in **temperature** create an **electrified state** (**static electricity**) resulting in the **polarity** of the **crystal**, meaning that one end will *repel* while the other end *attracts*.

PYRO-ELECTRICITY

Body temperature, when holding or "laying-on-of-stones," *activates* the principles of **pyro-electricity**.

PIEZO-ELECTRICITY

The *re-absorption* of electrons creates **piezo-electricity**, a form of **light**. The energetic exchange of **atoms** is dictated by the **atoms** of the **crystal** and the **atoms** of the person holding it. **Positive** and **negative charges**, which are *symmetrical* within the **crystal,** cause the connection to be **electrically** *neutral*. When **stress** is applied to the **crystal**, the **symmetry** is slightly **broken**, and this creates **voltage**. Every **crystal** on **earth** has this ability, but **crystals** from the **quartz** family are the most powerful **generators** and "healing amplifiers" on earth due to their unique **helical form**. They are said to bring the "energy of the stars into the soul." Like **natural computers**, they store, sort and access information to facilitate *memory* and **concentration**, and this makes them the most *effective* crystals for **programming**. They *attune* their *vibration* to each **situation** as needed, and work from the energy of *homeostasis* to *absorb*, *store* and *release* energy and **thoughts**, thus facilitating *memory* and **concentration** and **removing** blocks to encourage *flow*.

DOUBLE TERMINATED QUARTZ CRYSTALS

Double terminated quartz crystals are multi-functional because the energy moves outward in **either** direction or in **both** directions concurrently with the capacity to *draw* or transmit energy through both **ends**. They symbolize *patience* and *perseverance*, and are capable of moving *negative energies* from any **body**, *neutralizing* any *dis-order*, and *transmuting negative energy* to perfect **structure**.

FIVE EASY STEPS FOR CHARGING CRYSTALS TO CLEANSE WATER

1. ALIGN YOUR ENERGY

Bodies function much like **binary computers** (binary meaning one of two *choices*) – in this case, **weak** or **strong**. Turn your senses inward to go to *singularity* and connect to the *whole*. Put energy into your **spine**. This is the **hard drive** of your **computer**. *EU ... WEAK AND STRONG, Pg. 514*

2. CONNECT WITH YOUR CRYSTAL

Release your *mind* out to a *black whole* and feel the **pyroelectric** and **piezoelectric** *effect* as **you** and your **crystal's atoms** merge into one living being. Hold your **crystal** to your **heart** and feel the **life force energy** pulse through both your **veins**.

3. PUT YOUR HIGH-TECH EQUIPMENT TO USE

Your **crystal** is a "living being," so picture it with a **spine**. Allow your **spine** and the **crystal's spine** to *merge* into one. Connect with your **crystal's vein** and *feel* the **beat** from deep within the **womb** of the **earth**.

4. THE POWER OF SPIN

Feel the **physical potential** at the **base** of your **spine**. Connect the **water** within your **body**, and the **physical potential** at the **base** of your **spine** as well as your **crystal's spine** to the *effect* of *black wholes* and *white wholes*. Release **waste** from your **body** and the **earth's body** of **waters** to a *black whole*.

Spin out *accumulations* of *traumas*, **poisons**, **toxins**, **chemicals** and **radiation** on the **physical** level to the *black whole*.

Spin out *associated fears*, *limiting beliefs*, *expectations* and misinformation on the *mental*, *emotional* and *psychological* level to the *black whole*.

Spin out any *karmic*, *psychic* or *spiritual* **need** to *suffer*, *struggle* or to have to keep "paying the price" for **humanity** as stewards of the **earth** to the *black whole*.

Transmute beneficial properties through the *white whole*.

Spin oxygen, nutrition, trace carbon, nitrogen and the perfect **structure** of the **universe** into the **cells** of your **body** and the **bodies** of **water** on **earth** through the *white whole*.

Spin in the *calm* from the **pulse** of your **heartbeat** and the *rhythm* of the **earth's drum** in perfect *synchronization*.

5. PLACE THE CRYSTAL IN A BODY OF WATER

Place the **crystal** into a **body** of **water** along with the intention that every splash and every ripple in the **water's atoms** will *merge* with the **crystal's energy** and spread it out to all the **waters** of the **earth** and beyond. Strengthen that *effect* to the **quantum particles** of every **cell** throughout your **body**.

There are no isolated **systems** in **nature**. You can follow the infinite potential of a **crystal** placed in a **body** of **water** as the **water** flows **south**. The **evaporation** *generates* clouds that head **north** due to the **Coriolis Effect**, thus creating *free energy* in the form of **rain** and **snow** that **purifies** the **air** and the **waters** with your *intention* for a *universal cleanse*.

THE "GOOD NEWS" IS:

People are becoming more *aware* of the importance of **water** and their duty to keep it pristine for future generations. Even a tiny **crystal** can generate a lot of **voltage**, and is a natural **conductor** for cleansing the **waters** of the **earth** in **alignment** with that *intention*.

THE "BAD NEWS" IS:

Most people in developed countries have a "bad" *attitude* and take access to **clean water** for granted. They squander it, while too many children in the *dimension* of the "third world" and all other **beings** on the **planet** are *struggling* and *suffering* the **consequences** or their **ignorance**.

NUGGET OF WIZDOM FROM THE VECTOR

THE PREVAILING ATTITUDE THAT HUMANS ARE MORE SIGNIFICANT THAN ANY OTHER OF THE DIVERSE FORMS OF LIFE ON THIS PLANET IS DANGEROUSLY RIDICULOUS! THIS IS A FALSE ASSUMPTION, PERPETUATED THROUGH WILLFUL IGNORANCE, THAT WILL LEAD TO CONSEQUENCES OF EPIC PROPORTIONS. IT IS ESSENTIAL THAT THE COLLECTIVE CONSCIOUSNESS GRASPS THE IMPORTANCE OF AN EQUITABLE SYSTEM TO PROVIDE CLEAN WATER FOR EVERY BEING ON THIS PLANET. THE SOONER, THE BETTER.

WEAK AND STRONG

Energetically speaking, your **body** functions much like a **binary computer**, **binary** which means you have **one** of **two** *choices*. In this case, the choices are **weak** or **strong**; in other words, your energy is either **strong** to support the steps of *actions* or **words** you *choose* to use, or it is **weak** and not in energetic *alignment* to support your **goals**. Creating a beneficial **reality** requires minimum *effort* when your **goals** are energetically **aligned** with your absolute **potential**, as opposed to "forcing yourself" to **produce** by ploughing forward through energetic **weaknesses**.

All the information gathered by every **cell** in your **body** has been and is being recorded and stored in your **CNS**, the **hard drive** of your **computer**. Every *past*, *present* and *future experience*, as well as your **ancestors'**, **descendants'** and even potential **descendants' physical**, *mental*, *emotional*, *psychological*, *spiritual* and *psychic experiences*, are documented in the *memory* of your **spinal cord**, **cerebral spinal fluid**, **inner** and **outer meninges**, and in the **structure** of the **spine** itself. The **Higher Self Network** (**H.S.N.**), similar to **MSN**, is the internet accessing all information in the *unified field*, including **illnesses**, **dis-ease**, **cultural** and **religious** *experiences*.

Humans are multi-faceted beings who operate at multiple levels of *influence*, *consciousness*, *existences* and *dimensions*. Each and every human being has the ability to go **inward** to connect their *intuition* to their *perception*, to access the most **applicable answer** that will change any given **situation**, and to create **opportunities** out of **challenges**. The first step towards reclaiming this *insight* is to identify what **weak** energy *feels* like for you. It is much more important to identify the *sensations* of **weak** energy because, if something is already **strong**, there is no **need** for an *energetic upgrade*, although it is possible to boost **strong energy** to strengthen an even better result. Many people *feel* **nothing** at all when their energy is **strong**, but have a lot of **resistance** to *feeling* weak energy because they confuse the negative connotations of **being** "weak" with *feeling judgment* and **criticism**. In any given moment there are likely to be thousands of *external* and *internal forces* that can **weaken** people's energy, especially when they are moving out of their "comfort zone" and into their infinite potential. It is **not** a *judgement.* If you feel **nothing** when you are **strong**, it can actually simplifies things greatly because you can then focus explicitly on what **weak** feels like for you.

The easiest way to define **weak** energy is by *consciously* telling yourself simple untruths and very quickly, in a second or less, identifying what you *feel*. Make simple statements that you know are false, such as "my name is Donald Duck," "the ceiling is black (when it is white)," "one plus one equals (wrong number)" "the carpet is green (when it is brown)" etc. If you are still unable to *feel* the **weak** energy, you can create a *negative association* by **pinching** yourself every time you tell yourself an **untruth** and use that as your **baseline** for now. It is not important **what** you *feel*, but it is important that you *feel* something to use as a **baseline**. When you are working with energy, it is imperative to always get a **baseline** for how you are *feeling* so that your *mind* does not trick you into running around in circles like a dog chasing its tail. The more you pay attention to how **weak** energy feels to you, the more quickly you will identify when you are **not** in *alignment*. Once you identify that there is a **weakness** in any given moment, you can **delete** the *memories* and *attachments* that are *limiting* you from your optimum **potential** by performing an energetic *shift*.

Some people do *feel* both **weak** and **strong energy**, and may find it confusing. A simple way to define the **difference** is to connect with your **heart**, turn your **feet** with your **toes** pointed **inward** (like a duck), put *tension* in your *spine*, and put your **tongue** on the **roof** of your **mouth**. Notice how it *feels* in and around your **body** when you do this. Then, turn your **toes** out like a ballet dancer, **drop** your **tongue** from the **roof** of your **mouth**, let your **mouth** "hang open," and *relax* your **spine**. Once again, take notice of how this *feels*. The first position is **strong** because you are pulling your energy **inwards** to the **core** and connecting yourself to **source** through the connection of your **tongue** on the **roof** of your **mouth**. The second position is **weak**. When you allow your energy to "leak out," and disconnect yourself from *source* by **dropping** your **tongue** from the **roof** of your **mouth** and *relaxing your* connection to the **CNS**, the **hard drive** of your **computer** slows down.

If you *feel* yourself going **weak** to what is being **said** by you or to you or through your *action* or the *actions* of others, it is time to *align* your **energy**. *Feel* your **heart** and connect with its *beat*. Flip the switch from **weak** to **strong** by running the *energy* very quickly, in less than a second, from the **base** of your **spine** to the **top** and **back** down like a **zipper**.

There are subtle differences in how each of us *experiences* energy, and many **physical** and **non-physical** reasons the *ability* to "get in touch" with *feeling* **weak**, or *feeling* both **weak** and **strong**, is slightly different for every person. Some people are very **visual** and will see **colors**, or a **light** running up and down the **spine**, while others *feel* their bodies gravitate **forward** when they are **strong** or **backward** when they feel **weak**. Some have a sense of "coming together" when they *feel* **strong**, and a feeling of "falling apart" or a "dissipating" of their energy when they *feel* **weak**. Then there are those who are better able to *feel* **weak** and **strong** energy through their **hearts,** and they describe it as an "opening" or an "expansion" of energy when they *feel* **strong**, and a "closing" of the **heart** when they *feel* **weak**. Feeling the *sensations* other people *experience* when they have *thoughts* about someone they love, about babies, puppies and kittens and other enjoyable *thoughts,* inspires "heart openings," whereas *feelings* of hatred, "getting caught in a traffic jam," and other **negative** *associations* triggers a "heart closing." Generally children find it much easier to differentiate between the two because they are **innocent** and don't let their *minds* get in the way of their **hearts**.

Over the years I have worked with thousands of people to show them how to get in touch with **what** they are *feeling*, and they can become very *frustrated* when they cannot *feel*. *Frustration* is a combination of the *sensations* of *fear* and *anger*. The *mind* will tell you what you *want*, not what your *soul* **needs** to make your **heart** sing. There can be a lot of **resistance** from the *mind* because it likes to have its own way, and many people have become **de-sensitized** by focusing on **false obligations** rather than on a *balanced* approach to bring out every **aspect** of their *whole being*. If you are having difficulty *feeling* energy, it is not because you are unable to do so; it is because you **need** to rein your *mind* in and **re-train** it to work **for you** rather than against you. It is well worth it because, with every energetic *shift*, you raise the bar for yourself and for all of humanity. Optimizing the performance of your **body**, *soul* and *spirit* in every aspect of life creates a win, win, win, benefiting you, others around you, and the entire universe.

THE "GOOD NEWS" IS:

Happy *thoughts*, turning your **toes** in, **circles** and **circular motions**, putting your **tongue** on the **roof** of your **mouth** and **vertical lines** are all strengthening. If you to take part in an important conversation, it is very beneficial to strengthen yourself by putting your **tongue** on the **roof** of your **mouth**, feeling your **heart**, turning your **toes** in, and putting *tension* into your **spine** before *speaking*.

THE "BAD NEWS" IS:

There are many weaknesses held in the *collective consciousness*, such as *unhappy thoughts*, **walking** and **standing** with the **toes** facing **out**, **squares** and **linear lines**, **fists** and **horizontal lines**. For instance, in North America it is challenging to find boys' and men' shirts that do not have **horizontal stripes**. *Sub-consciously*, **vertical stripes** strengthen people and **horizontal stripes** weaken people unless they *shift* it. This is why **pinstriped suits** are still seen as a symbol of **power**, and why, in the old days, prisoners were given **horizontally striped** uniforms.

NUGGET OF WIZDOM FROM THE VECTOR

IN ANY GIVEN MOMENT, THERE ARE UNIQUE OPPORTUNITIES TO DELETE WEAKNESSES AND STRENGTHEN POTENTIAL. IT TAKES LESS THAN A SPLIT SECOND TO APPLY YOURSELF TO CLEAR ENERGY. DON'T WAIT ... TURN PROBLEMS INTO OPPORTUNITIES.

ABOUT COLETTE MARIE STEFAN

Colette Marie Stefan is a magical speaker, author and artist, with a great sense of humor, who shares universal life-transforming information, and provides results that inspire you to soar with her to new heights (in the ways of the dragons) at seminars around the globe. She has been the featured guest on many radio shows and tele-summits, as well as on all social media. Currently, Colette is captivating the air waves with her hit radio show, "The Truth Is Funny ... shift happens" which is, among other things, an open invitation for you to call in and receive life-transforming energetic upgrades. Colette has joined forces with her colleague Marc Kettenbach to provide state-of-the-art Energetic Upgrade Seminars that they promise will shift you into pursuing your authentic desires.

RADIO WAVES

The radio show, "The Truth Is Funny ..." came about as an unexpected gift from the universe in the form of one powerhouse of a woman, Pat Baccili from the Dr. Pat Show and Transformation Talk Radio. I am blessed to have so many opportunities to connect with brilliant men and women from across the globe, people who are willing to share their expertise on what I call the Higher Self Network (H.S.N.) via the radio waves. I have focused on using the show as a platform to give every listener a chance to shift problems into creative solutions by joining forces with five of the strongest energetic practitioners I know at this time. The beauty of this is that, as callers shift out of their problems, people listening in at the time or to the archived shows at a later time, are also receiving the shifts that apply to them. I love that each and every one of the radio shows has its own unique flavour, depending on who calls in and on the style of each of the practitioners I am working with.

DR. PAT BACCILI

"Several years ago Dr. Mehmet Oz proclaimed, 'As we get better at understanding how little we know about the body, we begin to realize that the next big frontier in medicine is Energy Medicine.' He forgot to mention that the next big 'energy medicine' frontier is here now and is brilliantly presented to us by Colette Marie Stefan in her epic book 'The Truth is Funny.'

"Inspiring, uplifting powerful, and transformative are just a few of the words that describe this lifetime of work, wisdom, and wonder. This is literally a book for whatever ails you! Colette is masterful at pinpointing areas of life that not only keep us energetically stuck but she handily takes us on a healing journey of self-discovery at the body, the mind, and the spirit planes of 'Truth.' The Truth is Funny works off the premise: you have the power to change, improve your pathway, heal your physical and emotional wounds and live an epic life. That's not all! Colette tells you exactly how to do that with the flare, intellect, and delivery that is heard each week on her hit radio show. The Truth is Funny will give you both 'Good news' and 'Bad news' that when combined demonstrates that 'Shift Happens' and we are more powerful than we think we are. Each chapter invites us to experience an energetic upgrade as we follow the journey of others, understand how miracles happen through knowledge, willingness, and surrender, and shout a giant 'YES' to the world of unlimited possibilities.

"So, Dr. Oz. meet the next big frontier wonderfully known as, 'The Truth is Funny,' and sign up for your personal energetic upgrade."

Dr. Pat Baccili, host Dr. Pat Show Talk Radio To Thrive By!

PHIL FREE

I first met Phil at certification of the Yuen Method TM in 2008. I scanned the room to test for the strongest person there, and he was it. I contacted him by e-mail shortly afterwards, and we have been working together ever since.

Phil has the patience to break down any problem into smaller, manageable pieces. He is a wonderful father to his four daughters, and a talented musician.

His first album "Phil Free All One" is available for sale at *www.philfree.rocks*

MARC KETTENBACH

When we first connected while attending a seminar in Philadelphia in 2009, it was instantly apparent that were kindred souls, surfing the edge of reality. Marc and I have combined forces ever since, acquiring tools and inspiring each other to excel, and at times, pushing each other over the edge (only when necessary) to break through mediocrity.

It is our pleasure to share inclusive information and easy to use tools that we have acquired along the way to ease your experience as you shift your reality to live your authentic desires.

"Brilliant!
It is very hard, to say something about something that is this brilliant other than: brilliant! When I first met Colette in 2009 in Philadelphia, I instantly knew we are connected Souls and I couldn't wait to meet that charming and energizing woman. Years down the road I am still blown away by Colette and her ability to shift energy! This book you are holding in your hand right now is probably the best thing you could possibly buy in order to shift your life for the better. Years of knowledge and research, working with thousands of clients, holding seminars, exchanging knowledge with top healers and energy workers around the globe all came to be sorted and to be broken down to its pieces in order to be explained in this book. Read it, use it and work with it! I promise you will feel a difference faster than you could ever imagine."

Marc Kettenbach, author, co-founder Energetic Upgrade Seminars – www.marckettenbach.com

LEROY MALOUF

I was so pleased when LeRoy expressed an interest to work with me. Eventually this led to our traveling to Egypt to host a seminar together.

I arrived in Egypt ten days earlier before the seminar was scheduled to begin, and had arranged a tour of the Pyramids of Giza for noon of that day because LeRoy's flight had not arrived until the wee hours that morning. I informed our tour guide that LeRoy is eighty years old, the flight had been long, and that he may want to sleep in. She asked if she should book a walker. I giggled and assured her that it would not be necessary.

At nine a.m. that morning, LeRoy called my room, impatient. "Where are you? I have gone for my swim and have answered my emails, I am waiting to have breakfast with you. Why are we not at the pyramids?"

Shortly afterwards, we climbed Giza in forty-two degree heat. I climbed the ramp behind LeRoy and corrected every step the two of us took to be stronger and stronger until we reached the King's Chamber. Once there, I whispered under my breath, "Act old!" LeRoy asked, "What do you mean?" Ha! ha! He was SO funny! I had to explain that I wanted to have more time to be in the energy of the chamber. "Oh, oh … I get it!" he replied, and accommodated me. Soon after we were each taking turns lying in the sarcophagus of the King's Chamber in the pyramid.

I have come to realize that there are not that many people on the earth who have lain in the sarcophagus, and that is how it is with LeRoy and me, we always feel when it is time to connect and we always have each other's back …

"Colette has done an amazingly thorough and creative job of:

- *Describing our physical body, it's parts and systems, how it functions, and how it is impacted by our beliefs and the way we live.*

- *Picturing many ways in which we approach living our life and how these both help and hinder us.*

- *Capturing various aspects of our environment and they impact us.*

- *Describing numerous symptoms, diseases, and difficulties we encounter and root causes for them.*

- *Revealing with great wisdom how we can live long, rich lives to the great benefit of ourselves and others.*

"I do not know of any other books that so richly describe and integrate such a wealth of information.

"There are only a few books or references that truly capture what is needed to enable a person to regain and remain in optimum wellness and vitality. This is my "new best friend" for information that benefits me and clients with whom I work."

LeRoy Malouf, author, founder of EWBP – www.EWBP.com

KAREN CAMPBELL BETTEN

I connected with Karen in California at a seminar. We immediately bonded as women and mothers, and have worked with each other to be the best moms that we can be. The last time we physically met was in 2014, in New York. It was so awesome to be able to connect in person, even though it was only for a few hours. I always enjoy working with Karen! She is brilliant!

"This book has the unique one two punch gift of powerful insight and humor to rocket the world beyond what any of us think is possible.

"Whether it's illness, relationships or finance issues you are struggling with, this book is a bedside reference to shift you and support you to manifest your dreams into reality. A true gift to the world, both the book and the author.

Karen Campbell Betten, Founder of Intuitive Living New York – www.intuitivelivingny.com

CHARAN SURDHAR

Charan contacted me in 2013, and we have been working together ever since. It is so awesome to work with a colleague who is also a mother and has the scientific background in epigenetics to back up energetic shifting. She was brave enough to unleash Marc and me in her community, hosting the very first Energetic Upgrade Seminar in the U.K. We both felt so loved and welcomed by her and her community!

"Are you ready for a real transformation? Many books tell you about transformation and then you go away and wonder how you can bring that transformation into your life.

"This book is here to transform, shift and bring you into alignment to who you are here to be and can be. It's not something that is "out there" and can't be reached. It's here, right here. Just the energy of the book can bring about transformation. To me it's almost like a book out of Hogwarts, but here it's the energy of the divine/creator (within you) that jumps out of the book bringing about the transformation.

"Colette's book has been written to create a shift in you to align you with your true essence. If you're ready for that, then this book is for you."

Charan Surdhar, Epigeneticist UK – www.charansurdhar.com

RICH PETERSON

The financial strategies for success in this book are built upon the expertise of Rich Peterson. His lifelong passion for the study of the markets began by charting and selling stocks for one dollar after he returned from a trip to the New York Stock Exchange at the tender age of nine. By sixteen, he was an order clerk on the floor of the Midwest Stock Exchange. After giving a speech to investment executives at the age of seventeen, he was offered an opportunity to begin his daily market commentary on Channel 26 in Chicago, which led to a twenty year career, during which he appeared daily on financial television in Chicago, LA and San Francisco, while working as a futures broker with Shearson, Hayden Stone.

Rich has followed his heart's passion to serve humanity by successfully blending his financial brilliance with the spirituality of Kali Natha Yoga in a unique formula. In his quest for universal peace, he co-founded Ice Lotus, a non-profit organization dedicated to improving lives through spiritual yoga based on the teaching principles of Ma Jaya Sati Bhagavati.

"ACTION! Not lame commentaries, but a battle plan for action! Get ready to have the shift triggered out of you! Sometimes you will agree, sometimes it will be 'what the?' But, I guarantee you, Colette will get you thinking and challenge the shift out of some of our traditional ways of thinking – so get ready for the fast lane to 'expansion'. It's the perfect companion to experiencing Colette in person. Expect to be going back to the book time and again. Perhaps jot down some notes as you go through the manual. Then go back later and smile as you experience the ongoing shift in real-life!"

Richard Peterson. President, The Ice Lotus, Inc.

INDEX

CLIMAX

The dichotomy is this: the climax is an anti-climax. As you clear energetic blocks and put these tools into practice, you will remember what you have always known …

All the answers and healing are within you!

The joke is, the more seriously you take yourself, on this perfectly imperfect journey we call life, the more challenging it is.

It is highly unlikely that in any given moment you will not find an energetic weakness. This does not mean that you are weak; it means you are strong.

The more you clear energy, the faster the ride … like a roller coaster. As you chug up to the top, the thrill of the drop is not far from your mind. Once you reach the bottom, there is another loop to contend with. Sometimes you want to yell at the controller to let you off, and at other times you get off the ride and can't wait to purchase another ticket to go again …

The universe has a great sense of humor: the final words for this book were written on Mother's Day …

My oldest daughter was also brought into this world on Mother's Day. It took twenty-eight hours to safely deliver her into this life, which seem miniscule now, in comparison to the twenty-eight months to give life to this book.

Now, I lovingly cut the cord, and look forward to thinking less …
and feeling more!

Thank you for your time and energy!

Enjoy the Ride!

Your fun facilitator,

Colette

If you are strong to taking this book to the next level, you are welcome to explore the following products, radio show and seminars at:

www.thetruthisfunny.com
www.energeticupgrade.com
www.transformationtalkradio.com

AVAILABLE SOON …

www.tailsfromthevector.com
www.adventuresofanactivatedgoddess.com